W9-AXO-408

Applied Software Measurement

Other McGraw-Hill Books of Interest

0-07-000748-9	Aiken	*Data Reverse Engineering: Untying the Legacy Knot*
0-07-015840-1	Davis	*201 Principles of Software Development*
0-07-709118-3	Duffy	*From Chaos to Classes: Object-Oriented Software Development in C++*
0-07-037774-X	Levey	*Reengineering COBOL with Objects: Step by Step to Sustainable Legacy Systems*
0-07-039400-8	Lyu	*The Handbook of Software Reliability Engineering*
0-07-042948-0	Modell	*A Professional's Guide to Systems Analysis*, 2/e
0-07-052229-4	Pressman	*A Manager's Guide to Software Engineering*
0-07-709167-1	Zetie	*Practical User Interface Design*

To order or receive additional information on these or any other McGraw-Hill titles, please call 1-800-822-8158 in the United States. In other countries, contact your local McGraw-Hill representative.

WM16XXA

Applied Software Measurement

Assuring Productivity and Quality

Capers Jones

Second Edition

McGraw-Hill
New York San Francisco Washington, D.C. Auckland Bogotá
Caracas Lisbon London Madrid Mexico City Milan
Montreal New Delhi San Juan Singapore
Sydney Tokyo Toronto

Library of Congress Cataloging-in-Publication Data

Jones, Capers.
Applied software measurement : assuring productivity and quality / Capers Jones.—2d ed.
p. cm.
Includes index.
ISBN 0-07-032826-9
1. Computer software—Quality control. 2. Function point analysis. I. Title.
QA76.76.Q35J66 1996
005.1'4—dc20 96-8652
CIP

McGraw-Hill 
A Division of The McGraw-Hill Companies

Copyright © 1996, 1991 by Capers Jones. All rights reserved. Printed in the United States of America. Except as permitted under the United States Copyright Act of 1976, no part of this publication may be reproduced or distributed in any form or by any means, or stored in a data base or retrieval system, without the prior written permission of the publisher.

3 4 5 6 7 8 9 0 DOC/DOC 9 0 1 0 9 8

ISBN 0-07-032826-9

The sponsoring editor for this book was John Wyzalek, the editing supervisor was Caroline R. Levine, and the production supervisor was Pamela A. Pelton.

Printed and bound by R. R. Donnelley & Sons Company.

McGraw-Hill books are available at special quantity discounts to use as premiums and sales promotions, or for use in corporate training programs. For more information, please write to the Director of Special Sales, McGraw-Hill, 11 West 19th Street, New York, NY 10011. Or contact your local bookstore.

This book is printed on recycled, acid-free paper containing a minimum of 50% recycled de-inked fiber.

Information contained in this work has been obtained by The McGraw-Hill Companies, Inc. ("McGraw-Hill") from sources believed to be reliable. However, neither McGraw-Hill nor its authors guarantee the accuracy or completeness of any information published herein and neither McGraw-Hill nor its authors shall be responsible for any errors, omissions, or damages arising out of use of this information. This work is published with the understanding that McGraw-Hill and its authors are supplying information, but are not attempting to render engineering or other professional services. If such services are required, the assistance of an appropriate professional should be sought.

Contents

Preface

The first edition of *Applied Software Measurement* was written in 1990 and 1991 and the book itself was published in 1991. This second edition was started late in 1994 and the text was completed in the summer and autumn of 1995. There have been some significant changes in the software industry between the publication dates of the first edition and the second. Here are some of the notable changes that make a second edition worthwhile.

Expansion of Functional Metrics

Since 1991 when this book was first published, the function point metric has now become the dominant software metric in the United States and in at least 20 other countries. More than 2000 additional projects have been added to our knowledge base since the previous edition, and all have been measured using function points or reported by clients in function point form.

The usage of function points has expanded in breadth, as well as in numbers of users. Function point metrics originated as a tool for sizing, estimating, and measuring software projects. However, the utility of function point is expanding very rapidly as a general business metric. Following are some representative examples:

Function Points and Business Process Reengineering (BPR)

Once a company quantifies the volume of its software portfolio using the function point metric, it is obvious that segments of that portfolio service the operating components of the business. For example, in a typical manufacturing company, out of a portfolio of 1,000,000 function points, engineering might use 200,000 function points, manufacturing might use 350,000, marketing and sales might use 50,000, finance and administration might use 100,000, and so forth.

When BPR studies occur, the use of function point metrics provides a new and powerful tool for aligning the software capabilities of the company with the new or revised operating units.

Function Points and Outsource Analysis

The function point metric provides a new and useful way for evaluating outsource contracts. In fact several outsourcers are already including "cost per function point" as part of their contracts for diverse topics including but not limited to: (1) cost per function point for basic development projects, (2) cost per function point on a sliding scale for creeping improvements, (3) cost per function point for maintenace and enhancement work.

(Several international outsourcers in India are using the differential between their cost per function point and U.S. averages to leverage their business.)

Note that this second edition now breaks out contract and outsource software as a separate topic and shows comparative productivity rates of outsourced applications versus similar projects developed by the information systems community.

Function Points and Taxation

The Internal Revenue Service in the United States, and several equivalent groups abroad, are exploring function points for determining the taxable value of software assets. Function points are also being used for determining the assets value of software companies when they merge or are acquired. Since function point metrics are far more appropriate for economic analysis than the former "lines of code" metric this topic can be expected to grow in importance.

As this second edition is being prepared, at least half a dozen cases are in U.S. tax courts that involve function points as a tool for determining both the value of software, and part of the value of software companies when they are bought and sold.

Function Points and Tool Capacities

The function point metric is providing a new approach for evaluating CASE tools and other software tools. For example, it takes about 50,000 function points of tool capacity to fully equip a software engineer. Software project managers need about 10,000 function points, as do software quality assurance personnel.

The usage of function point metrics for examining tool capacities is already revealing some interesting points. Underequipped quality assurance personnel and underequipped project managers have severe problems in doing their jobs well.

The defect removal efficiency levels of companies that have sparse QA tool suites are around 10 percent lower than in companies with adequate tool sets, for example.

Function Points and Make Versus Buy Analysis

Basic software application packages such as spreadsheets can sometimes be purchased for as little as $0.25 per function point. More specialized niche packages in the domains of finance or stock market analysis can cost more than $300 per function point.

Information of this kind serves as a new way of evaluating the economics of make versus buy analysis. The costs of building and maintaining software applications can now be compared to the costs of purchasing and acquiring packages. For example, if you need to acquire 1000 copies of a package, and the effective cost is $1.00 per function point, or you can build the same application for $500 per function point, it is now possible to evaluate either side of the situation using the same terms.

Function Points and Software Quality

The function point metric is now rapidly becoming the preferred metric for software quality analysis. At the time of the first edition in 1991, U.S. norms indicated a total of about 5.0 bugs or defects per function point, coupled with a defect removal efficiency that averages about 85 percent. This means that about 0.75 bugs per function point were delivered with the first releases of new software packages.

Best-in-class organizations can drop below two defects per function point in total potentials, and eliminate more than 98 percent of all defects prior to delivery to clients.

The former "lines of code" metric made many defect classes difficult to study. Function points are now being used to explore defects levels found in:

Requirements (about 15 percent of all defects)

Specifications (about 35 percent of all defects)

Source code (about 40 percent of all defects)

User documents (about 5 percent of all defects)

Bad fixes or secondary defects (about 5 per cent of all defects)

The ability to explore all kinds of software defects is what makes function points such a powerful tool for quality research, as opposed to the former "lines of code" or LOC metric which had no utility for exploring front-end defects or errors in paper documents such as specifications.

Function Points and Programming Language Evaluation

The function point metric has been used to evaluate the level of programming languages, as well as the resulting productivity rates. For example, the phrase "high-level" languages is now applied to languages that take less than 50 statements to encode one function point. By contrast, "low-level" languages take more than 100 statements to encode one function point.

Information on the ratio of function points to source code is now available for more than 450 programming languages and dialects. Some of the modern programming languages are very powerful when evaluated on this scale.

Productivity rates for applications developed with high-level programming languages are normally significantly better than for applications developed with low-level languages such as assembly (320 statements per function point) and mid-level languages such as COBOL (108 statements per function point).

Productivity rates for applications developed using low-level languages and mid-level languages average less than 10 function points per staff month. Productivity rates for applications in modern data base and nonprocedural languages average more than 20 function points per staff month, and some applictions exceed 100 function points per staff month.

Function Points and Tool or Environment Analysis

One of the most powerful uses of function point metrics is to perform multiple-regression studies to explore the impact of tools such as Sybase, DataEase, Lotus Notes, CADRE, Teamwork, COGNOS, Visual Basic, and the like. When productivity studies include the tools utilized as well as the function point productivity data, it is possible to derive the impact of an ever-growing number of software development and maintenance tools. For example, design tools, testing tools, complexity analysis tools, CASE tools, reverse engineering tools, cost estimating tools, project management tools, and a host of others are now being evaluated via function point benchmark studies.

This book does not get to the level of evaluating individual tools, but the author and his company, Software Productivity Research (SPR), are frequently commissioned to perform studies of this type.

Explosion of the Client-Server Architecture

The client-server phenomenon has swept over the information systems community to such an extent that almost half of new IS applications in our knowledge base are now client-server based. This phenomenon has had an immediate and near term impact on software productivity rates, and will have a longer range impact on quality and maintenance costs.

The near term productivity impact of client-server projects has been positive, but the longer-range implications of client-server applications is troubling. The high complexity levels of client-server applications coupled with rather careless development practices has led to a reduction in quality levels, and this will lead to an increase in maintenance costs when the client-server applications become aging legacy systems.

The Emergence of the Object-Oriented Paradigm

The object-oriented paradigm has entered the main stream of the software world, and object-oriented analysis, design, and coding approaches are now being used for many sizes and kinds of applications. More than half our clients are now starting to use object-oriented approaches, and almost 20 percent of the new systems software projects in our knowledge base now represent object-oriented programming languages.

Unfortunately, the OO paradigm has such a steep learning curve that productivity usually declines for the first six months after adoption. Once the learning curve is overcome, productivity rates then climb above prior values.

The OO claims of increased volumes of reusable material are only partly true and currently limited primarily to code reuse. Whole classes of software deliverables have not yet been included in the OO paradigm. For example, there is nothing in the OO literature dealing with reusable user documentation, and very little dealing with reuse of test materials, requirements, plans, estimates, and other business information.

Software Reusability is Expanding

Software reusability is also becoming a main stream topic. (Surprisingly, reuse in the Visual Basic environment is now far greater than any other, even though Visual Basic is not part of the object-oriented domain.) There are 12 major software artifacts that are potentially reusable: architecture, requirements, design, plans, estimates, code, data, interfaces, screens, user manuals, test plans, and test cases. The overall value of reuse rises in direct proportion to the number and volume of reusable materials utilized. Although only a few of our clients have achieved such results, the top projects in terms of the volume of reusable material are now approaching 75 percent in terms of code reuse, and more than 25 percent reuse of all other deliverables. These projects are breaking former "world records" in terms of high productivity and shorter schedules.

Military Software Moves Toward Civilian Best Practices

In 1994, the U.S. Secretary of Defense, William Perry, issued a directive that the military services should no longer regard Department of Defense standards as being mandatory. The DoD community was urged to adopt civilian best practices. As this book is written, it is too soon to judge whether this new policy will be effective, but at least it is promising. U.S. military standards for software are not without virtues but created some results that made U.S. military software the most expensive and the least productive in the world. For example, the DoD 2167 quality standard triggered the creation of about three times the volume of software paperwork as found in civilian norms. The new DoD 498 standard is hopefully more flexible.

The challenge to the DoD community is to preserve the best features of the DoD standards while moving toward civilian best practices. A second challenge is to be sure that the phrase "best practice" is taken seriously and not confused with the latest fads.

Software Process Assessments and Benchmarks Become Common

The Software Engineering Institute (SEI) and Software Productivity Research (SPR) were both incorporated in 1984, and both began to offer software process assessment services in 1985. In addition to qualitative information about processes and methods, Software Productivity Research also collects quantitative benchmark data on software productivity, quality, schedules, costs, and staffing. Indeed, most of the information in this book is derived from the SPR assessment and benchmark studies. The rapid expansion of the SPR and SEI assessments, and the growing volume of accurate benchmark data are starting to allow correlation and multiple regression studies that can identify the effectiveness of tools, methodologies, programming languages, specialization, and even ergonomic factors such as office space and noise levels.

Acknowledgments

Special thanks to my wife, Eileen Jones, for her support during both editions and for her patience when I get involved in writing. Thanks also for her capable handling of all of my book publishing contracts.

Great appreciation is due to my colleagues at Software Productivity Research for their aid in gathering the data, assisting our clients, building the tools that we use, and for making SPR an enjoyable environment. Thanks to Mahshad Bakhtyari, Ed Begley, Barbara Bloom, Julie Bonaiuto, William Bowen, Kristen Brooks, Lynne Caramanica, Sudip Chakraborty, Craig Chamberlin, Mike Cunnane, Charles Douglis (SPR's president), Richard Gazoorian, Dave Gustafson, Bill Harmon, Steve Hone, Jan Huffman, Peter Katsoulas, Donna O'Donnel, Mark Pinis, Kevin Raum, Richard Tang-Kong, and John Zimmerman. (Thanks also to Debbie Chapman, Carol Chiungos, Shane Hartman, Wayne Hadlock, and Richard Ward for their help over many years when they were at SPR.) Special thanks to the families and friends of the SPR staff, who have had to put up with both travel and overtime.

Great appreciation to Ken Bowes and Dick Spann for their outstanding work as SPR directors.

Many other colleagues work with us at SPR on special projects or as consultants. Special thanks to Allan Albrecht, the inventor of function points, for his invaluable contribution to the industry and for his outstanding work with SPR. Without Allan's pioneering work in function points, the ability to create accurate baselines and benchmarks would probably not exist.

Appreciation is due also to the officers and employees of the International Function Point Users Group (IFPUG). This organization also started about 10 years ago and has grown to become the largest software measurement association in the history of software. When the affiliates in other countries are included, the community of function point users is the largest measurement association in the world.

Thanks also to Michael Bragen, Rich Desjardins, Ken Foster, Bob Kendall, and John Mulcahy for the work they do with us. Thanks also to Dale Hedrick and Susan Turner for their support in their various specialties.

Much appreciation is due to the client organizations whose interest in software assessments, benchmarks and baselines, measurement, and process improvements have let us work together. There are too many groups to name them all, but many thanks to our colleagues and clients at Amdahl, Andersen Consulting, AT&T, Bachman, Bellcore, Bell Northern Research, Bell Sygma, Bendix, British Air, CBIS, Church of the Latter Day Saints, Cincinnati Bell, CODEX, Credit Suisse, DEC, Dunn & Bradstreet, DuPont, EDS, Fidelity Investments, Ford Motors, Fortis Group, General Electric, General Motors, GTE, Hartford Insurance, Hewlett-Packard, IBM, Informix, Inland Steel, Internal Revenue Service, ISSC, JC Penney, Kozo Keikaku, Lotus, Mead Data Central, McKinsey Consulting, Motorola, Nippon Telegraph, NCR, Northern Telecom, Nynex, Pacific Bell, Ralston Purina, Sapiens, Sears Roebuck, Siemens-Nixdorf, Software Publishing Corportion, SOGEI, Sun Life, Tandem, TRW, UNISYS, U.S. Air Force, U.S. Navy Surface Weapons groups, US West, Wang, Westinghouse, and many others.

Capers Jones

Preface to the First Edition

Measurement has been the basis of all science and engineering progress except for software. Although software is a creature of the mid-twentieth century, when both economic metrics and other engineering metrics are well developed, it has followed a strange path all on its own and has existed for almost 50 years with very little quantification of either productivity or quality or the factors which influence them.

The book's title, *Applied Software Measurement*, defines the book's intent: to demonstrate that software is in fact capable of accurate measurements, and that the measurements have notable practical value to both the management and the technical community within the software industry.

Software has made some progress without measurement, of course, but its progress has been essentially that of an art form or craft rather than an engineering discipline. How has it happened that a major industry can exist without basic knowledge of the factors which influence it?

First, both computers and modern software originated in the closing years of World War II to aid the military in solving certain mathematical problems. Mathematics has never been a marketed commodity, nor has it ever been easy to measure either mathematical results or the work of mathematicians. Therefore, software had its origin as a subdiscipline of a science which was interested primarily in final results, but which had no history of measuring the speed or effort required to achieve those results. Mathematical solutions of military problems were obviously so time-consuming that both calculators and computer technology were desirable, but the original need for speed was based more on military necessity than on economics.

Second, the initial wave of software applications in the late 1940s and early 1950s tended to be complex ballistic and scientific calculations which had four significant characteristics: (1) Solving the problems themselves required substantial mental effort but not much in the way of paperwork. (2) The problems were fairly small and self-contained, so only one, or perhaps two persons were involved. (3) Both machine language and primitive assembly languages were so tedious and difficult to use that coding became both a focal point of and a bottleneck to moving problem solutions onto a computer. (4) Once the problems were solved and the solutions were encoded, they did not change very much afterward.

Thus, when measurement of early software projects did occur, it was fairly reasonable to express the measurements in the crude terms of "lines of code." There were no measurements that encompassed the pure mental work of programming, and the enormous volumes of specifications and user documents were not part of the first generation of software projects. Nor was maintenance a major consideration for the first 10 years or so of software production.

It should be noted that, as a commodity, software lagged behind computers by more than 10 years. For vacuum-tube-based computers and the early discrete transistor computers, the bulk of the costs were associated with the computer itself, and the software was normally bundled with the hardware and given away. There is certainly very little business incentive to measure a commodity that is given away, so there was no economic pressure for improved software metrics. When computers began to move into the domain of business applications and outside the solution of specialized military and systems problems, software began to break away from hardware and move toward becoming a separate subindustry.

Unfortunately, the subindustry carried with it the mindset from the 1940s and 1950s that measurements were either intrusive (derived from software's mathematical origins) or should be based on lines of code (derived from the exhaustion and frustration of working with machine language and primitive assembly languages). Thus, the origins of software and the nature of the early work neither demanded measurements nor supplied any overwhelming economic reasons to explore and improve measurement.

What happened next was the explosion of software and computing in the 1960s, 1970s, and 1980s. Computers evolved from being specialized military and academic curiosities into being the main driving force of modern business, industry, and government. The demand for computers exceeded the early IBM prognostications by more than a 1000 to 1, and the demand continues to grow. Software production changed from being the province of obscure and esoteric specialists into one of the largest occupations in human history.

With the enormous growth in the demand for software and the similar growth in the number of software professionals, economic necessity has made measurements imperative. The president of a large company might not have been greatly concerned about measuring the performance of a computer and a few specialists in the late 1950s. But by 1990, the company could not operate or compete successfully without computers and software, and the employed software professionals might constitute 10 percent of company's work force. The annual budgets for computers, peripherals, and professional staff might exceed $1 billion!

It is obvious that the need for accurate measurements of software productivity and quality is directly related to the overall economic importance of software to industry, business, and government. That means that measurement is now a mainstream software activity, and it is one that is on the critical path to corporate and national success.

The contents of the book are intended to cover all of the broad and most of the specific topics associated with starting a full corporate measurement program that encompasses productivity, quality, and human factors. Chapter 1, the Introduction, is an overview of all aspects of applied software measurement in modern corporations, including on-going project measures, annual baselines, productivity measures, quality measures, demographic measures, and production library measures. It introduces standard economic concepts and points out the advantages of functional metrics for economic studies.

Chapter 2, The History and Evolution of Functional Metrics, starts by explaining in detail the economic fallacies of lines-of-code metrics. It then discusses all of the major variations in functional metrics since the first public announcement of function points in 1979. Topics covered include function points, DeMarco bang metrics, feature points, the British Mark II function point method, the IFPUG method, and several others.

Chapter 3, United States Averages for Software Productivity and Quality, attempts to carve out the current overall national rates for all key software productivity and quality topics. It uses the backfire function point technique to create U.S. averages for software productivity and quality. It also discusses the reasons for productivity variations between MIS, systems, and military projects. It includes a retrospective historical study of software productivity at 10-year intervals from 1950 to 1995, with projections forward to 2000.

Chapter 4, The Mechanics of Measurement, discusses the work of starting a corporate software baseline for the very first time. It deals with both sociological and technical issues of introducing applied software measurements. A baseline must contain both accurate "hard" data and also reliable "soft" data to determine why projects vary.

Chapter 5, Measuring Software Quality and User Satisfaction, discusses the business significance of quality for international competition of high-technology products. It then discusses the closely intertwined topics of quality control and user satisfaction. The chapter introduces the measurement of defect origins, defect severities, and defect removal efficiency. Also discussed is the measurement of user-reported defects after release of software to customers. The chapter includes cautions about paradoxical measurements, such as "cost per defect," that are economically unsound.

Appendix A, Rules for Counting Procedural Source Code, gives the detailed rules developed by Software Productivity Research to ensure consistent counting of source code size.

Appendix B, Rules for Counting Function Points and Feature Points, illustrates and discusses the detailed rules necessary to ensure consistent counting of function points and feature points.

Appendix C, Example of a Fully Measured Software Project, shows the total volume of information that must be recorded to fully measure a project. The volume of information approximates the amount typically recorded for a human patient undergoing a complete medical examination. This appendix illustrates and discusses all of the salient data types, including soft data on the environment and methods, hard data on the tangible deliverables, and normalized data using functional metrics.

Appendix D, Example of an Annual Baseline Report, shows a full annual corporate software baseline report for a medium-size company. Such a baseline will be about the same size, and require about the same kind of effort, as the production of a corporate annual report to shareholders and investors. The appendix illustrates and discusses the kinds of aggregation and analysis needed to show productivity and quality trends at the corporate level.

Appendix E, Example of an Executive Briefing on a New Baseline, shows a typical report to senior management. Not only are baseline reports printed for management distribution but special executive summaries are normally prepared for senior management. The appendix illustrates and discusses a typical executive-level presentation on software strengths and weaknesses, productivity, and quality.

Chapter

1

Introduction

This new edition of *Applied Software Measurement* confirms the conclusion of the first edition, that measurement is a key technology for successful software development and maintenance. Indeed, measurements have been a pivotal component in the progress of the software industry in the years between the publication of the first and second editions. In particular, the usage of function point metrics has exploded across the software world.

In 1990, function points were just beginning to expand in usage. In 1996, function point metrics have become the dominant metric in the United States and about 20 other countries. Function point metrics are even being explored in countries such as Cuba and China, where software measurement technology has been delayed by lack of immediate access to current information.

Software development and maintenance have become major corporate concerns in the last half of the twentieth century. Although most companies could not survive or compete successfully without software and computers, senior executive management remains troubled by a set of chronic problems associated with software applications: long schedules, major cost overruns, low quality, and poor user satisfaction.

These problems have occurred so widely that it is fair to characterize them as a "corporate epidemic." Yet software is not out of control in every company. The companies that have been most successful in bringing software under control tend to share most of these seven characteristics:

1. They measure software productivity and quality accurately.
2. They plan and estimate software projects accurately.
3. They have capable management and technical staffs.

4. They have good organization structures.
5. They have effective software methods and tools.
6. They have adequate staff office environments.
7. They are able to reuse substantial volumes of software deliverables.

All seven characteristics are important, but the first is perhaps the most significant of all, since it tends to permeate and influence the others. Let us consider each of the seven in turn.

Applied software measurement

Measurement is the basis of all science, engineering, and business. Unfortunately, software developers lagged far behind other professions in establishing both standard metrics and meaningful targets. The phrase "applied software measurement" refers to the emerging discipline associated with the accurate and meaningful collection of information which has practical value to software management and staffs. The goal of applied software measurement is to give software managers and professionals a set of useful, tangible data points for sizing, estimating, managing, and controlling software projects with rigor and precision.

For many years, measuring software productivity and quality was so difficult that only very large companies such as IBM attempted it. Indeed, one of the reasons for IBM's success was the early emphasis the company put on the applied measurement of quality and productivity, which gave IBM the ability to use the data for corrective purposes. But stable metrics and accurate applied measurement of software have been possible since 1979, and now every company can gain the benefits and insights available from applied software measurement.

The problem today is not a deficiency in software measurement technology itself; rather, it is cultural resistance on the part of software management and staff. The resistance is due to the natural human belief that measures might be used against them. This feeling is the greatest barrier to applied software measurement. The challenge today is to overcome this barrier and demonstrate that applied software measurement is not harmful, but as necessary to corporate success as standard financial measurements.

What tends to separate leading-edge companies from trailing-edge companies are not only technical differences but cultural differences as well. Project managers in companies at the leading edge, such as Microsoft, IBM, Du Pont, and Hewlett-Packard, may have 10 times as much quantified, historical information available to them to aid in project planning as their peers in companies at the trailing edge.

Managers in leading-edge companies also have accurate demographic and morale information available, which is largely missing at the trailing edge. Not only is such information absent at the trailing edge, but the managers and executives within trailing-edge companies are often deluded into thinking their companies are much better than they really are!

Planning and estimation

Planning and estimation are the mirror images of measurement. The factors and metrics that were recorded during project development are now aimed toward the future of uncompleted projects. There is a perfect correlation between measurement accuracy and estimation accuracy: Companies that measure well can estimate well; companies that do not measure cannot estimate either. Commercial-grade estimation tools have been available since the middle 1970s, and they are now becoming widely deployed. Here too measurement is significant, since only companies with accurate historical data can validate estimates and judge their accuracy. Leading-edge enterprises normally do not attempt to estimate large projects by hand; instead, they use either proprietary tools based on their own history or commercial estimating tools based on general industry data.

Management and technical staffs

Leading-edge companies tend to attract and keep good managers and good technical staffs. What attracts such people appears to be exciting projects, excellent working conditions, and the pleasure of working with capable colleagues. Although it is outside the scope of this book, leading-edge companies such as IBM tend to go out of their way to measure employee satisfaction by means of annual corporate opinion surveys. Trailing-edge companies have trouble keeping capable management and staff. What causes the dissatisfaction are poorly conceived or canceled projects, inadequate working conditions, primitive tools and methods, and the lack of stimulating colleagues and effective project management. Trailing-edge companies are seldom aware of these problems because they lack any form of measurement or opinion survey.

Organization structures

Software in the 1990s is becoming specialized just as medicine and law have become specialized. As special technical skills are needed, such as those of database administrators, quality assurance specialists, human factors specialists, and technical writers, it becomes more and more important to plan organization structures carefully. Indeed, among the hallmarks of the larger leading-edge corporations are measurement specialists and measurement organizations. One of the useful by-products of measurement is the ability to judge the relative effectiveness of organization structures such as hierarchical vs. matrix management for software projects and centralization vs. decentralization for the software function overall. Here too, measurement can lead to progress and the lack of measurement can lead to expensive mistakes.

Methodologies and tools

The labor content of software projects is extraordinarily high. Very few artifacts require as much manual labor as a large software system. Many software methodology, tool, language, and CASE vendors claim to displace human effort through automation with 10- or 20-to-1 improvements in productivity. Are such claims justified? Generally, they are not. Only companies that measure software productivity and quality can find their way through the morass of conflicting assertions and pick a truly effective path. As it turns out, heavy investment in tools prior to resolving organizational and methodological issues is normally counterproductive and will improve neither quality nor productivity. Only accurate measurements can navigate a path that is both cost-effective and pragmatic.

The office environment

The final aspect of leading-edge companies is a surprising one: The companies tend to have adequate office space and good physical environments. It appears that, for knowledge workers such as software professionals, the impact of physical office environments on productivity may be as great as the impact of the tools and methods used. Open offices and overcrowding tend to lower productivity, whereas private offices and adequate space tend to augment it. Findings such as that are possible only from accurate measurements and multiple-regression studies of all the factors which influence human endeavors.

Art is normally free-form and unconstrained; business is normally under management control. In companies with no measurement practices, software projects are essentially artistic rather than business undertakings. That is, there is no way for management to make an accurate prediction of the outcome of a project or to exert effective control once the project has been set in motion. That is not as it should be. Software should be a normal business function with the same rigor of planning, estimating, risk, and value analysis as any other corporate function. Only measurement, carefully applied, can convert software production and maintenance from artistic activities into business activities.

Although many different sociological and technological steps may be needed to bring software under management control in a large company, all of them require accurate measurement as the starting point. That is true of all physical and social systems: Only measurement can assess progress and direction and allow feedback loops to bring deviations under control.

Reusability

A topic of growing importance to the software community is the ability to reuse a number of software artifacts. Because manual development of software applications is highly labor-intensive, the ability to reuse material is one of the critical steps that can improve both software quality and productivity simultaneously. Twelve software "artifacts" are potentially reusable, and a successful reuse program will include all twelve.

1. Reusable requirements
2. Reusable architecture
3. Reusable plans
4. Reusable cost estimates
5. Reusable designs
6. Reusable source code
7. Reusable data elements
8. Reusable interfaces
9. Reusable screens
10. Reusable user manuals
11. Reusable test plans
12. Reusable test cases

Software reusability was largely experimental when the first edition of this book was published, but under the impact of many new tools and also new programming languages such as Visual Basic and Object Oriented (OO) languages reuse is starting to enter the main stream.

The Essential Aspects of Applied Software Measurement

Three essential kinds of information must be considered when dealing with applied software measurement, or the measurement of any other complex process involving human action:

1. Hard data
2. Soft data
3. Normalized data

All three kinds of information must be recorded and analyzed in order to gain insights into productivity or quality problems.

Hard data

The first kind of information, termed "hard data," refers to things that can be quantified with little or no subjectivity. For the hard-data elements, high accuracy is both possible and desirable. The key hard-data elements that affect software projects are:

- The number of staff members assigned to a project
- The effort spent by staff members on project tasks
- The schedule durations of significant project tasks
- The overlap and concurrency of tasks performed in parallel
- The project document, code, and test case volumes
- The number of bugs or defects found and reported

Although hard data can in theory be measured with very high accuracy, most companies are distressingly inaccurate in the data they collect. Factors such as unpaid overtime by professional staff members, management costs, user involvement, and frequent project accounting errors can cause the true cost of a software project to be up to 100 percent greater than the apparent cost derived from a normal project-tracking system. That fact must be evaluated and considered when starting a serious corporate measurement program: It will probably be necessary to modify or replace the existing project cost-tracking system with something more effective.

The solution to inaccurate tracking accuracy is not technically difficult, although it may be sociologically difficult. It is only necessary to establish a standard chart of accounts for the tasks which will normally be performed on software projects and then collect data by task.

The sociological difficulty comes in recognizing that current tracking systems tend to omit large volumes of unpaid overtime, user effort on projects, managerial effort, and often many other activities. Senior executives and software project managers must have access to an accurate accounting of what the true cost elements of software projects really are.

One of the most frequent problems encountered with project historical data that lowers data accuracy is a simple lack of granularity.

Instead of measuring the effort of specific activities, companies tend to accumulate only "bottom line" data for the whole project without separating the data into meaningful subsets, such as the effort for requirements, design, and coding. Such bottom-line data is essentially worthless because there is no real way to validate it.

For purposes of schedule and management control, it is common to break software projects into somewhere between 5 and 10 specific phases such as "requirements, design, coding, testing, and installation." Such phase structures are cumbersome and inadequate for cost measurement purposes. Too many activities, such as production of user documentation, tend to span several phases, so accurate cost accumulation is difficult to perform.

Table 1.1 is an example of the standard chart of accounts used by Software Productivity Research[1] when collecting the project data shown in the later sections of this book. It illustrates the kind of granularity by activity needed for historical data to be useful for economic studies. This chart of accounts is based on activities rather than phases. An "activity" is defined as a bounded set of tasks aimed at completing a significant project milestone. The milestone might be completion of requirements, completion of a prototype, or completion of initial design. As can easily be seen, variations in the activities that are usually performed are one of the primary reasons why productivity varies from industry to industry and class to class of software.

Although Table 1.1 uses 25 standard activities, that does not imply that only 25 things must be done to develop a software project. The 25 activities are accounting abstractions used to accumulate costs in a convenient manner. Any given activity, such as "requirements," obviously consists of a number of significant subactivities or specific tasks. Indeed, even small software projects may require hundreds of specific tasks in a full work breakdown structure; large projects may require many thousands. A task-level chart of accounts, although capable of high precision, tends to be very cumbersome for cost accumulation, since project staff must record times against a very large number of individual tasks.

The 25 activities listed in Table 1.1 illustrate the level of granularity needed to gain economic insights into the major costs associated with software.

Unless a reasonably granular chart of accounts is used, it is difficult to explore economic productivity in ways that lead to insights. For example, it has been known for many years that military software projects typically have lower productivity rates than civilian software projects of the same size. One of the key reasons for that can easily be seen by means of a granular chart of accounts.

TABLE 1.1 Example of Standard Software Charts of Accounts for Six Domains

Activities performed	End user	MIS	Outsource	Commercial	Systems	Military
1. Requirements		X	X	X	X	X
2. Prototyping	X	X	X	X	X	X
3. Architecture			X	X	X	X
4. Project plans		X	X	X	X	X
5. Initial design		X	X	X	X	X
6. Detail design		X	X	X	X	X
7. Design reviews			X	X	X	X
8. Coding	X	X	X	X	X	X
9. Reuse acquisition	X		X	X	X	X
10. Package purchase		X	X		X	X
11. Code inspections				X	X	X
12. Independent verification and validation						X
13. Configuration management		X	X	X	X	X
14. Formal integration		X	X	X	X	X
15. User documentation	X	X	X	X	X	X
16. Unit testing	X	X	X	X	X	X
17. Function testing		X	X	X	X	X
18. Integration testing		X	X	X	X	X
19. System testing		X	X	X	X	X
20. Field testing				X	X	X
21. Acceptance testing		X	X		X	X
22. Independent testing						X
23. Quality assurance			X	X	X	X
24. Installation and training		X	X		X	X
25. Project management		X	X	X	X	X
Activities	5	15	20	21	22	25

MIS projects normally perform only 15 of the 25 standard activities; systems software projects perform about 22; and military projects normally perform all 25. The need to perform almost twice as many activities explains why military projects are usually quite low in productivity compared to civilian projects.

Soft data

The second kind of information, termed "soft data," comprises topics in which human opinions must be evaluated. Since human opinions will vary, absolute precision is impossible for the soft data. Nonetheless, it is the soft data, taken collectively, which explains variations in project outcomes. The key soft data elements that affect software projects are:

- The skill and experience of the project team
- The constraints or schedule pressures put on the team
- The stability of project requirements over time
- User satisfaction with the project
- The expertise and cooperation of the project users
- Adequacy of the tools and methods used on the project
- The organization structure for the project team
- Adequacy of the office space for the project team
- The perceived value of the project to the enterprise

Although soft data is intrinsically subjective, it is still among the most useful kinds of information that can be collected. Soft data is the major source of information that can explain the variations in productivity and quality without which a measurement program cannot lead to insights and improvements. Therefore, in a well-designed applied software measurement program, much effort and care must be devoted to selecting the appropriate sets of soft factors and then developing instruments that will allow this useful data to be collected and analyzed statistically. That is the most difficult intellectual task associated with measurement programs.

Normalized data

The third kind of information, termed "normalized data," refers to standard metrics used for comparative purposes to determine whether projects are above or below normal in terms of productivity or quality. This form of information was very troublesome for the software industry, and more than 40 years went by before satisfactory normalization metrics were developed.

The historical attempts to use lines of code for normalization purposes failed dismally because of the lack of international standards that clearly defined what was meant by a "line of code" in any common language and because of serious mathematical paradoxes. Indeed, lines-of-code metrics are technically impossible for studying economic productivity, which is defined as the "goods or services produced per unit of labor expense." Lines of code are neither goods nor services, and for many large software projects less than 20 percent of the total effort is devoted to coding.

The mathematical paradoxes and the reversal of apparent economic productivity associated with lines-of-code metrics totally negate the validity of such data for statistical analysis. The most troubling aspect of the paradox is the tendency for lines-of-code productivity rates to penalize high-level languages. The reason for this paradox was first described by the author in 1978 in the *IBM Systems Journal.*[2] However, the fundamental mathematics of the paradox had been worked out during the industrial revolution, and the basic reason for the problem has been known by economists and industrial engineers for more than 200 years!

In any manufacturing process in which fixed costs are significant, a reduction in the number of units constructed will raise the average cost per unit. For software, more than half of the project costs can go to noncoding tasks such as requirements, specifications, documentation, and testing. These noncoding tasks tend to act like fixed costs, raise the cost per source line, and lower the source lines per person-month rates for projects written in high-level languages.

Table 1.2 illustrates the paradox of an increase in real economic productivity but a decline in source lines per person-month for high-level languages. Assume that two projects are identical in functionality, but one is written in a low-level language such as Assembler and the second written in a high-level language such as Ada. The noncoding tasks stay constant between the two examples and tend to act as fixed costs. The reduction in the number of source code statements in the Ada example, therefore, tends to act like a reduction in manufactured units.

Note that although the Ada version required only 4 person-months of total effort and the Assembler version required 6 person-months, the lines-of-code metric appears to be twice as good for the Assembler

TABLE 1.2 Example of the Mathematical Paradox Associated with Lines-of-Source-Code Metrics

	Assembler version	Ada version
Lines of source code in project	7500	2500
Noncoding effort in person-months	3	3
Coding effort in person-months	3	1
Total project effort in person-months	6	4
Net source lines per person-month	1250	625

version. That violates the standard economic definition of productivity and common sense as well.

Since October 1979, when A. J. Albrecht of IBM first publicized function points,[3] the new function-based metrics, such as function points for MIS projects and feature points for systems software, are becoming the preferred choice for software normalization. They have substantially replaced the older lines-of-code metric for purposes of economic and productivity analysis.

Function points will be described in detail in Chap. 2. The function-based metrics are derived from counts of the externally visible aspects of a software project that are significant to its users. The basic IBM function point metric uses weighted counts of five parameters: inputs, outputs, inquiries, logical files, and interfaces. (The feature point metric, developed for real-time and systems software, uses the same five parameters and also enumerates the number of algorithms. Other parameters, such as counts of entities and relationships, also are used by some of the function-based metrics.)

The essential aspects of function points apply empirical weights to the five basic factors that comprise an application. For example, the function point total for the projects shown in Table 1.2 might be as shown in Table 1.3.

Note that function points are independent of lines of code, so the function point total for both the Assembler and the Ada versions would be the same: 35 function points in this case. Measures based on function points, such as cost per function point and function points per staff-month, are much more reliable than the older lines of code for economic purposes.

Functional metrics are artificial business metrics equivalent perhaps to cost per square foot in home construction or the Dow Jones stock indicator. Contractors do not build houses a square foot at a time, but nonetheless cost per square foot is a useful figure. Software

TABLE 1.3 Example of Basic Function Point Counts

Element	Number		Weights		Total
Inputs	2	×	4	=	8
Outputs	2	×	5	=	10
Inquiries	0	×	4	=	0
Logical files	1	×	10	=	10
Interfaces	1	×	7	=	7
Total					35

Note: Chapter 2 discusses adjustments to the basic counts.

TABLE 1.4 Example of the Mathematical Validity Associated with Function Point Metrics

	Assembler version	Ada version
Number of function points in project	35.0	35.0
Noncoding effort in person-months	3.0	3.0
Coding effort in person-months	3.0	1.0
Total project effort in person-months	6.0	4.0
Net function points per person-month	5.83	8.75

professionals do not build software one function point at a time, but cost per function point is a useful economic metric.

As mentioned, both function points and feature points are totally independent of the number of source code statements, and they will stay constant regardless of the programming language used. Table 1.4 illustrates the same pair of example programs as shown in Table 1.2, only this time productivity is expressed in function points per person-month. Since both the Assembler version and the Ada version are identical in functionality, assume that both versions contain 35 function points.

Observe how the function point metric agrees with both common sense and the economic definition of productivity, since the same quantity of an economic unit (35 function points) has been produced for less labor in the Ada example.

Now that function points have been in use for more than 15 years, some interesting findings have occurred. Indeed, whole new kinds of studies that were previously difficult are now being carried out on a routine basis.

To illustrate the economic advantages of using the function point metric for large-scale studies, Fig. 1.1 shows the approximate U.S. norms or averages for software productivity in 1990 using data form the first edition, and then the averages for 1995. The interesting "bulge" in productivity for the 1995 curve is due in large part to the fact that end-user software applications are now so common that they are included in this second edition.

In the first edition, the overall U.S. average based on the cumulative results of some 4300 software projects was about 5.0 function points per staff-month. The current U.S. average is now about 5.7 function points per staff-month based on the cumulative results of roughly 6700 software projects.

Expressed another way, the average as presented in the first edition implied that each function point required more than 26 hours of human effort. By contrast, the average in this second edition implies a need for only about 24 hours per function point.

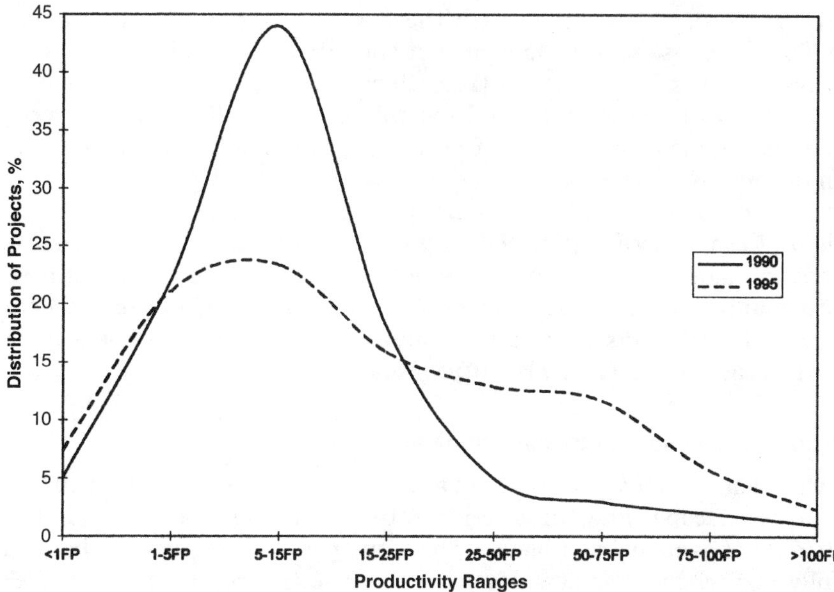

Figure 1.1 Average U.S. software project productivity expressed in function points per staff-month.

However, the overall ranges contained in the author's data are very broad: from a low of about 0.13 function point per staff-month (more than 1000 work hours per function point) to a high of more than 200 function points per staff-month (0.66 work hour per function point).

These wide variances can be explained by careful analysis of the major factors that influence software productivity: (1) overall sizes of the applications; (2) variations in the activities performed; (3) variations in the "soft" factors associated with software development such as tools, languages, and processes.

For example, the arithmetic mean or average of the six major kinds of software discussed in the second edition of this book are as follows:

	Function points per staff-month	Work hours per function point
End-user software	49.5	2.7
Outsourced software	8.4	15.7
Information systems	7.8	16.9
Commercial software	5.3	24.7
Systems software	4.2	31.4
Military software	1.8	73.3

The averages associated with these six categories would be unexplainable unless it were known that the average size of military software projects is almost 25 times larger than the average size of end-user software projects, and the volume of specifications and written material is more than 200 times larger in the military domain than in the end-user domain.

In other words, it is not enough just to have accurate quantitative data. It is also necessary to collect enough information about the factors that influence the data to explain *why* the results vary. Quantitative benchmark data without "soft" assessment data is insufficient to deal with the variations that occur. Conversely, process assessment data without quantification is also insufficient.

Assignment scopes and production rates

Two secondary measures that are extremely useful are those termed "assignment scope" and "production rate." An assignment scope is the amount of some deliverable for which one person will normally be held fully responsible. For new development projects, programmers are normally assigned between 50 and 100 function points as typical workloads.

For the purposes of maintaining existing software (fixing bugs and making small changes), an ordinary programmer will normally be responsible for perhaps 300 to 500 function points if the application is in a normal language such as Cobol. That is a particularly useful statistic, because most large companies have production libraries that total from 200,000 to more than 1 million function points. The average maintenance assignment scope is a key factor for predicting future maintenance staffing requirements.

Once assignment scope data is collected, the assignment scope is a key metric in determining how many technical staff members will be needed for both development and maintenance projects. Dividing the total size of a new project by the average assignment scope derived from a historical project will generate a useful estimate of the average staff size to be required.

The production rate is the amount of some deliverable which one person can produce in a standard time period such as a work-month. The previously mentioned U.S. average of about five function points per staff-month is an example of a production rate. The production rate is a key metric in determining how much effort will be needed in terms of person-months, since the total size of the project divided by the average production rate will generate the amount of effort needed. Thus a project of 50 function points in size divided by an average rate of five function points per person-month should require a total of 10 person-months to be completed.

Once the staffing and person-month of effort values have been created for a project, the approximate schedule can quickly be determined by simply dividing the effort by the staff. For example, a 24-person-month project to be completed by a staff of four people should take about 6 calendar months. Once their logic has become assimilated, assignment scopes and production rates lead to very useful quick-estimating capabilities.

Strategic and Tactical Software Measurement

In military science, strategy is concerned with the selection of overall goals or military objectives, whereas tactics is concerned with the deployment and movement of troops toward those goals. There is a similar dichotomy within corporations that affects the measurement function. A corporate strategy will concern the overall business plan, target markets, competitive situations, and direction of the company. Corporate tactics will concern the specific steps and movement taken to implement the strategy.

For the purposes of measurement, strategic measurements are normally those which involve the entire corporation and the factors which may influence corporate success. Tactical measurements are those which concern specific projects, and the factors which can influence the outcomes of the projects (Table 1.5).

TABLE 1.5 Strategic and Tactical Software Measures

Kind of data	Strategic measures	Tactical measures
Hard	Total staff size	Staffing by activity or task
	Occupation groups	Effort by activity or task
	Portfolio size	Costs by activity or task
	User support	Project deliverables
	Market share studies	Defect rates and severities
	Profitability studies	Function or feature points
	Cancellation factors	Staff assignment scopes
	Annual software costs	Staff production rates
	Annual hardware costs	Project risk analysis
	Annual personnel costs	Project value analysis
Soft	Morale surveys	User satisfaction
	Incentive plans	Effectiveness of tools
	Annual education	Usefulness of methods
	Corporate culture	Appropriate staff skills
	Executive goals	Environment adequacy
	Competitive analysis	Project constraints
Normalized	Total function points	Project size
	Annual function points	Productivity rate(s)
	Function points per user (consumption)	Defect rate(s)
		Cost rate(s)

A full applied software measurement program will include both strategic and tactical measurements. Some of the more common forms of strategic measurement include an annual survey of total data processing expenses vs. competitive companies, an annual survey of staff demographics and occupation groups vs. competitive companies, and an annual survey of the size, mix, quality, current status, and backlog associated with the corporate portfolio.

For productivity itself, sometimes the differences between the strategic concept of productivity and the tactical concept can be surprising. For example, when companies start to think in terms of productivity measurement, most of them begin tactically by measuring the efforts of the direct staff on a set of successfully completed projects. That might generate a number such as an average productivity rate of perhaps eight function points per person-month for the projects included in the tactical study. Tactical project measures are a reasonable way to measure successfully completed projects, but what about projects that are canceled or not successfully completed? What about indirect staff such as executives, administrators, and secretarial people whose salaries are paid by the software budget but who are not direct participants in tactical project work?

A strategic or corporate productivity measurement would proceed as follows: The entire quantity of function points delivered to users in a calendar year by the software organization would be counted. The total software staff effort from the senior software vice president down through secretarial support would be enumerated, including the efforts of staff on canceled projects and the staff on incomplete projects that are still being built. Even user effort would be counted if the users participated actively during requirements and project development. The strategic or corporate productivity metric would be calculated by dividing the total quantity of delivered function points in a calendar year by the total number of person-months of effort expended by the whole organization. This, of course, will generate a much lower number than the previous tactical rate of five function points per person-month, and a normal strategic corporate rate might be only from one to three function points per person-month. The current average is about 1.85.

Both strategic and tactical measurements are important, but they tend to give different insights. The strategic measures tend to be very important at the CEO and senior executive levels; the tactical measures tend to be very important at the group, unit, and project levels.

Plainly, a corporation must pay the salaries and expenses of its entire software organization from the vice presidents downward. It must also pay for canceled projects and for projects that are under development but are not yet complete. The strategic form of productivity measurement tends to be a very useful indicator of overall corporate

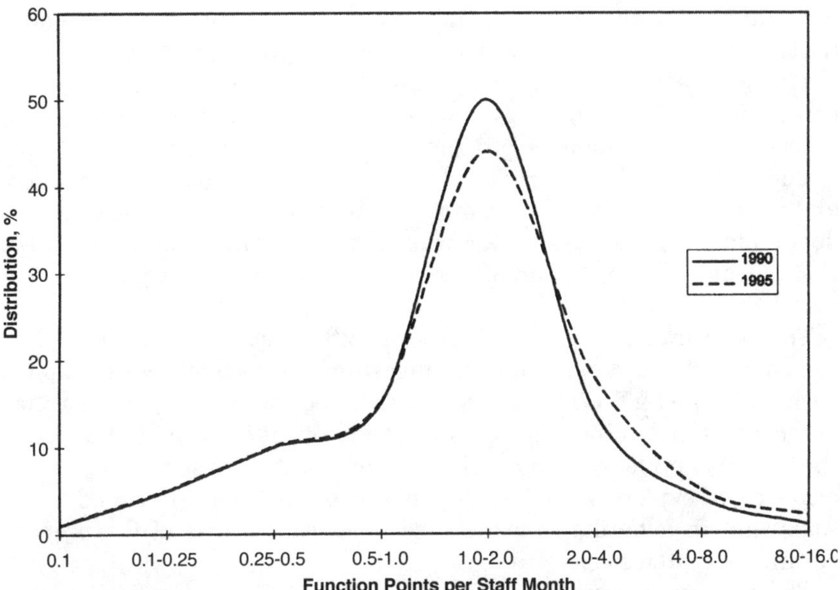

Figure 1.2 U.S. enterprise productivity in 1990 and 1995.

efficiency in the software domain. Figure 1.2 shows average U.S. productivity at the strategic or enterprise level for 1991.

It cannot be overemphasized that both the strategic and tactical forms of measurement are useful, but each serves its own purpose. The strategic form is of great interest to senior executives, who must pay for all software staff and expenses. The tactical form is of great interest to project and divisional managers.

Prior to the advent of function points, it was not technically possible to carry out large-scale strategic measurement studies at the corporate, industry, or national level. Now, however, the functional metrics have been widely deployed, and it is possible to make at least the first steps in exploring productivity differences by company, by industry, and by nation.

Current Measurement Experiences by Industry

The leading high-technology companies that produce both computers and software, such as IBM, Hewlett-Packard, Tandem, and DEC, tend to measure both software productivity and quality and to use the data to make planned improvements. They are also very good at measuring user satisfaction and they are comparatively good at project estimating. The trailing companies within this segment produce only partial quality measurements and little or nothing in the way of productivity measurement. Sociologically, quality tends to receive greater emphasis in high-technology companies than elsewhere because the success of such companies' products demands high quality.

There seems to be a fairly good correlation between high technology and measurement, and the companies that have active research and development programs under way in technical areas, such as Du Pont, General Electric, and Motorola, are often innovative in software measurements too.

The telecommunications manufacturing business, on the whole, has been one of the leaders in software measurement technology. Companies such as ITT, AT&T, GTE, and Northern Telecom have long known that much of their business success depends on quality, and they have therefore been pioneers in quality and reliability measures. Most have also started exploring productivity measures, although they tend to lag somewhat in adopting function-based metrics because of the preponderance of systems software.

The telecommunication operating companies such as Pacific-Bell, on the other hand, have tended to be quite sophisticated with productivity measurements and were early adopters of function points, perhaps because, with thousands of software staff members, productivity is a pressing concern.

When airlines and automotive manufacturers were extremely profitable, neither software productivity nor measurement tended to be emphasized. In the wake of deregulation and reduced earnings for airlines, and in the wake of enormous overseas competition in the automotive segment, both kinds of manufacturers are now attempting to make up for lost time by starting full quality and productivity measurement programs. Airlines such as Delta, American, Quantas, and British Air are taking active steps to enter the software measurement arena, as are automotive manufacturers such as Ford.

Energy and oil production companies, also in the wake of reduced earnings, are now starting to move quickly into the domain of productivity measurement and are beginning to move toward measures of quality and user satisfaction as well. Companies such as Exxon and Amoco were early students of software productivity measurement, and they have been moving into quality and user satisfaction as well.

When the first edition of this book was published in 1991, the pure software houses such as Microsoft and Computer Associates were lagging other industry segments in terms of software measurement technology. However, as the overall size of commercial software begins to approach the overall size of mainframe software, the commercial software world is moving rapidly toward full measurements of both software quality and software productivity. With large systems now being developed for personal computers, the commercial software world has as many problems with schedules as any other industry segment, so topics such as cost estimating are now increasingly important in the commercial software domain.

One of the most impressive advances in software measurement technology is that of the contract and outsource domain. When the first edition of this book was published in 1991, measurements were used for internal purposes within major outsource vendors such as Andersen, Electronic Data Systems (EDS), Keane, and IBM's ISSC division. However, now that global competition is heating up, most of the major outsourcers are making rapid strides in software measurement technology. This is true internationally as well as domestically, and offshore outsourcers such as TATA in India are also advancing rapidly into full software productivity and quality measurements. Indeed, the use of function point measurements is now a global competitive weapon among international outsource vendors. Within the United States, the outsource community is now one of the most sophisticated of any segment in terms of software measurement technology.

Management consulting companies such as Software Productivity Research; DMR Group; Peat, Marwick & Mitchell; Nolan; Norton & Company; and Ernst & Young have often been more effective than universities both in using metrics and in transferring the technologies of measurement throughout their client base.

The defense industry has long been active in measurement, but in part because of government requirements, often attempts to both measure and estimate productivity by using the obsolete lines-of-code metric with unreliable results. Even the measurement initiatives in defense research establishments such as the Software Engineering Institute (SEI) tend to lag behind the civilian sectors. SEI has not yet adopted any of the economically sound function-based metrics, although Watts Humphrey of SEI's attempts to measure the stages of software maturity are attracting much attention.[7] The defense segment is also spotty and incomplete in terms of quality measurement. That is unfortunate, given the size and resources of the defense community. The defense community is among the world leaders in terms of estimating automation, however, and most large defense contractors have professional estimating staffs supported by fully automated software-estimating packages. That does not, of course, mean that the defense industry has an excellent record of estimating accuracy, but it does mean that estimating is taken seriously.

The leading insurance companies, such as Hartford Insurance, UNUM, USF&G, John Hancock, and Sun Life Insurance, tend to measure productivity, and they are now stepping up to quality and user satisfaction measures as well. The trailing companies within the insurance segment seem to measure little or nothing. There is a general correlation with size, in that the larger insurance companies with several thousand software professionals are more likely to use measures than the smaller companies. Insurance is a very interesting industry because it was one of the first to adopt computers and one of the few in which there have been significant correlations between effective measurements and overall corporate profitability.

Banking and financial companies for many years tended to lag in terms of measurement, although there were some exceptions. In the wake of increased competition and dramatic changes in banking technology, the financial institutions as a class are attempting to make up for lost time, and many are mounting large studies in attempts to introduce productivity, quality, and user satisfaction measures as quickly as possible. Interestingly, Canadian banks such as CIBC and the Bank of Montreal may be ahead of U.S. banks such as the Bank of America in software measurement.

In the manufacturing, energy, and wholesale-retail segments, the use of software productivity measurement appears to be proportional to the size of the enterprise: The larger companies with more than 1000 software professionals, such as Sears Roebuck and J.C. Penney, measure productivity, but the smaller ones do not. Quality and user satisfaction measurement are just beginning to heat up within these industry segments.

Such public utilities as electric, water, and some telephone operating companies have started to become serious students of measurement in the wake of deregulation, and they are taking productivity measurement quite seriously. Such companies as Consolidated Edison, Florida Power and Light, and Cincinnati Gas and Electric are becoming fairly advanced in those measurements. Here too, however, quality and user satisfaction measures have tended to lag behind.

In the publishing business, the larger newspapers such as *The New York Times* have tended to be fairly active in both estimating and measurement, as have publishers of specialized documents such as telephone directories. Book publishers, on the other hand, have tended to be very late adopters of either measurement or estimation. It is surprising that some of the leading publishers of software engineering and measurement books are not in fact particularly innovative in terms of their own software methods and metrics!

Federal, state, and local government agencies have not as a rule spent much energy on measuring either software productivity or quality. That is perhaps due to the fact that they are not in a competitive environment. There are some interesting exceptions at the state level, where such government agencies as Human Resources in Florida are starting to measure and estimate well, but by and large government tends to lag behind the private sector in these concepts. At the national or federal level, it is interesting that the internal revenue services in both the United States and Australia tend to be fairly active in both software measurement and software estimating technologies.

Academic institutions and universities are distressingly far behind the state of the art in both intellectual understanding of modern software measurements and the actual usage of such measurements in building their own software. The first college textbook on function points, Dreger's text on *Function Point Analysis,*[8] was not published until 1989, a full 10 years after the metric was placed in the public domain by IBM. Even so, the author is employed by Boeing and is only a part-time faculty member. The number of major U.S. universities and business schools that teach software measurement and estimation concepts appears to be minuscule, and for the few that do the course materials appear to be many years out of date. The same lag can be observed in England and Europe. Interestingly, both New Zealand and Australia may be ahead of the United States in teaching software measurement concepts at the university level.

Using function-based metrics for large-scale industrial studies

A final illustration of how function-based metrics can be used for large-scale studies is illustrated by Table 1.6, which shows a provisional ranking of strategic or corporate software productivity rates for some 40 industrial and governmental segments. The data in the table has a high margin of error and does not actually support two decimal place precision. Table 1.5 is included to show the kinds of large-scale studies that can now be accomplished. Although partial data from more than 400 companies and government agencies is included, that is not a sufficient sample. Also,the raw data itself is highly suspect, since many of the enterprises had notable gaps and errors in their available data. The normalized data is derived primarily by backfiring from source-code metrics to feature points.

The rates in Table 1.6 are based on the total number of person-months for all direct and indirect software staff including executives, administrators, and nonproject support. Rates were estimated by dividing the total delivered feature points by the total accumulated number of person-months for all staff from vice presidents downward. Both direct technical staff and indirect workers such as secretarial support and administrative support are included. The effort amounts also include work expended on canceled projects and on projects which were still under development but not yet ready for delivery. The data in Table 1.5 is not derived from individual projects; it reflects the gross

TABLE 1.6 Ranking of Industries for Gross Software Productivity (Total Function Points Divided by Total Annual Effort)

Overall industry rankings	1991	1995	Difference	Percent
Software consulting groups	3.45	3.85	0.40	11.59
Entertainment (TV, films, games)	3.00	3.70	0.70	23.33
Banking and finance	3.20	3.50	0.30	9.37
Insurance companies	3.40	3.35	−0.05	−1.47
Oil and gasoline production	3.35	3.30	−0.05	−1.49
Telecommunication operating companies	3.20	3.30	0.10	3.12
Commercial software houses	3.50	3.25	−0.25	−7.14
Computer manufacturers	3.38	3.17	−0.21	−6.21
Sports (pro football, baseball)	3.00	3.15	0.15	5.00
Security and commodity brokers	2.80	3.15	0.35	12.50
Chemical and plastic production	2.75	2.75	0.00	0.00
Hotel chains	2.65	2.65	0.00	0.00
Restaurant chains	2.65	2.65	0.00	0.00
Electronics manufacturing	2.50	2.60	0.10	4.00
Aerospace manufacturing	2.25	2.35	0.10	4.44
General manufacturing	2.15	2.15	0.00	0.00
Agricultural production	2.00	2.00	0.00	0.00
Metals fabrication	1.85	1.85	0.00	0.00
Wholesale and retail	1.65	1.60	−0.05	−3.03
Conglomerates	1.50	1.50	0.00	0.00
Automotive manufacturing	1.35	1.35	0.00	0.00
Office equipment manufacturing	1.30	1.30	0.00	0.00
Appliance manufacturing	1.25	1.25	0.00	0.00
Metals and mining	1.20	1.25	0.05	4.17
Airlines	1.25	1.17	−0.08	−6.40
Public utilities (water, gas)	1.05	1.15	0.10	9.52
Universities and academic institutions	1.10	1.10	0.00	0.00
Railroad transportation	1.00	1.00	0.00	0.00
Trucking and warehousing	1.00	1.00	0.00	0.00
Hospitals and health care	0.90	0.90	0.00	0.00
Paper and allied products	0.85	0.90	0.05	5.88
Telecommunications manufacturing	0.65	0.75	0.10	15.38
Food processing	0.60	0.60	0.00	0.00
Printing and publishing	0.55	0.55	0.00	0.00
Defense contractors	0.50	0.55	0.05	10.00
City, county governments	0.50	0.50	0.00	0.00
State governments	0.45	0.50	0.05	11.11
Federal government (civilian)	0.40	0.40	0.00	0.00
Federal government (military)	0.30	0.35	0.05	16.67
Average	1.81	1.86	0.05	3.09

output of an industry divided by the total number of person-months employed by the software functions.

The sequence of industries in Table 1.6 is interesting, and especially so in the light of changes between 1990 and 1995. The major losers in terms of productivity between 1990 and 1995 are the commercial software houses and the computer manufacturers. The commercial software houses are sagging in productivity because the size of modern Windows-based applications is now pushing 5000 function points, while the DOS-based applications were generally below 1000 function points in size. The computer manufacturers have declined because the massive layoffs at IBM, Digital Equipment, Data General, and the like terminated a significant number of projects in middevelopment.

The major winners between 1990 and 1995 are the games and entertainment companies and the commercial outsource vendors. The game community now has a lot of very sophisticated tools available, and quite a few top-notch programmers. The outsource community has the largest volume of reusable material of any industry, and very capable staffs too.

It should be noted that neither the author nor his company perform benchmark studies in every industry every year. For some of the industries that show no change between 1990 and 1995, the reason is that SPR has not been commissioned to gather fresh data.

Factors associated with midrange industries tend to be mixed. Some of these industries may be short of discretionary capital; others may not have compensation rates or environments that attract sufficient quantities of top professionals. For the industries in the lower third of the productivity range, there are at least three possible correlations: (1) unavailability of funds for adequate tooling and support because of low profitability of the industry, (2) excessive volumes of paperwork caused by government or military requirements, (3) industries in which unpaid overtime is not present in any significant amount.

Measurement and the Software Life Cycle

An effective project management measurement system adds value to all of the major phases of software life cycles. Figure 1.3 illustrates the major kinds of measurements associated with each phase. For projects that are enhancements or replacements of existing systems, which in the 1990s comprise the majority of all projects, the structure, complexity, and defect rates of the existing software should be analyzed. It is at this point that the normal project cost tracking system should be initialized for enhancements.

During the requirements phase, function or feature points are enumerated and then the first formal cost estimate is normally prepared.

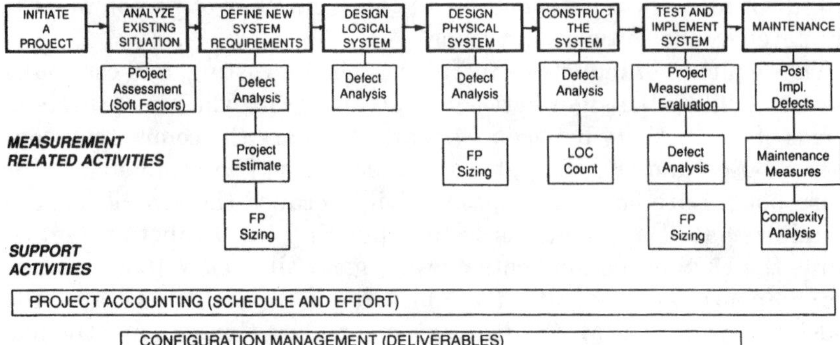

Figure 1.3 Measurement activities and the software life cycle.

For new projects, the requirements phase is the normal point at which the project cost tracking system should be initialized. It is also appropriate to initialize the project defect and quality tracking system, since requirements problems are often a major source of both expense and later troubles.

As the requirements are refined, the next aspect of measurement deals with whether the project should be in the form of a custom application or in the form of a package that is acquired and modified. The risks and value of both approaches are considered.

If the decision is to construct the project, then a second estimate should be prepared in conjunction with the logical design of the application. Since from this point on defect removal can be the most expensive element, it is imperative to utilize reviews and inspection and record defect data. A second and more rigorous cost estimate should be prepared at this time. During physical design, reviews and inspections are also valuable and defect data will continue to accumulate.

The coding or construction phase of an application can be either troublesome or almost effortless depending upon the rigor of the preceding tasks. A third formal cost estimate should be prepared; it will be very rigorous in accumulating costs to date and very accurate in estimating costs to the completion of the project. Defect and quality data recording should also be kept during code reviews or inspections. Complexity measures of the code itself can now be performed as well.

The testing phase of an application can range from a simple unit test by an individual programmer to a full multistage formal test suite that includes function test, integration test, stress test, regression test, independent test, field test, system test, and final acceptance test. Both the defect data and the cost data from the testing phase should be measured in detail and then analyzed for use in subsequent defect prevention activities.

During the maintenance and enhancement phase, both user satisfaction measures and defect measures should be carried out. It is at this point that it becomes possible to carry out retrospective analyses of the defect removal efficiencies of each specific review, inspection, and test and of the cumulative efficiency of the overall series of defect removal steps. A useful figure of merit is to strive for 95 percent cumulative defect removal efficiency. That is, when defects found by the users and defects found by the development team are summed after the first year of usage, the development team should have found 95 percent of all defects.

The Structure of a Full Applied Software Measurement System

A full applied software measurement system for an entire corporation or government agency is a multifaceted undertaking that will include both quality and productivity measures and produce both monthly and annual reports. Figure 1.4 shows the overall schematic of a full enterprise software measurement system. Let us consider the essential components of a full measurement system for software.

Quality measures

Starting at the left of Fig. 1.4, there are two major components of a quality measurement program: user satisfaction measures and defect

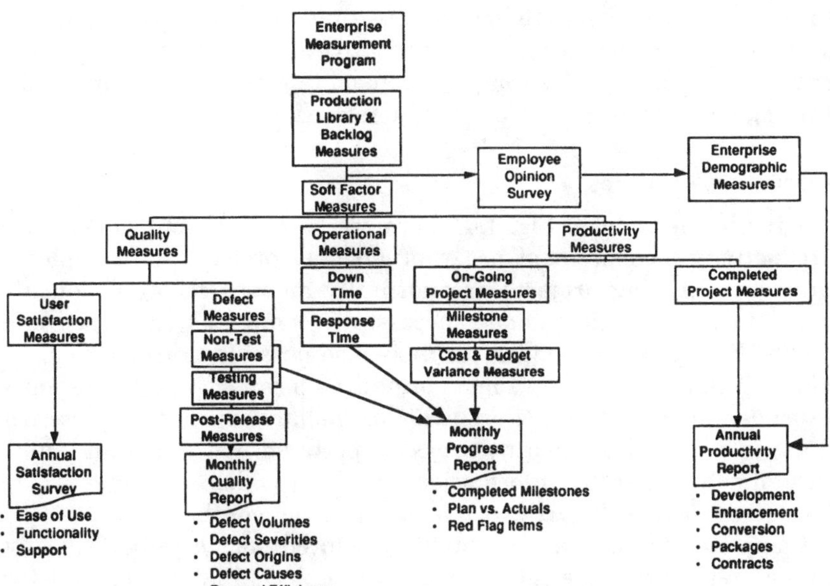

Figure 1.4 Enterprise software measurement system.

measures. User satisfaction is normally assessed once a year by means of interviews; actual users are asked to give their opinions of operational applications. User satisfaction is by definition a soft measure, since opinions are the entire basis of the results.

The second quality factor or defect counts are continuously recorded during project life cycles starting as early as requirements reviews and continuing through maintenance. Defect measures are normally reported on a monthly basis. In a well-planned measurement program, defect counts are one of the key hard-data measures. In trailing-edge companies, either quality in terms of defects is not measured at all or the measurements start so late that the data is woefully incomplete.

One of the most useful by-products of defect measurement is termed "defect removal efficiency." This is defined as the ratio of bugs found prior to installation of a software application to the total number of bugs in the application. Leading-edge enterprises are able to find in excess of 95 percent of all bugs prior to installation, whereas trailing-edge enterprises seldom exceed 70 percent in defect removal efficiency. There appears to be a strong correlation between high defect removal efficiency and such other factors as user satisfaction and overall project costs and schedules, so this is a very important metric indeed.

The measurement of defect removal efficiency is a sure sign that a company is at the leading edge, and only a handful of major corporations such as IBM and AT&T have carried out these powerful measures. Such companies are aware that most forms of testing are less than 30 percent efficient or remove less than one bug of every three, so they have long been augmenting testing with full reviews and inspections. Here too, accurate quantitative data gives the managers and staff of leading-edge companies insights which their peers in the trailing-edge companies do not even know exist!

Productivity measures

Moving to the right in Fig. 1.4, there are two major components of a productivity measurement program: ongoing projects and completed projects. Ongoing projects are normally measured, on a monthly basis, in terms of milestones successfully completed or missed and planned vs. actual expenditures. It is also possible to measure accumulated effort and cost in some normalized form such as "work-hours expended to date per function point" or "dollars expended to date per function point." The monthly project reports normally contain a mixture of soft subjective information such as problem statements and hard data such as dollars expended during the month.

Completed projects are normally measured once a year. Typically, in the first quarter of a calendar year all projects that were completed and installed in the previous year will be measured and analyzed.

This annual measurement of completed projects provides an ever-growing database of historical data and becomes the heart of the enterprise measurement program. Once an enterprise completes its first annual productivity report, it can use that as the baseline for judging improvements over time.

In producing an annual productivity report, all of the relevant soft factors need to be included, and the hard data for the project in terms of deliverables, schedules, staffing, and so forth should be extremely accurate. It is also desirable to convert the hard data into normalized form, such as cost per function point, for comparative purposes.

The annual productivity report will contain both strategic and tactical data, just as a corporate annual report will contain both. Indeed, companies such as IBM, ITT, and Pacific Bell tend to create their annual software productivity reports on the same schedules as the corporate annual reports to stockholders and even to adopt similar formats and production techniques such as the use of high-quality paper, professional graphics, and excellent layouts.

Because new development projects, enhancement projects, maintenance projects (defect repairs), package acquisition projects, and projects involving contract personnel tend to have widely different productivity profiles, it is desirable to segregate the annual data very carefully. This is the area where normalization is most important and where function-based metrics are starting to provide new and sometimes surprising insights into productivity and quality topics.

Production library and backlog measures

Large corporations tend to own many thousands of small programs and some hundreds of large systems, ITT, a major international corporation, surveyed its production library in the early 1980s and found that it owned some 65 million lines of source code, which was equivalent to about 520,000 function points. This software was spread over more than 50 subsidiary corporations and was apportioned among some 28,000 small programs and 2000 large systems. The replacement cost for the production library was in excess of $2 billion.

The ITT backlog of potential applications awaiting development consisted of approximately 65 large new systems and more than 3500 small new programs. In addition, more than 150 large systems and about 5000 small programs were awaiting updates and enhancements. The backlog size was equivalent to about 18 million source code statements or 170,000 function points. This backlog would have taken about four calendar years to implement and about 8500 labor-years. The costs for building the backlog would have approximated $600 million.

An interesting but seldom performed form of production library measurement study is that of the usage patterns of programs and systems, as described by Kendall and Lamb.[5] From a year-long analysis of IBM's data centers, they found that less than 5 percent of the company's applications used more than 75 percent of its machine capacity. Not only that, but standard packages such as the operating systems, sorts, and commercial databases utilized more machine capacity than all custom applications put together. An even more surprising finding was that, of the custom applications owned by IBM, more than two-thirds appeared to be dormant and were not executed at all in the course of the year.

That kind of strategic information is becoming increasingly vital as companies all over the world depend upon computing and software for their operational control and their new products as well. Production library and backlog analyses should become standard strategic measures in all medium-size to large corporations and should be performed on an annual or semiannual basis.

Soft-factor measures

Even accurate recording of quality and productivity data cannot answer questions about why one project is better or worse than another. To answer such questions, it is necessary to come to grips with one of the most difficult aspects of measurement: how to capture soft factors or subjective opinions in a way that can lead to useful insights. Soft-data collection is a necessary adjunct to both quality and productivity measures, and it can be stated that without effective soft-data measurement, the hard data will be almost useless.

This topic of measuring soft factors devolves into two related subtopics: (1) What soft factors should be measured? (2) What is the best way to collect soft data?

Every known factor that can influence software productivity and quality, of which there are more than 200, is a potential soft factor for measurement purposes. The primary soft factors are those which have the greatest known impacts, and this set of primary factors includes the skill and experience of staff, the cooperation of users during requirements and design, schedule or resource constraints, methods employed on the project, tools available, appropriate choice of programming language(s), problem complexity, code complexity, data complexity, project organization structures, and the physical environment.

Although the soft data is subjective, it must be recorded in a way that lends itself to statistical analysis. Since free-form text responses are difficult to analyze, this requirement normally leads to the creation of a multiple-choice questionnaire, so that all of the recorded information can be analyzed by computer. Following is an example of a typical soft-factor multiple choice question to illustrate the principle:

User involvement during development?

1. User involvement is not a major factor.
2. Users are heavily involved during early stages.
3. Users are somewhat involved during early stages.
4. Users are seldom involved during early stages.
5. User involvement is not currently known.

A normal soft-factor questionnaire will contain from 10 to more than 200 questions, such as the one developed by Software Productivity Research.[4]

Operational measures

Operational measures are those which concentrate on the adequacy and responsiveness of the computing environment. They normally include measures of (1) computer availability and downtime, (2) response time for users and development staff, (3) data storage volumes, (4) data storage access, and (5) telecommunications traffic, if any.

Operational measures have traditionally been the first form of metrification used by companies, because computer room efficiency has been studied since the 1950s. Most of the operational measures consist of hard data, but the more sophisticated companies augment simple monthly reports with personal interviews of users to collect soft data on user satisfaction with turnaround and computer room performance. Operational measures are normally considered to be tactical.

Enterprise opinion survey

Leading-edge companies are aware that taking good care of employees pays off in both higher productivity and lower voluntary attrition rates. A normal part of taking good care of employees is an annual opinion survey, which is normally conducted by a personnel group. This, of course, is one of the purest forms of soft data, since it deals primarily with subjective opinions. Opinion surveys are also strategic measures, since staff feelings and opinions have a wide and pervasive influence. It is important that, once such a survey has been conducted, change should follow swiftly. Nothing is more debilitating to morale than an opinion survey followed by inaction. Some of the kinds of topics included in the opinion survey include satisfaction with salary and benefits plans, physical office environments, company polices, and overall management direction. Although by their nature opinion surveys deal with soft or subjective opinions, they differ from the project-related tactical soft-factor studies in that they concentrate on issues that are general or corporate in nature.

Enterprise demographic measures

Now that software is approaching 50 years of age as an occupation, the same kind of specialization is occurring for software professionals that manifested itself for other knowledge workers such as doctors, attorneys, and engineers. It is highly desirable to perform an annual census of the kinds of software specialists needed and employed by the enterprise. This is one of the most useful kinds of strategic hard data that a company can collect for long-range planning purposes.

Some of the kinds of specialists that might be included are quality assurance specialists, technical writers, database administrators, estimating specialists, maintenance specialists, systems programmers, application programmers, human factors specialists, performance specialists, testing specialists, and planning specialists.

In all human activities that have been measured accurately, specialists tend to outperform generalists. Among large corporations with more than 1000 software professionals employed, those with generalists often lag behind those with specialists in terms of software productivity. An annual demographic survey can become a significant tool leading to improvement.

The Sociology of Software Measurement

Establishing an applied measurement program for software requires sensitivity to cultural and social issues. The normal reaction to a measurement program by both project management and staff is apprehension, and only when it is shown that the data will be used for beneficial purposes rather than punitive purposes will the apprehension subside.

The sociology of measurement implies a need for high-level corporate sponsorship of the measurement program when the program is first begun, since the normal reactions of subordinate managers whose projects will actually be measured are dismay, resistance, and apprehension. Normally, either the CEO or an executive vice president would be the overall measurement sponsor and would delegate responsibilities for specific kinds of measures to those lower down in the hierarchy. Indeed at such companies as IBM in the 1960s, ITT in the 1970s, and Hewlett-Packard in the 1980s, it was the demand for accurate measures from the CEO level that started the corporate measurement programs in the first place. The IBM corporate software measurement program has not yet been fully described for external publication, but a description of the Hewlett-Packard software measurement system has been published by Grady and Caswell.[6]

In a well-designed applied measurement program, staff and management apprehension or opposition is very transitory and lasts for only a month or so prior to start-up, after which the real value of accurate measures makes the system expand spontaneously. At Hewlett-Packard, for example, a small experiment in software project measurement was so useful and so successful that over a period of several years it expanded on a voluntary basis into a major international study including virtually all of Hewlett-Packard's software development laboratories. Indeed, the internal measurements have proved to be so valuable that in 1989 Hewlett-Packard began to offer the same kind of software project measurement services to their customers.

What causes the transition from apprehension to enthusiasm is that a well-designed applied measurement program is not used for punitive purposes and will quickly begin to surface chronic problems in a way that leads to problem solution. For example, excessive schedule pressures, inadequate office space, and insufficient computer turnaround may have been chronic problems for years and yet been more or less invisible. But a good measurement program can spot the impact of such problems and quantify the benefits of their solution.

It is an interesting phenomenon that new commercial software measurement tools have been entering the market at almost monthly intervals during the years from 1993 through 1995. A significant percentage of such tools are from start-up companies founded by former employees of companies such as AT&T, IBM, Hewlett-Packard, Motorola, or other companies with well-developed in-house measurement programs.

The rationale for these start-ups is that measurements were so valuable when they exist that the commercial marketing of measurement tools should be profitable. The general growth and success of the measurement subindustry to date make it look as if this rationale is a valid one.

The sociology of data confidentiality

In many companies, corporate politics have such prominence that project managers and some executives will be afraid to submit their data to a corporate measurement group unless the confidentiality of their data is guaranteed by the measurement group. That is, each manager will want to find out personally how his or her data compares to the corporate or group average but will not want that data distributed to other project groups or to "rival" managers.

Although it is sometimes necessary for reasons of corporate culture to start a measurement program on a confidential basis, the approach is both sociologically and technically unsound. In a mature and well-managed enterprise, software productivity and quality measurements are normal business tools and should have about the same visibility and the same security classification as corporate financial data. A branch sales manager, for example, could hardly insist on the confidentiality of the branch's quarterly profit-and-loss data.

Group, divisional, and corporate executives should receive productivity and quality reports on all projects and units within their scope of responsibility, just as they receive profit-and-loss reports or normal financial reports. A well-designed software measurement program will not be a punitive weapon; it will identify all weaknesses that need correction and point out all strengths that need encouragement.

Another disadvantage of data confidentiality is that it tends to lower the credibility of the measures themselves. For the first year of ITT's corporate measurement program in 1980, the data was held in confidence. The consequence was that no one really cared about the results. In the second year, when the projects were explicitly identified, acceptance of the measurements as important to managers and executives increased dramatically.

The sociology of using data for staff performance targets

Once a company begins to collect software productivity and quality data, there is a natural tendency to want to use the data to set staff performance targets. That, of course, is one of the reasons for apprehension in the first place. Leading-edge companies such as IBM and Hewlett-Packard do set performance targets, but for sociological and business reasons the targets should be set for executives at the director and vice presidential level, rather than for the technical staff.

The major reason for that is that executives are in a much better position to introduce the changes necessary to achieve targets than are technical staff members or first-line managers. Neither the technical staff nor subordinate managers are authorized to purchase better tools and workstations, stop work and receive necessary education, or introduce new practices such as full design and code inspections. Executives, on the other hand, can do all those things.

A secondary reason for establishing executive targets is likely to become more and more important in the future: Corporate officers have a legal and fiduciary duty to achieve professional levels of software quality, and if they do not, both their companies and themselves may find expensive lawsuits and perhaps even consequential damages in their futures!

Perhaps the single event that more than any other made IBM a leader in software quality for many years was the establishment in

1973 of numeric quality targets for software executives and the inclusion of those targets in their performance and bonus plans. Prior to that time, IBM, like many other companies, talked about achieving high quality, but when the pressure of business caused a choice between opting for high quality or skipping something like inspections to try to shorten delivery dates, quality seldom won. Once IBM's vice presidents and directors had quality goals in their performance plans, however, quality was no longer just being given lip service but became a true corporate incentive.

The sociology of measuring one-person projects

More than half of all software projects in the world are small projects that are carried out by a single programmer or programmer-analyst. This situation requires special handling, since it is obvious that all data collected on one-person projects can easily be used for appraisal purposes. The delicacy of measuring one-person projects is especially sensitive in Europe, where some countries prohibit the measurement of an individual worker's performance either because of national law, as in Sweden, or because the software staffs are unionized and such measurements may violate union agreements, as in Germany.

The normal solution to this problem in large companies such as IBM and ITT can be one or more of several alternatives: The basic alternative is to establish a cutoff point of perhaps two person-years and simply not measure any project that is smaller. This solution tends to concentrate the measurements on the larger and more costly projects, where, indeed, the value of measurement is greatest. A second solution is to collect one-person project data on a voluntary basis, since many programmers are perfectly willing to have their work measured. It is, however, tactful to ask for volunteers. A third solution, possible only in very large companies, is to aggregate all small one-person projects and then create an overall set of small-project statistics that does not drop below the division or laboratory level.

Of course, it is also possible to bite the bullet and use one-person project data for appraisal purposes, and some companies indeed do that. It is, however, very likely to lead to morale problems of a significant nature and perhaps even to lawsuits by indignant staff members who may challenge the measurements in court.

The sociology of MIS vs. systems software

Many large high-technology corporations produce both management information systems (MIS) projects and also systems software, such as operating systems or telecommunication systems. Some also produce other kinds of software as well: process control, scientific software, mathematical analysis, and so on.

Generally speaking, the MIS staffs and the systems software staffs have such difficulty communicating and sharing technical ideas that they might as well inhabit different planets. The dichotomy will affect measurement programs too, especially since systems software productivity is normally somewhat lower than MIS productivity because of the larger number of tasks performed and the effect of the soft factors. The natural reaction by the systems software groups to this fact is to assert that systems software is much more complex than MIS applications. Indeed, many systems software producers have rejected function-based metrics for two reasons: Function points originated in the MIS domain, and MIS projects normally have higher productivity rates.

This kind of dispute occurs so often that companies should plan remedial action when beginning their measurement programs. There are several possible solutions, but the most pragmatic one is simply to segregate the data along clear-cut lines and compare MIS projects primarily to other MIS projects and systems software primarily to other systems software. A more recent solution is to adopt the feature point metric for systems software productivity measures, since the built-in assumptions of feature points about algorithmic complexity tend to generate higher totals for systems software than for MIS projects.

Whatever solution a company decides on, the problem of needing to be sensitive to the varying software cultures needs attention right from the start.

The sociology of measurement expertise

The managers and technical staff workers who embark on a successful measurement project are often surprised to find permanent changes in their careers. There is such a shortage of good numerical information about software projects and such enormous latent demand by corporate executives that, once a measurement program is started, the key players may find themselves becoming career measurement specialists. This phenomenon has affected careers in surprising ways. From informal surveys carried out by Software Productivity Research, almost half of the measurement managers are promoted as a result of their work. About a third of the managers and technical staff workers who start corporate measurement programs work in the measurement area for more than 5 years thereafter. Both A. J. Albrecht and the author began their measurement careers with short measurement projects intended to last for less than 2 months. In both cases, the demand for more measurement information led to long-term careers.

Justifying and Building an Applied Software Measurement Function

For most U.S. companies other than those at the very leading edge such as IBM, Hewlett-Packard, AT&T, and a few others, a software measurement program will be a new and perhaps exotic concept. It will be necessary to justify the costs of measurement and to plan the staffing and sequence of establishing the measurement function with great care. The following are the major topics that must be considered.

The value of applied software measurement programs

It is, of course, not possible to perform direct productivity or quality comparisons between companies that measure and companies that do not, since only the ones that measure have any data. This phenomenon creates a trap of circular reasoning within companies that do not measure: Executives tend to say "prove to me that measurements will be valuable." But since the same executives have no idea of their current levels of productivity, quality, or user satisfaction, there is no baseline against which the proofs can be made.

Project managers and executives in companies that do not measure software numerically actually have a vested interest in preventing measurements from occurring. They suspect, rightly, that their performances will not be shown in a favorable light if measurements occur, and so they tend to obstruct metrics work rather than support it.

To make an initial case for the value of measurements, it is often necessary to depend on such indirect factors as market share, user satisfaction, and profitability. It is also necessary to gain the support of executives high enough in the company, or secure enough in self-esteem, that they will not feel threatened by the advent of a measurement program.

Software measurement is a very powerful defect prevention technology, and also can assist in raising defect removal efficiency. Software measurement can minimize poor investments and optimize good investments. As a result, software quality measurements have one of the best returns on investment of any software technology, and software productivity measurements are useful also.

Following are the approximate returns on each $1 invested in 10 current technologies. The investments are the results after 4 years of usage of the technology. This data is extracted from the author's book *Assessment and Control of Software Risks* (Prentice-Hall, 1994).

Technology	Return on investment, $, for each $1 after 4 years of usage
Full software reusability	30
1-CASE	25
Software quality measurements	17
Software estimation tools	17
Formal design inspections	15
Formal code inspections	15
Object Oriented programming	12
Software productivity measurements	10
Software process assessment	10
Functional metrics	8

Software quality measurements provide one of the highest ROIs of any technology and are far easier to get started than a full reusability program or a full I-CASE development environment.

Let us consider the value of measurement to a specific major corporation that has measured for many years: IBM. It is often said that "knowledge is power," and perhaps no other company in history has had available so much knowledge of its software. One of the major reasons for IBM's long dominance of the computer industry is that its founder, Thomas Watson, Sr., was personally insistent that IBM strive for the highest levels of quality and user satisfaction possible, and he introduced quality measures very early in the corporation's history. Both Watson, his son Thomas Watson, Jr., and the other IBM chairmen have continued that trend. It is revealing to consider some of the kinds of measurement data available within IBM but not necessarily available to most of IBM's major competitors.

IBM's quality data includes full defect recording from the first requirements review through all forms of inspection and all forms of testing and then all customer-reported bugs as well. IBM probably knew the measured efficiencies of every kind of software review, inspection, and test before any other corporation in the world, and it was able to use that data to make net corporate software quality improvements of about 5 to 1 during the late 1960s and early 1970s. Although IBM put much of this data into the public domain, very few competitors bothered to replicate IBM's findings! Of course, even IBM puts out some low-quality products and makes mistakes. But in terms of the percent of all products in the market that have high quality, few companies can equal IBM's overall rates.

IBM was also the first company to discover that software quality and software productivity were directly coupled and that the projects with the lowest defect counts by customers were those with the shortest schedules and the highest development productivity rates. This phenomenon, discovered by IBM in the early 1970's and put in the public domain in May 1975, is still not understood by many other software-producing enterprises that tend to think that quality and productivity are separate issues.

IBM's customer-reported defect database is so powerful and sophisticated that IBM can produce reports showing the origins and severities of defects for any product, for any month of any year, in any country, and in every major city. The data can also be sorted by industry as well. Software managers and senior executives in IBM receive such data monthly, and they also receive cumulative trends that show long-term progress for each product, each laboratory, each division, and the corporation as a whole.

IBM's user satisfaction surveys also revealed, long before most other companies realized this point, that user satisfaction and numeric defect rates were directly correlated. Projects with low defect counts tended to be high in user satisfaction; projects with high defect counts tended to be low in user satisfaction. This discovery also was made in the early 1970s.

IBM's employee demographic and opinion survey data can identify all technical occupation groups within the company and both the current and past morale history of every laboratory, branch office, and manufacturing location within the corporation. It is also possible for IBM executives to gain other kinds of useful information, such as the annual attrition rates of each location by occupation group within the company.

In addition to these software and demographic measurements, IBM managers and executives have an enormous quantity of economic and market data available to them, including the histories of the economic trends of all countries, demographic and population statistics of all cities in more than 100 countries, and the sales statistics of every IBM product in every geographic region of the world, every industry, and every time period for more than 15 years in the past and projected forward for more than 10 years in the future.

IBM's software productivity measures included systems, military, and MIS software projects. The multiple regression techniques used by Felix and Walston of IBM's Federal Systems Division[9] were published in 1977 as a landmark study which showed the factors that influenced software productivity. The analysis of the mathematical errors of lines of code was first published by the author in the *IBM Systems Journal* in 1978[2]; it proved conclusively that lines of code could never match economic productivity assumptions. Function points were invented within IBM for MIS projects by A. J. Albrecht of IBM's Data Processing Services Division and placed in the public domain in October 1979.[3] The insights and correlations based on that metric have been used by IBM to make far-reaching improvements in software methods and tools.

Of course, even with all of this data IBM can sometimes make mistakes and can sometimes be surprised, as by the success of the original personal computer or by the decline in large mainframe sales in the middle 1980s. Nonetheless, IBM managers and executives tend to have at least 10 times as much valid measurement-based data available to them as do equivalent managers and executives in most other companies, and IBM's long-term success is in large part due to that wealth of factual information.

Another well-known company that is beginning to become aware of the value of software measurement is Microsoft. Now that Microsoft's products have grown from small applications of a few hundred function points up to more than 5000 function points for EXCEL and Microsoft Word, and more than 50,000 function points for Windows 95, Microsoft is moving very rapidly into the software measurement arena. For example, as of 1995, Microsoft has one of the best quality and defect measurement systems in the software world.

The only lagging portion of Microsoft's measurement program is the lack of widespread support for function point metrics. The reason for this, perhaps, is that Microsoft has been one of the most productive companies for small applications in the world. Therefore, productivity measurements were more or less irrelevant, since there was no serious competitor to be compared against.

Now that Microsoft is developing applications that involve hundreds of personnel and require several years of development, it may be that productivity measurements based on function points will become as important in Microsoft as elsewhere in the software world.

The costs of applied software measurement programs

Accurate and complete measurements of software are not inexpensive; indeed, the costs can approximate the costs of a corporate cost accounting function. In the companies that have full applied measurement programs for software, the annual costs can sometimes exceed 4 to 5 percent of the total software budget, with about 2 percent being spent on measuring productivity and 2 to 3 percent spent on measuring quality and user satisfaction. By coincidence, the same breakdown often occurs in soft- and hard-data collection: about 2 percent for collecting the soft factors and about 2 to 3 percent for collecting the hard data from completed projects on an annual basis.

Very large corporations such as IBM, Hewlett-Packard, and AT&T can have permanent corporate measurement staffs in excess of a dozen individuals, regional or laboratory measurement staffs of half a dozen at each major site, and intermittent involvement in measurements by several hundred managers and staff members. The companies that have full software measurement programs are also the companies with the best track records of success in terms of both bringing software projects to completion and achieving high levels of user satisfaction afterwards. They also tend to be industry leaders in respect to morale and employee satisfaction.

The skills and staffing of a measurement team

Most universities and academic institutions have no courses at all in the measurement of software quality, productivity, or user satisfaction, so it is seldom possible to hire entry-level personnel with anything like an adequate academic background for the work at hand. Business schools and MBA programs also are deficient in these topics, so most companies are forced to substitute on-the-job training and industry experience in software management for formal credentials.

Some of the skills available in measurement teams such as those at IBM, AT&T, Du Pont, Hewlett-Packard, and ITT include a good knowledge of statistics and multivariate analysis, a thorough grounding in the literature of software engineering and software project management, a knowledge of software planning and estimating methods and the more powerful of the available tools, a knowledge of forms design, a knowledge of survey design, a knowledge of quality control methods including reviews, walk-throughs, inspections, and all standard forms of testing, a knowledge of the pros and cons of all software metrics including the new function-based metrics, and knowledge of accounting principles.

The special skills and knowledge needed to build a full measurement program are so scarce in the United States as a whole that many companies begin their measurement programs by bringing in one or more of the management consultants who specialize in such tasks. Once the consulting group assists in the start-up phase, the corporate measurement team takes over the future studies and measurements.

The placement and organization of the measurement function

Measurement of software productivity, quality, and user satisfaction works best with a dedicated staff of professionals, just as cost accounting and financial measurement works best with a dedicated staff of professionals. Leading-edge companies that recognize this fact will normally establish a corporate measurement focal point under an executive at about the level of a director or third-line manager. This focal point will often report to someone at the level of a vice president, executive vice president, or chief information officer (CIO). The corporate measurement group will coordinate overall measurement responsibilities and will usually produce the annual productivity report. As with finance and cost accounting, the larger units and subordinate organizations within the corporation may have their own local measurement departments as well.

The raw data collected from tracking systems, in-depth studies, surveys, interviews, and other sources should be validated at the source prior to being sent forward for aggregation and statistical analysis. However, some wrong data seems to always slip by, so the corporate group must ensure that all incoming data is screened, and questionable or incorrect information must be corrected. The raw data itself can either be collected by local personnel on the scene, by traveling data collection specialists from the unit or corporate measurement function, or even by outside consultants if the enterprise is just getting started with measurement.

If the corporation has a formal quality assurance (QA) function, the defect-related data will normally be collected by QA personnel. Quality data can, of course, be reported separately by the QA staff, but it should also be consolidated as part of the overall corporate reporting system.

User satisfaction data for commercial software houses and computer companies is often collected by the sales and marketing organization, unless the company has a human factors organization. Here too, the data can be reported separately as needed, but it should be consolidated as part of the overall corporate reporting system.

If the company does not have either a sales and marketing organization or a human factors organization, it would be normal to bring in a management consulting group that specializes in user satisfaction measurements to aid during the start-up phase.

The sequence of creating an applied software measurement program

For sociological reasons, measurement programs are often established in a sequence rather than as an attempt to measure all factors simultaneously. As a rule of thumb, companies at the extreme leading edge such as IBM will have all nine measurements deployed. To be considered a leading-edge enterprise at all, a company will have at least five of the nine measurement classes operational. Trailing companies will usually have no more than the first two forms of measurement deployed. At the extreme rear of the trailing edge are the unfortunate companies that have no measurements at all. They tend to be short-lived organizations whose future is not likely to be happy, and they stand a good chance of failing or being acquired by better-managed competitors.

The time span for creating a full software measurement program will vary with the urgency and executive understanding of the value of measurement. IBM's measurement program tended to evolve naturally over many years, and it started with opinion surveys even before the computer era. IBM got into quality measures even before software and computers became prominent in its product line, and it was perhaps the first U.S. company to actually measure software quality. Its software quality measures were started in 1964 for commercial and systems software, and it added productivity measures in 1968. Function points were invented within IBM's DP Services Division in about 1975 and placed in the public domain in October 1979. Thus, for more than 30 years, IBM's management and executives have had useful data available to aid in improving software quality and productivity.

ITT, on the other hand, had very few software measures of any kind other than an annual demographic survey prior to 1980. In 1981, ITT entered into a crash measurement program and implemented both quality and productivity measurements in less than a single calendar year. That is about as fast as a large company can enter the measurement arena.

The observed sequence of measurement in successful large enterprises tends to follow this pattern:

1. *Operational measures:* Historically, operational measures have been first. Most companies already record the key operational measures of computer utilization, downtime, and response time. These measures may be used for charge-backs, and they normally serve to keep tabs on the overall health of the computing complex. Operational measures have been common since the 1950s.

2. *Ongoing project measures:* Many large companies already require monthly status reports from project managers on accomplished milestones or planned vs. actual expenditures. Informal monthly ongoing project measures are common, but they are not always very effective as early warning indicators because of a natural human tendency to conceal bad news if possible. On-going project measures have been fairly common since the 1950s in large or very large corporations.

3. *Production library and backlog measures:* When the CEO and senior executives of corporations begin to sense how much money is tied up in software, they naturally want to find out the true dimensions of the corporation's investment. When they ask the CIO or senior software vice president, the initial answer is likely to be "I don't

know." This embarrassing exposure quickly tends to trigger a full production library and backlog study which will often be performed by an outside management consulting group that specializes in such tasks.

4. *User satisfaction measures:* The next measurement that companies tend to implement is that of user satisfaction. It is a basic metric for enterprises that market software and an important metric for internal information systems as well. Effective measurement of user satisfaction normally requires actual interviews with users. Forms and questionnaires alone are seldom sufficient to find out what really needs to be known, although such information is certainly helpful. User satisfaction surveys for software and computing products started in the late 1950s and 1960s.

5. *Completed project measures:* Now that function-based metrics have become widespread, many companies have started counting the function point totals of completed projects and accumulating resource data as well. This form of measurement can be useful, but neither function points nor resource data alone can deal with the issue of why some projects succeed and others fail. Nonetheless, it is a sign of growing sophistication when a company begins to collect accurate hard data and functional metrics from completed projects. Although some companies such as IBM have been measuring since the 1960s, completed project measures have only started to become common during the 1980s as a by-product of the development of function-based metrics.

6. *Soft-factor measures:* When a company begins to strive for leadership, it is natural to want to know everything that is right and everything that is wrong about the way it does business. At this point, such a company will start an in-depth survey of all of the soft factors that influence software projects. That is, it will perform a project-by-project survey of the methods, tools, skills, organization, and environment available for software development and maintenance. The soft factors can be used to eliminate weaknesses and augment strengths. The soft factors and the completed project data can be collected at the same time, and they can even be part of the same survey questionnaire or instrument. Soft-factor measures started to undergo serious study in the 1970s, and they matured in the 1980s.

7. *Software defect measures:* Only the true industry leaders such as IBM have stepped up to the task of measuring software defect rates, and this is a partial explanation of IBM's long-term success. Since the cost of finding and fixing bugs has historically been the largest software cost element, quality control is on the critical path to productivity control. Also, there is a strong observed correlation between defect levels and user satisfaction; users seldom give favorable evaluations to software products with high defect rates. Only a handful of U.S. companies have accurate measures of software defect rates

and defect removal, and they tend to dominate their industry segments. The leading-edge U.S. companies began their defect measures in the 1960s, but for many others, this will be a topic of the 1990s.

8. *Enterprise demographic measures:* Very few companies realize how important their employees truly are to corporate success. Those that do tend to perform annual demographic surveys of exactly how many employees they have in the skill classes that are relevant to corporate goals. The data can then be used for long-range projections over time. Unfortunately, some otherwise very sophisticated companies have not been able to carry out demographic surveys because of their tendency to lump all staff members under such job titles as "member of the technical staff." Since more than 40 kinds of specialists are associated with software, it will become increasingly important to include demographic measures as part of the overall corporate measurement program in the future. The military services and some government agencies have been keeping track of job categories since prior to World War II, but for many companies this will be a task for the 1990s.

9. *Enterprise opinion survey:* An opinion survey is last on the list not because it is least important, but because it requires the greatest amount of lead time and is the greatest change in corporate culture to begin implementation. Opinion surveys, of course, affect all employees and not just the software staffs, so it is necessary to have support and backing from the entire executive ranks. It is also necessary to have the survey instruments acquired or produced by personnel experts, or the results at best will be misleading and at worst may be harmful. Finally, it is necessary for the company to face reality and try to solve any major problems which the opinion survey uncovers. Opinion surveys are, of course, older than the computer era, and industry leaders have been using them since the 1950s. For many companies, opinion surveys must be a topic to be addressed in the 1990s.

Applied Software Measurement and Future Progress

Progress in all scientific and engineering work has been closely coupled to accurate measurements of basic phenomena. Without the ability to measure voltage, resistance, and impedance, there could be no electrical engineering. Without the ability to measure temperature, blood pressure, and blood types, medical practice could scarcely exist. Without the ability to measure barometric pressure, wind velocity, and wind direction, meteorology would be even more imperfect than it is today.

Software is at a pivotal point in its intellectual history. For the first 45 years of existence, it achieved a notorious reputation as the worst-measured engineering discipline of the twentieth century. Now that accurate and stable software measures are possible, the companies that seize the opportunity to base their improvements on quantified, factual information can make tremendous progress.

The companies that wish to improve but do not measure are at the mercy of fads and chance. Progress may not be impossible, but it is certainly unlikely. Only when software engineering is placed on a base of firm metrical information can it take its place as a true engineering discipline rather than an artistic activity, as it has been for much of its history. Measurement is the key to progress, and it is now time for software to learn that basic lesson.

Suggested Readings

Arthur, Jay, *Measuring Programmer Productivity and Software Quality,* Wiley Press, 1985. Jay Arthur is a software engineering researcher at U.S. West. In his book he discusses the pros and cons of various measurement techniques from the standpoint of how real companies are likely to use the information.

Conte, S. D., H. E. Dunsmore, and V. Y. Shen, *Software Engineering Metrics and Models,* The Benjamin/Cummings Publishing Company, Inc., Menlo Park, Calif., 1986, 396 pages. This book contains descriptions of most of the relevant metrics that can be used on software projects, together with suggestions for their applicability. It also contains discussions of statistical sampling, validation of data, and other useful information. Although aimed more at software engineering than at management information, it nonetheless covers the field in more depth than almost any other source. It is a good book for anyone getting started in metrics selection or evaluation.

Jones, Capers, *Program Quality and Programmer Productivity,* Technical Report TR 02.764, IBM Corporation, San Jose, Calif., 1977, 96 pages. This report reveals as much as IBM has ever chosen to reveal about the internal measurements of large systems software projects within the company. It includes data on a number of related topics, including productivity, quality, machine utilization, and the technologies which IBM had concluded were beneficial or harmful. For competitors of IBM, it is significant to note that the report, although published in 1977, contained more than 10 years worth of historical information which had already been available within the company.

———, *Assessment and Control of Software Risks,* Prentice-Hall, Englewood Cliffs, N.J., 1994. This book discusses some 65 risk factors noted during SPR's software process assessments. The risks are both technical and social in nature. Technical risks include those of poor quality, long schedules, and inadequate planning and estimating. Social risks include friction between clients and software groups, and the very serious situation of friction between software executives and corporate executives. For each risk, there is a discussion of how the risk might be prevented or controlled. Other information includes discussions of the return on investment in various software technologies.

———, *Patterns of Software System Failure and Success,* Thomson International, Boston, Mass., 1996. This book is based on research into two extreme conditions at opposite ends of the spectrum: (1) projects that set new records for software quality and productivity; (2) projects that failed totally and were canceled without being completed. Both technical and social factors contributed to both conditions. Poor management practices tended to outweigh technical factors for canceled projects, with planning, estimating, and quality control approaching or exceeding malpractice thresholds. Successful projects, as might be expected, were much better at estimation, planning, and quality control. They also tended to have reduced levels of creeping requirements and larger volumes of reusable materials.

———, *A History of Software Engineering in IBM from 1972 to 1977,* Software Productivity Research, Inc.; Burlington, Mass., 1989, 25 pages. This report is the history of a critical 5-year period in IBM, during which time software evolved from a relatively low-key support function for hardware devices into a true strategic product line. In 1972, software projects had grown enormously in size and complexity, but IBM's methods of managing and measuring progress were still groping with the changes. Each year during the period, a major problem was addressed and brought under control. In every case, the availability of measured data provided a background of facts which enabled IBM's senior management to make usually sound business decisions.

———, *A 10 Year Retrospective of Software Engineering within ITT from 1979 to 1989,* Software Productivity Research, Inc., Burlington, Mass., 1989, 35 pages. This report shows the evolution of software engineering methods within a major corporation, and it illustrates how measurement data became one of the most powerful tools for making rapid improvements in both quality and productivity of software projects. It also discusses the creation and functions of the well-known ITT Programming Technology Center, which was one of the premier R&D laboratories for software in the United States prior to ITT's sale of several divisions to Alcatel.

Sayward, F. G., and M. Shaw, *Software Metrics,* MIT Press, Cambridge, Mass., 1981, 399 pages. Fred Sayward was one of the researchers at the well-known ITT Programming Technology Center. This book is yet another of the dozen or so written or edited by researchers of that organization. It contains a very useful discussion on the design of experiments and on ensuring that measured data is not biased by accident or poor collection techniques. It also contains useful discussions of many standard software engineering metrics.

References

1. Jones, Capers, *U.S. Industry Averages for Software Productivity and Quality,* Version 4.0, Software Productivity Research, Inc., Burlington, Mass., December 1989, 37 pages.
2. Jones, Capers, "Measuring Programming Quality and Productivity," *IBM Systems Journal,* 17, no. 1, 1978, vol. IBM Corporation, Armonk, N.Y., pp. 39–63.
3. Albrecht, A. J., "Measuring Application Development Productivity," *Proceedings of the Joint SHARE, GUIDE, and IBM Application Development Symposium, October 1979.* Reprinted in Capers Jones, *Programming Productivity—Issues for the Eighties,* IEEE Press, Catalog Number EHO239-4, 1986, pp. 35–44.
4. Software Productivity Research, Inc., *CHECKPOINT™ Questionnaire,* Version 1.2, Software Productivity Research, Inc., Burlington, Mass., 1989, 55 pages.
5. Kendall, R. C., and E. C. Lamb, "Management Perspectives on Programs, Programming, and Productivity," presented at *GUIDE 45,* Atlanta, Ga., 1977. Reprinted in Capers Jones, *Programming Productivity—Issues for the Eighties,* IEEE Press, Catalog Number EHO239-4, 1986, pp. 35–44.
6. Grady, R. B., and D. C. Caswell, *Software Metrics: Establishing a Company-Wide Program,* Prentice-Hall, Englewood Cliffs, N.J., 1987, 288 pages.
7. Humphrey, W., *Managing the Software Process,* Addison-Wesley, Reading, Mass., 1989, 489 pages.
8. Dreger, J. Brian, *Function Point Analysis,* Prentice-Hall, Englewood Cliffs, N.J., 1989, 185 pages.
9. Walston, C., and C. P. Felix, "A Method of Programming Measurement and Estimation," *IBM Systems Journal,* vol. 10, no. 1, 1977. Reprinted in Capers Jones, *Programming Productivity—Issues for the Eighties,* IEEE Press, Catalog Number EHO239-4, 1986, pp. 60–79.

Chapter

2

The History and Evolution of Functional Metrics

The Invention and First Publication of Function Points

Between the publication of the first edition in 1991 and this second edition, function point metrics have become the dominant measurement instrument for software in the United States, Canada, Australia, New Zealand, South Africa, and much of Europe. Function point measurements are also expanding rapidly in the Pacific Rim, India, and South America.

As noted in Chap. 1, function points were invented by A. J. Albrecht of IBM in the middle 1970s.[1] A function point is a synthetic metric that is comprised of the weighted totals of the inputs, outputs, inquiries, logical files or user data groups, and interfaces belonging to an application. Once an application's function point total is known, the metric can be used for a variety of useful economic purposes, including:

1. Studies of software production
   - Function points per person-month
   - Work-hours per function point
   - Development cost per function point
   - Maintenance cost per function point
2. Studies of software consumption
   - Function points owned by an enterprise
   - Function points needed by various kinds of end users

- Build, lease, or purchase decision making
- Contract vs. in-house decision making
- Software project value analysis

3. Studies of software quality

- Test cases and runs required per function point
- Defects discovered per function point

To make an abstract topic concrete, Fig. 2.1 illustrates the essential topics that function points seek to enumerate. An average software application will normally have inputs and outputs that affect the end users, and many applications will also have inquiry capabilities. The application will normally also have data storage capabilities whereby information of interest to users can be kept and updated. Finally, the application may be part of a system, or it may share data with external applications.

After being used internally within IBM for several years, function points were discussed publicly for the first time in October 1979 in a paper which Albrecht presented at a joint SHARE/GUIDE/IBM conference held at Monterey, California.[2]

When he invented function points, Albrecht was working for IBM's Data Processing Services group. He had been given the task of measuring the productivity of a number of software projects. Because IBM's DP Services group developed custom software for a variety of other organizations, the software projects were written in a wide variety of languages: Cobol, PL/I, RPG, APL, and assembly language, to name but a few, and some indeed were written in mixed languages.

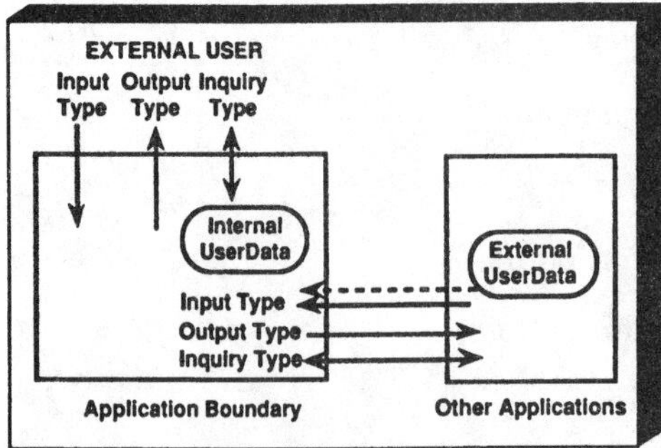

Figure 2.1 A basic application and its function point parameters.

Albrecht knew, as did many other productivity experts, that it was not technically possible to measure software production rates across projects written in different levels of language with the traditional lines-of-code measures.

Other researchers knew the problems that existed with lines-of-code measures, but Albrecht deserves the credit for going beyond those traditional and imperfect metrics and developing a technique that can be used to explore the true economics of software production and consumption.

Albrecht's paper on function points was first published in 1979 in the conference proceedings, which had only limited circulation of several hundred copies. In 1981, with both IBM's and the conference organization's permission, the paper was reprinted in the IEEE tutorial entitled *Programming Productivity: Issues for the Eighties* by the author.[3] This republication by the IEEE provided the first widespread circulation of the concept of function point metrics outside IBM.

The IEEE tutorial brought together two different threads of measurement research. In 1978, the author had published an analysis of the mathematical problems and paradoxes associated with lines-of-code measures.[4] That article, also included in the 1981 IEEE tutorial, proved mathematically that lines of code were incapable of measuring productivity in the economic sense. Thus it provided strong justification for Albrecht's work on function point metrics, which were the first in software history that could be used for measuring economic productivity.

It should be recalled that the standard economic definition of productivity is: "Goods or services produced per unit of labor or expense." A line of code is neither goods nor services in the economic sense. Customers do not buy lines of code directly, and they often do not even know how many lines of code exist in a software product. Also, lines of code are not the primary deliverables of software projects, so they cannot be used for serious studies of the production costs of software systems or programs.

The greatest bulk of what is actually produced and what gets delivered to users of software comprises words and paper documents. In the United States, sometimes as many as 400 English words will be produced for every line of source code in large systems. Often more than 3 times as much effort goes into word production as goes into coding. Words are obviously not economic units for software, since customers do not buy them directly, nor do they have any real control over the quantity produced. Indeed in some cases, such as large military systems, far too many unnecessary words are produced.

As already mentioned, customers do not purchase lines of code either, so code quantities have no intrinsic value to users. In most instances customers neither know nor care how much code was written or in what language an application is embodied. Indeed, if the same functionality could be provided to users with less code by means of a higher-level language, customers might benefit from the cost reductions.

If neither of the two primary production units of software (words and code) is of direct interest to software consumers, then what exactly constitutes the "goods or services" that make software a useful economic commodity? The answer, of course, is that users care about the functions of the application.

Prior to Albrecht's publication of the function point metric, there were only hazy and inaccurate ways to study software production, and there was no way at all to explore the demand or consumption side of the software economic picture.

Thus, until 1979 the historical problem of measuring software productivity could be stated precisely: "The natural units of software production (words and code) were not the same as the units of software consumption (functions)." Economic studies require a standard definition of both what is produced and also of what is consumed.

Since neither words nor lines of code are of direct interest to software consumers, there was no tangible unit that matched the economic definition of goods or services that lent itself to studies of software's economic productivity.

A function point is an abstract but workable surrogate for the goods that are produced by software projects. Function points are the weighted sums of five different factors that are of interest to users:

- Inputs
- Outputs
- Logical files (also called user data groups)
- Inquiries
- Interfaces

Function points are defined by Albrecht to be "end-user benefits," and they are actually starting to serve as the economic units which customers wish to purchase or to have developed. That is, function points are beginning to be used in contract negotiations between software producers and their clients.

Clients and developers alike can discuss an application rationally in terms of its inputs, outputs, inquiries, files, and interfaces. Further, if requirements change, clients can request additional inputs or outputs after the initial agreement, and software providers can make rational predictions about the cost and schedule impact of such additions, which can then be discussed with clients in a reasonable manner.

Function points, unlike lines of code, can also be used for economic studies of both software production costs and software consumption. For production studies, function points can be applied usefully to effort, staffing, and cost-related studies. Thus, it is now known that the approximate U.S. average for software productivity at the project level is 5 function points per person-month. At the corporate level, where indirect personnel such as executives and administrators are included as well as effort expended on canceled projects, the U.S. average is about 1.5 function points per person-month. Function points can also be used to explore the volumes and costs of software paperwork production, a task for which lines of code were singularly inappropriate.

For consumption studies, function points are beginning to create an entirely new field of economic research that was never before possible. It is now possible to explore the utilization of software within industries and the utilization of software by the knowledge workers who use computers within those industries. Table 2.1 shows the approximate quantity of function points utilized by selected enterprises in the United States. The data were derived from studies of the production libraries of representative companies.

Although the margin of error in Table 2.1 is high, this kind of large-scale study of the volumes of software portfolios required by industries could not easily be performed prior to the advent of the function point metric. Although lines of code might be attempted, the kinds of companies shown in Table 2.1 typically use up to a dozen or more different languages: Cobol, C, Assembler, SQL, and so on.

TABLE 2.1 Approximate Number of Function Points Owned by Selected U.S. Enterprises

Enterprise type	Function points in production library
Small local bank	125,000
Medium commercial bank	350,000
Large international bank	450,000
Medium-size life insurance company	400,000
Large life insurance company	550,000
Large telephone operating company	450,000
Large telephone manufacturing company	600,000
Medium-size manufacturing company	200,000
Large manufacturing company	375,000
Large computer manufacturer	1,650,000

TABLE 2.2 Approximate Number of Function Points Utilized by Selected Occupations in the United States

Occupation group	Function points used to support job performance
Airline reservation clerk	30,000
Travel agent	35,000
Corporate controller	20,000
Bank loan officer	15,000
Insurance claims adjuster	5,000
Aeronautical engineer	25,000
Electrical engineer	25,000
Telecommunications engineer	20,000
Software engineer	15,000
Mechanical engineer	12,500
First-line project manager (software)	3,500
Second-line project manager (software)	3,500

Table 2.2 shows yet another new kind of consumption analysis possible from the use of function points. It illustrates the approximate number of function points required to support the computer usage of selected occupation groups in the United States. Here too the margin of error is high and the field of research is only just beginning. But research into information-processing consumption was not technically possible prior to the advent of the function point metric. It appears that function points may be starting to shed light on one of the most difficult economic questions of the century: how to evaluate the business value of software applications.

Since software economic consumption studies are only just starting, the information in Tables 2.1 and 2.2 must be regarded as preliminary and as containing a high margin of error. Nonetheless, it is a powerful illustration of the economic validity of function points that such studies can be attempted at all.

In conclusion, although function points are an abstract and synthetic metric, they are no less valid for economic purposes than many other standard economic metrics which also are abstract and synthetic, such as the Dow Jones stock indicator, cost per square foot for construction projects, accounting rates of return, internal rates of return, net present value, and the formulas for evaluating the net worth of an enterprise. Function points are starting to point the way to the first serious economic analyses of software production and software consumption since the computer era began.

Problems with and Paradoxes of Lines-of-Code Metrics

One of the criticisms sometimes levied against function points is that they are subjective whereas lines of code is objective. It is true the function point counting to date has included a measure of human judgment, and therefore includes subjectivity. (The emergence of a new class of automated function point tools is about to eliminate the current subjectivity of functional metrics.) However, it is not at all true that lines of code is an objective metric. Indeed, as will be shown, in all of human history there has not been a metric as subjective as a line of code since the days when the yard was based on the length of the arm of the king of England!

To understand the effectiveness of function points, it is necessary to understand the problems of the older lines-of-code metric. Regretfully, most users of lines of code have no idea at all of the subjectivity, randomness, and quirky deficiencies of this metric.

As mentioned, the first complete analysis of the problems of lines-of-code metrics was the previously mentioned study by the author in the *IBM Systems Journal* in 1978.[4] In essence there are three serious deficiencies associated with lines of code.

1. There has never been a national or international standard for a line of code that encompasses all procedural languages. (See Appendix A for an example of what such a standard might look like.)
2. Software can be produced by such methods as program generators, spreadsheets, graphic icons, reusable modules of unknown size, and inheritance, wherein entities such as lines of code are totally irrelevant.
3. Lines-of-code metrics paradoxically move backward as the level of the language gets higher, so that the most powerful and advanced languages appear to be less productive than the more primitive low-level languages. That is due to an intrinsic defect in the lines-of-code metrics. Some of the languages thus penalized include Ada, APL, C++, Objective-C, SMALLTALK, and many more.

Let us consider these problems in turn.

Lack of a standard definition for lines of code

The software industry will soon be 50 years of age, and lines of code have been used ever since its start. It is surprising that, in all that time, the basic concept of a line of code has never been standardized.

Counting physical or logical lines. The variation that can cause the greatest apparent difference in size is that of determining whether a line of code should be terminated physically or logically. A physical termination would be caused by the ENTER key of a computer keyboard, which completes the current line and moves the cursor to the next line of the screen. A logical termination would be a formal delimiter, such as a semicolon, colon, or period.

For languages such as Basic, which allow many logical statements per physical line, the size counted by means of logical delimiters can appear to be up to 500 percent larger than if lines are counted physically. On the other hand, for languages such as Cobol, which utilize conditional statements that encompass several physical lines, the physical method can cause the program to appear perhaps 200 percent larger than the logical method. From informal surveys of the clients of Software Productivity Research carried out by the author, it appears that about 35 percent of U.S. project managers count physical lines, 15 percent count logical lines, and 50 percent do not count by either method.

Counting types of lines. The next area of uncertainty is which of several possible kinds of lines should be counted. The first full explanation of the variations in counting code was perhaps that published by the author in 1986,[5] which is surprisingly recent for a topic almost 45 years of age. Most procedural languages include four different kinds of source code statements:

1. Executable lines (used for actions, such as addition)
2. Data definitions (used to identify information types)
3. Comments (used to inform readers of the code)
4. Blank lines (used to separate sections visually)

Again, there has never been a U.S. standard that defined whether all four or only one or two of these possibilities should be utilized. In typical business applications, about 40 percent of the total statements are executable lines, 35 percent are data definitions, 10 percent are blank, and 15 percent are comments. For systems software such as operating systems, about 45 percent of the total statements are executable, 30 percent are data definitions, 10 percent are blank, and 15 percent are comments.

From informal surveys of the clients of Software Productivity Research carried out by the author, it appears that about 10 percent count only executable lines, 20 percent count executable lines and data definitions, 15 percent also include commentary lines, and 5 percent even include blank lines! About 50 percent do not count lines of code at all.

Counting reusable code. Yet another area of extreme uncertainty is that of counting reusable code within software applications. Informal code reuse by programmers is very common, and any professional programmer will routinely copy and reuse enough code to account for perhaps 20 to 30 percent of the code in an application when the programming is done in an ordinary procedural language such as C, Cobol, or Fortran. For object-oriented languages such as SMALLTALK, C++, and Objective C, the volume of reuse tends to exceed 50 percent because of the facilities of inheritance that are intrinsic in the object-oriented family of languages. Finally, some corporations have established formal libraries of reusable modules, and many applications in those corporations may exceed 75 percent of the total volume of reused code.

The problem with measuring reusability centers around whether a reused module should be counted at all, counted only once, or counted each time it occurs. For example, if a reused module of 100 source statements is included five times in a program, there are three variations in counting:

1. Count the reused module at every occurrence.
2. Count the reused module only once.
3. Do not count the reused module at all, since it was not developed for the current project.

From informal surveys of the clients of Software Productivity Research carried out by the author, about 25 percent would count the module every time it occurred, 20 percent would count the module only once, and 5 percent would not count the reused module at all. The remaining 50 percent do not count source code at all.

Applications written in multiple languages. The next area of uncertainty, which is almost never discussed in the software engineering literature, is the problem of using lines of code metrics for multilanguage applications. From informal surveys of the clients of Software Productivity Research, it appears that about a third of all U.S. applications include more than one language and some may include a dozen or more languages. Some of the more common language mixtures include:

- Cobol mixed with a query language such as SQL
- Cobol mixed with a data definition language such as DL/1
- Cobol mixed with several other special-purpose languages
- C mixed with Assembler
- Basic mixed with Assembler
- Ada mixed with Assembler

- Ada mixed with Jovial and other languages

Since there are no U.S. standards for line counting that govern even a single language, multilanguage projects show a great increase in the number of random errors associated with lines-of-code data.

Additional uncertainties concerning lines of code. Many other possible counting variations can affect the apparent size of applications in which lines of code are used. For example:

- Including or excluding changed code for enhancements
- Including or excluding macro expansions/including or excluding job control language (JCL)
- Including or excluding deleted code
- Including or excluding scaffold or temporary code that is written but later discarded

The overall cumulative impact of all of these uncertainties spans more than an order of magnitude. That is, if the most verbose of the line-counting variations is compared to the most succinct, the apparent size of the application will be more than 10 times larger! That is an astonishing and even awe-inspiring range of uncertainty for a unit of measure approaching its fiftieth year of use!

Unfortunately, very few software authors bother to define which counting rules they used. The regrettable effect is that most of the literature on software productivity which expresses the results in terms of lines of code is essentially worthless for serious research purposes.

Size variations that are due to individual programming style. A minor controlled study carried out within IBM illustrates yet another problem with lines of code. Eight programmers were given the same specification and were asked to write the code required to implement it. The amount of code produced for the same specification varied by about 5 to 1 between the largest and the smallest implementation. That was due not to deliberate attempts to make productivity seem high, but rather to the styles of the programmers and to the varying interpretations of what the specifications asked for.

Software functions delivered without producing code

A large-scale study within ITT[6] in which the author participated found that about 26 percent of the approximately 30,000 applications owned by the corporation had been leased or purchased from external vendors rather than developed internally. Functionality was being delivered to the ITT software users of the packages, but ITT was obviously not producing the code. Specifically, about 140,000 function points out of the corporate total of 520,000 function points had been delivered to users in the form of packages rather than being developed by the ITT staff. The effective cost per function point of unmodified packages averaged about 35 percent of the cost per function point of custom development. However, for packages requiring heavy modification, the cost per function point was about 105 percent of equivalent custom development. Lines-of-code metrics are essentially impossible for studying the economics of package acquisitions or for make-vs.-buy productivity decisions.

The advent of the object-oriented languages and the deliberate pursuit of reusable modules by many corporations is leading to the phenomenon that the number of unique lines of code that must actually be hand-coded is shrinking, whereas the functional content of applications continues to expand. The lines-of-code metric is essentially useless in judging the productivity impact of this phenomenon. The use of inheritance and methods by object-oriented languages, the use of corporate reusable module libraries, and the use of application and program generators makes the concept of lines of code almost irrelevant.

As the 1990 decade progresses, an increasing number of graphics or icon-based "languages" will appear, and in them application development will proceed in a visual fashion quite different from that of conventional procedural programming. Lines of code, never defined adequately even for procedural languages, will be hopeless for graphics-based languages.

The paradox of reversed productivity for high-level languages

Although lack of standardization is the most visible surface problem with lines of code, the deepest and most severe problem is a mathematical paradox that causes real economic productivity and apparent productivity to move in opposite directions! This phenomenon was introduced and illustrated in Chap. 1, but its importance makes it deserve a more elaborate explanation.

The paradox manifests itself under these conditions: As real economic software productivity improves, metrics expressed in both lines of source code per time unit and cost per source line form will tend to move backward and appear to be worse than previously. Thus, as real economic productivity improves, the apparent cost per source line will be higher and the apparent lines of source code per time unit will be lower than before even though less effort and cost were required to complete an application.

Failure to understand the nature of this paradox has proved to be embarrassing to the industry as a whole and to many otherwise capable managers and consultants who have been led to make erroneous recommendations based on apparent productivity data rather than on real economic productivity data. The fundamental reason for the paradox has actually been known since the industrial revolution, or for more than 200 years, by company owners and manufacturing engineers. The essence of the paradox is this: If a product's manufacturing cycle includes a significant proportion of fixed costs and there is a decline in the number of units produced, the cost per unit will naturally go up.

For software, a substantial number of development activities either include or behave like fixed costs. For example, the applications requirements, specifications, and user documents are likely to stay constant in size and cost regardless of the language used for coding. This means that when enterprises migrate from a low-level language such as assembly language to a higher-level language such as Cobol or Ada, they do not have to write as many lines of source code to develop applications but the paperwork costs are essentially fixed. In effect, the number of source code units produced declines in the presence of fixed costs.

Since so many development activities either include fixed costs or behave like fixed costs, the cost per source line will naturally go up. Examples of activities that behave like fixed costs, since they are independent of coding, include user requirements, analysis, functional design, design reviews, user documentation, and some forms of testing such as function testing.

Table 2.3 is an example of the paradox associated with lines of source code metrics in a comparison of Assembler and Ada. Assume

TABLE 2.3 The Paradox of Lines-of-Code Metrics and High-Level Languages

	Assembler version	Ada version	Difference
Source code size	100,000	25,000	−75,000
Activity, in person-months:			
Requirements	10	10	0
Design	25	25	0
Coding	100	20	−80
Documentation	15	15	0
Integration and testing	25	15	−10
Management	25	15	−10
Total effort	200	100	−100
Total cost	$1,000,000	$500,000	−$500,000
Cost per line	$10	$20	+$20
Lines per month	500	250	−250

$5000 per month is the fully burdened salary rate in both cases. Note that Table 2.1 is intended to illustrate the mathematical paradox, and it exaggerates the trends to make the point clearly visible.

As shown in Table 2.4, with function points the economic productivity improvements are clearly visible and the true impact of a high-level language such as Ada can be seen and understood. Thus, function points provide a better base for economic productivity studies than lines-of-code metrics.

To illustrate some of the more recent findings vis-à-vis the economic advantages of high-level languages as explored by function points, Fig. 2.2 shows the comparative productivity rates for a number of language categories. Data such as that shown in Fig. 2.2 is technically and mathematically impossible with lines-of-code metrics.

To summarize, economic productivity deals with the amount of effort required to produce goods or services that users consume or utilize. Studies of productivity, therefore, can be divided into those which concentrate on production efficiencies and those which concentrate on demand or consumption.

Table 2.3 highlights the failure of lines of code to measure economic productivity or even to make common sense. As the examples clearly show, the Ada version took only half the effort of the Assembler version and cost only half as much. This is a 50 percent improvement in

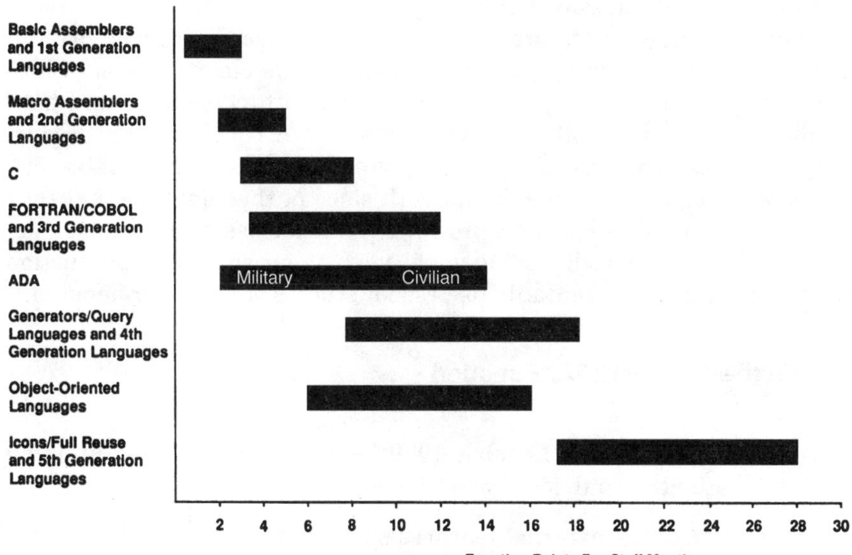

Figure 2.2 Productivity rates associated with language levels when measured with function points.

TABLE 2.4 The Economic Validity of Function Point Metrics

	Assembler version	Ada version	Difference
Source code size	100,000	25,000	−75,000
Function points	300	300	0
Activity, in person-months:			
Requirements	10	10	0
Design	25	25	0
Coding	100	20	−80
Documentation	15	15	0
Integration and testing	25	15	−10
Management	25	15	−10
Total effort	200	100	−100
Total cost	$1,000,000	$500,000	−$500,000
Cost per function point	$3,333	$1,666	−$1,667
Function points per person-month	1.5	3.0	−1.5

real economic productivity, or the ability to produce goods or services for a given level or labor and expense. But when lines-of-code metrics are used, the economic gains attributable to a high-level language disappear and the low-level language seems, erroneously, to be more productive. This paradox caused no end of confusion and error for the first 45 years of software's history.

When function points are used, however, economic productivity improvements are no longer concealed but become clearly visible. Since the two preceding examples provide the same functionality and both can be assumed to be 300 function points in size, consider their productivity results measured in function point form as shown in Table 2.4. Function points can be applied to both sides of the equation, and they are useful for exploring both production efficiencies and customer demand. The lines-of-code metric is paradoxical for studies of production efficiency, and it is essentially useless for studies of customer demand.

Albrecht's Original 1979 Function Point Methodology

When first published in October 1979,[2] Albrecht had created function points as a metric that could meet these five goals:

1. It dealt with the external features of software.
2. It dealt with features that were important to users.
3. It could be applied early in a product's life cycle.

4. It could be linked to economic productivity.
5. It was independent of source code or language.

When the function point metrics were first published, they consisted of four significant questions that could be answered easily for any software product, plus an adjustment for complexity. The 1979 function point method looked as shown in Table 2.5.

To use the 1979 IBM function point method, it was only necessary to count the number of inputs, outputs, inquiries, and logical master files that were associated with the application being measured. The counts were then multiplied by empirically derived weighting factors. The unadjusted total was then raised or lowered by as much as ± 25 percent for complexity, and the final result was the adjusted function point total. The metric could be applied as early as the requirements phase, and compared to the older lines-of-code metric, function points were a much better indicator of economic productivity.

The 1979 IBM function point marked the first point in the history of software where the true economic value of high-level languages could be directly measured. The early studies of 24 projects by Albrecht himself and published at the October conference in 1979 contained the first tangible evidence in software engineering history that languages such as Cobol, PL/I, and RPG yielded higher economic productivity rates than assembly languages. Until that time, the whole issue of direct measurement of high-level languages had been virtually impossible other than by the circuitous method of converting the sizes of all projects studied into basic assembly language.

However, it soon became evident that the way complexity was handled by the early function point technique needed to be modified to solve two problems: (1) Complexity was totally subjective. (2) Plus or minus 25 percent was not a broad enough range for the observed impact of complexity on real-life projects.

TABLE 2.5 The 1979 Version of the IBM Function Point Metric

Significant parameters	Weighting factors		Unadjusted total
Number of inputs	× 4	=	______
Number of outputs	× 5	=	______
Number of inquiries	× 4	=	______
Number of master files	× 10	=	______
Unadjusted total			______
Complexity adjustment (up to ± 25%)			______
Adjusted function point total			______

As function points started to be widely used outside IBM, Albrecht and his colleagues next addressed the need to make the complexity adjustments more objective and more pervasive in impact. These changes would be released later, in the 1984 IBM revision.

Worldwide Publication of Function Points in 1981

At the joint IBM/SHARE/GUIDE conference in 1979, Albrecht's paper attracted considerable attention among the participants. One of the other speakers, the author, who had been carrying out complementary research in software measurement, recognized the economic validity of the function point metric and made plans to include the topic in a new book that was in planning.

In 1981, with both IBM's and the conference organization's permission, Albrecht's paper was reprinted in the IEEE Tutorial entitled *Programming Productivity: Issues for the Eighties.*[3] This publication by the IEEE provided the first widespread circulation of the concept of function point metrics outside IBM and began to attract users on a global basis.

The 1981 IEEE tutorial also included other research on the paradoxes associated with lines-of-code metrics. While working for IBM in 1978, the author had published an analysis of the mathematical problems and paradoxes associated with lines-of-code measures in the *IBM Systems Journal.*[4] That article, also included in the 1981 IEEE tutorial, proved that lines of code were incapable of measuring productivity in the economic sense. Thus the work of the author and Albrecht could be viewed as opposite sides of the same coin: the author was able to demonstrate the fallacy of lines of code for economic purposes; Albrecht was able to create an economically valid metric for the first time in software history. Albrecht's own external publication of the function point metric occurred in 1984 when IBM published his famous guidelines.[7]

DeMarco's 1982 Publication of the "Bang" Functional Metric

Albrecht and the author were certainly not the only researchers who were attempting to go beyond the imperfect lines-of-code metric and move toward functional metrics. In 1982, Tom DeMarco published a description of a different kind of functional metric which he initially termed the "bang metric."[8] This unusual name was derived from the vernacular phase, "getting more bang for the buck." A less jocular name for the metric would be the "DeMarco functional metric."

Although DeMarco and Albrecht were acquainted with each other and their metrics were aimed at the same problem, the bang metric and the function point metric are somewhat different in form and substance. (The two appear to be totally independent inventions, incidentally.) DeMarco's consulting had often taken him into the domain of systems software and some of the more complex forms of software engineering, rather than pure MIS projects. His bang metric was the first attempt to apply functional metrics to the domain of systems and scientific software. In the metric, the basic elements to be counted are the following:

1. Functional primitives
2. Modified functional primitives
3. Data elements
4. Input data elements
5. Output data elements
6. Stored data elements
7. Objects (also termed "entities")
8. Relationships
9. States in a state transition model of the application
10. Transitions in a state transition model
11. Data tokens
12. Relationships involving retained data models

As can be seen, the DeMarco bang metric is a considerable superset of the Albrecht function point metric, and it contains such elements as data tokens and state transitions which are normally associated with the more complex forms of systems software such as operating systems and telecommunication systems.

The full set of things which can be counted by using the bang metric is of imposing if not intimidating length. However, DeMarco has pointed out that applications can be conveniently segregated into those that are "function strong" and those that are "data strong." That is, most applications will emphasize either functionality or files and data.

It is not impossible to relate the bang metric to function points. Since DeMarco has stated that subsets are acceptable, it is possible to select an exact match of bang and function point parameters. However, complexity adjustments of the two methods would still be different because the IBM adjustments are rule-driven and the DeMarco method is largely subjective.

Although the DeMarco bang metric is technically interesting and can lead to valuable insights when utilized, it fell far behind the Albrecht function point metric in terms of the numbers of users and practitioners once IBM began to offer function point courses as part of its data processing education curriculum. The metric also fell behind in convenience when numerous software packages that could aid in the calculation of IBM's function point metrics began to be marketed while the bang metric still required manual methods. Although the CADRE tool set contains support for the bang metric, there are now more than 20 vendors with tools which facilitate function point counting.

Finally, the DeMarco metric fell behind in the ability to evolve when the International Function Point User's Group (IFPUG) was formed. There is no equivalent for bang metrics to the IFPUG Counting Practices Committee, which serves to both enhance function points and provide standard definitions and examples. It would not be impossible, of course, to create a bang metric subcommittee within IFPUG, but that has not yet been done.

Albrecht's 1984 Revision of the IBM Function Point Methodology

In 1984, Albrecht and IBM published a major revision of the function point method[7] that significantly revised the technique. It is the basis of the current IBM function point methodology. Also in 1984, IBM started to include courses in function points as part of its data processing education curriculum, which created a quantum leap in overall utilization of the technique.

In the 1984 revision, the impact of complexity was broadened so that the range became approximately 250 percent. To reduce the subjectivity of dealing with complexity, the factors that caused complexity to be higher or lower than normal were specifically enumerated and guidelines for their interpretation were issued. Instead of merely counting the number of inputs, outputs, master files, and inquiries as in the 1979 function point methodology, the current methodology requires that complexity be ranked as low, average, or high. In addition, a new parameter, interface files, has been added. The current IBM implementation of function points looks as shown in Table 2.6.

With the 1984 IBM implementation, each major feature such as external inputs must be evaluated separately for complexity. In order to make the complexity evaluation less subjective, Albrecht developed a matrix for each feature that considers the number of file types, record types, and/or data element types. For example, Table 2.7 shows a matrix dealing with the complexity of external inputs.

The treatment of complexity is still subjective, of course, but it is now supported by guidelines for interpretation. Examples of inputs in-

TABLE 2.6 IBM's 1984 Revision of the Function Point Metric

Significant parameter	Low complexity	Medium complexity	High complexity
External input	× 3	× 4	× 6
External output	× 4	× 5	× 7
Logical internal file	× 7	× 10	× 15
External interface file	× 5	× 7	× 10
External inquiry	× 3	× 4	× 6

TABLE 2.7 Adjustment Weights for External Inputs

File types referenced	Data element types		
	1–4	5–15	⇒ 16
0–1	Low	Low	Average
2	Low	Average	High
⇒ 3	Average	High	High

TABLE 2.8 Adjustment Weights for External Outputs

File types referenced	Data element types		
	1–5	6–19	⇒ 20
0–1	Low	Low	Average
2–3	Low	Average	High
⇒ 4	Average	High	High

clude data screens filled out by users, magnetic tapes or floppy disks, sensor inputs, and light-pen or mouse-based inputs. The adjustment table for external outputs is shown in Table 2.8, and it is similar to the input adjustment table.

Examples of outputs include output data screens, printed reports, floppy disk files, sets of checks, or printed invoices. The adjustment table for logical internal file types is shown in Table 2.9, and it follows the same pattern.

Examples of logical internal files include floppy disk files, magnetic tape files, flat files in a personal computer database, a leg in a hierarchical database such as IBM's IMS, a table in a relational database such as DB2, and a path through a net in a network-oriented database. Table 2.10 shows the adjustments for external interfaces, and it follows the same pattern as the others.

TABLE 2.9 Adjustment Weights for Logical Internal Files

File types referenced	Data element types		
	1–19	20–50	⇒ 51
0–1	Low	Low	Average
2–5	Low	Average	High
⇒ 6	Average	High	High

TABLE 2.10 Adjustment Weights for Interface Files

File types referenced	Data element types		
	1–19	20–50	⇒ 51
0–1	Low	Low	Average
2–5	Low	Average	High
⇒ 6	Average	High	High

TABLE 2.11 Adjustment Weights for Inquiry Input Portions

File types referenced	Data element types		
	1–4	5–15	⇒ 16
0–1	Low	Low	Average
2	Low	Average	High
⇒ 3	Average	High	High

TABLE 2.12 Adjustment Weights for Inquiry Output Portions

File types referenced	Data element types		
	1–5	6–19	⇒ 20
0–1	Low	Low	Average
2–3	Low	Average	High
⇒ 4	Average	High	High

Examples of an interface include a shared database and a logical file addressable from or to some other application. The last parameter is inquiries, which is similar to the others but is divided into the two subelements of the input portion and the output portion, as shown in Tables 2.11 and 2.12.

Examples of inquiries include user inquiry without updating a file, help messages, and selection messages. A typical inquiry might be illustrated by an airline reservation query along the lines of "What Delta flights leave Boston for Atlanta after 3:00 p.m.?" as an input portion. The response or output portion might be something like "Flight 202 at 4:15 p.m."

Function point abbreviations and nomenclature

The IBM 1984 revision of the function point counting rules introduced yet another change that is minor in technical significance but important from a human factors standpoint. It adopted a set of standard full-length descriptions and standard abbreviations for the factors and variables used in function point calculations. Since examples and discussions of function points by experienced users tend to make use of those abbreviations, novice users of function point should master them as soon as possible.

Inputs, outputs, inquiries, logical files, and interfaces obviously comprise many different kinds of things, so the generic word "type" was added to the 1984 full nomenclature. However, since it is necessary to use some of the terms many times when giving examples, the revision introduced standard abbreviations as well. The changes in nomenclature and abbreviations are shown below:

1979 nomenclature	1984 nomenclature	1984 abbreviations
Inputs	External input type	IT
Outputs	External output type	OT
Logical files	Logical internal file type	FT
Interface	External interface file type	EI
Inquiries	External inquiry type	QT

Other abbreviations that were created in the 1984 IBM revision include the following:

DET	Data element type
FTR	File types referenced
RET	Record types
L	Low (for complexity)
A	Average (for complexity)
H	High (for complexity)

The terminology of function points has tended to change frequently, although the fundamental concepts have been remarkably consistent. Unfortunately, novices tend to be put off by the complexity of the terms, even though the terms are no more difficult, for example, than those associated with stocks or corporate finance.

The 14 influential adjustment factors

Another significant change in the 1984 IBM revision was an expansion in the range of complexity adjustments and the rigor with which the adjustments are carried out. Recall that, in the original 1979 version, complexity was a purely subjective adjustment with a range that spanned ± 25 percent. In the 1984 revision, it is derived from the overall impact of 14 influential factors, and the total range of adjustment of the complexity multiplier runs from 0.65 to 1.35.

The 14 influential complexity factors are evaluated on a scale of 1 to 5 (with a 0 being used to eliminate factors that are not present at all). The 14 influential complexity factors are assigned shorthand identifiers that range from C1 to C14 for accuracy and convenience when referencing them.

C1	Data communications
C2	Distributed functions
C3	Performance objectives
C4	Heavily used configuration
C5	Transaction rate
C6	On-line data entry
C7	End-user efficiency
C8	On-line update
C9	Complex processing
C10	Reusability
C11	Installation ease
C12	Operational ease
C13	Multiple sites
C14	Facilitate change

In considering the weights of the 14 influential factors, the general guidelines are these: score a 0 if the factor has no impact at all on the application; score a 5 if the factor has a strong and pervasive impact; score a 2, 3, 4, or some intervening decimal value such as 2.5 if the impact is something in between. This is, of course, still subjective, but the subjectivity is now spread over 14 different factors.

IBM's tutorial materials (9) provide the following general suggestions for assigning weights to the 14 influential factors:

0 Factor not present or without influence
1 Insignificant influence
2 Moderate influence
3 Average influence
4 Significant influence
5 Strong influence

Let us consider the maximum ranges of the 14 influential factors and look in detail at the scoring recommendations for the first two:

C1 data communication. Data communication implies that data and/or control information would be sent or received over communication facilities. This factor would be scored as follows:

0 Batch applications
1 Remote printing or data entry
2 Remote printing and data entry
3 A teleprocessing front end to the application
4 Applications with significant teleprocessing
5 Applications that are dominantly teleprocessing

C2 distributed functions. Distributed functions are concerned with whether an application is monolithic and operates on a single contiguous processor or is distributed among a variety of processors. The scoring for this factor is as follows:

0 Pure monolithic applications
1 Applications that prepare data for other components
2 Applications distributed over a few components
3 Applications distributed over more components
4 Applications distributed over many components
5 Applications dynamically performed on many components

C3 performance objectives. Performance objectives are scored as 0 if no special performance criteria are stated by the users of the application and scored as 5 if the users insist on very stringent performance targets that require considerable effort to achieve.

C4 heavily used configuration. Heavily used configuration is scored as 0 if the application has no special usage constraints and as 5 if anticipated usage requires special effort to achieve.

C5 transaction rate. Transaction rate is scored 0 if the volume of transactions is not significant and 5 if the volume of transactions is high enough to stress the application and require special effort to achieve desired throughputs.

C6 on-line data entry. On-line data entry is scored 0 if none or fewer than 15 percent of the transactions are interactive and 5 if all or more than 50 percent of the transactions are interactive.

C7 end-user efficiency. Design for end-user efficiency is scored 0 if there are no end users or there are no special requirements for end users and 5 if the stated requirements for end-user efficiency are stringent enough to require special effort to achieve them.

C8 on-line update. On-line update is scored 0 if there is none and 5 if on-line updates are both mandatory and especially difficult, perhaps because of the need to back up or protect data against accidental change.

C9 complex processing. Complex processing is scored 0 if there is none and 5 in cases requiring extensive logical decisions, complicated mathematics, tricky exception processing, or elaborate security schemes.

C10 reusability. Reusability is scored 0 if the functionality is planned to stay local to the current application and 5 if much of the functionality and the project deliverables are intended for widespread utilization by other applications.

C11 installation ease. Installation ease is scored 0 if this factor is insignificant and 5 if installation is both important and so stringent that it requires special effort to accomplish a satisfactory installation.

C12 operational ease. Operational ease is scored 0 if this factor is insignificant and 5 if operational ease of use is so important that it requires special effort to achieve it.

C13 multiple sites. Multiple sites is scored 0 if there is only planned using location and 5 if the project and its deliverables are intended for many diverse locations.

C14 facilitate change. Facilitate change is scored 0 if change does not occur, and 5 if the application is developed specifically to allow end users to make rapid changes to control data or tables which they maintain with the aid of the application.

Using the 14 influential factors for complexity adjustment

When all of the 14 factors have been considered and scores assigned individually, the sum of the factors is converted into a final complexity adjustment by the following procedure:

1. Multiply the sum of the factors by 0.01 to convert the sum to a decimal value.
2. Add a constant of 0.65 to the decimal value to create a complexity multiplier.
3. Multiply the unadjusted function point total by the complexity multiplier to create the final adjusted function point total.

It can be seen that the 14 influential factors yield a multiplier that has a range of from 0.65 to 1.35. If none of the factors were present at all, the sum would be 0, so only the constant of 0.65 is used as the multiplier. If all 14 factors were strongly present, their sum would be 70. Using the procedure of 70*0.01 + 0.65 = 1.35, the final multiplier in this case is 1.35.

Here is an example of the calculation sequence used to derive a function point total by using IBM's current method. Assume an average project with 10 inputs, 10 outputs, 10 inquiries, 1 data file, and 1 interface. Assume average complexity for the five primary factors and a range of weights from 0 to 5 for the 14 influential factors, so that the sum of the 14 influential factors totals to 40 influence points.

Basic counts	Elements		Weights		Results
10	Inputs	×	4	=	40
10	Outputs	×	5	=	50
10	Inquiries	×	4	=	40
1	Logical file	×	10	=	10
1	Interface	×	7	=	7
Unadjusted total					147

The influential factor calculations are as follows:

Data communications	0
Distributed functions	0
Performance objectives	4
Heavily used configuration	3
Transaction rate	3
On-line data entry	4
End-user efficiency	4
On-line update	2
Complex processing	3
Reusability	0
Installation ease	4

Operational ease	4
Multiple sites	5
Facilitate change	4

The sum total of the influential factors is 40. Then,

40*0.01 = 0.40 + 0.65 [constant] = 1.05 [complexity multiplier]

The final adjustment is:

147 [unadjusted total]*1.05 [complexity multiplier]
= 154 [adjusted function points]

Although the steps with the IBM method can be time-consuming, the calculation sequence for producing function points is fairly simple to carry out. Not quite so simple is reaching a clear agreement on the exact number of inputs, outputs, inquiries, data files, and interfaces in real-life projects. When first starting with function points by using the IBM method, users should be cautioned not to get bogged down in rules and determinations of exact weights. If you think clearly about the application, your counts are likely to be acceptably accurate. In summary form, here are the basic concepts used when counting with function points.

1. *Inputs:* Inputs are screens or forms through which human users of an application or other programs add new data or update existing data. If an input screen is too large for a single normal display (usually 80 columns by 25 lines) and flows over onto a second screen, the set counts as 1 input. Inputs that require unique processing are what should be considered.

2. *Outputs:* Outputs are screens or reports which the application produces for human use or for other programs. Note that outputs requiring separate processing are the units to count: In a payroll application, an output function that created, say, 100 checks would still count as one output.

3. *Inquiries:* Inquiries are screens which allow users to interrogate an application and ask for assistance or information, such as HELP screens.

4. *Data files:* Data files are logical collections of records which the application modifies or updates. A file can be a flat file such as a tape file, one leg of a hierarchical database such as IMS, one table within a relational database, or one path through a CODASYL network database.

5. *Interface:* Interfaces are files shared with other applications, such as incoming or outgoing tape files, shared databases, and parameter lists.

As can be seen, the current IBM function point methodology is substantially more rigorous than the original 1979 implementation, but the rigor has added considerably more work before an application's function points can be totaled. The effort involved to count the function points of a large system by using the current IBM methodology amounts to several days, sometimes spread out over several weeks.

Counting function points by using the current IBM method also requires trained function point specialists to ensure consistency of the counts. Both IBM and consulting companies such as Software Productivity Research are now providing both function point training and assistance in getting started with function points.

When first starting out with function points, formal training is definitely recommended; an example is the original function point workshop provided by IBM itself,[9] or the new function point workshop prepared by Albrecht for Software Productivity Research,[10] or one of the other consulting company offerings. It is interesting that most universities and academic institutions have not yet added courses in function point analysis to their curriculums and hence are some years behind the actual state of the art of software measurement.

Generally speaking, adopting the current IBM function point implies a serious commitment to good measurement and a willingness to devote staff, skills, and time. The payoff is the most reliable metric in software history, coupled with the ability to share productivity data with other enterprises.

The 1985 Software Productivity Research Method

In October 1985, Software Productivity Research introduced a new way to calculate function points as part of the SPQR/20 Software Productivity, Quality, and Reliability estimating model[11] and later as part of the SPQR SIZER/FP tool[12] and the CHECKPOINT™ measurement and estimation tool.[13] The SPR function point variation simplified the way complexity was dealt with and reduced the human effort associated with counting function points. The SPR function point methodology yields function point totals that are essentially the same as those by the current IBM function point method. In repeated trials, it produced counts that averaged within 1.5 percent of the IBM method, with a maximum variation of about 15 percent.

The SPR function point methodology attempts to meet three additional goals over and above the five goals that the IBM method was intended to meet. The additional SPR goals are:

6. To create function point totals easily and rapidly and to be able to create function points prior to the availability of all of the IBM factors in a normal project life cycle

7. To predict source code size for any known language
8. To retrofit function points to existing software

The primary difference between the IBM and SPR function point methodologies is in the way the two deal with complexity. The IBM techniques for assessing complexity, discussed in the preceding section, are based on weighting 14 influential factors and evaluating the numbers of field and file references. The SPR technique for dealing with complexity is to separate the overall topic of "complexity" into three distinct questions that can be dealt with intuitively:

1. How complex are the problems or algorithms facing the team?
2. How complex are the code structure and control flow of the application?
3. How complex is the data structure of the application?

This simplification of the way complexity is treated allows the SPR method to backfire function points. If the source code size of an existing application is known, then the SPR function point technique and its supporting software can automatically convert that size into a function point total.

With the SPR function point method, it is not necessary to count the number of data element types, file types, or record types as it is with the current IBM method. Neither is it necessary to assign a low, average, or high value to each specific input, output, inquiry, data file, or interface or to evaluate the 14 influential factors as defined by the IBM method.

As a result of the reduced number of complexity considerations, the SPR method can also be applied somewhat earlier than the IBM method, as during the preliminary requirements phase. The effort required to complete the calculations also is reduced, and that can be significant for manual calculations. However, the effort-reduction aspect is less significant if function point calculation software is used.

The three SPR complexity parameters deal with the entire application rather than with the subelements of the application. Mathematically, the SPR function point methodology has a slightly broader range of adjustments than the IBM methodology (from 0.5 to 1.5), and it produces function point totals that seldom differ by more than a few percent from the IBM methodology. The three SPR complexity questions for a new application look like this:

Problem complexity? ______

1. Simple algorithms and simple calculations
2. Majority of simple algorithms and calculations

3. Algorithms and calculations of average complexity
4. Some difficult or complex calculations
5. Many difficult algorithms and complex calculations

Code complexity? ______

1. Nonprocedural (generated, spreadsheet, query, etc.)
2. Well structured with reusable modules
3. Well structured (small modules and simple paths)
4. Fair structure, but some complex modules and paths
5. Poor structure, with large modules and complex paths

Data complexity? ______

1. Simple data with few variables and low complexity
2. Numerous variables, but simple data relationships
3. Multiple files, fields, and data interactions
4. Complex file structures and data interactions
5. Very complex file structures and data interactions

For fine tuning, the SPR complexity questions can be answered with decimal values, and answers such as 2, 2.5, and 3.25 are all perfectly acceptable.

The SPR function point questions themselves are similar to IBM's 1979 questions in that only one set of empirical weights is used. The SPR function point questions are shown in Table 2.13.

Since the SPR function point method is normally automated, manual complexity adjustments are not required when using it. For those who might wish to use it manually, the SPR algorithm for complexity adjustment uses the sum of the problem complexity and data complexity questions and matches the results to the values shown in Table 2.14.

Note that Table 2.14 shows only integer values for the complexity sum. For decimal results between integer values, such as 3.5, the SPR software tools calculate a fractional adjustment factor. For example, if the complexity sum were in fact 3.5, the adjustment multiplier would be 0.75.

It may be asked why *code complexity* is one of the questions posed by the SPR method but omitted from the SPR adjustment calculations.

TABLE 2.13 The 1985 SPR Function Point Method

Significant parameter		Empirical weight	
Number of inputs?	______	× 4 =	______
Number of outputs?	______	× 5 =	______
Number of inquiries?	______	× 4 =	______
Number of data files?	______	× 10 =	______
Number of interfaces?	______	× 7 =	______
Unadjusted total			______
Complexity adjustment			______
Adjusted function point total			______

TABLE 2.14 The SPR Complexity Adjustment Factors

Complexity sum	Adjustment multiplier
1	0.5
2	0.6
3	0.7
4	0.8
5	0.9
6	1.0
7	1.1
8	1.2
9	1.3
10	1.4
11	1.5

The code complexity factor is not required by the logic of the function point metric when producing normal forward function point counts. However, for retrofitting or backfiring function points to existing software, code complexity is an important parameter, as will be seen later.

The SPR function point method attempts to meet the five goals of the original IBM function point method and three additional goals as well, as discussed below.

High-speed function point calculations

The SPR methodology is normally automated rather than manual, and in typical use, it does not require manual calculations at all. Because it deals with complexity in terms of only three discrete and intuitive parameters and does not require segmentation of individual factors into low, average, and high complexity, it can create function point totals very rapidly. Users who are generally familiar with function point principles and who also know an application well enough to state how many inputs, outputs, inquiries, data files, and interfaces are involved can generate function point totals in less than a minute by using the automated SPR methodology.

Source code size prediction for any language

The SPR function point calculation method was released in October 1985, and it was the first available methodology to provide automatic source code size prediction. Although only 30 common languages were initially sized, the mathematical logic of the SPR size prediction technique can be applied to any or all of the 500 to 1000 or so existing languages and dialects.

Size prediction is based on empirically derived observations of the level of languages and on the number of statements required to implement a single function point. The history of source code size prediction is older than function points themselves, and the coupling of these two fields of research has been very synergistic. Prior to the invention of function points, the problems of using lines-of-code metrics had been explored by the author at IBM's San Jose programming laboratory in the late 1960s and early 1970s. This research led to a technique of normalizing productivity rates by expressing all values in terms of "equivalent Assembler statements." For example, if a project were coded in Fortran and required 1000 source code statements and 2 months of effort, the productivity rate in terms of Fortran itself would be 500 statements per month.

However, the same functionality for the application, had it been written in basic assembly language, would have required about 3000 source code statements, or three times as much code as was actually needed to do the job in Fortran. Dividing the probable 3000 assembly statements by the 2 months of observed effort generated a productivity rate of 1500 "equivalent Assembler statements" per month.

The purpose of this conversion process was to express productivity rates in a constant fashion that would not be subject to the mathematical anomalies and paradoxes of using lines of code with the languages of varying power. In a sense, basic assembly language served as a kind of primitive form of function point: The number of assembly statements that might be required to produce an application stayed constant, although the actual number would fluctuate depending upon which language was actually used.

In working with it, it was realized that the normalization technique provided a fairly rigorous way of assigning a numeric level to the power of a language. In the 1960s and 1970s, the terms "low-level language" and "high-level language" had become widespread but "level" had never been mathematically defined.

The level of a language was defined at IBM as the number of basic assembly language statements it would take to produce the functionality of one statement in the target language. Thus Cobol is considered to be level-3 because it would take about three assembly language statements to create the functionality of one Cobol statement. Fortran also was considered a level-3 language, since it took about three assembly language statements to encode functionality available in one Fortran statement. PL/I was considered a level-4 language because it took about four assembly language statements to replicate the functions of one PL/I statement.

The simple mathematics associated with levels allowed very rapid size conversion from one language to another. For example, if a program was 10,000 statements in basic assembly language, then dividing 10,000 by 3 indicated that the same application would have taken about 3333 Fortran statements. Dividing 10,000 by 4 indicated that about 2500 PL/I statements might have been required.

By the middle 1970s, the author, at IBM, had assigned provisional levels to more than 50 languages and could convert source code sizes back and forth among any of them. However, source code size conversion is not the same as source code size prediction. It was still necessary to guess at how many statements would be required to build an application in any arbitrary language. Once that guess was made, size conversion into any other language was trivial.

After the publication of the function point metric in 1979, the situation changed significantly. Several researchers, including Albrecht himself and the author, began to explore function point totals and source code size simultaneously. The research quickly led to a new definition of language level: "The number of source code statements required to encode one function point." Since function point totals can be enumerated as early as the requirements phase, the new definition implied that true source code size prediction would now be possible.

Software Productivity Research merged the new definition of "level" with the old definition and produced a list of some 300 common languages[14] that showed both the average number of source code statements per function point and the number of assembly statements necessary to create the functionality of one statement in the target language. Thus, for example, Cobol remains a level-3 language and two facts can now be asserted: (1) An average of three statements in basic assembly language would be needed to encode the functions of one Cobol statement. (2) An average of 105 Cobol statements would be needed to encode one function point.

Empirically, languages of the same level require the same number of source code statements to implement one function point, but the complexity of the application and its code have a strong impact. Although Cobol, for example, averages about 105 source statements per function point, it has been observed to go as high as 160 source code statements per function point and as low as 50 source code statements per function point.

Because of individual programming styles and variations in the dialects of many languages, the relationship between function points and source code size often fluctuates widely, sometimes for reasons that are not currently understood. Nonetheless, the relation between function points and source code statements is an extremely interesting and useful new form of research that no doubt will continue for many years. The average levels and ratios of source statements to function points for more than 450 general language categories are shown in Table 2.15.

For language classes that contain many different dialects and variations, such as "third generation," a default value is provided. The default is intended to be the approximate average level of languages within that class, and it is useful when attempting to place other languages within the table. The data in Table 2.15 comes from several sources. For common languages such as Cobol, many hundreds of projects have now been evaluated by actual counts in terms of both function points and source code size. For some languages, textbooks provide simultaneous implementations of the same algorithms in various languages. For other languages, only a few programs have yet been enumerated.

The range of statements per function point is quite broad: several hundred percent in some cases because of variations in individual programming styles and unknown causes. The data is presented to illustrate general trends, and it has a very large margin of error. In Table 2.15, the term "default" is used to show the generic value that should be considered when there are a number of languages approximately the same in level. For example, "third generation" or "fourth generation" has been an umbrella term for many languages.

It should be recalled that when Mendeleev first published the periodic table of atomic elements in 1869, some elements were in the wrong place and some had not even been discovered. The organizing principle of the periodic table, however, added considerably to the ability of chemists and physicists to explore useful relationships. Very likely some of the languages in Table 2.15 are in the wrong place, and it is obvious that hundreds of other languages could be added. Here

TABLE 2.15 Programming Language Levels and Ranges of Source Code Statements per Function Point

Language or dialect	Level	Min.	Mode	Max.
1. Natural language	0.10	1800	3200	5000
2. Machine language	0.50		640	
3. First generation default	1.00	200	320	400
4. Assembly (basic)	1.00	237	320	416
5. Autocoder	1.00	225	320	400
6. Basic assembly	1.00	200	320	450
7. SPS	1.00		320	
8. JCL	1.45		220	
9. Assembly (macro)	1.50	170	213	295
10. DCL	1.50		213	
11. Macro assembly	1.50	130	213	300
12. CPL	2.00		160	
13. Applesoft Basic	2.50		128	
14. Aztec C	2.50		128	
15. C (default value)	2.50	60	128	170
16. C86Plus	2.50		128	
17. DOS Batch Files	2.50		128	
18. Fortran 66	2.50	75	128	160
19. Fortran II	2.50	75	128	160
20. High C	2.50		128	
21. HP Basic	2.50		128	
22. Interpreted C	2.50		128	
23. Lattice C	2.50		128	
24. Liana	2.50		128	
25. Microsoft C	2.50		128	
26. Quick C	2.50		128	
27. Snobol 2-4	2.50		128	
28. TRS80 Basic II, III	2.50	80	128	170
29. Turbo C	2.50		128	
30. WATCOM C	2.50		128	
31. WATCOM C/386	2.50		128	
32. Waterloo C	2.50		128	
33. BASIC A	2.50	70	120	165
34. LOTUS Macros	3.00		108	
35. Second generation default	3.00	55	107	165
36. Algol 68	3.00		107	
37. Algol W	3.00		107	
38. ANSI Cobol 74	3.00	65	107	170

TABLE 2.15 Programming Language Levels and Ranges of Source Code Statements per Function Point (*Continued*)

Language or dialect	Level	Min.	Mode	Max.
39. Ariel	3.00		107	
40. BALM	3.00		107	
41. BLISS	3.00		107	
42. CHILI	3.00		107	
43. CHILL	3.00	60	107	143
44. CMS2	3.00	70	107	135
45. CORAL 66	3.00		107	
46. EUCLID	3.00		107	
47. Fortran 77	3.00	65	107	150
48. Fortran default	3.00	75	107	160
49. IBM VS Cobol	3.00		107	
50. Interpreted Basic	3.00	70	107	160
51. JOSS	3.00		107	
52. JOVIAL	3.00	70	107	165
53. MESA	3.00		107	
54. Oscar	3.00		107	
55. Procedural default	3.00	50	107	175
56. PROSE	3.00		107	
57. PROTEUS	3.00		107	
58. RM Cobol	3.00		107	
59. RM Fortran	3.00		107	
60. SAIL	3.00		107	
61. UNIX Shell Scripts	3.00		107	
62. VECTRAN	3.00		107	
63. Cobol	3.00	65	106.7	150
64. GW Basic	3.25	63	98	135
65. IBM Advanced Basic	3.25		98	
66. AAS Macro	3.50		91	
67. ANSI Cobol 85	3.50		91	
68. Berkeley Pascal	3.50		91	
69. Better Basic	3.50		91	
70. C Set 2	3.50		91	
71. CBASIC	3.50		91	
72. IBM Compiled Basic	3.50	60	91	130
73. IBM VS Cobol II	3.50	57	91	134
74. MS Compiled Basic	3.50	60	91	130
75. Pascal default	3.50	50	91	125
76. PL/S	3.50	47	91	143

TABLE 2.15 Programming Language Levels and Ranges of Source Code Statements per Function Point (*Continued*)

Language or dialect	Level	Min.	Mode	Max.
77. Professional Pascal	3.50		91	
78. RATFOR	3.50		91	
79. RM Basic	3.50		91	
80. SBASIC	3.50		91	
81. Strongly typed default	3.50	45	91	125
82. Tandem Access Language	3.50		91	
83. UCSD Pascal	3.50		91	
84. Waterloo Pascal	3.50		91	
85. WATFOR	3.50		91	
86. WHIP	3.50		91	
87. ZBASIC	3.50		91	
88. WATFIV	3.75		85	
89. Third generation default	4.00	45	80	125
90. CLASCAL	4.00		80	
91. COMAL	4.00		80	
92. Concurrent Pascal	4.00		80	
93. Fortran 90	4.00		80	
94. ICON	4.00		80	
95. Microfocus Cobol	4.00	45	80	127
96. MODULA 2	4.00	70	80	90
97. OGL	4.00		80	
98. PL/I	4.00	65	80	95
99. REXX (MVS)	4.00		80	
100. RPG I	4.00	50	80	115
101. Turbo Pascal 1–4	4.00	55	80	115
102. Turbo PROLOG	4.00		80	
103. TURING	4.00		80	
104. Turbo Pascal 4–5	4.50		72	
105. Ada 83	4.50	60	71	80
106. APT	4.50		71	
107. COGO	4.50		71	
108. DYANA	4.50		71	
109. ESPL/I	4.50	55	71	95
110. Fortran 95	4.50		71	
111. ICES	4.50		71	
112. JANUS	4.50		71	
113. LILITH	4.50		71	
114. NASTRAN	4.50		71	

TABLE 2.15 Programming Language Levels and Ranges of Source Code Statements per Function Point (*Continued*)

Language or dialect	Level	Min.	Mode	Max.
115. PL/M	4.50		71	
116. Problem-oriented default	4.50	50	71	90
117. SCEPTRE	4.50		71	
118. STRESS	4.50		71	
119. AMPPL II	5.00		64	
120. ANSI Basic	5.00	35	64	100
121. Arity PROLOG	5.00		64	
122. Associative default	5.00	35	64	85
123. COMIT II	5.00		64	
124. Common LISP	5.00		64	
125. CONNIVER	5.00		64	
126. FORTH (default)	5.00	27	64	85
127. Golden Common LISP	5.00	25	64	80
128. KCL	5.00		64	
129. KL	5.00		64	
130. KLO	5.00		64	
131. LAMBIT/L	5.00		64	
132. LISP default	5.00	25	64	80
133. macFORTH	5.00		64	
134. microFORTH	5.00		64	
135. MSL	5.00		64	
136. muLISP	5.00		64	
137. OBJECT Assembler	5.00		64	
138. PLANNER	5.00		64	
139. polyFORTH	5.00		64	
140. PROLOG default	5.00	35	64	90
141. Quick Basic 1	5.00	45	64	105
142. SYMBOLANG	5.00		64	
143. TCL	5.00		64	
144. TREET	5.00		64	
145. TREETRAN	5.00		64	
146. True Basic	5.00		64	
147. VULCAN	5.00		64	
148. XLISP	5.00		64	
149. ZLISP	5.00		64	
150. Quick Basic 2	5.25	40	61	100
151. CLARION	5.50		58	
152. HLEVEL	5.50		58	

TABLE 2.15 Programming Language Levels and Ranges of Source Code Statements per Function Point (*Continued*)

Language or dialect	Level	Min.	Mode	Max.
153. INTERLISP	5.50		58	
154. IQLISP	5.50		58	
155. KRL	5.50		58	
156. LOGLISP	5.50		58	
157. OPS5	5.50		58	
158. POP	5.50		58	
159. POPLOG	5.50		58	
160. PRO-IV	5.50		58	
161. QBasic	5.50		58	
162. Quick Basic 3	5.50	38	58	90
163. RPG II	5.50	40	58	85
164. RT-Expert 1.4	5.50		58	
165. SOLO	5.50		58	
166. VAX ACMS	5.50		58	
167. Extended Common LISP	5.75		56	
168. RPG III	5.75	37	56	80
169. TRANSLISP PLUS	5.75		56	
170. C++ (default value)	6.00	40	55	140
171. Centerline C++	6.00		55	
172. SCHEME	6.00		54	
173. BASE SAS	6.00		53	
174. CSP	6.00		53	
175. ED-Scheme 3.4.	6.00		53	
176. English-based default	6.00	35	53	90
177. FOIL	6.00		53	
178. INTELLECT	6.00		53	
179. LYRIC	6.00		53	
180. MAPPER	6.00		53	
181. MENTOR	6.00		53	
182. MS C++V.7	6.00		53	
183. NATURAL	6.00	43	53	77
184. Nroff	6.00		53	
185. PDP-11 ADE	6.00		53	
186. PILOT	6.00		53	
187. PLANIT	6.00		53	
188. PLATO	6.00		53	
189. TURBO C++	6.00	23	53	80
190. TUTOR	6.00		53	

TABLE 2.15 Programming Language Levels and Ranges of Source Code Statements per Function Point (*Continued*)

Language or dialect	Level	Min.	Mode	Max.
191. YACC	6.00		53	
192. YACC++	6.00		53	
193. Ada 95	6.50		49	
194. AI shell default	6.50	30	49	65
195. AI SHELLS	6.50		49	
196. AML	6.50		49	
197. ARC	6.50		49	
198. ARITY	6.50		49	
199. ART	6.50		49	
200. CAST	6.50		49	
201. CSL	6.50		49	
202. CxPERT	6.50		49	
203. EASY	6.50		49	
204. Eclipse	6.50		49	
205. ESPADVISOR	6.50		49	
206. EXSYS	6.50		49	
207. G2	6.50		49	
208. Guru	6.50		49	
209. INSIGHT2	6.50		49	
210. KBMS	6.50		49	
211. KEE	6.50		49	
212. KNOWOL	6.50		49	
213. NEXPERT	6.50		49	
214. NIAL	6.50		49	
215. Power Basic	6.50		49	
216. QNIAL	6.50		49	
217. TURBO EXPERT	6.50		49	
218. Turbo PASCAL >5	6.50		49	
219. TWAICE	6.50		49	
220. Visible C	6.50		49	
221. ART Enterprise	7.00		46	
222. ART-IM	7.00		46	
223. ASK Windows	7.00		46	
224. CELLSIM	7.00		46	
225. CICS	7.00		46	
226. CSSL	7.00		46	
227. DTABL	7.00		46	
228. DTIPT	7.00		46	

TABLE 2.15 Programming Language Levels and Ranges of Source Code Statements per Function Point (*Continued*)

Language or dialect	Level	Min.	Mode	Max.
229. DYNAMO-III	7.00		46	
230. FLEX	7.00		46	
231. GML	7.00		46	
232. GPSS	7.00		46	
233. OPS	7.00		46	
234. REALIA	7.00		46	
235. REXX (OS/2)	7.00		46	
236. SIMSCRIPT	7.00	35	46	60
237. SIMULA	7.00		46	
238. SIMULA 67	7.00		46	
239. Simulation default	7.00	30	46	65
240. STYLE	7.00		46	
241. ENFORM	7.00		45	
242. ADR/DL	8.00		40	
243. Artemis	8.00		40	
244. CA-dBFast	8.00		40	
245. CLIPPER DB	8.00		40	
246. CLOUT	8.00		40	
247. Database default	8.00	25	40	55
248. Dataflex	8.00		40	
249. dBase III	8.00	25	40	47
250. DEC-RALLY	8.00		40	
251. DL/1	8.00		40	
252. Erlang	8.00		40	
253. ESF	8.00		40	
254. FOCUS	8.00		40	
255. FOXPRO 1	8.00		40	
256. IBM CICS/VS	8.00	30	40	50
257. IDMS	8.00		40	
258. IMPRS	8.00		40	
259. INFORMIX	8.00		40	
260. INGRES	8.00		40	
261. KAPPA	8.00		40	
262. Keyplus	8.00		40	
263. MACH1	8.00		40	
264. MANTIS	8.00		40	
265. MARK IV	8.00		40	
266. Miranda	8.00		40	

TABLE 2.15 Programming Language Levels and Ranges of Source Code Statements per Function Point (*Continued*)

Language or dialect	Level	Min.	Mode	Max.
267. NOMAD2	8.00	30	40	55
268. OMNIS 7	8.00		40	
269. ORACLE	8.00		40	
270. PACE	8.00		40	
271. PPL (Plus)	8.00		40	
272. RAMIS II	8.00	30	40	50
273. RALLY	8.00		40	
274. RDB	8.00		40	
275. Realizer 1.0	8.00		40	
276. RELATE/3000	8.00		40	
277. SYBASE	8.00		40	
278. TESSARACT	8.00		40	
279. VAX ADE	8.00		40	
280. Visible Cobol	8.00		40	
281. Visual Basic DOS	8.00		40	
282. WARP X	8.00		40	
283. Access	8.50		38	
284. Haskell	8.50		38	
285. Model 204	8.50	23	37	43
286. Visual Basic 1	8.50	25	37	45
287. Application Manager	9.00		36	
288. BMSGEN	9.00		36	
289. CodeCenter	9.00		36	
290. Cofac	9.00		36	
291. COGEN	9.00		36	
292. COGNOS	9.00		36	
293. Ladder Logic	9.00		36	
294. MDL	9.00		36	
295. PC FOCUS	9.00		36	
296. dBase IV	9.00		35	
297. Decision supplement default	9.00	20	35	40
298. EXPRESS	9.00		35	
299. EZNOMAD	9.00		35	
300. FAME	9.00		35	
301. FileMaker Pro	9.00		35	
302. MARK V	9.00		35	
303. Nonprocedural default	9.00	23	35	40
304. Notes VIP	9.00		35	

TABLE 2.15 Programming Language Levels and Ranges of Source Code Statements per Function Point (*Continued*)

Language or dialect	Level	Min.	Mode	Max.
305. PARADOX/PAL	9.00		35	
306. PROGRESS V4	9.00		35	
307. Realizer 2.0	9.00		35	
308. SIMPLAN	9.00		35	
309. SPEAKEASY	9.00		35	
310. Spinnaker PPL	9.00		35	
311. STRATEGEM	9.00		35	
312. SUPERBASE 1.3	9.00		35	
313. System-W	9.00		35	
314. UFO/IMS	9.00		35	
315. Visual Basic 2	9.00	23	35	40
316. VZ Programmer	9.00		35	
317. FOXPRO 2.5	9.50		34	
318. GFA Basic	9.50		34	
319. Visual C++	9.50		34	
320. AMBUSH	10.00		32	
321. APL 360/370	10.00	12	32	45
322. APL default	10.00	10	32	45
323. APL*PLUS	10.00		32	
324. CLI	10.00		32	
325. IFPS/PLUS	10.00		32	
326. S-PLUS	10.00		32	
327. SAS	10.00		32	
328. SPSS	10.00		32	
329. Statistical default	10.00	20	32	40
330. UHELP	10.00		32	
331. Visual Basic 3	10.00	20	32	37
332. VS-REXX	10.00		32	
333. FLAVORS	11.00		29	
334. DELPHI	11.00		29	
335. EASEL	11.00		29	
336. Ensemble	11.00		29	
337. FactoryLink IV	11.00		29	
338. FlexGen	11.00		29	
339. Foundation	11.00		29	
340. Object LISP	11.00		29	
341. Object LOGO	11.00		29	
342. Object PASCAL	11.00		29	

TABLE 2.15 Programming Language Levels and Ranges of Source Code Statements per Function Point (*Continued*)

Language or dialect	Level	Min.	Mode	Max.
343. Object-Oriented default	11.00	13	29	40
344. OODL	11.00		29	
345. Symantec C++	11.00		29	
346. Topspeed C++	11.00		29	
347. Acumen	11.50		28	
348. CA-EARL	11.50		28	
349. GUEST	11.50		28	
350. Quickbuild	11.50		28	
351. RapidGen	11.50		28	
352. Wizard	11.50		28	
353. AWK	15.00		27	
354. CLOS	15.00		27	
355. Genascript	12.00		27	
356. KSH	12.00		27	
357. Objective-C	12.00	17	27	38
358. PERL	12.00		27	
359. Pro-C	12.00		27	
360. ObjectVIEW	13.00		25	
361. ACTOR	15.00		21	
362. EIFFEL	15.00		21	
363. LOOPS	15.00		21	
364. MAGIK	15.00		21	
365. MAKE	15.00		21	
366. PDL Millenium	15.00		21	
367. SHELL	15.00		21	
368. SMALLTALK 286	15.00		21	
369. SMALLTALK 80	15.00		21	
370. SMALLTALK/V	15.00	12	21	30
371. VisualAge	15.00		21	
372. Fourth generation default	16.00	10	20	30
373. ADR/IDEAL/PDL	16.00	14	20	30
374. ADS/Batch	16.00		20	
375. ADS/Online	16.00		20	
376. Application Builder	16.00		20	
377. APTools	16.00		20	
378. CDADL	16.00		20	
379. COBRA	16.00		20	
380. Datatrieve	16.00		20	

TABLE 2.15 Programming Language Levels and Ranges of Source Code Statements per Function Point (*Continued*)

Language or dialect	Level	Min.	Mode	Max.
381. EPOS	16.00		20	
382. Facets	16.00		20	
383. IBM ADF I	16.00		20	
384. MicroStep	16.00		20	
385. Visual Cobol	16.00		20	
386. ACCEL	17.00		19	
387. AS/SET	17.00		19	
388. CLIPPER	17.00		19	
389. CMSGEN	17.00		19	
390. CORVET	17.00		19	
391. CYGNET	17.00		19	
392. DNA-4	17.00		19	
393. GENIFER	17.00		19	
394. IBM ADF II	18.00		19	
395. MUMPS	17.00		19	
396. NETRON/CAP	17.00		19	
397. SYNON/2E	17.00		19	
398. VHDL	17.00		19	
399. ZIM	17.00		19	
400. Forte	18.00		18	
401. Synchroworks	18.00		18	
402. APS	19.00		17	
403. 1032/AF	20.00		16	
404. ABAP/4	20.00		16	
405. GAMMA	20.00		16	
406. GeODE 2.0	20.00		16	
407. Huron	20.00		16	
408. INSTALL/1	20.00		16	
409. M	20.00		16	
410. MAESTRO	20.00		16	
411. MAGEC	20.00		16	
412. PowerBuilder	20.00		16	
413. Program generator default	20.00	10	16	20
414. SAPIENS	20.00		16	
415. TELON	20.00	13	16	20
416. UNIFACE	20.00		16	
417. Visual Objects	20.00		16	
418. CorVision	22.00		15	

TABLE 2.15 Programming Language Levels and Ranges of Source Code Statements per Function Point (*Continued*)

Language or dialect	Level	Min.	Mode	Max.
419. GENEXUS	21.00		15	
420. PACBASE	22.00	12	15	24
421. QMF	22.00		15	
422. QUIZ	22.00		15	
423. TRANSFORM	22.00		15	
424. IEF	23.00	10	14	22
425. IEW	23.00	11	14	23
426. LINC II	23.00		14	
427. POWERHOUSE	23.00		14	
428. SoftScreen	23.00		14	
429. TI-IEF	23.00	10	14	22
430. ANSI SQL	25.00		13	
431. ANSWER/DB	25.00		13	
432. ASI/INQUIRY	25.00		13	
433. CULPRIT	25.00		13	
434. EASYTRIEVE+	25.00		13	
435. GENER/OL	25.00		13	
436. INQUIRE	25.00		13	
437. IQRP	25.00		13	
438. QBE	25.00		13	
439. Query default	25.00	9	13	20
440. SAVVY	25.00		13	
441. SQL	25.00	7	13	15
442. THEMIS	25.00		13	
443. EDA/SQL	27.00		12	
444. SEQUAL	27.00		12	
445. SQL-Windows	27.00		12	
446. Visicalc 1	35.00	5	9	15
447. PLANPERFECT 1	45.00		7	
448. MOSAIC	45.00		7	
449. BOEINGCALC	50.00		6	
450. EXCEL 1-2	51.00		6	
451. EXCEL 3-4	55.00		6	
452. FRAMEWORK	50.00	4	6	10
453. LOTUS 123 DOS	50.00	4	6	12
454. LUCID 3D	51.00		6	
455. QUATTRO	51.00		6	
456. QUATTRO PRO	51.00		6	

TABLE 2.15 Programming Language Levels and Ranges of Source Code Statements per Function Point (*Continued*)

Language or dialect	Level	Min.	Mode	Max.
457. Reuse default	60.00	3	6	8
458. Screen painter default	57.00		6	
459. Spreadsheet default	50.00	3	6	9
460. SURPASS	50.00		6	
461. THE TWIN	50.00		6	
462. EXCEL 5	57.00		5.5	
463. MATHCAD	60.00		5	
464. Fifth generation default	70.00	2	4	6

too, the organizing principle may be useful enough to compensate for errors in the individual placements.

Many applications are written in mixed languages, so the question that arises is how sizing might be performed in applications that are partially implemented in two, three, or any number of languages.

For example, suppose the application contains 1000 source code statements in Cobol and 1000 source code statements in a database development language such as DL1. Cobol is a level-3 language which will average about 105 statements per function point; DL1 is a level-8 language which will average about 40 statements per function point. To calculate a function point approximation for the combination, it is only necessary to divide the source code size by the average expansion factors, which will yield about 9.5 function points for the Cobol and 25 function points for the DL1. The application as a whole will contain 34.5 function points and will have an average expansion of about 58 source code statements per function point, giving the language combination an effective level of about 5.5.

The calculation sequence for mixed languages is shown below:

1000 Cobol statements\105 = 9.5 Cobol function points

1000 DL1 statements\40 = 25.0 DL1 function points

2000 total statements   total function points

2000 total statements\34.5 = 57.97 statements per function point

320 Assembler statements\57.97 = 5.52 effective language level

The calculations for mixed languages are tedious if carried out by hand or with a calculator for more than two languages. However, it is very easy to construct a spreadsheet or a simple program that can perform the calculations for any number of languages. (The maximum number of languages observed in one application in recent years is 11, so a tool that could calculate up to a dozen languages should be sufficient.)

Backfiring function points for existing software

Many enterprises have enormous portfolios of applications and systems written, in some cases, years before function points were even invented. For historical purposes and consistency, it is often desirable to be able to calculate function point totals for existing applications.

It is possible, of course, to count the function point parameters by hand in existing software. But those who have actually attempted to do that find that several days of effort may be required, and the work is often unpleasant. In extreme cases, even the documentation that describes the application may be missing or incomplete and the original programming staff no longer works at the enterprise.

The SPR function point method supports retrofitting of function points to existing software as its eighth goal beyond the five basic IBM function point targets. This retrofitting of function points is termed "backfiring." Backfiring of function points is possible because the SPR algorithms are bidirectional. If function points, code complexity, and the source language are the inputs, then the algorithms will predict source code size. If the inputs are source code size, code complexity, and source language, the algorithms will predict function points. The time required to retrofit function points to existing applications with the backfire method is usually less than a minute, assuming source code counts are available.

Once a relation between function points and source code size is established for a language such as Cobol, it becomes possible to backfire function points to older applications for which source code size is known by simply dividing the source code size by the appropriate function point expansion factor. For example, the function point total for an application of 10,000 Cobol source statements can be found by simply dividing 10,000 by the average expansion rate of 105 Cobol statements per function point, which yields a total of 95 function points.

However, it is at this point that *code complexity* becomes an important factor in function point calculations and rejoins *problem complexity* and *data complexity* in calculations. Highly complex code tends to require more source statements per function point than extremely simple code. Thus, very complex Cobol may require 150 statements to implement one function point, whereas very simple Cobol may require only 65 statements per function point.

The approximate range of adjustments in how many statements are required to implement one function point is illustrated by Table 2.16. For backfiring, first refer to Table 2.15 for the average number of statements per function point. For example, if you have 10,500 Cobol statements in your application, then dividing by the average expansion factor of 105 indicates that you have a total of 1000 function points for a project of average complexity. Next, divide the initial function point total by the adjustment factor shown in Table 2.16. Thus, if your application is of simple overall complexity, say a complexity sum of 6, divide by 0.85 to create a probable function point total of 1176.

If, on the other hand, your application is complex, say a complexity sum of 12, divide by 1.15 to create a probable function point total of 869. The implications of these calculations lead to a concept termed "the conservation of function points." In essence, it takes fewer statements to implement one function point for simple applications than it does for complex ones. This concept is also true in reverse: When function points are backfired, highly complex code will contain fewer function points than the same volume of simple code. This concept is counterintuitive, but it appears to be empirically correct.

For normal forward function point calculations, complexity adjustments also are desirable. To use the information in Table 2.16 in for-

TABLE 2.16 Adjustment Factors for Source Code Size Prediction

Sum of problem, code, and data complexity	Code size adjustment multiplier
3	0.70
4	0.75
5	0.80
6	0.85
7	0.90
8	0.95
9	1.00
10	1.05
11	1.10
12	1.15
13	1.20
14	1.25
15	1.30

ward mode, first sum the values of the three SPR complexity factors (problem, code, and data), which will create a total that ranges from 3 to 15. Next refer to Table 2.15 for the language and average number of statements per function point that you are interested in. Third, refer to Table 2.16 and select the source code size multiplier that matches your complexity sum. Fourth, multiply the average number of statements per function point by the adjustment factor from Table 2.16.

For example, if you are interested in Cobol the average number of statements per function point can be seen to be 105 by referring to Table 2.15. If the sum of your complexity factors is 12, multiply 105 by 1.15 to create a new value of 120.75 as the probable number of source code statements per function point in your application, adjusted for complexity.

Although the adjustments in Table 2.16 seem to give good results, it should be noted that the overall impact of complexity on source code size is not yet an exact science. It is quite possible for projects to behave very differently from the results shown here.

Function Points for Maintenance and Enhancement Projects

In 1990, somewhat more than 50 percent of the programmers in the United States were working on maintenance and enhancement of existing software.[15] Plainly, function points should be useful for those projects too. Indeed, the need to use function points for maintenance adds a ninth goal:

9. The metric should be useful for maintenance and enhancements.

Albrecht's 1984 revision to the IBM function point technique added the capability for using function points on maintenance and enhancement projects. For such projects there are three steps in using function points: (1) The function point total of the project before the changes are made is calculated. (2) The function point total for the update itself is calculated. (3) The function point total for the new release after the revision is calculated.

When used for maintenance and enhancements, function points can provide some useful insights into overall costs. There is a useful figure of merit that is starting to receive serious study: the maintenance assignment scope. An *assignment scope* is the amount of work for which one person is normally responsible in the course of a year. For maintenance purposes, it is an interesting topic to discover how many function points one maintenance programmer can comfortably handle. For modern well-structured software in a language such as Cobol, a maintenance programmer can be responsible for maintaining in excess of 1500 function points. For poorly structured, poorly documented aging software, the assignment scope seldom rises above 500 function points. Many enterprises average around 1000 function points as their normal assignment scopes. Restructuring and geriatric care for aging software can raise the assignment scope dramatically.

The 1986 Formation of the International Function Point Users' Group (IFPUG)

By 1986, several hundred companies, many but not all of them clients of IBM, had been using function points. The association of IBM's commercial clients, GUIDE, had established a working group on function points in 1983, but by 1986 a critical mass of function point users had occurred. It was then decided to form a new nonprofit organization devoted exclusively to the utilization of function points and the propagation of data derived from function point studies.

The new organization was named the International Function Point Users Group. Because of the length of the name, the organization is more commonly identified by the abbreviation, IFPUG, as it quickly came to be called. IFPUG has evolved from its informal beginnings into a major new association concerned with every aspect of software measurement: productivity, quality, complexity, and even sociological implications.

The IFPUG counting practices committee has become a de facto standards group for normalizing the way function points are counted, and it has done much to resolve the variations in terminology and even the misconceptions that naturally occur when a metric gains wide international use.

The IFPUG organization originated in Toronto, Canada. The organization moved its headquarters to the United States in 1988 and became a nonprofit U.S. corporation. Since this group is a nonprofit organization not affiliated with any vendor, as well as the worldwide focal point for function point metrics, it is appropriate to include the address and contact information:

IFPUG
Blendonview Office Park
5008-28 Pine Creek Drive
Westerville, Ohio 43081-4899

Phone (614) 895 7130
FAX (614) 895 3466

As this edition is being prepared, IFPUG is about to create a worldwide web home page on the Internet. The function point forum that communicates by E-mail over the Internet has more than 200 members as of the middle of 1995. There are also active function point forums and discussions on many information utilities such as CompuServe and America On-Line.

The 1986 Development of Feature Points for Real-Time and Systems Software

Function points were originally invented to solve the measurement problems of classical management information systems. This MIS origin means that function points are not necessarily perceived as optimal for real-time software such as missile defense systems, systems software such as operating systems, embedded software such as radar navigation packages, communications software such as telephone switching systems, process control software such as refinery drivers, engineering applications such as CAD and CIM, discrete simulations, or mathematical software.

When function points are applied to such systems, they, of course, generate counts, but the counts perhaps appear to be misleading for software that is high in algorithmic complexity but sparse in inputs and outputs. From both a psychological and practical vantage point, the harder kinds of systems software seem to require a counting method that is equivalent to function points but is sensitive to the difficulties brought on by high algorithmic complexity. The need to support real-time and systems software can be formally stated as a tenth goal for metrics:

10. The metric should work equally well with all MIS applications, systems software, real-time software, embedded software, and all other types of software.

In 1986, Software Productivity Research developed an experimental method for applying function point logic to system software such as operating systems and telephone switching systems.[16] To avoid confusion with the IBM function point method, this experimental alternative was called *feature points.* Since the initial results of using feature points have been favorable, the method has been experimentally applied to many kinds of software: systems software, embedded software, real-time software, CAD, AI, and even MIS software.

The SPR feature point metric is a superset of the IBM function point metric. It introduces a new parameter, algorithms, in addition to the five standard function point parameters. The algorithms parameter is assigned a default weight of 3. The feature point method also reduces the empirical weights for logical data files from IBM's average value of 10 down to an average value of 7 to reflect the somewhat reduced significance of logical files for systems software vis-à-vis information systems.

As can be seen, for applications in which the number of algorithms and logical data files are the same, function points and feature points will generate the same numeric totals. But when there are many more algorithms than files, which is not uncommon with systems software, the feature points will generate a higher total than function points. Conversely, if there are only a few algorithms but many files, which is common with some information systems, feature points will generate a lower total than function points. When feature points and function points are used on classical MIS projects, the results are often almost identical. For example, one small MIS project totaled 107 function points and 107 feature points. However, when applied to the harder forms of system software, the feature point counts are significantly higher. For a PBX telephone switch, the function point total was 1845 but the feature point total was 2300 because of the high algorithmic complexity of the application.

Although both the DeMarco bang metric and feature points are aimed at systems and scientific software, feature points differ from the DeMarco bang metric in these ways:

1. Feature points are intended to be mathematically mappable to function points. The bang metric does not aim at such equivalence, although it may be possible to convert counts from a subset of the DeMarco parameters into function points.
2. Feature points are intended to preserve the essential simplicity of the SPR counting concepts; the DeMarco bang metric opts for high precision at the cost of fairly substantial counting effort.

Since feature points are driven by algorithmic complexity, a definition of "algorithm" is appropriate. An algorithm is defined as the set of rules which must be completely expressed in order to solve a significant computational problem. For example, both a square root extraction routine or a Julian date conversion routine would be considered algorithms.

The SPR feature point method is similar in concept to function points, as can be seen from Table 2.17.

The SPR feature point method and the IBM function point method are obviously similar in concept, but what about pragmatic results? As of 1990, the feature point technique is still experimental and is still undergoing field trials. Some of the results to date are as follows: When feature points and function points are used on classical MIS projects, the results are often almost identical; as mentioned above one project totaled 107 function points and 107 feature points. The

TABLE 2.17 The 1986 SPR Feature Point Method

Significant parameter		Empirical weight	
Number of algorithms?	______	× 3 =	______
Number of inputs?	______	× 4 =	______
Number of outputs?	______	× 5 =	______
Number of inquiries?	______	× 4 =	______
Number of data files?	______	× 7 =	______
Number of interfaces?	______	× 7 =	______
Unadjusted total			______
Complexity adjustment			______
Adjusted feature point total			______

function point and feature point values usually converge. But when used on real-time and systems software, feature points often generate higher totals than function points. In one small real-time project, the total was 45 function points but 70 feature points.

Counting and weighting algorithms

Since the most visible difference between function points and feature points is the new parameter for "algorithms," it is worthwhile to discuss algorithmic concepts and how algorithms can be counted. An algorithm is defined in standard software engineering texts as the set of rules which must be described and encoded to solve a computational problem. Some examples of typical algorithms include calendar date routines, square root extraction routines, and overtime pay calculation routines. For feature point counting purposes, an algorithm can be defined in the following terms: "An algorithm is a bounded computational problem which is included within a specific computer program."

Algorithms obviously vary in difficulty and complexity, and the SPR treatment of algorithms assumes a range of perhaps 10 to 1 for algorithmic difficulty (the absolute range in real life is no doubt as great as 1000 to 1, but ranges of that magnitude are difficult to encompass). Algorithms requiring only basic arithmetic operations or a few simple rules would be assigned a minimum value of 1. Algorithms requiring complex equations, matrix operations, and difficult mathematical and logical processing might be assigned a weight of 10. The default weight for a normal algorithm using ordinary mathematics would be 3.

Although more than 50 software engineering books that describe and discuss algorithms are in print, it is interesting that there is no available taxonomy for classifying algorithms other than purely ad hoc methods based on what the algorithm might be used for. There is a need for a taxonomy based on complexity, and hopefully the feature point research can move toward that goal.

The basis for the provisional weights for algorithms is twofold: (1) the number of calculation steps or rules required by the algorithm and (2) the number of factors or data elements required by the algorithm. Since the feature point method is still experimental, the approach to weighting algorithms is still under evolution. For provisional purposes, Table 2.18 shows approximate equivalence between weights, rules, and factors currently being considered. Powers of 2 provide the basis of Table 2.18, as can be seen.

To illustrate the terms "rule" and "factor," consider the following example taken from an algorithm that selects activities in a software estimating tool: "If class is equal to 'military' and size is ⇒100 feature points, then independent verification and validation will be performed." The example is a single rule, and it contains two factors: class and size.

There are some supplemental rules for determining what algorithms are countable and significant:

1. The algorithm must deal with a solvable problem.
2. The algorithm must deal with a bounded problem.
3. The algorithm must deal with a definite problem.
4. The algorithm must be finite and have an end.

TABLE 2.18 Provisional Algorithm Weights, Rules, and Factors

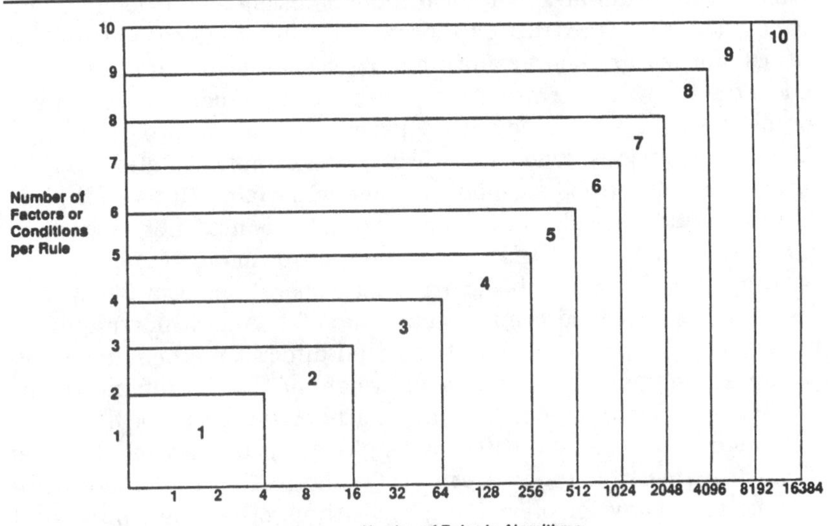

5. The algorithm must be precise and have no ambiguity.
6. The algorithm must have an input or starting value.
7. The algorithm must have output or produce a result.
8. The algorithm must be implementable in that each step must be capable of execution on a computer.
9. The algorithm can include or call upon subordinate algorithms.
10. The algorithm must be capable of representation via the standard structured programming concepts of sequence, if-then-else, do-while, CASE, etc.

These factors are currently being tuned and evaluated, since feature points are still experimental. However, research is underway to develop a more rigorous taxonomy and weighting scale for algorithms.

Examples of typical algorithms

Although the software engineering literature is plentifully supplied with illustrations and examples of algorithms, there is currently no complete catalog of the more common algorithms which occur with high frequency in software applications. Since it is always more useful to have tangible examples of concepts, the following are discussions of some common algorithm types:

Sorting. Sorting is one of the earliest forms of algorithm created during the computer era. Although physical sorting of records and files has been carried out for thousands of years, it was not until mechanical tabulating equipment was developed that sorting became anything other than a brute force manual task. With the arrival of electronic computers, the scientific study of sorting began. Sorting itself and the development of ever faster sorting algorithms have been among the triumphs of the software engineering community. Prior to about 1950, sorting methods were primarily simple and ad hoc. During the 1960s, 1970s, and on through to today, whole new families of sorting methods and improved algorithms were developed, including selection sorts, insertion sorts, bubble sorts, quicksort, and radix sorting.

Searching. Two of the primary functions of computers in their normal day-to-day business applications are sorting and searching. Here again, physical files have been searched for thousands of years, and techniques for facilitating the storage and retrieval of information long outdate the computer era. However, it was only after the emergence of electronic computers that the study of searching algorithms entered a rigorous and formal phase. This new research into sorting methods led to the development of binary searches, tree searches, indirect tree searches, radix searches, and many others.

Step-rate calculation functions. Under the concept of the graduated income tax, a certain level of taxable income is related to a certain tax rate. Higher incomes pay higher tax rates; lower incomes pay lower tax rates. The same logic of dealing with the dependent relations of two variables is perhaps the commonest general form of algorithm for business software. This logic, termed a "step rate calculation function," which is used for income tax rates, can also apply to the rates for consuming public utilities such as electricity and water, for salary and performance calculations, and dividends.

Feedback loops. Feedback loops of various kinds are common algorithms in process control applications, hospital patient monitoring applications, and many forms of embedded software such as that for fuel injection, radar, and navigation. Classic feedback loops are much older than the computer era, of course, and one of the clearest examples is provided by the automatic governors on steam engines. Such governors were normally rotating metal weights whose rotation was driven by escaping steam. As the velocity of the steam increased when pressures went higher, the governors opened more widely and allowed excess steam to escape. This same concept of feedback between two variables is one of the major classes of algorithms for sensor-based applications.

Function point calculations. It is appropriate to conclude the discussion of representative algorithms with the observation that the calculation sequence for function points is itself an algorithm. Let us consider two practical examples. Suppose you were writing a computer program to calculate function points by using IBM's original 1979 methodology. The calculation sequence would be to multiply the raw data for inputs, outputs, inquiries, and master files by the empirical weights Albrecht derived, thus creating a subtotal of unadjusted function points. You would then multiply the unadjusted subtotal by a user-specified complexity factor to create the final adjusted function point total. This entire calculating sequence would comprise only one algorithm, the "function point calculation algorithm." Since the calculations consist of only five simple multiplications and two additions, the weight for this algorithm can be viewed as minimal and be assigned a weighting value of 1.

Now let us suppose you were writing a computer program to calculate function points by using IBM's methodology as it was revised in 1984 and currently exists in 1990. The calculation sequence today would be to first multiply and sum the file and data element references to determine high, low, or medium complexity of the five input parameters. You would then multiply raw data for inputs, outputs, inquiries, data files, and interfaces by the separate values for high, low, and medium complexity to quantify the unadjusted function point total.

Then the 14 influential factors would be summed and multiplied by 0.01 and the constant 0.65 would be added to create the influence multiplier weight. Finally, the unadjusted function points would be multiplied by the influence weight to yield the adjusted function point total. Calculating the function point total is still, of course, a single algorithm, but now the weight would appropriately be set at 3 to reflect the increased difficulty of the calculation sequence. Thus, the original 1979 version of IBM's function points could be programmed with a single algorithm having a total algorithmic weight of 1. The 1984 revisions of IBM's function point method now require a more normal weight of 3. As can be seen from the two examples, as the algorithmic complexity of an application moves up the difficulty scale, the feature point technique can follow closely.

Additional considerations in the domain of algorithms include whether the algorithm in question lends itself to sequential or parallel processing. In addition, it is desirable to consider these aspects of algorithms:

1. Uniqueness
2. Correctness
3. Computational complexity
4. Length
5. Performance
6. Sensitivity
7. Selectivity

The research centering around the practical applications of feature points has opened up some interesting and potentially significant gaps in the software engineering literature. Notably, there seems to be no standard taxonomy for classifying algorithms, and there is no standard weighting scale for judging their difficulty or complexity.

From discussions with companies, such as DEC, Tektronix, and Motorola, that are experimenting with the feature point method, the most common question asked concerns the level of granularity of the algorithms to be counted. If the basic concept is held in mind that an "algorithm" should be bounded and complete and should perform a fairly significant business or technical function, then some practical illustrations of algorithms can be given. For example:

- In telephone switching systems, call routing is an appropriate algorithmic topic.
- In PC operating systems, floppy disk formatting is an example of an algorithm.

- In payroll programs, the calculations for hourly, exempt, managerial, and contractor pay are examples of normal algorithms.
- In process control applications, pressure monitoring and feedback are examples.

To give a somewhat more detailed example of typical algorithms and the weights assigned to them, Table 2.19 shows the major algorithms and the assigned weights in a software resource, cost, and quality estimating program as analyzed by the author.

As can be seen from Table 2.19, the level of granularity of typical algorithms is reasonably fine but not excessively so. (From examining the actual source code of the project used to provide the data of Table 2.19, the algorithms weighted 1 all took fewer than 25 statements in C to implement, the level-2 weighted algorithms usually took less than 50 C statements, the level-3 weighted algorithms usually took fewer than 100 C statements, and so on.)

It may be of interest to see some representative results. Table 2.20

TABLE 2.19 Examples of Algorithms in a Software Estimating Program

Algorithm	Algorithm weight
1. Defect potential prediction	3
2. Defect removal prediction	2
3. Function point calculation	2
4. Source code size prediction	2
5. Backfire function point prediction	2
6. Document size prediction	3
7. Test case and test run prediction	2
8. Reliability prediction	2
9. Paid overtime impact on project	1
10. Unpaid overtime impact on project	2
11. Development staff, effort, and schedule prediction	4
12. Activity schedule overlap prediction	3
13. Annual maintenance effort and staff prediction	3
14. Annual enhancement effort and staff prediction	3
15. Overall aggregation of project effort and costs	2
16. Overall calculation of project schedule	2
17. Effort and cost normalization	1
18. International currency conversion	1
19. Inflation rate calculation	1
20. Normalization of data to selected base metric	1

TABLE 2.20 Selected Project Results When Using the Feature Point Metric

Project type	Size range in feature points	Productivity range in feature points
1. Airline reservation	25,000–50,000	0.5–5.0
2. Billing systems	2,500–7,500	3.0–20.0
3. CAD software	600–2,500	1.0–6.5
4. Integrated CASE tools	1,000–15,000	2.5–17.5
5. Public switches	4,000–25,000	0.3–4.5
6. Compilers	600–2,000	2.5–25.0
7. Insurance claims handling	9,000–25,000	3.0–18.0
8. Operating systems	5,000–50,000	0.5–6.5
9. PBX switches	1,000–5,000	1.0–5.5
10. Project planning tools	250–1,500	3.0–12.0
11. Spreadsheet packages	1,000–3,000	2.0–10.0
12. Word processing packages	500–3,500	4.5–12.5

gives the ranges of a dozen project types, including sizes and overall productivity results that occur when using the feature point metric and backfiring data.

Choosing function points or feature points

For applications in which the number of algorithms is uncertain or in which algorithmic factors are not significant, function points would be the appropriate choice for a metric. Many business applications fall within this category, perhaps accounting software, customer information systems, and marketing support systems.

For applications in which the number of algorithms is countable, and in which algorithmic factors are significant, feature points would be the appropriate choice for a metric. Many scientific, engineering, and systems applications fall within this category, perhaps telephone switching systems, process control systems, and embedded software such as fuel injection.

Although the feature point method is still experimental and comparatively sparse data are available for it, the results of some early side-by-side comparisons between function points and feature points are interesting. Table 2.21 illustrates the experimental ratios between function points and feature points for sample kinds of software.

When the first edition of this book was published in 1991, standard IFPUG function points had been used very seldom for real-time and embedded software. Now that function points are the dominant soft-

TABLE 2.21 Ratios of Feature Points to Function Points for Selected Application Types

Application	Function points	Feature points
Batch MIS projects	1	0.80
On-line MIS projects	1	1.00
On-line database projects	1	1.00
Switching systems projects	1	1.20
Embedded real-time projects	1	1.35
Factory automation projects	1	1.50
Diagnostic and prediction projects	1	1.75

ware metric in much of the world, usage is increasing for every kind of software.

The basic IFPUG function point metric actually works very well for real-time and embedded software. However, it is necessary to expand some of the definitions of "inputs" and "outputs" to encompass things such as sensor-based information, hardware interrupt signals, voltage changes, and so forth.

Standard IFPUG function points have been successfully applied to military software such as the Tomahawk cruise missile, the software on board Aegis-class naval vessels, fuel injection systems in Ford automobiles, software embedded in medical instruments such as CAT scan equipment, both public and private telephone switching systems, and computer operating systems such as IBM's MVS and Microsoft's Windows 95.

The success of standard function points for real-time and embedded software has reduced the need for specialized variations such as feature point metrics. However, the overall IFPUG literature needs to be revised and expanded to facilitate the use of function points for applications other than information systems.

As a historical note, the inventor of function points, Allan Albrecht, is an electrical engineer by training and has always envisioned function points as a general-purpose metric for all kinds of software. The historical accident that function points were first applied to information systems led to the misconception that the metric was only suitable for information systems.

The 1987 Merger of Function Points and Halstead Metrics

In 1987, Don Reifer published a description[17] of a metric that was based on the concept of merging the Albrecht function point technique with the older Halstead software science metric.[18] The latter is based on the work of the late Dr. Maurice Halstead of Purdue University. Like many researchers, Halstead was troubled by the ambiguity and paradoxical nature of "lines of code." His technique was an attempt to resolve the problems by looking at the specific subelements of lines of code. He divided code into two atomic units: the executable or command portion (which he termed "operators") and the data descriptive portion (which he termed "operands"). The Halstead metric centers around counts of four separate values:

1. The total number of unique operators
2. The total number of unique operands
3. The total quantity of operators in an application
4. The total quantity of operands in an application

From those four counts, a number of supporting metrics are derived including:

1. The program's vocabulary (sum of unique operators and operands)
2. The program's length (sum of total operators and total operands)

There are a number of conceptual and practical difficulties about attempting to merge function points with the Halstead software science technique. From a conceptual standpoint, function points are intended to be independent of the programming language used and capable of being applied early in a project's life cycle, as during requirements and design. Since the Halstead software science metric is basically only a more sophisticated way of counting lines of code, it appears to be a poor choice for metrics applied early in the life cycle and also to be counter to the essential philosophy of function points as being language-independent.

The practical difficulties lie in the ambiguities and uncertainties of the Halstead software science metric itself. An attempt by ITT statisticians in 1981[19] to replicate some of the published findings associated with the Halstead software science metric uncovered anomalies in the fundamental data and a number of questionable assertions. The final conclusion was that the Halstead software science metric was so intrinsically ambiguous and studies using it were so poorly constructed and controlled that the results were useless for serious economic study purposes.

There are also a few problems of an historical nature with the fundamental assertions of the software science metric. For example, the software science literature has made the correct assertion that there is a strong relation between the length and vocabulary of a program.

That is, large systems will use a richer set of operator and operand constructs than small programs.

Although that observation is correct, it had actually been noted in 1935 by the linguist George Zipf for natural languages such as English and Mandarin Chinese. Indeed, Zipf's law on the relation of vocabulary and length covers the topic. As it happens, there appears to be a constant relation between length and vocabulary that would be true even if the language consisted of random characters divided into words or random lengths!

Unfortunately, few of the software science articles and reports build on those findings from conventional linguistics, and it is fair to say that the whole software science concept suffers from a tendency to be unfamiliar with conventional linguistics, even though the two domains are covering the same grounds. If the software science community had included the ideas published by linguists such as Zipf, Whorf, and Chomsky, the software science concept would not appear to be on such shaky intellectual ground.

The 1988 Publication of the British Mark II Function Point Method

In January 1988, Charles Symons, of Nolan, Norton & Company in London, published a description of his Mark II Function Point metric in the *IEEE Transactions on Software Engineering*.[20] Although Symons' work had started in the early 1980s and was announced in England in 1983, it was not well known in the United States prior to the IEEE publication in 1988.

Symons had been carrying out some function point studies at Xerox and other companies in the United Kingdom, and he had formed the opinion that the 1984 IBM method might perhaps be modified. The essence of Symons' concerns were four:

1. He wanted to reduce the subjectivity in dealing with files by measuring entities and relations among entities.
2. He wanted to modify the function point approach so that it would create the same numeric totals regardless of whether an application was implemented as a single system or as a set of related subsystems.
3. He wanted to change the fundamental rationale for function points away from value to users and switch it to the effort required to produce the functionality.
4. He felt that the 14 influential factors cited by Albrecht and IBM were insufficient, and so he added six factors.

When carried to completion, Symons' modifications of the basic function point methodology were sufficiently different from IBM's to merit the "Mark II" nomenclature. When counting the same application, the resulting function point totals differ between the IBM and Mark II by sometimes more than 30 percent, with the Mark II technique usually generating the larger totals.

Viewed objectively, Symons' four concerns are not equal in their impact, and his modifications have pros and cons. His first concern, introducing entities and relationships, does add a new dimension of rigor to function point counting, and his suggestion is starting to find widespread acceptance. His second concern, wanting total function point counts to stay constant regardless of whether an application is monolithic or distributed, is debatable and questionable. For example, in a construction project involving physical objects such as living space, there will be very significant differences in providing 1500 ft^2 of housing in the form of 10 single-family homes or in the form of 10 apartments in a single large building. It is obvious to architects and contractors that very different quantities of lumber, cement, roofing, and so on, will be required depending upon which construction choice is made.

In a parallel fashion, an application developed as an integrated, monolithic system will certainly have different needs and requirements than if the same functionality is implemented in 10 independent programs. At the very least, the interfaces will be quite different. Therefore, attempting to generate a constant function point count regardless of whether an application is monolithic or distributed seems hazardous.

Symon's third concern, wishing to change the basis of the function point method from "user value" to "development effort," appears to be a step in a retrograde direction. To continue with the parallel of the building trade, the value of a home is only partly attributable to the construction costs. The other aspects of home value deal with the architectural and design features of the home, the charm of the site, the value of surrounding homes, convenience of location, and many other topics.

In Albrecht's original concept, function points were analogous to the work of an architect in home construction: The architect works with the clients on the features and design that satisfy the clients' needs. In other words, the architect works with the client on the functionality required. In Symons' Mark II concept, function points become analogous to the work of a contractor in home construction: The contractor brings in equipment and workers and constructs the home. In other words, the contractor builds the functionality required.

Albrecht's original concept of function points appears to be preferable to the Mark II concept: Function points measure the size of the features of an application that users care about. The costs, schedules, and efficiency with which those features are built is a separate topic and should not be mixed up with the features themselves.

Symons' fourth modification, adding to IBM's 14 supplemental factors, is in keeping with his overall philosophy of switching function points from a metric dealing with value and size to a metric also including effort. The factors added by Symons are:

- Software with major systems software interfaces
- Software with very high security considerations
- Software providing direct access for third parties
- Software with special documentation requirements
- Software needing special user training
- Software needing special hardware

The additional factors considered by Symons are in real life often significant. The disadvantage in the context of function points is twofold: (1) If additional factors that influence a project are considered thoroughly, 6 is insufficient and more than 100 such factors might be added; (2) whenever such factors are added as complexity adjustments, they typically drive up the function point totals compared to the IBM standard. As more factors are added, the function point total will tend to creep up over time for reasons that appear unjustified under the assumptions of the original IBM assertions.

A practical business difficulty also stands in the way of utilizing the Mark II function point method conveniently. Unlike the IBM method, which is in the public domain, the Mark II method is a proprietary technique of the consulting group of Nolan, Norton & Company, which is a subsidiary of the larger international consulting company of Peat, Marwick, & Mitchell. Any form of automation of the Mark II method would at the moment require a licensing arrangement from the owners, which is a disadvantage in gaining widespread acceptance.

The 1989 Publication of the Dreger Function Point Tutorial

Function points were first publicly discussed in October 1979. The first college-level introductory text on function points, Dreger's *Function Point Analysis,*[21] was published in the autumn of 1989, almost exactly 10 years after the initial public presentation. Dreger's book assumes no prior knowledge of function points, and it is intended to take the reader step-by-step through the rules and regulations associated with counting function points by using the standard IBM 1984 methodology. The book succeeds quite well in accomplishing its goals, with the minor exception that Dreger tends to count slightly differently than Albrecht in a few situations. Notably, Dreger tends to accumulate slightly more kinds of things for inputs, outputs, and inquiries than would be normal when using the regular IBM method. The variations can be ignored by experienced function point users, and they are not likely to occur frequently in any case.

For first-time users of function points who would like a gentle introduction to the concept with plentiful examples and useful illustrations, the Dreger book succeeds admirably.

The 1990 IFPUG Standard Counting Practices Manual

As the number of users of function points continued to grow, more and more variations started to appear. The International Function Point Users Group (IFPUG) was created in 1986, and by 1990 it had more than 250 organizations as members. Since many of the function point users in the United States and Europe belonged to it, IFPUG became a natural focal point for function point standardization. It created several special interest groups and committees to deal with the expansion of function points into new domains. Of particular importance has been the work of the Counting Practices Committee, which is the working group charged with creating standard guidelines and resolving inconsistencies.

The task of the Counting Practices Committee has not been easy, since each person who created a variation in function point counting techniques naturally would want his or her particular variation endorsed by the committee. However, after several false starts and many drafts and revisions, the committee published the first version of the new counting practices manual in April 1990 at the Orlando IFPUG conference.[22]

The IFPUG counting practices generally follow the IBM 1984 standards, although a number of variations and extensions have occurred. A minor but noticeable variation concerns the nomenclature and abbreviations used by IFPUG for inputs, outputs, inquiries, and so on. Since any reasonably large case study or set of examples must repeat some of the terminology many times, the most common practice is to simply abbreviate the widely utilized terms. The following are the variations between the 1984 IBM terminology and the 1990 IFPUG terminology for the same concepts:

1984 IBM nomenclature	1990 IFPUG nomenclature
External input type (IT)	External inputs (EI)
External output type (OT)	External outputs (EO)
Logical internal file type (FT)	Internal logical files (ILF)
External interface type (EI)	External interface files (EIF)
External inquiry type (QT)	External inquiries (EQ)

At a technical level, the 1990 IFPUG counting rules both extend and somewhat modify the 1984 IBM standard. Here are brief examples of the 1990 IFPUG variations:

External inputs. The IFPUG rules count duplicate inputs twice, whereas the IBM rules count the input only once. For example, a banking system which accepts a deposit via an ATM or via manual methods would count the deposit as two inputs by using the 1990 IFPUG rules but one input by using the 1984 IBM rules.

External outputs. The IFPUG rules count duplicate outputs for each occurrence, whereas the IBM rules are not specific. For example, an output report that can either be printed on paper or sent to a disk-based print file would be counted twice under the 1990 IFPUG rules.

Internal logical files. The IFPUG rules on internal files generally agree with IBM, but they offer some extensions and additional refinements. For example, if a logical file is maintained by several applications, the 1990 IFPUG rules permit it to be counted by each application. The 1984 IBM rules do not mention this point at all and hence might be open to alternative interpretations.

External interface files. The potential variations between IBM and IFPUG are perhaps greatest in the way external interface files are counted. The 1990 IFPUG rules count external interfaces in behalf of the "receiving" application but not in behalf of the "sending" application. The 1984 IBM rules, on the other hand, credit the interface file to both the sender and the receiver. The reason for the variation is that the sending application may have no knowledge of what is happening to the interface data once it exits; it may never be received, for example. However, an application must clearly understand incoming or received interface data.

External inquiries. Inquiries have long been among the most troublesome factors when counting function points, because of the need to consider both the input and output portions. The 1990 IFPUG rules provide significantly expanded sets of examples dealing with queries. Indeed, some of the 1990 IFPUG examples are based on factors, such as context-sensitive HELP screens, which barely existed in 1984. Under the new IFPUG rules, context-sensitive HELP screens count as inquiries as do several other forms of HELP. The 1990 IFPUG rules differ from the 1984 IBM rules in some other respects as well. For example, the new IFPUG rules state that menu screens which provide both screen and data selection should be counted as inquiries, which differs from the IBM 1984 interpretation.

Although the differences among the function point methods are noticeable, it is highly encouraging that the IFPUG counting practices committee exists at all: For almost 50 years, lines-of-code metrics have been used without the review of any standardization body of any kind. The IFPUG counting practices committee is starting to provide a true international forum for serious discussions about functional metrics, and thus will benefit the software community as a whole.

The 1990 IEEE Draft Standard on Productivity Measurement

Function points provide only part of the information needed for software productivity measurement. The other key factors include a standard set of tasks or chart of accounts and descriptions of the tools, methods, and approaches used on the projects being measured. The productivity measurement committee of the software engineering subgroup of the IEEE has been charged with drafting an international standard for software productivity measurement. The draft IEEE standard[23] existed when this book was being written, but it had not yet been voted on. Fortunately, the IEEE productivity measurement committee has been in communication with the IFPUG counting practices committee, and it appears that the function point metric will be included in the IEEE standard and endorsed by the IEEE.

The 1990 SPR Approximation Method

Function points are starting to create such an explosion of new research and new findings that it will probably be necessary to support the function point method with its own journal simply to handle the volume of new concepts that are emerging. For example, SPR has addressed the problem of attempting to create accurate function point counts in the absence of full knowledge of an application.[24] Although at first this seems like an impossible task, the approximation method has considerable merit and appears to be leading to some powerful new capabilities.

Early in a project's requirements, it may not be possible to state with certainty the exact number of inputs, outputs, inquiries, logical files, and interfaces which will comprise the application. Knowledge about a project is not homogeneous. Some topics are explored earlier than others. This method is based on discovering and utilizing relations between the factors that are known with some precision early and the "hidden" factors that have not yet been worked out in detail. The method is based on observable ratios of inputs, outputs, inquiries, files, and interfaces derived from various kinds of software. For example, when considering an application type such as accounting systems, observe that a pattern such as the following might occur:

Factor	Percentage of functionality
Inputs	30
Outputs	20
Inquiries	5
Logical files	40
Interfaces	5
Total	100

It is a reasonable assumption that other accounting systems might well follow the pattern expressed by this one. As a corollary observation, accounting systems seem to be driven by inputs and file structures, so they would probably be the first topics explored in detail. Assuming that the two assertions are correct, once a single factor (such as the inputs) has been explored in detail, it is possible to extrapolate and make reasonable assumptions about the missing or unexplored factors.

This research is now moving into the task of identifying the relevant patterns associated with application classes and types such as insurance claims processing, banking transactions, process control applications, and switching systems. Preliminary results are both interesting and encouraging, and they show both the versatility of the function point method and the burst of intellectual excitement that permeates the software industry now that workable metrics exist.

The 1990 Albrecht Terminology Revision

In 1989, A. J. Albrecht retired from IBM after many years of service. His retirement did not, of course, end his interest in function points, and he put together a new and comprehensive tutorial[10] on function points which was based not only on IBM's research but also on the work of IFPUG, Software Productivity Research, and others as well.

The new tutorial includes the rules for counting function points in the IBM, IFPUG, and SPR fashions, and it also encompasses the SPR feature point concept. Although the tutorial was constructed in 1989, it has been available in the United States only since early 1990.

The purpose of the tutorial is to broaden the appreciation of functional metrics as a general-purpose technique that can be applied to systems and scientific software as well as to classic management information systems. The tutorial has the advantage of building on the past 15 years of functional metric research, and so it is able to encompass many topics that were not previously dealt with in function point training, such as explaining the rationale behind the major function point "flavors" and dealing with the differences in productivity rates between systems software and management information systems.

The tutorial marks the first educational attempt to integrate the major forms of functional metrics and to show the similarities and differences among them. Thus, the tutorial not only includes pragmatic case studies of counting techniques but also includes comparative discussions of the entire domain of functional metric research. As part of the tutorial material, Albrecht adopted a slightly different nomenclature and a revised set of abbreviations for the five function point parameters. For comparison, here are the key terms and concepts for the four major "flavors" of function point and feature point terminologies:

1984 IBM nomenclature	1990 IFPUG nomenclature
External input type (IT)	External inputs (EI)
External output type (OT)	External outputs (EO)
Logical internal file type (FT)	Internal logical files (ILF)
External interface type (EI)	External interface files (EIF)
External inquiry type (QT)	External inquiries (EQ)
1990 Albrecht nomenclature	**1986 SPR feature point nomenclature**
Input type (IT)	Inputs (IT)
Output type (OT)	Outputs (OT)
Internal user data group (IU)	Logical files (FT)
External user data group (EU)	Interfaces (EI)
External inquiries (QT)	Inquiries (QT)
	Algorithms (AT)

When all of the terminologies are displayed simultaneously, it can easily be seen that they describe the same constructs. However, for users familiar with one terminology, it would be distracting to see data displayed with one of the others. One of the events of 1991 was a standardization of terms and abbreviations for all of the various concepts associated with functional metrics.

The 1992 Creation of Permanent IFPUG Committees

Membership in the International Function Point Users Group (IFPUG) has been increasing at about 50 percent per year, so this is now a very large association with hundreds of companies and thousands of individual members. The IFPUG concept is to be a nonprofit association whose officers are volunteers. However, as membership increased it has been necessary to establish some permanent committees and working groups to deal with increasing needs of an expanding membership. These committees have appeared intermittently since about 1988, but 1992 is a convenient point for discussing the full set.

The counting practices committee (CPC) is the oldest (circa 1988) and perhaps the most controversial portion of IFPUG. This is the group that publishes the "standard" interpretation of how function points should be defined and counted. The CPC is a hard-working committee with a job that tends to generate many complaints and only sparse praise. Although the committee has some political polarization and blind spots, it is fair to say that without this committee function point measurements would be chaotic and far too ambiguous to be useful.

The education curriculum committee (ECC) was formed in 1992 and is responsible for various aspects of education and training in the function point domain, including but not limited to workshops, conferences, and the certification of function point courses for academic and public use.

The certification committee (CC) has the important role of administering the certification examination to prospective function point counters. IFPUG is to be commended for realizing that certification is a necessary prerequisite in order to keep function point variations within safe and tolerable bounds. (This committee was formed in 1991.)

The management reporting committee (MRC) deals with the topic of how function point data should be utilized for reporting productivity and quality information to higher management. Unfortunately, the vision of this committee seems to lag the actual usage of function points in the business world. (This committee was formed in 1991.)

The new environments committee (NEC) deals with the expanded usage of function points for embedded software, object-oriented (OO) software, real-time software, multimedia applications, graphical user interfaces (GUI), and other emerging concepts. It is an important point that IFPUG is not a static organization pointed toward the past, but a dynamic and future-oriented group that is attempting, with reasonable success, to make function point metrics useful for all kinds of software as quickly as they emerge. (This committee was actually formed circa 1989.)

The benchmarking committee (BC) was created in 1993 and is attempting to develop a standard way of expressing software productivity and quality data. It is also concerned with creating an IFPUG database of measured projects, which would be a significant accomplishment. Unfortunately, the work of this committee tends to lag in dealing with some of the pragmatic problems that occur when attempting to summarize large volumes of data that encompass various kinds of applications, many different industries, and software that range from large and complex military weapons systems of 100,000 function points through small and simple end-user applications of 10 function points. Also, the work of this committee tends to be at odds with the practices of companies that actually have sizable collections of quantitative data using function points, such as the Gartner Group, Howard Rubin Associates, and Software Productivity Research (SPR). For example, this book uses the benchmarking practices of SPR when dealing with activity-based software productivity, with software quality, with software occupation groups, and with burden rates and software cost data.

Some of the notable differences between how SPR deals with benchmarks and how IFPUG deals with benchmarks include:

- The SPR taxonomy of software classes and types used to differentiate various kinds of software such as military software, commercial software, embedded software, real-time software, etc., is more extensive than what IFPUG uses.
- The SPR chart of accounts for activity-based cost studies is a superset of what IFPUG recommends. The SPR chart of accounts is intended to encompass military and systems software as well as information systems.
- The SPR taxonomy of five software defect origins (requirements, design, code, user documents, and bad fixes) is a superset of what IFPUG recommends. SPR also measures "defect removal efficiency," which is not used by IFPUG.
- The SPR collection of "soft" data, or factors that influence the outcomes of software projects, is not only a superset of what IFPUG collects but is also more extensive than the Software Engineering Institute (SEI) assessment method.

However, it is significant the IFPUG is also working with the

International Standards Organization (ISO) to create a new standard on software measurement based on function points. Unfortunately, this new standard is not yet available as the second edition of this book is being published.

The 1994 IFPUG Release 4.0 Counting Rules

In January of 1994 IFPUG issued Release 4.0 of the *Function Point Counting Practices Manual.* The fourth release was made in response to many user requests for counting rules that could be applied to client-server projects and to graphical user interfaces (GUI) which did not exist when function points were first developed.

The most significant change included with the Release 4.0 rules is the change in how error messages are treated. In previous *Counting Practice Manual* releases from 2.0 through 3.4, error messages were counted as outputs and dealt with as a significant independent category. Of course, for many batch applications there are comparatively few error messages, so this was not a notable topic.

With any modern Windows or Macintosh application, there are typically a host of error messages and hence the prior method of counting them tends to expand the function point count, perhaps artificially. Under the Release 4.0 counting practices, error messages are viewed as a basic part of a transaction and not counted separately.

For batch applications and for applications with comparatively few error messages, there may be no perceptible difference in the function point totals regardless of whether they are counted using the Release 3 or Release 4 counting rules. For modern Windows, Macintosh, or graphical user interface (GUI) software with quite a few messages, the pragmatic result is that function point totals counted using Release 4 can be 20 to 30 percent lower than if the same application were counted under the Release 3 rules.

The change in rules between Release 3 and Release 4 presented a problem to organizations with large volumes of data derived from legacy systems, such as the Gartner Group and Software Productivity Research. Many of our reports and publications, such as the first edition of this book, were based on the older IFPUG counting rules. If we adopted the Release 4 rules retroactively, then we would have to revise and perhaps republish information that was perfectly correct when it came out prior to the January 1994 Release 4.0 rules.

Both Gartner Group and SPR have adopted a policy of phasing in new data based on Release 4 rules, but not doing any retroactive modifications to older published data. The data contained in this second edition of *Applied Software Measurement,* therefore, is primarily based on the older Release 3 through 3.4 counting practices. For some of the data, such as military software and systems software, the differences between Releases 3 and 4 are likely to be imperceptible.

For commercial software, information systems, outsource and contract software, and end-user applications the results of the Release 4 rules would have the probable effect of reducing the stated sizes by about 20 percent, and hence also reducing apparent productivity by the same amount. The logical problem of dealing with the differences between the Release 3 and Release 4 counting rules is no different than dealing with variations in currency exchange rates, interest rates, or any other value that is not actually a physical constant.

Future Technical Developments in Functional Metrics

Functional metrics have made remarkable progress over the past 15 years. There is now a major international society of functional metric users. A working standards committee exists, and it is actively addressing both extensions to the methodology and clarification of the topics that require it. The functional metric techniques have spread from their origins in management information systems and are starting to be used for systems and scientific software as well. Exciting new developments in functional metrics are occurring on almost a daily basis. It is apparent that the following evolution of the functional metrics concepts should occur over the next few years.

Automatic derivation of function or feature points from design

Since the major factors which go into function point and feature point calculations are taken from the design of the application, it is an obvious step to forge a direct connection between design tools and a function point calculation tool. This desirable step should enable automatic and nonsubjective counts of the basic functional metric parameters. Complexity adjustments, however, may still require some form of human intervention. It is not impossible to envision that even complexity adjustments may eventually become precise and objective as a by-product of research getting under way. Software Productivity Research, for example, has begun a study of more than 150 specification and design methodologies with a view to extracting the basic function point parameters from the standard design representations or, alternatively, making minimal modifications to the standard design representations in order to facilitate direct extraction of function point or feature point parameters.

Automatic backfiring of function points and feature points from source code

Now that function points are becoming a de facto standard metric for productivity studies, there is significant interest in retrofitting function points to aging applications that might have been created even before function points were invented or, in any case, which did not use function points during their development cycles. Since backfiring of function points or converting source code size into function point totals is already possible, it is an obvious next step to automate the process. That is, it is technically possible to build a scanning tool that would analyze source code directly and create function point totals as one of its outputs.

Automatic conversion from function points to feature points, Mark II function points, DeMarco bang metrics, and other variations

One unfortunate aspect of the rapid growth of functional metrics has been the proliferation of many variations, each of which uses different counting methods and creates different totals. It appears both technically possible and also desirable to establish conversion factors which will allow data to be mathematically changed from method to method. Such conversion techniques exist between the IBM function point method and the SPR function and feature point methods, and indeed have been done automatically by the CHECKPOINT® software tool.[13] However, conversion factors for the DeMarco bang metric, the Reifer merger with software science, and the British Mark II method have not yet been published.

Extension and refinement of complexity calculations

It has been pointed out many times that the possible Achilles heel of functional metrics in general and function points in particular is the way complexity is treated. In the original 1979 version of function points, complexity was purely subjective and covered a very small range of adjustments. In the 1984 revision, the range of adjustments was extended and the rigor of complexity analysis was improved, but much subjectivity still remains. This assertion is also true of the other flavors of functional metrics, such as the SPR function and feature point techniques.

There are several objective complexity metrics, such as the McCabe cyclomatic and essential complexity methods,[25] that appear to be promising as possible adjuncts to functional metrics. Other researchers, such as Wayne Smith of Computer Power, have started exploring possibilities for extending and refining business complexity concepts for use with functional metrics. SPR has identified 20 different forms of complexity that are possible candidates for future coupling with functional metrics, including computational complexity, semantic complexity, entropic complexity, and many others.[26] In any event, complexity research in the context of functional metrics is undergoing energetic expansion.

Publication of estimating templates based on functional metrics

From 1979 through 1996, function points had been applied to thousands of applications. Now that so many applications have been explored, a new form of research is starting to emerge: Patterns or "templates" of function point totals for common application types are discovered. It can be anticipated that the next decade will witness the publication of standard guidelines, empirically derived, for many different kinds of applications. These templates will allow very early estimating.

Utilization of functional metrics for studies of software consumption

During the first decade of the growth of functional metrics, almost all the studies were aimed at exploring software development or production. However, functional metrics have very powerful, and currently only partly explored, capabilities for studying software consumption as well. It can be anticipated that the next decade will see a host of new studies dealing with usage patterns and the consumption patterns of software functions.

Utilization of functional metrics for software value analysis

Assessing or predicting the value of software has been one of the most intractable measurement and estimation problems of the software era. Since the previous lines-of-code metric had essentially no commercial value and was neither the primary production unit nor the primary consumption unit of large software projects, it was essentially useless for value analysis. Although functional metrics are only just starting to be applied to value analysis, the preliminary results are encouraging enough to predict much future progress in this difficult area.

Overall prognosis for functional metrics

The software industry suffered for more than 45 years from lack of adequate measurements. Now that functional metrics have made adequate measurements technically possible, it can be anticipated that the overall rate of progress in both software productivity and software quality will improve. Measurement alone can focus attention on areas of strength and weakness, and now that software can be measured effectively, it can also be managed effectively for the first time since the software industry began!

Applying Functional Metrics to a Case Study

It is almost always easier to understand concepts from examples than from rules. Following are six examples of functional metric counting for the same application. The first example illustrates IBM's 1979 function point method, followed by IBM's 1984 function point method, then SPR's 1985 function point method, SPR's 1985 backfire method in both average and adjusted flavors, and finally SPR's 1986 feature point method.

The basic application in the example

The application to be sized in all four examples is an elementary one. The task is to write a personal computer program that automates the calculations for generating function points. The language used for the application is compiled Quick Basic™ on an IBM personal computer. The specific form of function point calculations for this application is similar to the original 1979 version of Albrecht and IBM. The sample application is only to calculate function points for new projects, not for enhancement or maintenance projects.

1. The application has one input screen through which users enter the name of the project being sized and also enter the number of inputs, outputs, data files, and inquiries and the user-specified complexity adjustment for a project for which the function points are to be calculated.
2. The application has one output screen, identical to the input screen except for the calculated outputs, that gives the results of the function point calculations.
3. The application also has the capability of printing out a one-page report showing the function point questions and the calculated results, so there are two outputs from the application. (*Note:* It is obvious that a standard print-screen function would suffice for this application, but assume that the application will develop its own print function.)
4. The application can save the inputs to a floppy disk if the user requests, so there is a single very simple data file involved with the application.
5. The application has no inquiry capabilities or any interfaces to other applications.

6. The processing logic consists of multiplying the four function point parameters by the standard weights, summing the results, and adjusting for subjective complexity. These processing steps comprise only a single algorithm of negligible complexity, and hence the algorithmic weight is 1.

7. The application is written in a compiled Microsoft Quick Basic™, and it required 600 logical source code statements, excluding remarks. Analysis of the source code revealed that 35 percent of the code was used to format and construct the input/output screens, including range and validity checking of inputs, 30 percent was used for formatting and printing the output, 25 percent was used for disk save and retrieve operations, and only 10 percent was used for the arithmetic calculations themselves.

8. The application's input and output screens are the same; they are shown here.

FUNCTION POINT CALCULATOR

APPLICATION NAME ____________

FUNCTION POINT FACTORS	RAW COUNT	EMPIRICAL WEIGHT	UNADJUSTED TOTALS
NUMBER OF INPUTS?	______	× 4 =	______
NUMBER OF OUTPUTS?	______	× 5 =	______
NUMBER OF INQUIRIES?	______	× 4 =	______
NUMBER OF DATA FILES?	______	× 10 =	______
NUMBER OF INTERFACES?	______	× 7 =	______
UNADJUSTED TOTAL			______
COMPLEXITY MULTIPLIER (0.65 TO 1.35)			______
FINAL ADJUSTED FUNCTION POINT TOTAL			______
PRINT RESULTS (Y/N)?	______		
SAVE FILE TO DISK (Y/N)?	______		
RUN PROGRAM AGAIN (Y/N)?	______		

Counting Function Points with the 1979 IBM Method

In the original 1979 version of function points, only four parameters were used. The complexity adjustment was purely subjective, and it covered a range of only ± 25 percent, which is not broad enough to handle the real-life impacts of complexity on software.

Parameter	Count		Weight		Total
Number of inputs	1	×	4	=	4
Number of outputs	2	×	5	=	10
Number of inquiries	0	×	4	=	0
Number of master files	1	×	10	=	10
Unadjusted total				=	24
Complexity adjustment (± 25%)				=	−6
Adjusted total				=	18

In considering the implications of the 1979 version of function points for this very simple application, two problems are evident: (1) The empirical weight of 10 for master files seems excessive for merely storing data on a floppy disk. (2) The complexity adjustment is purely subjective and does not cover a very broad range. The −25 percent complexity weight was the maximum allowed under the 1979 conventions, and it was established by nothing more than guesswork.

Counting Function Points with IBM'S 1984 Revision (Equivalent to IFPUG Method)

In the 1984 revision, the range of complexity adjustments was extended from a subjective ± 25 percent to a more objective technique that allows adjustments spanning a range of ± 125 percent. The revisions include both range adjustments in the standard empirical weights and processing adjustments based on 14 influential factors as illustrated below.

Parameter	Low complexity	Medium complexity	High complexity	Total
External inputs	1 × 3 = 3	0 × 4 = 0	0 × 6 = 0	3
External outputs	2 × 4 = 8	0 × 5 = 0	0 × 7 = 0	8
Logical files	1 × 7 = 7	0 × 10 = 0	0 × 15 = 0	7
Interfaces files	0 × 5 = 0	0 × 7 = 0	0 × 10 = 0	0
Inquiries	0 × 3 = 0	0 × 4 = 0	0 × 6 = 0	
Unadjusted total				18

Once the basic parameters have been enumerated, multiplied by the empirical weights, and summed to create the unadjusted total, the next step is to evaluate the influence of 14 factors on the application.

These factors are evaluated on a scale that runs from 0 to 5, with the following definitions:

0	The factor is not present or has no influence
1	Insignificant influence
2	Moderate influence
3	Average influence
4	Significant influence
5	Strong influence

For the simple application being used in the case study, the results of the 14 influential factors are as follows:

Data communications	0
Distributed functions	0
Heavily used configuration	0
Transaction rate	0
On-line data entry	2
End-user efficiency	3
On-line update	2
Complex processing	0
Installation ease	0
Operational ease	3
Multiple sites	0
Facilitated change	0
Total influence sum	= 10

After the 14 influential factors have been totaled, they must be converted into a complexity multiplier by using the following formula:

$$(\text{Sum}*0.01) + 0.65 = \text{multiplier}$$

Applying the formula yields these results:

$$(10*0.01) + 0.65 = 0.75$$

As can be noted, the range of possible adjustments with the above formula is from a low of 0.065 (assuming all 14 factors are zeros) to a high of 1.35 (assuming all 14 factors are fives). The final step in generating a function point total by using the revised IBM method is to multiply the unadjusted function points by the adjustment multiplier:

Unadjusted function point total	18
Processing adjustment multiplier	0.75

Adjusted function point total 13.5

Since function points are normally dealt with as integers, it would be appropriate to round the results to the nearest integer value, so the final adjusted function point total would be 14.

(The IBM 1984 revision formed the basis of the IFPUG method through 1995.)

Counting Function Points with SPR'S 1985 Method

The SPR method of counting function points differs from the 1984 IBM method primarily in the way complexity is handled. The SPR method does not ask you to evaluate the complexity of individual inputs, outputs, inquiries, data files, and interfaces as does the IBM method, nor does it require the counting of data elements and file types. It divides the topic of complexity into three distinct questions: (1) How complex is the logic or the problems the application must deal with? (2) How complex is the code that must be written? (3) How complex is the data structure of the application? From the answers to those three questions, the SPR method develops an overall complexity weight that covers the same range as the IBM technique and returns essentially the same adjusted function point totals.

Problem complexity? 1

1. Simple algorithms and simple calculations
2. Majority of simple algorithms and calculations
3. Algorithms and calculations of average complexity
4. Some difficult or complex calculations
5. Many difficult algorithms and complex calculations

Code complexity? 3

1. Nonprocedural (generated, spreadsheet, query, etc.)
2. Well structured with reusable modules
3. Well structured (small modules and simple paths)
4. Fair structure but with some complex modules and paths
5. Poor structure with large modules and complex paths

Data complexity? 1

1. Simple data with few variables and low complexity

2. Numerous variables but simple data relationships
3. Multiple files, fields, and data interactions
4. Complex file structures and data interactions
5. Very complex file structures and data interactions

The sum of problem complexity and data complexity is used directly for function point calculations, and in this case it is a 2. The code complexity parameter is used for backfiring function points, and it is discussed in subsequent sections. By referring to the following table, it can be seen that in this instance the sum of 2 for problem complexity and data complexity will be associated with a multiplier of 0.6.

Sum of logic and data complexity	Complexity multiplier
2	0.6
3	0.7
4	0.8
5	0.9
6	1.0
7	1.1
8	1.2
9	1.3
10	1.4
Complexity sum = 2	
Net SPR complexity multiplier = 0.6	

Next, the complexity multiplier is applied to the unadjusted total, as follows:

Parameter	Raw data		Weight		Total
Number of inputs	1	×	4	=	4
Number of outputs	2	×	5	=	10
Number of inquiries	0	×	4	=	0
Number of data files	1	×	10	=	10
Number of interfaces	0	×	7	=	0
Unadjusted total					24
Complexity multiplier					0.6
Adjusted function point total					14.4
Integer value of adjusted total					14.0

Since function points are normally rounded to integer values, the final adjusted function point total with both the SPR and IBM counting methods is 14. The SPR and IBM methods use different mathematical techniques to handle complexity adjustments, but in trials of more than 100 projects the average results are within 1.5 percent of being equal. The maximum variation under controlled conditions has been only about 15 percent.

Incidentally, the code complexity question asked by the SPR method is not used for normal function point calculations and could even be omitted. Code complexity is used when retrofitting function points to existing software by using the backfire mode of calculating function points directly from source code size.

Counting with SPR'S 1985 Backfire Method

To use the 1985 SPR Backfire method, it is first necessary to know both the language and the quantity of source code statements that were used to implement the application. In this case, the language was stated to be compiled Quick Basic™, which is a level-5 language and requires an average of about 64 statements per function point. Since the source code quantity was stated to be 600 statements, a first approximation by using the backfire technique can be made by simply dividing the source code count by the average ratio of statements to function points, as follows:

600 statements/64 statements per function point = 9.37 function points

With normal rounding, the backfire method would indicate a total of 9 function points. This is the fastest form of function point calculation, although it is certainly not the most precise. However, it is also possible to adjust the average backfire ratio to account for the complexity of the application. But to do that, additional information and calculations are required. First, it is necessary to sum the applications problem, code, and data complexity by using the standard five-point SPR scale.

In this example, problem complexity is a 1, code complexity is a 3, and the value of data complexity is a 1, so the sum total equals 4. By referring to Table 2.16, it can be seen that this sum is associated with an adjustment multiplier of 0.80. Applied to the case study at hand, the adjustment factor would be used by multiplying the average number of statements per function point for this language by the adjustment rate, as follows:

64	average statements per function point
0.80	complexity adjustment factor
51.20	statements per function points

If we now divide the 600 source code statements by the 51.2 statements per function point, the result is 11.7 function points. Using normal rounding to the next integer value, the total is 12 function points for this calculation sequence. Thus, backfiring with adjusted complexity offers the advantages of relatively high speed calculations with reasonable accuracy. Backfiring is a very useful way of applying function points to aging software when it may be too difficult or too expensive to create function point totals by normal counting methods.

Counting with SPR'S 1986 Feature Point Method

Feature points, it may be recalled, were developed to give the benefits of the function point method to real-time software, embedded software, systems software, and telecommunications software (and to other types of software with high algorithmic complexity). That is why feature points introduce the new "algorithm" parameter, which is quite significant for software outside the realm of management information systems. However, feature points can be used with MIS projects too.

The feature point method uses the SPR conventions for dealing with complexity, and it also lowers the empirical weight for data files from a 10 down to a 4 to reflect the typical situation that I/O and data file operations are not usually as significant outside the MIS world as they are within it. The following are the feature point results:

Problem complexity? 1

1. Simple algorithms and simple calculations
2. Majority of simple algorithms and calculations
3. Algorithms and calculations of average complexity
4. Some difficult or complex calculations
5. Many difficult algorithms and complex calculations

Code complexity? 3

1. Nonprocedural (generated, spreadsheet, query, etc.)
2. Well structured with reusable modules
3. Well structured (small modules and simple paths)
4. Fair structure but some complex modules and paths
5. Poor structure with large modules and complex paths

Data complexity? 1

1. Simple data with few variables and low complexity
2. Numerous variables but simple data relationships
3. Multiple files, fields, and data interactions
4. Complex file structures and data interactions
5. Very complex file structures and data interactions

Sum of logic and data complexity	Complexity multiplier
2	0.6
3	0.7
4	0.8
5	0.9
6	1.0
7	1.1
8	1.2
9	1.3
10	1.4
Sum of logic and data complexity = 2	
Net SPR complexity multiplier = 0.6	

Parameter	Raw data		Weight		Total
Number of algorithms	1	×	1	=	1
Number of inputs	1	×	4	=	4
Number of outputs	2	×	5	=	10
Number of inquiries	0	×	4	=	0
Number of data files	1	×	10	=	7
Number of interfaces	0	×	7	=	0
Unadjusted total					22
Complexity multiplier					0.6
Adjusted feature point total					13.2

With normal rounding to integer values, the final adjusted feature point total would be 13. Note that, since the feature point method is still experimental, the weight adjustment for algorithms has only a provisional default value of 3; it can be reset to any appropriate value over the normal range of 1 to 10. For a simple algorithm such as this example, a nominal value of 1 for the weight of the algorithm seems appropriate.

The basic rationale of the feature point method is that algorithmic complexity is an independent and significant variable. The numerical total of 13 feature points vs. the total of 14 function points is due to the simplicity of the algorithmic complexity of the application and the essentially trivial data file implications. The low feature point total may actually come closer to matching the reality of the application than function points.

Feature points are somewhat more flexible than function points, and the implementation of feature points allows for easy modification of all weighting factors. To summarize, for average applications in which algorithms and file structures are equal in number, the function point and feature point totals will be identical. For intuitively simple applications with few or very simple algorithms, feature points will generate lower counts than function points, and for intuitively complex applications with many algorithms or very complex algorithms, feature points will generate significantly higher counts than function points.

Comparison of the Case Study Results

The six versions' functional metric totals for the same application tend to illustrate the evolution of function points. Function points started as a useful but somewhat limited normalizing metric. As their value became clear, function points evolved in the direction of increasing flexibility and closer coupling to real economic productivity.

Since the IFPUG method is directly based on the IBM 1984 revision, this simple example would stay more or less the same through any of the IFPUG versions including version 4.0. The following table illustrates the overall results of the six cases, and the approximate results of some of the other common function point calculation approaches published over the past 15 years when applied to the same sample problem.

Method	Raw data	Adjustments	Adjusted totals
1979 IBM method	24	0.75	18
1982 DeMarco bang method	22	0.80	18
1984 IBM method	18	0.75	14
1985 SPR method	24	0.60	14
1986 SPR backfire (without adjustment)	9	0.00	9
1986 SPR backfire (with adjustment)	9	1.44	13
1986 SPR feature point method	22	0.60	13
1987 Reifer method	23	0.90	21
1988 Mark II method	20	0.80	16
1990 IFPUG method Versions 1, 2, and 3	18	0.75	14
1994 IFPUG Version 4.0	18	0.75	14
1994 Boeing 3D method	20	0.80	16

It would be very interesting to perform a controlled study of the results of function point counting that used all of the major methods and counted the same applications in these domains:

- Information systems software
- Embedded, real-time software
- GUI-based client-server software
- Object-oriented software

Unfortunately, this kind of side-by-side comparison is seldom performed by any of the function point organizations or function point metric developers.

The 1979 IBM function point method is no longer in use, and it is included to provide a baseline for the newer techniques. The 1979 IBM method is easy to use, but it is limited in flexibility and is absolutely subjective in its treatment of complexity. The 1984 IBM function point method, owing to the new and more flexible way of quantifying the five basic parameters, has the lowest total of the raw data counts of any of the methods. It is probably closest to the intuitive judgment that the example is really quite simple. The IBM 1984 method of adjusting for complexity by means of 14 influential factors has the dual effect of both increasing the range of such adjustments and adding rigor to the adjustment process.

The 1985 SPR function point method provides an adjusted count identical to that of the 1984 IBM method for this example. However, the SPR and IBM methods achieve their results somewhat differently.

The SPR method has a higher raw total but a more dramatic adjustment reduction.

Both the 1984 IBM function point method and the 1985 SPR method provide much greater ranges of adjustment for complexity than did the IBM 1979 technique, and hence they yield lower adjusted function point totals. The 1985 SPR backfire method has two flavors: unadjusted averages and complexity adjusted averages. The unadjusted average method, which merely requires looking up values in Table 2.15, is plainly very quick, but it is not highly accurate. The method cannot be recommended for serious studies of function points, but it is certainly adequate for tutorial and educational purposes and for special situations in which absolute precision is not a major concern.

However, when the backfire technique is adjusted for complexity, its accuracy improves to very acceptable levels. Thus the backfire method supported by automated tools for complexity adjustment will probably find a useful niche in aiding function points to be applied historically to aging software that did not use function points when it was first being developed.

The 1986 SPR feature point method yields the lowest adjusted count for the case study, and intuitively it comes closest to matching the reality of the very simple application used. The SPR feature point method is the most flexible of any, since all of the parameters can be adjusted to two decimal places. The inclusion of the new algorithm parameter in feature points also makes the SPR feature point method suitable for real-time systems and embedded software. However, the SPR feature point method is still experimental and undergoing field trials.

The 1988 Mark II function point method is used in the United Kingdom primarily, although there are a few users of this method in Canada. The author is not aware of any U.S. users of the Mark II function point method.

The IFPUG methods have become the de facto standard for counting function points throughout much of the world. This trend started in 1990 with Version 1, and each version of the IFPUG counting practices manual has seen both a refinement of the approach and an expansion of the users of this method. Since IFPUG is working with the International Standards Organization (ISO) it is probable that the IFPUG method will become a true international standard in the future, probably based on Version 4.0 counting rules and perhaps combined with portions of the Mark II approach.

The Boeing 3D method surfaced in 1994 and appears to be an amalgamation derived from the early DeMarco bang functional metric, with some features from the British Mark II function point metric. The stated purpose of this metric is to give more weight to the functionality of applications that are high in algorithmic density, as opposed to being high in data. To a certain degree, the Boeing 3D variation overlaps the SPR feature point metric.

Neither 3D function points nor feature points have extensive user communities, although a number of companies in the systems and embedded software domains use one or the other of these two methods.

The variations among the illustrated methods are significant, and care must be used when discussing productivity rates to know which method was actually used in generating the totals. (If the unillustrated British Mark II or the DeMarco bang method were used, the ranges would be even greater.) However, the ranges associated with functional metrics are trivial in comparison to the ranges of uncertainty associated with the older lines-of-code metric, whereby variations of more than 200 percent in apparent size are quite common because of the lack of standard definitions of how the code was counted.

In the future, it can be predicted the variations in counting with functional metrics will be reduced, under the influence of the IFPUG and its counting practices committee.

Selecting a Chart of Accounts for Resource and Cost Data

The function point and feature point methods are normalizing metrics whose primary purpose is to display productivity and quality data. To be meaningful, the effort and the cost data itself must be collected to a standard chart of accounts for all projects. One of the major problems with measuring software projects has been the lack of a standard chart of accounts. For example, the simplest and most primitive chart of accounts would merely be to accumulate all costs for a project without bothering to identify whether those costs were for requirements, design, coding, testing, or something else. This kind of data is essentially impossible to validate, and it is worthless for economic studies or any kind of serious exploration.

A slightly more sophisticated way to collect data would be to use a five "cost bucket" chart of accounts that segregated effort and costs among these five elements:

1. Requirements
2. Design
3. Development
4. Testing
5. Management

This technique is better than having no granularity at all, but unfortunately it is insufficient for serious economic studies. Consider, for example, the testing cost bucket. The smallest number of tests performed on a software project can be a single perfunctory unit test. Yet some large projects may carry out a 12-step series that includes a unit test, function test, stress test, performance test, independent test, human factors test, integration test, regression test, system test, field test, and user acceptance test. If all testing costs are simply lumped together under a single cost bucket labeled "testing" there would be no serious way to study the economics of multistage test scenarios.

The smallest chart of accounts that has sufficient rigor to be used effectively with MIS projects, systems software, and military software contains 25 cost elements, with the total project serving as the twenty-sixth cost accumulation bucket. Software Productivity Research has produced such a uniform chart of accounts[7] suitable for all types of software and for carrying out studies of software economics.

The IBM 1984 function point chart of accounts,[29] being derived primarily from MIS projects, uses a 20-task chart of accounts that is not really suitable for military projects or systems software projects. For example, the IBM chart of accounts excludes quality assurance, independent verification and validation, independent testing, design and code inspections, and many other activities that are common outside the MIS world but not within it. The IBM chart of accounts also excludes tasks associated with really large systems, such as system architecture and project planning.

It should be clearly understood that because from 20 to 25 cost buckets are available for recording staffing, effort, schedule, and cost information, that does not imply that every project will in fact carry out all of the tasks. Indeed, MIS projects routinely perform only from 6 to 12 of the 25 tasks. Systems software projects tend to perform from 10 to 20 of the 25 tasks. Military projects tend to perform from 15 to all 25 of the tasks, which is one of the reasons for the high costs of military projects. When a project does not carry out one or more of the specific tasks in the chart of accounts, that task is simply set to contain a zero value. The following are the IBM and SPR charts of accounts for comparative purposes:

SPR chart of accounts	IBM chart of accounts
1. Requirements	1. Project management
2. Prototyping	2. Requirements
3. System architecture	3. System design
4. Project planning	4. External design
5. Initial analysis and design	5. Internal design
6. Detail design and specification	6. Program development
7. Design reviews and inspections	7. Detail design

SPR chart of accounts	IBM chart of accounts
8. Coding	8. Coding
9. Reusable code acquisition	9. Unit test
10. Purchased software acquisition	10. Program integration
11. Code reviews and inspections	11. System test
12. Independent verification and validation	12. User documentation
13. Configuration control	13. User education
14. Integration	14. File conversion
15. User documentation	15. Standard task total
16. Unit testing	16. Studies
17. Function testing	17. Package modification
18. Integration testing	18. Other
19. System testing	19. Nonstandard task total
20. Field testing	20. Development total
21. Acceptance testing	
22. Independent testing	
23. Quality assurance	
24. Installation and user training	
25. Project management	
26. Total project costs	

Note that the two charts shown above are essentially top-level charts. The SPR chart of accounts, for example, expands into a full work-breakdown structure encompassing more than 150 subordinate tasks. Use of a standard chart of accounts is of sufficient importance to merit an eleventh goal for function point metrics:

11. Hard project data (schedules, staff, effort, costs, etc.) should be collected by using a standard chart of accounts.

Because the SPR chart of accounts is a superset of IBM's, projects measured by using the SPR chart of accounts can be subset for direct comparison against projects using the IBM chart of accounts on an activity by activity basis. Note that, because of its MIS origins, the IBM chart of accounts excludes several activities that are significant and expensive for military and systems software (such as independent verification and validation). It may not be advisable to use the standard IBM chart of accounts for projects other than normal MIS applications. Be especially cautious of attempting direct comparisons of costs or productivity between MIS projects and systems or military projects comparisons.

The data collected with the standard chart of accounts is the unambiguous hard data that is not likely to be colored by subjective personal opinions:

- The size of the staff for each activity
- The total effort for each activity
- The total cost for each activity
- The schedule for each activity
- The overlap or concurrency of activity schedules
- The deliverables or work products from each activity

If, as often happens, a project did not perform every activity in the standard 25 activity chart of accounts, those cost buckets are simply filled with zero values. If, as also happens, additional activities were performed below the level of the standard 25 activity chart of accounts, subordinate cost buckets can be created. Productivity studies have sometimes been carried out by using as many as 170 cost buckets for a chart of accounts.

It is dismaying and astonishing that in almost 50 years of software history, there has never been an industry standard for the chart of accounts that should be used to collect software project resource data! Now that functional metrics are becoming the new standard, it is hoped that the importance of standardizing a chart of accounts will soon be addressed.

Summary of and Conclusions about Functional Metrics

Functional metrics in all their forms provide the best capability for measuring economic productivity in software history. Although training is necessary before starting and care must be exercised to ensure consistency, function points and feature points are worth the effort. It is appropriate to recapitulate all of the 11 essential goals of the function point and feature point concepts and to add a final twelfth goal regarding the soft information that should also be captured in order to explain variations in hard project results:

The 12 essential goals of functional metrics

1. The metric should deal with software's visible features.
2. The metric should deal with factors important to users.
3. The metric should be applicable early in the life cycle.

4. The metric should reflect real economic productivity.
5. The metric should be independent of source code.
6. The metric should be easy to apply and calculate.
7. The metric should assist in sizing all deliverables.
8. The metric should retrofit to existing software.
9. The metric should work for maintenance and enhancements.
10. The metric should work with all software types including MIS projects, systems software projects, real-time and embedded software projects, and military software projects.
11. Hard project data (schedules, staff, effort, costs, etc.) should be collected by using a standard chart of accounts.
12. Soft project data (skills, experience, methods, tools, etc.) should be collected in an unambiguous fashion that lends itself to multiple regression analysis.

Function points and feature points are new metrics, and they are still in evolution. Both methods are providing new and clear insights into software productivity and quality. They are key steps leading to the development of software engineering as a true engineering profession.

In conclusion, measurement is the key to progress in software. Without accurate measurements in the past, the software industry has managed through trial and error to make progress, but the progress has been slower than is desirable and sometimes erratic. Now that accurate measurements and metrics are available, it can be asserted that software engineering is ready to take its place beside the older engineering disciplines as a true profession, rather than an art or craft as it has been for so long.

References

1. IBM Corporation, *DP Services Size and Complexity Factor Estimator,* DP Services Technical Council, 1975.

2. Albrecht, A. J., "Measuring Application Development Productivity," *Proceedings of the Joint SHARE, GUIDE, and IBM Application Development Symposium, October 1979,* pp. 83–92.

3. Jones, C., *Programming Productivity—Issues for the Eighties,* IEEE Computer Society, Catalog No. 391, 1981, Revised 2nd edition, 1986, 462 pages.

4. Jones, C., "Measuring Programming Quality and Productivity," *IBM Systems Journal,* vol. 17, no. 1, 1978, pp. 39–63. (Reprinted in Reference 3, above.)

5. Jones, C., *Programming Productivity,* McGraw-Hill, New York, 1986, 282 pages.

6. Jones, C., *A 10 Year Retrospective of Software Engineering within ITT,* Software Productivity Research, Inc., Burlington, Mass., February 1989, 25 pages.

7. Albrecht, A. J., *AD/M Productivity Measurement and Estimate Validation,* IBM Corporate Information Systems, IBM Corp., Purchase, N.Y., May 1984.

8. DeMarco, T., "Developing a Quantifiable Definition of Bang," in *Controlling Software Projects,* Yourdon Press, New York, 1982, pp. 92–110.
9. IBM Function Point Workshop Tutorial Materials, IBM Corp., available through IBM education centers in the United States, 1987.
10. Albrecht, A. J., and D. Herron, *A Functional Metric Course,* Software Productivity Research, Inc., Burlington, Mass., 1990, 400 pages.
11. User Guide to SPQR/20, Software Productivity Research, Inc., Burlington, Mass., October 1985, revised January 1987, 65 pages.
12. *User Guide to SPQR SIZER/FP,* Software Productivity Research, Inc., Burlington, Mass., July 1987.
13. *User Guide to CHECKPOINT™*, Software Productivity Research, Inc., Burlington, Mass., May 1989, revised April 1990, 125 pages.
14. Jones, Capers, *Preliminary Table of Languages and Levels,* Software Productivity Research, Inc., Burlington, Mass., May 1989, 18 pages.
15. Jones, Capers, *Introduction to Software Measurement and Estimation,* Software Productivity Research, Inc., Burlington, Mass., June 1988, 40 pages.
16. Jones, Capers, *A Short History of Function Points and Feature Points,* Software Productivity Research, Inc., Burlington, Mass., June 1986, 65 pages.
17. Reifer, Don, Private communication and correspondence with Capers Jones, 1987.
18. Halstead, Maurice, *Elements of Software Science,* Elsevier, New York, 1977.
19. Hamer, Peter, *Analysis of Software Science Metrics,* ITT Standard Telephone Laboratories, Harlow, England, 1982, 55 pages.
20. Symons, Charles, "Function Point Analysis—Difficulties and Improvements," *IEEE Transactions on Software Engineering,* January 1988, vol. 14, no. 1, pp. 2–11.
21. Dreger, J. Brian, *Function Point Analysis,* Prentice-Hall, Englewood Cliffs, N.J., 1989, 185 pages.
22. *IFPUG Counting Practices Manual,* Release 3.0, International Function Point User's Group, Westerville, Ohio, April 1990, 73 pages.
23. IEEE Software Productivity Measurement Committee, Draft Standard; IEEE Computer Society, 1990.
24. Herron, Dave, "Proposal for Ratio-Based Function Point Calculations," unpublished communication, April 1990.
25. McCabe, Tom, "A Complexity Measure," *IEEE Transactions on Software Engineering,* SE-2,4, December 1976, pp. 308–320.
26. Jones, Capers, *Forms of Complexity that Affect Software Engineering,* Software Productivity Research, Inc., Burlington, Mass., March 1990, 5 pages.
27. Jones, Capers, *Selecting a Chart of Accounts,* Software Productivity Research, Inc., Burlington, Mass., May 1988, 5 pages.
28. Ragland, Robin (ed.), *Function Point Counting Practices Manual,* Release 4.0, International Function Point User's Group, Westerville, Ohio, January 1994.

Chapter

3

United States Averages for Software Productivity and Quality

Introduction

The first version of *Applied Software Measurement,* published in 1991, was based primarily on data gathered between 1985 and 1990, although it included older data too. This edition of the book includes almost 5 years of new findings. More than 2000 new software projects have been analyzed by the author and his company between 1991 and 1996. This brings the author's available volume of software project data up to more than 6700. This knowledge base continues to grow at a rate of 30 to 40 projects each month.

This new edition contains both data on new projects, and also some new data items. For example, costs are included in this edition and ranges of various topics will also be shown. Both "function points per staff month" and "work hours per function point" are now included.

Although the volume and quality of data on software projects has improved between the first and second editions, it is still far from perfect. Few projects have consistent, accurate, and complete data associated with them. As mentioned in the first edition, software measurement resembles an archaeological dig. One shifts and examines large heaps of rubble, and from time to time finds a significant artifact.

Many important technological changes have occurred in the software industry over the past 5 years. On the whole, these changes have benefited software productivity and reduced software schedules in every software domain. Software quality, on the other hand, has declined in some segments such as information systems. However, the quality of commercial software (i.e., the packages sold over the counter such as spreadsheets or word processors) has improved and overall results are better than in 1991.

Table 3.1 shows the approximate net changes in U.S. average productivity and quality rates between 1990 and 1995. [Since the 1990 data was expressed using version 3.0 of the function point counting rules developed by the International Function Point Users Group (IFPUG) the new 1995 average is also based on the version 3.0 rules rather than the newer version 4.0 counting rules.]

The upper data in Table 3.1 shows the average results from the overall SPR knowledge base, i.e., cumulative results through 1990 and the cumulative results through 1995. Although newer projects are more productive than older ones, the overall national averages cannot change with much rapidity. The lower portion of Table 3.1 illustrates projects that were put into production in calendar year 1990 and those that entered production in 1995. By limiting the results to a single year, it is easier to see the rate of progress because prior data is excluded.

Unfortunately, averages tend to be deceptive no matter how the information is displayed since the ranges are so broad. The ranges of observed productivity in 1990 ran from a low of 0.13 function point per staff month to a high of about 140 function points per staff month for prototypes and small applications. In 1995, the ranges ran from a low of 0.35 up to a high of more than 200 function points per staff month for prototypes and small end-user applications with substantial reuse. (Note that Table 3.1 excludes end-user applications.) The reasons and details for such wide ranges are discussed later in this chapter. Suffice it to say there is still a high margin of error, and readers are cautioned that "averages" are often misleading and should not be used for serious business purposes such as contracts or cost estimates.

The overall productivity gains between 1990 and 1995 can be attributed to the growth of the object-oriented paradigm, to better tool suites, to the explosive growth of client-server applications, and to

TABLE 3.1 Comparison of 1990 and 1995 Overall U.S. Productivity and Quality Levels (Data Expressed Using IUG Version 3.0 Function Points)

	U.S. productivity average	U.S. defect potential average	U.S. defect removal average, %	U.S. defect delivery average
1990 (cumulative)	5.00	5.00	85	0.75
1995 (cumulative)	5.66	4.74	92	0.38
1990 (only)	5.60	4.85	87	0.63
1995 (only)	8.45	4.60	93	0.32

continued expansion of high-level programming languages and application generators within the software world. Software reusability is also becoming a contributor, and especially so within specific domains such as outsourcing and commercial software. Better measurements are also a major contributor since as more companies use function points the pool of available data is becoming larger.

The quality gains between 1990 and 1995 can be attributed to continued progress within the systems and military software domains, to improved quality control within the commercial software domain, and to greater recognition of the need for software quality as a by-product of the ISO 9000 standards and the Software Engineering Institute's capability maturity model. Defect tracking tools and test management tools are also growing in numbers and sophistication. The down side of software quality is that client-server applications are often worse than prior quality levels during the monolithic mainframe era. In quality too, better measurements have been a major contributor by providing expanding pools of information. As the software industry continues to evolve, the overall impetus is positive and indicates that continued improvements should occur throughout the remainder of the twentieth century and well into the twenty-first century.

Sources of Possible Errors in the Data

Readers should be aware that this study has the potential of a high error content. The raw data, although better than that available for the first edition, remains partial and inconsistent in respect to the activities included, and it is often known to be incomplete and even wrong (i.e., the widespread failure to measure unpaid overtime).

Many different companies and government data has been examined. There are no current U.S. or international standards for capturing significant data items or for including the same sets of activities when projects are measured. For costs and financial data, there are not even any recognized, standard accounting practices for dealing with the overhead or burden rates which companies typically apply. This fact is troublesome within the United States, and even more troublesome for international cost comparisons where there are major differences in compensation, where currency exchange rates must be dealt with, and where burden rate variances can be many hundred percent.

Since the data has such as high potential for error, it is reasonable to ask why it should be published at all. The reason for publication is the same as the reason for publishing any other scientific results based on partial facts and provisional findings. Errors can be corrected by subsequent researchers, but if the data is not published there is no incentive to improve it.

For example, when the Danish astronomer Olaus Roemer first attempted to measure the speed of light his results only indicated 227,000 km/s, which differs from today's value of 299,792 km/s by more than 24 percent. However, prior to Roemer's publication in 1676 most scholars thought the speed of light was infinite. Even Roemer's incorrect results started scientists along a useful path.

It is hoped that even if the data shown here is later proved wrong, its publication will at least be a step toward new and correct data that will benefit the overall software community. The software industry should not lurch into the twenty-first century without a solid quantified foundation for software costs, schedules, quality, and other tangible matters.

There are three major kinds of error that can distort the results published here:

1. Errors in determining the size of the projects
2. Errors in determining the effort or work content applied to the projects
3. Statistical or mathematical errors in aggregating and averaging the results

Let us consider the implications of these three sources of error in turn.

Sizing Errors

The data contained in this book consists of four major categories in descending order of precision: (1) projects actually measured by the author or by consultants employed by the author's company; (2) projects measured by clients of the author's company and reported to the author; (3) legacy systems where function point sizes were backfired by direct conversion from lines-of-code (LOC) data; (4) projects collected from secondary sources or from the general software literature.

In the first edition, about 75 percent of the data was originally recorded in terms of "lines of code" and the function point totals were derived via backfiring. In this edition, the distribution among the four sizing methods is approximately the following: (1) about 30 percent of the size data was measured by Software Productivity Research personnel who are certified function point counters; (2) about 15 percent of the data came from SPR clients who asserted that the sizes were derived using certified function point counters; (3) about 35 percent of the size data was derived from backfiring or direct conversion from the original LOC counts; (4) about 20 percent of the data was derived from secondary sources, such as studies reported to the International Function Point Users Group (IFPUG) or published in the function point literature.

The actual sizes of the projects used to produce this book could vary, and possibly vary significantly. The normal precision of function point counting when performed by certified counting personnel is about plus or minus 10 percent. The normal precision of "backfiring" is only about plus or minus 25 percent, although exceptional cases can vary by more than 50 percent.

The mixture of data from four discrete sources means that the actual sizes of the projects could vary from the stated sizes by a significant but unknown value. Hopefully, although this is uncertain, the possible errors from the four sources are not all in the same direction and hence may partially cancel out.

Effort, Resource, and Activity Errors

The second source of error concerns possible mistakes in collecting the effort and costs associated with software projects. It is a regrettable fact that most corporate tracking systems for effort and costs (dollars, work hours, person months, etc.) are incorrect and manage to omit from 30 to more than 70 percent of the real effort applied to software projects. Thus most companies cannot safely use their own historical data for predictive purposes. When SPR personnel go on site and interview managers and technical personnel, these errors and omissions can be partially corrected by interviews. For secondary data, the errors are not so easily corrected.

The most common omissions from historical data, ranked in order of significance, include the following:

Sources of cost errors	Magnitude of cost errors
1. Unpaid overtime by exempt staff	Up to 25% of reported effort
2. Charging time to the wrong project	Up to 20% of reported effort
3. User effort on software projects	Up to 20% of reported effort
4. Management effort on software projects	Up to 15% of reported effort
5. Specialist effort on software projects	Up to 15% of reported effort
Human factors specialists	
Database administration specialists	
Integration specialists	
Quality assurance specialists	
Technical writing specialists	
Education specialists	
Hardware or engineering specialists	
Marketing specialists	
6. Effort spent prior to cost tracking start-up	Up to 10% of reported effort

Sources of cost errors	Magnitude of cost errors
7. Inclusion and exclusion of nonproject tasks	Up to 5% of reported effort
Departmental meetings	
Courses and education	
Travel	
Overall error magnitude	Up to 110% of reported effort

Not all of these errors are likely to occur on the same project, but enough of them occur so frequently that ordinary cost data from project tracking systems is essentially useless for serious economic study, for benchmark comparisons between companies, or for baseline analysis to judge rates of improvement. A more fundamental problem is that most enterprises simply do not record data for anything but a small subset of the activities actually performed. In carrying out interviews with project managers and project teams to validate and correct historical data, the author and the consulting staff of SPR have observed the following patterns of incomplete and missing data, using the 25 activities of the standard SPR chart of accounts as the reference model:

Activities performed	Completeness of historical data
1. Requirements	Missing or incomplete
2. Prototyping	Missing or incomplete
3. Architecture	Incomplete
4. Project planning	Incomplete
5. Initial analysis and design	Incomplete
6. Detail design	Incomplete
7. Design reviews	Missing or incomplete
8. Coding	Complete
9. Reusable code acquisition	Missing or incomplete
10. Purchased package acquisition	Missing or incomplete
11. Code inspections	Missing or incomplete
12. Independent verification and validation	Complete
13. Configuration management	Missing or incomplete
14. Integration	Missing or incomplete
15. User documentation	Missing or incomplete
16. Unit testing	Incomplete
17. Function testing	Incomplete
18. Integration testing	Incomplete
19. System testing	Incomplete

Activities performed	Completeness of historical data
20. Field testing	Incomplete
21. Acceptance testing	Missing or incomplete
22. Independent testing	Complete
23. Quality assurance	Missing or incomplete
24. Installation and training	Missing or incomplete
25. Project management	Missing or incomplete
26. Total project resources, costs	Incomplete

When SPR personnel collect data, at least we ask the managers and personnel to try to reconstruct any missing cost elements. Reconstruction of data from memory is plainly inaccurate, but it is better than omitting the missing data entirely. Unfortunately, the bulk of the software literature and many historical studies only report information to the level of complete projects rather than to the level of specific activities. Such gross "bottom line" data cannot readily be validated and is almost useless for serious economic purposes.

For the six software subindustries or domains included in this edition, the overall performance in terms of resource and cost tracking accuracy is as follows:

Software subindustry	Resource and cost tracking accuracy
Military software	Most complete cost data, although unpaid overtime is often missing. Usually has the most detailed activity costs
Systems software	Fairly complete data, although unpaid overtime is often omitted. Management effort and some specialist effort may be omitted. Activity data is often good for testing and quality control
Outsource and contract software	Fairly complete cost data, although unpaid overtime is often omitted. Seldom any real granularity in terms of distribution of effort by activity, although most activities are captured
Commercial software	Fairly complete in large companies such as Microsoft. Cost data may not exist at all for small independent software vendors. Unpaid overtime is usually omitted. Activity costs not always shown
Management information systems	Woefully incomplete with many major errors and omissions; among them are unpaid overtime, management costs, user costs, and many specialists such as quality assurance (if any) or database administration

Software subindustry	Resource and cost tracking accuracy
End-user software	Usually no cost or resource data or any kind. Only the fact that developers of end-user applications can reconstruct their time from memory makes any conclusions in this domain possible at all

The primary impact of the missing and incomplete data elements is to raise *apparent productivity* and hence cause results to seem much better than they truly are. For example, SPR and a benchmarking competitor were both commissioned to study the productivity levels of the same corporation and compare them against our respective benchmarks within the same industry (financial services). The SPR benchmark for that industry averaged about 8 function points per staff month, but the other company's benchmark for the same industry averaged more than 20 function points per staff month.

The reason for the difference was that the SPR data had used on-site interviews to correct and compensate for missing effort that was not part of normal cost-tracking system results. The competitive benchmark database, on the other hand, was based on surveys distributed by mail. There was no mechanism for validating the reported results by means of on-site interviews with project personnel to correct for missing or incomplete data elements. Since cost and resource tracking systems routinely omit from 30 to more than 70 percent of the total effort devoted to software projects, the apparent results can easily top 20 function points per staff month.

In real life there are projects that can top 20 function points per staff month, and even 100 function points per staff month. However, any project larger than 1000 function points that reports productivity rates higher than 10 function points per staff month needs to be validated before the data can be accepted as legitimate.

Given that the majority of activities in corporate tracking systems are missing or incomplete, the question arises as to just what value tracking systems have to American businesses. When used for cost control purposes, many tracking systems are so inaccurate that they seem to have no positive business value at all. Indeed, they are a source of major cost and schedule overruns because they provide such inaccurate data that when project managers attempt to use the data to predict new project outcomes, they place their projects in jeopardy.

Software schedule ambiguity

Schedule data is also very troublesome and ambiguous. Considering how important software schedules and time to market considerations are, it is surprising that this topic has had very little solid, hard data in print for the past 50 years.

Even more surprising is the fact that so few companies track software development schedules, since this topic is visibly the most important to software managers and executives. Failure to measure software schedules means that at least 85 percent of the software managers in the world jump into projects with hardly a clue as to how long they will take. This explains the phenomenon that about half of the major disasters associated with missed schedules and overruns can be traced back to the fact that the schedules were not competently established in the first place.

From collecting schedule information on historical projects, it happens that establishing the true schedule duration of a software project is one of the trickiest measurement tasks in the entire software domain. When a software project is shipped is often fairly clear, but when it originated is the hardest and most imprecise data point in the software industry.

For most software projects, there is an amorphous and unmeasured period during which clients and software personnel grope with fundamental issues such as whether to build or buy, and what is really needed. Of several thousand software projects analyzed over the past 10 years by the author and his colleagues, less than 1 percent had a clearly defined starting point. To deal with this ambiguity, our pragmatic approach is to ask the senior software manager for a project to pick a date as the starting point, and simply use that. If the project had formal, written requirements it is sometimes possible to ascertain the date that they started, or at least the date shown on the first printed version.

Surprisingly, more than 15 percent of software projects are also ambiguous as to when they were truly delivered. Some of the sources of ambiguity are whether to count the start of external beta testing as the delivery point or wait until the formal delivery when beta testing is over. Another source of ambiguity is whether to count the initial delivery of a software product, or whether to wait until deferred functions come out a few months later in what is usually called a "point release" such as "Version 1.1." For determining the delivery of software, our general rule is to count the first formal release to paying customers or to users that are not participants in beta testing or prerelease field testing.

Not only are both ends of software projects ambiguous and difficult to determine, but the middle can get messy too. The confusion in the midportion of software projects is because even with the "waterfall model" of development there was always overlap and parallelism between adjacent activities. As a general rule of thumb, software requirements are usually only about 75 percent defined when design starts. Design is often little more than 50 percent complete when coding starts. Integration and testing can begin when coding is less than

20 percent complete. User documentation usually starts when coding is about 50 percent done, and so forth. Owing to overlap and parallelism, the end-to-end schedule of a software project is never the same as the duration of the various activities that take place.

The newer spiral and iterative models of software development are even more amorphous, since requirements, design, coding, testing, and documentation can be freely interleaved and take place concurrently. The schedule interval in this book runs from the nominal "start of requirements" until the "first customer ship" date of the project. The activities included in this interval are those of the 25 standard activities that SPR utilizes that are actually performed.

Software cost ambiguity

Although productivity measurements based on human effort in terms of work hours or work months can now be measured with acceptable precision, the same cannot be said for software costs, and prices as well. There are several major problems in the cost domain that have existed for more than 50 years but which escaped notice so long as software used inaccurate metrics like lines of code that tended to mask a host of other important problems. These same problems occur for other industries besides software, incidentally. They tend to be more troublesome for software than for most other industries because software is so labor-intensive.

A fundamental problem with cost measures is the fact that salaries and compensation vary widely from job to job, worker to worker, company to company, region to region, industry to industry, and country to country. For example, among SPR's clients in the United States the basic salary of "senior systems programmer engineers" averages about $75,000 per year, and ranges from a low of about $40,000 per year to a high of over $100,000 per year. When international clients are included, the range for the same position runs from less than $10,000 per year to more than $120,000 a year. The more expensive countries such as Belgium, Sweden, and Switzerland can average from 150 to 170 percent of United States norms. Countries such as Germany and Austria may be roughly equivalent to slightly higher than U.S. norms. However, countries such as China, India, and Russia may be as little as 15 to 20 percent of U.S. norms.

Industries vary too. For software executives such as chief information officers (CIO) the banking industry pays more than twice as much (close to $200,000) as public utilities or education ($82,000) but all industries pay more than government service. There are also major variations associated with the sizes of companies. As a rule, large companies pay more than small companies. However, some small start-up companies offer equity to founding employees, and that can translate into substantial money that is difficult to evaluate. (Microsoft is a famous example, since their employee stock option plan created more millionaires than any other company in history.) Geographic regions vary too. Major urban areas such as New York and San Francisco have compensation packages that are about 30 percent higher than rural areas in the West and South.

Other software-related positions have similar ranges. This means that in order to do software cost studies it is necessary to deal with geographic differences in costs, industry differences in costs, size of company differences, and a number of other complicating factors. Table 3.2 shows some of the SPR findings on software positions and typical compensation packages for the United States for the years 1994 and 1995. Note that many companies offer employees stock option plans. The "equity" column in Table 3.2 refers to significant options whose cash value might very well exceed a year's compensation when exercised.

Most higher-paying software positions are managerial or executive in nature. However, a few technical jobs have rather good compensation packages associated with them. These are positions such as "chief scientist" and "research fellow." Normally positions such as this are found in companies that have major research laboratories such as AT&T's Bell Labs or IBM's Research Division. There are usually very few incumbents in these senior technical positions, but the fact that they exist at all is an interesting phenomenon.

Another and equally significant problem associated with software cost studies is the lack of generally accepted accounting practices for determining the burden rate or overhead costs that are added to basic salaries to create a metric called "the fully burdened salary rate" which corporations use for determining business topics such as the charge-out rates for cost centers. The fully burdened rate is also used for other business purposes such as contracts, outsource agreements, and return on investment (ROI) calculations. Some representative items that are included in burden or overhead rates are shown in Table 3.3, although the data is hypothetical and generic.

The components of the burden rate are highly variable from company to company. Some of the costs included in burden rates can be social security contributions, unemployment benefit contributions, various kinds of taxes, rent on office space, utilities, security, postage, depreciation, portions of mortgage payments on buildings, various fringe benefits (medical plans, dental plans, disability, moving and living, vacations, etc.), and sometimes the costs of indirect staff (human resources, purchasing, mail room, etc.). Some former components of the burden rate are being discontinued by companies in the modern era of downsizing and cost reduction. For example, 10 years

TABLE 3.2 Approximate 1995 U.S. Software Compensation

Occupation	Annual salary, $	Bonus, $	Total, $	Equity
President of a software company	185,000	31,450	216,450	Yes
Chief scientist (software)	150,000	18,750	168,750	Yes
VP, software engineering	112,500	16,875	129,375	Yes
Chief information officer (CIO)	105,000	15,750	120,750	Yes
Software research fellow	100,000	15,000	115,000	No
VP, information systems	95,000	14,250	109,250	Yes
VP, software quality assurance	90,000	11,250	101,250	No
Director of networks	90,000	11,250	101,250	No
Director of systems development	87,000	13,050	100,050	Yes
Software business unit manager	87,000	13,050	100,050	Yes
Director of software testing	85,000	10,625	95,625	No
Director of operations	85,000	10,625	95,625	No
Director of customer support	85,000	10,625	95,625	No
Director of software quality assurance	83,000	9,960	92,960	No
Software project manager	75,000	9,000	84,000	No
Director of data administration	75,000	9,000	84,000	No
Software architect	77,000	5,775	82,775	No
Senior systems programmer	75,000	7,500	82,500	No
Senior systems analyst	67,000	6,700	73,700	No
Systems programmer	60,000	3,000	63,000	No
Systems analyst	55,000	2,750	57,750	No
Computer operations manager	55,000	1,925	56,925	No
Network administrator	50,000	5,000	55,000	No
Database analyst	52,000	2,600	54,600	No
Data security analyst	52,000	2,600	54,600	No
Programmer/analyst	50,000	2,500	52,500	No
LAN manager	47,000	4,700	51,700	No
Quality assurance specialist	49,000	2,450	51,450	No
Testing specialist	49,000	2,450	51,450	No
Software planning specialist	50,000	1,250	51,250	No
Software metrics specialist	50,000	1,250	51,250	No
Software estimating specialist	50,000	1,250	51,250	No
Database administrator	50,000	1,250	51,250	No
Manager of software publications	47,000	1,175	48,175	No
Application programmer	42,000	2,100	44,100	No
Business analyst	40,000	2,000	42,000	No
Software technical writer	40,000	1,000	41,000	No
Customer support specialist	37,000	1,850	38,850	No
PC technical support	35,000	1,750	36,750	No
Computer operator	30,000	1,500	31,500	No
Average (arithmetic mean)	69,280	7,047	76,328	
Weighted average	51,889	3,201	55,090	

TABLE 3.3 Generic Components of Typical Burden or Overhead Costs in Large and Small Companies

	Large company		Small company	
	$	%	$	%
Average annual salary	50,000	100.0	50,000	100.0
Personnel burden:				
Payroll taxes	5,000	10.0	5,000	10.0
Bonus	5,000	10.0	0	0.0
Benefits	5,000	10.0	2,500	5.0
Profit sharing	5,000	10.0	0	0.0
Subtotal	20,000	40.0	7,500	15.0
Office burden:				
Office rent	10,000	20.0	5,000	10.0
Property taxes	2,500	5.0	1,000	2.0
Office supplies	2,000	4.0	1,000	2.0
Janitorial service	1,000	2.0	1,000	2.0
Utilities	1,000	2.0	1,000	2.0
Subtotal	16,500	33.0	9,000	18.0
Corporate burden:				
Information systems	5,000	10.0	0	0.0
Finance	5,000	10.0	0	0.0
Human resources	4,000	8.0	0	0.0
Legal	3,000	6.0	0	0.0
Subtotal	17,000	34.0	0	0.00
Total burden	53,500	107.0	16,500	33.0
Salary + burden	103,500	207.0	66,500	133.0
Monthly rate	8,625		5,542	

ago many large corporations offered moving and relocation packages to new managerial and senior technical employees that included features such as:

- Payment of real estate commissions
- Moving fees for household goods
- Settling-in allowances
- Hotels or rent while searching for new homes

These moving and living packages are now in decline, and some companies no longer offer such assistance at all.

As can be seen from the right side of Table 3.3, small companies that are self-funded may have burden or overhead rates that are only a fraction of the amount shown in Table 3.2. On the other hand, some corporations can have burden rates that top 300 percent because they allocate their whole cost of doing business into the burden; i.e., travel, marketing, sales can also be apportioned as part of this structure.

One of the major gaps in the software literature as of 1995, and for that matter in accounting literature as well, is the almost total lack of international comparisons of the typical burden rate methodologies used in various countries. So far as can be determined, there are no published studies that explore burden rate differences between countries such as the United States, Canada, India, the European Union countries, Japan, China, etc.

Among SPR's clients, the range of average burden rates runs from a low of perhaps 15 percent of basic salary levels (for start-up companies operating out of the owner's homes) to a high of approximately 300 percent. In terms of dollars, that range means that the fully burdened compensation rate for a senior software engineer in the United States can run from a low of under $50,000 per year to a high of $250,000 per year.

There are no apparent accounting or software standards for what constitutes an "average" burden rate. Among SPR's clients, several companies include the entire costs of operating their businesses as part of their burden rate structure. For these two, their fully burdened monthly costs are in excess of $25,000. This is close to five times greater than the actual average compensation levels, and reflects the inclusion of all indirect personnel, buildings, medical costs, taxes, utilities, and the like.

When the combined ranges of basic salaries and burden rates are applied to software projects in the United States, they yield about a 5 to 1 variance in costs for projects where the actual number of work months or work hours are identical! When the salary and burden rate ranges are applied to international projects, they yield about a 15 to 1 variance between countries such as India or Pakistan on the low end, and Germany or Switzerland or Japan on the high end.

Hold in mind that this 15 to 1 range of cost variance is for projects where the actual number of hours worked is identical. When productivity differences are considered too, there is more than a 100 to 1 variance between the most productive projects in companies with the lowest salaries and burden rates and the least productive projects in companies with the highest salaries and burden rates.

Expressed in terms of cost per function point, the observed range for software projects spans amounts that run from less than $50 per function point on the low end to more than $10,000 per function point on the high end. Although it is easily possible to calculate the arithmetic mean, harmonic mean, median, and mode of software costs, any such cost value would be dangerous to use for estimating purposes when the ranges are so broad. This is why SPR is reluctant to publish general software cost data, and instead uses work hours or person months for productivity studies.

Two other cost matters also are important. For long-term projects that may span several years, inflation rates need to be dealt with. Many commercial estimating and measurement tools, such as the CHECKPOINT® tool the author's company markets, have inflation rate adjustments as standard features.

For international software projects, currency conversions must be dealt with. Here too, commercial software cost estimating tools such as CHECKPOINT® may have built-in currency conversion features. However, fluctuations in exchange rates are essentially daily topics and are not stable over long periods.

When clients ask for data on "average cost per function point," the only safe answer is that costs vary so much owing to compensation and burden rate differences and to inflation that it is better to base the comparison on work effort. Cost data is much too variable for casual comparisons. Cost comparisons are possible, but they need a lot of preparatory work before they can be accurate.

Software work period ambiguity

One of the chronic problems of the software industry has been ambiguity in the various work periods such as work days, work weeks, work months, and work years applied to software projects. The calendar year is 365.25 days long, and there are 52 weeks and 12 calendar months each year. These are essentially the only constant, unambiguous values associated with software work periods, and even these are not really constant because leap years occur every 4 years.

Consider calendar year 1996 in terms of week days and holidays since 1996 is a leap year:

Months	Days	Week days	U.S. public holidays
January	31	23	2
February	29	21	1
March	31	21	0
April	30	22	1
May	31	23	1
June	30	20	0
July	31	23	1

Months	Days	Week days	U.S. public holidays
August	31	22	0
September	30	21	1
October	31	23	1
November	30	21	1
December	31	22	1
Totals	366	262	10

Since there are 366 calendar days and 262 week days, the average work month will be slightly longer than a non-leap year and will consist of 21.83 work days. Of course we don't really work every week day, and this is where the ambiguity begins.

In the United States, the normal work week runs from Monday through Friday, and consists, nominally, of five 8-hour days, often cited somewhat humorously as "9 to 5." However, because lunch periods and coffee breaks are standard in the United States, many companies compensate for this by having 9-hour business days, such as opening at 8:30 A.M. and closing at 5:30 P.M.

Although we may be physically at work for 8 or 9 hours a day, very few of us can or would want to work solidly for 8 hours every day. The exact amount of time used for coffee breaks, lunch, rest breaks, and social matters varies from company to company but can be assumed to average about 2 hours per day. If we assume that we are in fact working for 6 hours each day, and there will be 22 working days each month, then the monthly total would be 132 work hours each month. If we assume that we are going to work 7 hours each day, the total jumps to 154 work hours each month. However, the actual amount of work time is a very ambiguous quantity and simple assumptions are not accurate. Let us consider some of the reasons for variance.

Since there are 52 weeks in a year, that indicates 104 Saturdays and Sundays, leaving a residue of 261 business days when we subtract 104 from 365. At this point, by dividing 261 days by 12 months, there would be an average of 21.75 working days each month. If you round 21.75 up to 22, and multiply by 6 work hours each day, you arrive at the value of 132 hours each month, which is a common default value used for rough cost and effort estimating purposes. However, there are also national and some state public holidays, vacation days, sick days, special away due to weather, and non-work days for events such as travel, company meetings, and the like. This is where the bulk of the ambiguity arises.

The major public holidays where business offices are typically closed in the United States total to about 10 days each year. This includes both national holidays such as the Fourth of July and Veterans Day and state holidays, which vary from state to state.

In the United States, the entry-level vacation periods are normally only 5 to 10 days per year. For journeymen with more than 5 years of work experience, the average is about 15 days per year. There are also senior personnel with extensive longevity who may have accrued vacation periods of 20 days per year. Let us assume that vacations average 15 days per year in the United States.

Vacations are difficult to deal with when estimating software projects. On "crunch" projects vacations may be deferred or prohibited. Even during ordinary projects, vacations may be temporarily put on hold until the project is over, or at least until the portions of the project are stable. Therefore, vacations tend to come between projects and assignments, rather than in the midst of them. However, on large-scale multiyear projects vacations must be considered.

Summing both 10 public holidays and 15 vacation days and subtracting them from an annual 261 business days yields 236 days remaining. At this point there would be an average of 19.66 working days per month. Rounding 19.66 up to 20 and multiplying by 6 hours a day yields a result of 120 work hours per month.

It is also necessary to consider sick leave, and days when companies are closed owing to conditions such as snowstorms or hurricanes. Let us assume an average of three sick days per year, and two days for unscheduled office closures due to weather conditions. Subtracting five more days brings us down to 231 working days in a year, which is equivalent to 19.25 working days per month. Rounding 19.25 down to 19 and multiplying by 6 hours each day yields a result of 114 work hours per month.

There are also days devoted to education, company meetings, appraisals, interviewing new candidates, travel, and other activities that are usually not directly part of software projects. These extraneous activities are difficult to generalize. However, let us assume that they total to 16 days per year. This now reduces the number of work days to 215 per year. Dividing by 12 months, the number of work days per month is now 17.9. Rounding this to 18 and multiplying by 6 hours a day, the number of nominal work hours per month would be only 108.

Another source of great ambiguity is the amount of unpaid overtime applied to software projects. Software personnel, as a class, are a pretty hard-working group, and unpaid overtime is very common. For example, an average of about 60 minutes every night during the week and half a day or 4 hours every weekend is a common value for unpaid overtime.

For "crunch" projects, vacations and some holidays may be suspended. There is also a tendency to work harder and take fewer breaks during the day. This means that projects under severe schedule pressure might accrue 7.5 hours of regular time and 2 hours of unpaid overtime during the week. On weekends, another 12 hours of unpaid overtime might be worked. Thus for "crunch" projects there might be as many as 165 regular work hours each month, and a total of perhaps 88 hours of unpaid overtime. This would amount to a combined value of 253 work hours per month. This is a difference of 121 hours, or 92 percent, compared to the nominal 132 hours per month that is frequently used.

The range of the calculations shown here indicates that the number of work hours per month in the United States can vary from a low of 108 to a high of 253. While intervening values such as 120 or 132 can be used as rough assumptions for estimation, the ambiguity of the situation is large enough so that "averages" are bound to be wrong and misleading. SPR and the author recommend a careful analysis of the available work periods for each project, rather than simply utilizing default or average values.

Table 3.4 shows some observations on the normal patterns of work time and unpaid overtime for the six subindustries covered in this book. With so much variability, it is easy to see why SPR recommends exploring the specifics of real software projects and attempting to match the actual pattern, rather than depending upon abstract averages.

When international data is considered, variations in work periods are large enough to require careful handling. For example, the Japanese work week normally includes 5½ days and much more overtime than U.S. norms; i.e., it runs to almost 50 hours a week. The Canadian work day fluctuates between summer and winter, is only about 7.5 hours as opposed to the U.S. norm of 8 hours, and also has somewhat less unpaid overtime than U.S. or Japanese norms. European vacations are much longer than U.S. norms and may average more than 20 days. On the other hand, vacations in Mexico are shorter than U.S. norms and average less than 10 days. Variations such as these require careful handling for international comparisons to be valid.

TABLE 3.4 Representative Software Work Hours per Day in Six Subindustries

	Work hours per 8-hour day	Unpaid overtime per day	Total work hours per day
End user	3.5	0.0	3.5
MIS	5.5	1.0	6.5
Outsource	7.0	1.5	8.5
Commercial	7.0	2.0	9.0
Systems	6.0	1.0	7.0
Military	6.5	1.0	7.5
Average	5.9	1.1	7.0

When examining the literature of other scientific disciplines such as medicine, physics, or chemistry, about half of the page space in journal articles is normally devoted to a discussion of how the measurements were taken. The remaining space discusses the conclusions that were reached. The software engineering literature is not so rigorous, and often contains no information at all on the measurement methods, activities included, or anything else that might allow the findings to be replicated by other researchers. The situation is so bad for software that some articles even in refereed journals do not explain the following basic factors of software measurement:

- Which activities are included in the results; i.e., whether all work was included or only selected activities
- The assumptions used for work periods such as work months
- The programming language or languages used for the application
- Whether size data using lines of code (LOC) is based on:
  1. Counts of physical lines
  2. Counts of logical statements
- Whether size data using function points is based on:
  1. IFPUG function point rules (and which version)
  2. Mark II function point rules (and which version)
  3. Other rules such as Boeing, SPR, DeMarco, IBM, or something else
- How the schedules were determined, i.e., what constituted the "start" of the project and what constituted the "end" of the project.

It is professionally embarrassing for the software community to fail to identify such basic factors. The results of this lack of rigor in measurement reporting leads to very wide apparent variances on top of very wide real variances. These false variances based on miscounting, missizing, or misstating can approach or exceed a 10 to 1 range. The real variances based on accurate and consistent measurements can also vary by about a 10 to 1 range. The overall permutations of these two ranges can lead to apparent productivity and quality differences of 100 to 1. This is far too broad a range to be acceptable for an occupation that aspires to professional status.

Statistical and Mathematical Errors

The statistical and mathematical methods used in the first edition of this book were mixed and not carefully controlled. That same criticism can be applied to this edition as well. The overall set of projects used in producing the data contained here is clearly biased. This is because the author and his company are management consultants rather than academics. We collect data when we are commissioned to do so by specific clients. This means that there are significant gaps in the data, and the sizes of applications we study tend to be much larger than the probable distribution in the United States as a whole. Table 3.5 shows the approximate numbers of software projects for this second edition. By contrast, Table 3.6 shows what the author regards as the approximate distribution of software project types in the United States as a whole, compared to the SPR knowledge base.

As can easily be seen, the SPR knowledge base underrepresents every software domain except systems software in terms of relative percentages. The most severe underrepresentation is the domain of end-user software, where SPR has never been commissioned to perform any formal assessments or benchmark studies. Only the fact that many of the author's personal friends and colleagues (and the author himself) write end-user applications provides any data at all.

The net results of the visible bias in the SPR knowledge base is that overall averages based on our knowledge base will appear to be *lower* than true national averages based on a perfect representation of software projects. Systems software is comparatively low in software productivity, while end-user applications are comparatively high in software productivity. If U.S. norms were calculated based on a more

TABLE 3.5 Summary of SPR Knowledge Base Contents

Size of project, function points	End user	MIS	Outsource	Commercial	Systems	Military	Other	Total	Percent
<1	20	50	3	30	40	10	50	203	3.01
1–10	75	75	2	15	130	20	30	347	5.14
11–100	50	325	5	75	270	30	125	880	13.03
101–1,000	3	915	90	255	1325	75	415	3078	45.58
1,001–10,000	0	465	50	155	950	90	280	1990	29.47
10,001–100,000	0	50	20	25	110	20	30	255	3.78
Total	148	1880	170	555	2825	245	930	6753	100.00
Percent	2.19	27.84	2.52	8.22	41.83	3.63	13.77	100.00	

TABLE 3.6 Comparison of SPR Knowledge Base and U.S. Distribution of Software Projects

	End user	MIS	Outsource	Commercial	Systems	Military	Other	Total
SPR percent	2.19	27.84	2.52	8.22	41.83	3.63	13.77	100.00
U.S. percent	17.50	30.00	5.50	9.00	12.50	11.50	14.00	100.00
Difference, %	−15.31	−2.16	−2.98	−0.78	29.33	−7.87	−0.23	0.00

representative match of the distribution of projects, the probable results would be close to 9 or 10 function points per staff month rather than the 5.66 function points per staff month shown in Table 3.1. The situation is compounded by the fact that small projects of less than 100 function points in size comprise only about 21 percent of the SPR knowledge base, and systems larger than 1000 function points in size constitute more than 33 percent of the SPR knowledge base.

The probable distribution of projects in the United States as a whole would be that more than 60 percent of all projects are less than 100 function points in size, while less than 10 percent are larger than 1000 function points in size. Here too, the net result is to make averages derived from the SPR knowledge base appear lower than might occur from a closer match to the true pattern of occurrence. If the SPR knowledge base matched the true size ranges, then the probable averages for the United States would be more than 12 function points per staff month, or about twice the value of 5.66 function points per staff month shown in Table 3.1.

These biases are unfortunate. However, so far as can be determined there is no national database that is a perfect representation of either U.S. software patterns or those of any other country either. A very relevant question is whether the sum total of the SPR knowledge base is even large enough to be statistically valid for a country the size of the United States. The answer is that the SPR knowledge base is probably not large enough for statistical validity. Even so, if the results of the author's analysis were not published, there might be no incentive for other researchers to expand their knowledge bases or challenge and correct the author's conclusions.

Table 3.7 shows the relationship between the SPR knowledge base and the estimated numbers of software projects that might be studied in

TABLE 3.7 Total U.S. Software Projects and SPR Knowledge Base

Domains	U.S.	SPR	SPR %
End-user	4,200,000	148	0.00
MIS	7,000,000	1880	0.03
Outsource	1,260,000	170	0.01
Commercial	2,100,000	555	0.03
Systems	2,870,000	2825	0.10
Military	2,660,000	245	0.01
Other	3,220,000	930	0.03
Total	23,310,000	6753	0.03

the United States if 100 percent of all operational software projects were examined. So far as can be determined as of 1995, no known U.S. software knowledge base is probably valid either. It is even questionable if the sum of all major U.S. software knowledge bases would be large enough to be statistically valid (i.e., the sum of the data maintained by the U.S. Air Force, by Gartner Group, by IFPUG, by Quantitative Software Management, by Howard Rubin Associates, by the Software Engineering Institute, and by Software Productivity Research).

Age ranges of the Software Productivity Research knowledge base

The author and his colleagues are often asked about the ages of the projects in the SPR database. SPR began software productivity and quality data collection in volume in 1985 (see Table 3.8). However, the author had been involved in software measurement work long before SPR was formed. He was part of various groups in IBM that collected productivity and quality data from 1968 through 1979. He was also part of the ITT corporate group that collected software quality and productivity data from 1979 through 1983. He also worked at the consulting company of Nolan, Norton & Company during 1983 and 1984 in a consulting practice devoted to software data collection.

The SPR knowledge base is not a constant number, however. SPR is averaging about two baseline data collection efforts in the United States each month, and another two overseas. Each study will typically collect data on between 10 and 20 software projects, so between 30 and 40 new projects are being added on a monthly basis. As interest in software baselines and assessments continues to rise, these numbers will be increasing in 1996 and beyond.

Because of the large number of legacy applications contained in the SPR knowledge base, it is also of interest to consider the distribution of projects that are new, that consist of enhancements to existing applications, or that are concerned with maintenance or defect repairs

TABLE 3.8 Age Ranges of Data in the SPR Knowledge Base

Time period	Number of projects (approximate)	Percent of projects
1951–1960	100	1.5
1961–1970	500	7.5
1971–1980	1000	15.0
1981–1990	2550	38.0
1991–1995	2550	38.0
Total	6700	100.0

for existing applications. Table 3.9 gives the approximate overall distribution of the SPR knowledge base in three categories. As the software industry moves past the 50-year mark (which occurred in 1993) the number of legacy applications that are being enhanced or maintained will grow slightly larger every year.

Another frequent question to the author concerns how the knowledge base reflects various programming languages of interest. Here there is far too much data to represent it all. The author and his colleagues at Software Productivity Research developed and market the CHECKPOINT® software cost estimation and measurement tool. One of our standard features is "support for all known programming languages." In order to back up this assertion, we have been producing an annual report of software programming languages. Version 8 of SPR's *Table of Programming Languages and Levels* is in preparation as this book is being written. Version 8 contains a total of 470 programming languages and dialects. Since this document is more than 50 pages long, only a few selected languages are shown in Table 3.10.

TABLE 3.9 Distribution of SPR Knowledge Base into New, Enhancement, and Maintenance Projects

Project type	End user	MIS	Outsource	Commercial	Systems	Military	Other	Total	Percent
New	111	470	51	150	848	61	372	2063	30.54
Enhancement	22	1128	85	278	1554	147	419	3632	53.78
Maintenance	15	282	34	128	424	37	140	1058	15.67
Total	148	1880	170	555	2825	245	930	6753	100.00

TABLE 3.10 Distribution of SPR Knowledge Base for Selected Programming Languages

Languages	End user	MIS	Outsource	Commercial	Systems	Military	Other	Total	Percent
4GL's	0	188	26	0	0	0	140	353	5.23
Ada	0	0	0	11	45	86	0	142	2.10
Assembly	0	19	5	6	339	2	47	417	6.18
Basic	22	0	0	17	0	0	19	57	0.85
C	3	23	17	111	1130	5	56	1344	19.91
COBOL	0	940	85	28	0	6	47	1105	16.36
FORTRAN	0	28	3	6	37	7	74	156	2.30
Generators	0	132	14	85	0	0	56	286	4.23
Object oriented	15	75	9	72	283	7	37	498	7.37
Query language	3	226	22	17	28	5	28	328	4.86
Visual language	30	38	7	56	0	0	93	223	3.29

TABLE 3.11 Distribution of SPR Knowledge Base Associated with Selected Technologies

Project type	End user	MIS	Outsource	Commercial	Systems	Military	Other	Total	Percent
Object oriented	22	71	8	45	263	31	56	495	7.33
Client-server	0	188	20	60	0	0	37	306	4.52
Distributed	0	376	39	29	0	12	102	559	8.27
JAD	0	508	46	28	650	49	140	1420	21.02
RAD	0	94	5	0	28	0	74	202	2.99
QFD	0	0	0	3	14	0	0	17	0.25
ISO 9000	0	4	5	8	85	0	15	116	1.72
TQM	0	113	10	39	226	7	19	414	6.13
SEI CMM 2-4	0	24	1	0	42	6	11	84	1.24
Information engineering	0	282	34	33	0	0	0	349	5.17
Inspections	0	94	19	111	1130	54	140	1547	22.91
Prototypes	99	846	94	250	1257	86	279	2910	43.10
Multiplatform	0	113	20	28	565	51	84	861	12.75
Reengineering	0	169	26	0	0	0	0	195	2.88
CASE	0	376	43	111	848	37	186	1600	23.69
Embedded	0	0	5	0	203	49	11	269	3.98
Reused material	104	376	102	278	848	56	279	2042	30.24

The author is often asked about how the available software projects in the knowledge base relate to various technologies, such as client-server projects or those using object-oriented methodologies. Table 3.11 gives the approximate numbers of software projects associated with selected technologies that are currently of interest to the software community. Here too, new information is coming in essentially on a daily basis. For example, if there is yet another release of this book, then technologies such as OLAP, data warehouses, and virtual reality projects might be available in sufficient numbers to display the percentages.

Variations in data representation and averaging techniques

The first edition of this book utilized powers of 2 for graphing the results. The first edition also did not display specific results for applications larger than 10,240 function points in size. This revised edition has switched over from powers of 2 to powers of 10. It also extends the upper range of displayed data up to 100,000 function points.

One of the many problems of exploring software productivity and quality is that of attempting to calculate "averages" in a way that makes sense and does not give misleading results. There are of course a number of techniques for establishing "average" values, i.e., the arithmetic mean, the harmonic mean, the geometric mean, the mode, or the median. There is also the interquartile range, or the set of values within which half of the results might be found. There are also standard deviations and various tests of statistical precision. The software world is not very sophisticated when it uses the word "average." From examination of the software literature, the most common usage of "average" appears to be nothing more than the arithmetic mean of the results. Table 3.12 is a set of 10 sample projects to illustrate some of the results that might occur based on which approaches are used to quantify averages.

The arithmetic mean of 18 function points per staff month is dominated by the large number of small, high-productivity projects. The arithmetic mean is suitable if the purpose of the average is to explore the central tendency of productivity rates. The accompanying stan-

TABLE 3.12 Examples of Means, Mode, and Median for 10 Software Projects

Project	Function points	Effort (months)	Productivity (function points per staff month)	Productivity (work hours per function point)
A	10	0.30	33.33	3.96
B	10	0.50	20.00	6.60
C	12	0.60	20.00	6.60
D	15	0.60	25.00	5.28
E	30	1.50	20.00	6.60
F	50	3.30	15.15	8.71
G	60	4.00	15.00	8.80
H	80	5.30	15.09	8.75
I	100	6.60	15.15	8.71
J	500	100.00	5.00	26.40
Totals	867	122.70		
Arithmetic mean			18.37	9.04
Standard deviation			7.43	6.32
Harmonic mean			14.60	7.18
Geometric mean			16.74	7.88
Median			17.58	7.66
Mode			20.00	6.60
Weighted average			7.07	18.68

dard deviation of 7.43 reflects a fairly broad range of productivity rates, which indeed is a common occurrence.

Note that if the arithmetic mean is used by companies that do not compensate for the approximate 50 percent "leakage" of effort noted with cost tracking systems in the United States, the apparent average productivity rate would be about 36 function points per staff month. If the arithmetic mean is used by companies whose software measurements are built around "design, code, and unit test" or DCUT activities, which constitute only about 25 percent of total software development effort, the apparent productivity would be about 72 function points per staff month. The arithmetic mean is dangerously misleading even if used with full project data, and it becomes more so when applied to the partial project data that is so common in the software world.

The harmonic mean of 14.6 function points per staff month is more balanced than the arithmetic mean, but is still dominated by the smaller projects, which utilized very little overall effort and had the highest productivity rates.

The geometric mean of 16.53 function points per staff month is derived by multiplying the 10 productivity values together, and then extracting the tenth root. The geometric mean is seldom encountered in software studies, although it often is used for population studies.

The mode of 20 function points per staff month and the median of 17.58 function points per staff month are seldom encountered in the software literature, although both are useful in certain situations and are used from time to time in this book.

The weighted average is probably of greatest interest to financial and executive personnel, who are concerned with overall expenses for software. It is the somewhat pessimistic weighted average results of 7 function points per staff month derived from dividing total function points (867) by total effort (122.7 months) that often causes executives to move toward outsourcing arrangements on the grounds that productivity is too low. This is an important point, because a few large systems that are sluggish or unsuccessful can make a hundred successful small projects invisible in the eyes of senior executives. Software managers, executives, and technical workers should realize that many successful small projects are not as significant to corporate management as one huge disaster. Therefore, the weighted average is a relatively important business metric, more so, in fact, than the arithmetic mean.

Suppose there had been another large project the same size as project J, project K, which was canceled and not delivered. Assume that this canceled project was also 500 function points in size and 100 months of effort were devoted to it prior to termination. The function points for this failed project would not be part of the normal productivity results since it was incomplete and not delivered. However, it is perfectly reasonable to record the 100 months of effort because they were actually utilized. Including 100 months of effort for a failed project affects the arithmetic only slightly: it drops from 18 to 16.36 function points per staff month. However, the inclusion of the additional 100 months of effort drives the weighted mean down to a dismal 3.9. It is highly likely that corporate management would wish to do this, and would probably invite various outsource vendors in for serious discussions as well.

The software industry has not been very careful or very conscientious in these measurement and statistical attributes:

- For 50 years the software industry has used a metric (lines of code) that was never standardized and violates the basic assumptions of economic productivity.
- For 50 years the software industry has tried to make do with gross project-level data, and it has no standard chart of accounts or standard activity descriptions for activity-based costing.
- The software industry has failed to validate raw data prior to publication, and hence tends to overstate productivity and understate costs by using partial data.
- The software industry has seldom bothered to identify in print the nature of the statistical methods used to produce reports, benchmarks, and baseline studies.

The United States and other countries too should have national databases of software productivity and quality information. Since the first edition of this book was published, the U.S. Air Force has been attempting to establish a national database, with encouraging but not totally satisfactory results. The Australian Software Metrics Association (ASMA) has also attempted to quantify local results. The International Function Point Users Group (IFPUG) is also attempting this, although they must depend upon members to contribute information. There is a new and fairly active function point interest group on the Internet, and several CompuServe forums (i.e., CASE, computer language, cost estimating, and information management) discuss function point results from time to time. There are also a number of proprietary or semiprivate databases owned by commercial companies such as Gartner Group, Quantitative Software Management (QSM), and Software Productivity Research.

However, a true national database would probably exceed the volume of all known databases to date. A true national database for software projects in the United States would probably need to contain data from about 5000 organizations and perhaps 75,000 software projects. This is about three times larger than the sum of all known data on software productivity and quality.

It would also be highly useful to establish both industry databases and individual company databases for software quality and productivity information. At the corporate level, several hundred U.S. companies now have at least rudimentary information on software topics, and rather accurate function point counts (even if their cost and resource data is suspect). There is nothing to speak of at the industry level, although it would appear reasonable for software-intensive industries such as insurance, banking, and telecommunications to wish to do this.

Significant Software Technology Changes between 1990 and 1995

Following are short summaries of the major technological changes between 1990 and 1995 that have affected overall national averages for software.

Benchmarking

Benchmarking, or comparing software productivity, quality, schedules, salaries, methodologies, etc., between companies, was rare when the data for the first edition of this book was assembled. Since 1990, benchmarking has been on an explosive growth path. The author's company is now doing about two or three benchmark studies each month, and many other companies are also facilitating benchmark studies. The probable reason for the accelerating interest is the fact that the function point metric makes benchmarking much more accurate and the data much more useful than was possible in the former "lines of code" (LOC) era. In any case, now that hundreds of companies are measuring software productivity and quality, the impact is beneficial in terms of leading to improvements in the factors that are measured.

There are still problems with inconsistencies and incompatibilities among the various benchmarking consulting companies, and the published results. For example, SPR and Gartner Group have different averages for several industries. The probable reason for the difference is the fact that the SPR data is derived from on-site interviews which correct some of the anomalies and missing items that are normally omitted from software cost and resource tracking systems. Benchmarking does not have a direct, near-term impact on software quality or productivity rates. However, benchmarks are usually preludes to some kind of planned improvement program and hence almost always on the critical path for companies that do make improvements in software productivity and quality.

End-user programming

The first edition of this book did not deal with end-user programming at all. However, the numbers of knowledge workers who are computer literate and can program is going up at double-digit rates. The tools and programming languages for end-user development have exploded under the impact of Visual Basic and its competitors. Even the macro languages for spreadsheet applications have become more user-friendly and less arcane.

There are now enough end-user applications and their typical productivity rates are high enough (in excess of 50 function points per staff month) to actually elevate national averages when end-user data is included. End-user programming is not always safe and effective, however, as will be discussed later in this book.

Somewhat surprisingly, the volume of reusable material in the end-user programming domain now tops every other owing to the huge numbers of Visual Basic controls now being marketed by third-party vendors. This phenomenon is very significant.

Client-server applications

When this book was first published, scarcely 100 projects out of more than 4000 were client-server projects. Yet roughly 500 client-server projects have been explored in the past 5 years. Client-server software productivity rates are typically about double mainframe Cobol productivity rates (i.e., 16 function points per staff month versus 8 function points per staff month). However, client-server software complexity is high and quality is not as good as for mainframe applications. About twice as many defects or bugs are present at delivery as were found in mainframe applications. The implication is that maintenance costs will be much higher for client-server software than for mainframe software, as today's client-server applications become tomorrow's legacy systems.

However, a new subindustry is emerging of quality control tools for client-server applications. Hopefully, this subindustry will grow and prosper, or maintenance costs may go out of control in the client-server domain.

Commercial software

When this book was first published in 1991, the quality levels of commercial software were not very impressive. Productivity was high, in large part because of massive bouts of unpaid overtime on the part of many commercial software engineers. Since commercial software houses as a class are sensitive to public opinion, the major players such as Microsoft, Lotus, and Computer Associates have been trying energetically to improve their quality levels but not reduce their productivity or lengthen their schedules. They appear to have been generally successful, and the progress of commercial software is significant in overall national results.

Typical Windows-based commercial software packages such as spreadsheets and word processors are now between 1000 and 5000 function points in size and can be purchased for prices in the range of $295 per copy (or less). Therefore, the cost per function point of packaged applications can be as low as $0.15. Packages are occupying increasingly large percentages of corporate portfolios. The commercial software business is now a significant component of the United States balance of trade.

Downsizings and layoffs

The author has been in the software business for more than 30 years. Yet the period between 1990 and 1995 has been the most traumatic in terms of layoffs and downsizings of major corporations. A number of the author's clients such as Digital Equipment, IBM, Wang, and Data General are now much smaller than they were 10 or even 5 years ago.

The immediate near-term impact of downsizings is a sharp reduction in productivity and an overall reduction of quality levels within the affected company, in part because often the best technical and quality assurance personnel jump ship or are let go. If the enterprise survives, it can eventually regain its former productivity and quality levels. Indeed, it may even exceed them, since average project sizes tend to decline during layoffs and downsizing operations.

In a curious way, downsizings have contributed to long-range national U.S. productivity gains. The reasons are threefold: (1) more and more software is now being done by outsourcers, who are usually more productive than their clients; (2) as large companies shrink, average project sizes shrink too; (3) the reduction in number of large companies building software means that smaller companies construct a larger percentage of total applications. Small companies are often more productive than large corporations. Also, during bouts of downsizings and layoffs, large companies seldom tackle the high-risk applications whose frequent failures tend to bring down corporate and national productivity averages.

Function point expansion

When this book was first published, usage of function point metrics was growing but still a minority among the major software houses of the United States and abroad. Membership in the International Function Point Users Group (IFPUG) has been steadily expanding at about 50 percent per year. By about 1993, function point metrics became the most widely used software metric in the United States and IFPUG was the largest software measurement association.

The European software community is also adopting function point metrics rapidly, and function points are making significant progress in India and Japan as well. This rapid expansion of function point metrics means an exponential growth in the availability of software productivity and quality data.

A major change in function point counting rules occurred in 1994, when the version 3.0 rules were replaced by the version 4.0 rules. Version 4.0 does not count error messages and hence has the effect of reducing the overall volume of function points by a total of about 20 percent. Because the first edition of this book utilized version 3.0, this new edition does too. See Chap. 2 for general rules for converting between IFPUG versions.

As function points expand, a number of variants have occurred. The major variances now include the IFPUG methods, the British Mark II method, the Boeing 3D method, and the SPR feature point method. Another variant is the DeMarco function point method. (The DeMarco method was developed independently during the same time that Albrecht was developing the original IBM function point in the 1970s. The simultaneous research of Albrecht and DeMarco somewhat resembles the simultaneous discovery of evolution by Charles Darwin and Alfred Wallace. Since Albrecht published first, he is the equivalent to Darwin in this analogy.)

The function point metric is contributing to software productivity and quality improvements in an interesting way. The older "lines of code" metric focused industry attention on the task of coding. The high costs associated with the production of more than 50 paper documents surrounding software was essentially invisible using LOC metrics. Also invisible were bugs found in requirements, specifications, and user documents. Function point metrics have thrown a spotlight on a topic that had not been examined, and revealed that software paperwork often costs more than source code. Also, defects in requirements and specifications outnumber coding defects, and cannot easily be found by testing.

ISO 9000-9004 standards

The international standards organization (ISO) has assumed a new and major importance in the context of the evolution of the European Union. The ISO 9000-9004 quality standards are now being implemented on a worldwide basis and are affecting both hardware and software products. In particular ISO 9001 is affecting software projects.

Unfortunately, the ISO quality standards are not particularly effective for software projects and have managed to omit a number of important software quality topics. However, the ISO quality standards have had the beneficial impact of making quality an important business issue and raising the global awareness of the importance of quality. There is no solid evidence that demonstrates that ISO certification actually improves software quality levels. Software defect potentials and defect removal efficiency levels are approximately the same in certified companies and in similar companies that are not certified.

Object-oriented paradigm

Since this book was published in 1991, the object-oriented paradigm has emerged from cult status to become a mainstream methodology (although many of the OO conferences retain an interesting flavor of eccentricity and cultishness). Productivity rates of OO projects using languages such as Objective C, Smalltalk, and C++ are generally significantly higher than those of similar projects developed using procedural languages such as C, Fortran, or Pascal: 10 to 12 function points per staff month as opposed to 4 to 6 function points per staff month. This means that the rapid expansion of the OO paradigm is having some impact on quantitative results and especially so for systems and commercial software where the OO paradigm is farthest up the learning curve. The OO analysis and design domain has had such a steep learning curve that the near-term impact is negative for productivity.

As more companies move along the OO learning curve, and as class libraries of reusable objects improve in quantity and quality, it can be hypothesized that the OO domain will continue to expand in volume and in impact. (Surprisingly, however, the volume of reusable material available for the Visual Basic programming language currently exceeds the volume for any known OO language.)

Outsourcing

The outsourcing subindustry has continued to grow and prosper in both the United States and abroad. In the 1991 edition of this book, outsourced or contract software projects were subsumed under the general headings of information systems, systems software, or military software.

The growth rate of the outsourcing domain and the comparatively high productivity and quality levels of the outsource community deserve to have outsource projects shown as a separate category. Since many outsourcers are in fact superior to their clients in software development methods, the overall results of the outsource domain contribute to the general improvements in software productivity and quality reflected in this edition. In terms of work-hours per function point, the outsource world typically excels their clients by somewhere between 15 and 50 percent. Of course, outsource charges and costs are higher so the costs per function point are similar.

The outsourcing community that serves particular industries such as banking, health care, and insurance tends to accumulate substantial volumes of reusable material within those industries. Part of the reason for higher productivity levels achieved by major outsourcers is the large volumes of reusable specifications, source code, test cases, and user manual sections for software within specific industries.

Software reusability

Software reuse was largely a theoretical topic in 1991 when this book was first published. It is still not a pervasive technology in terms of day-to-day reuse by large numbers of corporations. However, reusability is now beginning to grow to significant proportions. Successful reuse covers many artifacts, and not just source code. Reusable plans, estimates, specifications, data, user documentation, and test materials are some of the other reusable materials. An emerging subindustry of tools and vendors is beginning to coalesce around reuse. It is time that this technology is emphasized in terms of its pragmatic results.

It is an interesting observation that software projects that approach or exceed productivity rates of 100 function points per staff month typically use in excess of 50 percent reusable code and also have high levels of other reusable material such as specifications, test materials, and sections of user manuals.

Software Engineering Institute (SEI) capability maturity model (CMM)

The SEI CMM was in its infancy when the first edition of this book was published. Now it has almost 10 years of continuous usage, and several years of evolution and modification. In the past, the author of this book has been critical of the SEI CMM as being incomplete, arbitrary, and totally devoid of effective quantification of results. These problems still remain, but the SEI has not been idle. New features are being added to the CMM, and the penetration of the CMM continues to grow.

In 1991, less than 10 percent of the author's clients had even heard of SEI or the CMM and less than 2 percent had used the SEI assessment method. By 1995, more than 50 percent of the author's clients have heard about the SEI, and about 10 percent have experimented with an SEI-style assessment.

In spite of its many faults, the SEI CMM concept has at least raised the awareness levels of many software houses about topics such as process improvement, quality, measurement, and metrics. Thus the

SEI has become a minor contributor to the progress of software in the United States, and even abroad. Hopefully, the SEI will continue to improve on the original very primitive CMM concepts and will eventually adopt modern quantitative metrics such as function points instead of the flawed "physical lines of code" or LOC metrics they first endorsed.

A study of software quality performed by the author's company in 1994 found some overlap among the SEI CMM levels. The best software produced by level 1 organizations actually had higher quality levels than the worst produced by level 3 organizations. However, there was also evidence to suggest that average quality levels and also productivity levels went up with each maturity level.

Changes in the structure, format, and contents of the second edition

In the first edition of this book in 1991 this chapter on U.S. national averages showed overall data from approximately 4300 projects as a series of simple graphs and tables. Selected portions of the data were broken down into three subcategories:

1. Management information systems
2. Systems software
3. Military software

That approach was acceptable at the time, because there was no other comparable collection of quantitative data available. Now that software measurements and benchmarking are entering the mainstream of software technologies, many companies and many industries have significant amounts of data on their own performance. Therefore this second edition will display the data in a much more detailed and granular, although complicated, fashion.

In this edition, data from six subindustries or domains will be shown separately. The six subindustries are:

1. End-user software produced for personal use by the developers themselves
2. Information systems produced for internal business use within enterprises
3. Contract or outsourced software systems produced for some other enterprise
4. Commercial software produced for licensing or sale to clients
5. Systems software that controls physical devices such as computers
6 Military software produced under various Department of Defense standards

TABLE 3.13 Approximate 1995 Numbers of Software Personnel in the United States

Subindustry	Managers	Programmers	Ancillary	Total
MIS	136,800	760,000	152,000	1,048,800
Outsource	22,950	127,500	25,500	175,950
Commercial	15,113	85,000	22,950	123,063
Systems	64,770	340,000	91,800	496,570
Military	66,560	320,000	96,000	482,560
Other	13,725	75,000	16,500	105,225
Subtotal	319,918	1,707,500	404,750	2,432,168
End users	0	8,000,000	0	8,000,000
Total	319,918	9,707,500	404,750	10,432,168

These six categories are not the only kinds of software produced. However, they are the most common types of software development projects in North America, South America, Europe, Africa, India, the Middle East, and the Pacific Rim.

A seventh category identified as "other" is shown in some of the tables. This seventh category is a catch-all for various kinds of software where SPR has not done enough assessment and baseline studies to display detailed information or reach overall conclusions; i.e., the computer game industry, the software used for entertainment such as the animation sequence of Jurassic Park, the music software industry, specialized medical and scientific software, and the like. The approximate 1995 populations of personnel in these various categories are shown in Table 3.13.

The column labeled "Ancillary" refers to the large and growing numbers of software specialists that are now a major component of the overall software industry. Examples of the ancillary occupations include software quality assurance specialists, database administrators, software technical writers, software measurement specialists, software testing personnel, and a host of others. Lumping all of the end-user programmers into the "Programmers" column is a compromise. Many of the end-user programmers are managers themselves, and indeed some are executives, scientists, attorneys, physicians, or members of any other profession. However, the purpose of the table is to show the approximate numbers of personnel in a software context.

Following are short discussions of what each of the six categories means in the context of this book.

End-user software

The phrase "end-user software" refers to applications written by individuals who are not programmers or software engineers as their normal occupations. Many knowledge workers such as accountants, physicists, medical doctors, managers, and other professionals have the technical ability to write software if they choose to do so or have the time to do so. There are currently about 110,000,000 workers in the United States. The author estimates that there are perhaps 8,000,000 managers, engineers, architects, accountants, and other knowledge workers who know enough about programming to build end-user applications using tools such as spreadsheets, Quick Basic, Visual Basic, and Realizer.

The upper limit of applications which end users can build, using current technologies, is approximately 100 function points in size. The average size for end-user applications is closer to 10 function points in size. There is no exact census of the number of companies where end users have developed applications, but SPR estimates the U.S. total to be in the range of 50,000 companies including a host of smaller companies that employ no professional software personnel at all.

Similar ratios of professional software personnel to end-user software personnel are found in the other industrialized countries. On a global basis, there are perhaps 12,000,000 professional software personnel but more than 25,000,000 end users outside the United States who can program.

Interestingly, the end-user population seems to be growing at more than 10 percent per year, while the professional software population is now down to single-digit growth rates and even declining within some industries. The population of end users who can program constitutes one of the largest markets in the world, and a host of vendors led by Microsoft are bringing out tools and products at an accelerating rate.

As this new edition of the book is written, there are more questions about the quality, value, and economics of end-user-developed software than there are answers. Nonetheless, it is a topic of growing importance because knowledge of computer programming is becoming a fairly common business skill.

Management information systems (MIS)

The phrase "management information systems," or MIS, refers to the kinds of applications which enterprises produce in support of their business and administrative operations: payroll systems, accounting systems, front and back office banking systems, insurance claims handling systems, airline reservation systems, and the like. Many government agencies also produce management information systems, such as the various kinds of taxation software produced at local, state, and national levels; social security benefit tracking systems; and drivers license and vehicle registration systems.

The class of information systems constitutes a very broad range of application sizes and types, including but not limited to large mainframe systems in excess of 50,000 function points at the upper end of the spectrum, and small personal computer applications of less than 100 function points at the low end of the spectrum. The information systems community in the United States is far and away the largest employer of professional software personnel: more than 1,000,000 personnel out of an approximate U.S. total of 2,400,000 work in the domain of information systems. More than 25,000 U.S. organizations employ information systems personnel.

The large employment of information systems personnel is also true for every industrialized country in Europe, South America, and the Pacific Rim. The global information systems community is the largest in every industrialized country. The exceptions to this rule include China, Russia, and other countries which have lagged in the usage of computers for business and service-related purposes, as opposed to military and manufacturing purposes.

The major employers of information systems software personnel are the industries that were early adopters of mainframe computers: banks, insurance companies, manufacturing companies, government agencies, and the like. Insurance, for example, has at least a dozen major companies that employ many thousands of software personnel: Aetna, Travelers, CIGNA, Hartford, Sun Life, etc.

Of course, many large corporations that are better known for other kinds of software also produce information systems in significant volumes: AT&T, IBM, and Boeing Computer Services are also information systems producers. For that matter, the DoD and the military services produce huge volumes of information systems.

A number of CASE and methodology vendors have also specialized or concentrated on the MIS domain: Bachman, Oracle, Intersolv, LBMS, KnowledgeWare, SQA, James Martin, Texas Instruments, and many more. Essentially all of the vendors that specialize in topics such as RAD, information engineering, client-server technologies, and database technologies are aiming at the MIS world. There are also MIS specialists in the consulting business, just as there are also specialized consulting companies in the systems and military software domains.

The information systems community is strongly allied with the concepts of databases, repositories, and data warehouses. The bulk of all database tools, languages, and methods are aimed squarely at the management information systems domain.

Outsourced and contract software

The phrase "outsourced software" refers to software produced under a blanket contract by which a software development organization agrees to produce all, or specific categories, of software for the client organization. The phrase "contract software" refers to a specific software project that is built under contract for a client organization. There are a number of forms under which the contract might be negotiated: time and materials, fixed cost, and work for hire to name but three. Note that this book deals with civilian contracts and civilian outsourcing primarily in the information systems domain. The military world has unique standards and procurement practices, and even a body of special contract law that does not apply in the civilian world (although parts of it may show up in civilian contracts with the U.S. federal government).

The systems software domain also has some extensive contract and outsource experiences, and indeed is more likely to go abroad for outsourcing than any other domain. However, in the United States the large outsource vendors such as ISSC, EDS, and Keane tend to concentrate on the information systems market.

The contract and outsource houses are more likely to be hired for major applications than for small ones. The upper limit of the outsource size range is well in excess of 100,000 function points. As pointed out in another of the author's books, *Patterns of Software System Failure and Success* (International Thomson, 1995), the outsource community has a better record of success for large systems than do their clients (although no domain can build large systems without some kind of problems or troubles occurring).

Contract software and outsourced software are alike in that the work is performed by personnel who are not employees of the client organization, using terms and conditions that are mutually agreed to and covered by contractual obligations. Contract software and outsourced software differ in the overall scope of the arrangement. Contracts are usually for specific individual projects, while the outsource arrangement might encompass hundreds or even thousands of projects under one general contractual umbrella.

The software outsourcing community is growing rather rapidly. The diversity of organizations within the outsource and contract community runs from a host of one-person individual contractors up to the size of Electronic Data Systems with perhaps 40,000 software professionals. The total number of contract and outsource software personnel in the United States is roughly about 175,000 out of a total software employment of about 2,400,000. Some of the major outsource and software contracting organizations include Andersen, Keane, EDS, ISSC, Computer Sciences Corporation, and a host of others.

The volume of domestic outsourcing agreements between large information systems clients and outsource contractors is quite significant: Currently about 10 percent of all information systems software in the United States is produced under contract or outsource agreements, and that volume is increasing rather rapidly. As of 1995, the total volume of IS software from the United States that is being outsourced internationally seems to be less than 1 percent of total IS applications, based on preliminary data collected during assessments performed by Software Productivity Research. Should the percentage rise significantly, the United States and other industrialized countries might face significant layoffs among IS software personnel. In fact, the domestic U.S. outsource companies could also face significant problems too, unless they establish international subsidiaries.

The United States is not the only country that is exploring international software outsource arrangements. Most countries with high labor costs, such as Japan, Sweden, the United Kingdom, and Germany are also interested in software development or maintenance in countries with lower labor costs.

Commercial software

Commercial software was not broken out as a separate category in the previous edition of this book. The phrase "commercial software" refers to applications that are produced for large-scale marketing to hundreds or even millions of clients. Examples of commercial software include word processors such as Word Perfect or Microsoft Word, spreadsheets such as Lotus, Quattro, and Excel, accounting packages such as Pacioli, project management tools such as Timeline, Microsoft Project, or Checkpoint, and a myriad of other kinds of software. Some commercial software houses are more specialized, and aim at niches rather than broad-based general populations. For example, companies such as Bellcore serve the communications industry.

The commercial software domain employs about 120,000 software personnel out of a current U.S. total of perhaps 2,400,000. Although more than 3000 companies produce commercial software in the United States, the major players are getting bigger and rapidly acquiring the smaller players. The larger commercial software players include the pure software shops such as Microsoft, Computer Associates, Oracle, Knowledgebase, Symantec, and Lotus. The larger players also include many hybrid companies that build hardware as well as software: IBM, DEC, Unisys, SUN, Apple, AT&T, and many others. There are also a host of specialized niches within the commercial software world: accounting software companies, game software companies, CASE companies, and many more.

Although commercial software packages are built throughout the world, the United States is currently the dominant player in global markets. Software Productivity Research estimates that about 85 percent of the commercial packages running in the United States originated here, and that about 40 percent of the commercial software everywhere in the world has a U.S. origin. This is perhaps the most one-sided balance of trade of any U.S. industry.

As personal computers become more powerful, the size range of commercial software applications is exploding. In the DOS era, typical PC applications were in the size range of 200 to 1000 function points. Now that Windows 95, Windows NT, and OS/2 have unlocked the painful size restrictions on memory and addressability, modern PC applications are as large as mainframe systems of a decade ago. Indeed, Windows 95, Windows NT, and OS/2 are in the 50,000 function point range and compare to MVS, UNIX, and other massive applications.

Many commercial word processors, spreadsheets, and other standard Windows applications are now in excess of 5000 function points in size. This explains why 8 to 16 megabytes of memory, gigabyte hard drives, or quad-speed CD ROM drives are now the preferred equipment for running modern PC Windows-based applications.

There is a great deal of diversity in the commercial software domain, and this is due in part to the need to support diverse operating systems and multiple hardware platforms, i.e., UNIX, DOS, Windows, OS/2, MVS, VMS, etc. A common aspect of the commercial software domain is that the applications are built to appeal to a mass market rather than being built upon commission for a specific client or a small number of clients with explicit requirements. The commercial software domain needs to balance a number of factors in order to be successful in the marketplace: the feature sets of the products, the quality levels of the delivered software, and the time to reach the relevant market.

Systems software

In the context of this book "systems software" is defined as that which controls physical devices. The original archetype of systems software were operating systems such as CPM, DOS, OS/2, MVS, Windows NT, or UNIX that controlled computer hardware. Other examples of systems software include telephone switching systems such as AT&T's ESS5 central office switching systems, smaller private branch exchange (PBX) switches, and local area net (LAN) controllers. Also included under the general definition of systems software would be software that controls automobile fuel injection systems, civilian aircraft flight control software, medical instrument software, and even the software embedded in home appliances such as microwaves and clothes dryers.

The systems software world tends to build very large applications that are sometimes in excess of 200,000 function points in size. This domain also builds applications that may control complicated and expensive hardware devices where failures might be catastrophic, i.e., aircraft, spacecraft, telephone switching systems, manufacturing equipment, weapons systems, medical instruments, and the like.

The dual need for methods that can build large systems with high reliability has given the systems software world some powerful quality control approaches. Systems software is not very good in terms of productivity but is a world leader in terms of quality. The systems software domain in the United States contains about 500,000 professional software personnel and managers, or roughly 25 percent of the approximate total of 2,400,000 U.S. software personnel. The number of companies that produce systems software total to more than 2500 and include some of the largest employers of software in the world. For example, both AT&T and IBM have more than 25,000 software personnel, and roughly half are in the systems software domain. Many other companies have 10,000 or more software personnel, such as Digital Equipment and Hewlett-Packard.

Other examples of systems software producers include automotive manufacturers such as Ford, Chrysler, and General Motors; aircraft manufacturers such as Boeing, and a host of well-known computer and telecommunication companies such as Motorola, Sun, Unisys, and GTE. Pure software companies such as Microsoft also produce systems software, although Microsoft is discussed under the topic "Commercial Software."

Systems software is often built for custom hardware platforms and may use custom or proprietary operating systems. Systems software also tends to utilize the UNIX operating system to a higher degree than other software classes. The systems software domain is also the main user of high-end development workstations. As a result of the special needs of systems software, the vendors serving this community are often quite distinct from those serving the information systems domain or the military domain.

Military software

The phrase "military software" refers to software produced for a uniformed military service such as a nation's Air Force, Army, or Navy, or software produced for the Department of Defense (or the equivalent in other countries). This broad definition includes a number of subclasses, such as software associated with weapons systems, with command, control, and communication systems (usually shortened to C3 or C cubed), with logistical applications, and also with software virtually identical to civilian counterparts such as payroll applications or benefits tracking applications.

The military software domain employs more than 475,000 software professionals in the United States, out of a total of about 2,400,000.

There are about 1500 defense contracting companies in the United States, although probably 85 percent of all defense contract dollars go to the top 50 of these groups. The Department of Defense and the uniformed military services alone are reported to employ more than 70,000, although that number is partly speculative. (The annual software conferences sponsored by the Air Force's Software Technology Support Center attract about 3000 attendees and rank as one of the largest pure software conferences in the United States.)

The major defense and military employers are predominantly large corporations such as Lockheed Martin, Grumman Northrop, AT&T, Hughes, SAIC, Litton, Computer Sciences Corporation, GTE, Loral, and Logicon. The U.S. defense industry is currently going through a downsizing and shrinking phase. This is producing some reduction in the defense software community. However, software is so important to modern military weapons systems that the reductions will hopefully not erode U.S. defense software capabilities. The military software world has built the largest software systems in human history. Some have exceeded 250,000 function points in overall size.

The United States is far and away the major producer and consumer of military and defense software in the world. The volume and sophistication of U.S. military software is actually a major factor of U.S. military capabilities. All those pictures of cruise missiles, smart bombs, and Patriot missiles destroying Scuds that filled television news during the Gulf War had an invisible background: It is the software and computers on board that make such weapons possible.

Since the NATO countries tend to use many weapons systems, communication systems, logistics systems, and other software systems produced in the United States, it appears that the volume of U.S. defense and military software may be larger than that of the next five countries put together (Russia, China, Germany, United Kingdom, and France). Many countries produce military and defense software for weapons and communications systems that they use or market, such as Israel, Brazil, South Korea, Sweden, and Japan.

The total of military software personnel outside of the United States is estimated by SPR to be about 900,000. The bulk of these are in Russia, the Ukraine, and China, but there are also active military software projects and defense contractors in Brazil, Argentina, Mexico, the United Kingdom, Canada, France, Israel, Sweden, Germany, Egypt, Turkey, Vietnam, Poland, Cuba, Iraq, Iran, and essentially every country with a significant military establishment.

Over the years the U.S. defense community has evolved an elaborate set of specialized standards and practices which differ substantially from civilian norms. Although these military practices and Department of Defense standards are not without merit, they have tended to be so cumbersome and baroque that they sometimes served more as impediments to progress rather than benefiting either the defense contractors or the DoD itself.

Since the United States is the world's largest producer and consumer of military software, the way the United States goes about the production of military software is of global importance. In the United States in 1994, William Perry, the Secretary of Defense, issued a major policy statement to the effect that DoD standards no longer needed to be utilized. Instead, the armed services and the DoD were urged to adopt civilian best current practices. This change in policy is in the early stages of implementation, and it is too soon to know how effective or even how pervasive the changes might be.

Variations in Software Development Practices among Six Subindustries

The six different subindustries included in this new edition vary significantly in productivity rates, quality levels, schedules, and many other quantitative matters. The quantitative differences are really reflections of some very significant variations in how software is built within each of the six domains.

Variations in activities performed

One of the most visible differences that can easily be seen from SPR's assessment and baseline studies is the variations in the activities that are typically performed. SPR's standard chart of accounts for software baselines includes 25 activities. Only large military projects perform all 25, and the variances from project to project and company to company are both interesting and significant.

The end-user software domain averages performing four activities and in some cases may perform only a single activity, coding.

The management information systems domain averaged from 12 to 18 activities for mainframe software. Client-server projects are averaging only 6 to 12 activities, which explains in part why quality has declined in the MIS domain.

The outsource domain is somewhat more rigorous than the MIS domain, and runs from 15 up to perhaps 20 activities.

The commercial software, systems software, and military software domains all perform more than 20 activities on average, and the military usually performs all 25. Since many of the activities in these domains are quality-related, it can be seen why the quality control results are typically better than the rudimentary MIS domain.

Table 3.14 shows two important factors:

TABLE 3.14 Software Development Activities Associated with Six Subindustries (Percentage of Staff-months by Activity)

Activities performed	End user	MIS	Outsource	Commercial	Systems	Military
1. Requirements		7.50	9.00	4.00	4.00	7.00
2. Prototyping	10.00	2.00	2.50	1.00	2.00	2.00
3. Architecture		0.50	1.00	2.00	1.50	1.00
4. Project plans		1.00	1.50	1.00	2.00	1.00
5. Initial design		8.00	7.00	6.00	7.00	6.00
6. Detail design		7.00	8.00	5.00	6.00	7.00
7. Design reviews			0.50	1.50	2.50	1.00
8. Coding	35.00	20.00	16.00	23.00	20.00	16.00
9. Reuse acquisition	5.00		2.00	2.00	2.00	2.00
10. Package purchase		1.00	1.00		1.00	1.00
11. Code inspections				1.50	1.50	1.00
12. Independent verification and validation						1.00
13. Configuration management		3.00	3.00	1.00	1.00	1.50
14. Formal integration		2.00	2.00	1.50	2.00	1.50
15. User documentation	10.00	7.00	9.00	12.00	10.00	10.00
16. Unit testing	40.00	4.00	3.50	2.50	5.00	3.00
17. Function testing		6.00	5.00	6.00	5.00	5.00
18. Integration testing		5.00	5.00	4.00	5.00	5.00
19. System testing		7.00	5.00	7.00	5.00	6.00
20. Field testing				6.00	1.50	3.00
21. Acceptance testing		5.00	3.00		1.00	3.00
22. Independent testing						1.00
23. Quality assurance			1.00	2.00	2.00	1.00
24. Installation and training		2.00	3.00		1.00	1.00
25. Project management		12.00	12.00	11.00	12.00	13.00
Total	100.00	100.00	100.00	100.00	100.00	100.00
Activities	5	16	20	21	22	25

1. The most common activities that are likely to be performed
2. The approximate percentage of effort devoted to each activity

Since there are major variations in activity patterns associated with project size as well as with domain, assume that Table 3.14 is derived from software projects that are nominally 1,500 function points in size. The data in Table 3.14 should not be used as a cost estimating template. Whenever data is shown using percentages, note that the inclusion or removal of any activity would throw off all of the percentages. Table 3.13 illustrates the fact that the six domains have significant variances in the processes usually followed for building software.

Even a cursory examination of Table 3.14 shows why productivity variations are so large from domain to domain: Variations in the number of activities performed is sufficient to cause significant productivity differences. A more careful examination also sheds light on why quality variations occur, too. Note the percentages of effort devoted to quality control, inspections, and testing in the systems and military domains compared to the percentages in the end-user and MIS domains.

Variations in defect potentials, defect prevention, defect removal, and quality control

There are notable differences in the sets of defect prevention and defect removal activities among the six domains. In order to give a context to these differences, three important concepts need to be understood: (1) defect potentials, (2) defect prevention, (3) defect removal.

The concept of "defect potential" refers to the sum total of possible errors in software from five separate sources: (1) errors in requirements, (2) errors in design, (3) errors in source code, (4) errors in user documentation, (5) errors associated with "bad fixes" or secondary errors introduced while fixing a primary error.

The defect potentials of software applications have been derived from long-range studies of software defect reports over periods of several years. The first such studies known to the author were carried out at IBM during the 1960s and 1970s on products such as the OS/360 operating system and the IMS database.

All defect reports were accumulated from requirements through development and out into the field for several years of maintenance and enhancement. The defect origins were also explored, to see how many errors could be traced back to requirements, to design, to code, to user manuals, or to poor quality control during the defect repair process.

The current range of potential defects is from a low of less than 1 defect per function point to a high of more than 10 defects per function point, as will be shown later in this chapter. However, the function point metric provides a fairly useful approximation for overall defect potentials: Raise the function point total of the application to the 1.25 power and the result will give a rough estimate of the total volume of errors or bugs that may be encountered.

Table 3.15 illustrates the overall distribution of software errors among the various categories of origin points. The concept of "defect prevention" is the most difficult to study and quantify. Here is an example of how assumptions on defect prevention are derived.

TABLE 3.15 Percentage of Software Defect Origins for Six Domains

Defect Origin	End user	MIS	Outsource	Commercial	Systems	Military	Average
Requirements bugs	0.00	15.00	20.00	10.00	10.00	20.00	12.50
Design bugs	15.00	30.00	25.00	30.00	25.00	20.00	24.17
Source code bugs	55.00	35.00	35.00	30.00	40.00	35.00	38.33
User document bugs	10.00	10.00	10.00	20.00	15.00	15.00	13.33
Bad fix bugs	20.00	10.00	10.00	10.00	10.00	10.00	11.67
Total bugs	100.00	100.00	100.00	100.00	100.00	100.00	100.00

Assume that you have two projects of the same size and nominal complexity, say 1000 function points. Assume that one of the projects developed a prototype while the other project did not. When the defects for the two projects are accumulated, assume that design reviews found 200 bugs or errors in the project that did not build a prototype and only 100 bugs or errors in the project that did build a prototype. It can be hypothesized that the prototype had the effect of preventing 100 potential bugs or errors that might otherwise have occurred.

Of course, one example is not enough to really form such a hypothesis. But if 50 projects that built prototypes were compared to 50 similar projects that did not, and the number of design defects had a 2 to 1 average difference in favor of prototypes, then the hypothesis would be reasonable.

The concept of defect removal efficiency is very important for quality control and quality assurance purposes. Defect removal efficiency is normally calculated on the anniversary of the release of a software product. Suppose that during development, a total of 900 bugs or errors were found. During the first year of use, customers found and reported another 100 bugs. On the first anniversary of the product's release, the 900 bugs found during development are added to the 100 bugs customers reported, to achieve a total of 1000 bugs for this example. Since the developers found 900 out of 1000, their defect removal efficiency can easily be seen to be 90 percent.

The measurement of defect removal efficiency levels is one of the signs of a "best in class" software producer. Not only do best in class organizations measure defect removal efficiency levels, but they average more than 95 percent removal efficiency levels for their entire software portfolio. It is comparatively easy to go above 95 percent in defect removal efficiency levels for small applications of less than 100 function points in size. As the size of the application grows, defect removal efficiency levels typically decline unless very energetic steps are taken.

For applications larger than 10,000 function points and especially for those approaching 100,000 function points defect removal efficiency levels in excess of 95 percent are only possible by using a multistage set of pretest removal activities such as formal inspections, coupled with an extensive suite of formal testing stages. A simple rule of thumb can approximate the number of discrete defect removal operations needed to go above 95 percent in cumulative defect removal efficiency: Raise the size of the application in function points to the 0.3 power and express the result as an integer:

Function points	Defect removal stages
1	1
10	2
100	4
1,000	8
10,000	16
100,000	32

Table 3.16 illustrates the variations in typical defect prevention and defect removal methods among the six domains. Table 3.16 oversimplifies the situation, since defect removal activities have varying efficiencies for requirements, design, code, documentation, and bad fix defect categories. Also, each defect removal operation has a significant range of performance. Unit testing by individual programmers, for example, can range from less than 20 percent efficient to more than 50 percent efficient.

Overall, formal inspections have the highest average efficiency levels: Both design and code inspections average about 50 percent in efficiency and can go above 70 percent. Inspections are higher in efficiency than any known form of testing, with one exception. The exception is the kind of high-volume beta testing practiced by Microsoft, where more than 10,000 clients test a software package concurrently.

Another useful rule of thumb is that any given defect removal operation will find about 30 percent of the bugs that are present. This fairly low level of average defect removal efficiency explains why it takes up to 18 discrete defect removal operations to top 99 percent in cumulative defect removal efficiency levels.

Exploring activity-based costing

Table 3.17 shows the overall ranges of software productivity expressed in two complementary formats: (1) function points per staff-month; (2) work hours per function points.

One of the purposes of the second edition of this book is to move

TABLE 3.16 Patterns of Software Defect Prevention and Removal Activities for Six Software Subindustries, Percentages

Prevention activities:	End user	MIS	Outsource	Commercial	Systems	Military
Prototypes	20.00	20.00	20.00	20.00	20.00	20.00
Clean rooms					20.00	20.00
JAD sessions		30.00	30.00			
QFD sessions					25.00	
Subtotal	20.00	44.00	44.00	20.00	52.00	36.00
Pretest removal:						
Desk checking	15.00	15.00	15.00	15.00	15.00	15.00
Requirements review			30.00	25.00	20.00	20.00
Design review			40.00	45.00	45.00	30.00
Document review				20.00	20.00	20.00
Code inspections				50.00	60.00	40.00
Independent verification and validation						20.00
Correctness proofs						10.00
Usability labs				25.00		
Subtotal	15.00	15.00	64.30	89.48	88.03	83.55
Testing activities:						
Unit test	30.00	25.00	25.00	25.00	25.00	25.00
New function test		30.00	30.00	30.00	30.00	30.00
Regression test			20.00	20.00	20.00	20.00
Integration test		30.00	30.00	30.00	30.00	30.00
Performance test				15.00	15.00	20.00
System test		35.00	35.00	35.00	40.00	35.00
Independent test						15.00
Field test				50.00	35.00	30.00
Acceptance test			25.00		25.00	30.00
Subtotal	30.00	76.11	80.89	91.88	92.69	93.63
Overall efficiency	52.40	88.63	96.18	99.32	99.58	99.33
Number of activities	3	7	11	14	16	18

further toward the concept of activity-based costing of software projects. Software data that is collected only to the levels of complete projects or to the levels of six to eight software development phases is not accurate enough for either serious economic analysis or cost estimating of future projects.

The arithmetic mean of the data in Table 3.17 is not very useful information. The cumulative results, on the other hand, are actually both interesting and useful. Experience has shown that the concept of

TABLE 3.17 Maximum, Minimum, and Modal Productivity Ranges for Software Development Activities

	Function points per month			Work hours per function point		
Activities performed	Minimum	Mode	Maximum	Maximum	Mode	Minimum
1. Requirements	50.00	175.00	350.00	2.64	0.75	0.38
2. Prototyping	25.00	150.00	250.00	5.28	0.88	0.53
3. Architecture	100.00	300.00	500.00	1.32	0.44	0.26
4. Project plans	200.00	500.00	1500.00	0.66	0.26	0.09
5. Initial design	50.00	175.00	400.00	2.64	0.75	0.33
6. Detail design	25.00	150.00	300.00	5.28	0.88	0.44
7. Design reviews	75.00	225.00	400.00	1.76	0.59	0.33
8. Coding	15.00	50.00	200.00	8.80	2.64	0.66
9. Reuse acquisition	400.00	600.00	2000.00	0.33	0.22	0.07
10. Package purchase	350.00	400.00	1500.00	0.38	0.33	0.09
11. Code inspections	75.00	150.00	300.00	1.76	0.88	0.44
12. Independent verification and validation	75.00	125.00	200.00	1.76	1.06	0.66
13. Configuration management	1000.00	1750.00	3000.00	0.13	0.08	0.04
14. Formal integration	150.00	250.00	500.00	0.88	0.53	0.26
15. User documentation	20.00	70.00	100.00	6.60	1.89	1.32
16. Unit testing	70.00	150.00	400.00	1.89	0.88	0.33
17. Function testing	25.00	150.00	300.00	5.28	0.88	0.44
18. Integration testing	75.00	175.00	400.00	1.76	0.75	0.33
19. System testing	100.00	200.00	500.00	1.32	0.66	0.26
20. Field testing	75.00	225.00	500.00	1.76	0.59	0.26
21. Acceptance testing	75.00	350.00	600.00	1.76	0.38	0.22
22. Independent testing	100.00	200.00	300.00	1.32	0.66	0.44
23. Quality assurance	30.00	150.00	300.00	4.40	0.88	0.44
24. Installation and training	150.00	350.00	600.00	0.88	0.38	0.22
25. Project management	15.00	100.00	200.00	8.80	1.32	0.66
Cumulative results	1.90	6.75	13.88	69.38	19.55	9.51
Arithmetic mean	133	284.8	624	2.78	0.78	0.38

cumulative results is difficult to grasp, so a simple example may clarify the situation.

Suppose we were building a simple application of 100 function points in size, and we spent 1 month in coding the application and 1 month in testing the application. Our productivity rate for coding is obviously 100 function points per month, and our productivity rate for testing is also 100 function points per month. Therefore the arithmetic mean of our work is also 100 function points per month, since we performed two activities at the same rate. However, the sum of our work on coding and testing was 2 months of effort. Therefore, our real productivity for this project is 50 function points per staff month using the cumulative results. This is easily calculated by dividing the 100 function points in our application by the total amount of effort expended.

Assuming that there are 132 productive working hours in a month, we can perform the same analyses using work hours per function point. Our effort devoted to coding was 132 hours, and our effort devoted to testing was 132 hours. Since the project is 100 function points in size, each activity amounted to 1.32 work hours per function point. Therefore, the arithmetic mean of our two tasks was also 1.32 work hours per function point. Here too, our total effort summed to 2 months, so our real productivity using the harmonic mean is 2.64 hours per function point. This is because we spent a total of 264 hours on this 100 function point project, i.e., 264 hours divided by 100 function points.

Software Productivity Improvement Rates

Cumulative results do not change very rapidly, because the weight of past experience tends to act as a damper. In order to see how productivity changes over time, it is interesting to aggregate projects by decade, by half decade, or by year. For example, it is interesting to compare all projects that entered production in 1995 against all projects that entered production in 1990, 1985, and 1980, and so on back into the past.

The author has had the good fortune of having access to software productivity and quality data for almost 30 years. While working for IBM in the 1960s and 1970s on various productivity and quality improvement programs, all of IBM's internal data was readily available. In addition, the author served as an IBM liaison to various customers on productivity and quality matters, so quite a bit of external data was also available. The author also had access to internal and external data associated with ITT and with many clients of the Nolan & Norton consulting company. The author's own company, Software Productivity Research, has hundreds of clients and hence data on thousands of software projects.

As an experiment, the author "backfired" selections from his available historical data as far back as 1945 and plotted the results at 5-year intervals using, when possible, projects entering production in each specific year. To complete the experiment, the author also projected the data forward to the year 2000 A.D. This experiment has a high margin of error, and especially so for data collected prior to 1975. The results are interesting even if unreliable (Table 3.18). It is particularly interesting to see the impact of end-user software projects on overall results.

TABLE 3.18 U.S. Software Productivity Rates and 5-Year Intervals (Productivity Expressed in Terms of Function Points per Staff-Month)

Year	End user	MIS	Outsource	Commercial	Systems	Military	Average
1945						0.10	0.10
1950		1.00			0.50	0.30	0.60
1955		1.50			0.60	0.40	0.83
1960		2.00		1.50	1.00	0.50	1.25
1965		3.00		2.50	1.50	0.70	1.93
1970		4.00		3.50	2.00	1.00	2.63
1975	9.00	5.00	5.00	6.00	2.50	1.50	4.83
1980	12.00	5.50	6.00	6.50	3.50	2.25	5.96
1985	20.00	6.00	7.00	7.00	4.00	2.50	7.75
1990	35.00	8.75	9.25	7.75	4.50	3.00	11.38
1995	49.00	12.00	13.00	7.50	6.00	3.50	15.17
2000	65.00	15.00	19.00	9.50	9.00	5.00	20.42
Average	31.67	5.80	9.88	5.75	3.19	1.73	6.07

The overall rate of improvement is fairly significant, and especially so when end-user applications are added to national results. The author is of two minds about the inclusion of end-user projects in national results. On the pro side, end-user software applications are a significant part of the U.S. software world. End-user applications will grow in volumes and sophistication as computer literacy improves among knowledge workers.

On the con side, end-user applications are not usually "owned" by corporations or government agencies. They have a short life expectancy and can appear and disappear at random intervals based on job changes. End-user applications are not part of formal software portfolios, are not under formal configuration control, and usually have no quality assurance reviews of any kind. They also introduce significant bias into other results, because end-user software lacks requirements, specifications, test plans, test libraries, and often user documentation. Hence productivity levels are high enough to dominate averages if end-user results are included.

A graph can illustrate the results more intuitively than a table of numbers. Figure 3.1 gives a visual representation of the data in Table 3.18 so that the impact of end-user software applications can easily be perceived. The rate of progress without end-user software is actually fairly good: Productivity has tended to double at less than 10-year intervals. However, when end-user applications are included and projected forward to 2000 A.D., the rate of progress is much better than might be anticipated.

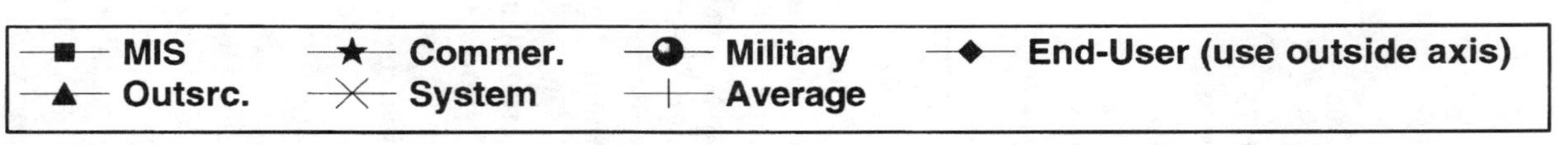

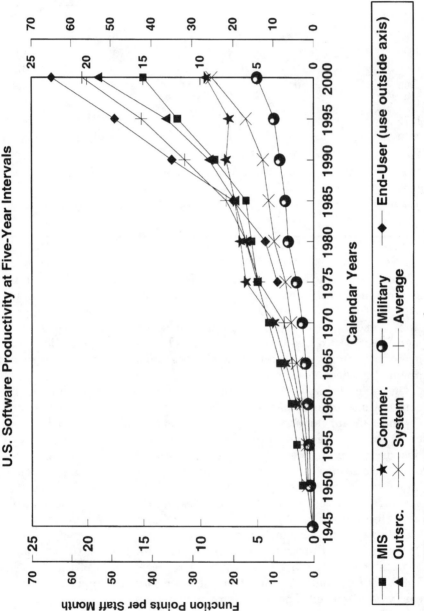

Figure 3.1 U.S. software productivity rates at 5-year intervals.

A final caution about end-user software is that essentially *all* end-user applications are less than 100 function points in total size. The other domains of software have applications whose sizes run up to more than 100,000 function points. There is a tendency in the software press to assert that because end-user productivity rates are high compared to anything else, end-user development will put professional software personnel out of business. This is a distorted and untrue hypothesis. Large systems cannot be done at all by end users. For any application where quality, reliability, or formal change management is necessary, end-user development is a poor choice.

End-user development is also a poor choice for situations where there are whole classes of users, such as the class of project managers or the class of insurance sales personnel. It would be sheer folly to have 1000 managers or 2000 salespeople each attempt to develop end-user applications in the same general domain.

The chapter heading "U.S. Averages for Software Productivity and Quality" is probably an exaggeration when all of the sources of error are considered. However, as stated earlier, if preliminary results remain unpublished there is no incentive to correct errors and improve on those results because other researchers do not have access to the information. This second edition of the information on U.S. averages might have the following results:

- Development of international guidelines for what constitutes "national averages." This guideline should address important topics such as whether end-user applications should or should not be included in national results.

- A meeting or conference where all organizations with national databases or knowledge bases of software productivity, schedule, and quality data can meet and discuss the differences and similarities of their contents. Right now the Gartner Group, the Air Force, Quantitative Software Management (QSM), the Software Engineering Institute (SEI), The Software Productivity Consortium (SPR), Howard Rubin Associates, the Australian Software Metrics Association (ASMA), the International Function Point User's Group (IFPUG), the British Mark II Function Point Users Group, and Software Productivity Research (SPR) all have significant volumes of data, but the results vary by as much as several hundred percent for unknown reasons. Since all of these groups are more or less in competition with one another, a general council of software data collection groups would need to be sponsored by a neutral organization such as the IEEE, DPMA, or perhaps the emerging National Software Council. The goal is to move toward common data collection and analysis practices.

- An international standard for software benchmarking that would define the activities to be included, the kinds of influential "soft" factors to be collected, and the kind of statistical analysis that should be performed on the results.

- Conversion rules among the various flavors of function point metrics, i.e., how to convert data from IFPUG to Mark II to Boeing 3D to SPR feature points. At the moment the various function point associations are somewhat narrow and parochial and tend to ignore rival methods.
- General agreement on the ranges and values to utilize when "backfiring" or converting data between the older "lines of code" metric and the newer family of function point metrics.
- A methodology for determining the taxable value of software that is not so fraught with errors and ambiguity as the current approach used by the U.S. Internal Revenue Service (IRS) and the equivalent organizations in other countries.

Ranges, Averages, and Variances in Software Productivity

This second edition of *Applied Software Measurement* includes four significant and visible changes in the way data is represented compared to the first edition:

1. This edition uses powers of 10 rather than powers of 2 for showing size ranges.
2. This edition shows six subindustries as well as overall U.S. averages.
3. This edition uses more tables and fewer graphs than the previous edition.
4. In some tables, end-user software is now included (which raises the averages).

A major factor in exploring software productivity, quality, schedules, or other tangible matters is that the range of possible outcomes is very broad. This is not an uncommon phenomenon. For example, the range in the height or weight of adult humans is also very broad. Similarly, per capita incomes, the time required to run one mile, and many other phenomena have broad ranges.

For software, an interesting question is "what is the probability that a given software project will achieve a specific productivity rate? Table 3.19 gives the probabilities based on application size as reflected from the SPR knowledge base. In Table 3.19, the mode or most likely productivity range is underscored so that it can be easily seen. For the most common size ranges of software projects, i.e., projects

TABLE 3.19 Productivity Probability Ranges for Selected Software Application Sizes, Percentages (Productivity Expressed in Terms of Function Points per Staff-month)

Productivity	1	10	100	1000	10,000	100,000
>100	10.00	7.00	1.00	0.00	0.00	0.00
75–100	20.00	15.00	3.00	1.00	0.00	0.00
50–75	34.00	22.00	7.00	2.00	0.00	0.00
25–50	22.00	33.00	10.00	3.00	0.00	0.00
15–25	10.00	17.00	35.00	20.00	2.00	0.00
5–15	3.00	5.00	26.00	55.00	15.00	20.00
1–5	1.00	1.00	10.00	15.00	63.00	35.00
<1	0.00	0.00	8.00	4.00	20.00	45.00
Total	100.00	100.00	100.00	100.00	100.00	100.00

between 10 and 1000 function points in size, the overall range is from less than 1 to more than 100 function points per staff month.

Another way of looking at the data examines the probabilities of achieving various productivity rates based on the domain or subindustry. Table 3.20 shows information similar to Table 3.19, only based on the six software domains that are now dealt with separately. As with Table 3.19, the mode or most likely productivity range is underlined so that it stands out from the other information.

When viewed as independent data collections, each of the columns in Tables 3.19 and 3.20 produces more or less normal bell-shaped curves. However, the two tables tend to peak at different places because the sizes of typical applications vary with the class of application. That is, military software projects are usually larger than civilian projects, and end-user software projects are usually smaller than any other category.

TABLE 3.20 Productivity Probability Ranges for Selected Software Domains, Percentages (Productivity Expressed in Terms of Function Points per Staff-month)

Productivity	End user	MIS	Outsource	Commercial	Systems	Military
>100	7.00	1.00	3.00	3.00	0.00	0.00
75–100	15.00	4.00	8.00	7.00	0.00	0.00
50–75	40.00	7.00	12.00	10.00	1.00	0.00
25–50	22.00	12.00	16.00	15.00	10.00	2.00
15–25	10.00	18.00	22.00	20.00	17.00	8.00
5–15	5.00	35.00	27.00	25.00	33.00	15.00
1–5	1.00	18.00	10.00	15.00	27.00	55.00
<1	0.00	5.00	2.00	5.00	12.00	20.00
Total	100.00	100.00	100.00	100.00	100.00	100.00

Another significant variance that changes with both size and domain of the application is the overall distribution of effort into major activities. Table 3.21 shows four overall categories of work: (1) work associated with production of paper documents, (2) work associated with production of source code, (3) work associated with finding and eliminating bugs or defects, (4) work associated with project management tasks.

As can be seen from Table 3.21, coding is the dominant activity for projects below 1000 function points in size, but coding is by no means the most expensive activity for large software applications more than 1000 function points in size. Table 3.22 presents the same kinds of variations, only now the variances are based on domain or software subindustry. Note that here too, coding is not the dominant activity for applications other than end-user software. Software paperwork and software defect removal are often more expensive than coding. Surprisingly, for some projects, even managerial tasks can outweigh coding costs. This phenomenon occurs primarily in the military domain and is due to the extensive oversight and managerial work associated with defense contracts.

TABLE 3.21 Variations in Software Effort Associated with Software Size Ranges, Percentages

Function points	Management	Paperwork	Defect removal	Coding	Total
1	5.00	5.00	20.00	70.00	100.00
10	10.00	7.00	18.00	65.00	100.00
100	12.00	15.00	23.00	50.00	100.00
1,000	15.00	25.00	30.00	30.00	100.00
10,000	16.00	31.00	35.00	18.00	100.00
100,000	17.00	35.00	36.00	12.00	100.00
Average	12.50	19.67	27.00	40.83	100.00

TABLE 3.22 Variations in Software Effort Associated with Software Classes, Percentages

Software	Management	Paperwork	Defect removal	Coding	Total
End user	0.00	10.00	40.00	50.00	100.00
MIS	12.00	22.00	33.00	33.00	100.00
Outsource	12.00	24.00	34.00	30.00	100.00
Commercial	11.00	26.00	36.00	27.00	100.00
Systems	13.00	38.00	33.00	16.00	100.00
Military	16.00	47.00	25.00	12.00	100.00
Average	10.67	27.83	33.50	28.00	100.00

Because the ranges are so broad in Tables 3.19 through 3.22 it is obvious that quite a large number of factors are influencing the overall outcomes. Two have already been discussed: (1) size, (2) domain or class of software such as the six categories shown here. However, more than 100 other factors can influence the final results, including but not limited to:

- Novelty or difficulty of the application
- Volumes of reusable material available
- Volumes of paper documents produced
- Volumes of defects or errors encountered
- Experience levels of technical staff and project management
- Rate of "creeping requirements"
- Programming languages used
- Tools used
- Processes and methodologies used
- Geographic dispersal of software team
- Physical office environment for software team

Because it is easier to perceive trends from charts than from graphs, Fig. 3.2 shows the overall ranges of software productivity from the SPR knowledge base.

The variances in software productivity rates are obviously greater at the small end than at the large end of the spectrum. Small projects have considerable latitude in methods, tools, and languages. Really

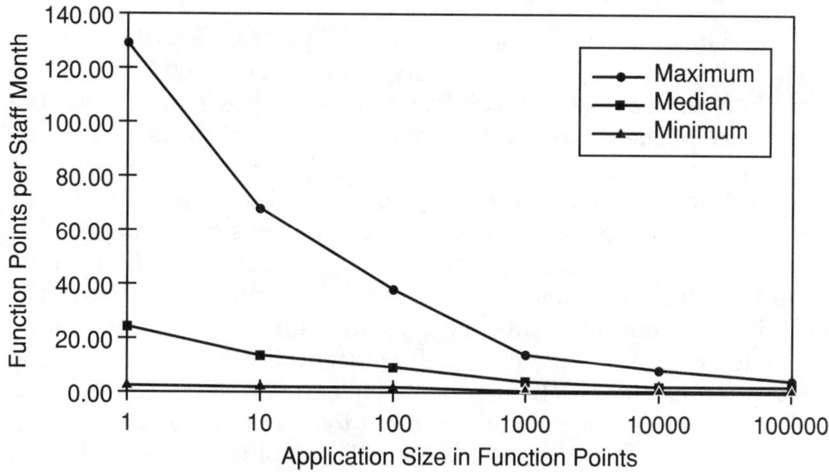

Figure 3.2 Overall ranges of U.S. software productivity levels.

large systems, on the other hand, tend to follow similar patterns or tend to run out of control and get canceled.

Before turning to the tables and charts that contain overall results, following are brief summaries of six "zones" of productivity information for each of the subindustries included in this edition: end-user software, management information systems, outsourcers or contractors, commercial software, systems software, and military software.

Zone of End-User Software Projects

End-user software was not included in the first edition of this book. However, the increase in journal articles on this topic, the very significant increase in the numbers of end users who program, and the improved tools available for this task make the subject worthy of inclusion.

End-user applications have the highest productivity rates of any domain. However, end user applications are almost always less than 100 function points in size. The "average" end-user application (mode) hovers around 15 function points in size. End-user productivity rates usually run from less than 25 to more than 150 function points per staff-month and average about 35 function points per staff-month. However, end-user applications do not perform many of the work activities of the other classes of software shown in this book, i.e., no formal requirements, no formal specifications, no formal integration or configuration control, no quality assurance, and usually no manuals or user information. Productivity is high because the amount of work performed is low.

Zone of Management Information Systems (MIS) Projects

The MIS domain produces software than ranges from less than 1 function point in size up through applications in excess of 100,000 function points in size. Because the MIS domain is sharply segmented into the subdomains of "new" projects and "enhancement" projects it is not as easy to present overall result. The "average" size (mode) of new MIS projects that are started from scratch is about 250 function points. However, the average size of enhancement projects that add new features to existing software applications is only about 50 function points.

The MIS domain is undergoing rapid transformation owing to the pervasive influence of client-server architecture. This also makes averages and overall results difficult to present, because the client side and the server side of client-server applications may have different productivity rates and even use different tools and languages.

Average productivity rates for new MIS applications in standard Cobol are in the range of 8 to 10 function points per staff-month. For client-server applications using generators or object-oriented projects, productivity rates are about 16 function points per staff-month. Other MIS approaches include information engineering, which average about 14 function points per staff-month, and rapid application development (RAD), which averages about 20 function points per staff-month.

For enhancements to aging legacy systems, productivity varies sharply based on the size, age, structure, and decay of the application being updated. Assuming that 50 function points of new and changed material are being added to a 500 function point application that is moderately high in complexity, the productivity rate would average about 6 to 9 function points per staff-month.

The MIS domain is generally competent and effective for applications that run up to about 5000 function points in size. For very large systems and especially for applications that approach or exceed 50,000 function points in size, the MIS domain has many more failures and disasters than successes. The MIS domain has been experimenting with a host of interesting technologies, including but not limited to joint application design (JAD), rapid application development (RAD), computer aided software engineering (CASE), information engineering (IE), reverse engineering, reengineering, generators, reusability, and many more. The overall impact of these technologies runs from slightly negative to very positive. However, all of the technology factors that affect MIS projects will be discussed after the basic quantitative averages are given.

Zone of Contract and Outsource Software Projects

The contract and outsource community first came to the author's attention about 10 years ago when doing a benchmark study within the New England banking community. Several projects stood out from the rest because they were about twice as productive as others of the same size and complexity levels. These projects were done by a well-known software contract house that specialized in the financial services industry. Productivity rates for the contract work were about 16 function points per staff-month, while similar projects produced by the employees of the various banks averaged about 8 function points per staff-month.

Four contributing factors explained the doubled productivity:

- Clients were less likely to change requirements with contractors than with their own staff.
- The contractors had done similar jobs for other banks and knew the application areas very well.

- The contractors had quite a lot of reusable material available for banking applications.
- The contractors worked quite a few extra hours that did not get charged back to the client.

As a general rule, the performance of outsource and contract houses is better than the typical results of their clients. If this were not the case, the contract and outsource business would eventually wither away. As the situation now stands, the contract and outsource business is growing rapidly. Contract and outsource vendors can work on any size application, but their main strength seems to be applications that are large enough and complex enough to cause severe troubles if their clients attempted them, i.e., applications from 5000 to more than 100,000 function points in size.

An "average" software contract will be for an application of about 1000 function points in size. Productivity rates by contractors and outsourcers are typically 25 percent or so higher than their client's nominal rates; i.e., average about 5 to 8 function points per staff-month. In specific industries where outsourcers and contractors serve many clients and hence have substantial volumes of reusable material available, outsource productivity rates can average close to 20 function points per staff-month. (Note that there are exceptions to the rule that outsourcers do better than their clients. Outsourcers and contractors can fail as embarrassingly as anyone else.)

Zone of Commercial Software Projects

The commercial software world is being transformed by hardware and platform changes. As recently as 10 years ago, all large commercial software projects were on mainframes or at least minicomputers. Personal computers were limited to 64 kbytes of memory, puny hard disks (if any), and were not suitable for applications larger than around 500 function points in size.

That was true in 1985. Today's personal computers are approaching an average of 16 megabytes of memory, hard drives with more than 1 gigabyte of capacity, and processing speeds that are moving toward 200 megahertz. Essentially today's personal computers are as powerful as the mainframes of a generation ago.

Many windows and UNIX applications are now well over 5000 function points in size. Both Windows NT and Windows 95 top 50,000 function points in size. (Based on Microsoft's ads stating that Windows 95 contained more than 11,000,000 lines of source code, Windows 95 might be in the range of 85,000 function points or roughly the same as IBM's mainframe MVS operating system.)

As personal computer software balloons in size, the software development methods of companies such as Microsoft are edging closer to those of the traditional mainframe software producers such as AT&T and IBM in both methods and results. Even Microsoft has had trouble with their Windows NT and Windows 95 projects, and hence is beginning to use mainframe approaches such as inspections and formal defect tracking systems.

The commercial software world is now dominated by Microsoft, with other major players being Computer Associates, IBM, and a host of niche companies such as the SAS Institute, Oracle, KnowledgeWare, and many others. When the first edition of this book came out in 1991, an "average" commercial software package on a personal computer was about 500 function points in size. The average size for mainframe packages was about 5000 function points. As this second edition is being prepared, the average size of Windows-based PC applications is approaching 5000 function points in size, or very nearly the same as the mainframe domain.

Typical commercial software productivity rates are in the range of about 4 to 10 function points per staff-month. This comparatively low rate is because the commercial software domain requires significant volumes of user manuals, HELP screens, and other amenities that are not always part of in-house software projects.

Zone of System Software Projects

The definition of systems software in this book is that it controls physical devices. This definition is broad enough to encompass operating systems, switching systems, fuel injection systems, aircraft flight control systems, medical instrument controls, and robotic manufacturing control systems.

Systems software applications are often large and complex. An "average" systems software package will be about 5000 function points in size and will have development productivity rates of somewhere between 3 and 6 function points per staff-month. Really major systems software projects, such as IBM's MVS operating system, can easily top 100,000 function points.

The object-oriented paradigm is moving rapidly through the systems software world. Some OO projects within this domain are achieving productivity rates in excess of 20 function points per staff-month. Because systems software controls physical devices that are usually expensive and may be dangerous to human life and safety if the software fails, the systems software domain has long been the top-ranked industry segment in terms of quality control. The systems software world builds some very complex applications but usually manages to remove in excess of 95 percent of the bugs prior to delivery. The systems software quality emphasis explains why more systems houses use formal inspections that any other subindustry.

The systems software world ranks second to the military world in the production of *very* large sets of specifications and planning documents. Paperwork is therefore a major component of systems software production.

Zone of Military Software Projects

Military software has long been dominated by Department of Defense (DoD) standards. A secondary effect of DoD standards has been the production of amazingly large volumes of software specifications, planning documents, change requests, user manuals, and other paper deliverables.

Military software costs are driven more by paperwork than by any other factor. This phenomenon was almost invisible when "lines of code" or LOC metrics were used for productivity analysis. However, the function point metric clearly points out the magnitude of software paperwork costs for military projects.

Military software is the overall laggard in terms of productivity rates. This is not due to poor coding productivity, since coding results using both Ada83 and Ada95 compare very favorably to civilian norms. The poor productivity can be attributed to massive volumes of paperwork and the expensive oversight requirements associated with military contracts. An "average" military contract project will be about 5000 function points in size and will run from 1 to about 5 function points per staff-month in overall productivity levels.

The world of military software has many subdivisions, including but not limited to embedded real-time software, command, control, and communication (C3) software, logistics and supply software, personnel software, strategic and tactical simulation software, ordinary management information systems, and many kinds of tools and support software.

U.S. Software Staffing Levels

The first topic of significance is the staffing required to build software applications. This issue has considerable flexibility, since adding or subtracting staff members is one of the few changes that can be accomplished while a project is actually underway, even if sometimes the changes are difficult or intrusive. Table 3.23 shows the approximate overall staffing levels for U.S. software projects.

When a technology evolves and matures, a point is reached where one practitioner can no longer encompass all of the information need-

TABLE 3.23 Average Staffing Levels for United States Software Projects

Function points	End user	MIS	Outsource	Commercial	Systems	Military	Average
1	0.25	0.50	0.50	0.50	0.60	0.75	0.52
10	0.50	1.00	1.00	1.25	1.50	1.75	1.17
100	1.00	1.25	1.15	1.75	2.00	3.00	1.69
1,000	0.00	9.00	8.00	10.00	11.00	15.00	10.60
10,000	0.00	70.00	65.00	80.00	90.00	120.00	85.00
100,000	0.00	750.00	700.00	775.00	900.00	1300.00	885.00

ed to work effectively on every kind of problem that occurs. When this point occurs, the most effective response is specialization. Instead of generalists who can deal with any topic within the scope of the technology, there will be those who are particularly experienced and knowledgeable in selected areas and who may know other areas only slightly. This phenomenon has been true for medical practice, legal practice, chemistry, physics, biology, mathematics, and most forms of engineering.

The software industry reached the point of needing specialists as long as 20 years ago. As the end of the twentieth century approaches, many kinds of software specialists are working in large software-intensive enterprises. For some large enterprises, there may be more than 100 different occupation groups within a general software organization, and various kinds of specialists can exceed one-third of total employment. As of 1995 there are more questions than answers in the domain of specialization, but this is an important topic that will become more important as we near the end of the century.

From the consulting engagements my company performs with various clients, some preliminary observations are accumulating on the numbers and kinds of specialists associated within enterprises of specific sizes and types. Following are short discussions of the kinds of specialists encountered.

Very small enterprises with less than 10 software professionals

Enterprises whose entire software staff is less than 10 normally have no formal specialties at all in terms of job titles. However, there are de facto specialties based on the needs of the organization. For example, a major role in quality assurance and testing may devolve to one or more of the staff. Another key role is maintenance of prior versions, and here too the work may be concentrated in a few individuals. Good technical writing is not a very common skill, so if anyone in a department has such a skill they tend to accumulate much of the writing tasks that may occur. Since small enterprises can only build small to medium applications (although they can maintain large systems) the lack of formal specialists is not a major problem.

Small enterprises with up to 100 software professionals

By the time an enterprise approaches 100 software personnel, they usually have several kinds of specialists on board. Some of the specialists observed include within this size range (in alphabetic order):

Customer support specialists

Database administration specialists

Maintenance and enhancement specialists

Network specialists (local, wide area)

Quality assurance specialists

Systems software support specialists

Technical writing specialists

Testing specialists

The percentage of the overall software population which these specialists occupy would average about 10 to 25 percent with perhaps 15 percent being the median value.

Medium enterprises with up to 1000 software personnel

The domain of medium software organizations with up to about 1000 total software personnel is one of the most troublesome in the United States in terms of cost overruns, missed schedules, and other kinds of software problems. Organizations within this size range need specialization fairly urgently in order to perform the work at hand, but quite a few still maintain a preference for a generalist slant. This is one of the reasons why midsized companies often have the lowest productivity rates and the worst quality levels of any size range. The more sophisticated enterprises within this size range have quite a range of specialties, however:

Configuration control specialists

Cost estimating specialists

Customer support specialists

Database administration specialists

Function point counting specialists

Maintenance and enhancement specialists

Measurement specialists

Network specialists (local, wide area)

Quality assurance specialists

Systems software support specialists

Technical writing specialists

Testing specialists

The range of specialization within this size group runs from perhaps 15 to 35 percent, with about 25 percent being a median value.

Large enterprises with up to 10,000 software personnel

By the time an enterprise is large enough to employ in the range of 10,000 software personnel they need a host of different kinds of specialists. In fact, one of the reasons why quality levels and productivity levels in very large companies can exceed those of midsized companies can be attributed to the specialists that are available in large corporations. Following are some of the kinds of specialists observed in major corporations and large government groups:

Architecture specialists

Configuration control specialists

Cost estimating specialists

Customer support specialists

Database administration specialists

Education and training specialists

Function point counting specialists

Human factors specialists

Information systems specialists

Integration specialists

Maintenance and enhancement specialists

Measurement specialists (customer satisfaction)

Measurement specialists (productivity)

Measurement specialists (quality)

Network specialists (local, wide area)

Package acquisition specialists

Performance specialists

Planning specialists

Process improvement specialists

Quality assurance specialists

Reusability specialists

Standards specialists

Systems software support specialists

Technical writing specialists

Technology specialists (object-oriented methods, GUI, client-server, etc.)

Testing specialists

Tool development specialists

The range of specialists within large enterprises runs from a low of perhaps 20 percent to a high of more than 40 percent, with about 30 percent being a median value. In large enterprises within this size range, specialization is definitely the norm. Note that the same phenomenon stays true for even larger enterprises in the 20,000 to 40,000 software personnel range.

Ratios of specialists to general software personnel

One of the major topics in the domain of specialization is how many specialists of various kinds are needed to support the overall work of the software community. This topic was only just starting to be explored in depth in 1995, so the ratios in Table 3.24 have a high margin of error. Indeed, for some kinds of specialization no normative ratios are yet available. Table 3.24 lists specialists in descending order of the numbers encountered.

Unfortunately, research into software specialization is such a new topic that ratios are not yet available for quite a few software specialists. Because the numbers of technical staff members and the kinds of specialists can change independently, the overall ranges of software personnel are extremely broad. Table 3.25 illustrates the observed ranges in total software staffing levels.

Software staffing patterns are highly flexible. There is a tendency to staff to maximum levels of software projects that have considerable schedule pressure behind them. The fact that excessive staffing may slow things rather than speed things up is understood in theory but seldom considered in practice.

TABLE 3.24 Ratios of Technical Specialists to General Software Populations

Specialist occupation	Specialists to generalists in typical populations		
Maintenance and enhancement specialists	1	to	3
Testing specialists	1	to	8
Technical writing specialists	1	to	15
Database administration specialists	1	to	25
Quality assurance specialists	1	to	25
Configuration control specialists	1	to	30
Systems software support specialists	1	to	30
Integration specialists	1	to	50
Measurement specialists	1	to	50
Network specialists (local, wide area)	1	to	50
Function point counting specialists	1	to	75
Architecture specialists	1	to	75
Performance specialists	1	to	75
SEI CMM specialists	1	to	100
Reusability specialists	1	to	100
Cost estimating specialists	1	to	100
Human factors specialists	1	to	100
ISO 9000-9004 specialists	1	to	125
Package acquisition specialists	1	to	150
Process improvement specialists	1	to	200
Education and training specialists	1	to	250
Standards specialists	1	to	300

TABLE 3.25 United States Ranges for Software Staffs (Technical + Management)

Function points	Minimum	Median	Maximum
1	0.14	0.52	1.03
10	0.40	1.17	2.57
100	0.72	1.69	3.38
1,000	5.30	10.60	20.14
10,000	43.35	85.00	153.00
100,000	486.75	885.00	1548.75

U.S. Software Schedule Ranges

Of all known factors associated with software, schedules stand out as being the most troublesome and the most frequent source of executive dissatisfaction with the software community. The schedules shown here run from the nominal "start of requirements" up to the nominal "first customer ship" date of software projects. The starting point of software projects is usually ambiguous and difficult to determine. The starting points used in Table 3.26 were simply derived by querying the responsible project managers. Delivery dates are sometimes ambiguous too. The assumption in Table 3.26 is for delivery to the first paying customer rather than delivery to beta test or field test customers.

Software schedules, like staffing patterns, are highly variable. In part schedules are determined by the number of personnel assigned, in part by the amount of overtime (both paid and unpaid), in part by the volume of creeping user requirements, and in part by the tools, technologies, and languages utilized.

The most troublesome aspect of software schedules is the major difference between the real schedules of software projects and the anticipated or desired schedules as determined by clients or senior executives. Figure 3.3 illustrates the typical pattern of differences between the initial schedule established for the project during requirements and the final delivery of the software. Note how the gap between anticipation and reality grows steadily wider as the applications increase in size and complexity.

Figure 3.3 represents what is probably the most severe and chronic complaint about software from corporate executives and high government and military officials: Large systems are often later than requested. They are often later than when the software managers promised too, which is one of the reasons why the software management community is not highly regarded by senior executives as a rule.

The large gap between the actual delivery date and the anticipated

TABLE 3.26 Average Software Schedules In Calendar Months

Function points	End user	MIS	Outsource	Commercial	Systems	Military	Average
1	0.05	0.10	0.10	0.20	0.20	0.30	0.16
10	0.50	0.75	0.90	1.00	1.25	2.00	1.07
100	3.50	9.00	9.50	11.00	12.00	15.00	10.00
1,000	0.00	24.00	22.00	24.00	28.00	40.00	27.60
10,000	0.00	48.00	44.00	46.00	47.00	64.00	49.80
100,000	0.00	72.00	68.00	66.00	78.00	85.00	73.80

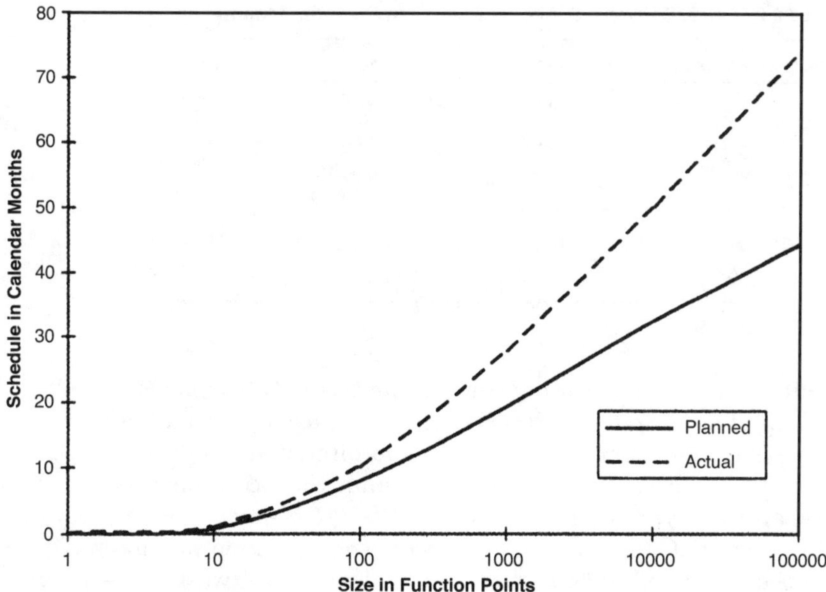

Figure 3.3 Differences between planned and actual software schedules.

delivery date is the cause of more friction between the software world, corporate executives, and clients than any other known phenomenon. This gap is also the cause of a great deal of expensive litigation. Some of the factors that explain this gap are due to creeping user requirements. However, a problem of equal severity is malpractice in the way the original schedule estimates were developed. Often schedules are set by decree or client demand rather than being carefully planned based on team capabilities.

Arbitrary schedules that are preset by clients or executives and forced on the software team are called "backward loading to infinite capacity" in project management parlance. The essence of the phrase is that irrational schedules trigger more disasters than any other known phenomenon.

The presence of this gap between anticipation and reality is one of the reasons why a subindustry of commercial software estimating tools has emerged. As this book is written, at least 50 specialized commercial software cost estimation tools are on the market in the United States. There are more than 100 general-purpose project planning or "project management" tools on the market too.

Table 3.27 illustrates the overall ranges of software schedules. Note how wide a range can exist between "best in class" and "worst in class" results. The minimum column can occur only for software projects that are at state-of-the-art levels in terms of reusability, manage-

TABLE 3.27 U.S. Software Schedule Ranges in Calendar Months

Function points	Minimum	Average	Maximum
1	0.03	0.16	0.40
10	0.32	1.07	2.35
100	3.00	10.00	19.00
1,000	16.56	27.60	44.16
10,000	29.88	49.80	84.66
100,000	44.28	73.80	132.84

ment methods of planning and estimating, staff experience levels, tools, and development processes. In fact, excellence in all of these attributes is necessary to move toward minimum schedules with a good chance of success. The maximum column can occur on projects that are careless with quality control, that fail to control creeping requirements, or that make any of a host of other common mistakes. There are thousands of ways to mess up or damage software projects, and only a few ways to do them well.

U.S. Ranges in Creeping User Requirements

Because creeping requirements contribute to the gap between planned and actual schedules, it is appropriate to consider that topic next. Table 3.28 shows the approximate volumes of creeping requirements that occur after the completion of the nominal requirements phase. The contents of the original "official" requirements are assumed to constitute 100 percent. The growth rate in Table 3.28 is expressed as a percentage change to the original full set of requirements.

TABLE 3.28 Average Volumes of Creeping Requirements After Requirements Phase, Percentage

Function points	End user	MIS	Outsource	Commercial	Systems	Military	Average
1	0.03	0.07	0.06	0.08	0.10	0.23	0.09
10	0.25	0.53	0.54	0.80	0.63	1.50	0.71
100	1.75	6.30	5.70	8.80	6.00	11.25	6.63
1,000	0.00	16.80	13.20	19.20	14.00	28.50	18.34
10,000	0.00	33.60	26.40	36.80	23.50	48.00	33.66
100,000	0.00	50.40	40.80	52.80	39.00	63.75	49.35
Average	0.68	17.95	14.45	19.75	13.87	25.54	15.37

Another way of expressing requirement creep is the average monthly rate during the activities of design and coding, where creeping requirements are most likely to occur:

Domain	Average monthly rate of creeping requirements, %
End-user software	0.5
Management information systems	1.0
Outsource software	1.0
Commercial software	3.5
System software	2.0
Military software	2.0

Creeping requirements were difficult to measure during the "lines of code" or LOC era. However, one of the useful features of the function point metric is the ability to perform direct and rather accurate measures of the rate at which requirements changes occur.

Assume that you reach an initial agreement with a client to build an application 1000 function points in size. Any change to the features of the application will almost certainly affect the function point total. By comparing the size in function points at the time of the initial agreement with the size at delivery, the rate of change can be measured directly and accurately.

U.S. Software Effort Ranges

Table 3.29 shows approximate averages expressed in terms of staff months of effort. The table assumes software engineers or programmers, and also the many ancillary occupations such as quality assur-

TABLE 3.29 Average Software Effort in Person-Months (Assumes 132 Work Hours per Person-Month)

Function points	End user	MIS	Outsource	Commercial	Systems	Military	Average
1	0.01	0.05	0.05	0.10	0.12	0.23	0.09
10	0.25	0.75	0.90	1.25	1.88	3.50	1.42
100	3.50	11.25	10.93	19.25	24.00	45.00	18.99
1,000	0.00	216.00	176.00	240.00	308.00	570.00	267.50
10,000	0.00	3,360.00	2,860.00	3,680.00	4,230.00	7,680.00	4,362.00
100,000	0.00	54,000.00	47,600.00	51,150.00	70,200.00	110,500.00	66,690.00

TABLE 3.30 Ranges of Software Effort in Person-Months

Function points	Minimum	Average	Maximum
1	0.01	0.09	0.41
10	0.14	1.42	6.02
100	2.60	18.99	64.28
1,000	64.87	267.50	876.49
10,000	1,079.42	4,362.00	12,952.98
100,000	21,553.29	66,690.00	205,735.95

ance, database administration, and testing. Project management is assumed to be present also. The assumption in the table is that an average work month contains approximately 132 working hours. Note that Table 3.29 shows averages for the rows, but not for the columns. It is easy to average columns of numbers, but the arithmetic average of projects that span a range from 1 to 100,000 function points is so misleading that it is better not to even bother. The situation is even more troublesome when the ranges of effort are considered, as will be seen in Table 3.30.

Table 3.30 shows the overall ranges that occur in this important topic. A host of factors are associated with the extreme conditions, such as reusability, experience, programming languages, and tools. Only an expert human estimator or one of the better expert-system software cost estimating tools can sort through all of the contributing factors and develop an accurate estimate for where any particular project is likely to fall. The minimum side of the table can occur only with state-of-the-art technologies and expert technical and management personnel. The maximum side of the table can occur whenever too many mistakes are made. As always, there are many ways to fail and only a few ways to succeed.

U.S. Software Productivity Averages and Ranges for New Projects

The first edition of this book utilized "function points per staff-month" as the primary normalizing metric for expressing productivity. This edition continues to use that metric but also adds the complementary metric "work hours per function point." In this book, the two are roughly equivalent if you assume that a staff-month contains 132 work hours.

Table 3.31 assumes all activities from the start of requirements through delivery to the first external customer. As many as 25 activities can be performed, including many that have nothing at all to do with coding, such as creation of paper documents (i.e., specifications, user manuals, plans, etc.). Also assumed in Table 3.31 are activities such as quality assurance, testing, and project management. This data is much lower than several other national databases of software productivity data. So far as can be determined, the primary reason for the differences is that the SPR knowledge base attempts to include *all* activities. Many other productivity data collections center on "design, code, and unit test" and these activities amount to only about 25 percent of total effort expended on software projects.

Note that the averages displayed with Table 3.31 are merely the arithmetic means of the columns, the weighted average, or total function points divided by total effort. Table 3.32 presents the same information, only expressed in terms of work hours per function point rather than function points per staff-month.

The two forms of data in Tables 3.31 and 3.32 are mathematically equivalent under the assumption that there are 132 work hours, on average, in a calendar month. The ranges of software productivity in

TABLE 3.31 U.S. Average Productivity in Function Points per Staff-Month

Function points	End user	MIS	Outsource	Commercial	Systems	Military	Average
1	80.00	20.00	20.00	10.00	8.33	4.44	23.80
10	40.00	13.33	11.11	8.00	5.33	2.86	13.44
100	28.57	8.89	9.15	5.19	4.17	2.22	9.70
1,000	0.00	4.63	5.68	4.17	3.25	1.75	3.90
10,000	0.00	2.98	3.50	2.72	2.36	1.30	2.57
100,000	0.00	1.85	2.10	1.96	1.42	0.90	1.65
Average	49.52	8.61	8.59	5.34	4.14	1.81	9.17

TABLE 3.32 U.S. Average Productivity in Work Hours per Function Point

Function points	End user	MIS	Outsource	Commercial	Systems	Military	Average
1	1.65	6.60	6.60	13.20	15.84	29.70	12.27
10	3.30	9.90	11.88	16.50	24.75	46.20	18.76
100	4.62	14.85	14.42	25.41	31.68	59.40	25.06
1,000	0.00	28.51	23.23	31.68	40.66	75.24	35.31
10,000	0.00	44.35	37.75	48.58	55.84	101.38	57.58
100,000	0.00	71.28	62.83	67.52	92.66	145.86	88.03
Average	3.19	29.25	26.12	33.81	43.57	76.30	39.50

TABLE 3.33 U.S. Productivity Ranges in Function Points per Staff-Month

Function points	Minimum	Average	Maximum
1	129.36	23.80	2.44
10	71.62	13.44	1.66
100	38.46	9.70	1.56
1,000	15.41	3.90	1.14
10,000	9.26	2.57	0.77
100,000	4.64	1.65	0.49

TABLE 3.34 U.S. Productivity Ranges in Work Hours per Function Point

Function points	Minimum	Average	Maximum
1	1.02	12.27	53.99
10	1.84	18.76	79.51
100	3.43	25.06	84.85
1,000	8.56	35.31	115.70
10,000	14.25	57.58	170.98
100,000	28.45	88.03	271.57

the United States are very broad. Table 3.33 shows the range in function points per staff-month.

Table 3.34 displays the equivalent information using the metric "work hours per function point."

It is obvious from the ranges in Tables 3.31 through 3.34 that many factors are simultaneously affecting the results: size, domain, tools, methods, experience, and so forth.

U.S. Software Productivity Averages and Ranges for Enhancement Projects

New software projects that are started with requirements and entail complete development are fairly easy to characterize and measure. Enhancements, on the other hand, are much more complicated and much harder to deal with.

In addition to the other factors that influence results, such as experience, tools, and languages, enhancement projects are influenced to a very large degree by these factors:

- The structure or complexity of the base legacy system that is being updated
- The number of latent defects still residing in the base or legacy system
- The structure or complexity of the new code that is to be added
- The structure or complexity of any changed code
- The structure or complexity of any deleted code

The best case is the simple addition of new features to a well-structured existing application, with few latent bugs, and with no inner structural changes of any kind. The worst case is scattered updates and internal changes to a poorly structured existing application with many latent bugs or errors still remaining.

Another aspect of enhancement productivity measurement is difficult to explain but is based on empirical evidence. Unlike new software projects where smaller projects are more productive than large, small enhancements are very unproductive. The reason for this is that the overhead of these activities drags down productivity at the low end:

- Regression testing the base or legacy application
- Recompiling the base or legacy application
- Rewriting the specifications and user manuals in part
- Reshipping the entire product

Enhancement productivity tends to peak in a fairly narrow band, where the size of the enhancement is roughly 5 percent of the size of the existing application. This phenomenon tends to lead to the concept of fixed release intervals, with the interval roughly coinciding with a volume of changes that approximates 5 percent. For personal computer software less than 1000 function points in size, the optimal release interval is about every 6 to 9 months. For large applications above 5000 function points in size, the optimal release interval is roughly every 12 to 18 months.

A simple graph can clarify the situation (Fig. 3.4). Assume that an existing application of 1000 function points in size is to be modified. If the size of the enhancement is about 5 percent (50 function points), productivity will tend to peak.

Although it is not a law of nature and some exceptions occur, most enhancements are much smaller than the base legacy application that is being updated. This means that a table of productivity data will appear to have some null records, for situations where the enhancement is larger than the base.

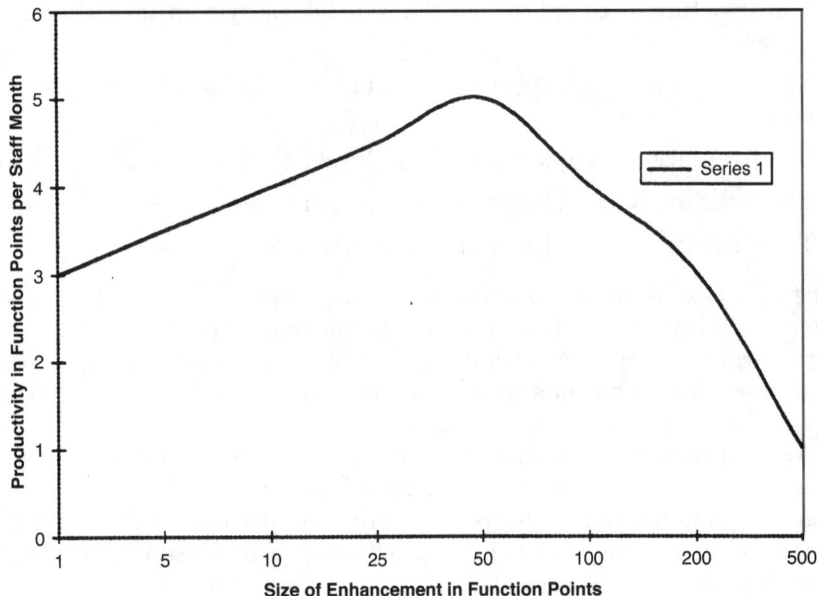

Figure 3.4 Productivity variations for enhancing a 1000 function point application.

Figure 3.5 shows what happens when enhancements vary from 1 function point upward, and the base system size also increases. To read Fig. 3.5, note that the upper left corner represents adding 1 function point to a 1 function point application. The lower right corner represents the productivity of enhancing 100,000 function point systems. Figure 3.5 has some seeming anomalies in the rates, until it is recalled that productivity tends to peak for enhancements that are neither very large nor very small but about 5 percent of the size of the original application.

U.S. Averages for Software Maintenance (Defect Repair) Productivity

In ordinary usage the word "maintenance" is highly ambiguous and can mean almost any change to a software application after it goes into production. In this book, the word "maintenance" is used in a narrower, more restricted sense as meaning only defect repairs. The reason for this is a practical one. The costs of defect repairs are usually absorbed by the developing organization, while the costs of adding new features or enhancements are often billed out to customers.

Some geriatric conditions, such as restructuring aging legacy systems, can be funded by either clients or the developing organization,

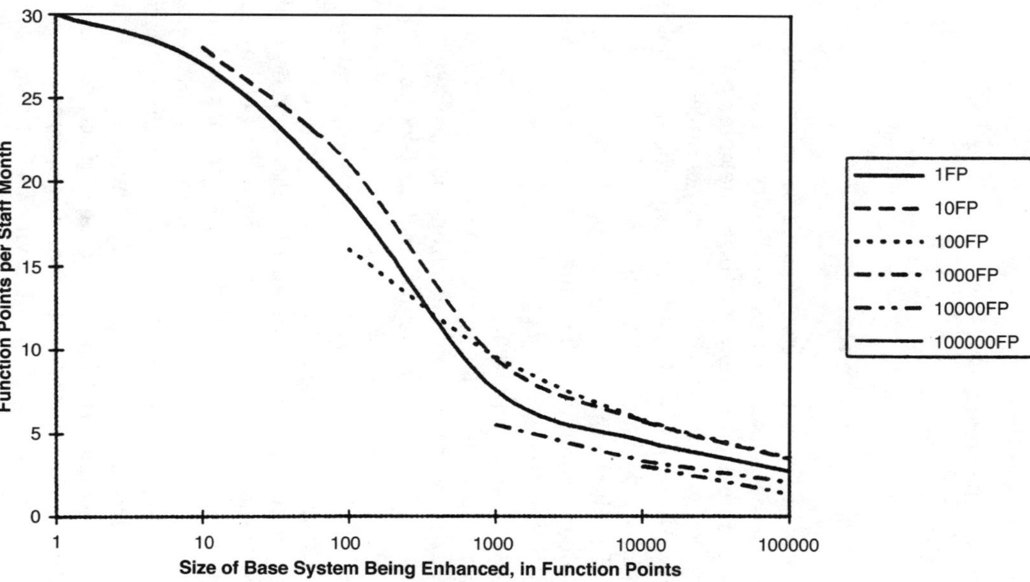

Figure 3.5 Relationship of enhancement size, base system size, and productivity.

depending upon various conditions. In this book, the effort devoted to maintenance is primarily that of finding and fixing bugs in the source code. There are, of course, a host of other aspects of software maintenance that are expensive, including but not limited to:

Customer support organizations

Field service organizations

On-site maintenance teams

Maintenance management

Maintenance of user manuals

Litigation associated with defects

Maintenance productivity is a complicated topic and also difficult to measure. One of the reasons for the difficulty is that the repairs for many software defects are very small: Sometimes only one or two lines of source code are in error. These small changes exceed the normal precision of function point metrics (one line of Cobol is roughly equivalent to only 0.01 function point).

The costs of maintenance are not really driven by the volume of code that is added or modified. The major maintenance cost driver is associated with the size, age, and complexity, and latent defects of the application that is being repaired.

Complexity is a difficult topic in its own right. For day-to-day practical purposes, the most common measurement of software complexity is the McCabe "cyclomatic complexity" metric (McCabe, 79).[1] The cyclomatic complexity metric is a measure of the control flow of an application. It is derived from a graph of the application, and the general formula is that cyclomatic complexity equals the number of edges on the graph minus the number of nodes on the graph, plus 2. Perfectly structured source code with no branches of any kind has a cyclomatic complexity of 1. There will be a beginning and ending node for the graph, and one line that connects them (i.e., $1 - 2 + 2 = 1$).

In practice, cyclomatic complexity levels of less than 10 are normally considered fairly well structured. Cyclomatic complexity levels from 10 to 20 are considered fair or average structure. Levels higher than 20 are considered hazardous or poorly structured.

Figure 3.6 shows the overall productivity for a typical defect repair scenario where the entire volume of code modified is equal to or less than 1 function point in size. The base system being modified will vary from 1 function point (an unlikely occurrence) up to 100,000 function points. The complexity levels will vary from low through average up to high.

Note that in Fig. 3.6 the unit of measure is "work hours per function point" rather than "function points per staff-month." For activi-

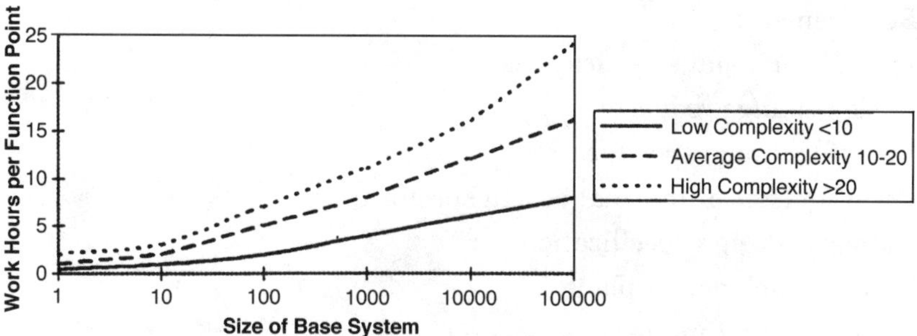

Figure 3.6 Maintenance productivity variances due to size of base system and cyclomatic complexity levels.

ties such as finding and fixing bugs that are asynchronous and for which and each occurrence may take only a few hours, this form of data representation seems to be a better fit for representing the situation than "function points per staff-month." The latter metric tends to imply some kind of continuous effort, and bug repairs are typically performed one by one using bursts of very intense effort.

There are no significant differences in the effort devoted to finding and fixing bugs among the six domains discussed in this book. That is, end-user software, information systems, systems software, commercial software, and military software are all subject more or less equally to the problems of size, age, latent defects, and complexity levels.

U.S. Averages for Volumes and Ranges of Software Paperwork

Software is an extraordinarily paper intensive industry. The overall volume of paper documents surrounding software projects is one of the largest of any manufactured product in human experience. The author has been a direct participant in projects where the volume of specifications alone exceeded 60,000 pages. For very large military software projects, the total volume of paper documents can exceed 1,000,000 pages. What is astonishing about paperwork volumes for very large systems is that the specifications and technical documents may be large enough to go beyond the normal lifetime reading speed of a single analyst! Assuming a technical reading speed of about 200 words per minute, there are some systems where an employee could work for an entire 40-year career doing nothing but reading plans and specifications without ever finishing.

The overall sets of paper documents for software projects include but are not limited to:

Requirements
Initial functional specifications
Design change requests
Final functional specifications
Program logic or internal design specifications
Database design specifications
Project development plans
Project cost estimates
Project milestone reports
Project cost variance reports
Review and inspection plans
Test plans
User manuals
Maintenance manuals
Internal defect reports
Customer defect reports

Table 3.35 gives the overall volume of pages per function point for the aggregated sum of major document types produced. The table assumes normal U.S. paper stock (8.5 by 11 inches) with about 400 words per page.

The volume of paperwork varies with both size and domain. The smallest volumes of software paper documents are obviously associated with small end-user software applications, where there may be none at all. The largest volumes of paper documents are associated with large military applications, where the amount of effort devoted to producing paper can exceed 50 percent of total software budgets.

TABLE 3.35 Sum of Pages per Function Point in Software Project Plans, Specifications, and User Manuals

Function points	End user	MIS	Outsource	Commercial	Systems	Military	Average
1	0.50	0.50	0.60	1.00	1.00	2.00	0.93
10	0.60	1.50	1.60	2.00	2.00	4.00	1.95
100	0.75	2.50	2.60	3.00	3.00	6.00	2.98
1,000	0.00	4.00	4.25	5.50	6.00	9.00	5.75
10,000	0.00	5.00	5.25	6.50	7.00	12.00	7.15
100,000	0.00	6.00	6.50	7.50	8.00	15.00	8.60
Average	0.62	3.25	3.47	4.25	4.50	8.00	4.01

Although the phrase "paperwork" is used in this book, it is actually a misnomer. Quite a lot of textual and graphical material is available on-line. For example, this manuscript was prepared using Microsoft Word for Windows. The on-line HELP screens for this application total to more than 100 pages of text.

The author and his company have not yet been commissioned to explore the impact of CD ROM or hypertext on paperwork volumes. The effort to produce documents for these technologies is expected to be somewhat greater than producing simple text and graphics materials on paper, however.

We have been commissioned to explore the costs of translating information from one national language to another. Indeed, both the screens, HELP text, and user manuals for the CHECKPOINT® product which the author's company markets have been translated into French. A rule of thumb is that translation into a second national language takes about 35 percent of the effort of creating the materials in the original language.

U.S. Average Risk of Project Failure and Cancellation

The author and his company have been studying opposite ends of the software spectrum for many years. One end of the spectrum consists of projects that set new records for productivity, quality, or other tangible accomplishments. The opposite end of the spectrum consists of projects that were terminated owing to cost and schedule overruns, failure to meet requirements, or other causes associated with poor planning, estimating, quality control, or excessive requirements creep.

Table 3.36 shows the overall probability that software projects will be terminated prior to completion. A larger research study on this

TABLE 3.36 Percentage of U.S. Average Probability of Software Project Termination prior to Completion

Function points	End user	MIS	Outsource	Commercial	Systems	Military	Average
1	1.00	0.10	0.10	0.10	0.10	0.10	0.25
10	5.00	1.00	1.00	2.00	1.00	2.00	2.00
100	15.00	6.00	6.00	5.00	5.00	7.00	7.33
1,000	100.00	17.00	14.00	9.00	12.00	15.00	27.83
10,000	100.00	45.00	40.00	45.00	25.00	33.00	48.00
100,000	100.00	80.00	45.00	70.00	40.00	55.00	65.00
Average	53.50	24.85	17.68	21.85	13.85	18.68	25.07

project is described in another of the author's books, *Patterns of Software System Failure and Success.*[2]

None of the six domains is fully successful for large systems above 10,000 function points in size. Applications approaching or exceeding 100,000 function points are one of the most risky business ventures of the modern world. However, the systems software domain and the outsource domain have a somewhat better probability of finishing really large systems than do the other domains. The military software domain is in third place.

The root causes identified for failed or canceled projects are too extensive to detail here but include the following:

Poor quality control

Inadequate project planning

Inadequate project estimating

Inadequate milestone tracking

Inadequate measurement methods

Excessive schedule pressures

Excessive requirements creep

Project management malpractice

Poor cooperation between clients and development team

The overall probability of a software project's being terminated is shown graphically in Fig. 3.7. As can easily be seen, small projects are comparatively "safe" in terms of premature mortality, but large software systems are one of the most hazardous and failure prone constructs of any industrial product. The high failure rate on large systems is one of the key reasons why senior corporate executives seldom consider software executives as candidates for high-level corporate positions. There is a general distrust and even dislike of the software community within many companies and government agencies. What fosters this dislike is the feeling that software is not fully under control and hence that software executives are not as capable as other kinds of executives who have fewer visible disasters in sight.

U.S. Averages for Software Life Expectancy

Once a software project reaches its clients, it is an interesting question how long the project will be utilized prior to being replaced by another product. As a general rule, the life expectancy of software is somewhat proportional to size and also varies by domain or subindustry. Table 3.37 shows the approximate averages that are currently

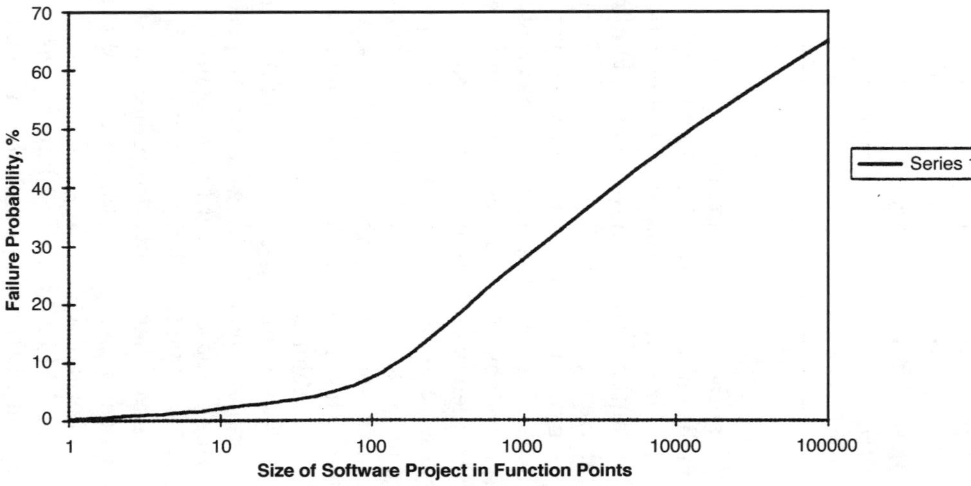

Figure 3.7 Probability of software project termination without completion.

TABLE 3.37 Average Software Life Expectancy of Software Projects in Production(Calendar Years Until Modified or Replaced)

Function points	End user	MIS	Outsource	Commercial	Systems	Military	Average
1	0.50	0.50	0.60				0.53
10	1.00	1.50	1.50	2.00	2.50		1.70
100	2.50	3.50	3.00	4.00	5.00	5.00	4.10
1,000		6.00	5.00	5.00	8.00	9.00	6.60
10,000		11.00	10.00	9.00	14.00	17.00	12.20
100,000		15.00	13.00	16.00	18.00	23.00	17.00
Average	1.33	6.25	5.52	7.20	9.50	13.50	7.02

known. Neither the author nor his company have been commissioned to explore very small projects, so there are some gaps in the data for the lower end of the size ranges. Note that the blanks in Table 3.37 are areas where the author does not have enough data to perform any kind of meaningful averages.

It is an interesting question why large software systems have very long life expectancies. The probable reason is that replacement is too expensive for large systems, whereas small projects are more or less disposable. By coincidence, the life expectancy patterns of software projects more or less resemble a totally unrelated topic. The life expectancy of animals is generally proportional to their overall body weight. Small animals such as chipmunks, squirrels, and rabbits seldom live more than a few years, while larger animals such as horses and cows can live more than 20 years.

Information on software life expectancy is useful data for planning maintenance and enhancement staffing over long periods. A useful rule of thumb for this purpose is that it takes about one full-time person to keep from 500 to 2000 function points of software running and operational. This means that a software project of 10,000 function points in size may need a perpetual staff of 5 to 20 personnel to fix bugs and perform minor updates.

Well-structured applications with few latent bugs, with adequate comment densities, and with excellent maintenance materials need the fewest personnel. Poorly structured systems with many bugs and marginal or missing maintenance materials need the largest support staffs.

The comparative labor intensiveness of software maintenance and enhancements over long time periods explains why there is a growing subindustry of companies providing geriatric tools and services for aging legacy systems. Some of the components of the software geriatric care business include:

Complexity analysis tools
Code restructuring tools
Defect tracking tools
Maintenance cost estimating tools
Configuration control tools
Reverse engineering tools
Reengineering tools
Maintenance workbenches

The overall effectiveness of an active geriatric program is rather high. The author has observed a tripling of maintenance assignment scopes on legacy systems in less than 4 years (i.e., function points supported by one person) as a direct result of formal geriatric programs that reduced complexity via restructuring and reengineering.

U.S. Average for Annual Enhancement Volumes

Once software goes into production, it normally continues to grow and add features for much of its useful life. Since changes are made in response to new user requests, to changes in regulations or statutes, or to improved aspects of the current application it is difficult to characterize the nature of enhancements succinctly.

Table 3.38 gives the approximate annual volumes of new and changed features, compared against the function point totals. That is, an annual rate of "8 percent" would imply that for a 100 function

TABLE 3.38 Average Percentage of Annual Enhancements (New + Changed Features) (Percentages are Based on Changes to Base Application Function Point Totals)

Function points	End user	MIS	Outsource	Commercial	Systems	Military	Average
1							
10	12.00	5.00	4.00				7.00
100	10.00	7.00	7.00	10.00	7.00	7.00	8.00
1,000		6.00	6.50	9.00	6.50	8.00	7.20
10,000		7.50	6.50	7.00	8.00	9.00	7.60
100,000		4.00	4.50	4.50	4.00	6.50	4.70
Average	11.00	5.90	5.70	7.63	6.38	7.63	7.37

point application, 8 new or changed function points were added during the year. The blanks in Table 3.38 are for topics where the author does not have enough data to form meaningful averages.

Average values such as those in Table 3.38 don't really tell the whole story. The maximum changes observed in applications for a single year can approach 100 percent when, for example, a mainframe application migrates to become a client-server application or when a DOS produce is ported to Windows. SPR has noted several companies where the volatility of their software projects is running in excess of 25 percent per year. That is, about one-fourth of the total quantity of function points in the application at the beginning of a year will be modified or added before the year is out. Applications dealing with volatile business topics tend to change very rapidly. Conversely, SPR has noted a few projects where the volatility hovers around 0 percent; that is, for various business reasons, the software is not modified.

U.S. Averages for Software Costs

As mentioned previously in this chapter, software costs are extremely variable. Staff compensation for identical jobs varies from country to country, industry to industry, region to region, and company to company. Even more variable are the overhead costs or burden rates applied on top of compensation for benefits, rent, depreciation, and the like.

Table 3.39 gives the approximate "average" compensation levels among the six domains discussed in this book. However, both compensation levels and burden rates can change independently over ranges of about 3 to 1 in the United States, and 8 to 1 abroad.

Using the cost profiles shown in Table 3.39, Table 3.40 shows the approximate cost per function point for the six domains, and the overall averages for the United States by size range. Table 3.40 shows the fully burdened costs, i.e., salary + burden.

Because abstract metrics such as cost per function point don't make it easy to visualize the real magnitude of software costs, Table 3.41 shows the approximate total costs for building software applications in various size ranges for the six domains discussed in this book assuming fully burdened cost structures.

TABLE 3.39 U.S. Average Staff Compensation and Burden Rate Levels

	End user	MIS	Outsource	Commercial	Systems	Military	Average
Salary, $	6000	4750	4500	5000	5250	4500	4875
Burden, %	60.00	60.00	200.00	60.00	60.00	225.00	101.25
Salary + burden, $	9600	7600	13,500	8000	8400	14,625	9811

TABLE 3.40 Average Cost per Function Point (Salary + Burden), Dollars

Function points	End user	MIS	Outsource	Commercial	Systems	Military	Average
1	120	380	675	800	1,008	3,291	1,046
10	240	570	1,215	1,000	1,575	5,119	1,620
100	336	855	1,475	1,540	2,016	6,581	2,134
1,000	0	1,642	2,376	1,920	2,587	8,336	3,372
10,000	0	2,554	3,861	2,944	3,553	11,232	4,829
100,000	0	4,104	6,426	4,092	5,897	16,161	7,336
Average	232	1,684	2,671	2,049	2,773	8,453	3,389
Median	240	1,248	1,925	1,730	2,302	7,459	2,753
Mode	180	1,022	1,689	1,487	2,059	6,679	2,587

TABLE 3.41 Average Cost to Construct Software Applications (Salary + Burden), Dollars

Function points	End user	MIS	Outsource	Commercial	Systems	Military	Average
1	120	380	675	800	1,008	3,291	1,046
10	2,400	5,700	12,150	10,000	15,750	51,188	16,198
100	33,600	85,500	147,488	154,000	201,600	658,125	213,385
1,000	0	1,641,600	2,376,000	1,920,000	2,587,200	8,336,250	3,372,210
10,000	0	25,536,000	38,610,000	29,440,000	35,532,000	112,320,000	48,287,600
100,000	0	410,400,000	642,600,000	409,200,000	589,680,000	1,616,062,500	733,588,500
Average	12,040	72,944,863	113,957,719	73,454,133	104,669,593	289,571,892	130,913,156

As can be seen from Table 3.41, software is a major business expense for U.S. business, military, and government operations. Very few other parts of U.S. industry are simultaneously so expensive, so troublesome, and yet so necessary for success. It is also of interest to consider the cost per function point using only basic salary or compensation levels, without including the burden rates. Table 3.42 gives the average cost per function point without applying the burden; i.e., only basic salary rates are included.

The data in Table 3.42 is interesting but not really relevant, since most organizations apply their burden rates when performing cost studies. What makes Table 3.42 interesting is the fact that the relative efficiency levels of outsource contractors and their clients (MIS development groups) favor the outsource organizations when burden rates are removed.

TABLE 3.42 Average Cost per Function Point Using Only Salary Levels without Burden Rates, Dollars

Function points	End user	MIS	Outsource	Commercial	Systems	Military	Average
1	75	238	225	500	630	1,013	447
10	150	356	405	625	984	1,575	683
100	210	534	492	963	1,260	2,025	914
1,000	0	1,026	792	1,200	1,617	2,565	1,200
10,000	0	1,596	1,287	1,840	2,221	3,456	1,733
100,000	0	2,565	2,142	2,558	3,686	4,973	2,654
Average	145	1,053	890	1,281	1,733	2,601	1,284

TABLE 3.43 U.S. Average Costs per Function Point with and without Burden Rates, Dollars

	Unburdened	Fully burdened
End-user software	150	250
Information systems software	600	1000
Outsource software	550	1500
Commercial software	1000	1700
Systems software	1200	2000
Military software	2500	5000
Average	1000	1908

The author receives more than half a dozen requests each month for data on "average cost to build a function point." Sometimes these requests are due to fairly serious business situations such as contract litigation or tax litigation. The ranges are so broad for cost per function point that the author usually declines to provide "average" data and suggests instead that each company use its own specific compensation and burden rate levels. Somewhat reluctantly, Table 3.43 reflects the author's judgment of what the most common (or mode) would be for average U.S. cost per function point in the six domains included in this book, using round numbers to reflect the general lack of precision of the concept.

The averages shown in Table 3.43 are the arithmetic means of the two columns and hence should be used only with caution.

It should be recalled that the cost information shown here is an attempt to reflect 100 percent of the work effort associated with software. The costs start with requirements and include all development activities. Quality assurance, production of user manuals, and project management are included as well as normal design, code, and testing activities. The costs are much higher than might be observed under two other conditions:

- For companies whose measurements are centered around design, code, and unit test (commonly abbreviated to DCUT), your costs will appear to be only about 25 percent of the costs shown in these cost tables.
- For companies whose measurements are based on normal cost tracking systems which typically "leak" an average of about 50 percent of the real effort on software projects (i.e., unpaid overtime, time spent prior to turning on the tracking systems, specialists such as quality assurance, etc.), your costs will appear to be only about 50 percent of the costs shown in these tables.

On the whole, the cost of software is one of the most troublesome, ambiguous, and poorly recorded aspects of the entire software world.

U.S. Averages for Defect Potentials

The "defect potential" of a software application is the sum of all defects found during development and out into the field when the application is used by clients or customers. The kinds of defects that comprise the defect potential include five categories:

Requirements defects

Design defects

Source code defects

User documentation defects

"Bad fixes" or secondary defects found in repairs to prior defects

The information on potential defects in this book is derived from observations of software projects that utilized formal design and code inspections plus full multistage testing activities. Obviously the companies also had formal and accurate defect tracking tools available.

There are normally several gaps in software defect statistics: (1) desk checking or defects found privately by development personnel; (2) defects found during unit testing by the programmers themselves; (3) defects found during informal reviews by friends or colleagues of development personnel.

From time to time, companies perform experiments and ask for volunteers to provide data on defects found during these gaps in conventional defect statistics. Indeed, the author has been such a volunteer and has kept records of the numbers of errors found in his own software while desk checking and unit testing.

TABLE 3.44 U.S. Average Defect Potentials (Requirements, Design, Code, Document, Bad Fixes) (Data Expressed in Terms of "Defects per Function Point")

Function points	End user	MIS	Outsource	Commercial	Systems	Military	Average
1	1.00	1.00	1.00	1.00	1.00	1.00	1.00
10	2.50	2.00	2.00	2.50	3.00	3.25	2.54
100	3.50	4.00	3.50	4.00	5.00	5.50	4.25
1,000	0.00	5.00	4.50	5.00	6.00	6.75	5.45
10,000	0.00	6.00	5.50	6.00	7.00	7.50	6.40
100,000	0.00	7.25	6.50	7.50	8.00	8.50	7.55
Average	2.33	4.21	3.83	4.33	5.00	5.42	4.53

Table 3.44 gives the approximate U.S. average results in terms of defect potentials. Note that this kind of data is clearly biased, since very few companies actually track life-cycle defect rates with the kind of precision needed to ensure really good data on this topic.

Software development is a very difficult intellectual undertaking that is high in complexity and hence prone to a variety of bugs or errors. As a general rule, the major cost and schedule drivers associated with civilian software are those associated with defect removal activities, which cost more than anything else. (For military software, paperwork costs more than anything else.)

The overall ranking of U.S. software expense and schedule elements is of interest, since coding is only in fourth place:

Defect removal operations

Paperwork in all forms

Meetings and communication

Code development

Software quality cannot be ignored for projects that want to minimize costs and schedules. If quality control is not excellent upstream during requirements, design, and specification phases, then the downstream effort, schedule, and costs that accrue during testing can be of major proportions.

U.S. Averages for Cumulative Defect Removal Efficiency

The defect potential is not of course the quantity of errors or bugs delivered to customers. The potential defects are reduced by a series of reviews, inspections, and test steps so that only a fraction of the potential defects reach software clients. Since each defect removal step, on average, is only about 30 percent efficient in finding bugs or errors, it is obvious that quite a few steps are needed in order to eliminate software errors.

Table 3.45 reflects the average "cumulative defect removal efficiency" or percentage of software defects found and eliminated prior to delivery of software to its intended users. Note that defect removal efficiency declines with the overall sizes of software applications. There are also significant variations among the six subindustries or domains included in this book.

As a general rule, the best industries for software quality control are those where software controls large and complicated physical devices such as computers, switching systems, weapons systems, aircraft, and medical instruments. The best industries overall in terms of software defect removal efficiency include:

Telecommunication manufacturers

Computer manufacturers

Aircraft manufacturers

Medical instrument manufacturers

Defense weapons systems manufacturers

Commercial software manufacturers

The larger commercial software houses such as Microsoft are now starting to achieve results that compare favorably to the traditional large-systems houses such as AT&T and IBM. Now that Windows NT and Windows 95 are approaching the size and complexity levels of software such as IBM's MVS operating system or AT&T's ESS5 switching system, Microsoft is beginning to utilize similar quality control approaches.

TABLE 3.45 U.S. Averages for Cumulative Defect Removal Efficiency Before Release, Percentage

Function points	End user	MIS	Outsource	Commercial	Systems	Military	Average
1	95.00	97.00	99.90	99.90	99.90	99.90	98.60
10	90.00	97.00	99.00	98.00	99.50	99.00	97.08
100	70.00	90.00	95.00	96.00	98.00	96.00	90.83
1,000	0.00	83.00	87.00	92.00	94.00	93.00	89.80
10,000	0.00	75.00	85.00	90.00	93.00	91.00	86.80
100,000	0.00	65.00	80.00	88.00	90.00	89.00	82.40
Average	85.00	84.50	90.98	93.98	95.73	94.65	90.81

U.S. Averages for Delivered Software Defects

If the defect potentials and defect removal efficiency levels are known, it is straightforward to predict the numbers of software defects still latent at the time of software release. Table 3.46 shows the approximate numbers of software errors still present at delivery to software clients.

Because abstract metrics such as "defects per function point" do not make it easy to visualize the actual quantities of software errors likely to remain in software at the time of delivery, Table 3.47 shows the overall probable quantity of delivered software defects. From the rather significant volumes of defects still present at the time of delivery, it is easy to see why software producers have such large customer support staffs and such a significant maintenance or defect repair budget for many years after the delivery of software to clients.

Note that not all defects are of equal importance or equal severity. The software industry usually categorizes customer-reported defects using some kind of weighting factor. A very common schema for this purpose is the four-level severity scale originally developed by IBM in the early 1960s:

TABLE 3.46 U.S. Averages for Delivered Defects per Function Point

Function points	End user	MIS	Outsource	Commercial	Systems	Military	Average
1	0.05	0.03	0.00	0.00	0.00	0.00	0.01
10	0.25	0.06	0.02	0.05	0.02	0.03	0.07
100	1.05	0.40	0.18	0.20	0.10	0.22	0.39
1,000	0.00	0.85	0.59	0.40	0.36	0.47	0.56
10,000	0.00	1.50	0.83	0.60	0.49	0.68	0.84
100,000	0.00	2.54	1.30	0.90	0.80	0.94	1.33
Average	0.45	0.90	0.48	0.36	0.29	0.39	0.53

TABLE 3.47 U.S. Average Volumes of Latent Defects in Software at Delivery

Function points	End user	MIS	Outsource	Commercial	Systems	Military	Average
1	0	0	0	0	0	0	0
10	3	1	0	1	0	0	1
100	105	40	18	20	10	22	39
1,000	0	850	585	400	360	473	556
10,000	0	15,000	8,250	6,000	4,900	6,750	8,448
100,000	0	253,750	130,000	90,000	80,000	93,500	132,880
Average	36	44,940	23,142	16,070	14,212	16,791	23,654

TABLE 3.48 U.S. Averages for Delivered Defects by Severity Level

Function points	Severity 1 (critical)	Severity 2 (significant)	Severity 3 (minor)	Severity 4 (cosmetic)	Total
1	0	0	0	0	0
10	0	0	1	0	1
100	1	4	14	20	39
1,000	6	78	222	250	556
10,000	127	1,225	4,224	2,872	8,448
100,000	2,658	15,946	66,440	47,837	132,880
Average	465	2,875	11,817	8,497	23,654
Percent	1.97	12.16	49.96	35.92	100.00

Severity 1 Critical problem (software does not operate at all)

Severity 2 Significant problem (major feature disabled or incorrect)

Severity 3 Minor problem (some inconvenience for users)

Severity 4 Cosmetic problem (spelling errors in messages; no effect on operations)

Table 3.48 shows the approximate overall distributions of software defects by severity level at the time of delivery to customers. As can be seen, most of the really serious severity 1 and severity 2 defects are eliminated before delivery. However, for large systems, the number of latent high-severity software defects is very troublesome. The example of the long delays in opening up the Denver Airport due to software defects in the luggage handling system illustrates the point very clearly.

U.S. Averages for Potential and Actual Software Reusability

Software reuse is an emerging technology of major importance. Reuse holds the promise of making larger quality and productivity improvements for software than any other technology to date. However, reuse encompasses much more than just reusing source code. SPR is now beginning to collect information on 12 categories of reusable software artifacts, as seen in Table 3.49.

While the literature on software reuse is expanding, as are tools that support reuse, a number of major elements are underreported. For example, there is little current information in print on reusable user manuals, reusable cost estimates, or reusable test materials. As this book is being written, the outsource software community and the

TABLE 3.49 Observed Volumes of Reuse in Software Applications, Percentage

	End user	MIS	Outsource	Commercial	Systems	Military	Average
Requirements			20	20	20		20
Architecture			20	30	10	10	18
Plans			25	20	10		18
Estimates		10	25	20	10	10	15
Design	15	15	25	30	15	10	18
Source code	15	20	35	35	25	15	24
Data	15	30	30	20	15	15	21
Interfaces		30	30	40	10	10	24
Screens		15	25	35	15	10	20
User manuals			15	25	10		17
Test plans			20	30	20	10	20
Test cases		15	25	30	20	10	20
Average	15	19	25	28	15	11	20

commercial software community tend to be somewhat ahead in overall volumes of reusable material. However, reuse is such an important topic that essentially every domain concerned with large software projects is mounting some kind of research and development program into reusable artifacts. Table 3.49 shows the approximate percentages of reusable artifacts by domain, with a very high margin of error.

From discussions and conversations with reusability researchers, it is apparent that much more reuse would be theoretically possible than has in fact been achieved to date. The author's view of the maximum potential for reuse of these 12 artifacts would be:

Software artifacts	Potential reuse, %
1. Reusable requirements	30
2. Reusable architecture	35
3. Reusable plans	30
4. Reusable cost estimates	30
5. Reusable designs	45
6. Reusable source code	75
7. Reusable data elements	60
8. Reusable interfaces	50
9. Reusable screens	50
10. Reusable user manuals	25
11. Reusable test plans	35
12. Reusable test cases	55
Average (arithmetic mean)	43

If pushed to optimum levels, the volume of reusable material would more than double today's averages. This would be a notable step toward reducing the costs and improving the quality of the software industry. The use of percentages is imprecise, and indicates the following: When you examine a software artifact such as a test plan or test library, what percentage of the volume of material for the current application has been used with other applications?

In order for reusability to be effective, it requires a very high level of quality control. Reusing garbage or defective components is not a viable strategy. Therefore, effective reusability programs must be associated with effective software quality assurance programs. The strong coupling of reuse and quality limits the applicability of reuse to enterprises that are somewhat better than average.

The Impact of Technology on Software Productivity and Quality Levels

One of the main uses of the Software Productivity Research knowledge base is to provide a research vehicle for judging the effects of various tools, programming languages, and methodologies on software productivity, quality, schedules, costs, and maintainability. The usual mode of this research is to measure a sample of projects that used the topic in question (i.e., a particular CASE tool, programming language, or some other new technology) and compare the results against a sample of similar projects that did not use the same approach.

This methodology allows fairly granular analyses that can actually distinguish fairly small differences in tools, languages, and methods. However, due to the very large numbers of specific vendors, it is more convenient to express the results at the levels of "classes" of technologies, i.e., lump all OO programming languages together rather than discuss C++, Objective C, Eiffel, Actor, etc., separately.

Since new languages, tools, and approaches appear frequently and at random intervals, this kind of research essentially never ends and is a continuous study. In the time between the first and second editions of this book, quite a number of new technologies have emerged, and some older technologies such as the object-oriented paradigm have expanded into new prominence.

There are far too many tools and approaches in the software world to deal with each one individually, so of necessity the information in this book will deal with classes of technologies rather than specific instances. The overall numbers of software technologies that might be considered are far too large for a company the size of the author's, or really for any company or university, to deal with all of them. Even large software research houses such as Auerbach, Gartner Group, and Meta Group can only deal with small samples of the available software tools and technologies:

Approximate Numbers of U.S. Software Tools and Methods Circa 1995

Technology domain	Number of commercial tools
Client-server tools	20
Configuration control tools	20
Document support tools	25
Software metrics and measurement tools	35
Software defect removal methodologies	40
Commercial software CASE and I-CASE tools	50
Commercial software cost estimating tools	50
Object-oriented programming tools	50
Software methodologies	65
Project management tools	100
Programming languages and dialects	500
Stand-alone software tools	3000

Not only are many tools and methods currently available, but the creation of new tools and methods is expanding as the software industry matures and becomes more sophisticated. For example, a new commercial software cost-estimating tool entered the market almost every month of 1993, 1994, and 1995. The author's company has been keeping a table of programming languages since 1986. New languages have been entered into this table almost every week since it was started. The total number of languages in the table is now about 470, and there is no apparent end to the creation of new programming languages and new dialects.

One of the problems of evaluating software technologies is to measure exactly what changes, and how to express the results. The method the author selected for this chapter encompasses eight aspects of acquiring and using new tools or methods:

1. The approximate learning curve in months to became familiar with the approach
2. The initial productivity impact during the learning curve
3. The long-range productivity impact after the technology is fully understood
4. The impact on defect potentials, if any
5. The impact on defect removal efficiency, if any

6. The impact on software schedules, if any
7. The approximate return on investment
8. Cautions or counterindications for situations where the approach may be hazardous

Five of these eight factors can be expressed as a percentage change compared to "average" results. This is not a very accurate method, but it has the virtue of being consistent across any kind of tool, method, or programming language.

The learning curve is expressed in terms of calendar months required to study the new method and use it long enough to become comfortable with it. This information is derived from interviewing practitioners about their experiences.

The course length is expressed in terms of business days required to take a normal introductory course to the topic in question. This information is derived from scanning the course catalogs of commercial software education groups and the in-house catalogs of large corporations such as AT&T and IBM. (University education operating on a semester or trimester basis is too sluggish for most software professionals.)

Almost every significant technology reduces productivity temporarily while software professionals learn how to use the new method and begin to ascend the learning curve. This fact is true outside of software, of course, but the software literature does not accurately reflect the short-term loss of productivity while the learning curve is being ascended. This information is derived from benchmark and assessment studies.

One of the most visible instances of a steep and protracted learning curve is that associated with various flavors of object-oriented analysis and design. The learning curve for OO analysis and design is so steep that roughly 50 percent of the projects attempting to use this approach for the first time abandon it before completion, or bring in older methods to supplement the OO approach in order to complete the project. After a few months to a year, when the new technology is fully absorbed, it is interesting to see what kinds of long-range improvements (if any) result from its utilization.

Two flavors of software quality improvements are considered: (1) reduction in defect potentials; (2) improvements in defect removal efficiency. Both are important, and some technologies can benefit both aspects simultaneously. The information is derived from SPR assessment and benchmark studies.

An excellent example of a technology that benefits both defect prevention and defect removal is the use of formal inspections. Not only are inspections about twice as efficient in finding bugs as most kinds of testing, but participants in inspections rapidly improve their own work from being exposed to common problems in their colleagues' work.

Schedule reduction is one of the most important topics in the software world, so any attempt to evaluate new or emerging technologies must be sensitive to this topic. Unfortunately, this topic is heavily impacted by exaggerated claims and false assertions. The information is derived from long-range analysis over a multiyear period of companies that have adopted various approaches (and also have adopted good measurement practices).

The return on investment is the most complex issue. What constitutes "value" from a new approach can really comprise six different dimensions:

1. Cost reductions when building software initially
2. Cost reductions when supporting or maintaining software
3. Speed improvements or shortening of development schedules
4. Quality improvements in terms of reduced defect potentials
5. Quality improvements in terms of elevated defect removal efficiency
6. Morale improvements on the part of management or staff

In this edition, these six factors have been amalgamated by the author into a single overall value dimension:

Excellent	>20% tangible improvements
Very good	>15% tangible improvements
Good	>10% tangible improvements
Fair	>5% tangible improvements
Poor	No tangible improvements
Very poor	Negative or harmful results

Needless to say, this approximation is not very accurate and has a high margin of error. Even so, the results are interesting and hopefully may have some utility.

The topic of counterindications is also very complicated. For example, the classes of application generators and fourth-generation languages often benefit productivity and can be very helpful. Yet these approaches would not be recommended for embedded, real-time software such as air traffic control or the target sensing routines on board the Patriot missile.

Another example of a counterindication deals with "rapid application development," or RAD. RAD approaches can be very useful for small projects, and especially so for small information systems. Yet the RAD approach can also be hazardous for applications larger than a few thousand function points in size, or for those like military weapons systems or large systems software projects where quality and reliability are of prime importance.

The technologies ranking as "excellent" typically produce significant benefits, and sometimes in more than a single factor. For example, inspections improve defect removal more than anything else but also have a positive impact on defect prevention, schedules, and productivity rates. Five technologies are in the excellent category: inspections, prototypes, reusable code and reusable design, and achieving a level of 5 on the SEI CMM scale.

At the opposite end of the spectrum are technologies that are harmful, or which return zero or negative value. Obviously there is little value from being a "1" on the SEI CMM scale. Two rather popular methods return negative value, however: using "physical lines of code" or LOC as a normalizing metric; and the use of logical statements as a normalizing metric.

Perhaps the worst software technology of all time was the use of physical lines of code. Continued use of this approach, in the author's opinion, should be considered professional malpractice. Physical lines of code have no economic validity and hence cannot be used for serious economic studies. While logical statements can at least be converted into function point metrics by means of the "backfiring" approach, there are no published algorithms for doing this based on physical lines of code.

The end result is that neither software productivity nor software quality can actually be measured using physical lines of code, and companies attempting to do this are essentially wasting far more than $1 for every $1 they spend. The primary loss is simply spending money for measurement without getting any useful data. The more serious hidden loss is the fact that concentrating primarily on LOC metrics blinds researchers, managers, and software staff to many important issues associated with the costs, schedules, and quality implications of noncode activities.

Coding is not the major cost driver for large-system development. Defect removal and the construction of paper documents (specifications, plans, user manuals, etc.) cost much more than the code itself. These major cost drivers can be measured directly using function point metrics but cannot be measured using physical LOC metrics. Hence the use of physical LOC metrics tends to blind researchers to perhaps 80 percent of all known software cost elements!

Between these extreme conditions of "excellent" and "very poor" are a number of technologies that do return positive value in at least one dimension. It should be noted that there is no "silver bullet" or single technology that can yield 10 to 1 improvements in productivity, quality, or any other tangible factor.

Table 3.50 shows a sample of some of the technologies which the au-

TABLE 3.50 Overall Rankings of Software Technologies on Productivity, Schedules, and Quality Levels

Technology	Learning curve, (months)	Course lengths, (days)	Initial productivity results, %	Final productivity results, %	Defect potential results, %	Defect removal results, %	Schedule reduction results, %	Return on investment
Reusable code	6.00	3.00	−10.00	25.00	−12.50	10.00	−20.00	Excellent
Reusable design	6.00	2.00	−10.00	25.00	−15.00	10.00	−17.50	Excellent
Quality estimating	1.00	2.00	2.50	7.50	−20.00	20.00	−7.50	Excellent
Formal inspections	1.00	2.00	10.00	20.00	−20.00	35.00	−15.00	Excellent
Measurement	2.00	2.00	−2.50	12.50	−20.00	20.00	−12.50	Excellent
Prototypes	1.00	0.00	12.50	18.00	−15.00	10.00	−10.00	Excellent
SEI CMM level 5	18.00	5.00	−5.00	20.00	−12.50	17.50	−10.00	Excellent
Cost estimating	1.00	2.00	5.00	12.50	−5.00	5.00	−12.50	Very good
Function points	3.00	2.00	−2.50	10.00	−4.50	7.50	−10.00	Very good
Restructuring	1.00	1.00	7.50	15.00	−20.00	7.50	−5.00	Very good
OO programming	6.00	5.00	−15.00	25.00	−10.00	10.00	−7.50	Very good
I-CASE	6.00	4.00	−12.50	15.00	−5.00	10.00	−7.50	Very good
Risk management	2.00	2.00	−1.00	5.00	−5.00	5.00	−5.00	Very good
QFD	3.00	3.00	−3.00	5.00	−10.00	10.00	−5.00	Very good
Reusable tests	3.00	2.00	−5.00	10.00	0.00	10.00	−5.00	Very good
SEI CMM level 4	12.00	4.00	−5.00	15.00	−10.00	12.50	−5.00	Very good
Formal structures	2.00	2.00	7.50	12.50	−12.50	10.00	−5.00	Very good
JAD	1.00	1.00	7.50	12.50	−15.00	5.00	−7.50	Good
RAD	4.00	3.00	15.00	20.00	10.00	−2.50	−15.00	Good
Visual languages	3.00	2.00	5.00	15.00	−10.00	5.00	−10.00	Good
Information engineering	6.00	3.00	−7.50	12.50	−7.50	5.00	−7.50	Good
4GL's	4.00	2.00	−2.50	10.00	−10.00	5.00	−7.50	Good

Ada95	3.00	4.00	−5.00	10.00	−10.00	10.00	−5.00	Good
SEI CMM level 3	6.00	3.00	−5.00	10.00	−7.50	10.00	−5.00	Good
Reusable documents	2.00	2.00	−2.50	5.00	−5.00	10.00	−2.50	Good
Project management	1.00	1.00	−2.50	5.00	0.00	0.00	−2.50	Good
Configuration control	2.00	1.00	2.50	7.50	−10.00	5.00	−2.00	Good
Defect tracking	1.00	1.00	−2.50	2.50	−2.50	5.00	−1.00	Good
Complexity analysis	1.00	1.00	0.00	2.50	−12.50	7.50	−1.00	Good
Reengineering	1.00	2.00	−5.00	7.50	−2.50	2.50	0.00	Good
CASE	3.00	3.00	−10.00	7.50	0.00	5.00	−5.00	Good
SEI CMM level 2	3.00	2.00	−5.00	5.00	−5.00	5.00	−2.50	Good
Client-server	6.00	3.00	−10.00	10.00	15.00	−10.00	−20.00	Fair
TQM	6.00	5.00	−5.00	5.00	5.00	5.00	0.00	Fair
OO design	6.00	3.00	−20.00	12.50	−5.00	10.00	5.00	Fair
ISO 9000-9004	4.00	3.00	−10.00	5.00	−5.00	5.00	7.50	Fair
SEI CMM level 1	2.00	0.00	−2.50	0.00	0.00	0.00	0.00	Poor
LOC metrics, logical	1.00	1.00	0.00	0.00	0.00	0.00	0.00	Poor
LOC metrics, physical	1.00	0.00	0.00	−5.00	0.00	0.00	0.00	Very poor
Cumulative results	141.00	89.00	−91.50	413.00	−274.50	297.50	−241.50	
Average	3.62	2.28	−2.35	10.59	−7.04	7.63	−6.19	Good

thor and his colleagues have examined and are continuing to examine. The overall cumulative results are interesting but not terribly useful. They do indicate that if a company plans on absorbing several technologies more or less concurrently, they should plan to spend quite a bit of time on education. They should also expect fairly substantial initial productivity reductions while ascending the learning curve.

Both the need for education and the rather lengthy learning curves required to get up to speed in the more complicated technologies tend to be ignored by vendors of technologies and are underreported in the software literature as well. The averages of the overall results are not totally useful either. However, they do make clear an important point: There is no "silver bullet" or single technology that, by itself, will create order-of-magnitude improvements. However, dealing with the simultaneous and concurrent results from multiple technologies is a very difficult topic for measurement and benchmark studies. Since no single technology, by itself, is likely to achieve really impressive results, the next topic of interest is how to express the results that might occur from *combinations of technologies.*

One of the basic uses of this kind of information is to put together patterns of best current practices observed in various software domains. Table 3.51 is built from the information in Table 3.50 and illustrates the current "best in class" patterns of technologies associated with the six domains.

It is significant and interesting that not every software technology is appropriate for every kind of application. For example, the very successful "joint application design" approach requires that users participate during the JAD sessions. This limits the usefulness of the JAD approach to applications where the users are known, and hence for applications such as Windows NT or OS/2 with the potential of millions of unknown users, JAD cannot really be applied.

Because the management information systems (MIS) population is larger than any other software domain, more vendors, tools, and methodologies are available for information systems than for any other kind of software. Of course, outsourcers and contractors who build information systems have access to the same kinds of approaches. The effective software technologies that are used across all six domains are general-purpose methods that are widely applicable to any kind of software situation. Those that are used only in a few of the domains are more narrow in focus and more specialized.

Note that several technologies, such as the use of "physical lines of code" as a normalizing metric are "worst current practices" and should not be used within any domain under almost any circumstances since the end results are usually harmful. The overall patterns of technology usage reflect those found in leading companies

TABLE 3.51 Patterns of Best Current Practices in Six Software Domains

	End user	MIS	Outsource	Commercial	Systems	Military
Reusable code	Yes	Yes	Yes	Yes	Yes	Yes
Reusable design	Yes	Yes	Yes	Yes	Yes	Yes
Quality estimating		Yes	Yes	Yes	Yes	Yes
Formal inspections		Yes	Yes	Yes	Yes	Yes
Measurement		Yes	Yes	Yes	Yes	Yes
Prototypes	Yes	Yes	Yes	Yes	Yes	Yes
SEI CMM level 5				Yes	Yes	Yes
Cost estimating		Yes	Yes	Yes	Yes	Yes
Function points		Yes	Yes	Yes	Yes	Yes
Restructuring		Yes	Yes			
OO programming	Yes	Yes	Yes	Yes	Yes	Yes
I-CASE		Yes	Yes	Yes	Yes	Yes
Risk management		Yes	Yes	Yes	Yes	Yes
QFD		Yes	Yes		Yes	Yes
Reusable tests		Yes	Yes	Yes	Yes	Yes
SEI CMM level 4					Yes	Yes
Formal structures	Yes	Yes	Yes	Yes	Yes	Yes
JAD		Yes	Yes			
RAD		Yes	Yes			
Visual languages	Yes	Yes	Yes	Yes		
Information engineering		Yes	Yes			
4GL's	Yes	Yes	Yes			
Ada95				Yes	Yes	Yes
SEI CMM level 3		Yes	Yes	Yes	Yes	Yes
Reusable documents		Yes	Yes	Yes	Yes	Yes
Project management		Yes	Yes	Yes	Yes	Yes
Configuration control		Yes	Yes	Yes	Yes	Yes
Defect tracking		Yes	Yes	Yes	Yes	Yes
Complexity analysis		Yes	Yes	Yes	Yes	Yes
Reengineering		Yes	Yes			
CASE	Yes	Yes	Yes			
SEI CMM level 2						
Client-server		Yes	Yes			
TQM		Yes	Yes	Yes	Yes	Yes
OO design		Yes	Yes	Yes	Yes	Yes
ISO 9000-9004				Yes	Yes	
SEI CMM level 1						
LOC metrics, logical						
LOC metrics, physical						

and government agencies. No single company and certainly no government agency is likely to use all of these best practices at the same time. However, if you perform assessments and baseline studies are hundreds of good to excellent companies, you can begin to see the patterns emerge.

You can also observe one of the distressing aspects of the software industry. Some companies neither explore best practices nor make any serious attempt to use them. For example, the author and his colleagues have done several consulting studies for large MIS shops with huge portfolios of aging legacy systems written in Cobol. It is obvious that a whole suite of geriatric tools and services might be useful for such companies, including but not limited to complexity analyzers, restructuring tools, reengineering tools, reverse engineering tools, etc. Yet many times the managers within the MIS domain have made no effort to acquire such technologies, and they are sometimes even surprised to find that geriatric tools are commercially available.

Evaluating the Productivity Impact of Multiple Technologies

Evaluating the simultaneous impact of multiple technologies is one of the most difficult research problems in the entire software world. Even though the author and his company have more data than most, it is still not an easy task. After experiments with several ways of displaying the data derived from Software Productivity Research's multiple regression studies, an interesting method has been to show how four kinds of technologies or social factors interact with one another.

This method involves limiting the selection to no more than four different approaches, and then showing the extreme conditions that can result from moving from "best" to "worst" for each factor alone, and then for all combinations and permutations of factors. The reason that this method is limited to four approaches is that the 16 combinations that result are about the largest number that can be expressed in a table of convenient length. Each time a factor is added, the number of combinations doubles, so that five factors would yield 32 combinations, six factors would yield 64 combinations, and so on.

Table 3.52.1 shows the interactions of four technical factors: (1) the experience levels of the staff in the kind of application being developed and the tools used; (2) the usage or lack or usage of formal structured development methods; (3) the usage of integrated or I-CASE tools, or their lack; (4) the usage of high-level or low-level programming languages.

The data is based on more than 800 software projects explored between 1987 and 1995. The size range of the projects runs from a low of

50 function points to a high of 1000 function points, and hence excludes large systems. This size range is roughly equivalent to projects that run between 5000 and 100,000 source statements in normal procedural languages such as Fortran and Cobol. The data includes military software, civilian systems software, and management information system (MIS) software. Included although not named are results derived from more than a dozen CASE and I-CASE tools.

The phrase "experienced staff" implies personnel who are familiar with both the domain of the application and also with the tools being utilized.

The phrase "structured methods" implies usage of one of the formal software methodologies such as the Yourdon structured design approach, the Warnier-Orr approach, and the Information Engineering (IE) approach.

The phrase "I-CASE tools" implies usage of one of many commercial tools including but not limited to Amdahl's HURON tools, Bachman's ANALYST tools, Cadre's TEAMWORK tools, CGI's PACBASE tools, Texas Instruments' Information Engineering Facility (IEF) tools, Sapiens, and Unisys' LINC tools, etc.

The phrase "high-level languages" implies programming languages which require less than 50 statements to encode one function point. Examples of such languages include object-oriented languages such as Smalltalk, C++, and Objective C. Also included are both fourth-generation languages and application generators, such as GAMMA, PowerSoft, and TELON.

The phrase "low-level languages" implies programming languages which require more than 100 statements to encode one function point. Examples of such language include Cobol (averaging 106.7 statements per function point), Fortran, C, and of course assembly language.

Note that midrange languages are excluded from Table 3.52.1. These languages require somewhere between 50 and 100 statements to encode one function point. Examples of excluded midrange languages are Ada, PL/I, and Pascal.

TABLE 3.52.1 Productivity Range of 16 Permutations of 4 Software Technology and Social Factors (Data Expressed in Terms of Function Points per Staff-month)

	Worst-case scenario		
	Lowest	Median	Highest
1. Inexperienced staff Unstructured methods Ordinary tools Low-level languages	0.25	2.50	5.00

The purpose of the table is to illustrate that a single factor or technology, by itself, is not sufficient to make major improvements in software productivity. What is required is a combined approach with many concurrent improvements.

The four factors illustrated are only some of the topics that are known to impact software productivity and quality in favorable ways. Not shown because of space limitations are the impacts of reusability, object-oriented analysis and design, quality control methods such as inspections and quality function deployment, and many others. Each time a factor is included, the number of permutations doubles, so four factors is the maximum convenient number for a journal article.

Although not the prime purpose of the table, it is significant that military software projects clump toward the low side, MIS projects toward the high side, and civilian systems software toward the central column of the data reported in Table 3.52.1.

Table 3.51 illustrates the worst of the worst, where primitive tools are utilized by inexperienced technical personnel coding in low-level languages using chaotic and unstructured processes. Table 3.52.2 illustrates the impact of changing each of these four factors individually. Table 3.52.3 illustrates the six combinations that are possible from changing two of the factors concurrently.

It is an interesting observation that most of the data on the two-fac-

TABLE 3.52.2 Productivity Range of 16 Permutations of 4 Software Technology and Social Factors (Data Expressed in Terms of Function Points per Staff-month)

	Single-factor changes		
	Lowest	Median	Highest
2. Inexperienced staff Unstructured methods CASE tools Low-level languages	0.30	3.50	6.00
3. Inexperienced staff Structured methods Ordinary tools Low-level languages	0.50	4.00	7.00
4. Experienced staff Unstructured methods Ordinary tools Low-level languages	0.75	4.50	8.00
5. Inexperienced staff Unstructured methods Ordinary tools High-level languages	1.00	5.00	9.50

TABLE 3.52.3 Productivity Range of 16 Permutations of 4 Software Technology and Social Factors (Data Expressed in Terms of Function Points per Staff-month)

	Two-factor changes		
	Lowest	Median	Highest
6. Inexperienced staff Structured methods CASE tools Low-level languages	1.50	6.00	10.00
7. Inexperienced staff Unstructured methods CASE tools High-level languages	2.00	7.00	12.00
8. Experienced staff Unstructured methods CASE tools Low-level languages	3.00	8.00	12.50
9. Inexperienced staff Structured methods Ordinary tools High-level languages	3.50	8.50	13.00
10. Experienced staff Structured methods Ordinary tools Low-level languages	4.00	9.00	14.00
11. Experienced staff Unstructured methods Ordinary tools High-level languages	5.00	10.00	15.00

tor changes shown in Table 3.52.3 closely approximate the U.S. norms illustrated earlier. In fact, the actual practices of many U.S. companies can be represented by the combinations in the table. About half of all companies in the United States can probably be found within the table's range.

Table 3.52.4 illustrates the impact of changing three of the factors concurrently. Here the observed results are quite respectable. Data in the table reflects projects and companies which constitute about 15 percent of the ones examined by Software Productivity Research.

The final results in Table 3.52.5 show the best of the best, where all four factors are set to optimum levels. The results here are indeed impressive, although only about 3 percent of the projects measured by Software Productivity Research have achieved them. There are also other factors at play which are not shown here, such as high levels of reusability. However, each additional factor would double the number of permutations and so reasons of space cause them to be excluded.

TABLE 3.52.4 Productivity Range of 16 Permutations of 4 Software Technology and Social Factors (Data Expressed in Terms of Function Points per Staff-month)

	Three-factor changes		
	Lowest	Median	Highest
12. Experienced staff Structured methods CASE tools Low-level languages	6.00	12.00	20.00
13. Inexperienced staff Structured methods CASE tools High-level languages	6.50	14.00	25.00
14. Experienced staff Unstructured methods CASE tools High-level languages	7.00	18.00	30.00
15. Experienced staff Structured methods Ordinary tools High-level languages	10.00	25.00	50.00

TABLE 3.52.5 Productivity Range of 16 Permutations of 4 Software Technology and Social Factors (Data Expressed in Terms of Function Points per Staff-month)

	Best-case scenario		
	Lowest	Median	Highest
16. Experienced staff Structured methods CASE tools High-level languages	20.00	40.00	100.00

As may be seen from the flow of information shown in Tables 3.52.1 through 3.52.5, no single approach by itself is adequate to make large gains in software productivity. But multiple, concurrent improvements can create impressive results.

The margin of error in the tables is high, and the results have also been converted to integer values to simplify presentation. However, the overall flow of the information does reflect the results derived from hundreds of software projects in scores of companies and government agencies. What Tables 3.52.1 through 3.52.5 do not address, however, is the time and cost needed to make multiple concurrent improvements. If a company's technology base is as primitive as the one illustrated by the first plateau of Table 3.52.1 through 3.52.5 it can be

3 to 5 years and many thousands of dollars per staff member before the results shown in the sixteenth plateau can be achieved.

Evaluating the Quality Impact of Multiple Technologies

The same approach for dealing with the impact of multiple technologies on software productivity can also be used to illustrate the impact of various approaches on software quality. It is obvious that no single defect removal operation is adequate by itself. This explains why "best in class" quality results can only be achieved from synergistic combinations of defect prevention, reviews or inspections, and various kinds of test activities. Companies that can consistently average more than 95 percent in defect removal efficiency levels and keep defect potentials below about 3.0 per function point are moving toward "best in class" status.

The four quality factors selected for inclusion are these:

Formal design inspections by small teams (usually 3 to 5) of trained personnel. Formal inspections have the highest defect removal efficiency levels of any method yet studied. Design problems may outnumber code problems, so design inspections are a key technology for large systems. Inspections are used by essentially all "best in class" companies.

Formal code inspections by small teams (usually 3 to 5) of trained personnel. Formal code inspections differ from casual "walkthroughs" in that defect data and effort data is recorded and used for statistical purposes. Note that the defect data is *not* used for appraisal or personnel purposes.

Formal quality assurance by an independent QA team, hopefully containing one or more certified QA analysts. The purpose of the formal QA team is to ensure that suitable defect prevention and removal operations have been selected and that relevant standards are adhered to.

Formal testing by trained testing specialists. Testing is a teachable skill, although not many software development personnel have access to adequate training. Most of the "best in class" companies have established formal test departments that take over testing after unit test and deal with the more difficult topics of stress testing, regression testing, integration testing, system testing, and the like.

As with productivity, a useful way of showing the combined impacts of various defect removal operations is to show the permutations that result from using various methods singly or in combination. Since four factors generate 16 permutations, the results show that high quality levels need a multifaceted approach. Table 3.53.1 shows the

TABLE 3.53.1 Defect Removal Efficiency of 16 Combinations of 4 Defect Removal Methods

	Worst-case results, %		
	Worst	Median	Best
1. No design inspections No code inspections No quality assurance No formal testing	30	40	50

TABLE 3.53.2 Defect Removal Efficiency of 16 Combinations of 4 Defect Removal Methods

	Single-factor results, %		
	Worst	Median	Best
2. No design inspections No code inspections Formal quality assurance No formal testing	32	45	55
3. No design inspections No code inspections No quality assurance Formal testing	37	53	60
4. No design inspections Formal code inspections No quality assurance No formal testing	43	57	66
5. Formal design inspections No code inspections No quality assurance No formal testing	45	60	68

cumulative defect removal efficiency levels of all 16 permutations of four factors.

Table 3.53.1 illustrates the "worst of the worst," which unfortunately is far too common in the software world. The essential message is that organizations that take no formal action to improve quality will probably not exceed 50 percent in overall defect removal efficiency. Table 3.53.2 shows the impact of changing each factor individually. As before, no single change will yield results that are other than marginal improvements.

Table 3.53.3 shows the overall combinations of changing two factors at a time. As before, there are six combinations that might result.

The two-factor results approximate U.S. averages, and many companies and government groups are probably in this zone. The three-

TABLE 3.53.3 Defect Removal Efficiency of 16 Combinations of 4 Defect Removal Methods

	Two-factor results, %		
	Worst	Median	Best
6. No design inspections No code inspections Formal quality assurance Formal testing	50	65	75
7. No design inspections Formal code inspections Formal quality assurance No formal testing	53	68	78
8. No design inspections Formal code inspections No quality assurance Formal testing	55	70	80
9. Formal design inspections No code inspections Formal quality assurance No formal testing	60	75	85
10. Formal design inspections No code inspections No quality assurance Formal testing	65	80	87
11. Formal design inspections Formal code inspection No quality assurance No formal testing	70	85	90

TABLE 3.53.4 Defect Removal Efficiency of 16 Combinations of 4 Defect Removal Methods

	Three-factor results, %		
	Worst	Median	Best
12. No design inspections Formal code inspections Formal quality assurance Formal testing	75	87	93
13. Formal design inspections No code inspections Formal quality assurance Formal testing	77	90	95
14. Formal design inspections Formal code inspections Formal quality assurance No formal testing	83	95	97
15. Formal design inspections Formal code inspections No quality assurance Formal testing	85	97	99

TABLE 3.53.5 Defect Removal Efficiency of 16 Combinations of 4 Defect Removal Methods

	Best Case Results, %		
	Worst	Median	Best
16. Formal design inspections Formal code inspections Formal quality assurance Formal testing	95	99	99.99

factor results begin to achieve respectable levels of defect removal efficiency, as shown in Table 3.53.4. (See p. 251.)

For best of the best results, all defect removal operations must be present and performed capably, as shown by Table 3.53.5.

As may be seen from the progression through the 16 permutations, achieving high levels of software quality requires a multifaceted approach. No single method is adequate. In particular, testing alone is not sufficient; quality assurance alone is not sufficient; inspections alone are not sufficient.

Technology Warnings and Counterindications

One important topic associated with software that is essentially never discussed in the literature is warnings, hazards, and counterindications. The topic deals with situations where various technologies might be counterproductive or even hazardous. Following are observations derived from SPR assessments about selected technologies which can do harm in special situations:

Capability maturity model (CMM) developed by the Software Engineering Institute (SEI) originally covered less than a third of the factors known to impact software productivity and quality. For example, recruiting, compensation, and tools were not discussed at all. Further, the SEI CMM lacked any quantification of quality or productivity rates, so the whole concept could not be mapped to any empirical results. In addition, the SEI asserted that quality and productivity improved long before the method had been tested under field conditions. The end result is that climbing to a particular CMM level such as level 2 or level 3 does not guarantee success. The Navy has reported receiving software from a CMM level 3 contractor that had excessive defect levels. If the CMM is used only as a general scheme, it is fairly benign. If it is used rigidly, as for determining contract eligibility, it is visibly defective and imperfect.

Client-server architecture is much more complex than traditional monolithic architectures for software applications. The increase in complexity has not yet been accompanied by an increase in defect prevention or defect removal methods. The end result is that client-server applications typically have about 20 percent more potential defects than traditional applications, and remove about 10 percent fewer of these defects before deployment. The result is twofold: (1) near term quality and reliability problems; (2) long-range elevations in maintenance costs as the client-server applications age to become legacy systems.

Computer aided software engineering (CASE) has two current deficiencies: (1) CASE tools seldom cover the "complete life cycle" of software projects in spite of vendor claims; (2) CASE tools typically have a steep learning curve. The end result is that CASE tools have just about as great a chance to have zero or negative impacts on software costs and schedules as they do to have positive impacts. Any company that expects to achieve positive value from investments in CASE technology should prepare to spend about $1 in training on the tool's capabilities for every $1 spent on the tool itself.

ISO 9000-9004 standards tend to create volumes of paperwork that compare alarmingly with DoD 2167A. However, the author has not been able to find any solid empirical evidence that the ISO standards actually improve software quality. When this fact was broadcast via CompuServe and the Internet, the most surprising response was that "the ISO standards are not intended to improve quality but only to provide a framework so that quality improvements are feasible." The current end result of ISO certification for the software world is primarily an increase in paperwork volumes and costs, and very little other tangible change. Of course, ISO certification is necessary for sale of some products in the European markets.

Lines of code metrics come in two flavors: (1) logical statements; (2) physical lines. Neither metric is suitable for economic studies or for serious quality analysis. However, the use of logical statements is marginally better, because there are published rules and algorithms for converting logical statements into function points. There are no known rules for converting physical lines into function points, because of the random variations associated with individual programming styles interacting with hundreds of possible languages.

Over and above mere random variances and enormous variations, there are much deeper problems. The most important problem with LOC metrics of either kind is that the measured results run in the opposite direction from real results. That is, as economic productivity and quality improve, apparent results measured using LOC metrics will decline. It is this problem that causes the LOC metric to be assigned a "professional malpractice" label by the author.

Object-oriented analysis and design in all varieties tends to have a very steep and lengthy learning curve. The end result is that roughly half of the projects which use OO analysis and design for the first time either abandon the approach before completion or augment OO analysis and design by means of older, more familiar methods such as Warnier-Orr design, information engineering, or conventional structured analysis. If a company can overcome the steep learning curve associated with such a major paradigm shift, the use of OO analysis and design eventually turns positive. Don't expect much tangible improvement in the first year, however.

Rapid application development (RAD) has been generally beneficial and positive for applications below about 1000 function points in size. For really large systems above 5,000 function points in size some of the shortcuts associated with the RAD concept tend to increase potential defects and reduce defect removal efficiency levels. The end result is that RAD may not be appropriate for large systems or for applications where quality and reliability are paramount such as weapons systems and systems software.

Using Function Point Metrics to Set "Best in Class" Targets

One of the useful by-products of the function point metric is the ability to set meaningful targets for "best in class" accomplishments. For the data shown here, no single company has been able to achieve all of the targets simultaneously. These "best in class" results are taken from companies that rank among the top 10 percent of the author's clients in terms of software productivity and quality levels in the various domains. As with any software data, there is a significant margin of error.

Note that the productivity targets are based on the standard SPR chart of accounts, which includes 25 development activities. (See Table 3.14 for examples of the sets of activities that are assumed here.)

Table 3.54 indicates best in class software productivity rates expressed in terms of "function points per staff-month." The same information is presented in terms of "work hours per function point" in Table 3.55.

Any organization that can consistently approach or better the data shown in Tables 3.54 and 3.55 is very capable indeed However, a strong caution must be given: The data in the tables assume *complete and accurate* historical data for all activities starting with requirements and running through delivery to a real customer or client. If

TABLE 3.54 Best in Class Development Productivity Targets (Function Points per Staff-Month)

Function points	End user	MIS	Outsource	Commercial	Systems	Military	Average
1	300.00	200.00	250.00	250.00	175.00	100.00	212.50
10	250.00	150.00	175.00	175.00	125.00	65.00	156.67
100	150.00	100.00	125.00	100.00	75.00	50.00	100.00
1,000	0.00	50.00	65.00	60.00	45.00	30.00	50.00
10,000	0.00	12.00	13.50	11.00	8.50	6.00	10.20
100,000	0.00	5.50	6.50	5.00	4.50	4.00	5.10
Average	233.33	86.25	105.83	100.17	72.17	42.50	106.71

TABLE 3.55 Best in Class Software Development Productivity Targets (Work Hours per Function Point)

Function points	End user	MIS	Outsource	Commercial	Systems	Military	Average
1	0.44	0.66	0.53	0.53	0.75	1.32	0.71
10	0.53	0.88	0.75	0.75	1.06	2.03	1.00
100	0.88	1.32	1.06	1.32	1.76	2.64	1.50
1,000	0.00	2.64	2.03	2.20	2.93	4.40	2.84
10,000	0.00	11.00	9.78	12.00	15.53	22.00	14.06
100,000	0.00	24.00	20.31	26.40	29.33	33.00	26.61
Average	0.62	6.75	5.74	7.20	8.56	6.48	5.89

you compare only coding against the tables, it is easy to achieve the results. If you use data from cost tracking systems that "leak" half or more of the actual effort, it is not very difficult to approach the levels shown in these tables either.

Note that maintenance and enhancement projects in real life will have somewhat different results from those shown in the tables. However, when dealing only with "best in class" targets, these differences are small enough to be negligible. When using these tables for maintenance and enhancement projects, note that it is the size of the enhancement or update, and not the size of the base application, that should be the point of comparison.

Because software schedules are of such critical importance to the software industry, let us now consider best in class schedule results in

Table 3.56. These schedules are not easy to achieve, and if your organization can approach them you can be justifiably proud of your accomplishments.

The best in class results for software quality don't differ quite so much from domain to domain. They do differ substantially with the size of the software application, however. For small projects of less than 100 function points, zero-defect levels are possible in terms of the numbers of delivered defects. For systems larger than 1000 function points, and especially for software systems larger than 10,000 function points, zero-defect levels are theoretically possible, but in fact the author has never seen it accomplished in more than 30 years.

Table 3.57 gives the "best in class" results in two flavors: (1) with the data normalized to a "per function point" basis; (2) the absolute or total numbers of defects that are likely to be encountered.

TABLE 3.56 Best in Class Software Development Schedule Targets (Calendar Months)

Function points	End user	MIS	Outsource	Commercial	Systems	Military	Average
1	0.05	0.06	0.06	0.06	0.07	0.07	0.06
10	0.25	0.50	0.40	0.60	0.70	1.00	0.58
100	3.00	6.00	5.50	6.50	7.00	9.00	6.17
1,000	0.00	13.00	11.00	12.00	14.00	14.50	12.90
10,000	0.00	28.00	24.00	26.00	30.00	36.00	28.80
100,000	0.00	52.00	46.00	46.00	45.00	58.00	49.40
Average	1.10	16.59	14.49	15.19	16.13	19.76	13.88

TABLE 3.57 Best in Class Software Quality Results

	Defects per function point			Absolute defect levels		
Function points	Defect Potential	Defect Removal	Delivered Defects	Defect Potential	Defect Removal	Delivered Defects
1	1.00	100.00	0.00	1	100.00	0
10	1.00	99.99	0.00	10	99.99	0
100	1.50	99.50	0.01	150	99.50	1
1,000	2.50	99.00	0.03	2,500	99.00	25
10,000	3.00	98.00	0.06	30,000	98.00	600
100,000	4.00	97.25	0.11	400,000	97.25	11,000
Average	2.17	98.96	0.03	72,110	98.96	1,938

The data in Table 3.57 includes five classes of defects (requirements, design, code, user manuals, and bad fixes) and all four standard severity levels for software defects; i.e.,

Severity 1	Total failure of application (1% of delivered defects)
Severity 2	Failure of a major function (10% of delivered defects)
Severity 3	Minor failure (50% of delivered defects)
Severity 4	Cosmetic error (39% of delivered defects)

In summary, software measurement is being rapidly transformed by the usage of function point metrics. The former lines of code (LOC) metric was reasonably effective during the early days of computing and software when low-level assembly language was the only major programming language in use. For assembly language programs and systems, code was the dominant cost driver.

More powerful languages changed the productivity equation and reduced the overall proportion of time and effort devoted to coding. With modern object-oriented programming languages, visual languages, and application generators, software can be built with coding effort dropping below 15 percent of the total work. In the modern world, usage of lines of code is ineffective and indeed harmful, since this metric does not reveal the main cost drivers of modern software.

However, programming languages do not reduce the quantity of paper documents in the form of plans, specifications, and user manuals. The synthetic function point metric is now opening up new kinds of analyses and successfully showing the economic improvements associated with better tools, better programming languages, and better quality control approaches.

This chapter has a high margin of error, but it is encouraging that trends can be seen at all. Hopefully other researchers can correct any errors included here and expand the information as new and better data becomes available.

References

1. McCabe, T. J., "A Complexity Measure," *IEEE Transactions on Software Engineering*, SE-2, no. 4, pp. 308–320.
2. Jones, Capers, *Patterns of Software Systems Failure and Success*, International Thomson Press, Boston, 1995.

Chapter

4

The Mechanics of Measurement: Building a Baseline

Introduction

Between the publication of the first edition in 1991 and this second edition, the related concepts of assessments, baselines, and benchmarks have entered the mainstream of software development.

- "Assessments" are structured evaluations of software processes, methods, and other influential factors using on-site interviews with software managers and staff.
- "Baselines" are quantitative evaluations of an enterprise's current productivity and quality levels, to be used as a starting point for measuring rates of improvement.
- "Benchmarks" are quantitative evaluations of two or more enterprises to discover how each participant performs certain activities or achieves specific results.

These three are not mutually exclusive, and indeed using all three simultaneously results in the best understanding of software practices and how those practices impact quantitative results.

Software Assessments

A basic form of software qualitative measurement is an *assessment* performed by an independent, impartial team of assessment specialists. Software assessments have exploded in frequency under the impact of the well-known assessment technique developed by the

Software Engineering Institute (SEI). SEI is a government-funded research institute located on the campus of Carnegie Mellon University in Pittsburgh, Pennsylvania.

The SEI assessment method is neither the first nor the only software assessment method used for software. But is has become the best known owing to widespread coverage in the software press and from the publication of a well-known book, Watts Humphrey's *Managing the Software Process,*[1] which described the assessment method used by the Software Engineering Institute (SEI). A second book dealing with software assessments was the author Capers Jones' *Assessment and Control of Software Risks,*[14] which describes the results of the assessment method used by Software Productivity Research (SPR).

Both the SEI and SPR assessments are similar in concept to medical examinations. That is, both assessment approaches try to find everything that is right and everything that may be wrong with the way companies build and maintain software. Hopefully not too much will be wrong, but it is necessary to know what is wrong before truly effective therapy programs can be developed.

The SEI assessment approach has been in use since 1986. It was originally developed as a tool for exploring the capabilities of large defense contractors. The name of this assessment approach, the "capability maturity model" or CMM, is now well known throughout the industry, and SEI-style assessments can be found in Europe, the Pacific Rim, South America, and essentially all over the world.

Using the SEI CMM approach, software managers and staff are interviewed about the processes and methods deployed on software projects. The overall goal of the SEI CMM approach is to improve the sophistication or "maturity" with which software is built. To this end, the SEI has developed a five-plateau maturity scale (see below):

As can be seen, about 75 percent of all enterprises assessed using the SEI approach are at the bottom level, or "initial." SEI asserts that it takes about 18 months to move up a level, so software process improvement is a long-range goal.

SEI Capability Maturity Model (CMM) Scoring System

CMM level	Frequency, %	Approximate definition
1 = initial	75.0	Primitive and random processes
2 = repeatable	15.0	Some standardized methods and controls
3 = defined	8.0	Well-structured methods with good results
4 = managed	1.5	Very sophisticated, with substantial reuse
5 = optimizing	0.5	State of the art, advanced approaches

A complete discussion of the SEI scoring system is outside the scope of this book. The SEI scoring is based on patterns of responses to a set of about 150 binary questions. The higher SEI maturity levels require "yes" answers to specific patterns of questions. For example, an SEI question dealing with quality assurance might look like this:

Does your organization have a formal software quality assurance organization?

Software Productivity Research also has an assessment approach that is somewhat older than the SEI assessment approach. The SPR assessment approach also uses a five-point scale, but the results run in opposite directions.

An example of an SPR question that deals with quality assurance overlaps the same topic as the SEI question shown above, although the formats are different. The SPR questionnaires use multiple-choice forms rather than the binary question formats used by SEI. One of the SPR questions associated with software quality is:

Quality assurance function (select one choice)_______

1. Formal QA group with adequate resources
2. Formal QA group but understaffed (< 1 to 30 ratio)
3. QA role is assigned to development personnel
4. QA role is performed informally
5. No QA function exists for the project

Like the SEI approach, the SPR assessment method also uses site visits and structured interviews covering several hundred factors that can influence the outcomes of software projects. The answers to the SPR questionnaires are input directly into a proprietary tool which performs a statistical analysis of the results and shows the mean values and standard deviations of all factors.

Table 4.1 is the SPR scoring system, and the approximate percentages of results noted within five industry groups: commerical software, outsource contractors, military software, systems software, and management information systems software. As can be seen, most organizations are "average" in most topics covered. However, the systems, commerical, and outsource communities have a higher frequency of "good" and "excellent" responses than do the MIS and military communities.

Because the SPR assessments produce typical bell-shaped curves and the SEI assessments have a skewed distribution, a simple inver-

TABLE 4.1 Distribution of Results Using the SPR Assessment Methodology, Percentage

	MIS	Outsource	Commercial	Systems	Military	Average
1 = excellent	1.00	2.00	2.00	2.00	1.00	1.60
2 = good	12.00	22.00	23.00	24.00	16.00	19.40
3 = average	62.00	60.00	55.00	52.00	57.00	57.20
4 = poor	19.00	15.00	18.00	20.00	21.00	18.60
5 = very poor	6.00	1.00	2.00	2.00	5.00	3.20
	100.00	100.00	100.00	100.00	100.00	100.00

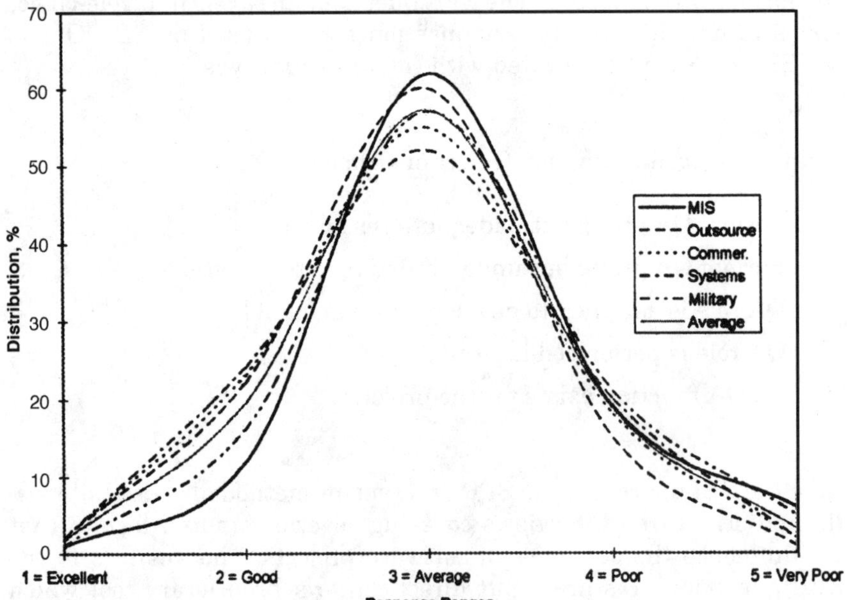

Figure 4.1 SPR software process assessment distribution of results.

sion of the two scales is not sufficient to correlate the SPR and SEI results. Figure 4.1 illustrates the kinds of distribution associated with the SPR assessment results. However, by using both inversion and mathematical compression of the SPR scores, it is possible to establish a rough equivalence between the SPR and SEI scales. In order to achieve roughly the same distribution as the SEI results, some of the SPR scoring data has to be condensed, as follows:

SPR scoring range	Equivalent SEI score	Approximate frequency, %
5.99–3.00	1 = initial	80.0
2.99–2.51	2 = repeatable	10.0
2.01–2.50	3 = defined	5.0
1.01–2.00	4 = managed	3.0
0.01–1.00	5 = optimizing	2.0

The inversion and compression of the SPR scores is not a perfect match to the SEI assessment distributions but is reasonably close.

A full and formal software assessment is a very good starting place for any kind of process improvement program. Since none of us can see our own faults clearly, a careful, independent assessment by trained specialists is the software world's equivalent of a complete medical examination. A software assessment should find everything we do wrong in building and maintaining software, and also everything we do that is right or better than average.

Software assessments normally take from a few weeks to a maximum of about 2 months. The larger, longer assessments are those of multinational organizations with many different labs or locations that are in different cities or countries. A basic assessment of a single location should not require much more than a month to collect the data and produce an assessment report.

However, an assessment by itself is not sufficient. The qualitative data collected during the assessment must be melded and correlated with "hard" productivity and quality data for optimum results. Therefore, a software assessment should not be a "stand alone" event but should be carefully integrated with a baseline study, a benchmark study, or both.

Software Baselines

A software "baseline" analysis is the collection of hard, quantitative data on software productivity and quality levels. Both a baseline and an assessment are the normal starting points of long-range software process improvement programs. The fundamental topics of a software baseline include these elements:

Software Baseline Topics Common in 1996

- Basic productivity rates for all classes and types of software projects

- Comparative productivity rates by size of applications
- Comparative productivity rates by programming language
- Comparative productivity rates associated with various tools and methodologies
- Basic quality levels for all classes and types of software projects
- Comparative quality levels by size of software applications
- Schedule intervals for software of all classes and types of software projects
- Comparative schedules by size of applications
- Comparative schedules associated with various tools and methodologies
- Measurement of the total volume of software owned by your enterprise
- Measurement of the volumes of various kinds of software owned
- Measurement of software usability and user satisfaction levels

Unlike assessments, where external and independent assessment teams are preferred, software baseline data can be collected by an enterprise's own employees. However, some strong cautions are indicated, since there is no value from collecting erroneous data.

- Your software cost tracking system (if any) probably "leaks," and therefore you should validate the data before using it for baseline purposes.
- You can validate your resource and cost data by the straightforward method of interviewing the participants in major software projects and asking them to reconstruct the missing elements, such as unpaid overtime or work performed before the tracking system was initialized for the project.
- If you use function points for normalizing your data, you will need to have one or more certified function point counters available to ensure that your counts are accurate. (Many function point courses are available in every part of the United States. The International Function Point Users Group, or IFPUG, offers several certification examinations each year.)
- You cannot reconstruct missing quality data (although you can reconstruct missing cost and productivity data). Therefore, you may not be able to get really accurate quality data for perhaps a year after you start your baseline measurements. However, you can "model" your missing quality data using any of several commercial quality estimation tools.

Your initial baseline should probably contain information on somewhere between 10 and 30 software projects of various sizes and kinds. You will want to include all of the major kinds of software projects that are common, i.e., new work, enhancements, projects done by contractors, projects starting with packages, etc.

Expect it to take between a month and about 6 weeks to collect the initial baseline data if you do the work yourselves.

Software Benchmarks

Software benchmark studies compare how two or more enterprises carry out the same activities, or compare their quantitative quality and productivity results. Sometimes benchmarks involve direct competitors, and they should always involve enterprises that are producing similar kinds of software.

Since benchmarks involve at least two separate enterprises, and sometimes many enterprises, the work of collecting the data is normally performed by an external, independent group. For example, many management consulting companies have benchmark practices. However, some companies have in-house benchmarking departments and executives.

For commercial software, there are usually independent user associations that can sometimes perform benchmarks involving hundreds or even thousands of users of the same software. Some software journals and commercial benchmark companies also perform and publish software benchmark studies.

The most common forms of software benchmarks in 1995 include:

- Benchmark comparisons of aggregate software expenditures
- Benchmark comparisons of total software portfolio sizes
- Benchmark comparisons of software staff compensation levels
- Benchmark comparisons of software productivity using function points
- Benchmark comparisons of software schedule intervals
- Benchmark comparisons of software quality
- Benchmark comparisons of user satisfaction
- Benchmark comparisons of development processes
- Benchmark comparisons of software specialization
- Benchmark comparisons of software assessment results, such as SEI's CMM

The term "benchmark" is far older than the computing and software professions. It seemed to have its origin in carpentry as a mark of standard length on work benches. The term soon spread to other domains. Another early definition of benchmark was in surveying, where it indicated a metal plate inscribed with the exact longitude, latitude, and altitude of a particular point. Also from the surveying domain is the term "baseline," which originally defined a horizontal line measured with high precision to allow it to be used for triangulation of heights and distances.

When the computing industry began, the term benchmark was originally used to define various performance criteria for processor speeds, disk and tape drive speeds, printing speeds, and the like. This definition is still in use, and indeed a host of new and specialized benchmarks have been created in recent years for new kinds of devices such as CD ROM drives, multisynch monitors, graphics accelerators, solid-state flash disks, and high-speed modems.

As a term for measuring the relative performance of organizations in the computing and software domains, the term benchmark was first applied to data centers in the 1960s. This was a time when computers were entering the mainstream of business operations and data centers were proliferating in number and growing in size and complexity. This usage is still common for judging the relative efficiencies of data center operations.

In the 1970s the term benchmarking also began to be applied to various aspects of software development. There are several flavors of software development benchmarking; they use different metrics and different methods and are aimed at different aspects of software as a business endeavor.

Cost and resource benchmarks are essentially similar to the classic data center benchmarking studies, only transferred to a software development organization. These studies collect data on the annual expenditures for personnel and equipment, number of software personnel employed, number of clients served, sizes of software portfolios, and other tangible aspects associated with software development and maintenance. The results are then compared against norms or averages from companies of similar sizes, companies within the same industry, or companies that have enough in common to make the comparisons interesting.

In very large enterprises with multiple locations, similar benchmarks are sometimes used for internal comparisons between sites or divisions. The large accounting companies and a number of management consulting companies can perform general cost and resource benchmarks.

Project-level productivity and quality benchmarks drop down below the level of entire organizations. These benchmark studies accumulate effort, schedule, staffing, cost, and quality data from a sample of software projects developed and/or maintained by the organization that commissioned the benchmark. Sometimes the sample is as large as 100 percent, but more often the sample is more limited. For example, some companies don't bother with projects below a certain minimum size, or they exclude projects that are being developed for internal use as opposed to projects that are going to be released to external clients.

Project-level productivity and quality benchmarks are sometimes performed using questionnaires or survey instruments that are mailed or distributed to participants. Such studies can also be performed via actual interviews and on-site data collection at the client site.

To avoid "apples to oranges" comparisons, companies that perform project-level benchmark studies normally segment the data so that systems software, information systems, military software, scientific software, and other kinds of software are compared against projects of the same type. Data is also segmented by application size, to ensure that very small projects are not compared against huge systems. New projects and enhancement and maintenance projects are also segmented.

Activity-based benchmarks are even more detailed than the project-level benchmarks already discussed. Activity-based benchmarks drop down to the level of the specific kinds of work that must be performed in order to build a software application. For example, the 25 activities used by Software Productivity Research include requirements, prototyping, architecture, planning, initial design, detail design, design reviews, coding, reusable code acquisition, package acquisition, code inspections, independent verification and validation, configuration control, integration, user documentation, unit testing, function testing, integration testing, system testing, field testing, acceptance testing, independent testing, quality assurance, installation, and management.

Activity-based benchmarks are more difficult to perform than other kinds of benchmark studies, but the results are far more useful for process improvement, cost reduction, quality improvement, schedule improvement, or other kinds of improvement programs. The great advantage of activity-based benchmarks is that they reveal very important kinds of information that the less granular studies can't provide. For example, for many kinds of software projects the major cost drivers are associated with the production of paper documents (plans, specifications, user manuals) and with quality control. Both paperwork costs and defect removal costs are often more expensive than coding. Findings such as this are helpful in planning improvement programs and calculating returns on investments. But in order to know the major cost drivers within a specific company or enterprise, it is necessary to get down to the level of activity-based benchmark studies.

Software personnel and skill inventory benchmarks in the context of software are a fairly new arrival on the scene. As the twentieth century comes to a close, software has become one of the major factors in global business. Some large corporations have more than 25,000 software personnel of various kinds, and quite a few companies have more than 2500. Over and above the large numbers of workers, the total complement of specific skills and occupation groups associated with software is now approaching 100.

Large enterprises have many different categories of specialists in addition to their general software engineering populations, for example, quality assurance specialists, integration and test specialists, human factors specialists, performance specialists, customer support specialists, network specialists, database administration specialists, technical communication specialists, maintenance specialists, estimating specialists, measurement specialists, function point counting specialists, and many others. There are important questions in the areas of how many specialists of various kinds are needed, how they should be recruited, trained, and perhaps certified in their area of specialization. There are also questions dealing with the best way of placing specialists within the overall software organization structures.

Benchmarking in the skill and human resource domain involves collecting information on how companies of various sizes in various industries deal with the increasing need for specialization in an era of downsizing and business process reengineering. A number of methodologies are used to gather the data for benchmark studies. These include questionnaires that are administered by mail or electronic mail, on-site interviews, or some combination of mailed questionnaires augmented by interviews.

Benchmarking studies can also be "open" or "blind" in terms of whether the participants know who else has provided data and information during the benchmark study. In a fully open study, the names of all participating organizations are known and the data they provide is also known. This kind of study is difficult to do between competitors and is normally performed only for internal benchmark studies of the divisions and locations within large corporations.

One of the common variations of an open study is a limited benchmark, often between only two companies. In a two-company benchmark, both participants sign fairly detailed nondisclosure agreements and then provide one another with very detailed information on methods, tools, quality levels, productivity levels, schedules, and the like. This kind of study is seldom possible for direct competitors but is often used for companies that do similar kinds of software but operate in different industries, such as a telecommunications company sharing data with a computer manufacturing company.

In partly open benchmark studies, the names of the participating organizations are known, even though which company provided specific points of data is concealed. Partly open studies are often performed within specific industries such as insurance, banking, and telecommunications. In fact, studies of this kind are performed for a variety of purposes besides software topics. Some of the other uses of partly open studies include exploring salary and benefit plans, office space arrangements, and various aspect of human relations and employee morale.

In blind benchmark studies, none of the participants know the names of the other companies that participate. In extreme cases, the participants may not even know the industries from which the other companies were drawn. This level of precaution would be needed only if there were very few companies in an industry, or if the nature of the study demanded extraordinary security measures, or if the participants are fairly direct competitors.

Overall, the most accurate and useful kind of information is usually derived from benchmark studies that included at least a strong sample of on-site interviews, and where the benchmark study is at least partly open. Because each of the different kinds of benchmark approaches can generate useful information, some companies use several different kinds concurrently. For example, very large corporations such as AT&T and IBM may very well commission data center benchmarks, cost and resource benchmarks, assessment benchmarks, and either project-level or activity-based productivity and quality benchmarks concurrently.

Software benchmarking is continuing to expand in terms of the kinds of information collected and the number of companies that participate. Based on the ever-growing amount of solid data, it can be said that benchmarking is now a mainstream activity within the software world.

The objective of applied software measurement is insight. We don't measure software just to watch for trends; we look for ways to improve and get better. It should never be forgotten that the goal of measurement is useful information, and not just data, and that the goal of information is improvement. A medical doctor would never prescribe medicines or therapies to patients without carrying out a diagnosis first. Indeed, any doctor who behaved so foolishly could not stay licensed. Software is not yet at this level of professionalism: Consultants and vendors prescribe their tools or methods without any diagnosis at all.

A good measurement program is a diagnostic study that can identify all software problems that need therapies. The therapies themselves can often be derived from the measurements. For example, if

20 projects are measured in a company and all 20 project teams report "crowded, noisy office conditions" as an environmental factor, it is a fair conclusion that improvements in office space are needed.

Measurement can take place at the strategic or corporate level or at the project or tactical level. Both are important, but the greatest insights are normally available by careful tactical measurement on a project-by-project basis. If such a study is carried out annually, it will allow a company to create a measured baseline of where it was at a given point in time and to use that baseline to judge its rate of improvement in the future.

Once baseline measurements begin, they normally become such valuable corporate assets that they quickly become standard annual events. This implies full-time staffing and adequate support, both of which are desirable. However, the very first baseline a company carries out is a special case. It differs from a normal annual software productivity survey in several key respects:

1. The measurement team that collects the data is new, and it may be external management consultants.
2. The concept of measurement is new, and the company is uncertain of what measurement is all about.
3. The managers of the projects to be measured are probably apprehensive.
4. There is no prior model to work from, in terms of what data to include or even what the report might look like.
5. The timing and effort required for the baseline may be somewhat greater than in future baselines because of the need to climb up the learning curve.

Unless consultants are used, the first annual baseline will probably be staffed on a short-term basis by people who are fairly new to measurements and who are exploring metrics concepts. This also is a normal situation. An interesting phenomenon is that about 15 to 25 percent of the staff members who become involved with a company's initial baseline analysis become so intrigued with measurement technology that they enter new career paths and will wish to stay with measurement work permanently! That is a good sign for the software industry, since when metrics and measurements become serious enough for a career change, it indicates that a term like "software engineering" is becoming real instead of a painful misnomer.

The daily work of a physician involves diagnosis and treatment of patients. The daily work of a tactical measurement specialist involves diagnosis and treatment of projects. The project is the basic unit of study for tactical software measurement purposes. Although the term "project" is a common one, it is seldom defined. For the purposes of measurement, a project is defined as a set of coordinated tasks that are directed at producing and delivering a discrete software program, component, or system. The project team is assumed to consist of at least one manager and a varying number of technical staff members ranging from one to several hundred. The project team is also assumed to have a reasonably homogeneous set of methods and tools, which can encompass tools for requirements, design, coding, defect removal, and documentation.

Practical examples of what is meant by the term "project" include the following: an accounts payable system, an Ada compiler, a PBX switching system, a new release of a commercial software product such as WordPerfect Release 5, Lotus Release 3, or CHECKPOINT® Releases 1 and 2, an order entry system, or a personnel benefits tracking system. All of these are "projects" in the measurement sense that the components and programs were part of a single overall scheme or architecture, the staff ultimately reported to a single executive, and a homogeneous tool set was employed.

Very large systems, such as IBM's MVS operating system, would normally consist of quite a few separate projects such as the scheduler component, the supervisor component, and the access methods. The practical reason for considering these technically related components to be separate projects is that they were developed in different cities under different managers who used different methods and tool sets. For the purposes of gaining insights, it is necessary to measure the tasks of each of the groups separately if for no other reason than because some were in California and others were in New York. Obviously, the final measures can be consolidated upward, but the data itself should be derived from the specific projects within the overall system.

An annual baseline measurement study is a well-defined and thorough diagnostic technique that can be administered either by professional consultants or by the measurement team that a company creates by using its own employees. To establish a baseline initially, a reasonable sample of projects is required. Normal annual baselines include all projects above a certain size that went into production in the preceding year. Thus, a company's 1997 baseline would include all of its 1996 delivered projects.

However, the very first annual baseline is usually somewhat of an experiment, and so it may not contain 100 percent of the prior year's projects. Indeed, the very first baseline may contain projects whose completions span many years. Yet, a reasonable sample is necessary to gain insights about software issues. Normally from 10 to 30 projects will constitute the volume of an initial baseline. The projects themselves should be a mixture of new development, enhancements, and special projects (such as package acquisitions or contract projects) that reflects the kinds of software work the company actually carries out.

The baseline measurement study will examine all of the factors present in an enterprise that can affect the enterprise's software development, enhancement, and maintenance by as much as 1 percent. The baseline study can cover more than 200 soft environmental factors, and it is an attempt to bring the same level of discipline to bear on software as might be found in a thorough medical examination. As with medical examinations, a software baseline study is a diagnostic study aimed at finding problems or, in some cases, the lack of problems. After a careful diagnosis, it is possible to move toward a cure if problems are discovered. But before appropriate therapies can be prescribed, it is necessary to know the exact nature of the condition.

Why a Company Will Commission a Baseline

There are four common reasons why a company will commission a productivity analysis, and the measurement team should be very sensitive to them:

1. The company is interested in starting a software measurement program, and it wants both reliable information on current productivity and assistance in selecting and starting a software improvement program of which measurement is a key component.
2. The company wants to reduce the overall costs of software, data processing, and computing expenses with the enterprise and is looking for ways to economize.
3. The company wants to shorten software development schedules and provide needed functions to users more quickly.
4. The company has already achieved high software productivity, and it is seeking an independent validation of that fact which will be credible with enterprise management and the users of data processing.

The ethics of measurement

Regardless of the company motivations for commissioning a baseline analysis, the staff involved in it has an ethical obligation to make the analysis accurate and valuable. There is no value, and there can be considerable harm, in incomplete or inaccurate information presented to higher management. Management has a fiduciary duty to run the enterprise capably. The measurement team has an ethical duty to give the executives accurate data and clear explanations of the significance of the data.

It is important that both company management and the measurement team have a clear understanding of what results will come from a baseline study and what will not. What will result is a very clear picture of the software strengths and weaknesses of the enterprise that commissioned the study. For any weaknesses that are noted, possible therapies can be prescribed. What will not result is an instantaneous improvement in productivity. After the analysis is over, it can take from a month to a year to implement the therapies, and sometimes more than a year after that before tangible improvements can begin to show up. Very large corporations with more than 1000 software professionals should extend their planning horizons out to 3 years or more.

It is unfortunate that Americans tend to like quick, simple solutions to difficult and complicated problems. Improving software productivity and quality in a large company is a difficult and complicated problem, and an annual baseline tactical analysis is a very important part of the entire process.

The Methodology of the Baseline Analysis

The exact methods and schedules for carrying out the baseline analysis depend upon the number of projects selected and on whether the analysis will be performed at a single location or carried out at multiple locations and cities. Defense contractors, and other kinds of companies as well, may start their baseline work with a self-assessment procedure developed by the Software Engineering Institute at Carnegie Mellon University and published by Watts Humphrey.[1] This self-assessment procedure evaluates a number of technological factors and then places the company on a "software maturity grid." The results of the self-assessment are interesting and useful, but the SEI process is not detailed enough to serve as the basis for an accurate diagnosis of deeper conditions, nor does it tend to suggest appropriate therapies.

The normal cycle for a full annual baseline analysis runs from 2 to 3 calendar months. The methodology for the full baseline described here is based on the concepts first used at IBM and ITT and subsequently adopted by other companies such as AT&T, DEC, and Hewlett-Packard. The SPR methodology described here differs from the SEI approach in a fashion that is analogous to a full medical examination vs. a self-checking procedure to be carried out at home. The SPR methodology is intended to be administered by professional consultants assisted by statistical analysis and multiple-regression techniques. The volume of information collected by using the SPR method may be more than an order of magnitude greater than the SEI method; it takes more time but leads to a fuller set of diagnoses and expanded therapies. Examples of the kinds of results that are possible are shown here in Appendices C, D, and E. Other results were also published in the author's books *Programming Productivity*[2] and *Assessment and Control of Software Risks.*[14]

The very first time a full baseline is attempted, the additional startup work can stretch out the cycle to 6 months or more. Following are the general patterns:

Executive sponsorship

As pointed out in Chap. 1, the natural initial reaction to a baseline study is apprehension and fear, with the most severe alarms being felt by the managers whose projects will be measured. Therefore, an annual baseline study will probably require an executive sponsor at the vice presidential level, or even higher, the first time it is carried out.

Selection of the measurement team

Set aside one or two months for the critical task of assembling a measurement team. No modern company would dream of turning its finances and corporate accounting over to well-intentioned amateurs without professional qualifications; yet many companies attempt to start measurement baseline programs with personnel whose only qualification is that they are between assignments and hence are available. That is not as it should be: The measurement manager selection should be based on capabilities, as should selection of the rest of the measurement team.

The first time a company performs a baseline, the managers and staff will normally be somewhat inexperienced, but the situation is quite transient. Surprisingly, measurement technology is so interesting that perhaps 15 to 25 percent of the initial staff will decide to pursue measurement as a permanent career. As of 1996, no academic courses are available to software measurement specialists, but a new career is definitely emerging.

For the initial selection of a team, the manager should have a very good grounding in software methods and tools and sufficient knowledge of statistics to know how to apply statistics to practical problems. The measurement team should include at least one person with a good background in statistics, and all of the team should be experienced in software tools and methods.

Designing the data collection instruments

The first time a company starts to create an annual baseline, it is faced with the necessity of either acquiring or constructing questionnaires or survey forms. It is also faced with the necessity of acquiring or constructing software tools that can aid in the analysis and interpretation of the collected data. A minimum of about 6 months should be allotted if the company decides to construct its own instruments and tools. About 2 to 3 months should be allotted for selecting a consulting group if the company decides on the second option.

Some of the management consulting companies offering baseline services as part of their consulting practice include (in alphabetic order) A.D. Little; Arthur Andersen; Computer Power; DMR; Gartner Group; Index Group; Peat; Marwick & Main; Nolan, Norton & Company; Roger Pressman Associates; Reifer Associates; Rubin Associates; and Software Productivity Research. Just as medical doctors do not diagnose patients by mail, a baseline study cannot be effectively carried out by means of mail surveys. Experienced, knowledgeable consultants must conduct face-to-face interviews with the project managers and team members to gain the really valuable insights that can occur.

Nonprofit Associations with Function Point Baseline and Benchmark Data

Now that the function point metric has become the dominant software metric throughout much of the world, a growing number of nonprofit measurement associations have come into existence that collect data from their members. A sample of these nonprofit organizations as of 1996 includes:

Country or region	Acronym	Name
Australia	ASMA	Australian Software Metrics Association
Quebec	CIM	Centre d'interet sur les metriques
Germany	DASMA	Deutschprachise Anwendergruppe für Software Metrik und Aufwandschutzung
Europe	EFPUG	European Association of Function Point Users Groups
France	FFPUG	French Function Point Users Group
Italy	GUPPI	Gruppo Utenti Function Point Italia
Netherlands	NEFPUG	Netherlands Function Point Users Group
New Zealand	SMANZ	Software Metrics Association of New Zealand
United Kingdom	UFPUG	UK Function Point Users Group
United States	IFPUG	International Function Point Users Group
	NSC	National Software Council

Associated with the emerging National Software Council in the United States is the national software benchmark database sponsored by the

U.S. Air Force. This database is somewhat primitive and does not get to the level of activity-based costing, but it does support function point metrics in addition to the inadequate physical and logical "lines of code" metrics. In addition to these existing nonprofit associations, function point users are beginning to coalesce and form associations in many other countries such as Brazil, China, India, Japan, Russia, and South Korea.

"Vertical" associations of function point users are also beginning to form within specific industries such as banking, insurance, telecommunications, software, and health care. These special-interest groups usually get together at the general conferences held for software practitioners within the industries. There are also very active on-line function point metric discussions on the Internet, and also on various forums such as the Compuserve CASE forum, computer language forum, and cost estimating forums.

Although lagging somewhat owing to conservatism, the major software professional associations such as the IEEE Computer Society and the Data Processing Management Association (DPMA) are at least inviting speakers to discuss functional metrics at selected conferences. Even the very conservative Software Engineering Institute (SEI) has joined IFPUG and is finally awake to the power of functional metrics.

Introductory session prior to commencing the annual baseline

The first public event of the baseline analysis begins with a 1- to 3-h seminar on the rationale of the baseline and what is going to be accomplished. If available, it is helpful to show what other companies in the same line of business have been learning from their baselines or what is currently known about software productivity and quality in the industry as a whole. The purposes of the introductory session are to inform all staff and management of the intent of the baseline and to gain feedback about the natural apprehensions and concerns. Although this task takes less than one day, at least a month of lead time is required to schedule the event. Also, if the session is to be given in more than one city or country (for multinationals) additional time will be required.

Preliminary discussions and project selection

Plan on at least a week, and probably 2 weeks, for project selection. After the introductory session, the next step is to select from 10 to 30 specific projects to be examined, with 12 being the average number selected. This is a delicate process in terms of corporate politics. Since the normal management reaction will be apprehension, there is sometimes a tendency to select only projects considered to be "successful." That is not as it should be. What is best is to select projects that are representative of what is really going on: good projects, bad projects, development projects, enhancement projects, completed projects, and unfinished projects are all candidates for measurement.

Scheduling the project interviews

Once the projects are selected, the first schedules will be set for the individual project analyses. A complete baseline analysis for 12 projects usually takes about 2 calendar months to complete, involves about 25 days of consulting time (16 of them on site at the project locations), and requires roughly 60 h of client staff and management time to complete the questionnaires. Each interview session of a project team will range from about 2 h to a maximum of about 4 h. The participants will include the project manager and some or all of the project team, with a limit of perhaps six people in all. The limit of six people is not absolute, but it does represent the upper bounds of meetings that can be conversational without being discursive.

Individual project analysis

Each project selected by the company should be analyzed by using a standard technique so that the data is comparable. For example, the data collection instrument used by Software Productivity Research is a tactical project evaluation questionnaire that covers a total or more than 200 factors dealing with the projects themselves, the methods and tools used, the documents produced, the languages, the specialists and the organization structure, the defect prevention and removal techniques, and so forth.

Each project analysis requires from 2 to 4¼ h. The participants for each analysis include the consultant, the manager of the project being analyzed, and several technical personnel: usually a design specialist, one or more programmers and one or more technical writers if they were used for the project. If the project uses quality assurance, a quality assurance specialist should be part of the interview session. Thus, each analysis requires an investment by the project team of from 6 to perhaps 24 staff-hours.

All the participants in each analysis receive copies of the data collection questionnaire, which they are free to annotate during the analysis and to keep when the session is over. The master copy of the baseline questionnaire is kept with the actual project data by the consultant performing the analysis.

It is not uncommon for individuals on a project to have different opinions, and these ranges should be noted. Indeed, based on several hundred projects, it can be stated that managerial responses are normally about half a point more optimistic than technical staff responses when it comes to the usefulness of various methods and processes.

Although some apprehension is normal prior to the interview sessions, the apprehension vanishes almost immediately. Indeed, on the whole the managers and staff enjoy the interviews tremendously, and for perfectly valid sociological reasons:

1. They have never before had the opportunity to discuss their views of the tools, methods, and approaches in a serious and nonthreatening way, and they enjoy it.
2. The interviews are a clear and definite sign that the company is starting to take software seriously. This is, of course, an encouraging fact for software professionals, who have long considered themselves to be outside the scope of their company strategy.
3. The interviews provide a rare opportunity for people working on the same project to discuss what they are doing in a well-structured manner that includes, without exception, every facet that can influence the outcome of the project.

If the company is using automated tools for data collection and analysis, then before each analysis session is over, it may sometimes be possible to give the project manager a preliminary report that shows the responses for that project. Indeed, for unfinished projects it is possible to carry out a full cost estimate. However, if paper questionnaires are used, it is not convenient to provide immediate feedback.

Aggregation of data and statistical analyses

Set aside at least 10 working days for aggregation and analysis of the collected data. When all the selected projects have been individually analyzed, the combined data is aggregated and analyzed statistically. Hopefully, powerful statistical tools will be available to facilitate this aggregation. The factors that are significant include those in respect to which:

- All projects noted deficiencies or weaknesses.
- All projects noted successes or strengths.
- There were inconsistencies among projects, such as instances of some projects using formal inspections whereas similar projects did not.

Before production of the final reports, client management will be alerted to any significant findings that have emerged. The information can take the form of either an informal presentation or a draft report.

Preparation of the baseline presentation

There are two standard outputs from an annual baseline survey:

1. A presentation to executives on the findings
2. The full baseline report itself

The presentation to executives will normally be in the form of either overheads or 35-mm slides, depending upon your corporate protocols. The presentation, which may run up to 100 screens or slides, will discuss the background of the study, the weakness and strengths identified, the numerical hard data, and any possible therapies that appear to need immediate management attention. For preparation of the draft, about a week will normally be required. Production of slides and overheads may take up to 2 weeks depending upon the nature and speed of your production facilities.

For large companies, the time required to go through the presentation can range to more than half a day. The audience for the presentation will normally be senior executives, often including the CEO. The presentation will be given initially to the senior management of the company, but the normal protocols in business are such that it is highly advantageous to put on a road show and give the presentation to all company locations and managers who have any software responsibilities at all. Thus, in large corporations such as AT&T, Hewlett-Packard, ITT, and IBM, the annual baseline presentation may be given in more than 25 different cities.

Preparation of the baseline annual report

After the full analysis of the data, the final results of the baseline are prepared under the supervision of the senior baseline measurement manager. The final report, typically 70 to 100 pages in length, contains the detailed results of the productivity analysis. Appendix D discusses and gives an example of a corporate annual report.

In companies such as IBM and ITT, the annual baseline reports are prepared on the same time scale as the corporate annual reports. Indeed, the annual software report tends to be about the same size and to more or less resemble in substance a true corporate annual report. The production of a true corporate annual report for a company such as IBM, however, is about a 3-month undertaking with costs that exceed $1 million for content, layout, and production. The cost and time of a software baseline is not in that league, of course, but about 2 to 3 weeks of effort to produce the draft, followed by 1 to 2 weeks of production would be normal. The published report will differ from the slide or screen presentation in these respects:

- It will have explanatory text that discusses the significance of the findings.
- It will normally have more detail than the presentation.

The final reports vary in content with the specifics of each company, but they always include the following items:

1. An executive summary of significant diagnostic findings
2. Specific problems diagnosed in the areas of management, organization, staff specialization, policies, physical environment, methodologies, tools, the production library, and the applications backlog
3. Raw and normalized data on the projects and interpretation of the results
4. Suggested therapies that the enterprise should explore to overcome the noted problems

Overall scope and timing of the baseline

The normal scope of a baseline analysis generally runs from the initial meeting through the delivery of the final report. Although there are wide variances depending on the number of projects selected by the client, number of cities to be visited, and the like, a typical productivity analysis will take about 25 to 50 consultant days: 1 introductory day, 10 to 15 days of on-site data collection, 4 to 6 days of data analysis, 5 to 7 days of presentation creation, 4 to 7 days of written report preparation, 2 days of internal review among the measurement staff, ½ day with the senior company management for the preliminary report, 1 day for last-minute changes and corrections, and 1 full day with senior management to present the findings of the final report.

Follow-on Activities After the Baseline Is Complete

The baseline analysis will diagnose all software problems and all software strengths in an enterprise, with essentially no exceptions. As with medical diagnosis, the diagnostic stage must be followed by a therapy stage in order to cure the condition. Exactly what follow-on activities will be needed varies from client to client. There is no single pattern that always emerges, just as medical therapy varies from patient to patient and illness to illness. There are, however, five general action items which often occur as a result of a productivity analysis.

Site visits. A very frequent adjunct to a productivity analysis are site visits by client personnel to enterprises that have already achieved high levels of productivity. There are a number of leading-edge enterprises, already well ahead of U.S. averages in terms of software productivity, that allow or encourage visitors. To cite but two, the IBM Santa Teresa Programming Center in San Jose, California, and the Hartford Insurance Company in Hartford, Connecticut, frequently receive visitors from other enterprises who are interested in seeing what has been accomplished. Site visits give client enterprises an opportunity to see real companies in action, and they are very effective in showing the pragmatics of software productivity.

Tool acquisition. Many enterprises are found to be deficient in software tooling, such as numbers of workstations and graphics and text design packages. A very common follow-on activity is the acquisition and installation of new tools. Tool acquisition is not inexpensive, and from $3000 to more than $25,000 per software engineer may sometimes be committed.

Methodology selection. Enterprises which lack technology exploration functions such as development centers or software research labs may be several years out of date in terms of methodology. A frequent result of a baseline analysis is the selection of and experimentation with such new methodologies as joint application design (JAD), high-speed prototyping, time-box prototyping, object-oriented languages, and inspections. Methodological changes do not require as heavy a capital investment as tool upgrades, but they do require time and educational commitments. Method upgrades can involve as much as several weeks of education time per software engineer and from $500 to $5000 per staff member in training expenses.

Policy formation. Changes in enterprise policies and cultures are the most difficult follow-on activities after a productivity analysis. For example, implementing a dual-compensation plan, installing opinion surveys, creating an open-door policy, and changing employment contracts are major topics that involve not only the software and data processing management but also the senior management of the enterprise up to the boards of directors, together with such other functions as personnel and legal staffs.

Permanent measurement departments. The baseline analysis itself will introduce metrics such as the function point technique and the McCabe Complexity Metrics to the enterprises that commission an analysis. The analysis will also introduce the soft and hard data collection principles and many other useful metrics.

A very frequent follow-on activity to the initial baseline is the establishment by the enterprise of a permanent software measurement program, which will continue to measure software development and maintenance productivity and create annual software state-of-the-art reports. This is a significant step, but it is not an inexpensive one. A permanent measurement focal point requires at least one full-time expert, and the continuing costs of a measurement function can total several person-years each calendar year.

Organizational changes. Upgrading the organization structure of an enterprise is a relatively common follow-on activity. The establishment of formal maintenance departments occurs fairly often in large enterprises after a productivity analysis. Other organizational changes may be the creation of a quality assurance function, a development center, an information center, a measurement department, and the like. Less visible changes, such as substituting hierarchical management structures for the less effective matrix structures, may also occur from time to time.

Identification of Problems beyond the Current State of the Art

In the practice of medicine there are many diseases for which there is no current cure. In carrying out baseline analyses, there will be situations for which software engineering has no effective remedy. The following are examples of conditions for which no really effective therapies exist.

Irrational scheduling. Unfortunately, in the United States more than half of the large projects are scheduled in an irrational manner: A predetermined end date is selected, and it is forced on the project by arbitrary decree. If the selected date exceeds staff capabilities by more than about 25 percent, the consequences are a potential disaster. The magnitude of the disaster can include attrition of staff, whose members may leave in disgust, catastrophic cost overruns, and, of course, no reasonable hope of making the irrational schedule.

The baseline analysis will point this situation out, but once an irrational schedule has been committed to a client or, even worse, published to the outside world, there is no easy solution. There are, of course, excellent commercial estimating tools available, but less than 15 percent of U.S. companies use such tools today. Once a schedule has been committed to a client, it is embarrassing to admit that it was arbitrary. In the long run, baseline measurements will provide accurate schedule information to prevent future occurrences. However, the first creation of a baseline will probably encounter projects with the distressing problem of having irrational schedules forced upon them.

Incompetence of management and staff. As of 1996, software engineering and software management have no formal procedures for monitoring the equivalent of medical malpractice. A small but distressing number of projects will be found to be incompetently managed or developed. The situation seldom occurs in the context of baseline analyses for the pragmatic reason that companies with significant incompetence at the executive levels will probably not carry out baseline measurements at all. If the situation does occur, there is no easy therapy.

Aging non-Cobol production libraries. For aging Cobol software, restructuring and renovation services and products can extend the useful lives of aging software by automatically restructuring, redocumenting, and isolating dead code. For other languages such as Assembler, Fortran, and PL/I, there were no commercially available automatic restructuring facilities in 1996. Clients with such software either have to redevelop it, replace it, or continue to live with it. Note that automatic restructuring is theoretically possible with other languages, but the companies that provide the service have chosen not to apply their methods to non-Cobol software. That may change in the future.

Layoffs or drastic reductions in force. Enterprises that are faced with heavy competition, declining markets, or severe cash flow problems and have been forced to lay off substantial percentages of their work force may seek a baseline analysis in order to see if reduced staffing can continue to provide acceptable software functions and operations. Because so many of the powerful software technologies require upfront capital investment and substantial training expenses, clients with this situation should be warned that the set of available therapies not requiring some initial investment is neither large nor dramatically effective.

Large systems after the design phase. From time to time, clients commission a baseline analysis because they are in the middle of a major effort (more than 5,000 function points or 500,000 source statements) that seems to be out of control and the schedules are stretching to unacceptable lengths. Unfortunately, if the key requirements and design phases are already past, there are no technologies that can dramatically reduce the rest of the cycle. New languages usually cannot be prescribed, since their performance may not be adequate for large systems. There are techniques, such as design and code inspections that can improve quality significantly and productivity slightly, but once the design phase is passed, options become few.

Context of the Baseline and Follow-on Activities

After the final report is presented and accepted by the client, the productivity analysis is normally complete. Whether or not the analysis leads to follow-on work depends upon the nature of the diagnosis, the kinds of therapies recommended, and the capabilities of the company organization.

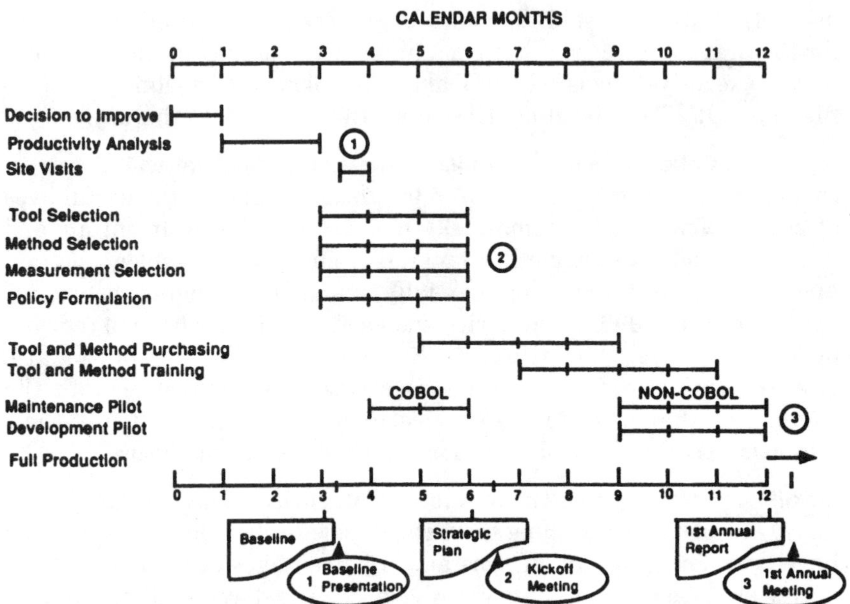

Figure 4.2 Chronological sequence of baseline analysis and follow-on improvements.

A baseline analysis is often followed by changes in policy, methodologies, tools, staffing patterns, measurements, expectations, or any combination of the above. To demonstrate how a productivity analysis fits in context with the other activities, Fig. 4.2 shows the normal sequences of events.

As can be seen, a baseline analysis is on the critical path to improving software productivity, but it must be followed by many other activities and events. Some of the activities, such as site visits and methodology selection, can occur fairly rapidly. Others, such as tool selection, require more extended analysis because capital investment of significant amounts may be required. The really long-term changes involve policies and organizational changes. It is seldom possible for a large company to introduce policy changes, such as dual salary plans, without many months of deliberation. Similarly, major organization changes, such as the creation of separate test or maintenance groups, will also require substantial time for deliberation.

What a Baseline Analysis Covers

A software baseline analysis explores essentially all of the soft and hard tactical factors that impact software development and maintenance: the project itself, the tools, the methodologies, morale and policy issues, languages, customer constraints, purchased software, training, and many other things. The following is an overview of the major topics and their significance.

Project factors. First to be covered for each project studied are the attributes of the project itself. Whether the project is a new effort or an enhancement or a modification to an existing program is a key item, since productivity rates for enhancements are dramatically lower than for new development. The scope of the project also is important; notably different results will accrue depending upon whether the project is a prototype, a stand-alone program, a component of a large system, or a large system itself.

Also significant at the project level are any constraints against the project by users or enterprise management, i.e., schedule constraints, budgetary constraints, staffing constraints, and the like. Severely constrained projects are likely to run into difficulties, and are also difficult to analyze because of the large proportion of unpaid overtime that is typical on constrained projects.

In the United States, most software professionals are exempt from overtime payments, and yet they work 48 to 52 h/week, which means that 8 to 12 h/week (20 to 30 percent) of the total project effort can be in the form of unpaid overtime. Unless this factor is explored and understood, productivity measurements cannot be accurate or meaningful. The impact of unpaid overtime is also significant in doing productivity comparisons internationally. In the United States, 40-h workweeks are the norm, but software professionals often work 48 to 52 h. In Japan, 44-h workweeks are the norm, but software professionals often work up to 60 h. In Canada, 35- to 37-h workweeks are the norm, but software professionals work 35 to 42 h. In any case, unpaid overtime is a major variable and must be analyzed.

Management factors. Achieving high productivity requires much more than just buying new tools and methods. The way employees are dealt with, the way morale issues are handled, and the way enterprises manage and organize software projects are very significant parameters. The software productivity analysis covers all of the critical managerial issues in depth. This portion of the baseline analysis may sometimes lead to the formulation of new policies and management practices.

Staff specialist factors. More than 100 occupations and specialist types are now identified in software projects: software engineers, systems analysts, quality assurance specialists, maintenance specialists, database administrators, and so on. The baseline analysis examines which specialist types are currently available within the enterprise and which additional specialists may be needed to meet the needs of future projects.

Physical environment factors. The availability of sufficient workspace for software development and maintenance staffs and the kinds of equipment and workstations installed are explored fully. Although few enterprises recognize the significance, the physical environment is one of the major determinants of software productivity.

Methodology factors. The word "methodology" covers a broad spectrum of methods, tools, and procedures applied to software projects. The methodology portion of the productivity analysis covers all procedures used by the enterprise for software, including the way requirements are developed, the specification and design methods used, the way documentation is handled, and all other methodological factors.

Package acquisition and modification factors. In many enterprises a significant percentage of applications is purchased from outside vendors. The baseline analysis explores enterprise methods for evaluating, acquiring, and modifying software packages. Package acquisition is often a productivity enhancement factor, but it can sometimes be a productivity reduction factor as well.

Programming language factors. With more than 500 languages available, most enterprises find it difficult to select a single language or a set of languages that is optimized for its needs. Part of the baseline analysis is to examine the future projects of the enterprise and diagnose the most effective language choices. The most appropriate languages can range across all generations. It is not accurate to prescribe fourth-generation languages exclusively, since they are not appropriate for many program and system types.

Defect removal and quality assurance factors. Eliminating bugs or defects is usually the most expensive single activity in the software world when all defect removal efforts are summed together. The baseline analysis also covers the methods and techniques used to find and remove errors: reviews, walk-throughs, inspections, all forms of testing, and proofs of correctness. For each project studied, the defect removal efficiency of the specific series of removal steps to be used is calculated. The overall effectiveness of enterprise defect removal is quantified as well. This portion of the productivity analysis often results in adoption of improved defect removal techniques.

Measurement and normalization factors. Most enterprises that commission a baseline analysis start with essentially no hard data at all on either productivity or quality. Therefore, a vital output from the analysis will be a solid benchmark of validated, hard productivity and quality data. The first baseline report will give most enterprises much better data than they have ever had or even knew was possible.

Standard design blueprints and reusable code. The baseline analysis explores whether or not standard designs, termed "blueprints," and reusable code would be appropriate technologies for the projects and enterprises studied. Reusability is one of the most effective technologies yet developed, but it is not applicable to all enterprises and project types.

Developing or Acquiring a Baseline Data Collection Instrument

Most of us have had complete physical examinations. In the course of the examination, we normally fill out a medical history form that runs to perhaps 10 pages and contains several hundred questions. A baseline measurement report is somewhat similar in logical content: It will be necessary to come to grips with several hundred factors, since software projects can be influenced by that many. This brings up an immediate need either to construct a data collection questionnaire or to acquire one from a commercial source. The questions used here to illustrate the concepts are taken from the proprietary CHECKPOINT® questionnaire developed by the author for Software Productivity Research for carrying out large-scale baseline studies.[3]

Regardless of its source, the data collection instrument must have these attributes: both hard data and soft data must be capable of statistical analysis. It is fairly straightforward to carry out statistical studies of the hard data, which is normally numeric in any case. The soft factors, on the other hand, present a special problem. Bear in mind that the soft factors are usually subjective things about which individuals may give widely differing responses. It is not sufficient to just ask for opinions, since the opinions cannot be analyzed statistically.

The approach which Software Productivity Research developed is to use multiple-choice questions built around a weighting scale, the software effectiveness level (SEL). The CHECKPOINT® questions that evaluate skill, experience, novelty, and so on, are based on the following rationale: They use a scale from 1 to 5, with 3 representing the approximate U.S. average. Numbers lower than 3 usually represent situations that are better than average; numbers higher than 3 usually represent situations that are hazardous or troublesome. The only exceptions to this rule are certain questions in which no risk or hazard at all is involved.

Consider the following question about project novelty as it occurs in the CHECKPOINT® questionnaire:

Project novelty?

1. Conversion or functional repeat of a well-known program
2. Functional repeat, but some new features
3. Even mixture of repeated and new features
4. Novel program, but with some well-understood features
5. Novel program, of a type never before attempted

It is easily seen that a 1 or 2 is less likely to be troublesome than a 4 or 5. The five possible answers somewhat resemble the Richter scale for earthquake magnitudes, in that as the numeric level of the answer goes up the potential for causing harmful situations also goes up.

The CHECKPOINT® questions are so organized that 3 represents the approximate U.S. average for the parameter in question. Thus, for the above novelty question an answer of 3, which means an even mixture of repeated and new features, is the approximate average for U.S. software. Since averages change over time, the SEL scale is recalibrated annually by Software Productivity Research.

To allow fine-tuning of client responses, the answers need not be integers, and up to two decimal places of precision can be used if desired. That is, answers such as 2.5 and 2.75 are perfectly valid and legitimate if the true situation falls between two points on the 5-point scale. Because the questionnaire is so set up that 3 represents the approximate U.S. average for most questions, it is relatively easy to evaluate projects by using the 5-point scale:

- Projects averaging less than 1.5 are generally at the very extreme leading edge of modern software methods and practices. (*Note:* This would be equivalent to a rating of 5 on the SEI maturity level scale.)
- Projects averaging between 1.5 and 2.5 are generally well ahead of norms in terms of methods and practices.
- Projects averaging between 2.5 and 3.5 are generally in the normal range in terms of methods and practices.
- Projects averaging between 3.5 and 4.5 are generally deficient in terms of methods and practices, and significant therapies may be indicated. (*Note:* This would be equivalent to a rating of 1 on the SEI maturity level scale.)
- Projects averaging more than 4.5 are generally so poorly equipped and are so backward in technology that they have a very high probability of being absolute failures that should be canceled.

Software Productivity Research carries out baseline studies as a standard consulting engagement, and it is interesting to see the strengths and weaknesses that occur with high frequency in the United States. Table 4.2 shows the 12 most common weaknesses and Table 4.3 the 12 most common strengths that were noted between 1990 and 1995.

TABLE 4.2 Most Common Software Weaknesses between 1990 and 1995 In the United States

1. Schedules set before project is defined
2. Excessive schedule pressure
3. Major requirements changes after the requirements phase
4. Inadequate project planning, tracking, measurement, and estimating methods
5. Inadequate pretest defect removal methods
6. Inadequate systems development methodology
7. Inadequate office space and poor environment
8. Inadequate training for management and staff
9. Inadequate support for reusable designs and code
10. Inadequate organizations and use of specialists
11. Too much emphasis on partial solutions such as the ISO 9000 standard or the SEI CMM
12. Attempting new technologies with inadequate training (00 methods, client-server projects, etc.)

TABLE 4.3 Most Common Software Strengths between 1990 and 1995 in the United States

1. Staff experience in the application area
2. Staff morale and cohesiveness
3. Staff experience with programming languages
4. Staff experience with support tools
5. Staff experience with computer hardware
6. Availability of workstations or terminals
7. Availability of support tools
8. Use of adequate testing methods
9. Use of project library control methods
10. Use of structured code methods
11. Usage of formal assessments
12. Usage of geriatric tools for aging legacy software

A cursory examination of the more common U.S. software weaknesses and strengths leads to the following conclusion: The problems are centered around managerial, sociological, environmental, and organizational issues. The strengths are centered around tool and technical staff skills.

There is a second form of multiple-choice question that also is useful for baseline analyses. In this second case, the 5-point rating scale is used to discover the opinions of the respondents about whether something ranges from excellent to very poor.

Figure 4.3 shows this technique for allowing managers and staff to evaluate how well they perform various kinds of defect removal operations.

Business and Legal Reviews	Excl		Avg		Poor
1 Patent or legal reviews	1	2	3	4	5
2 Import/export license reviews	1	2	3	4	5
Nontesting Defect Removal					
1 Joint application development (JAD)	1	2	3	4	5
2 Prototyping	1	2	3	4	5
3 Requirements review	1	2	3	4	5
4 Functional design review	1	2	3	4	5
5 Logic design review	1	2	3	4	5
6 Data structure design review	1	2	3	4	5
7 Module design review	1	2	3	4	5
8 User documentation review	1	2	3	4	5
9 Maintenance documentation review	1	2	3	4	5
10 Code review and inspection	1	2	3	4	5
11 Quality assurance review	1	2	3	4	5
12 Correctness proofs	1	2	3	4	5
13 Independent verification and validation	1	2	3	4	5
Testing Defect Removal					
1 Unit testing	1	2	3	4	5
2 New function testing	1	2	3	4	5
3 Regression testing					
4 Integration testing	1	2	3	4	5
5 Stress or performance testing	1	2	3	4	5
6 System testing	1	2	3	4	5
7 Field testing	1	2	3	4	5
8 User acceptance testing	1	2	3	4	5
9 Independent testing organization	1	2	3	4	5
Postrelease Defect Removal					
1 Error-prone module analysis	1	2	3	4	5
2 Automated restructuring	1	2	3	4	5
3 User satisfaction survey	1	2	3	4	5
4 Maintenance defect repair	1	2	3	4	5

Figure 4.3 Use of a 5-point scale for evaluating performance of multiple tasks.

Administering the Data Collection Questionnaire

A baseline analysis session is a sometimes intense and always candid exploration of the particular methods and tools used on a project. The participants in the session include the project manager or supervisor, one or more technical people from the project, and the consultant who is handling the analysis. From time to time, additional people may attend: quality assurance personnel, guests from other projects, and the like.

Each of the participants should have his or her own blank copy of the questionnaire, which is usually passed out about a week before the session begins but is sometimes passed out at the session itself. The participants may annotate their questionnaires if they wish. They can keep the questionnaires when the session is over, since the consultant administering the session keeps the master copy.

If, as in the case of the CHECKPOINT® questionnaire, the questions are in automated form, it is technically possible to enter the responses immediately into a computer and produce a report on the spot. Although desirable from one standpoint, the pragmatic result of having a computer in the room is not so good from a sociological standpoint. There is a tendency for the consultant who enters the data to get wrapped up in the mechanics of using the computer. There is also a certain unconscious intimidation attached to having the computer present which may discourage free conversation. On the whole, it seems preferable to use paper questionnaires for the sessions themselves and produce computerized versions later.

Some of the questions on the baseline questionnaire are general and deal with global enterprise issues, but more than two-thirds of them are quite specific and deal with individual tactical project attributes. Consultants are cautioned not to try to handle multiple projects simultaneously in workshop mode. That has occasionally been done, but the results are unsatisfactory for these reasons: (1) The large number of people in the room leads to side conversations and distractions. (2) It is difficult to keep the focus on any single project. (3) It is easy to mix up responses and make mistakes in filling out the master copy of the questionnaires.

The time allotted to a productivity analysis session is typically 3.5 h, although sessions are sometimes completed in 2 h or less and they may sometimes run as high as 6 h. If a single consultant is administering the sessions, then two sessions a day can usually be handled. The sessions are usually interesting to all concerned, and sometimes they are even enjoyable. They encourage both management and technical personnel to see that their problems and issues are being taken seriously, and the nature of the questionnaire and topics leads to very frank discussions of significant matters. Consultants and clients alike will learn a great deal from the productivity analysis sessions. The following are section-by-section discussions of a baseline questionnaire and the kinds of issues that are likely to come up during a productivity analysis session.

Recording the basic project identity

The first items to be recorded are the basic identities of the project and the participants:

- Security level
- Name and location of the company
- Name of the project
- Names, phone numbers, and locations of all of the participants in the session
- Date of the session
- Start date of the project (if known)
- Current status of the project (i.e., completed, canceled, or partially completed)
- Comments or free-form information

A small but important point is very significant: security level. Unless the client gives specific written permission, the data collected during a baseline analysis is normally confidential and cannot be distributed to anyone. Indeed, a nondisclosure agreement should accompany such a study if external consultants are used. For military and defense projects, even more stringent security may be required. Be sure to note the security requirements for the project being analyzed in order to protect confidentiality. For military projects, the security level should be applied to each page.

If the questionnaire is acquired from a management consulting group such as Software Productivity Research, it may ask about the optional standard industry classification or SIC code for the enterprise. This can, of course, be omitted for single-company internal studies. The U.S. Department of Commerce has developed a coding scheme for all major industries and service companies as an aid in producing statistical reports. The SIC code is included for large-scale multiclient studies to identify the industry of the clients and to aid in concealing the identity of the specific companies that participated. The remainder of the information simply serves to give a context to the study: who was present, who performed the interviews, when the interviews took place, and so forth.

Project natures, scopes, classes, and types

An annual baseline for a large company will deal with a highly heterogeneous set of projects: new projects, enhancements, prototypes, programs, systems, MIS, military, batch, on-line, and so on, are likely to be present.

It is absolutely necessary to record the specifics of the individual projects included. Software Productivity Research has developed a taxonomy for dealing with these factors which is shown in Fig. 4.4.

- The "nature" parameter identifies the five major flavors of software projects that are common throughout industry and which tend to have different cost and productivity profiles.
- The "scope" parameter covers the range of possibilities from disposable prototypes through major systems.
- Generally speaking, the "class" parameter is associated with the business aspects of a software project. Class determines the rigor and costs of project paperwork, and the volume of paperwork can be directly correlated to class number.
- The "type" parameter is significant in determining the difficulty and complexity of the code itself.

For statistical purposes, each of the 210 possible class-type combinations will have notably different productivity, quality, and skill "signatures" associated with them. Since the form of the questionnaire puts simple project attributes at the top and complicated attributes at the bottom, it is easy to predict (and easy to validate through measurement) that projects with low class-type numbers will be much more productive than those with high class-type numbers. And, indeed, projects of the class 1, type 1 form are the most productive in the United States and elsewhere. Projects of class 15 type 14 are the least productive in both the United States and elsewhere.

Fifteen classes are identified; they range from personal software through military contract software. Classes 1 and 2 are for personal software developed informally; class 3 is for software developed in an academic environment such as a university; classes 4 through 6 are for software developed by enterprises for their own internal use; and classes 9 through 15 are for software that will be delivered to external users, such as contract software, bundled software, and licensed software. The reason for recording class is that there are dramatic differences in productivity, quality, and technologies from class to class.

Consider the documentation, for example, that might be created to support a simple Cobol application program. If the program is developed for internal use (class 4) it might require 20 different supporting

Project Classification

Project Nature? ____
1 New program development
2 Enhancement (new functions added to existing software)
3 Maintenance (defect repair to existing software)
4 Conversion or adaptation (migration to new platform)

Project Scope? ____
1 Disposable prototype
2 Evolutionary prototype
3 Module or subelement of a program
4 Reusable module or macro
5 Complete stand-alone program
6 Program(s) within a system
7 Major system (multiple linked programs or components)
8 Release (current version of an evolving system)

Release Number ____

Project Class? ____
1 Personal program, for private use
2 Personal program, to be used by others
3 Academic program, developed in an academic environment
4 Internal program, for use at a single location
5 Internal program, for use at a multiple location
6 Internal program, developed by external contractor
7 Internal program, with functions used via time sharing
8 Internal program, using military specifications
9 External program, to be put in public domain
10 External program, leased to users
11 External program, bundled with hardware
12 External program, unbundled and marketed commercially
13 External program, developed under commercial contract
14 External program, developed under government contract
15 External program, developed under military contract

Project Type? ____
1 Nonprocedural (generated, query, spreadsheet)
2 Batch applications program
3 Interactive applications program
4 Batch database applications program
5 Interactive database applications program
6 Scientific or mathematical program
7 Systems or support program
8 Communications or telecommunications program
9 Process control program
10 Embedded or real-time program
11 Graphics, animation, or image-processing program
12 Robotics, or mechanical automation program
13 Artificial intelligence program
14 Hybrid project (multiple types)

For Hybrid Projects:
Primary Type? ____ Secondary Type? ____

Figure 4.4 Recording project nature, scope, class, and type.

documents totaling perhaps 30 English words for every line of source code. If it were developed to be leased to external users, then it would probably require more than 50 supporting documents totaling almost 80 English words for every line of source code. If the program were developed for the U.S. Department of Defense under military specifications, it would require more than 100 supporting documents totaling almost 200 English words for every line of source code. In short, class is a significant parameter to consider when it comes to prescribing therapies for software problems.

The next question, project type, has 14 possibilities. The first 13 cover standard types such as batch and interactive applications and database programs. Type 14 is reserved for hybrid projects where more than a single type will be present in the same system. When this occurs, the primary and secondary types should be noted (and perhaps other types as well).

Project goals and constraints

When projects begin, management and staff will receive either explicit or implicit marching orders that they are asked to follow on the project. These goals and constraints should be recorded for each project included in a baseline analysis. There are many variations and flavors of goals and constraints, but the essential breakdown is simple:

1. Most projects are directed to adhere to tight schedules, and this becomes the major goal and constraint. These projects have a dreadful tendency to become disasters.
2. A few projects, such as mission-critical ones or those dealing with human life, are directed to achieve very high levels of quality and reliability.
3. Some projects are in the middle ground, and they receive no goals or constraints at all.
4. Some projects are back-burner types that are being done as fill-in between more significant projects.

Early on during the baseline analysis, the participants should discuss any goals or constraints levied against the project. This will normally generate lively discussions, and it will be the first sign that something useful is going to come out of the baseline measurement study.

Goals and constraints are critical productivity and quality issues, and consultants should be very sensitive to them. In real life, most projects start out handicapped by constraints established by client demands, managerial decrees, or some other extrinsic source. The most common, and also the most hazardous, constraints are those dealing with delivery schedules: More than 50 percent of all software projects in the United States have delivery dates established before the project requirements are fully defined!

The next most common set of constraints concerns staffing. Projects often have a locked staff and skill mix that cannot be extended but is clearly insufficient for the work at hand. A third set of constraints, to be dealt with later, concerns such technical constraints as performance, memory utilization, and disk space.

Staff availability and work-habit factors

One of the most important factors in coming to grips with productivity is that of establishing accurate corporate profiles of availability and work-hours. Staff availability questions ask whether project personnel have worked full time on the project or divided their time among multiple projects. The normal assumption is that personnel will be assigned to a project 100 percent of the time, but sometimes this assumption is not correct. If the answer is something other than 100 percent, the staff should estimate the percent of time assigned. It is also important to ascertain what percent of the project technical staff is exempt from overtime pay and will not generally be paid overtime. In the United States, most software professionals, except for junior, entry-level personnel, are exempt from overtime.

Your corporate accounting department can probably supply you with the average workday, workweek, and workyear for your company. You must be very thorough in exploring how much effort was applied to the software project being analyzed. These are important questions from a measurement view, and also from an estimating standpoint. The normal U.S. workweek is 40 h, yet software professionals frequently work in excess of 50-h weeks. Thus, 20 to 30 percent of all effort applied to a project can be in the form of unpaid overtime, a very significant factor.

It is well known from time-and-motion studies that the productive time on software projects is much lower than the normal 40-h accounting week. What is not so well known is that individual corporate cultures can make the productive week vary significantly. Therefore, capturing productive time is important. Table 4.4 shows a typical profile of work habits for knowledge workers in the United States.

Assuming that only 6 h/day is productive work and there are a practical 185 working days for actual tasks, the U.S. norm would seem to be 1110 h/year applied to knowledge work. If the 24 days of meetings are included, then another 144 h can be added to the total, bringing the total up to 1254 h of work per year. Now consider the work habits associated with critical software projects. Table 4.5 shows a software engineering workyear on a schedule-driven project.

TABLE 4.4 Distribution of Staff Time During a Calendar Year

Time use	Average days
Normal working days	185
Weekdays (Saturdays and Sundays)	104
Meeting days	24
Vacation days	15
Public holidays	10
Slack days between tasks	7
Sick days	7
Business travel days	5
Education days	5
Conferences	3
Total	365

TABLE 4.5 Distribution of Software Staff Time During Critical Schedule-Driven Projects

Time use	Average days
Normal working days	197
Saturdays worked	40
Sundays worked	20
Nonworking weekends	44
Meeting days	24
Vacation days worked	10
Vacation days taken	5
Public holidays worked	6
Public holidays taken	4
Slack days between tasks	0
Sick days	0
Business travel days	5
Education days	0
Conferences	3
Total	365

The total number of project workdays, exclusive of meetings, is now up to 273 and includes many Saturdays, Sundays, some public holidays, and so forth. The average number of productive hours worked per day can also climb from 6 to 8, and the number of hours actually at work can climb from 8 to 10 or more. Thus, the probable number of work-hours on a critical software project can total to 2184, or to 2376 if meetings are included. This number represents more than 196 percent difference in the annual hours applied between ordinary knowledge work and critical software projects.

Obviously, this factor must be explored and studied in depth for software baselines to be accurate! Unfortunately, most corporate project-tracking systems do not record unpaid overtime. Therefore, one critical part of the baseline interview sessions is to get the software project managers and teams to reconstruct, from their memories, the real quantity of time they spent on their projects. It cannot be overemphasized that unless it captures such factors as unpaid overtime, tracking system data is essentially worthless for serious economic studies, and it is critical for accuracy to use the memories of the project team members.

Other related issues include use of contract personnel on the project and whether or not project personnel were dividing their time among several projects or were working on the project being studied in full-time mode. For contract personnel it is significant to ask what percent of the project team was comprised of contract personnel. The number can range from 0 to 100 percent. This topic is significant for both productivity and quality purposes. Generally speaking, projects developed by contract personnel are often higher in productivity and are produced with shorter schedules than similar projects developed by full-time salaried employees. However, because of contract billing rates, the projects may cost more.

Inflation rates can be significant for long-term projects that may take a number of years to develop. For example, the ITT System/12 electronic switching system started in 1976 and was not delivered until 1983, or after 7 years in development. Plainly, inflation will be significant over that span of years. For small projects that will typically take less than a year to develop, inflation rates can be omitted.

Determining the Size of the Project to Be Measured

Whether you use function points, feature points, lines of code, or something else, you will need to determine the size of an application if productivity studies are to be meaningful. There are no U.S. or world standards for counting source code, and there are very few enterprise or local standards. (Refer to Appendix A for the Software Productivity Research source-code-counting rules.) Therefore, when carrying out the first baseline analysis within a company, size information will be somewhat difficult to ascertain.

For example, on one of the first internal studies of software productivity carried out by the author at IBM in 1973, it was discovered that the major IBM divisions and labs were using six widely different conventions for counting source code size, which led to apparent differences of more than 300 percent in how large any given program or system would appear, depending on which rules were used. From that discovery, IBM standardized its source-code-counting rules and even developed an internal tool that automatically counted source lines in a consistent manner. Today, both function points and feature points provide size data independent of lines of source code. However, even though function and feature points are less variable than source code, there are still uncertainties in determining size.

More than half a dozen commercial tools that are available, such as Battlemap, Pathview, Inspector, and ACT, which means analysis of complexity, are capable of counting source code statements. There are also several tools that can aid in the calculation of function points and feature points, but as of 1990 there are no tools that can automatically backfire function points directly from source code even though this is not an excessively difficult accomplishment.

An emerging set of new tools may soon be able to predict function point and feature point totals as a by-product of design, but such methods are still experimental. Also new are tools such as the DMR function point enumerator, which enters into dialogs with a project manager about the nature and characteristics of the project and creates a function point total as a by-product.

Even today, however, many and perhaps most companies have not yet adopted functional metrics, nor have they as yet established counting rules, nor have they acquired a counting tool. Therefore, be very careful with project sizing when carrying out your first baseline assessment.

When ITT began its first baseline assessment in 1980,[4] the ITT companies were reporting size in an astonishing variety of ways, including source lines with more than a dozen rule variations, object lines, bytes, and function points. The total range of variations, assuming one project had been counted under all possible rules, was more than an order of magnitude! It is easy to see why ITT established standard counting rules as an immediate by-product of the first baseline study.

If you use a commercial questionnaire such as CHECKPOINT®, it will contain counting rules for source code, function points, and feature points. Size determination is a major topic for productivity analysis purposes, and especially so for large-scale studies involving different labs, divisions, or companies where it is quite unlikely that the projects will obey the same conventions. It is mathematically possible to convert source code counting rules from any set of counting rules into any other arbitrary set, but you must know the rules before you can do so. You can also convert size easily between source code and functional

TABLE 4.6 Variations in Apparent Size of Software That Are Due to Alternative Methods for Counting Source Code

Method	Apparent size in source lines
New executable lines only	100
New executable lines + data definitions	170
New executable lines, data definitions, comments	220
New + reused executable lines	250
New + reused executable lines + data definitions	430
New + reused executable lines + data definitions + commentary lines	500

metrics by using the backfire method explained in Chap. 2. Table 4.6 illustrates some of the possible size variations based on how lines of code might be counted in PL/I for a typical business application.

It cannot be overemphasized that in the absence of local standards, any and all variations will be used. The variations are not malicious, nor are they attempts to puff up sizes to make productivity look artificially high. It simply happens that size determination is too complicated an issue to be left to chance.

Although function points and feature points do not have the wide range of uncertainty that has always been associated with lines of code, even here there are many possible variations. So long as function point and feature point counting involves human judgment, there must necessarily be uncertainty. Table 4.7 shows the approximate

TABLE 4.7 Range of Variation Associated with Functional Metrics

Method	Automation available	Range of variation ± %
IBM 1979	No	50
DeMarco bang metric (1982)	Yes	50
Rubin variation (1983)	Yes	50
IBM 1984	Yes	20
SPR 1985	Yes	15
SPR backfire (1986)	Yes	35
SPR feature points (1986)	Yes	25
British Mark 11 (1988)	No	40
Herron approximation (1989)	Yes	35
IFPUG 1990 (Version 1-2)	Yes	20
IFPUG 1993 (Version 3)	Yes	20
IFPUG 1995 (Version 4)	Yes	25

ranges associated with the major flavors of function point counting. The data in Table 4.7 is based on a very small number of trials and experiments by the author as well as on secondhand reports, and must be regarded as premature for serious benchmarks. Additional projects and additional trials are needed.

Although it is hardly a valid mathematical procedure to aggregate and average the variations of unlike techniques, the average range of the entire set of methods in Table 4.7 is about 35 percent. Without multiplying examples, it can be seen that determining the size of projects for baseline purposes is not a trivial task. It requires both considerable effort and serious attempts at validation.

Standard Project Charts of Accounts

A chart of accounts is really nothing more than a convenient set of buckets into which cost and resource data can be placed. It is surprising that our industry has run for almost 50 years without any national or international standards, and very few corporate standards, on this topic. In the absence of a standard chart of accounts, many companies accumulate software project costs into a single cost bucket. Unfortunately, such an amorphous lump of data is worthless for serious economic studies because there is no way of validating it. The following sample illustrates the kinds of partial data that many companies have to utilize because they have no better:

Project	Schedule	Effort	Staff	Cost
Billing system	18 months	2000 h	3	$60,000

Note the missing elements in the above example: How much time was devoted to any particular task? What was the breakdown of the 2000-h total? Were there any missing tasks? What were the three staff members doing? There is no way to validate such amorphous data. Even worse, there is no way to gain insight from such data, which is the main purpose of measurement. The absolute minimum for a chart of accounts to have any value at all is five tasks and a total. Table 4.8 illustrates a minimal chart of accounts and the data elements to be recorded. Artificial data is inserted simply to give the chart the appearance of a completed one.

At least with a five-bucket chart of accounts, the tasks and the nature of the project begin to take on some semblance of reality. But five elements is by no means granular enough for real insight.

TABLE 4.8 Minimal Chart of Accounts for Software Projects

	Schedule, months	Effort, months	Staff	Cost, $
1. Requirements	1	1	1	5,000
2. Design	1	1	1	5,000
3. Code development	3	3	1	15,000
4. Integration and test	2	2	1	10,000
5. Project management	—	2	1	10,000
Project total	7	9	1.3	45,000

The CHECKPOINT® standard chart of accounts, illustrated in Chaps. 1 and 2, includes 25 development activities and a total, and it can be used for all current classes and types of software: civilian and military projects, large systems and small programs, new projects and enhancements, and so on.

That there are 25 tasks in a chart of accounts does not imply that every project performs all tasks. The set of 25 tasks is merely the smallest set that can be applied more or less universally. A good chart of accounts is revealing not only as a data collection tool but also as identifying tasks that should have been performed for a project but were not. For example, Table 4.9 illustrates the set of tasks performed for a PBX software project by a telecommunications company. It is based on interviews with the manager and staff.

TABLE 4.9 Chart of Accounts for a PBX System Software Project

	Schedule, months	Effort, months	Staff	Cost, $
1. Requirements	2	4	2.0	20,000
2. Initial design	2	6	3.0	30,000
3. Detail design	2	10	5.0	50,000
4. Code development	4	20	5.0	100,000
5. Unit test	1	5	5.0	25,000
6. Function test	2	10	5.0	50,000
7. Integration	2	2	1.0	10,000
8. System test	3	15	5.0	75,000
9. User documentation	3	6	2.0	15,000
10. Installation	1	3	3.0	15,000
11. Project management	—	15	1.0	75,000
Total project	22	96	4.4	480,000

Table 4.7 may appear to be reasonably complete and, indeed, useful, but it is highly significant that the following tasks which are useful for PBX software were not performed:

Prototyping

Project planning

Reusable code acquisition

Design reviews and inspections

Code reviews and inspections

Configuration control

Quality assurance

The project in question was one that overran its budget by more than 40 percent and its schedule by more than 6 months. It quickly became obvious when looking at the tasks performed vs. what would be normal for such applications that the project had been in rush mode since it started, and the attempts to shortcut it by skipping quality control development practices led to disaster. Specifically, skimping on quality control and rushing to start coding paved the way to major delays later, when it was discovered during test that the project had so many bugs that it could not work under normal operating conditions.

Note that exploration of factors which cause success or failure is possible when a granular chart of accounts is used, but it remains outside the scope of analysis when measures are less precise.

The most useful kind of chart of accounts is one which is derived from the full work breakdown structure of the project being explored. In developing such a chart of accounts, it is significant to consider whether a single level of detail is desired or a multilevel "exploding" chart of accounts is to be used. In a single-level chart of accounts, all costs are accumulated against a small set of cost buckets. Single-level charts of accounts are easy to develop and are not burdensome to use, but they are somewhat coarse in terms of data precision. The following is an example of a single-level chart of accounts for six activities:

1. Requirements
2. Design
3. Coding
4. Documentation
5. Testing
6. Management

In multilevel charts of accounts, costs are accumulated against a variety of fairly granular "buckets" and then summarized upward to create higher levels of cost accumulation. Multilevel charts of accounts are the normal mode for accurate cost accounting, but they require more effort to establish and are somewhat more burdensome in day-to-day use. The following is an example of a multilevel chart of accounts which expands on the preceding example:

1. Requirements
   1.1. Preliminary discussion
   1.2. Joint application design
   1.3. Requirements preparation
2. Design
   2.1. Initial functional design
   2.2. Initial data flow design
   2.3. Detailed functional design
   2.4. Detailed logic design
   2.5. Design reviews
3. Coding
   3.1. New code development
   3.2. Reusable code acquisition
   3.3. Desk checking
   3.4. Code inspections
4. Documentation
   4.1. Writing introduction
   4.2. Writing user's guide
   4.3. Writing operator's guide
   4.4. Writing maintenance manual
   4.5. Document editing
   4.6. Document printing
5. Testing
   5.1. Test planning
   5.2. Unit test
   5.3. Function test
   5.4. System test
   5.5. Acceptance test
6. Management
   6.1. Project planning and estimating
   6.2. Project milestone tracking
   6.3. Project reviews
   6.4. Project personnel management

There is no theoretical limit to the number of levels that can be used in a multilevel chart of accounts. In practice, more than 3 levels and more than about 200 subordinate tasks tend to become rather complicated. There are, of course, many commercial project management tools that can handle thousands of tasks, and large projects will normally utilize them.

It should be kept in mind that an appropriate level of granularity is one which provides meaningful information to project managers and the team itself. Data that is too coarse cannot lead to insights; data that is too granular will discourage both managers and staff alike because of the difficulty of recording the necessary information.

Identifying Occupation Groups and Staff Specialists

Now that software is becoming a full-fledged professional undertaking, many specialists are starting to become necessary for success. Just as medical practice has long been segmented into specialist areas, such as general practice, psychiatry, and neurosurgery, software is also starting to create special skill areas.

There are currently some 100 recognizable specialist skills in the area of software development and maintenance: application programmers, system programmers, database programmers, maintenance specialists, and so on. Small applications are usually done by individual programmers or software engineers; large applications not only require perhaps hundreds of workers but may also involve over dozens or even all 40 or so of the different occupation groups! Table 4.10 shows the numbers and kinds of the 10 most common software occupations typically engaged on business software applications of various sizes.

TABLE 4.10 Software Occupation Groups Related to Software Size

Staffing profile	Small projects	Medium-size projects	Large projects
Project managers	1	2	25
Systems analysts	3	25	
Application programmers	1	5	100
System programmers	1	10	
Project librarians	1	5	
Technical writers		1	20
Database administrators		1	5
Quality assurance		1	5
Test specialists			10
Performance specialists			5
Total staff	2	15	210

The significance of this section varies with the overall size of the enterprise being analyzed. As general rules of thumb, the following are the kinds of specialists usually found in various sizes of enterprises.

Small software staffs of fewer than 10 employees. Small shops typically run on the generalist principle, with dual-purpose programmer-analysts being the most widely encountered occupation group. When specialization does occur, it usually consists of segmenting the analysis work from the programming work and sometimes segmenting applications programming from systems programming.

Medium software staffs with 10 to 100 employees. When enterprises grow from small to medium, an increase in specialists is usually noted: Database programmers, sometimes network or communication programmers, and a definite split between system and application programming are frequent attributes.

Large software staffs with 100 to 1000 employees. Large enterprises enjoy the luxury of many specialists that smaller enterprises can seldom afford: professional writers for documentation, test specialists, maintenance specialists, tool and support specialists, and the like. From a productivity analysis point of view, large enterprises that do *not* have full specialization are candidates for staff structure improvements.

Very large software staffs with more than 1000 employees. Very large enterprises usually have all 100 of the major specialist types and sometimes other types unique to their own businesses as well. Very large organizations that do not have maintenance specialists, test specialists, documentation specialists, and so on, are candidates for staffing upgrades.

Superlarge software staffs with more than 10,000 employees. At the extreme end of the scale will be found enterprises such as AT&T, IBM, the Department of Defense, and a few other organizations with more than 10,000 software employees overall. The norm here is not only for full specialization but for planned organizations built around the needs of the specialists. The adoption of full specialization and the supporting apparatus for them is one way to explain the phenomenon that productivity rates may be higher at the extremely large end than in the middle, in terms of staff sizes.

The hazards of generalists. in specialist situations. In all human situations, so far as can be determined, specialists tend to outperform generalists. It is certainly true that in knowledge work the advance from amateur to professional status is marked by such an enormous increase in the knowledge content that one person can no longer absorb

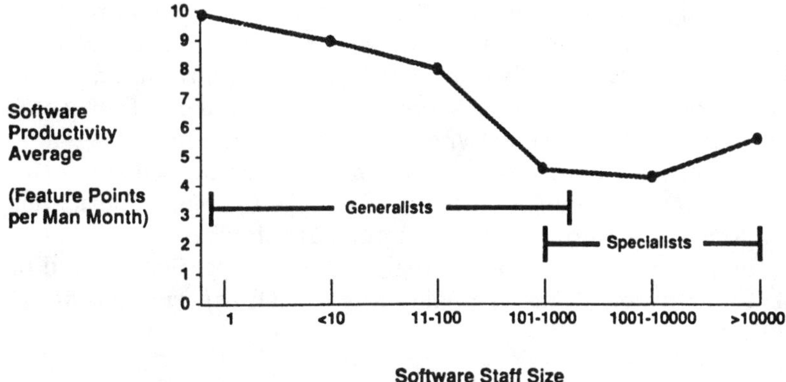

Figure 4.5 U.S. software productivity and total staff size.

all of it, and so specialization is a necessary adjunct to the growth of a profession. Consider the number of medical and legal specialties, for example.

As for software, this phenomenon has only started to be explored and measured. Figure 4.5 gives the results to date. As can be seen, enterprise software productivity rates sag notably as the number of members on a professional staff begins to climb. In really large companies, however, the rate starts to climb again. One of the main reasons for that climb is that really large companies, such as IBM, Hewlett-Packard, and ITT, have gone beyond generalists and have moved toward full specialization and the organizations needed to support specialists.

Staff Skill and Personnel Variables

Psychologists who have studied software success patterns, such as Curtis,[5] Schneiderman,[6] and Weinberg,[7] agree that experience is correlated with both productivity and quality. Breadth of experience is more important than length of time, incidentally.

Of all the variables known to affect software, "individual human variation" has the greatest known impact. In controlled studies, in which eight programmers were asked to develop identical applications, the participants varied by more than 20 to 1 in productivity and by more than 10 to 1 in errors.

Yet this variable is difficult to capture and evaluate, and it is one of the most subjective of all soft factors. Not only is the factor subjective, but it must be measured carefully to avoid injustice to the people themselves. One of the chronic problems of personnel management is a phenomenon termed "appraisal skew," which means that managers tend to habitually appraise staff in accordance with their personal patterns rather than objective facts. Some managers consistently appraise high; others consistently appraise low. (As a young programmer, one of the first serious programming tasks performed by the author was a project to measure appraisal skew of a large government agency.) Multinational companies must use extreme caution in measuring this parameter, since it is illegal in parts of Europe to record information about a worker's performance in a computerized database.

For the purposes of a baseline analysis, staff experience should be noted. There are eight major breakdowns of staff experience that are significant:

1. Experience in the application area
2. Experience with tools
3. Experience with methods
4. Experience with analysis and design
5. Experience with languages
6. Experience with reviews and inspections
7. Experience with testing techniques
8. Experience with the development hardware

Not only is staff experience significant, but, surprisingly, user experience and user cooperation provide two of the stronger positive correlations with productivity. There are three major user experience topics that should be recorded:

1. User experience with software in general
2. User experience with automation in his or her job area
3. User experience as a participant in software projects

Management Project and Personnel Variables

Management topics are among the most sensitive and important sets of questions in the entire baseline analysis. The questions in this section should explore the fundamental policy and morale issues of the enterprise as well as the specific management environment for the project being analyzed. Most enterprises are highly political internally. Managerial power struggles, disputes, and dislikes can be very significant productivity parameters. Major projects are sometimes canceled or significantly thrown off track because key managers are fighting about goals, methods, or status.

From a productivity improvement standpoint, the problems and issues which the managerial section can highlight are very difficult to treat or cure. Making changes in personnel and morale policies is outside the scope of authority of most software and data processing managers. Nonetheless, the managerial section is a critical one which will give both clients and consultants significant insights into enterprise cultural attributes.

Some of the topics to be explored in dealing with management issues include:

1. Management agreement or disagreement on project goals
2. Management authority to acquire tools or change methods
3. Management planning and estimating capabilities
4. Management commitment to quality or schedule constraints
5. The impact of corporate politics on the project

Of all of the factors which management can influence, and which management tends to be influenced by, schedule pressures stand out as the most significant. Some schedule pressure can actually benefit morale, but excessive or irrational schedules are probably the single most destructive influence in all of software. Not only do irrational schedules tend to kill the projects, but they cause extraordinarily high voluntary turnover among staff members. Even worse, the turnover tends to be greatest among the most capable personnel with the highest appraisals. Figure 4.6 illustrates the results of schedule pressure on staff morale.

It should be noted in conclusion that management has a much greater impact on both companies and projects than almost any other measured phenomenon. The leading-edge companies that know this, such as IBM, tend to go to extraordinary lengths to select managers carefully and to provide them with adequate training and support once they have been selected. Such companies are also careful to monitor manager performance and to find other work should a manager lack all of the attributes of successful management. Indeed, reverse appraisals in which staff members assess managers as well as management appraising staff members are utilized by leading-edge enterprises as part of their programs to ensure high management capabilities. A baseline study is not a direct tool for studying management capabilities, but those who have carried out baseline studies realize that it will point out strengths and weaknesses in this area.

Project Attribute Variables

The term "attribute" includes the impact of the physical office space for the software team and also the impacts of the workstations, tools, and methodologies in current use. Most of the attribute questions are

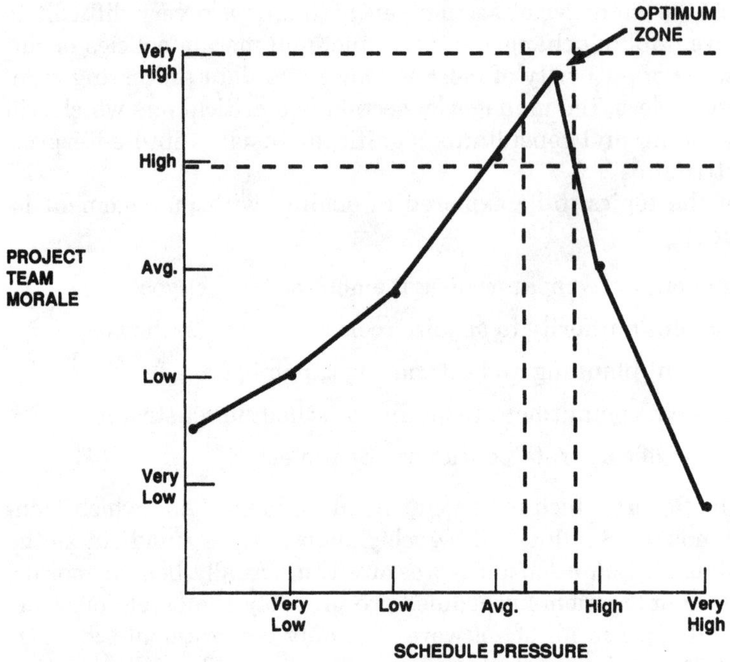

Figure 4.6 The impact of schedule pressure on staff morale.

reasonably self-explanatory, but the significance of the answers varies considerably. The most obvious kinds of attribute topics are concerned with the available tools and methods which the project team can use:

1. Requirements methods
2. Design methods and tools
3. Formal or informal system development methodologies
4. Formal or informal standards
5. Integration methods (discrete, continuous, etc.)

In recent studies such as those of Tom DeMarco and Tim Lister,[8] some unexpected findings and conclusions regarding the physical environment itself have turned up.

In a large-scale study involving more than 300 programmers, the DeMarco-Lister research noted the surprising finding that the programmers in the high quartile for productivity had office space that was approximately double the space available for programmers in the low quartile (more than 78 vs. 44 ft^2). In an older but even larger study by Gerald McCue[9] that was commissioned by IBM and involved more than 1000 programmers at the Santa Teresa Programming

Center, the physical environment with all programmers having 10-by-10 ft private offices resulted in productivity rates some 11 percent higher than the same personnel had achieved in their previous office buildings, which had 8-by-10-ft cubicles shared by two programmers.

These are significant and even poignant findings: Because of the rapid growth of numbers of computer professionals in most enterprises, lack of space is a national problem. Most companies allot scarcely more than 50 ft^2 of noisy space to their software professionals, with very unsatisfactory results. Unfortunately, physical space is one of the most expensive and difficult problems to solve. Poor available space is not quite an incurable problem, but it is among the most difficult problems in the industry.

Another aspect of environment is that of available computer resources and the impact of computer response time on development productivity. Thadani of IBM[10] explored this, and he concluded that slow response times (>1 s) exerted a disproportionate loss in productivity because programmers tended to lose concentration and drift off for several additional seconds before recovering their train of thought. All physical, social, and technological aspects of the environment should be explored as part of the baseline analysis. If a commercial-grade questionnaire is used, such as the CHECKPOINT® questionnaire, more than 50 environmental factors will be included.

From studying the environments of several hundred companies and government agencies in the United States, Canada, England, Australia, Europe, and Asia, quite a large number of chronic environmental and methodological problems have been noted. They appear to be endemic around the world.

- Requirements methodologies are deficient in more than 75 percent of all enterprises.
- Use of prototyping is starting to increase, but more than 85 percent of enterprises do not use prototype methods.
- Software design automation is almost totally lacking in more than 50 percent of all enterprises, and it is inadequate in more than 75 percent of all enterprises.
- Software documentation methods are inadequate in more than 85 percent of all enterprises.
- Office space and physical environment are inadequate in more than 80 percent of all enterprises.
- Management tools (estimating, tracking, planning) are inadequate in more than 60 percent of all enterprises.
- Software measurements are inadequate in more than 90 percent of all enterprises.

- Software defect removal methods are inadequate in more than 80 percent of all enterprises.

Consultants and clients should keep in mind that a baseline analysis is a diagnostic technique which will find environmental problems but will not cure them. The cures will come from upgrading the environmental deficiencies.

Yet another aspect of the environment to be considered is the sociological aspect. In this case, topics to be explored are whether the organization reacts positively or negatively to change and how long it might take to carry out some of the following changes:

- Introduce a new methodology such as inspections or JAD sessions.
- Acquire new tools such as workstations.
- Create a new department such as a quality assurance group, a measurement group, or a development center.
- React to competitive situations.

Surprising contradictions sometimes occur when sociological issues are explored. For example, in the early 1980s the stated goal of the ITT chairman was to improve software productivity rapidly. However, the executive charged with that task discovered that the purchase of a new tool required an average of eight approval signatures and more than 6 months of calendar time! Before it was possible to make rapid progress in software technologies, it was necessary to examine and streamline the purchasing process.

The topics of both bureaucratic friction and of change facilitation are normal parts of a baseline analysis. These topics are also supported by a substantial body of literature that deals not only with software but with other areas of human endeavor. Since the natural human response to new ideas is to reject them until someone else has proved that they work, this topic is quite significant.

Contract Project Variables (Optional)

In a baseline analysis, contract projects should be included if the company or agency utilizes contract personnel in any significant quantity. The questions that might be asked about contract projects are optional, and they are used only when the baseline analysis is actually studying a project which is being developed by a contracting organization. Contract software generally encompasses five different contractual arrangements:

1. Contracts with private individuals on a work-for-hire basis.

2. Contracts with consulting organizations for staff and services on site at the client locations.
3. Contracts with software houses or consulting organizations for custom packages: The work is performed at the contractor's location.
4. Contracts with civilian government agencies at local, state, or national levels.
5. Contracts with military services or the Department of Defense.

Each of these has different pros and cons, legal obligations, and the like.

Contract work can be surprisingly effective. A proprietary study of New England banking applications carried out by the author noted that contract projects averaged about twice the productivity, in function points per staff-month, of projects the same size and class developed by employees of the banks. There were four reasons for this phenomenon: (1) The banks were more careful in defining requirements with contractors than with their own staff; (2) the contractors were fairly experienced in the applications; (3) the contractors had access to reusable code from similar applications; and (4) the contractors worked substantial amounts of overtime that was not billed back to the clients.

Software Package Acquisition (Optional)

Software packages and acquired software are definitely mainstream topics for a baseline analysis. When ITT carried out its initial baseline in the early 1980s,[4] the team was surprised to discover that out of some 65,000 source code statements (equivalent to about 520,000 function points) some 26 percent of the total software owned by ITT had been acquired from vendors rather than developed by ITT personnel.

The questions about packages are optional, and they are used only when the baseline analysis is studying a project that included or was based on a purchased package. In real life, purchasing packages is often a cost-effective way to get functions into production rapidly. Indeed, in terms of function points delivered per unit of effort, packages exceed all other forms in overall productivity. Depending upon the size and evaluation concerned, productivity rates in excess of 1000 function points per staff-month are possible for packages. Cost per function point, on the other hand, may or may not be as favorable.

One major caution regarding packages should never be ignored: Package modification is a high-risk activity with a significant chance of failure and disaster. Not only is productivity normally low for modifying purchased packages, but if the vendors are reluctant to provide support, modification can easily be more expensive than custom development. As a rule of thumb, package modification is feasible only if the vendor is cooperative and supportive and if the package is well structured and well documented. Even then, changes that equal more than about 15 percent of the volume of the original software should be avoided. For older packages, poorly structured packages, and those for which vendor cooperation is minimal or even hostile, changes of more than 5 percent should be avoided. Indeed, searching for a second vendor or a more modern package should be considered.

Software Defect Removal Methods

Since software defect removal methods were inadequate in about 80 percent of all enterprises in 1990, a baseline analysis nearly always results in recommendations to upgrade defect removal methods via inspections, increased quality assurance funding, modernizing, testing, and the like.

A baseline analysis is not the only method for actually measuring quality, since it can take more than a year to accumulate enough quality data to calibrate defect removal efficiency. (Chapter 5 discusses the techniques for quality and user satisfaction measurement.) However, baseline analysis can and should provide context and background information on these topics:

1. Does the company really care about quality?
2. Are defect prevention methods adequate?
3. Are defect removal methods adequate?
4. Is a formal quality assurance organization in existence?
5. Is the quality assurance organization properly staffed and missioned?
6. Does the company measure quality numerically?
7. Are there any numeric quality targets for executives?

There are very significant differences in the kinds of defect removal activities practiced by companies on internal software, by vendors of commercial software, and by companies that work with the Department of Defense under military specifications. Defect removal for internal software is almost universally inadequate. Typically, enterprises use only perfunctory design reviews, no code inspections at all, no quality assurance, and a minimal test series that includes a unit test, function test, and customer acceptance test. The cumulative defect removal efficiency of the whole series seldom goes above 80 percent, which is why it takes a long time for most internal production software to stabilize: 20 percent of the bugs are still in it.

Defect removal for commercial software, at least that sold by major vendors such as IBM, is significantly more thorough than for internal software. Vendors usually have a formal quality assurance review, design and code inspections, and in many cases a separate test department. The test series for commercial software starts with unit testing and includes regression testing, system testing, and field testing with early customers. Typical defect removal efficiencies for commercial software run from 90 to 96 percent.

Defect removal for Department of Defense (DOD) software under military specifications is similar to that for commercial software, but it includes several activities unique to the DOD environment: independent validation and verification by an outside source, and independent testing by an outside source. Although DOD and military specification requirements add significantly to costs, there is no hard evidence that DOD software has either higher overall defect removal efficiencies or higher reliability than commercial software. Neither the DOD itself nor most contractors measure defect removal efficiency as a general rule, but the few that do seem to be about the same or slightly higher in efficiency than commercial houses: perhaps 85 to 95 percent cumulative efficiency. The baseline analysis methodology concentrates very heavily on defect prevention and removal methods for very pragmatic reasons:

1. Defect removal is often the most expensive single software activity.
2. It is not possible to make significant improvements in software productivity without first improving software quality.

An internal study within IBM in 1975 noted the impact of quality on productivity for marketed commercial software products. The study revealed that the products with the highest quality after delivery had also achieved the highest development productivity. This study was surprising at the time, but when the economics of the situation were explored, the results were easily predictable. Projects that paid attention to quality did not get hung up during integration and test, nor did they receive negative evaluations from the IBM quality assurance organizations. Such findings are in the public domain today, but in spite of that fact, very few companies really understand the linkage between quality and productivity.

Software Documentation Variables

There are 10 general classes of documentation that should be studied as part of a baseline analysis, and more than 100 different kinds of documents can be produced in support of software. Software is astonishingly paper-intensive: For software projects developed under military specifications and a DOD contract, paperwork will be the most expensive part of the project. DOD contract projects often generate more than 200 English words for every line of source code, and paperwork production can hit peaks of 60 percent of the entire project costs.

For commercial software produced by major vendors such as IBM, DEC, Hewlett-Packard, Raytheon, TRW, and Grumman, paperwork will usually be the second most expensive activity ranking just after defect removal. Here too, however, the costs are a significant proportion of overall expenses. Commercial software will typically generate around 75 English words for every line of source code, and paperwork costs can amount to 40 percent of the total project.

For internal software and information systems, paperwork can be significant, but nothing nearly as dramatic as the two preceding cases. Typically, in-house information systems will generate about 30 English words for every line of source code, and perhaps 25 to 30 percent of the total project costs will be devoted to paperwork.

Although paperwork costs are always in the top three expense categories for software, and often are number 1, most companies are totally unaware of the significance of this cost element. Baseline analyses carried out in computer companies and defense contractor environments almost always shock the managers and executives when they discover that 30 to 60 percent of their total software costs go to paperwork and less than 15 percent goes to coding. The 10 major classes of paperwork to be included in a baseline analysis include:

1. Planning documents
   - Development plans
   - Business plans

2. Business and financial documents
   - Requests for proposals (RFPs)
   - Cost estimates
   - Budgets
   - Capital expenditure requests

3. Control documents
   - Milestone reports
   - Monthly progress reports
   - Budget variance reports

4. Technical documents
   - Requirements
   - Initial functional specifications
   - Final functional specifications
   - Module design specifications

5. On-line documents
   - Help screens
   - Readme files
   - Hypertext links

6. User-oriented documents
   - Reference manuals
   - User's guides
   - Systems programmer's guides
   - Maintenance manuals

7. Tutorial documents
   - Introductions
   - Course materials

8. Marketing documents
   - Sales brochures
   - Advertisements

9. Quality and defect removal documents
   - Inspection reports
   - Quality assurance reports
   - Audit reports
   - Test reports
   - User bug reports

10. Correspondence and miscellaneous documents
    - Letters
    - Staff résumés
    - 35-mm slides
    - Overheads

One of the newer and very promising applications of the function point technique is the ability to predict and measure the volume of software paperwork: a task obviously beyond the capabilities of lines of code. Table 4.11 shows the use of function points for quantifying the volume of documents measured for a large commercial database product produced by a major computer company.

Maintenance and Enhancement Project Variables

The word "maintenance" is ambiguous in the software industry as of 1996, and it can mean either defect repairs of or the addition of new functions and enhancements to a software product. Not only that, but

TABLE 4.11 Normalized Volumes of Paperwork for a Commercial Software Package

Documents	Pages per function point	Pages per function point	Words per function point
Planning	0.275	0.188	113
Business	0.138	0.000	38
Control	0.188	0.000	80
Technical	7.125	1.250	2,250
On-line	1.500	0.750	125
User-oriented	6.250	1.875	2,188
Tutorial	1.250	1.250	625
Marketing	0.063	0.123	63
Quality control	15.000	0.313	3,750
Correspondence	2.500	0.625	1,250
Totals	34.300	6.375	10,450

for commercial software producers such as IBM, DEC, and Hewlett-Packard, "maintenance" can include delivery support, field service, hot-line support, and several other activities not usually found associated with internal software.

A baseline analysis will have quite a wide variance in scope for the maintenance area, depending on whether the client enterprise has commissioned the study for internal software, for commercial software, or for military software. In a baseline analysis, enhancements are generally treated as equivalent to new development and are studied as such, although their "hard" data should be broken out and shown separately because productivity rates for enhancements are quite different from new development. Specific maintenance questions should be included to cover defect repairs and the special considerations for commercial software, such as customer support and field service.

It is interesting that enhancement productivity follows a curve totally different from that for new projects. Enhancement productivity peaks, for example, when the size of the change is roughly 3 to 5 percent of the size of the system being modified. Smaller changes have high overhead costs associated with recompiling and regression testing, so productivity is low. Larger changes normally tend to damage the structure of the original system, so again productivity is low. Both enhancement and maintenance productivity are very sensitive to the structure of the base code being updated: Modifying well-structured code is more than twice as productive as modifying older unstructured software.

For maintenance or defect repairs of commercial software, totally new factors appear. Examples are "invalid" defect reports in which users report faults that in fact are caused by something other than the software itself, "duplicates" whereby several users report the same bug, and "abeyancies" whereby a problem found by a user cannot be replicated at the system repair center. The baseline analysis methodology should cover all of those aspects, but it varies significantly with the kind of software and client enterprise being analyzed.

A critical phenomenon often occurs when an industry approaches 50 years of age: It takes more workers to perform maintenance than it does to build new products. For example, by the time automotive production was 50 years of age, there were many more mechanics in the United States repairing automobiles than there were workers in Detroit and elsewhere building new cars.

Software will soon be 50 years of age, and we appear to be following a similar trend. Table 4.12 shows the approximate numbers of world programmers working on development, enhancements, and maintenance from 1950 through 1990, with projections forward to 2000. The data is partly empirical and partly extrapolation from client studies. The message of Table 4.12 is probably valid, but the reliability of the data itself is low.

Project Risk and Value Factors

A very important aspect of a baseline analysis is to try to come to grips with the value and also the risks of the projects that are included. Value and risks are opposite sides of a coin, so they should be studied simultaneously. The value factors to be explored include:

TABLE 4.12 Population of Development, Enhancement, and Maintenance Programmers at 10-year Intervals

Year	Programmers, new projects	Programmers, enhancement	Programmers, repairs	Total
1950	90	3	7	100
1960	8,500	500	1,000	10,000
1970	65,000	15,000	20,000	100,000
1980	1,200,000	600,000	200,000	2,000,000
1990	3,000,000	3,000,000	1,000,000	7,000,000
2000	4,000,000	4,500,000	1,500,000	10,000,000
2010	5,000,000	7,000,000	2,000,000	14,000,000
2020	7,000,000	11,000,000	3,000,000	21,000,000

1. Tangible value (cost reduction primarily)
2. Direct revenues (marketed software only)
3. Indirect revenues (hardware drag along)
4. Intangible value (enhanced capabilities, morale, etc.)
5. Competitive value

The risk factors to be explored include:

1. Risk of absolute failure or cancellation
2. Risk of excessive schedule pressure
3. Risk of unstable requirements
4. Risk of poor quality
5. Risk of inadequate staff or inadequate skills

Risk and value analyses are in rapid transition that should continue through the 1990s. The early forms of value analysis dealt only with tangible cost savings associated with software projects. It was realized during the 1980s that the strategic value of software was often greater than that of any other aspect, but the measurement of strategic value is a complex task. The most recent approach to measuring the value of software is to use function points and feature points to explore consumption patterns of software once the software is deployed. Risk analysis too is evolving, and we should see substantial progress. The Department of Defense is extremely interested in it, and so it will continue to be researched.

Complexity and Source Code Factors

Every project studied in a baseline analysis should be evaluated for complexity in at least three different forms: (1) the complexity of the underlying problem and algorithms, (2) the complexity of the source code, and (3) the complexity of the data and data structures. Although the questions that might be asked about complexity are usually self-explanatory, the implications of the answers are not. Software complexity analysis in 1990 is not an exact science. There are techniques, such as the McCabe cyclomatic complexity metric,[11] with which source code structural complexity can be measured.

The McCabe technique yields very useful insights and provides a good quantification of practical software complexity. Small well-structured programs with straight-line logic will have a "cyclomatic complexity" of 1; that is, they have no branching logic. Empirical studies reveal that programs with cyclomatic complexities of less than 5 are generally considered simple and easy to understand. Cyclomatic complexities of 10 or less are considered not too difficult. When the cyclomatic complexity is more than 20, the complexity is perceived as high. When the McCabe number exceeds 50, the software for practical purposes becomes untestable.

There are no measures at all of problem or algorithmic complexity, and empirical studies suggest that much of the observed complexity actually seen with source code is accidental or is caused by poorly trained programmers rather than by the problem itself. Data complexity is also generally unmeasured, although counting the entity types referenced by the program or system holds significant promise. (Entities are persons or objects whose attributes comprise the data the program is manipulating.)

One other gap in complexity theory also is notable: All of the complexity research on software to date has been based on new programs. There are no pragmatic studies on complexity when updating an existing system, although empirical evidence reveals that updates have perhaps 3 times the error potential of new code for equal volumes and that errors correlate with structure. When the major forms of complexity that affect software projects are considered, there are at least 20 of them. As of 1996, only about half of them have been measured objectively and numerically; the rest still await exploration. The 20 varieties of complexity include the following:

1. *Algorithmic complexity:* (deals with spatial complexity and algorithmic volumes). This form of complexity is one of the classic topics of software engineering. The basic concept is the length and structure of algorithms intended to solve various computable problems. Some algorithms are quite simple, such as one that finds the circumference of a circle, C = pi* diameter. Other problems, such as those involving random or nonlinear phenomena, may require extremely long algorithms. Problems with high complexity tend to be perceived as difficult by the humans engaged in trying to solve them. Examples of problems with high algorithmic complexity include radar tracking and target acquisition.

2. *Computational complexity:* (deals with chronological complexity and run time lengths). This form of complexity also is a classic topic of software engineering. The basic concern is the amount of computer time or the number of iterations required to solve a computational problem or execute an algorithm. Some forms of algorithms, such as those involving random or nonlinear phenomena, may require enormous amounts of computer time for solution. Examples of problems with high computational complexity include long-range weather prediction and cryptographic analysis.

3. *Informational complexity:* (deals with entities and relationships). This form of complexity has become significant with the rise of large database applications. The basic concern is with the kinds of entities about which information must be stored and with the relations among those entities. Examples of problems with high informational complexity include airline reservation systems, integrated manufacturing systems, and large inventory management systems.

4. *Data complexity:* (deals with numbers of entity attributes and relationships). This form of complexity, similar in concept to informational complexity, deals with the number of attributes that a single entity might have. For example, some of the attributes that might be used to describe a human being include sex, weight, height, date of birth, occupation, and marital status.

5. *Structural complexity:* (deals with patterns and connections). This form of complexity deals with the overall nature of structures. Highly ordered structures, such as crystals, are often low in complexity. Other forms of structure include networks, lists, fluids, relational data structures, planetary orbits, and atomic structures.

6. *Logical complexity:* (deals with combinations of AND/OR/NOR/NAND logic). This form of complexity deals with the kinds of logical operations that comprise syllogisms, statements, and assertions. It is much older than software engineering, but it has become relevant to software because there is a need for precise specification of software functions.

7. *Combinatorial complexity:* (deals with permutations and combinations). This form of complexity deals with the numbers of subsets and sets that can be assembled out of component parts. In any large software project, there are usually many different programs and components that require integration to complete the tasks of the application.

8. *Cyclomatic complexity:* (deals with nodes and edges of graphs). This form of complexity has been popularized by Tom McCabe. Its basic concern is with the graph formed by the control flow of an application. Unlike some of the other forms of complexity, this one can be quantified precisely. It is defined as the number of edges of a graph, minus the number of nodes, plus 2. Pragmatically, this is a significant metric for software, since modules or programs with high cyclomatic complexity are often difficult to maintain and tend to become error-prone.

9. *Essential complexity:* (deals with nodes and edges of reduced graphs). This form of complexity is similar in concept to cyclomatic complexity, but it deals with a graph after the graph has been simplified by the removal of redundant paths. Essential complexity has been popularized by Tom McCabe.

10. *Topologic complexity:* (deals with rotations and folding patterns). This form of complexity is explored widely by mathematicians

but seldom by software engineers. It deals with the various forms of rotation and folding that are permissible in a basic structure. The idea is relevant to software, since it can be applied to one of the intractable problems of software engineering: attempting to find the optimal structure for a large system.

11. *Harmonic complexity:* (deals with waveforms and Fourier transformations). This form of complexity is concerned with the various waveforms that together create an integrated wave pattern. The topic is very important in physics and engineering, but it is only just being explored by software engineers.

12. *Syntactic complexity:* (deals with grammatical structures of descriptions). This form of complexity deals with the structure and grammar of text passages. Although the field is more than 100 years old and is quite useful for software, it has seldom been utilized by software engineers. Its primary utility would be in looking at the observed complexity of specifications with a view to simplifying them for easier comprehension. It has a number of fairly precise quantifications, such as the FOG index and the Fleish index.

13. *Semantic complexity:* (deals with ambiguities and definitions of terms). This form of complexity is often a companion to syntactic complexity. It deals with the definitions of terms and the meaning of words and phrases. Unlike syntactic complexity, it is rather amorphous in its results.

14. *Mnemonic complexity:* (deals with factors affecting memorization). This form of complexity deals with the factors that cause topics to be easy or difficult to memorize. It is widely known that human memories have both a temporary and a permanent component. Memorization of text, verbal data, mathematics, and symbols normally involves temporary memory, which is quite limited in capacity. (A famous assertion holds that temporary memory can absorb only seven chunks of information at a time, plus or minus two.) Permanent memory is not fully understood, but it may involve some form of holographic distribution of engrams over the neural net of the brain. Visual data such as peoples' faces bypass temporary memory and are entered directly into permanent memory, which explains why it is easy to remember faces but not names.

15. *Perceptional complexity:* (deals with surfaces and edges). This form of complexity deals with the visual appearance of artifacts and whether they appear complex or simple to the human perceiver. Regular patterns, for example, tend to appear simpler than random configurations with the same number of elements.

16. *Flow complexity:* (deals with channels and fluid dynamics of processes). This form of complexity concerns fluid dynamics, and it is a major topic of physics, medicine, and hydrology. Since software sys-

tems also are dynamic and since information flow is a major aspect of design, this topic has a great relevance to software engineering. Within the past few years, a great deal of exciting research has taken place in the area of flow dynamics, and particularly in the area of turbulence. An entirely new subdiscipline of mathematical physics termed "chaos" has started to emerge, and it seems to have many interactions with software engineering.

17. *Entropic complexity:* (deals with decay and disorder rates). All known systems have a tendency to move toward disorder over time, which is equivalent to saying that things decay. Software, it has been discovered, also decays with the passage of time even though it is not a physical system. Each time a change is made, the structure of a software system tends to degrade slightly. With the passage of enough time, the disorder accumulates sufficiently to make the system unmaintainable. This form of complexity is very significant in physics and astronomy and is starting to be explored in software engineering.

18. *Functional complexity:* (deals with patterns and sequences of user tasks). When users of a software system call the system "complex," what exactly do they mean? This form of complexity concerns the user perception of the way functions within a software system are located, turned on, utilized for some purpose, modified if necessary, and turned off again.

19. *Organizational complexity:* (deals with hierarchies and matrices of groups). This form of complexity deals not with a software project directly, but with the organizational structures of the staff that will design and develop it. It has been studied by management scientists and psychologists for more than 100 years, but only recently has it been discovered to be relevant to software projects. A surprising finding has been that large systems tend to be decomposed into components that match the organizational structures of the developing enterprise rather than components that match the needs of the software itself.

20. *Diagnostic complexity:* (deals with factors affecting identification of malfunctions). When a medical doctor is diagnosing a patient, certain combinations of temperature, blood pressure, pulse rates, and other signs are the clues needed to diagnose specific illnesses. Similarly, when software malfunctions, certain combinations of symptoms can be used to identify the underlying cause. This form of complexity analysis is just starting to be significant for software projects.

Measuring the Hard Data for Software Projects

Each major task in a software project will produce some kind of a deliverable, and the volume of the deliverables should be measured as part of a baseline analysis. The normal kinds of deliverables for software projects can be divided into two sets: natural and synthetic. The natural deliverables of a software project are the tangible outputs of many tasks, and they include:

1. Pages of paper documents
2. Source code
3. Test cases

The synthetic deliverables of a software project are the volumes of abstract constructs, and they include:

1. Function points (in all variations)
2. Feature points

Although the synthetic functional deliverables are superior to the natural deliverables for economic studies, it is also useful to record the volumes of natural deliverables as well. Table 4.13 shows a typical set of hard data measurements using natural deliverables.

There are several equations developed by the author for software measurement that can be used interchangeably with both natural and synthetic deliverables. The equations are concerned with relationships between assignment scopes and production rates for software deliverables. An assignment scope is the amount of a deliverable for which one person is normally responsible. A "production rate" is the amount of a deliverable which one person can normally produce in an hour, day, week, or month.

The equations have several interesting attributes: (1) they allow software projects to be measured with reasonably low error; (2) they work equally well with function points, pages of documentation, and lines of source code; (3) they can be used with any source language; (4) they can be used for estimating as well as measurement; (5) they can be used for individual activities, complete programs, large systems, or entire enterprises; (6) they establish regular and predictable

TABLE 4.13 Measurement of Hard Data for Project Deliverables

Activity	Deliverable	Size	Assignment scope	Production rate per month
Requirements	Pages	100	50	25
Design	Pages	250	150	25
Coding	Statements	25,000	7,500	1,250
User documents	Pages	300	200	50
Unit test	Test cases	2,500	500	250
Function test	Test cases	750	250	125

relationships among the major attributes of software projects: staff sizes, human effort, schedules, and costs. There are three fundamental equations and three supplemental equations in the set. The fundamental equations are:

1. Staff size = product size/assignment scope
2. Effort = product size/production rate
3. Schedule = effort/staff size

Although simple in concept and use, the fundamental equations are surprising. They allow any real software project to be matched with very low error for the attributes of staff size, effort, and schedules.

The three supplemental equations are:

4. Cost = (effort*salary) + other costs
5. Assignment scope = product size/staff size
6. Production rate = product size/effort

It is surprising how useful equations as simple as these can be. Let us consider each one in turn. The first equation solves the troublesome question of how large staff sizes are likely to be for any given project. To repeat, the assignment scope is the average quantity of work for which an average staff employee is responsible on any given project. For example, on small to medium-size software projects, an average programmer might be responsible for completing 5000 lines of Cobol source code. Expressed in function points, the same assignment scope would be 47 function points.

Once an enterprise begins to think in terms of and measure assignment scopes, a great many troublesome points can be resolved. For example, in dealing with a natural deliverable such as lines of source code, once an enterprise knows that its average coding assignment scope is 3000, 4000, or 5000 lines (assignment scopes range up to 20,000 lines) then optimal staff sizes for new projects can easily be calculated. Assume an enterprise is planning a new 50,000-source-line Cobol system and its average coding assignment scope has been 5000 lines. Dividing product size (50,000 lines) by assignment scope (5000 lines) indicates that a staff of 10 programmers would be needed.

Assignment scopes can also be used with synthetic deliverables such as function points. For example, a typical maintenance assignment scope for a programmer who performs defect repairs and minor updates would be about 500 function points in size. In real life, assignment scopes vary in response to skill levels, source languages, product sizes, and environmental factors. But the assignment scope concept is worth understanding and using.

It is immediately apparent that the terms of the equation can be reversed. For example, to ascertain a typical coding assignment scope for historical projects that are completed, it is only necessary to divide product size (50,000 statements, for example) by the number of programmers (10, for example) to find the average assignment scope: 5000 in this example.

The second fundamental equation solves the problem of how much human effort will be required for a software project. In this equation, product size is once again used (and either lines of source code or function points will work). Product size is divided by production rate to find out how much human effort will be required. For example, in the 50,000 Cobol source-line system used in the previous example, a typical pure code production rate might be 2000 lines of source code per month. Dividing product size (50,000 Cobol statements) by production rate (2000 lines of source code per month) yields 250 person-months of effort to code the system.

Here too it is apparent that the terms of the equation can be reversed: To find the productivity rate for any completed project merely dividing product size by actual effort will give the productivity rate. The equation also works with function points or any other deliverable object such as documentation pages, test cases, or even bug reports.

Although the assignment scope parameter and the equations that use it are comparatively new to software engineering, the production rate factor has been in existence for many years.

The third fundamental equation solves the problem of development schedules. Effort (as calculated by the second equation) is divided by staff size (as calculated by the first equation) to yield the calendar time needed to develop the program. In the example already used, effort was calculated at 100 person-months and staff size was calculated at 10, so the schedule would be 10 calendar months.

The fourth equation, for cost, is not fundamental, but it is useful. Project cost is calculated by simply multiplying effort by average burdened salary. Assuming for the example discussed thus far that the average burdened salary rate per month is $5000, the basic product cost can be calculated by multiplying the 100 months of effort by $5000 to yield a basic product cost of $500,000.

Although this is a simplistic way to deal with costs, it is reasonably satisfactory. The remaining term of the fourth equation ("other costs") is to be used for cost items outside the scope of normal burdened salaries—heavy capital equipment investments, moving and living costs, real estate, and the like.

Of the six equations, only the first one, which introduces the assignment scope variable, is comparatively new to software engineering, having been used for project estimating since about 1984.

However, since assignment scope allows the problem of staff size prediction to be handled relatively unambiguously, it is the keystone of the equation set.

Measuring Project, Activity, and Task Schedules

Among the most difficult and taxing forms of hard data measurement is that of project and task schedules. The initial difficulty with schedule measurement is a basic one: identifying the starting point of any given project! Very seldom are projects started so crisply and precisely that a manager or user can assert "Project XYZ began on April 25, 1990." Usually there is a great deal of exploratory discussion and informal work, which can sometimes span a year or more, before an actual project finally coalesces.

Once an approximate start date for a project is identified, the next set of difficulties involves overlaps among tasks. The original waterfall model concept contained the naive assumption that a task would not begin until its predecessor ended, as shown in Fig. 4.7. It quickly became evident to all who worked on real projects that the assumption of waiting until a task ended before the next task began was unrealistic. Given normal schedule pressures and software work habits, it is quite common to start the next task in sequence long before a predecessor task is over. Indeed, from analysis of several thousand projects since 1985 it can be asserted that the approximate average overlap is 25 percent; that is, about one-fourth of any given task will remain unfinished at the time the next task in sequence is begun. That average is often exceeded, and overlaps of 50 or even 100 percent (which implies true concurrency) are frequently encountered.

Figure 4.8 shows how the waterfall model tended to be implemented in real-life terms. Although overlap is simple and easy to understand in

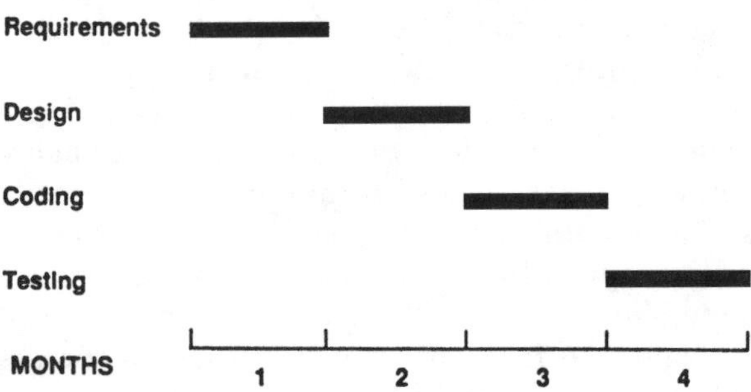

Figure 4.7 Original assumption of zero overlap with the waterfall model.

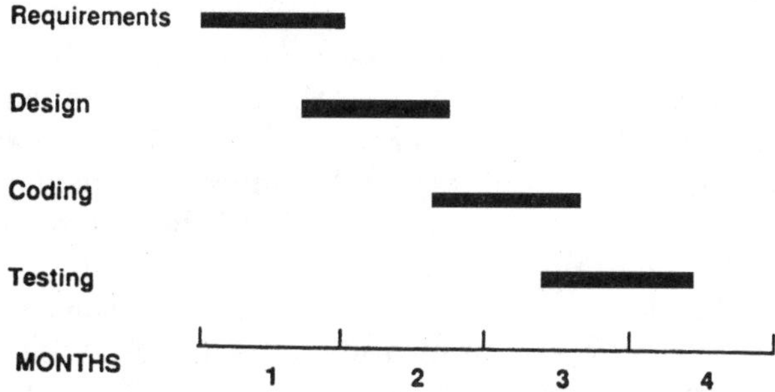

Figure 4.8 Revised assumption of 25 percent overlap with the waterfall model.

principle, it is quite difficult to measure in real life. The problems are not insoluble, however. If a formal project planning system is used, it will show not only the overlaps but the actual calendar dates as well.

If formal project planning systems are not used, it is seldom possible to reconstruct the actual dates from memory. A useful approximation, however, is to ask the project managers and staff to express overlap in percentage terms; i.e., "coding overlapped design by 50 percent." Unless overlaps are measured and included in historical data, it will be very difficult to use such data for predicting future projects. The gross schedule from the beginning to the end of a project is insufficient for accurate estimation.

Reusable Design and Code Factors (Optional)

Reusable designs are less common than reusable code, although they are no less important. Reusable code is one of the most powerful productivity techniques available. Leading-edge companies such as Toshiba and Hartford Insurance are able to develop new applications with up to 85 percent of the deliverable code coming from reusable sources. The topic of reusability should be included in all projects that actually make use of this technique—and in theory some 90 percent of all project could.

One of the reasons why design and development personnel should be part of the baseline analysis sessions is that they have a much better idea about reused code availability than most managers. An interesting study by Barry Silverman of reused code at NASA[12] found that managers thought that the reused code volumes in the projects studied totaled to less than 5 percent, whereas the programmers on the projects said that the volume approached 60 percent.

Whenever really high productivity rates occur (i.e., more than 5000 source code statements or 50 function points per person-month) there is a very strong probability that at least half of the code in question was reused. Prescribing reusability as a therapy will occur in quite a large number of enterprises. Consultants should definitely consider reusability when doing productivity analyses within all large enterprises with more than 200 programmers and analysts. Certain industry types are especially good candidates for reusability: aerospace, banking, computers, electronics, communications, insurance, public utilities, and telephone operating companies, for example. These enterprises do large numbers of very similar applications, and that is exactly the domain where reusability is most effective.

Base Code Factors for Maintenance and Enhancement Projects

For projects that either enhance existing software or perform major defect repairs, an exploration of base code is quite important. For new programs and systems the section should be omitted completely.

The long-range growth of software over time, and also the growth in entropy or complexity, can be modeled with high precision. Such modeling can lead to decisions on what interventions or therapies may be needed to slow down or reverse the decay normally associated with aging software. The 10-year evolution of software projects was described by the author in the *Journal of Software Maintenance Practice and Experience.*[13]

The costs, schedules, risks, and defect potentials of enhancing or modifying an existing system are dramatically different from those typical of entirely new software. Adding 1000 Cobol source lines to an aging, poorly structured, and partially undocumented system can easily be 3 times as expensive and take more than twice as long as writing a new program of 1000 Cobol statements. Moreover, because of the difficulty of updating aging software safely, the potential defects when updating old software can be 3 times higher than for new software, and the average defect removal efficiency is 5 to 10 percent lower for enhancement work than for new software.

It very often happens during a baseline analysis that clients want explicit advice and counsel on therapies that can improve aging software. Starting in 1980 a new software subindustry began to emerge that by 1996 appears to be generating many millions of dollars in annual revenues. It consists of the companies that provide "geriatric care" for aging software—automated restructuring services or products, and the even newer reverse engineering and reengineering products. By the end of the 1990s, this subindustry is likely to have 15 or

20 companies engaged with accumulated annual revenues exceeding $100 million.

The more sophisticated restructuring algorithms, such as those developed by Eric Bush of Language Technology or Chris Miller of Catalyst (now Peat, Marwick) are derived from graph theory and work surprisingly well. With few exceptions, interviews with more than a dozen users of the major restructuring tools indicate very high satisfaction levels for all Cobol systems restructured.

Not only is the code itself restructured well enough that the cyclomatic complexity number often drops to 1, but the code is also redocumented, dead code is identified, and various other minor improvements are made.

In 1986, the companies offering geriatric care (such as Language Technology, Systems and Programming Resources, and Peat, Marwick) were primarily supporting only Cobol software. That was for reason of business and not technology limitations: The fundamental mathematics of restructuring could also be applied to PL/I, Fortran, and other languages if the volume of business made the investment attractive.

The costs of restructuring range from perhaps 2 cents to more than $1 per source line depending on the volume of code, the service selected, and whether or not any manual intervention is required to perform such tasks as remodulatization that are normally performed by the restructuring tools. Most of the companies in the restructuring business have some kind of free trial arrangement under which up to 5000 source lines can be tried for nothing. If the baseline analysis turns up significant quantities of aging Cobol, restructuring is a recommended therapy. Unfortunately, many companies have aging libraries of programs in other languages that cannot be automatically restructured: Assembler, Fortran, PL/I, PLS, RPG, APL, and the like.

Two newer technologies, reverse engineering and reengineering, have recently joined the restructuring concept in providing geriatric care. Reverse engineering uses expert system techniques to extract the hidden design elements from the source code itself, with a view to performing either manual or automatic conversion once the design (long lost from human view) is recovered. Reengineering is concerned with the automatic migration of aging software to new platforms, new languages, or more robust forms. Both reverse engineering and reengineering are so new as this book is written that empirical evidence about them is scarce, although the technologies appear to be well formed and may be effective.

The set of therapies for non-Cobol source code is both limited in effectiveness and expensive to apply. Pragmatically, the most effective therapy yet observed for other languages is the manual removal of error-prone modules.

Internal studies by IBM in the 1970s indicated that software errors are not smoothly or randomly distributed throughout the modules of large software systems. The errors tend to clump in a very small number of very buggy modules. In the case of one of IBM's commercial software products, the IMS Data Base, 57 percent of all errors were found in only 5 percent of the modules. More than 60 percent of the modules had no errors at all. Other companies studying software errors have made similar findings.

It is possible to analyze production software manually, isolate the error-prone modules, and either redevelop the modules or upgrade them substantially. That is not a particularly easy task, and it requires highly skilled professional programmers who may be occupied for very long periods of time—a year or more—while the work is going on.

Some other therapies in the maintenance and enhancement area are also worth noting. As of 1996, most companies with fewer than about 200 total software professionals usually handle maintenance on an informal basis whereby development personnel fix bugs as the need arises. Companies with more than 200 software personnel often have separate maintenance departments staffed by professionals who concentrate on defect repairs and small enhancements.

Quite a few companies that had more than 200 professionals in 1996 only a few years before had 50 or fewer. Since organization structures typically change more slowly than staffs grow in size, it is often useful to consider the establishment of professional software maintenance units if the enterprise is of the right size and does substantial amounts of maintenance. These specialist groups are usually more productive than ad hoc maintenance by developers, and the separation of tasks allows both development and maintenance professionals to concentrate their skills.

Delta Code Factors for Maintenance and Enhancement Projects

The delta code examination is used only to cover the structure and complexity of enhancements of or modifications to existing systems. The distinction between delta code and new code is minor but significant: The delta code will be added to the existing system as discrete blocks or modules, will require internal changes to the existing source code inside the current program, or will be both added and changed simultaneously. Productivity rates, risks, potential bad fixes, costs, and schedules are significantly worse when the delta changes require updating existing code than they are when the delta code is merely added on top of the original program.

When delta code is added to an existing system, the new code will either utilize or modify the existing data structures of the original program. Since modifying an existing data structure is sometimes very intricate, it is significant to note this factor if it occurs. The phrase "bad fix" refers to an error accidentally inserted into a program or system while trying to fix a previous error. This is a surprisingly common occurrence, and an internal study within IBM revealed that a full 20 percent of the customer-reported bugs against the MVS operating system were bad fixes.

The probability of making bad fixes is directly proportional to the structure of the original code: For cyclomatic complexity numbers of less than 10, the probability is about 1 bad fix per 20 changes (i.e., a 5 percent bad fix probability). For cyclomatic complexity numbers of 20 to 30, the bad fix probability rises to about 20 percent, and for McCabe complexity numbers greater than 50, the bad fix probability is approximately 40 percent. In extreme cases, when the McCabe number approaches 100, bad fixes can hit 60 percent.

The therapies that minimize bad fix potentials include automatic restructuring (available for Cobol only), code inspections, and testing of all modifications before releasing the change. This last step, although intuitively obvious, is often not performed because of schedule pressures.

Descriptive Materials and Comments

The last set of topics of a baseline analysis is intended to explore specific information about the project that may require text and comments: the computers, operating systems, and tools used on the project, database packages if any, and the like. A section is also reserved for comments by the clients or consultants of any unusual aspects of the project being analyzed. Unusual aspects that can impact productivity and quality include, but are not limited to, the following:

- Transfer of the project from one city to another
- Physical movement of the project team from one location to another
- Significant expansion of requirements or project scope during mid-development
- Significant technical redirections or restarts
- Staff attrition rates higher than 20 percent per year
- Use of a new programming language or major new tool for the very first time
- Change in hardware or software environment after the project started

- Disasters, such as the California earthquake, fires in a data center or office building, and so on

When the last comments are recorded, the analysis of the project is completed. The consultant administering the questionnaire should use the comments section for recording the start and stop times of a session, as a planning aid for future sessions. Finally, the consultant should close by asking the participants if there are any factors or issues that have not yet been covered.

Since a full baseline analysis will include from 5 to 20 projects, the consultant might tell the participants how many other projects are being analyzed and what the approximate schedules are for the aggregation and statistical analysis of the entire set.

Analysis and Aggregation of the Baseline Data

Since Appendix C illustrates the kind of output that results from a baseline analysis, it is sufficient here to discuss the overall results from a human factors standpoint. The interview sessions themselves, and the kinds of information collected, are quickly perceived by all participants as benign and even helpful. This situation is natural and beneficial. Indeed, the results are favorable enough that spontaneous requests for additional interviews occur frequently.

The technology developed for carrying out software baseline analyses is thorough and accurate. Most enterprises have never before experienced such a detailed examination of their software policies, methods, tools, metrics, and environment. Although the practical results of a baseline analysis depend upon the specific diagnoses that are made, they often include the following improvements in client software environments:

- Establishment of a software metrics program and the adoption of leading-edge measurement techniques
- Enhanced credibility with users and enterprise management in terms of schedule and resource commitments
- Changes in the training and education made available to management and technical personnel
- Establishment of new policies dealing with morale and human relations issues
- Adoption of leading-edge software requirements and design techniques
- Adoption of leading-edge defect removal and quality assurance techniques

- Adoption of new technologies for restoration of aging software systems
- Changes in the physical environment, the supporting tools, and the workstations available for software professionals
- Measurable and validated increases in productivity and quality simultaneously

The overall goal of the baseline analysis technology is to inform all participants of the exact strengths and weaknesses that were discovered during the diagnosis. Only from the basis of firm diagnostic knowledge is it possible to plan effective therapies.

The specific therapies prescribed can encompass tools, policy changes, methodological changes, organization changes, staffing level changes, or all of the above simultaneously. The baseline analysis will diagnose all known problems affecting software, but therapy selection requires skilled and knowledgeable consultants and clients.

References

1. Humphrey, Watts, *Measuring the Software Process,* Addison-Wesley, Reading, Mass., 1989, 489 pp.

2. Jones, Capers, *Programming Productivity,* McGraw-Hill, New York, 1986, 279 pp.

3. SPR, CHECKPOINT®, "Data Collection Questionnaire," Software Productivity Research, Inc., Burlington, Mass., 1990, 35 pp.

4. Jones, Capers, "A 10 Year Retrospective of Software Engineering within ITT," Soft~ware Productivity Research, Inc., Burlington, Mass., 1989, 35 pp.

5. Curtis, B., *Human Factors in Software Development,* IEEE catalog number EHO229-5, 2d ed., IEEE Press, Washington, D.C., 1986, 730 pp.

6. Schneiderman, B., *Software Psychology—Human Factors in Computer and Information Systems,* Winthrop, Cambridge, Mass., 1980, 320 pp.

7. Weinberg, G., *The Psychology of Computer Programming,* Reinhold, New York, 1971, 288 pp.

8. DeMarco, T., and T. Lister, *Peopleware,* Dorset House, New York, 1987, 188 pp.

9. McCue, G., "IBM's Santa Teresa Laboratory—Architectural Design for Program Development," *IBM Systems Journal,* vol. 17, no. 1, 1978. Reprinted in C. Jones, *Programming Productivity—Issues for the Eighties,* IEEE catalog number EH02394, 2d ed., IEEE Press, Washington, D.C., 1986, 462 pp.

10. Thadani, A. J., "Factors Affecting Programmer Productivity During Development," *IBM Systems Journal,* vol. 23, no. 1, 1984, pp. 19–35.

11. McCabe, T., "A Software Complexity Measure," *IEEE Transactions on Software Engineering,* vol. 2, December 1976, pp. 308–320.

12. Silverman, B., "Software Cost and Productivity Improvements: An Analogical View," *Computer,* May 1985, pp. 86–96. Reprinted in C. Jones, *Programming Productivity—Issues for the Eighties,* IEEE catalog number EHO239-4, 2d ed., IEEE Press, Washington, D.C., 1986, 462 pp.

13. Jones, Capers, "Long-Range Enhancement Modelling," *Journal of Software Maintenance—Practice and Experience,* vol. 1, no. 2, 1990.

14. Jones, Capers, *Assessment and Control of Software Risks,* Prentice-Hall, Englewood Cliffs, N.J., 1994, 619 pp.

Chapter

5

Measuring Software Quality and User Satisfaction

Between the first edition in 1991 and this edition a number of quality-related topics have affected the software community. Among the more significant are:

The emergence of the ISO 9000-9004 quality standards

The emergence of data quality as a major topic

The expansion of the Software Engineering Institute (SEI) methods

The explosive growth of client-server software

The rapid growth of object-oriented (OO) paradigm

The rise (and fall) of total quality management (TQM)

ISO 9000-9004 Standards

The International Standards Organization (ISO) quality standards 9000 through 9004 became mandatory in 1992 for selling various products throughout the European Community. Since these standards have only a few years of field usage, there is still very little solid empirical data yet available. Unfortunately, the information that is available indicates that the ISO standards have very little tangible impact on software quality but do tend to elevate software costs in a noticeable way owing to increasing the volumes of paper material produced.

In the course of SPR assessment and baseline surveys between 1992 and 1995, a number of companies were contacted that were in the process of completing ISO certification or which had recently been certified. Similar companies were also studied which were not applying for certification. So far as can be determined from limited samples, there is not yet any tangible or perceptible difference in the quality levels of companies which have been certified and similar groups which have not. Of course, there is less than 4 years of history by which to judge.

As of 1996, there is still a remarkable lack of quantified results associated with the ISO 9000-9004 standard set. To date it does not seem to have happened that the ISO-certified groups have pulled ahead of the noncertified groups in some tangible way. The only tangible and visible impact of ISO certification appears to be the costs of the ISO certification process itself, the time required to achieve certification, and an increase in the volume of quality-related paper documents.

It is obvious that the ISO standards have had a polarizing effect on software producers, as well as on hardware manufacturers. Some companies such as Motorola have challenged the validity of the ISO standards, while others such as ViewLogic have embraced the ISO standards fully. The reaction to ISO certification among software groups to date has been somewhat more negative than hardware and electronic component manufacturing. However, in several industries contacted (fiber optics, electronics manufacturing) the overall results of ISO certification are viewed as ambiguous. Some of the reactions are negative. On the other hand, some companies are using ISO certification as a marketing opportunity.

Some ISO adherents have observed that it is not the place of the ISO 9000-9004 standards to actually improve quality. Their purpose is simply to ensure that effective practices are followed. They are not in and of themselves a compilation of best current practices. Indeed, some companies have pointed out that compliance is fairly easy if you already have a good quality control approach in place, and that ISO certification tends to raise the confidence of clients even if quantification is elusive.

On the whole, the data available from the ISO domain as of mid-1995 remains insufficient to judge the impact of the ISO standards on these topics: (1) defect potentials, (2) defect removal efficiency levels, (3) defect prevention effectiveness, (4) reliability, (5) customer satisfaction levels, (6) data quality.

Quite a bit of information about ISO 9000-9004 is available via the Internet and various information utilities such as CompuServe. Attempts to find empirical data that ISO standards improved software quality using these channels elicited no useful factual information. However, many ISO enthusiasts responded with the surprising message that the ISO standards were not actually intended to improve quality and hence should not be faulted if they failed to do so.

Data Quality and Data Metrics

The topic of data quality was not included in the original 1991 edition but has catapulted into significance in the world of data warehouses, repositories, on-line analytical processing (OLAP), and client-server applications. Unfortunately, as of 1995, research into data quality is handicapped by the fact that there are no known normalizing metrics for expressing the volume of data a company uses, the quality levels of the data, and the costs of creating data, migrating data from platform to platform, correcting errors, or destroying obsolete data.

There is so little quantified information on data quality that this topic is included primarily to serve as a warning flag that an important domain is emerging, and substantial research is urgently needed. It is suspected that the databases and repositories owned by major corporations are filled with errors, redundant data, and other significant sources of trouble. But with no effective data volume or quality metrics, researchers are handicapped in even determining averages and ranges of data quality.

Several commercial companies and Dr. Richard Wang of MIT have begun to address the topic of data quality, but to date there are no known published statistical studies that include the volumes of data errors, their severity levels, or the costs of removing data errors. There is not even any accepted standard method for exploring the "cost of quality" for data errors in the absence of any normalizing metrics. (Note that the author's company, Software Productivity Research, is now exploring the concept of a "data point" metric that can be mathematically related to the function point metric. This is a research project, and all technical contributions would be welcome.)

SEI Capability Maturity Model

The Software Engineering Institute (SEI) capability maturity model (CMM) concept is one of the most widely discussed topics in the software literature. SEI has claimed that software quality and productivity levels correlate exactly with maturity level. As of 1995, there is not yet a lot of solid empirical data which either supports or challenges these assertions. SEI itself is only just beginning to start data collection, so up until recently the assertions were purely theoretical.

During calendar year 1994 Software Productivity Research, Inc., was commissioned by the Air Force to perform a study of the economic impact of various SEI CMM levels. Raw data was provided to SPR on levels 1, 2, and 3 by an Air Force software location. In terms of quality, the data available to date indicated that for maturity levels 1, 2, and 3 average quality tends to rise with CMM maturity level scores. However, this study had a limited number of samples. By contrast, the Navy has reported a counterexample and has stated that at least some software produced by a level 3 organization was observed to be deficient in terms of software quality and had high defect levels.

There is clearly some overlap among the various SEI levels. Some of the software projects created by organizations at SEI CMM levels 1 and 2 are just as good in terms of quality as those created by SEI level 3. Not only that, but achieving SEI level 3 does not guarantee that all software projects will have exemplary quality. On the whole, the SEI CMM is in need of much more solid empirical data. Some of the results from ascending the SEI CMM are favorable, but the SEI approach is by no means a "silver bullet" that will solve all software quality problems.

Finally, there has been no quantitative comparison between software produced by the few hundred enterprises that have used the SEI maturity level concept and the more than 30,000 U.S. software producers that have not adopted the maturity concept at all. The topic of the exact costs and the value of the SEI maturity levels needs a great deal more research and quantification before definite conclusions can be reached. Ideally, what would be mounted is a large-scale survey involving perhaps 50 organizations and at least 250 projects at various SEI CMM levels. Since studies of this magnitude are routine for validating other kinds of defense systems, it is sadly typical of the software community that little effort is devoted to testing new concepts before they are deployed.

Client-Server Quality

The client-server phenomenon has been sweeping the software industry for more than 5 years. The growth of the client-server approach is one of the most rapid ever experienced by the software community:

- All major software journals have client-server articles in essentially every issue.
- New and specialized client-server journals are appearing at an accelerating rate.
- Technical bookstores are beginning to have entire sections of client-server books.
- New client-server conferences and client-server tracks are occurring almost daily.

No young technology is fully perfected when it first appears, and client-server is no exception. From talking to client-server users, developers, and listening to conversations at client-server conferences the following critical problem areas will need to be addressed by client-server tool vendors and developers in the future:

1. Client-server quality levels are suspect.
2. Client-server development methodologies are still immature.
3. Data consistency among client-server applications is questionable.
4. Client-server maintenance costs are essentially unknown in 1995 but may be steep.

Here are some preliminary observations.

- Since client-server applications are usually new, there is not a long history of quality data. Preliminary quality data from client-server applications is somewhat alarming, and indicates a need for pretest inspections and better quality control.
- Compared to the way mainframe applications have been built, the overall set of methods used for client-server software can only be characterized as "immature." Quite a bit more rigor is indicated.
- How client-server applications will impact corporate data administration, data dictionaries, and repositories has not yet been fully worked out. Initial findings are somewhat ominous. It is hard to escape the conclusion that client-server applications are starting to suffer from inconsistent data definitions, unique or quirky data elements, and carelessness in data design.
- Client-server applications are usually brand new in 1995, but they will not be brand new in 1999. How much it will cost a company to maintain client-server applications when they themselves are aging legacy systems is an important but totally unknown topic. It may be that total replacement of aging client applications might become common, but this is not so likely on the server side. The whole issue needs serious study.

Unlike stand-alone personal computer applications, client-server projects are distributed software applications that involve multiple computers, networks or linkages between mainframes and personal computers, and quite a bit of sharing and synchronization of the data residing in the server portion of the application. These factors means that client-server development is more complex than developing older monolithic applications. It also means that the operational complexity is higher.

Although the complexity of typical client-server applications is fairly high, development practices for client-server applications are often efficiency rates. Defect removal efficiency reflects the combined effectiveness of all reviews, inspections, and tests carried out on software before delivery. For example, if a total of 90 bugs are found during the development of a software project and the users find and report 10 bugs, then the defect removal efficiency for this project is 90 percent, since 9 out of 10 bugs were found before release.

The average defect removal efficiency for typical monolithic mainframe applications has been about 85 percent. (Note that best in class companies average above 95 percent.) To date, the equivalent results within the client-server domain has been less than 80 percent, although the data on this topic is very sparse and has a high margin of error.

When the mainframe defect potentials of about 4.5 bugs per function point are reduced by 85 percent, the approximate quantity of delivered defects can be seen to average about 0.675 defect per function point. For distributed client-server applications, the higher defect potential of 5.5 bugs per function point interacts in an alarming way with the reduced removal efficiency of 80 percent. The results indicate a defect delivery level of about 1.1 defects per function point, which is uncomfortably close to twice the typical amounts latent in mainframe software.

Although client-server quality is often marginal today, that does not mean that it will stay bad indefinitely. The same kinds of methods, tools, and approaches that have been used successfully by "best in class" software producers for many years can also be used with client-server applications. These approaches can be summarized in terms of defect prevention methods, defect removal methods, and quality tools.

Among the kinds of defect prevention approaches that work with client-server applications, the concept of joint application design, or JAD, can be very useful. The JAD approach calls for joint requirements development between the client organization and the software group. The overall impact of the JAD method is to reduce the rate of unplanned creeping requirements and to reduce the number of defects in the requirements themselves.

Also effective in the defect prevention domain are methods such as rapid application development, or RAD, prototyping, reusable components, some aspects of information engineering (IE), and a variety of rigorous specification approaches such as the Warnier-Orr method, the Yourdon methods, and many others. Structured programming and coding approaches are also helpful. Another very effective defect prevention approach, although one that takes several years to reach full power, is a quality measurement program.

In terms of defect removal, testing alone has never been sufficient to ensure high quality levels. All of the best in class software producers such as AT&T, Hewlett-Packard, Microsoft, IBM, Raytheon, or Motorola utilize both pretest design reviews and formal code inspections. Design reviews and code inspections can both be used with client-server applications and should make notable improvements in defect removal efficiency.

In terms of tools that can benefit client-server quality, any or all of the following tools have a useful place: (1) quality and defect estimating tools, (2) defect tracking and measurement tools, (3) complexity analysis tools, (4) design and code inspection support tools, (5) prototyping tools, (6) code restructuring tools, (7) configuration control tools, (8) record and playback test support tools, (9) test coverage analysis tools, (10) test library control tools.

Distributed client-server applications are now so numerous that by the end of the century they may constitute the major portion of the kinds of software which support business and government operations. Unfortunately, the elevated complexity levels of client-server applications coupled with somewhat careless quality control are leading to some significant problems with dissatisfied users and higher than anticipated maintenance costs.

Both problems can be solved, but they need to be brought to the attention of the software community before effective solutions can be deployed. As client-server software applications become more pervasive, there is an urgent need to explore the quality levels, inspection approaches, testing methods, and other topics of significance.

Object-Oriented Quality Levels

The object-oriented world has been on an explosive growth path. The usage of OO methods has now reached a sufficient critical mass to have created dozens of books, several OO magazines, and frequent conferences such as OOPSLA and Object World. Unfortunately, this explosion of interest in OO methodologies has not carried over into the domain of software quality. There are a number of citations on software testing, but little or no empirical data on actual software quality levels associated with the OO paradigm.

From very preliminary and provisional results, it appears that object-oriented languages such as C++ and Smalltalk may have reduced defect levels compared to normal procedural languages such as C or Cobol or Fortran. Defect potentials for OO languages are perhaps in the range of 1 per function point, as opposed to closer to 1.75 per function point for normal procedural languages. However, the defect potentials for object-oriented analysis and design have not yet showed any reduction, and indeed may exceed the 1.25 defects per function point associated with the older standard analysis and design approaches such as Yourdon, Warnier-Orr, and Gane & Sarson.

Unfortunately, OO analysis and design tend to have a high rate of abandonment, as well as projects which started with OO analysis and design but switched to something else in midstream. These phenomena make it difficult to explore OO quality. There is obviously a steep learning curve associated with most of the current flavors of OO analysis and design, and steep learning curves are usually associated with high levels of errors and defects.

There is not yet enough data available in 1995 to reach a definite conclusion, but there is no convincing published evidence that OO quality levels are dramatically better than non-OO quality levels for OO analysis and design. The data on OO languages is somewhat more convincing but still needs more exploration. On theoretical grounds it can be claimed that OO quality levels should be better, owing to inheritance and class libraries. However, that which is inherited and the class libraries themselves need to be validated carefully before theory and practice coincide.

Total Quality Management (TQM) for Software

When the first edition of this book was published in 1991, total quality management (TQM) was on an upswing in the software industry. Now that the second edition is being prepared, TQM appears to be declining in the software world, owing to the visible lack of success as a software QA approach. Unfortunately, only about half of the total quality management (TQM) experiments in the United States are successful and improve quality, and the other half are failures. The successful use of TQM correlates strongly with the seriousness of the commitment and the depth of understanding by executives and management. TQM works only if it is really used. Giving the TQM concepts lip service but not really implementing the philosophy only leads to frustration.

The TQM concept is not a replacement for more traditional software quality approaches. Indeed, TQM works best for organizations that are also leaders in traditional quality approaches. Specifically, some of the attributes of companies which are successful in their TQM programs include the following: (1) they also have effective software quality measurement programs which identify defect origins, severities, and removal efficiency rates; (2) they utilize formal reviews and inspections before testing begins; (3) their software quality control was good or excellent even before the TQM approach was begun.

Conversely, enterprises which lack quality metrics, which fail to utilize pretest defect prevention and removal operations, and which lag their competitors in current software quality control approaches tend to gain only marginal benefits, if any, from the adoption of the TQM method. Such enterprises are very likely to use TQM as a slogan, but not to implement the fundamental concepts.

The operative word for total quality management is *total*. Concentrating only coding defects, measuring only testing, and using the older KLOC metric violates the basic philosophy of total quality management. These approaches ignore the entire front end of the life cycle and have no utility for requirements problems, design problems, documentation problems, or any of the other sources of trouble which lie outside of source code.

It is obvious that there are three sets of factors which must be deployed in order for total quality management (TQM) to be successful with software:

1. Adopting a culture of high quality from the top to the bottom of an enterprise
2. Using defect prevention methods to lower defect potentials
3. Using defect removal methods to raise prerelease efficiencies

Synergistic combinations of defect prevention methods can reduce defect potentials by more than 50 percent across the board, with the most notable improvements being in some of the most difficult problem areas, such as requirements errors.

The set of current defect removal methods includes such things as formal inspections, audits, independent verification and validation, and many forms of testing. However, to bring TQM to full power in an organization, the culture of the management community must be brought up to speed on what TQM means and how to go about it.

In general, no one method by itself is sufficient, and a major part of the TQM approach is to define the full set of prevention and removal methods that will create optimal results. This in turn leads to the need for accurate measurement of defect potentials and defect removal efficiency.

How TQM will evolve for client-server software or object-oriented software is an unknown topic as of 1995. In theory, TQM should work in both domains and should be even more effective in an object-oriented domain because of class libraries and inheritance. In fact, the topic remains uncertain.

Quality Control and International Competition

There are four critical business factors which tend to determine successful competition in global markets:

1. Cost of production
2. Time to market
3. Quality and reliability
4. User satisfaction

All four are important, and all four depend upon careful measurement for a company to make tangible improvements. Cost of production has been a major factor for hundreds of years, and it has proved its importance in both natural products (agriculture, minerals, metals, and so on) and manufactured durable goods, as well as services. Indeed, cost of production was the first business factor to be measured and explored in depth.

Time to market has become progressively important in recent years as new manufacturing technologies and rapid communication make international competition more speed-intensive than the former durable goods economy. Time to market has been particularly important in the twentieth century; it is a key consideration for consumer goods and such personal electronics as Walkman-class radios, cassette players, and compact disc players. It is also a major factor for industrial and commercial products.

Only since the 1950s have quality, reliability, and user satisfaction been recognized as the major driving force for high-technology products and hence a key ingredient in long-range national and industrial success. Quality, reliability, and user satisfaction are turning out to be the driving force of competition for high-technology products, including automobiles, computers, telecommunications equipment, and many modern consumer products such as kitchen appliances and power tools.

It is primarily quality control, rather than cost of production or time to market, that explains the unprecedented success of Japan in modern high-technology competition. Indeed, the pioneering work of Deming[1] on quality measurement and statistical quality control that was widely adopted by Japanese industry has perhaps been the single most important factor in Japan's favorable balance of trade vis-à-vis the United States.

Further, in the specific case of software, quality control is on the critical path for reducing cost of production and shortening time to market. It is also important in determining user satisfaction. The importance of quality control cannot be overstressed: software producers who do not control quality risk being driven from their markets and perhaps out of business by competitors who do control quality! Before dealing with the measurement of quality, it is useful to consider the significance of this factor on high-technology products in general and on software in particular.

Since the reemergence of Japanese industry after World War II, Japan has followed one of the most successful industrial strategies in all human history. The basic strategy has two aspects:

1. Concentrate on high-technology products, since the value per shipped ton is greater than for any other kinds of product.
2. Compete by achieving quality levels at least 25 percent higher than those of U.S. and European companies while holding prices to within ± 1 0 percent of U.S. and European levels.

In research of the factors that contribute to market share of high technology products, the customer perception of quality has turned out to be the dominant factor for large market shares. For high technology products, quality and user satisfaction even outweigh time to market and cost of production in terms of overall market share and competitive significance.

A question that arises is why the widely publicized Japanese strategy has been so successful against U.S. and European companies when those companies can easily follow the same strategy themselves. The answer is that U.S. and European business strategies evolved more than 100 years ago during an earlier industrial era when factors such as least-cost production were dominant in creating market shares and quality was often a secondary issue. Many U.S. and European executives either ignored quality or perceived it to be an optional item that was of secondary importance. That was a mistake, and the United States and Europe are now paying the price for it.

The whole postwar generation of U.S. and European executives were playing by the rules of a 100-year-old game while Japanese executives were playing a modern high-technology game. The following is a list of 10 high-technology products the quality of which is the dominant factor leading to market shares:

1. Automobiles
2. Cameras
3. Compact disc players
4. Computers
5. Machine tools
6. Medical instruments
7. Stereo receivers
8. Telephone handsets
9. Television sets
10. Watches

Japan has become the world's largest producer of 5 of the 10 products and is a major producer of all of the others. The United States has steadily lost global market share in all of the areas except computers.

Another significant aspect of industry as the twentieth century draws to a close is that microcomputers and software are embedded in all 10 of the product types listed above. The 1997 model year automobiles, for example, included cars with as many as 12 separate onboard computers governing fuel injection, cooling and heating, audio equipment, odometers and tachometers, and other instruments!

As computers and software continue to expand into consumer product areas, companies must recognize that success in software is on the critical path to corporate survival. The future success of the United States against global competition requires that the CEOs of U.S. industries understand the true factors of global competition in the twenty-first century:

1. High-technology products are critical to U.S. success.
2. Quality is the dominant marketing factor for high-technology products.
3. High-technology products depend upon computing and software.
4. Quality is the key to success in computing and software.
5. Quality must start at the top and become part of the U.S. corporate culture.

By the end of the twentieth century, it can be seen that two new business laws may become operational and drive successful businesses and industries into the twenty-first century:

Law 1. Enterprises that master computers and software will succeed; enterprises that fall behind in computing and software will fail.

Law 2. Quality control is the key to mastering computing and software; enterprises that control software quality will also control schedules and productivity. Enterprises that do not control quality will fail.

Defining Quality for Measurement and Estimation

Readers with a philosophical turn of mind may have noticed a curious anomaly in this chapter so far. The term "quality" has been used many times on every page but has not yet been defined. This anomaly is a symptom of a classic industrial paradox which deserves discussion. Quality and quality control are agreed by all observers to be major international business factors, yet the terms are extraordinarily difficult to define precisely. This phenomenon permeates one of the finest although unusual books on quality ever written: *Zen and the Art of Motorcycle Maintenance,* by Robert Pirsig.[2] In his book, Pirsig ruminates that quality is easy to see and is immediately apparent when encountered. But when you try to pin it down or define what it is, you find the concept is elusive and slips away. It is not the complexity, but the utter simplicity of quality that defies explanation.

In the writings of software quality specialists, and in informal discussions with most of them, there are a variety of concepts centering around software quality. Here are the concepts expressed by several software specialists, in alphabetical order:

- Dr. Barry Boehm, formerly of TRW and now with DARPA, tends to think of quality as "Achieving high levels of user satisfaction, portability, maintainability, robustness, and fitness for use."
- Phil Crosby, the former ITT vice president of quality, has created the definition with the widest currency because of its publication in his famous book *Quality Is Free.*"[3] Phil states that quality means "Conformance to user requirements."
- W. Edwards Deming, in his lectures and writings, considers quality to be "striving for excellence in reliability and functions by continuous improvement in the process of development, supported by statistical analysis of the causes of failure."
- Watts Humphrey, of the Software Engineering Institute, tends to speak of quality as "achieving excellent levels of fitness for use, conformance to requirements, reliability, and maintainability."
- The author defines software quality as "the absence of defects that would make software either stop completely or produce unacceptable results. Defects can be traced to requirements, to design, to code, to documentation, or to bad fixes of previous defects. Defects can range in severity from minor to major."
- James Martin, in his public lectures, has asserted that software quality means being on time, within budget, and meeting user needs.
- Tom McCabe, the complexity specialist, tends to define quality in his lectures as "high levels of user satisfaction and low defect levels, often associated with low complexity."
- John Musa of Bell Laboratories, the well-known reliability modeler, states that quality means a combination of "low defect levels, adherence of software functions to user needs, and high reliability."[4]
- Bill Perry, head of the Quality Assurance Institute, has defined quality in his speeches as "high levels of user satisfaction and adherence to requirements."

Considered individually, each of the definitions has merit and raises valid points. Taken collectively, the situation resembles the ancient Buddhist parable of the blind men and the elephant: The elephant was described as being like a rope, a wall, or a snake depending upon whether the blind man touched the tail, the side, or the trunk. For practical day-to-day purposes, a working definition of quality must meet two criteria:

1. Quality must be measurable when it occurs.
2. Quality should be predictable before it occurs.

Table 5.1 lists the elements of the major definitions quoted above and indicates which elements meet both criteria.

Although Table 5.1 does not contain many surprises, it is important to understand the limitations for measurement purposes of two important concepts: conformance to requirements and user satisfaction. For software, Phil Crosby's widely quoted definition of quality as "conformance to requirements" suffers from two serious limitations:

1. Although this can be measured after the fact, there are no a priori estimating techniques that can predict the phenomenon ahead of time.
2. When software defect origins are measured, "requirements" is one of the chief sources of error. To define quality as conformance to a

TABLE 5.1 Predictability and Measurability of Quality Factors

Quality factor	Predictable	Measurable
Defect levels	Yes	Yes
Defect origins	Yes	Yes
Defect severity	Yes	Yes
Defect removal efficiency	Yes	Yes
Product complexity	Yes	Yes
Project reliability	Yes	Yes
Project maintainability	Yes	Yes
Project schedules	Yes	Yes
Project budgets	Yes	Yes
Portability	Yes	Yes
Conformance to requirements	No	Yes
User satisfaction	No	Yes
Fitness for use	No	Yes
Robustness	No	No

major source of error leads to problems of circular reasoning, and prevents either measurement or estimation with accuracy.

User satisfaction with software is certainly capable of being measured with high precision after the fact. But there are currently no effective estimating techniques that can directly predict the presence or absence of this phenomenon far enough ahead of time to take effective action. There are, however, very strong correlations between user satisfaction and factors that can be estimated. For example, there is a very strong inverse correlation between software defect levels and user satisfaction. So far as can be determined, there has never been a software product with high defect levels that was satisfactory to its users. The opposite situation, however, does not correlate so well: There are software products with low defect levels that are not satisfactory to users.

Another aspect of user satisfaction is an obvious one: Since this factor depends on users, it is hard to carry out early measurements. In the case of defects, for example, measurements can start as early as the requirements phase. As for user satisfaction, it is hard to begin until there is something to use. These considerations mean that, in a practical day-to-day measurement system, user satisfaction is a special case that should be dealt with on its own terms, and it should be decoupled from ordinary defect and removal metrics. The bulk of the other metrics in Table 5.1 meet the two criteria of being both predictable and measurable. Therefore, any or all of them can be used effectively for quality control purposes.

Five Steps to Software Quality Control

These five steps to software quality control have been observed in the course of software management consulting in leading corporations:

Step 1 Establish a software quality metrics program

Software achieved a notorious reputation during the first 50 years of its history as the high-technology occupation with the worst track record in terms of measurements. Over the last 15 years, improvements in measurement technology have enabled leading-edge companies to measure both software quality and productivity with high precision. If your company has not yet adopted leading-edge quality metrics for key products, you are headed for a disturbing future as your more advanced competitors pull ahead.

The significance of this step cannot be overstated: If you look inside the leading companies within an industry you will find full-scale measurements programs and hence executive abilities to receive early warnings and cure problems. For example, IBM and AT&T have had quality measurements since before World War II and software quality measurements since the 1960s. Quality measurement is a critical factor in high-technology products, and all the companies which have tended to become household words have quality measurement programs: DEC, Hewlett-Packard, IBM, and many others. The lagging enterprises which have no software measures also have virtually no ability to apply executive control to the software process.

Step 2 Establish tangible executive software performance goals

Does your enterprise have any meaningful software quality or productivity goals operational? The answer for many U.S. companies would be no, but for leading-edge companies such as IBM and Hewlett Packard it will be yes. Now that software can be measured, it is possible to establish tangible, pragmatic performance goals for both software quality and productivity. Since the two key aspects of software quality are defect removal efficiency and customer satisfaction, reasonable executive targets would be to achieve higher than 95 percent efficiency in finding software bugs and higher than 90 percent "good" or "excellent" customer satisfaction ratings.

Step 3 Establish meaningful software quality assurance

One of the most significant differences between leading and lagging U.S. enterprises is the attention paid to software quality. It can be strongly asserted that the U.S. companies that concentrate on software quality have higher productivity, shorter development schedules, and higher levels of customer satisfaction than companies that ignore quality. Since the steps needed to achieve high quality include both defect prevention and defect removal, a permanent quality assurance organization can facilitate the move toward quality control.

It is possible, in theory, to achieve high quality without a formal quality assurance organization. Unfortunately, the American psychology often tends to need the external prompting which a formal quality assurance organization provides. An effective, active quality assurance team can provide a continuous boost in the quality arena.

Step 4 Develop a leading-edge corporate culture

Business activities have a cultural component as well as a technological component. The companies that tend to excel in both market leadership and software engineering technologies are those whose corporate cultures reflect the ideals of excellence and fair play. If your corporate culture stresses quality, service to clients, innovation, and fairness to employees, there is a good chance that your enterprise is an industry leader. If your corporate culture primarily stresses only schedule adherence or cost control, as important as those topics are, you may not ultimately succeed. Am interesting correlation can be noted between corporate culture and quality control. Of the companies that produce software listed *The 100 Best Companies to Work for in America*[5] most have formal software quality programs.

There is no external source of corporate culture. The board of directors, the CEO, and the senior executives are the only people who can forge a corporate culture, and it is their responsibility to do it well. As Tom Peters has pointed out in his landmark book, *In Search of Excellence,*[6] the truly excellent enterprises are excellent from top to bottom. If the top is not interested in industry leadership or doesn't know how to achieve it, the entire enterprise will pay the penalty.

Step 5 Determine your software strengths and weaknesses

More than 200 different factors can affect software productivity and quality; they include the available tools and workstations, the physical environment, staff training and education, and even your compensation plans. In order to find out how your enterprise ranks against U.S. or industry norms and whether you have the appropriate set of tools and methods in place, it is usually necessary to bring in one of the many U.S. management consulting organizations that specializes in such knowledge.

This step is logically equivalent to a complete medical examination in a major medical institution. No physician would ever prescribe therapies without a thorough examination and diagnosis of the patient. The same situation should hold true for software: Do not jump into therapy acquisition without knowing what is right and wrong in all aspects of your software practice.

Software Quality Control in the United States

Computing and software have become dominant issues for corporate success and even corporate survival. As the twentieth century draws to a close, the enterprises that can master computing and software will probably be the key enterprises of the next century. The enterprises that do not master computing and software may not survive to see the next century!

Quality control is the key to mastering computing and software, and the enterprises that succeed in quality control will succeed in optimizing productivity, schedules, and customer satisfaction also. Following are short discussions of some of the quality control methods used in the United States.

Quality assurance organizations

Most United States commercial, military, and systems software producers have found it useful to establish formal quality assurance (QA) organizations. These QA organizations vary significantly in their roles, authorities, and responsibilities. The most successful of the QA organizations, which are typical of large computer manufacturers and major software vendors, are capable of serving as general models.

Quality assurance organization types. There are two common forms of QA organization; they might be termed "active" and "passive." Of these, the active QA organization is usually more successful, although more expensive as well.

Active quality assurance. The phrase "active quality assurance" means a formal quality assurance organization that plays an active part in software projects. This is the form of quality assurance most often practiced by leading-edge computer manufacturers, defense contractors, and other high-technology enterprises. This form is recommended above the passive form. Typical roles encompassed by active QA organizations include:

1. Moderating design and code inspections
2. Collecting and analyzing defect data
3. Developing and running test scenarios
4. Estimating defect potentials
5. Recommending corrective actions for quality problems
6. Teaching courses on quality-related topics

Active quality assurance groups normally start work on projects during or shortly after the requirements phase and are continuously engaged throughout a project's development cycle.

Because of the scope and amount of work carried out by active quality assurance groups, the staffing requirements are not insignificant: Most active QA organizations are in the range of 3 to 5 percent of the size of the software development organizations they support. Some, such as the IBM QA organization supporting commercial and systems software, approach 10 percent of the entire software staff. Active QA organizations normally are managerially independent of development, which is a pragmatic necessity to guarantee independence and avoid coercion by development project management.

Passive quality assurance. The phrase "passive quality assurance" refers to a group whose primary task is observation to ensure that the relevant quality standards and guidelines are in fact adhered to by development personnel. The passive QA organizations can, of course, be much smaller than the active ones, and typically they are in the range of I to 2 percent of the size of the development groups they support. However, the effectiveness of passive QA is necessarily less than that of the active form. Some of the roles performed by the passive QA organizations include:

1. Observing a sample of design and code inspections
2. Analyzing defect data collected by development personnel
3. Recommending corrective actions for quality problems

Passive QA organizations, like the active forms, are normally managerially independent of development, which is a pragmatic necessity to guarantee independence and to avoid coercion by development project management.

Reviews, walk-throughs, and inspections

Informal reviews have been held spontaneously since the earliest days of software, and the first such reviews may even have taken place prior to 1950. However, in the burst of really large system projects starting in the 1960s and 1970s, it became obvious that testing was too late in the development cycle, too inefficient, and not fully effective.

Several IBM researchers turned their attention to the review process, and three alternative approaches surfaced more or less at the same time: Design reviews and code reviews originated at the IBM San Jose laboratories in the early 1970s. Structured walk-throughs originated concurrently at the IBM Poughkeepsie laboratory. Formal design and code inspections originated slightly after walk-throughs; they were created at the IBM Kingston laboratory and were based on the analysis of Michael Fagan.

After considerable debate and trial, the formal inspection process tended to come out ahead in terms of overall rigor and efficiency and gradually moved toward becoming a standard technique within IBM. Indeed, inspections appear to be the most efficient form of defect removal yet developed, and only formal inspections tend to consistently exceed 60 percent in defect removal efficiency. External publication of the method in 1976 by Fagan[7] brought the inspection technique into more widespread use. IBM began to offer external training in inspections by 1979, and other companies such as ITT and AT&T adopted the method as an internal standard. By 1990, a dozen or more computer, consulting, and educational companies including SPR were teaching inspections, and the method continues to expand in 1996.

Formal inspections differ from reviews and walk-throughs primarily in the rigor of the preparation, the formal roles assigned, and the postinspection follow-up. To be deemed an "inspection" it is necessary to obey the following protocols:

1. The participants must receive training prior to taking part in their first inspection.
2. There will be sufficient time available for preparation before the inspection sessions take place.
3. In the inspection sessions, there will be at least the following staff present:
   - A moderator (to keep the discussions within bounds)
   - A reader (to paraphrase the work being inspected)
   - A recorder (to keep records of all defects)
   - An inspector (to identify any problems)
   - An author (whose work is being inspected)

All five (or more) may be present for large projects. For small projects dual roles can be assigned, so that the minimum number for a true inspection is three: moderator, author, and one other person.

4. The inspection sessions will follow normal protocols in terms of timing, recording defects, and polling participants.
5. There will be follow-up after the inspection process to ensure the identified defects are repaired.
6. The defect data will not be used for appraisal or punitive purposes.

The purpose of inspections is simply to find, early in the process, problems which if not eliminated could cause trouble later. It should be emphatically stated that the purpose of inspections is not to humiliate the authors, nor is it to fix the problems. Defect repairs take place later. The purpose, once again, is simply to find problems.

Inspections are not inexpensive, but they are highly efficient. Prior to first utilizing this method, there will be a natural reluctance on the part of programmers and analysts to submit to what may seem an unwarranted intrusion into their professional competence. However, this apprehension immediately disappears after the first inspections, and the methodology is surprisingly popular after the start-up phase.

Any deliverable can be inspected, and the method has been used successfully on the following:

- Requirements
- Initial and detailed specifications
- Development plans
- Test plans
- Test cases
- Source code
- User documentation
- Training materials
- Screen displays

For initial planning purposes, Table 5.2 shows the normal times required to prepare for and carry out inspections for typical deliverables. Table 5.2 is taken from the SPR inspection training materials[8] as updated for 1991. Note that the variations for both preparation and meeting effort can exceed ± 50 percent of the figures in Table 5.2, based upon individual human factors, interruptions, and the numbers of problems encountered. Normal single-column pages in a 10-pitch type with a normal volume of graphics are assumed: roughly 500 words per text page and about 150 words per page containing charts, diagrams, or illustrations. For source code, normal formatting of about 50 statements per page of listing and a single statement per physical line is the assumption.

The business advantages of inspections can be illustrated by two simple figures. Figure 5.1 shows the distressing gaps in the timing between defect introduction and defect discovery in situations where testing alone is used. Figure 5.2 shows the comparatively short intervals between defect creation and defect discovery that is associated with inspections.

Inspections tend to benefit project schedules and effort as well as quality. They are extremely efficient in finding interface problems between components and in using the human capacity for inductive rea-

TABLE 5.2 Typical Inspection Preparation and Execution Times

Deliverable	Preparation	Meeting
Requirements	25 pages/h	12 pages/h
Functional specification	45 pages/h	15 pages/h
Logic specification	50 pages/h	20 pages/h
Source code	150 LOC/h	75 LOC/h
User documents	35 pages/h	20 pages/h

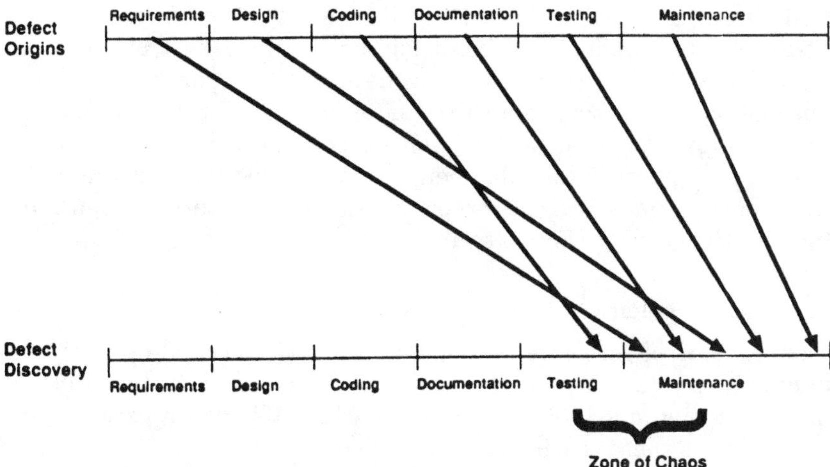

Figure 5.1 Delays between defect creation and discovery when testing is the primary removal method.

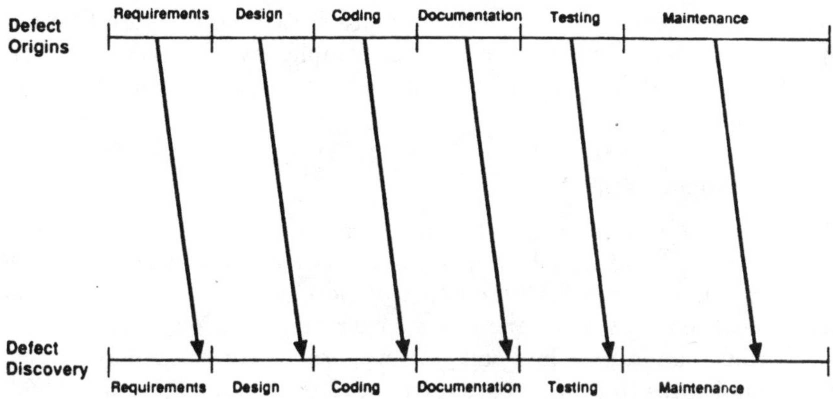

Figure 5.2 Reduced delays between defect creation and discovery associated with formal inspections.

soning to find subtle errors that testing will miss. They are not very effective, of course, in finding performance-related problems.

Quality circles

The technique of quality circles[9] became enormously popular in Japan, where many thousands of quality circles have been registered. The concept is that ordinary workers, given the opportunity and some basic training in cause-effect analysis, can provide a powerful quality assurance and productivity boost for their employers. Quality circles have demonstrated their value in manufactured goods, electronics, automotive production, and aircraft production. In Japan, at least, the technique has also worked well for software. Here in the United States, the approach has not been widely utilized for software, nor is there enough empirical data reported in the literature to even judge the effectiveness for U.S. software.

Zero-defect programs

The concepts of zero defects originated in aviation and defense companies in the late 1950s. Halpin wrote an excellent tutorial on the method in the mid-1960s.[10] The approach, valid from a psychological viewpoint, is that if each worker and manager individually strives for excellence and zero defects, the final product has a good chance of achieving zero defects. The concept is normally supported by substantial public relations work in companies which adopt the philosophy. Interestingly, some zero-defect software applications of comparatively small size have been developed. Unfortunately, however, most software practitioners who live with software daily tend to doubt that the method can actually work for large or complex systems. There is certainly no empirical evidence that zero-defect large systems have yet been built.

Proofs of correctness

The concepts of correctness proofs originated in the domain of systems software, and they have been made well known by such authors as Mills[11] and Martin.[12] Unfortunately, there is no empirical data that demonstrates that software proved correct has a lower defect rate under field conditions than software not proved correct. Anecdotal evidence indicates that proofs are fairly hard to create, and indeed there may be errors in a substantial number of the proofs themselves. Also, proofs are very time-consuming. On the whole, this technology lacks empirical validation.

Independent verification and validation

Military projects following military specifications such as 2167A and 498 are constrained to use outside specialists for reviewing major deliverables, and indeed for independent testing as well.[13] Independent verification and validation is normally termed "IV&V," since the whole name is too long for convenience. Although the concept seems sound enough, there is insufficient empirical evidence that military projects have significantly higher quality or reliability than ordinary systems software projects of the same size and complexity, which do not use IV&V. Mission-critical military projects seem to have reasonably high levels of quality and reliability, however.

There are also commercial IV&V companies which offer testing and verification services to their clients. Since testing is a technical specialty, these commercial testing houses often do a better job than the informal, "amateur" testing carried out by ordinary programmers who lack training in test methods.

Professionally staffed testing departments

In almost every human activity, specialists tend to outperform generalists. That is decidedly true of software testing, which is a highly sophisticated technical specialty if it is to be performed well. As a rule of thumb, companies that have testing departments staffed by trained specialists will average about 10 to 15 percent higher in cumulative testing efficiency than companies which attempt testing by using their ordinary programming staffs. Normal unit testing by programmers is seldom more than 25 percent efficient, in that only about 1 bug in 4 will be found, and most other forms of testing are usually less than 30 percent efficient when carried out by untrained generalists. A series of well-planned tests by a professionally staffed testing group can exceed 35 percent per stage, and 90 percent in overall cumulative testing efficiency. Microsoft is one of the strongest enthusiasts for professional testing groups, which are necessary for products such as Windows 95.

Clean-room development

The concept of clean-room development as described by Dr. Harlan Mills and his colleagues at IBM is based on the physically clean rooms used to construct sensitive electronic devices, where any impurity can damage the process. For software, clean-room development implies careful control of all deliverables prior to turning the deliverable over to any downstream worker. The clean-room method also envisions the usage of formal specification methods, formal structural methods, and also proofs of correctness applied to critical algorithms. The clean-room concept is new, and it is intuitively appealing. However, empirical evidence is scarce, and no large-scale successes have yet been reported. The federal and military support groups of the IBM corporation have been the most active U.S. adherents to the clean-room concept.

Prototyping

Prototyping is more of a defect prevention than a defect removal technique, although the impact on a certain class of defects is very high. Projects which use prototypes tend to reach functional stability earlier than those which do not. Therefore, prototyped projects usually add only 10 percent or less of their functions after the requirements phase, whereas unprototyped projects tend to add 30 percent or more of their functions after the requirements phase. Since the defect rates associated with late, rushed functions are more than twice as high as normal averages, it can be stated that prototyping is a very effective defect prevention method. It is most successful for midsize projects—between about 100 and 1000 function points. For very small projects, the project itself serves the same purpose as the prototype. For very large projects, it is not usually possible for the prototype to reflect all of the functionality.

Joint application design

The joint application design (JAD) methodology originated in Canada at the IBM Toronto programming laboratory, and it has now spread throughout the world. More than a dozen companies now teach JAD-like techniques and offer consulting services to facilitate JAD sessions. Like prototyping, the JAD technique is more of a defect prevention method than a defect removal method. It is an improved method of deriving the requirements for a software project by means of structured, joint sessions of user representatives and the software design team. The sessions follow a structured format, and they are facilitated by a trained moderator. As with prototypes, projects using the JAD approach reach functional stability earlier, and they usually add less than 10 percent of their final functionality as afterthoughts. It should be noted that the JAD method is synergistic with prototyping, and the two techniques together seem to be a very effective combination.

The JAD method originated in the domain of management information systems, and assumes that there will be an available set of users who can participate. Thus, for projects for which users are either not available or there may be thousands of them (as with spreadsheets or word processing software), the JAD method may not be useful.

Software complexity analysis

There is a strong and direct correlation between code complexity and software defect rates. Since code complexity can be directly measured by means of a dozen or so commercially available tools, a useful first step in improving quality is to analyze the complexity of existing software. The programs or components of systems that have dangerously high complexity levels can then be isolated and corrected.

Error-prone module removal

In all of the large software systems that have yet been studied by major corporations, including IBM, DEC, Wang, AT&T, and Hewlett-Packard, the bugs or defects have not been randomly distributed through the systems. Instead, they have clumped in surprisingly localized sections termed "error-prone modules." As a rule of thumb, about 5 percent of the modules in a large system may receive almost 50 percent of the total defect reports. Once such modules have been identified, the problems can often be corrected. Although high complexity and poor coding practices are often associated with error-prone modules, there are other factors too. Often error-prone modules are those added to the system late, after requirements and design were nominally finished. In many cases, the late arrival of the code led to the embarrassing situation of having no test cases created for it, since the test and quality assurance groups did not know the code had been added!

Restructuring, reverse engineering, and reengineering

In 1985, a new subindustry started to form; it comprised companies that offered various geriatric services for aging software. The first such services to be offered were automatic or semiautomatic restructuring of Cobol source code. The general results were favorable, in that the restructured code was easier to modify and maintain than the previous unstructured versions. However, restructuring did not change the size of the modules, so manual remodularization was often used as an adjunct to reduce the sizes of the modules down to manageable levels (fewer than 500 source code statements). Here too, the results have generally been favorable. Some companies, indeed, have experimented with using the restructuring techniques on new applications, since the standardized results make it easier for programmers to maintain applications other than those they wrote themselves. Here too, the results are favorable.

The impact of restructuring and remodularization on software quality is significant, but it is largely indirect. Restructuring and remodularization will find some bugs and dead code, of course, but the primary benefit is a reduction in the effort associated with defect repairs and enhancements once the transformation is finished. More recently, such companies as Bachman Associates, CGI, CADRE Technologies, and Language Technology have announced capabilities of expert systems which can analyze existing source code and create a synthetic specification from latent information present in the code itself. This process, termed "reverse engineering," is based on the thesis that the original specifications have long since fallen into decay, leaving the enterprise with nothing but aging source code and human knowledge to work from when updating applications. Obviously, aging source code is not a good starting point for major enhancements or updates of the application.

The next step beyond reverse engineering is reengineering, or semi-automatic conversion of an aging application into a modern one, perhaps by using different languages and running on a different platform. The concepts of reverse engineering and reengineering are appealing, but not enough empirical data exists at present to state whether they will be truly successful.

The Malcolm Baldrige awards

One does not ordinarily associate governments with quality, yet the government-sponsored Baldrige awards for quality have become a major factor in U.S. business and hopefully will remain so in the future. To win a Baldrige award, it is necessary to not only achieve high quality in real life but also to measure the results in a statistically valid way. Associated with the Baldrige concept are seven pillars, including measures, strategy, customer focus, human skill enhancement, process, and results. Thus far, the Baldrige awards have stirred up more action in the engineering world than in the software world, but several leading software producers are actually attempting a run at one of these prestigious awards. All of us in the software industry should wish them luck, since winning the award would benefit the entire industry. For the Baldrige awards to stay effective, great care must be exercised in whom they are given to. Nothing can damage the impact of such an award more quickly than giving to an enterprise that does not truly deserve it!

Measuring Software Defect Removal

The word "quality" has so many possible definitions for software that it has tended to become an intangible term. As already discussed, it can mean user satisfaction, conformance to requirements, or any combination of a host of concepts that end with "ility" such as reliability, maintainability, and portability. These abstract definitions can be measured subjectively, but the measurements are often vague and unsatisfying.

There is one major aspect of quality that can be measured in a tangible and convincing way. The hard, tangible aspect of quality is the measurement of defect removal. Not only can defect removal be measured with high precision, but this metric is one of the fundamental parameters that should be included in all corporate software measurement programs.

Projects that perform well in terms of defect removal often perform well with such other aspects of quality as conformance to requirements and user satisfaction. On the other hand, projects with inadequate defect removal are seldom successful in the other aspects of quality either.

Reporting frequency for defect measurements

The natural frequency for defect measurement is monthly. That is, every month a standard report that shows all of the defects found in the course of the prior month should be produced. The monthly report should contain at least the following sections:

1. Defects found by reviews and inspections
2. Defects found by testing
3. Defects found and reported by users

More sophisticated defect reports, such as those produced by large commercial software producers like IBM, are capable of showing this additional information:

4. Defects found by product and product line
5. Defects found by geographic region (country, city, state, etc.)
6. Defects found by customer
7. Defect found by industry (banking, insurance, etc.)

All of this data can be condensed and summarized on an annual basis, but the fundamental reporting frequency should be monthly.

Turning on the defect count "clock"

Productivity data can be reconstructed from the memories of the project teams. Indeed, such reconstructed data is sometimes better than the data that comes out of a tracking system because it lacks the errors of the typical tracking system.

Quality data, on the other hand, cannot be reconstructed. It must be measured, and it must be accumulated for quite some time before enough of it is available to be useful. If you start counting today, it can be more than a year before you accumulate enough data to really understand your company's quality levels. However, if you do not start today, or at least fairly soon, you may never understand your company's quality levels. Indeed, if your competitors measure quality and your company does not, they may very well put your company out of business before you can even know why! There are three natural starting places for beginning to count defect levels:

1. As early as possible, such as during requirements
2. When testing begins
3. When customers begin to use the software

less formal than for older mainframe applications. For example, formal inspections of specifications and source code are less common for client-server applications than for mainframe applications. The combined results of higher complexity levels and less rigorous development practices tend to have both a near-term and a long-term impact: In the near term, client-server quality is often deficient, and in the long term, client-server maintenance costs may well exceed those of traditional mainframe applications.

Although the data is still far from complete and has a high margin of error, it is of interest to consider some of the differences between monolithic mainframe applications and client-server applications.

Following is a typical defect pattern for monolithic mainframe applications, using the metric "defects per function point" for normalizing the data.

By contrast, following is the equivalent defect pattern for distributed client-server applications. The number of requirements problems is approximately equal between the two domains. However, owing to increased complexity levels associated with distributed software, design and coding defect rates are typically more numerous. Also more numerous is the category of "bad fixes," which are secondary defects or bugs accidentally introduced into software during fixing of previous bugs. The category of bad fixes is somewhat ominous since it will have an impact on the long-range maintenance costs of client-server applications.

As can be seen, client-server applications are generating more than 20 percent higher defect potentials than monolithic mainframe software.

Even more troublesome than the elevated defect potentials associated with client-server software are somewhat lower defect removal

Software Defect Pattern for Monolithic Mainframe Applications (Defects per Function Point)

Requirements defects	Design defects	Code defects	Bad fixes	Overall defect total
1.00	1.25	1.75	0.50	4.50

Software Defect Pattern for Distributed Client-Server Applications (Defects per Function Point)

Requirements defects	Design defects	Code defects	Bad fixes	Overall defect total
1.00	1.75	2.00	0.75	5.50

From consulting engagements with several hundred clients in large corporations, the norm (among those who measure defects at all) is, unfortunately, number 3. That is not as it should be. The true starting place, in order to gain insights that can make major improvements, is to start as early as possible. IBM, for example, starts its defect "clock" during the requirements phase and keeps it running through the entire life cycle. This kind of data is invaluable for insights and subsequent defect prevention.

Late starts with defect counting tend to obscure problems with requirements and design, which typically comprise the bulk of all problems for major systems. The earlier the counting begins, the better the insights that can be gained. Early starting, of course, involves cultural changes within a company and some careful preparation in order to make defect measures a useful corporate tool.

Definition of a software defect

A software defect is simply a bug which if not removed would cause a program or system to fail or to produce incorrect results. *Note:* The very common idea that a defect is a failure to adhere to some user requirement is unsatisfactory because it offers no way to measure requirements defects themselves, which constitute one of the larger categories of software error.

Defects can have five different origins in a software project, and it is normal to assign an origin code to each discovered defect. Examples of the five defect origins include requirements errors, such as accidentally leaving out a necessary input screen; design defects, such as a mistake in an algorithm; coding defects, such as branching to a wrong location; documentation defects, such as giving the incorrect command for starting a program; and bad fixes, such as making a fresh mistake while fixing a previous bug.

When measuring defect removal, it is normal to assign the responsibility for determining whether or not a given problem is a defect to the quality assurance manager. If the project does not have a quality assurance manager assigned, the project manager or supervisor should assign the origin code after the defect has been technically analyzed.

Some defects will be reported more than once, especially when the software has many users. Although duplicate reports of the same bug are recorded, the normal defect removal metric is based on a "valid unique defect," or the first report of any given bug. From time to time, defect reports that are submitted turn out, upon examination, to be either user errors or problems that are external to the software itself. These are termed "invalid defect reports," and they are excluded from the software defect measures. They are, however, recorded for historical and statistical purposes. There are also various plateaus of defect severity. The four-point severity scale used by IBM for software looks like this:

Severity 1	System or program inoperable
Severity 2	Major functions disabled or incorrect
Severity 3	Minor functions disabled or incorrect
Severity 4	Superficial error

An initial defect severity code is often assigned by the client or user of the software such as a tester. However, since users have a natural tendency to code most defects severity 1 or severity 2, the final severity level is usually determined by a quality assurance manager or an objective source. In summary, defects are counted as totals and then sorted into subcategories as follows:

Unique defect reports versus duplicate defect reports

Valid defect reports versus invalid defect reports

Defect reports by origin:

1. Requirements defects
2. Design defects
3. Coding defects
4. Documentation defects
5. Bad fixes

Defect reports by severity:

1. Severity 1 defects
2. Severity 2 defects
3. Severity 3 defects
4. Severity 4 defects

If you measure software defects by using these concepts, a typical distribution of valid unique defects for a medium to large system might look like the data shown in Table 5.3.

Note the interesting skew in the distribution in Table 5.3: For critical severity 1 defects, requirements errors are dominant; for severity 2 defects, design errors are dominant. Coding errors are in second place overall, but they do not comprise the largest source of error except for the comparatively unimportant severity 4 category. Of course, the table reflects the results of medium-size to large systems of 50,000 Cobol statements and larger. For small programs of 5000 Cobol statements or less, coding errors would comprise more than 50

TABLE 5.3 Distribution of Software Defect Origins and Severities

	Severity level				
Defect origin	1, %	2, %	3, %	4, %	Total, %
Requirements	5.0	5.0	3.0	2.0	15.0
Design	3.0	22.0	10.0	5.0	40.0
Coding	2.0	10.0	10.0	8.0	30.0
Documentation	0.0	1.0	2.0	2.0	5.0
Bad fixes	0.0	2.0	5.0	3.0	10.0
Total defects	10.0	40.0	30.0	20.0	100.0

percent of the total error density. In addition to the valid unique defects which the table reflects, you can expect an invalid defect for each valid defect. If you have multiple users of or clients for your software, you can expect one duplicate defect report for every five users.

Measuring Defect Removal Efficiency

Once a satisfactory encoding scheme for your basic defect counts has been adopted, the next stage is to measure the defects found by each removal activity. Typical MIS projects go through pretest requirements and design reviews, partial code walk-throughs, and from two to five testing steps depending on the size and nature of the project. A typical MIS defect removal series might look like this:

1. Requirements review
2. Design review
3. Desk checking by individual programmers (not measured)
4. Code walk-through
5. Unit testing by individual programmers (not measured)
6. Integration testing of entire program or system
7. Acceptance testing by users

At this point it should be noted that tasks 3 and 5 (desk checking and unit testing) are often not measured, since they are carried out by the individual programmers themselves. (However, some programmers have volunteered to record defects found during these activities, simply to complete the data necessary to evaluate a full defect removal series.) Assuming that you will measure only the public defect removal activities and not the private ones, your data might look like the information in Table 5.4 for a 50,000-source-statement Cobol application that also contained some 500 function points. Note that

TABLE 5.4 Software Defect Distributions by Removal Step

Removal activity	Defects found	Defects per KLOC	Defects per function point
Requirements review	125	2.5	0.25
Design review	250	5.0	0.50
Code inspection	500	10.0	1.00
Integration test	150	3.0	0.30
Acceptance test	100	2.0	0.20
Total defects	1125	22.5	2.25

Table 5.4 makes the simplifying assumption that it takes 100 Cobol statements to implement one function point. The average value is actually 105 statements per function point, but for tutorial purposes an even amount was selected.

At this point, you will not yet be able to complete the final set of quality measures. That requires collecting defect data reported by actual users of the project. You will normally collect data from users for as long as the project is in use, but after one year of production, and then annually for each additional year of use, you will be able to complete a very significant analysis of the defect removal efficiencies of your review, inspection, and test series. Assume that the first year of production by your users generated the number of defects shown in Table 5.5. You will now be able to calculate one of the most important and meaningful metrics in all software: your defect removal efficiency.

The general formula for defect removal efficiency is quite simple: It is the ratio of bugs found prior to delivery by your staff to the total number of bugs. The total number of bugs is found by summing bugs you discovered with the bugs your clients discovered in a predetermined time period. In this example, the bugs that your staff removed before delivery totaled 1125. The bugs found by your users in the first year totaled 400. If you add those two values together, the sum is 1525. That is equal to 30.5 bugs per KLOC, or 3.05 bugs per function point, which are middle-range values for Cobol applications of this size. (Leading-edge applications will total fewer than 15 bugs per KLOC, whereas the real disasters may go above 75 bugs per KLOC.)

TABLE 5.5 User-Reported Defects from One Year of Production Runs

Activity	Defects found	Defects per KLOC	Defects per function point
First-year user defect reports	400	8.0	0.8

Cumulative defect removal efficiency is defined as the percentage of bugs found by the development team before a software product is delivered to its users. Efficiency cannot be measured until after a predetermined time period has gone by, and the first year of use is a convenient interval for the first calculation. Of course, not all bugs will be found after only one year, so recalculation after 2 or even 3 years would also be useful.

In this example, finding 1125 bugs out of 1525 amounts to only 73.8 percent, which is a typical but mediocre result. The normal defect removal efficiency for MIS projects is somewhere between 50 and 75 percent when measured. Leading-edge MIS companies will find more than 90 percent of the bugs, while leading-edge commercial and military software producers will find more than 95 percent of the bugs.

Defect removal efficiency is a very important metric, because raising efficiency above 90 percent can improve quality, productivity, and user satisfaction at the same time. Indeed, a cumulative total of 95 percent appears to be one of the most powerful node points in all of software engineering, since schedules, quality, effort, and user satisfaction all tend to approach optimum levels when this target is achieved.

Not only can the cumulative defect removal efficiency of a series of removal steps be measured; it is also possible to measure the individual net efficiency of each step. In real life, each defect removal step will have a differential efficiency against each source of defect. Table 5.6 shows typical efficiencies against four defect origins for a variety of reviews, inspections, and tests. The efficiencies in Table 5.6 were calcu-

TABLE 5.6 Defect Removal Efficiencies by Defect Origin

	Defects by origin, %			
Removal step	Requirements	Design	Coding	Documentation
JAD	50	25	10	15
Prototyping	40	35	35	15
Requirements review	40	15	0	5
Design review	15	55	0	15
Code inspection	20	40	65	25
Subtotal	75	85	73	50
Unit test	1	5	20	0
Function test	10	15	30	5
System test	10	15	35	20
Field test	20	20	25	25
Subtotal	35	45	75	43
Cumulative	87	92	94	72

lated from empirical studies, although significant variations can and do occur.

The table of defect removal efficiencies actually matches real-life results fairly closely. Coding defects are the easiest to remove, and hence they have the highest overall efficiencies against them. Requirements defects are the most troublesome, and normally they have the lowest efficiencies. Although documentation defects are not intrinsically difficult to remove (journals such as *Scientific American* exceed 99.5 percent in net efficiency), most software projects simply do not use high-efficiency techniques such as copy editing by professional editors or proofreading by pairs of readers.

In terms of the removal methods themselves, detailed code inspections are the most efficient form of defect removal yet measured, whereas most testing steps are less than 35 percent efficient. That is, most forms of testing find less than one bug out of every three bugs that actually exist. Once you have measured a reasonably large sample of projects (more than 50), you will be able to use the data you've collected to make very accurate quality and reliability estimates.

Some of the implications of Table 5.5 deserve discussion. First, given the low efficiencies of testing, it is obviously impossible to achieve high levels of cumulative efficiency without up-front activities such as prototyping, reviews, or inspections. To be blunt, companies that only perform testing will never go much beyond 75 percent in cumulative defect removal efficiency; that is, they will deliver at least one out of every four bugs to their clients.

Second, testing ranges from moderate to useless in its ability to come to grips with front-end defects such as requirements and design. Indeed, it is surprising that testing can find requirements defects at all. Therefore, it is imperative to utilize the high-efficiency pretest activities in order to control these major sources of system problems.

Given the magnitude of defects associated with requirements and design, it is obvious that these important defect sources must be included in quality control planning. Even a cursory inspection of removal efficiencies demonstrates that JADs, prototyping, and up-front inspections are logically necessary to control front-end bugs.

Third, there are some special calculations needed to include bad fixes, or bugs accidentally introduced as by-products of fixing previous bugs. The total quantity of bad fixes averages about 5 to 10 percent, and it will be directly related to the complexity of the work product being repaired.

Fourth, given the low average efficiencies of most removal steps, it is obvious that to achieve a high cumulate efficiency, it will be necessary to use many steps. Commercial and military software producers, for example, may include as many as 20 to 25 discrete removal activities.

This is one of the key differences between systems software and MIS projects. MIS projects normally utilize only five to seven different kinds of removal, and they seldom utilize the rigorous inspection process.

Fifth, serious quality control requires a synergistic combination of multiple techniques, with each removal step aimed at the class of defects for which its efficiency is highest. Figure 5.3 illustrates a typical synergy among defect removal methods. The moral of the figure is quite simple: Choose the combination of defect removal steps that will achieve the highest overall efficiency for the lowest actual costs.

Here is a final point on defect measurement and defect removal in general. Finding and fixing bugs has been among the most expensive, if not the most expensive, activity for software since the industry began. Companies that do measure quality and defect removal have a tremendous competitive advantage against those who do not. Historically, certain industries such as computers and telecommunications paid serious attention to both hardware quality and software quality and introduced quality measurement programs, in some cases, more than 30 years ago. These industries have been capable of withstanding overseas competition much better than such industries as automotive construction, which learned about quality control far too late. Quality control is the key to corporate survival in the twenty-first century, and measurement is the key to quality control. Now is the time to start!

Finding and Eliminating Error-Prone Modules

In the late 1960s Gary Okimoto, a researcher at the IBM Endicott laboratory, carried out a study in which he looked at the distribution of defects within the OS/360 operating system. To his surprise, and to the surprise of everyone else who knew of the study, the defects were not smoothly or randomly distributed throughout the modules of the system. Instead, they clumped in a small number of very buggy modules. Some 4 percent of the modules contained 38 percent of the errors in the entire operating system. This study is perhaps the original discovery of the error-prone module concept. In any case, it is the first such study known to the author.

The study was replicated against other IBM software products, and it invariably produced striking results. For example, when west coast researchers at IBM's Palo Alto laboratory carried out a similar study on the IMS database product, some 57 percent of the errors were concentrated in only 31 modules, which constituted about 7 percent of the modules of the product and about 12 percent of the code.

Other companies, including AT&T, ITT, Wang, and Hewlett-Packard, have come to regard error-prone module analysis as a normal aspect of quality control. So far as can be determined from all of

	Requirements Defects	Design Defects	Code Defects	Document Defects	Performance Defects
Reviews/ Inspections	Fair	Excellent	Excellent	Good	Fair
Prototypes	Good	Fair	Fair	Not Applicable	Good
Testing (all forms)	Poor	Poor	Good	Fair	Excellent
Correctness Proofs	Poor	Poor	Good	Fair	Poor

Figure 5.3 Defect removal methods.

the studies yet carried out, error-prone modules are a very common phenomenon and will occur in all large systems unless deliberate corrective steps are taken. Fortunately, a number of corrective steps that can eliminate error-prone modules from software products are available. The most basic step is to measure defects down to the level of modules in inspections, testing, and maintenance. Any module with more than about ten defects per KLOC is a candidate for a full review to explore its status. From the error-prone modules that have been explored in depth, a number of causative factors have been identified. The most significant among them are:

1. Excessive schedule pressure applied to the developers
2. Excessive complexity that is due to either:
   - Failure to use proper structured techniques
   - Intrinsic nature of the problem to be encoded
3. Excessive size of individual modules (>500 statements)
4. Failure to test the module after code was complete

The first three factors are intuitive and even self-explanatory, but the fourth factor is something of a surprise. Even more surprising is the high frequency with which this phenomenon occurs. Normally, error-prone modules that have not been tested are those which were created very late in a product's development cycle, often while testing was nearing completion. These modules were rushed into production without bothering to update the specifications or the test case libraries! The solution to this problem is a rigorous module promotion process, which includes "locked" master copies of a software product with no way to add modules unless careful quality control procedures are followed.

Using Metrics to Evaluate Test-Case Coverage

As of 1995, there are perhaps 30 to 50 commercially available tools that can be used to assist in measuring test-case coverage. These tools normally trace the execution sequence of code when it is executing, and they can isolate and identify sequences that are not executed while testing. Although such tools are very useful, it should be clearly realized that there is a striking discontinuity between test coverage and testing efficiency. Even though a particular test step, such as function testing, for example, causes the execution of more than 90 percent of the instructions in a program, that does not imply that 90 percent of the bugs will be found. Indeed, normally less than 30 percent of the bugs will be found by function testing. The reason for the discontinuity is fairly straightforward: Just because instructions have been executed does not guarantee that they are doing what was actually intended.

It should also be noted that there is no guarantee that the test cases themselves are correct. Indeed, a study at IBM's Kingston laboratory in the middle 1970s found that test cases often had a higher error content than the products for which the test cases were constructed! Another surprising finding was that about one-third of the test cases appeared to be duplicates, which added nothing to testing rigor but quite a bit to testing costs.

Using Metrics for Reliability Prediction

Quality and reliability are logically related topics. Surprisingly, they are often decoupled in the software engineering literature. Many articles on quality do not mention reliability, and many articles on reliability do not mention quality.

The reliability domain has built up a large body of both theoretical and empirical models and a number of supporting metrics such as mean time to failure (MTTF) and mean time between failures (MTBF). A good overview of the reliability domain is provided by Musa, Iannino, and Okumoto.[4]

Because the topics of quality and reliability are so often separated, it is useful to show at least the crude correlations between them. Table 5.7 is derived from empirical data collected by the author at IBM in the 1970s for systems software written in Assembler. The data was collected from unit, function, component, and system test runs.

TABLE 5.7 Relation between Defect Levels and Reliability

Defect levels in defects per KLOC	Approximate mean time to failure (MTTF)
More than 30	Less than 2 min
20–30	4–15 min
10–20	5–60 min
5–10	1–4 h
2–5	4–24 h
1–2	24–160 h
Less than 1	Indefinite

Measuring the Costs of Defect Removal

Since the computing and software era began, the largest single identifiable cost element has been that of finding and fixing bugs. It is astonishing, therefore, that so few companies have measured this cost with accuracy. It is also embarrassing that attempts to measure defect removal have so often been paradoxical in economic terms.

The paradox of "cost per defect"

For perhaps 10 years, the most common unit of measure for assessing defect removal has been "cost per defect." At least 50 referenced journal articles and perhaps half a dozen software management books have contained the statement, "It costs 100 times as much to fix a bug in production as it does during design." The concept of cost per defect is to accumulate the total costs associated with defect removal for a particular activity class such as testing and then divide the cost by number of defects found. Thus, if a particular test step found 100 defects and cost $2500 to carry out, the cost per defect would be $25.

Unfortunately, as it is commonly calculated, cost per defect is one of the worst and most foolish metrics ever devised. It contains a built-in mathematical paradox that causes it to penalize high quality and to do so in direct proportion to the level of quality achieved. The best programs and systems with the fewest defects will look the worst and the most decrepit and bug-ridden applications will look the best!

To understand the nature of the problems with cost per defect, it is necessary to look at the detailed economic picture of removing defects in software. Every software defect removal activity, regardless of whether it is a review, an inspection, a test, or maintenance, will have three basic cost elements associated with it:

1. Preparation costs
2. Execution costs
3. Repair costs

Preparation costs consist of the things which must be performed prior to carrying out a specific form of defect removal. For example, prior to testing a program, it is necessary to create test cases. Prior to carrying out a design review, it is necessary to read the specifications. Preparation costs are essentially fixed; they will remain comparatively constant regardless of how many bugs are present. Thus, even for zero-defect software it will still be necessary to write test cases and read the descriptive materials. Execution costs are associated with the actual events of the defect removal activity. For testing, execution consists of running the application against the set of prepared test cases.

For reviews and inspections, execution is the cost of actually holding the review and inspection sessions. Execution costs are not fixed costs, but they are somewhat inelastic. That is, the cost of executing a review or test is only partly associated with the number of defects present. The bulk of the costs is associated with the mere mechanics of going through the exercise. Thus, even zero-defect applications will accumulate some costs for carrying out reviews and inspections and running test cases, and even zero-defect applications can have maintenance costs. That is surprising but true, since user errors and invalid defects will probably be reported against the product.

Defect repair costs are those associated with actually fixing any bugs or defects that were identified. Defect repairs are true variable costs, and they are the only cost elements that will drop to zero if zero bugs are present in a program or system. When quality improves, the cost per defect will tend to get higher rather than lower, since the fixed and inelastic preparation and execution costs will become progressively more important. Table 5.8 illustrates the paradox of cost per defect in the case of high quality for two applications in Ada, both of which were 150 function points, or 10,000 source statements, in size. Assume $5000 per person-month as the normal labor rate.

Consider the economic fallacy of cost per defect. The true costs of defect removal declined from $35,000 to only $10,000, or better than 70 percent. The costs of the critical defect repair component declined by a full 10 to 1 between the low-quality and high-quality examples. Yet while the real economics of defect removal improved tremendously, the "cost per defect" skyrocketed from $70 to $2000! It is obvious that if the high-quality product had achieved zero-defect status, there still would have been expenses for preparation and execution. In this

TABLE 5.8 The Paradox of Cost per Defect for Quality Measures

	Low-quality Ada application	High-quality Ada application
Size in KLOC	10	10
Size in function points	150	150
Defects found	500	5
Preparation costs	$5,000	$5,000
Execution costs	$25,000	$2,500
Defect repairs	$25,000	$2,500
Total removal cost	$35,000	$10,000
Cost per defect	$70	$2,000
Cost per function point	$233.33	$66.66

case, the cost per defect would have been infinity, since there would be tangible costs divided by zero defects!

Plainly, cost per defect is not a suitable metric for economic studies associated with software quality. Here too, function points are much better for economic purposes. Since both versions of the application contained 150 function points, it can be seen that the metric defect removal costs per function point matches economic assumptions perfectly. For the low-quality version, $233.33 per function point was spent for defect removal; for the high-quality version, only $66.66 was spent.

Collecting defect removal data

Although cost per defect is not valid in the way it is normally used—with preparation and execution simply clumped with repairs, the metric can be explored by time-and-motion studies and utilized in conjunction with functional metrics. Table 5.9 shows the effort associated with common forms of defect, removal in terms of preparation, execution, and defect repairs. Preparation and execution are measured in work-hours per function point, and repair (and only repair) is measured in hours per defect repaired. The final total of effort is normalized to person-hours per function point.

For economic study purposes, it is necessary to convert all of the final effort data into a per function-point basis. For example, assume that you are carrying out a design inspection with five participants on a project that totals 100 function points and in the course of the inspection you find 50 bugs that need repairs. From the data in Table 5.9, the preparation effort would amount to 25 h and the inspection sessions would amount to 50 work-hours (but only 10 clock hours). The 50 bugs would require 75 h. Thus the entire process totaled as follows:

Preparation		Execution		Repair		
25 h	+	50 h	+	75 h	=	150 h

The overall inspection, including preparation, execution, and repair, netted out to 1.5 work-hours per function point. In this example, the effort per bug would be 3.0 h per bug for the sum of preparation, execution, and repair. Consider the same basic example, only this time assume that only 10 bugs were found:

Preparation		Execution		Repair		
25 h	+	50 h	+	15 h	=	90 h

TABLE 5.9 Preparation, Execution, and Defect Repair Effort

Removal step	Preparation, hours per function point	Execution, hours per function point	Repairs, hours per defect
JAD	0.15	0.25	1.00
Prototyping	0.25	1.00	1.00
Requirements review	0.15	0.25	1.00
Design inspection	0.15	0.50	1.50
Code inspection	0.25	0.75	1.50
Unit test	0.50	0.25	2.50
Function test	0.75	0.50	5.00
System test	1.00	0.50	10.00
Field test	0.50	0.50	10.00

In this second situation, the overall inspection process amounted to only 0.9 h per function point, which is substantially below the previous rate of 1.5 h per function point. However, the "effort per bug" has now tripled and is up to 9.0 h per bug! As can easily be seen, the fixed and inelastic costs of preparation and execution tend to distort the per-bug metric so that it becomes paradoxically more expensive as quality improves. A metric that penalizes the very goal you are seeking is hardly suitable for serious economic studies.

The Cost-of-Quality Concept

Phil Crosby's famous book *Quality Is Free,*[3] made popular a cost collection method termed "cost of quality." Although this concept originated in the domain of manufactured products, it has been applied to software projects as well. It is fairly thorough in its approach, and it captures costs associated with rework, scrap, warranty repairs, complaint handling, inspections, and testing. There are three large cost buckets associated with the concept:

1. Prevention costs
2. Appraisal costs
3. Failure costs

Crosby's descriptions of these costs are based on manufactured products, and they are somewhat orthogonal to software. For software purposes, prevention would encompass methods that simplified complexity and reduced the human tendency to make errors. Examples of prevention costs include the costs of training staff in structured design and coding techniques. Joint application design (JAD) also comes under the heading of prevention, since it is one of the key by-products of the approach.

Appraisal costs for software include inspections and all forms of testing. For military projects, appraisal costs also include independent verification and validation, or IV&V, as it is called. In one sense, fixing bugs found by testing might be thought of as failure costs, but it seems more appropriate to count the costs as appraisal elements, since they normally occur prior to delivery of the software to its final customers. Failure costs of software are the costs associated with postrelease bug repairs: field service, maintenance, warranty repairs, and in some cases liability damages and litigation expenses.

Evaluating Defect Prevention Methods

Defect removal deals with tangible things such as bug reports that can be counted fairly easily. Defect prevention, on the other hand, is much harder to come to grips with. This phenomenon is true of other human activities as well. For example, the cost and efficacy of preventive medicine is much more uncertain than the cost and efficacy of treating conditions once they occur. The term "defect prevention" means the overall set of technologies that simplify complexity and minimize a natural human tendency to make errors while performing complex tasks. Examples of defect prevention technologies include prototypes, JAD sessions, graphic design methods, formal architectures, structured techniques, and high-level languages. Indeed, some defect removal methods, such as inspections, are also effective in terms of defect prevention because participants will spontaneously avoid making mistakes which they observe during the inspection sessions. Figure 5.4 illustrates some of the synergies among defect prevention methods.

Long-range monitoring of defect prevention and defect removal

After quality measurement programs get underway, they can be used to monitor long-term effects over a period of many years. For example, Table 5.10 illustrates a 10-year trend by a major computer manufacturer for both applications and systems software. The original data has been simplified and rounded to demonstrate the trends.

The overall combination of defect prevention and defect removal improvements led to a full order of magnitude improvement in defects as received by clients. It cannot be overemphasized that both defect prevention and defect removal need to be part of an effective quality

	Requirements Defects	Design Defects	Code Defects	Document Defects	Performance Defects
JAD's	Excellent	Good	Not Applicable	Fair	Poor
Prototypes	Excellent	Excellent	Fair	Not Applicable	Excellent
Structured Methods	Fair	Good	Excellent	Fair	Fair
CASE Tools	Fair	Good	Fair	Fair	Fair
Blueprints & Reusable Code	Excellent	Excellent	Excellent	Excellent	Good
QFD	Good	Excellent	Fair	Poor	Good

Figure 5.4 Defect prevention methods.

TABLE 5.10 Long-Range Improvements in Defect Prevention and Defect Removal

	1985	1986	1987	1988	1990	1995
Potential defects per function point	5.0	4.5	4.0	3.5	3.0	2.5
Removal efficiency, %	70	80	85	90	95	99
Delivered defects per function point	1.5	0.9	0.6	0.35	0.15	0.025

program: Neither is sufficient alone; together, they are synergistic. Finally, it cannot be overemphasized that without measurements carefully carried out over many years, none of the improvements would be either possible or visible.

Measuring Customer-Reported Defects

For many years, relations between defects actually delivered to customers and the number of defects found and reported back by customers has been known only to perhaps three or four major computer and telecommunication manufacturers. The relations are not intrinsically mysterious, but only a few companies had measurement systems that were sophisticated enough to study them. The fundamental problem posed by the situation is this: If you deliver a software product to a certain number of customers and it has 100 latent defects still present at the time of delivery, how many of those defects will be found and reported back by the customers in the first year? How many in the second year? The answers obey two general rules:

1. The number of defects found correlates directly with the number of users; the more users, the greater the number of defects found.
2. The number of defects found correlates inversely with the number of defects that are present; the more defects, the fewer the defects found.

The first rule is intuitive and easy to understand; the second is counter-intuitive and, at first glance, very hard to understand. It would seem that the more bugs present in software, the greater the number that would be found and reported, but that is not the case. As it happens, rule 2 tends to be in direct conflict with rule 1 for the following reason: Very buggy software cannot or will not be used. Therefore, if your company ships software with more than a certain quantity of bugs latent within it, those bugs will prevent the utilization of the software, will slow down sales, and will in general stretch out the time before the bugs are found and fixed.

Tables 5.11 and 5.12 illustrate these phenomena. They show the impacts of changing numbers of users and then the impact of changing numbers of latent defects with a specific number of users.

Table 5.11 illustrates the phenomenon that somewhere between about 20 and 95 percent of the bugs will normally be found in the first year of production, based on the number of users of the software. Since only high-volume production by large numbers of users can approach 100 percent in overall removal efficiency, it can clearly be seen that the greater the number of users, the higher the percentage of first-year bug removal.

Table 5.12 illustrates the counterintuitive phenomenon that the number of bugs found by users is inversely related to the number of bugs present. The unfortunate truth is that buggy software will not (and sometimes cannot) be put into high-volume production. The initial users of the software will generally have such a bad experience with buggy software that references are impossible. Indeed, if the software package and the vendor are of sufficient magnitude that

TABLE 5.11 Relations between Users and First-Year Defect Reports

	Case 1	Case 2	Case 3	Case 4
Number of users	1	10	100	1000
Defects present	100	100	100	100
Number of defects found in year 1	20	40	75	95
Percent of defects found in year 1	20	40	75	95
Number of defects remaining in year 2	80	60	25	5
Number of years to remove all defects	5	3	2.5	2

TABLE 5.12 Relations between Defect Quantities and First-Year Defect Reports

	Case 1	Case 2	Case 3	Case 4
Number of users	100	100	100	100
Number of delivered defects	100	200	300	400
Number of defects found in year 1	60	80	100	100
Percent of defects found in year 1	60	40	33	25
Number of defects after year 1	40	120	200	300
Number of years to the removal of all defects	2	4	5	7

user groups exist, word of the poor quality will spread like wildfire and will slow down subsequent sales.

The findings in Table 5.12 are counterintuitive, but they are derived from empirical studies with actual projects. The distressingly low rate of only 25 percent in the high-defect case 4 is due, in such situations, to the fact that users do not trust the products and will not use them except in the most timid and careful fashion. Only software with a low level of initial defects will go into fully productive use fast enough to flush out the latent defects in a short time.

The data in Tables 5.11 and 5.12 implies that a calculation of defect removal efficiency after one year of service will probably be artificially high, since not all of the bugs will have been found in only one year. That is true, and it explains why companies such as IBM will recalculate defect removal efficiency after two or more years.

One other aspect of customer-reported bugs also is counterintuitive, and that is the severity levels reported by users. In this case, the reason is that the reported data is simply wrong, because of business factors. Table 5.13 shows the numbers of customer-reported bugs for commercial grade software received by a major computer company.

What is counterintuitive about the table is the astonishing 47 percent shown in the left column for severity 2 levels. At first glance, it would seem that the manufacturer was seriously amiss in quality control. In this case, however, appearances are deceiving. What was happening is that the vendor tried to fix severity 1 bugs within a week and severity 2 bugs within 2 weeks. Severity 3 bugs were fixed within about a month, and severity 4 bugs were not fixed until the next normal release. Obviously, every customer wanted his or her bug report processed promptly, so this tended to create an artificial bulge

TABLE 5.13 Severity Levels of Customer-Reported Defects

Severity level	Percent of defect reports	Probable distribution, %
Severity 1 (system unusable)	3	3
Severity 2 (major function disabled)	47	15
Severity 3 (minor function disabled)	35	60
Severity 4 (no functions disabled: superficial problem)	15	22
Total	100	100

of severity 2 defects. The probable number of real severity 2 bugs was something approaching 15 percent, as shown in the second column.

Measuring Invalid Defects, Duplicate Defects, and Special Cases

Companies that produce commercial software are aware that they not only must deal with real bugs but must also deal with enormous quantities of bugs that are not really the fault of the software against which the bug was reported. For example, in a modern multivendor environment utilizing commercial operating systems, databases, query languages, and user applications, it is quite easy to mistake the origin of a defect. Thus, a customer can send in a bug report for a seeming error in a query language when it might actually be against the user application, the operating system, or something else. As a rule of thumb, software vendors will receive two invalid defect reports for every valid report of an actual bug.

An even more common problem is duplicate reports of the same bug. For example, when WordPerfect release 5.0 was first issued, a fairly simple bug in the installation procedure generated more than 10,000 telephone calls from users on the same day to report the same bug, temporarily shutting down phone service into Utah! The costs and effort to service the duplicate calls far exceeded the costs of actually fixing the bug itself. As a rule of thumb, about 70 percent of all commercial software bugs will be found by more than one user. About 15 percent will be found by many users.

A third problem that should be measured is that of "abeyant defects." This term is used for a bug such that the system repair center cannot recreate it or make the failure happen. Obviously, some special combination of circumstances at the user location is causing the bug, but finding out exactly what it is may require on-site assistance and considerable expense! As a rule of thumb, about 20 percent of commercial software bugs will require additional information because the bugs will not occur at the repair location. The collected costs of processing invalid bug reports, duplicates, and abeyant bug reports can exceed 25 percent of the total cost of fixing real bugs. That is too big an amount to ignore, and certainly too big to leave out of quality and maintenance plans.

Finally, the most expensive single aspect of mainframe commercial software has been field service. Companies, such as IBM, DEC, and Hewlett-Packard, that send service representatives on-site to customer locations to aid in defect identification and repair can for some products spend more effort and costs on field service than on the entire total of software development and internal maintenance!

Measuring User Satisfaction

Measurement of user satisfaction differs from measurement of software defects in a number of important respects:

1. User satisfaction measures are normally annual events; defect measures are normally monthly events.
2. User satisfaction data requires active effort in order to collect it; defect reports may arrive in an unsolicited manner.
3. The staff that measures user satisfaction is normally not the staff that measured defects.
4. The changes required to improve user satisfaction may go far beyond the product itself and may encompass changes in customer support, service policies, and corporate goals.

For commercial software, user satisfaction surveys are normally carried out by the vendor's sales force on an annual basis. The sales personnel will interview their clients and will then report the findings back to the sales organization, which in turn will pass them on to the development groups. It should be noted that many commercial software products have large user associations. In that case, the user satisfaction studies may even be carried out by the user's association itself. It should also be noted that for the most successful and widely used commercial software packages, user satisfaction surveys will probably be carried out by one or more of the major industry journals such as *Datamation, ComputerWorld,* and *Software.* These studies tend to include multiple vendors and multiple products at the same time, and they are exceptionally good sources of comparative information. For internal software such as MIS projects, user satisfaction surveys can be carried out by quality assurance personnel (assuming the company has any) or by designated staff assigned by software management.

Contents and topics of user satisfaction surveys

Because of the multiple kinds of information normally included on user satisfaction surveys, it is appropriate to give an actual example of some of the topics discussed. Following are actual excerpts from a user satisfaction survey[14] developed by Software Productivity Research. The survey questions included stress the major topics of the survey, but in order to concentrate on essential factors, they omit basic boilerplate information such as the name of the product and the name of the company.

Excerpts from the SPR User Satisfaction Questionnaire

Nature of product usage? _____

1. Job-related or business usage only
2. Mixture of job-related and personal usage
3. Personal usage only

Frequency of product usage? _____

1. Product is used continuously around the clock
2. Product is used continuously during business hours
3. Product is used as needed on a daily basis
4. Product is used daily on a regular basis
5. Product is used weekly on a regular basis
6. Product is used monthly on a regular basis
7. Product is used annually on a regular basis
8. Product is used intermittently (several times a year)
9. Product is used infrequently (less than once a year)

Importance of product to your job functions? _____

1. Product is mandatory for your job functions
2. Product is of major importance to your job
3. Product is of some importance to your job
4. Product is of minor importance to your job
5. Product is of no importance to your job

How product functions were performed previously? _____

1. Functions could not be performed previously
2. Functions were performed manually
3. Functions were performed mechanically
4. Functions were performed electronically
5. Functions were performed by other software

Primary benefits from use of current product? _____

1. Product performs tasks beyond normal human abilities
2. Product simplifies complex decisions
3. Product simplifies tedious calculations
4. Product shortens critical timing situations
5. Product reduces manual effort
6. Other: _____
7. Hybrid: product has multiple benefits

Primary benefit? _____

Secondary benefit? _____

Product user evaluation

Ease of learning to use product initially? _____

1. Very easy to learn
2. Fairly easy to learn
3. Moderately easy to learn, with some difficult topics
4. Difficult to learn
5. Very difficult to learn

Ease of installing product initially? _____

1. Little or no effort to install
2. Fairly easy to install
3. Moderately easy to install, with some difficult spots
4. Difficult to install
5. Very difficult to install

Ease of customizing to local requirements? _____

1. Little or no customization needed
2. Fairly easy to customize
3. Moderately easy to customize, with some difficult spots

4. Difficult to customize
5. Very difficult to customize

Ease of logging on and starting product? _____

1. Very easy to start
2. Fairly easy to start
3. Moderately easy to start, with some difficult spots
4. Difficult to start
5. Very difficult to start

Ease of product use for normal tasks? _____

1. Very easy to use
2. Fairly easy to use
3. Moderately easy to use, with some difficult spots
4. Difficult to use
5. Very difficult to use

Ease of product use for unusual or infrequent tasks? _____

1. Very easy to use
2. Fairly easy to use
3. Moderately easy to use, with some difficult spots
4. Difficult to use
5. Very difficult to use

Ease of logging off and exiting product? _____

1. Very easy to exit
2. Fairly easy to exit
3. Moderately easy to exit, with some difficult spots
4. Difficult to exit
5. Very difficult to exit

Product handling of user errors? ______

1. Very natural and safe error handling
2. Fairly good error handling
3. Moderately good error handling, but some caution needed
4. User errors can sometimes hang up system
5. User errors often hang up system or stop product

Product speed or performance in use? ______

1. Very good performance
2. Fairly good performance
3. Moderately good normal performance but some delays
4. Performance is sometimes deficient
5. Performance is unacceptably slow or poor

Product memory utilization when in use? ______

1. No memory utilization problems with this product
2. Minimal memory utilization problems with this product
3. Moderate use of memory by this product
4. Significant memory required to use this product
5. Product memory use is excessive and unwarranted

Product compatibility with other software products? ______

1. Very good compatibility with other products
2. Fairly good compatibility with other products
3. Moderately good compatibility with other products
4. Significant compatibility problems
5. Product is highly incompatible with other software

Product quality and defect levels? ______

1. Excellent quality with few defects
2. Good quality, with some defects

3. Average quality, with normal defect levels
4. Worse than average quality, with high defect levels
5. Poor quality with excessive defect levels

Product reliability and failure intervals? _____

1. Product has never failed or almost never fails
2. Product fails less than once a year
3. Product fails or crashes a few times a year
4. Product fails fairly often and lacks reliability
5. Product fails often and is highly unreliable

Quality of training and tutorial materials? _____

1. Excellent training and tutorial materials
2. Good training and tutorial materials
3. Average training and tutorial materials
4. Worse than average training and tutorial materials
5. Poor or unacceptable training and tutorial materials

Quality of user reference manuals? _____

1. Excellent user reference manuals
2. Good user reference manuals
3. Average user reference manuals
4. Worse than average user reference manuals
5. Poor or unacceptable user reference manuals

Quality of on-screen prompts and help messages? _____

1. Excellent and lucid prompts and help messages
2. Good prompts and help messages
3. Average prompts and help messages
4. Worse than average prompts and help messages
5. Poor or unacceptable prompts and help messages

Quality of output created by product? _____

1. Excellent and easy to use product outputs
2. Good product outputs, fairly easy to use
3. Average product outputs, normal ease of use
4. Worse than average product outputs
5. Poor or unacceptable product outputs

Functionality of product? _____

1. Excellent—product meets all functional needs
2. Good—product meets most functional needs
3. Average—product meets many functional needs
4. Deficient—product meets few functional needs
5. Unacceptable—product meets no functional needs

Vendor support of product? _____

1. Excellent—product support is outstanding
2. Good—product support is better than many
3. Average—product support is acceptable
4. Deficient—product has limited support
5. Unacceptable—little or no product support

Status of product versus major competitive products? _____

1. Clearly superior to competitors in all respects
2. Superior to competitors in many respects
3. Equal to competitors, with some superior features
4. Behind competitors in some respects
5. Clearly inferior to competitors in all respects

Value of product to you personally? _____

1. Excellent—product is highly valuable

2. Good—product is quite valuable
3. Average—product has acceptable value
4. Deficient—product is not valuable
5. Unacceptable—product is a loss

List the five best features of the product:

1. ______________________________
2. ______________________________
3. ______________________________
4. ______________________________
5. ______________________________

List the five worst features of the product:

1. ______________________________
2. ______________________________
3. ______________________________
4. ______________________________
5. ______________________________

List five improvements you would like to see in the product.

1. ______________________________
2. ______________________________
3. ______________________________
4. ______________________________
5. ______________________________

As can be seen, a full user satisfaction survey covers a wide variety of topics. This brings up a significant decision for software vendors:

1. Should user surveys be carried out by live interviews?
2. Should user surveys be carried out by mail survey?
3. Should user surveys include both live interviews and mail surveys?

The pragmatic answer to these options depends upon the number of users, the available staff, and the geographic scatter of the users themselves. Normally, for major mission-critical systems and large mainframe packages, it is desirable to carry out the survey in the form of live interviews. Mail surveys are appropriate under the following conditions:

1. The product has more than 1000 users. (That is the minimum number for which mail surveys will typically generate an adequate volume of responses.)
2. The product is distributed through secondary channels, such as distributors or by mail itself.
3. The customers are widely dispersed geographically.

A hybrid methodology that utilizes both mail questionnaires and live surveys is a technique frequently employed by computer manufacturers and large software houses. The mail surveys, normally somewhat simplified, will be widely distributed to several thousand customers. Sales personnel will then carry out in-depth user satisfaction surveys with perhaps a 5 percent sample of customers or with customers that meet certain prerequisites. Typical prerequisites might include number of copies of the product acquired by the customer, size of the customer's company, or other salient factors.

Combining User Satisfaction and Defect Data

Although user satisfaction data and defect data are collected at different intervals, by different staff, and for different purposes, it is an extremely useful undertaking to combine these two measurements at least once a year. A very useful technique for combining the two kinds of information is a simple scatter graph which shows user satisfaction on one axis and user-reported defect levels on the other axis. Figure 5.5 illustrates

USER SATISFACTION

	HIGH	LOW
HIGH DEFECT LEVELS	ZONE OF URGENT REPAIRS	ZONE OF URGENT REPLACEMENT
LOW DEFECT LEVELS	ZONE OF EXCELLENT APPLICATONS	ZONE OF FUNCTIONAL ENHANCEMENT

Figure 5.5 Scatter graph of user satisfaction and defect data.

such a combination graph. Obviously, the four different conditions shown by the figure can lead to four different business responses.

1 High levels of user satisfaction and low levels of defects. This situation implies an excellent product, and it is the desirable goal of all software. Companies that measure both user satisfaction and numeric defect levels quickly realize the strong correlation between the two phenomena. Software products with high defect levels never generate satisfactory levels of user satisfaction. Leading software vendors and computer manufacturers can achieve more than 90 percent of all products within this quadrant.

2 Low levels of user satisfaction and low levels of defects. Products falling within this quadrant have obviously missed the mark in some attribute other than pure defect levels. The most common factors identified for products in this quadrant are insufficient functionality, cumbersome human interfaces, and inadequate training or documentation.

3 High levels of user satisfaction and high levels of defects. This particular quadrant is included primarily for consistency, and it will normally have very few if any projects falling within it. Any software product that does fall here is a candidate for full inspections and quality upgrading. Typically, the only projects within this quadrant will be initial releases with fairly important new functionality.

4 Low levels of user satisfaction and high levels of defects. Products falling within this quadrant are candidates for emergency handling and perhaps replacement. The steps that can be handled on an emergency basis include searching for and eliminating error-prone modules, full inspections, and perhaps retesting. The longer-range solutions may include restructuring the product, rewriting the documentation, and including additional functions.

Since this quadrant represents project failure in its most embarrassing form, it is significant to note that a majority of products falling here were rushed during their development. Excessive schedule pressures coupled with inadequate defect prevention and removal technologies are the factors most often associated with projects in this quadrant.

Summary and Conclusions

The measurement of quality, reliability, and user satisfaction is a factor that separates the leading-edge companies from the laggards. On a global basis, high quality is the main driving force for high-technology products. The companies that recognize this basic fact are poised for success in the twenty-first century; the companies that do not recognize it may not last to see the twenty-first century!

Suggested Readings

Because quality control and user satisfaction are such major topics, it is desirable to conclude with a short reading list of some of the more notable books that expand upon the topics discussed here.

Japanese competitive methods

Walton, Mary, *The Deming Management Method,* Putnam, New York, 1986; 262 pages. No single individual in all history has had more impact on the global economic balance than W. Edwards Deming. Deming moved to Japan after World War II, and he was the primary source of Japan's manufacturing quality control methods. He returned to the United States, and he was belatedly being listened to by U.S. companies that refused his advice for more than 30 years.

Noda, Nabuo, *How Japan Absorbed American Management Methods,* Asian Productivity Organization Press, Tokyo, 1981, 37 pages. The Asian Productivity organization is sponsored by the national governments of Japan, Korea, Thailand, the Republic of China, and several other countries. This short pamphlet is an interesting chronology of the absorption of statistics-based quality control and psychology based management practices in Japan.

Matsumoto, Koji, *Organizing for Higher Productivity: An Analysis of Japanese Systems and Practices,* Asian Productivity Organization Press, Tokyo, 1982, 75 pages. This is yet another of the interesting studies of Japanese methods and techniques. The author is an official of the Ministry of International Trade and Industry (MITI), and he is in a good position to speak about Japanese industrial and management practices.

Ohmae, Kenichi, *The Mind of the Strategist: The Art of Japanese Business,* McGraw-Hill, New York, 1982, 283 pages. Kenichi Ohmae is a director of the prestigious McKinsey & Company management consulting organization. This book gives his observations as a leading business consultant to major Japanese corporations. Since strategic planning in Japan is often more sophisticated than in the United States, this book is quite valuable to U.S. readers.

Crocker, Olga, C. Charney, and J. S. L. Chiu, *Quality Circles,* Mentor, New York, 1984, 361 pages. Quality circles are derived from the work of the American W. Edwards Deming, but they are much more popular in Japan, where more than 7000 of them are registered with the Japanese national registry of quality control. The appealing concept of quality circles is that, given the chance and training, employees want to improve quality and help their employers. The quality circle methodology formalizes that concept, and this book shows managers and executives what they can do to tap this valuable resource.

Pascale, Richard Tanner, and A. G. Athos, *The Art of Japanese Management,* Warner, New York, 1982, 363 pages. This interesting book contrasts Matsushita from Japan and ITT from the United States. Both enterprises had charismatic senior executives and were introducing novel and exciting management principles, but each reflected the paradigm of the nation in which the enterprise developed.

Jones, Capers, *Software Productivity and Quality Today—The Worldwide Perspective,* Information Systems Management Group, 1993, 200 pages. This book is the first to attempt to quantify software productivity and quality levels on a global basis. Demographic information is included on the software populations of more than 90 countries and 250 global cities. Productivity data is ranked for systems software, information systems, military software, and other categories. This book is comparatively unique in that it uses the SPR Feature Point metric, rather than the more common Function Point metric. The book also discusses international variations in software effectiveness, quality control, and research programs.

Morita, Akio, E. M. Reingold, and M. Shimomura, *Made in Japan,* Penguin, New York, 1986, 343 pages. This is an autobiography of Akio Morita, the founder of Sony corporation. The book is interesting because it reveals not only the details of Sony's industrial growth but also the personality of its founder. Sony shared the typical high quality of other Japanese companies in product manufacture, but it also had an unusually perceptive sense of market trends.

Random, Michel, *Japan: The Strategy of the Unseen,* Aquarian, Wellingborough, England, 1987, 205 pages. This book, translated from the original French, is a tutorial for European, British, and American business travelers visiting Japan. It discusses the historical and philosophical background of Bushido, the code of the Samurai in medieval Japan. This is a major part of modern Japanese business practice, and Westerners who have no knowledge of Samurai history will be at a disadvantage.

Masuda, Yoneji, *The Information Society,* World Future Society, Bethesda, Md., 1981, 170 pages. This book is now somewhat dated, but in one sense that may add to its importance. It discusses some of the large-scale experiments carried out in Japan to explore the concepts of full computerization and communication capabilities in ordinary households. Entire villages were equipped with terminals and communication networks that allowed such functions as remote purchasing from stores, remote emergency medical advice, and even some direct participation in town government functions. Similar large-scale experiments have taken place in other countries such as Sweden, France, and Canada, but the Japanese experiments are perhaps the largest yet carried out.

Halberstam, David, *The Reckoning,* Avon, New York, 1987, 786 pages. This book is a massive history of the automotive industry that concentrates on Ford and Toyota, and it deals with both the companies and the executives who founded them. The major point of the book is that, through a combination of arrogance and ignorance, the mightiest industry in America was struck a damaging blow by Japanese competition. U.S. automotive executives ignored quality and disregarded its importance until it was almost too late to recover. They also were guilty of ethnocentrism and the naive assumption that U.S. technology would permanently dominate the postwar world.

Quality control and corporate excellence

Crosby, Philip B., *Quality Is Free,* Mentor, 1980, 270 pages. Phil Crosby was the ITT Vice President of Quality, and he was the person who introduced modern quality control practices into the ITT system. His famous book, long a best-seller, derives its title from the empirical observation that the economic advantages of quality control far overshadow the costs. Phil Crosby and W. Edwards Deming were two of the pioneers in this field of study.

Geneen, Harold, and A. Moscow, *Managing,* Avon, New York, 1984, 305 pages. Harold Geneen was the chairman and CEO that took ITT from a medium-size telecommunications company to the most diverse and largest conglomerate in U.S. history. His style was unique, but his observations on running very large enterprises are worthy of note. It is interesting that Phil Crosby dedicated his *Quality Is Free* to Harold Geneen, since Harold's support was vital to establishing statistical quality methods within ITT.

Peters, Tom, *In Search of Excellence,* Random House, 1985, 389 pages. This is one of the most widely discussed books of the 1980s. In it, Peters discusses the characteristics which tend to separate leading enterprises from laggards. Excellence in all its forms, human, cultural, and business, is part of the pattern of success.

Andrews, Dorine C., and Susan K. Stalick, *Business Reengineering—The Survival Guide,* Prentice Hall, Englewood Cliffs, 1994, 300 pages. Business process reengineering (BPR) has become a cult of the 1990s. When BPR is used to provide better customer service, it is often successful. However, BPR has become synonymous with massive layoffs and cutbacks and is sometimes a step to corporate disaster. This book covers the pros and cons of the topic from the point of view of someone who may have to live through a major BPR analysis.

Pirsig, Robert, *Zen and the Art of Motorcycle Maintenance,* In spite of the unusual title and the fact that it is a novel rather than a technical book, Pirsig's book is in fact a book on quality that is good enough to have been used by IBM as part of its quality assurance training.

The book deals with a cross-country motorcycle trip taken by Pirsig and his son. In the course of the trip, the author discusses the meaning of quality and the difficulty of coming to grips with this elusive concept. The fundamental points are that doing things well provides great satisfaction to the doer as well as to the beneficiary, and that quality is easy to experience but difficult to define.

Software engineering and software quality control

Jones, Capers, *Patterns of Software System Failure and Success,* International Thomson, Boston, 1995, 250 pages. This new book was published in December of 1995. The contents are based on large-scale studies of failed projects (i. e., projects that were either terminated prior to completion or had severe cost and schedule overruns or massive quality problems) and successful projects (i. e., projects that achieved new records for high quality, low costs, short schedules, and high customer satisfaction). On the whole, management problems appear to outweigh technical problems in both successes and failures. Other factors discussed include the use of planning and estimating tools, quality control approaches, experience levels of managers, staff, and clients, and stability of requirements.

Freedman, D., and G. M. Weinberg, *A Handbook of Walkthroughs, Inspections, and Technical Reviews,* Little, Brown, Boston, 1982, 450 pages. Daniel Freedman and Jerry Weinberg are two well-known consultants to the software industry. This book provides an excellent introduction to the various forms of review and inspection that have proved to be so effective for software projects. The book is in question-and-answer form, and it covers all of the topics that naturally occur to first-time participants of reviews and inspections.

DeMarco, Tom, and Tim Lister, *Peopleware,* Dorset House, New York, 1987, 188 pages. This book deals with the human side of software; it discusses the concept that so long as software is a human occupation, optimizing the treatment and conditions of software staff will be beneficial. The book goes beyond merely stating a point, however, and discusses large-scale empirical studies that buttress some of its conclusions. Among the most surprising observations was the discovery that the physical office environment had a direct correlation with software productivity: programmers in the high quartile had more than 78 ft^2 of office space, and those in the low quartile had either open offices or less than 44 ft^2. DeMarco was the recipient of the 1987 Warnier prize for outstanding contributions to computer and information science.

DeMarco, Tom, *Controlling Software Projects,* Yourdon Press, New York, 1982, 284 pages. This book gives the advice of one of the industry leaders in keeping software projects under control in terms of a variety of dimensions: quality, schedule, costs, and others. The book also introduced DeMarco's bang functional metric.

Boehm, Barry, *Software Engineering Economics,* Prentice-Hall, Englewood Cliffs, N.J., 1981, 767 pages. This book is perhaps the largest ever written on the costs associated with software projects. It certainly has one of the largest and most complete sets of references to the relevant literature. The book contains the original equations for the COCOMO estimating model, and it presents one of the few nonproprietary descriptions of how a software cost-estimating model might work. It has been a best-seller since it originally appeared.

Humphrey, Watts, *Managing the Software Process,* Addison-Wesley, Reading, Mass., 1989, 489 pages. Humphrey, formerly at IBM, was head of the prestigious Software Engineering Institute (SEI) associated with Carnegie Mellon University. This book contains both his observations on the software process and also his method for evaluating the five stages of maturing of software development organizations.

Biggerstaff, T., and A. Perlis, *Software Reusability,* Vols. 1 and 2, Addison-Wesley, Reading, Mass., 1989, Vol. 1, 424 pages; Vol. 2, 386 pages. Dr. Biggerstaff was part of the ITT Programming Technology Center. Together with Dr. Perlis of Yale, he was cochairman of the famous 1983 ITT conference on software reusability. This two-volume set builds upon a kernel of papers that were presented at that conference, but it brings the entire subject up to date. Biggerstaff heads the reusability project at the Microcomputer and Electronics Corporation (MCC).

Glass, Robert L., *Modern Programming Practices: A Report from Industry,* Prentice-Hall, Englewood Cliffs, N.J., 1982, 311 pages. Books on software engineering theory outnumber books on software engineering practices by at least 20 to 1. This one is based on interviews and empirical observations carried out within large companies—Martin Marietta, TRW, CSC, and others. Although somewhat dated, it is an interesting attempt to describe what goes on day-to-day when large companies build software.

Dunn, Robert, and Richard Ullman, *Quality Assurance for Computer Software,* McGraw-Hill, New York, 1982, 349 pages. This book is yet another that originated with research carried out within ITT. Dunn and Ullman were quality assurance specialists for one of ITT's divisions and later for the corporate offices. It summarizes, broadly, all of the major tasks and issues regarding setting up a quality assurance organization for modern software engineering projects.

Dunn, Robert, *Software Defect Removal,* McGraw-Hill, New York, 1984, 331 pages. Bob Dunn continues his explication of software quality methods with a broad-based survey of all of the major forms of defect removal. As with the preceding title, this book comprises part of the set of methods for quality assurance used within the ITT system.

Chow, Tsun S., *Software Quality Assurance,* IEEE Press, Catalog Number EH0223-8, 1984, 500 pages. Tsun Chow's tutorial volume is part of the IEEE series on software engineering. It contains some 50 articles by various authors covering all of the major software QA topics.

Myers, Glenford, *The Art of Software Testing,* Wiley, New York, 1978, 177 pages. Although this book is now approaching 20 years old, it is still regarded as a classic text on software testing and is still a textbook in many university and graduate school curricula. Myers is a multifaceted researcher who was also one of the originators of structured design and a contributor to computer architecture as well. He was the 1988 recipient of the Warnier prize for outstanding contributions to computer and information science.

Brooks, Fred, *The Mythical Man-Month,* Addison-Wesley, Reading, Mass., 1995, 195 pages. This book has sold more copies than any other book on a software topic since the industry began. (A revised new version came out in 1995 with many new insights.) Brooks was the IBM director who first developed the operating system software for the IBM System/360 computer line, which was one of IBM's first major efforts to run far beyond planned budgets and schedules. His report is a classic account of why even large and well-managed enterprises such as IBM run into trouble when building large software systems. The cover art of the book captures the problems exactly: giant prehistoric ground sloths struggling to free themselves from the La Brea tar pits! The message is that, once the problems of large systems get started, no amount of money or extra staff can easily recover the situation.

Pressman, Roger, *Software Engineering: A Practitioner's Approach,* McGraw-Hill, New York, 1982, 352 pages. This book, widely used as a college text, is an excellent introduction to all of the major topics of concern to both software engineers and software managers as well. It is organized chronologically and is based on the phases of a software life cycle. It is much broader in scope than many other software engineering texts in that it includes management topics such as planning, estimating, and measurement. It also covers requirements, design, coding, testing and defect removal, and maintenance. It would be difficult to find a more suitable introduction to all of the critical topics than is contained in this book.

References

1. Walton, Mary, *The Deming Management Method,* Perigree, New York, 1986, 262 PP.
2. Pirsig, R., *Zen and the Art of Motorcycle Maintenance,*
3. Crosby, Phil, *Quality Is Free: The Art of Making Quality Certain,* McGraw-Hill, New York, 1979.

4. Musa, J., A. Iannino, and K. Okumoto, *Software Reliability: Measurement, Prediction, Application,* McGraw-Hill, New York, 1987, 619 pp.
5. Levering, R., M. Moskowitz, and M. Katz, *The 100 Best Companies to Work for in America,* Addison-Wesley, New York, 1985, 396 pp.
6. Peters, Tom, *In Search of Excellence,* Random House, New York, 1985, 385 pp.
7. Fagan, M., "Design and Code Inspections to Reduce Errors in Program Development," *IBM Systems Journal,* vol. 15, no. 3, 1976, pp. 182–211.
8. SPR, "Software Design Inspections," Software Productivity Research, Burlington, Mass., 1990, 35 pp.
9. Crocker, 0., L. S. Charney, and J. S. L. Chieu, *Quality Circles,* Mentor, New York, 1984, 361 pp.
10. Halpin, J. F., *Zero Defects—A New Dimension in Quality Assurance,* McGraw-Hill, New York, 1966, 228 pp.
11. Mills, H., "The New Math of Computer Programming," *CACM,* vol. 18, January 1975, pp. 43–48.
12. Martin, J., *System Design That Is Provably Bug Free,* Prentice-Hall, Englewood Cliffs, N.J., 1985.
13. Deutsch, M., *Software Verification and Validation: Realistic Project Approaches,* Prentice-Hall, Englewood Cliffs, N.J., 1982.
14. SPR, "User Satisfaction Survey Questionnaire," Software Productivity Research, Burlington, Mass., 1989.

Appendix

A

Rules for Counting Procedural Source Code

Introduction

It is quite astonishing that in 50 years of software engineering and programming history, there has never been a true international standard that defined exactly what is meant by "a line of source code." The following rules for counting source code were created by Software Productivity Research. They are intended to provide at least minimal consistency with clients when discussing productivity issues in terms of "lines of source code."

Indeed, the rules have been embodied in a size conversion tool that can convert apparent size by using any arbitrary combination of rules into the equivalent size when some other combination is used. Such a tool is more or less necessary when an attempt is made to compare productivity between companies, departments, and even projects by using lines of source code.

The general principle of the following rules can be stated briefly: "Count as you think." Counting should come as close as possible to being intuitive and natural, and it should avoid being artificial and stilted. In the rules, the SPR standard is indicated by an asterisk, i.e., * The SPR standard is not necessarily the optimum choice, but in general it seems to be pragmatic and make sense.

* = SPR standard counting technique

Project Source Code Counting Rules

Multiple-language counting ______

*1. Each language is counted separately
2. All languages are lumped and counted together

Source code termination ______

*1. Delimiters
2. Physical lines

Source code counting ______

1. Executable statements only
*2. Executable statements + data definitions
3. Executable statements + data definitions + comments

Macro instruction and expansion counting ______

0. Project does not have macro instructions or expansions
1. Macro instructions and expansions are not counted
2. Macro instructions are counted, but not expansions
*3. Macro instructions and unique expansions are counted
4. Macro instructions and all expansions counted separately
5. Macro instructions and all expansions lumped with product

Reusable code counting ______

0. Project does not have reusable code
1. Reusable modules are not counted
*2. Unique reusable modules are counted separately
3. All uses of reusable modules are counted separately
4. Reused modules are lumped and counted with product code

Program and application generator counting ____

0. Project does not have generator statements
1. Generator statements are not counted
2. Generator input statements are counted
*3. Generator inputs and outputs are counted separately
4. Generator inputs and outputs are lumped together

Job control language counting ____

0. Project does not have job control language
1. Job control language is not counted
*2. Job control language is counted separately
3. Job control language is lumped and counted with product

Changed code counting ____

0. Project does not have changed code
1. Changed code is not counted
*2. Changed code is counted separately from new code
3. Changed code is lumped and counted with new code

Base code counting ____

0. Product does not have base code
1. Base code is not counted
*2. Base code is counted separately
3. Base code is lumped and counted with new and changed code

Deleted code counting ____

0. Project does not have deleted code
1. Deleted code is not counted
*2. Deleted code is counted separately
3. Deleted code is lumped with new and changed code

Scaffold code counting ______

0. Project does not have scaffold code
1. Scaffold code is not counted
*2. Scaffold code is counted separately from product code
3. Scaffold code is lumped and counted with product code

Support code counting ______

0. Project does not have support code
1. Support code is not counted
*2. Support code is counted separately from product code
3. Support code is lumped and counted with product code

Test case code counting ______

0. Project does not have test case code
1. Test case code is not counted
*2. Test case code is counted separately from product code
3. Test case code is lumped and counted with product code

General Rules for Counting Code within Applications

- Do not count commentary lines or information appended to executable lines for informational purposes.
- Count verbs or action statements, such as assignments, print commands, conditionals, and loops.
- Count equations and mathematical expressions.
- Count data definitions, including both variables and constants, and also type definitions.
- Count initialization of data definitions.
- Count procedure definitions.
- Count each formal parameter within a procedure.
- Count procedure labels.
- Count unexpanded macro calls if you are interested in development size.

- Count expanded macro instructions if you are interested in delivered size.
- Clearly identify and explain the specific counting rules you have selected.
- Be aware that individual human variation can and will cause notable differences in the sizes of programs that are logically identical. In a controlled study, eight programmers varied by 5 to 1 in the number of statements they used to implement the same algorithm.

Examples of the SPR Source Code Counting Rules

- Do not count commentary lines or statements that are used purely for information purposes; i.e., the following statement would not be counted:

```
REM THIS ROUTINE CALCULATES GROSS PAY
```

- For strongly typed languages, count data definitions statements as 1 statement; i.e., the following example counts as 1 statement:

```
WEEKDAY = (MONDAY, TUESDAY, WEDNESDAY, THURSDAY, FRIDAY, SATURDAY, SUNDAY)
```

- For weakly typed languages, count data definitions statements as 1 statement; i.e., the following example counts as 1 statement:

```
DATA = MONDAY, TUESDAY, WEDNESDAY, THURSDAY, FRIDAY, SATURDAY, SUNDAY
```

- Count assignment statements as 1 statement; i.e.,

```
A = B + C
```

- Count equations as you would treat them in mathematics; i.e., as a single unit or line. The following expression counts as 1 statement:

```
A = ( (B * C)/(D - E) ) + ( (F + G + H) * I) )
```

- For languages that allow multiple logical statements per physical line, count the logical statements. (This is the same as counting delimiters.) The following example counts as 3 statements:

```
BASE = 0: BASE = HOURS * RATE: PRINT BASE
```

Note: The two colons and the carriage return at the end of the line are the 3 delimiters.

- Count procedure or function calls as 1 statement; i.e.,

```
CALL PRINTDRV
```

- Count IF's and THEN's as separate statements; i.e., the following example would count as 2 statements:

```
IF A OCCURS
THEN UPDATE B
```

- Count IF's followed by GOTO's as separate statements; i.e., the following example would count as 2 statements:

```
IF A OCCURS THEN GOTO NEWSTART
```

- Count IF's, THEN's, and ELSE's as separate statements; i.e., the following example would count as 3 statements:

```
  IF A OCCURS
THEN UPDATE B
  ELSE UPDATE C
```

- Count CASE statements as separate statements; i.e., the following example would count as 5 statements:

```
SELECT CASE NUMBER$
  CASE ''ONE'': PRINT ''1''
  CASE ''TWO'': PRINT ''2''
  CASE ''THREE'': PRINT ''3''
  CASE ''FOUR'': PRINT ''4''
END SELECT
```

Count DO-WHILE constructions as 1 statement; i.e., the following example would count as 4 statements:

```
WHILE J >10 DO
  PRINT HEADER
  PRINT LINENUM
  PRINT MESSAGE
```

- Count FOR-NEXT constructions as 1 statement; i.e., the following example would count as 4 statements:

```
FOR J = 1 TO 10
  PRINT HEADER
  PRINT LINENUM
  PRINT MESSAGE
NEXT J
```

- Count REPEAT-UNTIL constructions as 1 statement; i.e., the following example would count as 4 statements:

```
REPEAT
  PRINT HEADER
  PRINT LINENUM
  PRINT MESSAGE
UNTIL INDEX >10
```

- Count nested constructions in accordance with the individual element rules; i.e., the following example would count as 8 statements:

```
FOR J = 1 TO 10
  PRINT HEADER
    FOR K = 1 TO 3
      PRINT NUMBER
      PRINT STREET
      PRINT CITY
    NEXT K
  PRINT LINENUM
  PRINT MESSAGE
NEXT J
```

Software Productivity Research Cobol-Counting Rules

Although Cobol is the most widely used language in the world and approximately 50 percent of all software is written in it, there are currently no national or international standards that actually define exactly what is meant by "a line of Cobol source code" for the purposes of measuring productivity.

The most basic problem with Cobol counting is the fundamental decision whether to count physical lines or logical lines. Among SPR clients, about 75 percent count physical lines, which is definitely the most convenient method since many library tools and Cobol compilers themselves can provide such data.

However, since the actual work required to produce an application correlates rather poorly with physical lines, it is often more useful for productivity studies to count logical lines. Because Cobol tends to have conditional statements that span several physical lines, a count of logical lines can reduce the apparent size of the application by more than 2 to 1. For productivity purposes, this is very troublesome—especially in light of the fact that few productivity authors actually state which rules they used for line counting!

If you do wish to count logical lines, you face two problems: (1) What are the exact rules that define logical lines? (2) How can logical lines be counted other than by a laborious manual analysis? It is remarkable that, after so many years of Cobol's history, these problems remain. The answer to both questions is the same: It is necessary to build or acquire a line-counting tool that embodies your corporate standards (since there are no global standards). Several Cobol-line-counting tools are commercially available, and they can be set to match your corporate rules.

The following rules by Software Productivity Research are a surrogate for a true standard, and they should be used with caution. *Note:* The Cobol rules are based on the general rules for procedural languages given in the preceding section.

As stated before, try to count as you think: If a statement represents a unit of thought, it should also represent a unit of work and hence deserves to be counted.

1. Statements within the IDENTIFICATION DIVISION are not counted by SPR, since they are essentially comments. If you choose to count them, suggested rules are as follows:

- PROGRAM ID and the ID itself count as 1 line.
- AUTHOR and the author's name count as 1 line.
- INSTALLATION and following text count as 1 line.
- DATE WRITTEN and following text count as 1 line.
- DATE COMPILED and following text count as 1 line.
- SECURITY and following text count as 1 line.
- COMMENTS and following text do not count, since commentary lines are normally excluded.

2. Statements within the ENVIRONMENT DIVISION are similar to comments in some ways, but because they are volatile and change when applications migrate, it is appropriate to count the FILE CONTROL SELECT statements.

3. Count statements within the DATA DIVISION in accordance with these rules:

- Each statement in the FILE section counts as 1 line, e.g., BLOCK, RECORD, and VALUE OF.
- COPY statements themselves count as 1 line each. The code that is actually copied from a source statement library is reused code and should be counted as such. If you are interested in development productivity, it can be ignored. If you are interested in delivery productivity, it should be counted.
- Each numbered FIELD or SUBFIELD statement (01, 02, 66, etc.) including the PICTURE clause counts as 1 line.
- Statements in the WORKING STORAGE section follow the same rules as for the FILE section.

4. Count statements within the PROCEDURE DIVISION in accordance with these rules:

- Count procedure labels as 1 line; i.e., MAIN-ROUTINE of END-OF-JOB routine would count as 1 line each.
- Count verbal expressions as 1 line; i.e., OPEN, WRITE, CLOSE, MOVE, ADD, etc., count as 1 line each.

- Count CALL statements as 1 line; i.e., CALL 'GRCALC' by USING CR-HOURS, CR-RATE, WS-GROSS counts as 1 line.
- Count PERFORM statements as 1 line; i.e., PERFORM RATE-LOOKUP THROUGH RATE-EXIT counts as 1 line.
- Count IF logic as separate statements; i.e., the following expression counts as 3 lines:

```
IF HOURS IS GREATER THAN 40
  SUBTRACT 40 FROM HOURS GIVING OVERTIME
  MULTIPLY OVERTIME BY 1.5 GIVING PREMIUM
```

- Count IF-ELSE-GO TO logic as separate statements; i.e, the following expression counts as 3 lines:

```
IF LINE-COUNT = 50 OR LINE-COUNT >50 GOTO PRINT-HEADINGS
  ELSE GO TO PRINT-HEADINGS-EXIT
```

Appendix

B

Rules for Counting Function Points and Feature Points

This appendix provides a set of quick reference rules and counting recommendations for both function points and feature points. The rules were prepared by A. J. Albrecht and Michael Cunnane, and they are current through the end of 1995. Rules such as those are revised from time to time in accordance with revisions by the IFPUG Counting Practices Committee (for function points) and the Software Productivity Research corporation (for feature points).

This set of rules is in the concise format suitable for a folding, pocket-size card. This format is very common, and it provides a convenient tool for staff and management personnel who are engaged in counting function or feature points at a number of diverse locations.

SPR METRIC ANALYSIS

REFERENCE CARD

Counting Rules for Function Points Feature Points

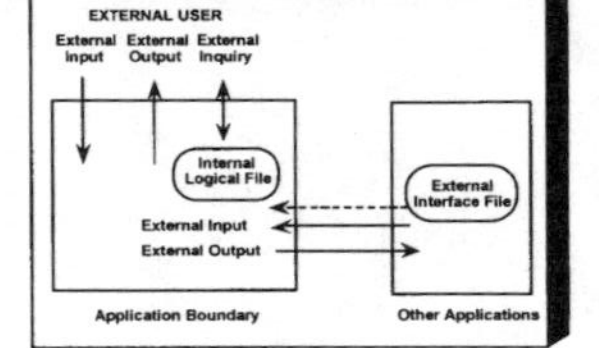

SOFTWARE PRODUCTIVITY RESEARCH

1 New England Executive Park
Burlington, MA 01803
(617) 273-0140

INTERNAL LOGICAL FILE (ILF)

Count each major logical group of user data or control information in the application as an internal logical file. Include each logical file, or within a database, each logical group of data from the viewpoint of the user that is generated, used, and maintained by the application. Count each logical group of data as viewed by the user and as defined in the external design or data analysis rather than on the physical implementation. ILFs maintained by more than one application are counted as ILFs by each.

COUNTING RECOMMENDATIONS

Do *not* include logical internal files that are *not* accessible to the user through external output or inquiry and that are not independently maintained.

Description	Count
• Logical entity or group of entities from user viewpoint	1 ILF
• Logical internal file generated or maintained by the application	1 ILF
• User maintained table(s) or files(s)	1 ILF
• File used for data or control by sequential (batch) application and maintained by application	1 ILF
• Attributive entity maintained only through main entity	0 ILF
• Associative entity, join or connection with only key attributes	0 ILF
• Intermediate or sort work file (temporary)	0 ILF
• File created only because of technology used (e.g., index file)	0 ILF
• A "master file" only read by application	0 ILF 1 EIF

EXTERNAL INTERFACE FILE (EIF)

Count each major logical group of user data or control information used by the application (but maintained by another application) which crosses the application boundary. Include each logical file or logical group of data from the viewpoint of the user.

COUNTING RECOMMENDATIONS

Count each major logical group of user data or control information that is extracted by the application from another application as an external interface file. The extract will not result in an update to any internal logical files. If an update occurs, count an EI not an EIF.

Description	Count
• File of records extracted from another application (used for reference only)	1 EIF
• Data base read from other applications	1 EIF
• Internal logical file from another application used as a transaction	0 EIF, 1EI
• System HELP, Security File, Error File read/referenced by the application from another application where files are maintained	EIFs

EXTERNAL INPUT (EI)

Count each *unique* user data or user control input type that enters the external boundary of the application being measured, and adds, changes, deletes or otherwise alters data (e.g., assign, transfer, add, update...) in an internal logical file. Also count control information which enters the application boundary and assures compliance with business function specified by the user. An external input should be considered unique if the external logical design requires processing logic different from other external inputs.

COUNTING RECOMMENDATIONS

The recommendation most closely describing each external input should be used in counting each external input.

Description	Count
• Data screen with add, change, and delete	3 EI
• Multiple screens accumulated and processed as one transaction	1 EI
• Two data screens with different order of data, but the same processing logic	1 EI
• Two data screens with the same format, but different processing logic	2 EI
• Data screen with multiple unique functions	1 EI/Funct.
• Automatic data or transactions from other applications	1 EI/ Trans type
• User application control input	1 EI
• Input forms (OCR) with one transaction	1 EI
• An update function following a query	1 EI, 1 EQ
• Individual selections on menu screen	0 EI
• Update of user maintained table or file	1 EI
• PF Key duplicate of a screen already counted as input	0 EI
• Light pen duplicate of a screen already counted as input	0 EI
• External input types introduced only because of the technology used	0 EI
• Selection of a field in list box (not a stand-alone function)	0 EI

EXTERNAL OUTPUT (EO)

Count each unique user data or control data that leaves the external boundary of the application being measured. An external output should be considered unique if it has different data, or if the external design requires a processing logic different from other external outputs. External outputs often consist of reports, output files sent to other applications, or messages to the user.

COUNTING RECOMMENDATIONS

The recommendations most closely describing each external output should be used in counting each external output.

Description	Count
• Data screen output	1 EO
• Batch report (e.g., scheduled)	1 EO
• Automatic data or transactions to other applications	1 EO
• Error messages returned as a result of an input transaction (new rule)	0 EO
• Backup files	0 EO
• Output to screen and to printer	2 EO
• Output files created for technical reasons	0 EO
• Bar chart as well as pie chart graphical displays	2 EO
• Inquiry with calculated information	1 EO, 0 EQ

EXTERNAL INQUIRY (EQ)

Count each unique input/output combination, where an input causes and generates an output, as an external inquiry. An external inquiry should be considered unique if it has different data elements from other external inquiry types in its output part, or if the external design requires a processing logic different from other external inquiries. See the IFPUG Counting Practices Manual for definitions.

COUNTING RECOMMENDATIONS

The recommendations most closely describing each inquiry type should be used in counting each inquiry type.

Description	Count
• On-line input and on-line output with no update of data in files (e.g., browse)	1 EQ
• Inquiry followed by an update input	1 EQ/1 EI
• Help screen input and output (per level)	1 EQ
• On-line input with immediate printed output of existing data and no update of data	1 EQ
• Pick List or Drop Down with dynamic data	1 EQ
• Pick List or Drop Down with static data	0 EQ
• Batch report request resulting in a report with no derived data	1 EQ

FEATURE POINT METHODOLOGY

The SPR Feature Point metric is a superset of the IFPUG Function Point metric and introduces a new element (algorithms) in addition to the five standard Function Point parameters. The Feature Point method also reduces the Internal Logical File from IFPUG's average value of 10 to an average value of 7.

Figure B.1. SPR metric analysis reference card. Sheet 1.

Since Feature Points include algorithmic complexity, a definition of "algorithm" is appropriate. An algorithm is defined as the set of user required rules which must be completely expressed in order to solve a significant computational problem. For example, a square root extraction routine, a missile firing calculation, or an overtime pay calculation routine are all considered algorithms.

FUNCTION POINT METHODOLOGY

The primary difference between the IFPUG and SPR Function Point methodologies is in the way they deal with complexity. The IFPUG techniques for assessing complexity are based on weighing 14 influence factors and evaluating the numbers of field and file references for transactions or the numbers of fields and record element types (user views) for data groups.

The SPR technique for dealing with complexity separates the overall topic of "complexity" into two distinct questions that can be dealt with intuitively: 1) How complex are the algorithms or equations or problems in the software?; 2) How complex is the data structure of the application? The SPR methodology is usually utilized at or prior to Requirements.

With the SPR Function Point method, it is not necessary to count the number of data element types, file types referenced, or record types. Neither is it necessary to assign low, average, or high values to each specific external input, external output, external inquiry, internal logical file or external interface file. The SPR complexity questions can be answered quickly by anyone familiar with an application, and they deal with the entire application, rather than with its elements. Obviously, the IFPUG Methodology is a more accurate sizing metric.

COMPLEXITY FACTOR

The complexity factor and multiplier is used to compute the Function Point Count measure. SPR also uses a "quick-fire" method which can adjust the function point count by ±40%.

IFPUG and SPR use the same principles to identify the five elements (six with Feature Points) of counting. IFPUG then applies a weighting factor of high, low, or average, depending on the number of data elements, file types referenced, and record types invoked. SPR's quick-fire method assumes average weight in its methodology.

To adjust the raw FP count, IFPUG looks at 14 variables of complexity that will adjust the count by ±35%. SPR simply requires answers to two questions which summarize the intent of IFPUG's 14 complexity factors; however, both SPR Function Point and Feature Point Counts may be enhanced by applying IFPUG's 14 General System Characteristics.

By answering 1 through 5 on both questions and adding the two values together, a complexity multiplier is then obtained using the simple chart provided.

IFPUG METHODOLOGY

Function Point Counting

Elements	Low	Average	High	Total
External Input	___ x 3 +	___ x 4 +	___ x 6 =	___
External Output	___ x 4 +	___ x 5 +	___ x 7 =	___
External Inquiry	___ x 3 +	___ x 4 +	___ x 6 =	___
ILF	___ x 7 +	___ x 10 +	___ x 15 =	___
EIF	___ x 5 +	___ x 7 +	___ x 10 =	___
	Total Unadjusted Function Points			___

(Low, Average, High under "Count Weights")

Input Complexity Matrix

FTRs	1-4 DETs	5-15 DETs	16+ DETs
0-1	Low	Low	Avg.
2	Low	Avg.	High
3+	Avg.	High	High

Output Complexity Matrix

FTRs	1-5 DETs	6-19 DETs	20+ DETs
0-1	Low	Low	Avg.
2-3	Low	Avg.	High
4+	Avg.	High	High

File Complexity Matrix

RETs	1-19 DETs	20-50 DETs	51+ DETs
1	Low	Low	Avg.
2-5	Low	Avg.	High
6+	Avg.	High	High

FTR = File Types (User Data Groups) Referenced
DET = Data Element Type (Field)
RET = Record Element Type (User View)

IFPUG METHODOLOGY (Cont.)

Fourteen General System Characteristics are rated from 0-5 based upon their degree of influence on the application. The fourteen characteristics are:

- Data Communication
- Distributed Function
- Performance
- Heavily Used Configuration
- Transaction Rates
- On-Line Data Entry
- Design for End-User Efficiency
- On-Line Update
- Complex Processing
- Reusability
- Installation Ease
- Operational Ease
- Multiple Sites
- Facilitate Change

The Unadjusted Function Point count of an application is adjusted by the total of the General System Characteristics using the following equation to determine the application Function Point count:

[.65+ (.01 x total of General System Characteristics)]
x [Unadjusted Function Point Count]

Users should refer to the IFPUG Counting Practices Manual for more complete definitions.

"BACKFIRE" METHOD

The "backfire" method for estimating Function Points is based on empirical relationships discovered to exist between source code and Function Points in all known languages. This method is based on tables of average values. It is useful for doing retrospective studies of projects completed long ago, and for easing the transition to Function Point metrics for people who are familiar with lines-of-code metrics.

Assembler	320*	DB Languages	40
C	128	Object Oriented	29
COBOL	107	Query Languages	25
Ada	71	Generators	16

*Statements per Function Point

SPR METHODOLOGY

Function Point Counting

Element	Count Weight		Total
External Input	___ x 4	=	___
External Output	___ x 5	=	___
External Inquiry	___ x 4	=	___
Internal Logical File	___ x 10	=	___
External Interface File	___ x 7	=	___
		TOTAL	___

OR

Feature Point Counting

Element	Count Weight		Total
External Input	___ x 4	=	___
External Output	___ x 5	=	___
External Inquiry	___ x 4	=	___
Internal Logical File	___ x 7	=	___
External Interface File	___ x 7	=	___
Algorithm	___ x 3	=	___
		TOTAL	___

Function/Feature Count (FC)

Total Unadjusted Function/Feature Points = ___

Complexity Factor and Multiplier

Problem Complexity?
1) Simple algorithms and simple calculations
2) Majority of simple algorithms
3) Algorithms and calculations of average complexity
4) Some difficult or complex algorithms
5) Many difficult algorithms and complex calculations

Data Complexity?
1) Simple data with few variables
2) Numerous variable, but simple data relationships
3) Multiple files, fields, and data intersections
4) Complex file structures and data intersections
5) Very complex file structures and data intersections

Sum of Problem and Data Complexity	2	3	4	5	6	7	8	9	10
Complexity Multiplier	.6	.7	.8	.9	1.0	1.1	1.2	1.3	1.4

FP Count Measure:
FC X Complexity Multiplier = ___

Figure B.2. SPR metric anlaysis reference card. Sheet 2.

Appendix

C

Example of a Fully Measured Software Project

Introduction

Between the first edition in 1991 and today, software measurement technology has begun to stabilize and center around the usage of function point metrics. This does not mean that software measurement is stagnant. Indeed, measurement technology has improved notably over the last 5 years.

When the first edition was published, there were few commercial software measurement tools and very little in the way of useful benchmark data. There are now a host of software measurement tools and a variety of software databases and software benchmark consulting groups.

As of 1995 the International Function Point Users Group (IFPUG) is working with the International Standards Organization (ISO) to develop an international standard for software productivity measurements based on function points. The standard is not available as this book is written but should be available by late 1996 or 1997.

The volume of useful information that can be collected about a software project is roughly in the same league with the volume of information collected about a patient who is undergoing a thorough medical examination. In the course of the latter, the patient will provide some of the information, such as a medical history; various diagnostic laboratories and equipment will provide some of the information, such as the results of blood tests; and the examining physicians will provide some of the information. The total volume of information in a full medical examination can exceed 200 pages.

In software projects, the term "full measurement" also includes multiple sources of information. The project manager provides some of the information; the project staff provides some; tracking tools and accounting systems provide some; quality assurance provides some; and the users themselves provide some. Here too the full volume of information can exceed 200 pages. However, that much data is difficult to utilize conveniently, so it is normal both to condense it and to select key highlights, such as factors by which the project was either well ahead in terms of technology, or perhaps somewhat behind. The purpose of measuring a software project in considerable detail is twofold, and it is very similar to the purpose of medical records:

1. Accurate measurements can be used as early warnings to head off problems.
2. Accurate measurement can be turned into powerful "templates" for estimating future projects.

Three kinds of information must be recorded if software project measurements are to actually be useful:

1. Hard data
2. Soft data
3. Normalized data

The hard data consists of the quantified facts about a project that can be measured with high precision and low ambiguity. Examples of hard data include the schedules of each task performed, the staffing required, the effort expended, the money expended, and the sizes of key deliverables such as specifications, source code, and test cases. The soft data consists of the facts about a project or its staff wherein subjective human opinions come into play. For examples of soft data, consider the clarity or ambiguity of the requirements, the usefulness of the tools and methods, the skills of the staff, the cooperation of the users, and the adequacy of the office space. The normalized data consists of selected hard-data elements converted into a standard metric for comparative purposes. For examples of normalized data, consider "cost per function point," "function points per staff-hour," and "cost per KLOC."

The following sample report of a fully measured project includes all three kinds of data. The data itself is taken from several actual projects, but it is melded together and rounded to ensure confidentiality of the sources of the information. Although the volume of data is large, the effort to fully measure a software project is not excessive. In round numbers, about 25 staff-hours is required. This is not a significant amount in a project such as the example, which totaled over 30 person-months of effort and more than 12 calendar months of time. Indeed, the effort devoted to this project's measurement is only slightly more than 0.5 percent.

Context and Background of the Example

The sample project is hypothetical, but it is based on a classic MIS application: a payroll program for exempt and hourly workers. The example application is written in Cobol on an IBM AS/400. The size of the application is about 29,000 new Cobol statements and 3000 reused ones for common processing functions, bringing the total size to 32,000 statements in all. In terms of function points, the overall size is 302.

The project is new rather than an enhancement. The scope of the project is that of a small application consisting of several linked components. The class is that of an internal project for use at a single location. The type is hybrid, being partly a batch application and partly an on-line database application using CICS.

The experience level of the staff for this kind of application is fairly high, and the staff is very experienced in the Cobol language, the hardware environment, and the software environment. The users themselves are also fairly experienced, and they are active participants during early JAD sessions as well as later. User time as well as development time should be recorded for completeness.

It might be of interest to illustrate two salient features of this measured project, since such information is seldom available: (1) the overall distribution of effort among the key tasks of the project when it is first developed and (2) the lifetime distribution of effort for both the initial release and 10 years of maintenance and enhancement. Table C. 1 shows the distribution of normal paid project effort among the key tasks.

Table C.1 shows a fairly average distribution for MIS projects of this size. Note that the code cost exceeds the cost of any other element. However, paperwork and testing are significant in their contribution to the project totals.

Table C.2 shows information that is even rarer: the lifetime total effort for a project including the initial release, 10 years of maintenance (defect repairs), and 10 years of enhancements (adding new features). In this case, the postrelease maintenance and enhancement costs are estimated and included to show the overall relative proportions. These proportions, however, are about average for MIS projects such as the example.

Measurement Tool Used

The data was collected by using Release 2.3 of the commercial CHECKPOINT® integrated measurement and estimation tool developed by Software Productivity Research. The tool operates in both measure-

TABLE C.1 Distribution of Project Effort among Key Tasks

Major task groups	Person-months of effort	Proportion, %
Paperwork-related effort (specification, user documents, etc.)	8.0	24.4
Code-related effort (coding, desk checking)	13.0	39.9
Testing-related effort (all test steps from unit to system test)	9.5	28.8
Management-related effort (first-line management only)	2.0	6.4
Miscellaneous activities (meetings, presentations, etc.)	0.2	0.5
Total	32.9	100.0

TABLE C.2 Lifetime Distribution of Effort for Initial Development and 10 Years of Maintenance and Project Enhancement

Lifetime activity	Person-months of effort	Proportion, %
Initial development	32.0	12.1
User involvement	5.0	1.9
10 years of maintenance	140.0	55.0
10 years of enhancement	80.0	31.0
Total	257.0	100.0

ment and estimation mode, and both modes were used to produce the following reports. The measurement mode was used for development data and the recording of project soft factors, and the estimating mode was used to predict the 10-year maintenance and enhancement data.

Contents of the Measurement Example

The example is divided into two main sections: (1) the input data provided by the project manager and staff and (2) the output reports and normalized data produced by the measurement tool.

One of the conveniences offered by such tools is the automatic conversion and normalization of hard data into useful metrics. For example, for a given task such as requirements it is only necessary for the user to enter raw data on the staff, effort, schedule, and deliverable outputs.

The tool itself will add the requirements data to the overall project totals and convert the data into normalized results such as requirements pages per function point and requirements cost per function point.

The input section of the measured project report

The input section shows the actual kinds of information supplied by the project managers and staff, and it includes these major topics:

1. Basic identity and security levels of the project.
2. Nature, scope, class, and type information for the project (i.e., is the project new or an enhancement, a small program or a large system, internal or external, batch or on-line, and so forth).
3. Goals or constraints levied against the project by higher management or user demands.
4. Work-hour and staff availability profiles.
5. Occupation groups and specialists needed.
6. Answers to any of the multiple-choice questions that define the tools, methods, experience, and environment for the project. (Not every question need be answered, but the more that are answered the more complete the historical data for future reference.)
7. Size information in the form preferred by the project manager or by company policy. Size can be expressed in function points, feature points, or lines of source code and in any language or combination of languages.
8. Information on the specific computers, operating systems, and support software used; also information on specific tools and methods used such as "Yourdon design method" or "Method/1."
9. Free-form commentary text in the form of notes attached to any input item to provide additional information over and above that provided by the multiple-choice questions.
10. Additional remarks on any special events or unique factors that might have impacted the project outcome, such as "the development laboratory was relocated due to earthquake damage."

The output sections of the measured project report

For this book, only the major output reports have been selected in order to conserve space and highlight the major results of the project. The output reports include:

1. A summary total for the project that includes development of the initial release, user effort, maintenance (defect repairs) for 10 years, and enhancements (adding features) for 10 years.
2. Detailed task-by-task information showing the resources and schedule for each task performed, which in this case consisted of 14 tasks out of the set of 25 possible tasks that could be measured by the tool utilized.
3. Normalized data for each task showing task performance in terms of both function points and source lines. (The sample project had a net development productivity rate of 10.5 function points, or 973 source lines, per staff-month, which is slightly above 1996 norms.)
4. Defect and quality data which is shown here in summary form to conserve space. (The project had a total defect quantity of 880 bugs of all levels of severity. A total of 531, or 71.5 percent, was removed prior to delivery.
5. Detailed task-by-task information showing the user resources and schedule for each task performed, which in this case consisted of three tasks out of the set of five common user tasks.
6. Maintenance effort and costs for up to 10 years after the initial release of the project. (*Note:* This is estimated data, since the project is new.)
7. Enhancement effort and costs, plus the growth in size of the project, for up to 10 years after the initial release. (*Note:* This is estimated data, since the project is new.)
8. The identified strengths and weaknesses that impacted costs, effort, quality, and productivity. A "strength" is defined as a factor in respect to which the project performed better than U.S. averages based on the SPR 5-point rating scale. A "weakness" is defined as a factor in respect to which the project performed worse than U.S. averages based on the same 5-point rating scale.
9. Printed notes, which were recorded during the measurement process. (When the tool is actually used with a computer, the notes are associated with specific factors they comment on and are displayed as optional windows.)
10. The page counts for the documents actually produced out of the total of 56 different possible documents which the tool can record.

Outputs excluded from the example. In order to conserve space and concentrate on normal project measurements, a variety of additional factors which might be recorded or estimated were deliberately omitted from this example. Some of the omitted outputs include:

1. Project assessment against U.S. norms for similar projects.
2. Specific defect removal efficiencies for each review, inspection, and test actually utilized. (Summary information was provided to conserve space.)
3. Alternative scenarios of what the project might have been like had different languages or technologies been utilized.

Summary of and Conclusions about Software Project Measurement

The volume of data that can and should be recorded on software projects is roughly equivalent to the volume of medical information that can and should be recorded about patients undergoing full physical examinations. In both cases, the information can be used to avoid serious problems by identifying them before they become serious. The data can also be used for future estimates and long-range diagnostic studies.

This kind of information about all or a significant sample of projects within an enterprise makes it possible to carry out a new and powerful kind of analysis. When large collections of soft and hard data are analyzed statistically, it becomes possible to identify strengths and weaknesses that affect not only individual projects but also departments, laboratories, divisions, companies, and eventually entire industries.

Measurement Input Section

The data in the following section is typical of the kinds of information provided by the project manager and the technical staff of the project.

Project identity. The basic identity of the project is established by recording both the project name and also a set of standard facts about the project. In this case, the project has these attributes:

- Its "nature" is that of a new project, rather than an enhancement.
- Its "scope" is that of a system comprised of several programs, rather than a single program.
- Its "class" is internal, and the project was intended for use at a single location rather than as a distributed application.
- Its "type" is hybrid; it consists of both on-line and batch components.
- Its "goal" as assigned by senior management was "to complete the project in the shortest possible time."

Project occupation groups

With about 100 different kinds of specialists to choose from, it is significant to record the kinds of staff that worked on the project. This is different from simply recording hours, since the goal is to identify any special skills that might have been utilized. For the project included here, a comparatively ordinary MIS project, the kinds of occupation groups used for development included:

Project management

Systems analysts

Application programmers

Database administrators

Tool specialists

Management consultant

The kinds of occupation groups identified for maintenance included:

Project management

Maintenance programmers

Customer support specialists

Staff availability and work patterns

It is very important to record whether or not the staff members on a project could devote their full time to the project, or were dividing their time among several projects. It is also very important to record the basic work-hour pattern that was applied. For the project shown here, the accounting day was the normal U.S. 8-h day. Only an average of 6 h/day was applied to the project, but there was an average of 1 h/day of unpaid overtime by the project staff. Unpaid overtime is a weak link in most project-tracking systems, and this kind of data requires actual interviews with the staff to explore how much unpaid time was really applied.

Complexity, functionality, and reusability

Several topics are closely interrelated and should be considered together: The overall complexity of the problems, code, and data structure for the project should be recorded. The function point totals should be recorded, assuming that the project uses function points. Finally, and perhaps the most difficult, the amount of reusable code should be noted.

For the project shown here, some 3000 Cobol statements were estimated to be reused by the project team, and that amounted to about 48 function points. The pattern for the reused code also should be noted.

In this case, the purposes of the reused code included, among others:

Date and calendar management

Report formatting

Printer control

Screen formats

Skill and environmental factors—The soft data

It is very important to record data on the skills, tools, methods, and environment that affected the project in a way that lends itself to statistical analysis. This requirement rules out straight text, and it implies some kind of a coding scheme. Since this project was measured by using the CHECKPOINT® tool, it should be recalled that its encoding scheme is a 5-point scale set up in general as follows:

1 Much better than U.S. norms
2 Better than U.S. norms
3 Approximately at the U.S. average level
4 Worse than U.S. norms
5 Much worse than U.S. norms

There are more than two hundred soft questions that can be answered by using the 5-point scale. That allows a number of interesting conclusions to be drawn via multiple-regression techniques. The sets of major soft-data factors that should be measured include:

Staff experience with tools and methods

User experience and participation during the project

Usefulness of tools and methods

Stability of requirements

Convenience or inconvenience of the physical office arrangement

Organization structures used on the project

Descriptive materials and remarks

It is not possible to record all significant information by using only multiple-choice questions. Therefore, project measurement and management tools should also include the ability to accept textual information in several forms:

- Names of specific vendors, tools, and people associated with the project
- Notes on random but important topics, e.g., the disruption caused by a physical event such as the California earthquake

Measurement Output Section

The inputs to a project measurement system are organized for convenience in collecting the data. The outputs, on the other hand, should be organized to make the insights and information from measurement clear and easy to grasp. The outputs shown here begin with the hard numerical information about the project and then give the supporting information derived from the soft factors in later sections.

Summary of total project effort, staffing, schedules, and costs

Since the first thing that senior management often asks for is the "bottom line" of a project, the first item reported is the overall cost, effort, and staffing for these major elements:

Development

User involvement

Maintenance (defect repairs)

Enhancements

This summary information is followed by other quick looks at important factors, such as quality and defect removal, all intended to give an overall view of the project from a high-level vantage point.

Detailed breakdowns of effort, staffing, schedules, and costs by activity

Although the summary presentation condenses information for executive purposes, the follow-on data should be quite granular. The schedule, effort, staff, and cost information should be recorded by activity. In the project shown here that means that 13 out of the 25 possible activities were performed and so had data collected for them.

When the data is recorded by using a software tool, derivative forms of information can be provided automatically. For example, the percentages of project effort and percentages of project schedule which each activity required can be automatically calculated.

Templates for using historical data in estimating. One of the most important of all applications for measured historical data is using the information to estimate future projects. In spite of the widespread desirability of this function, exactly what information should be used has been uncertain. The essence of converting historical data into estimating templates requires knowledge of four things:

1. The nature of the primary deliverable from each activity or task

2. The sizes of the deliverables in terms of "natural" units such as the page counts of specifications and the number of test cases
3. The "assignment scopes," or the amount of each deliverable which on the average is assigned to one staff member
4. The "production rates," or the amounts of each deliverable which one person actually produced in an hour, day, week, month, or year

With automatic measurement tools such as CHECKPOINT®, templates are a standard output.

Normalized data in function point, feature point, or lines of code

For purposes of comparison with other projects or with industry norms, it is necessary to convert the raw data into a standard metric. Although function points have started to replace lines of code for this purpose, both forms are widely utilized. With a software measurement tool, it is easy to have the data converted into either metric or, as shown here, into both metrics in a side-by-side form.

Defect and quality data

Since one of the most expensive tasks in all of software engineering history is the cost of finding and fixing bugs, it is quite desirable to record the number, origins, and severities of the bugs and the amount of effort required to find and fix them.

Documentation data

Since paperwork in all its forms (plans, requirements, specifications, user documents, and so on) is often much more expensive than coding, it is desirable to measure the sets of actual documents produced, their sizes, and the effort associated with their production. When computerized measurement software is used, some additional calculations that can be performed are interesting. For example, since ordinary typed pages contain an average of perhaps 500 words, it is easily possible to calculate the number of words produced in support of a software project.

User effort data

In MIS projects such as the example shown here, the users of the projects are often active participants. Users are almost always participants during requirements and frequently during prototyping. They take part in reviews, and in many cases users or staff personnel in the user organization will produce the final user documentation. They can have heavy involvement in acceptance testing, and in some cases they also participate in project management. Since they are not part of the development organization, the time and effort they devote to projects is seldom recorded. However, that is not as it should be. For purposes of both historical accuracy and economic validity, user cost should be recorded. With computerized measurement software, it is possible to record user effort separately and then add that effort to the overall project.

Maintenance and enhancement data

Project measurements should not, of course, stop with the first release of a new software project. It is desirable to continue the project cost accounting on a month-by-month or year-by-year basis for as long as the software is in production. The example shown here includes 10 years of maintenance and enhancements costs. Since the project used was new, the costs were estimated rather than measured, but as time passed, the estimated values would gradually be replaced by historical data.

It is significant for companies that do business with the Department of Defense that estimating tools are being asked to produce 20-year estimates of maintenance and enhancements. No one, least of all developers of estimating tools, actually believes that 20-year predictions will be accurate. Nonetheless, this kind of long-range information can certainly be produced.

It should be noted that "maintenance" as used here means defect repairs. Adding new features and meeting new requirements is defined as "enhancements." The dichotomy is more accurate from an accounting standpoint and also makes it easier to separate the widely differing productivity rates.

It should be noted again that software projects, like all physical systems, are subject to entropy. Entropy is, of course, a gradual increase in disorder over time. For software, each change made to the existing system will slightly degrade its original structure. Over long periods of time, these slight degradations in structure tend to accumulate until the system can ultimately become unmaintainable. Corrective actions, such as restructuring and reengineering, are possible. However, unless deliberate action is taken, the long-term growth in system complexity will go up, and that will reduce both the assignment scopes and production rates of future updates. Thus, if a given update required 1 person-month in 1990, by 1995 the complexity of the system might have increased so much that the same update would take 5 person-weeks. By 2000, the same update might require 2 person-months. One of the most useful by-products of long-range historical measurements, as an aid in planning corrective actions, is the ability to calculate the rates at which systems decay.

Project strengths and weaknesses

One of the convenient features of computerized measurement tools is the ability to carry out complex tasks that make it easy to gain insights into why projects are better or worse than expected. Since the soft environmental factors were recorded by using a 5-point scale with 1 and 2 being better and 4 and 5 being worse than U.S. averages, it is easy to separate a project's strengths from its weaknesses. In the example given here, strengths are defined as factors averaging 2.5 or less and weaknesses as factors averaging 3.5 or higher. The zone from 2.5 to 3.5 is the approximate U.S. average, and it can be presumed to not have a significant outcome on the project in question.

However, not every environmental factor influences every aspect of a project. With expert systems, it is easy to pick out the soft environmental factors that influence project characteristics of significance to managers. In the example given here, the factors that influenced those topics are shown:

Costs

Effort

Quality

Productivity

Schedules

Personnel

Environment

Notes and comments

Obviously, not every point of significance can be reduced to a multiple-choice question and a 5-point scale. Computerized measurement systems also provide the ability to record miscellaneous comments about whatever seems important to the staff or management.

Paperwork volumes

Not all projects produce the same set of written materials. It is desirable to record which specific documents were actually produced and compare that to an overall list of document types. In the example given here, 24 discrete kinds of documents were produced out of the set of 56 total possible kinds of documents.

Security level NONE 3/06/96 5:35:23pm
Project s:\tmp\mcgraw
Version label MIS EXAMPLE: 320 FUNCTION POINT PAYROLL PROGRAM
Location BOSTON, MASSACHUSETTS

Checkpoint(R) 2.3.1 REPORT(S)

MIS Example

Contents:

Security level NONE
Project s:\tmp\mcgraw
Version label MIS EXAMPLE: 320 FUNCTION POINT PAYROLL PROGRAM
Location BOSTON, MASSACHUSETTS

3/06/96 5:35:23pm
Page 1

TOTALS

Project Profile

Project nature	1]	New program development
Project scope	5]	Complete stand-alone program
Project class	4]	Internal: for use at a single location
Project type (primary)	5]	Interactive database applications
Project type (secondary)	2]	Batch applications
Project goals for estimating	1]	Standard estimate

Development and User		**Attributes**	**Assessment**	**Estimation**
Schedule Months	12.19*	Personnel	2.63	2.50
Person Months	33.65*	Technology	2.98	3.00
Staff Headcount	7.00*	Process	3.48	3.50
Cost $ Thousands	144.76*	Environment	2.56	2.46
Delivered FP3	302.00	Index	3.02	2.87
Base FP3	0.00	Risk	3.13	
Document pages	356.00*	Value	2.00	

Quality

Delivered defects	191.00*
Total defect removal efficiency	52.01*

Productivity

FP3 / person Month	8.98*

Cost and Effort

	Effort Months	Staff Headcount	Cost $ Thousands
Development	28.72*	5*	123.53*
User involvement	4.93*	2*	21.23*
Maintenance	139.73*	3*	839.13*
Enhancement	79.54*	1*	532.37*
Subtotal	252.92*	11*	1,516.26*
Other project costs			0.00*
Total cost			1,516.26*

Security level NONE
Project s:\tmp\mcgraw
Version label MIS EXAMPLE: 320 FUNCTION POINT PAYROLL PROGRAM
Location BOSTON, MASSACHUSETTS

3/06/96 5:35:23pm
Page 2

TOTALS (continued)

Quality

Defect potentials	398*
- Defects removed	239*
+ Bad fixes	32*
Delivered defects	191*
Potential defects per FP3	1.32*
Delivered defects per FP3	0.63*
Total defect removal efficiency	52.0* %
Removal cost per FP3 $ Thousands	0.12*
Removal effort per FP3 Months	0.03*

Reliability

Months to stabilization	6.89*
Mean CPU hours until failure	
At delivery	6.59*
At stabilization	135.48*

Size

Code Class	FP3	KLOC	Level	Source Lines per FP3
New	272	29.01*	3.00	106.67*
COBOL	272	29.01*	3.00	106.67*
Reused	30	3.04*	3.00	101.33*
COBOL	30	3.04*	3.00	101.33*
Prototyped	0	0.00	3.00	0.00
Base	0	0.00	3.00	0.00
Changed	0	0.00	3.00	0.00
Deleted	0	0.00	3.00	0.00
Delivered	302	32.05*		106.14*
Project	302	32.05*		106.14*

Security level NONE
Project s:\tmp\mcgraw
Version label MIS EXAMPLE: 320 FUNCTION POINT PAYROLL PROGRAM
Location BOSTON, MASSACHUSETTS

3/06/96 5:35:23pm
Page 3

TOTALS (continued)

Productivity

	Ratios
FP3 per person	43.14*
FP3 per person Month	8.98*
FP3 per calendar Month	24.78*

	Cost $ Thousands
Development cost per FP3	0.41*
User cost per FP3	0.07*
Maintenance cost per FP3	2.78*
Enhancement cost per FP3	1.76*
Other cost per FP3	0.00*
Total cost per FP3	5.02*

Security level NONE
Project s:\tmp\mcgraw
Version label MIS EXAMPLE: 320 FUNCTION POINT PAYROLL PROGRAM
Location BOSTON, MASSACHUSETTS

3/06/96 5:35:23pm
Page 4

DEVELOPMENT TASK ANALYSIS

Development Schedule / Effort / Cost

Activity	Begin Date	End Date	Schedule Months	Effort Months	Staff FTE	Cost $ Thousands
Dev project management	3/01/96*	3/06/97*	12.16*	1.84*	0.15*	7.90*
Requirements	3/01/96*	6/13/96*	3.42*	2.68*	0.80*	11.53*
Funct analysis/design	5/17/96*	6/29/96*	1.41*	1.09*	0.78*	4.69*
Detail design & specs	6/07/96*	6/30/96*	0.76*	0.60*	0.80*	2.56*
Coding	6/16/96*	11/19/96*	5.13*	11.46*	2.26*	49.26*
Reusable code acquis	7/09/96*	7/13/96*	0.13*	0.08*	0.58*	0.33*
Unit testing	7/24/96*	11/19/96*	3.88*	1.20*	0.31*	5.14*
Function testing	10/10/96*	12/11/96*	2.04*	2.99*	1.48*	12.83*
System testing	12/10/96*	2/18/97*	2.30*	3.41*	1.50*	14.64*
Acceptance testing	2/17/97*	3/07/97*	0.59*	0.65*	1.12*	2.86*
User/maintenance doc	7/09/96*	2/17/97*	7.33*	2.65*	0.37*	11.41*
Installation	2/17/97*	2/20/97*	0.10*	0.07*	0.68*	0.28*
User training	2/19/97*	2/20/97*	0.03*	0.02*	0.65*	0.09*
Total			39.26*	28.72*	5.00*	123.53*
Overlapped schedule			12.19*		2.39*	
Unpaid overtime				4.22*		

Security level NONE
Project s:\tmp\mcgraw
Version label MIS EXAMPLE: 320 FUNCTION POINT PAYROLL PROGRAM
Location BOSTON, MASSACHUSETTS

3/06/96 5:35:23pm
Page 5

DEVELOPMENT TASK ANALYSIS (continued)

Development Schedule / Effort Percentages

Activity	Schedule %	Effort %
Dev project management	99.7*	6.4*
Requirements	28.3*	9.3*
Funct analysis/design	11.6*	3.8*
Detail design & specs	6.2*	2.1*
Coding	42.0*	39.9*
Reusable code acquis	1.1*	0.3*
Unit testing	31.8*	4.2*
Function testing	16.7*	10.4*
System testing	19.1*	11.9*
Acceptance testing	5.1*	2.3*
User/maintenance doc	60.4*	9.2*
Installation	1.1*	0.2*
User training	0.3*	0.1*
Total	323.5*	100.0*

Development Paid / Unpaid Effort

Activity	Paid Effort Months	Unpaid Effort Months	Total Effort Months
Dev project management	1.57*	0.27*	1.84*
Requirements	2.29*	0.39*	2.68*
Funct analysis/design	0.93*	0.16*	1.09*
Detail design & specs	0.51*	0.09*	0.60*
Coding	9.77*	1.68*	11.46*
Reusable code acquis	0.06*	0.01*	0.08*
Unit testing	1.02*	0.18*	1.20*
Function testing	2.55*	0.44*	2.99*
System testing	2.91*	0.50*	3.41*
Acceptance testing	0.56*	0.10*	0.65*
User/maintenance doc	2.26*	0.39*	2.65*
Installation	0.06*	0.01*	0.07*
User training	0.02*	0.00*	0.02*
Total	24.5*	4.2*	28.7*

Security level NONE
Project s:\tmp\mcgraw
Version label MIS EXAMPLE: 320 FUNCTION POINT PAYROLL PROGRAM
Location BOSTON, MASSACHUSETTS

3/06/96 5:35:23pm
Page 6

DEVELOPMENT TASK ANALYSIS (continued)

Development Productivity

Activity	FP3 per Month	KLOC per Month	Cost $ Thousands per FP3	Cost $ Thousands per KLOC
Dev project management	164.49*	17.46*	0.03*	0.25*
Requirements	112.58*	11.95*	0.04*	0.36*
Funct analysis/design	276.90*	29.39*	0.02*	0.15*
Detail design & specs	507.45*	53.86*	0.01*	0.08*
Coding	26.36*	2.80*	0.16*	1.54*
Reusable code acquis	3,984.52*	422.90*	0.00*	0.01*
Unit testing	252.35*	26.78*	0.02*	0.16*
Function testing	101.16*	10.74*	0.04*	0.40*
System testing	88.67*	9.41*	0.05*	0.46*
Acceptance testing	463.00*	49.14*	0.01*	0.09*
User/maintenance doc	113.75*	12.07*	0.04*	0.36*
Installation	4,578.65*	485.96*	0.00*	0.01*
User training	14,388.34*	1,527.13*	0.00*	0.00*
Total	10.5*	1.1*	0.4*	3.9*

Development Sizes / Scopes / Rates

Task	Size	Deliverable	Assignment Scope	Production per Month
Personnel management	3.00*	People	3.00*	1.63*
Tradit requirmnts spec	109.00*	Internal Pages	109.00*	40.63*
Initl functional spec	76.00*	Internal Pages	76.00*	69.68*
Data design spec	20.00*	Internal Pages	20.00*	33.61*
Coding	29.01*	KLOC	9.67*	2.53*
Reusable code acquis	3.04*	KLOC	3.04*	40.11*
Unit testing	197.00*	Cases	65.67*	164.61*
New function testing	146.00*	Cases	73.00*	48.90*
System testing	61.00*	Cases	30.50*	17.91*
Acceptance testing	27.00*	Cases	13.50*	41.39*
Installation guide	7.00*	External Pages	7.00*	77.13*
User's guide	91.00*	External Pages	91.00*	154.27*
Product I/O screens	94.00*	Screens	94.00*	61.12*
On-line error messages	30.00*	Screens	30.00*	68.76*
Installation	32.05*	KLOC	32.05*	485.96*
User training	36.00*	External Pages	36.00*	1,715.17*

Security level NONE
Project s:\tmp\mcgraw
Version label MIS EXAMPLE: 320 FUNCTION POINT PAYROLL PROGRAM
Location BOSTON, MASSACHUSETTS

3/06/96 5:35:23pm
Page 7

DEVELOPMENT SCHEDULE / EFFORT / COST CHART

Development Schedule

Activity

Dev project management
Requirements
Funct analysis/design
Detail design & specs
Coding
Reusable code acquis
Unit testing
Function testing
System testing
Acceptance testing
User/maintenance doc
Installation
User training

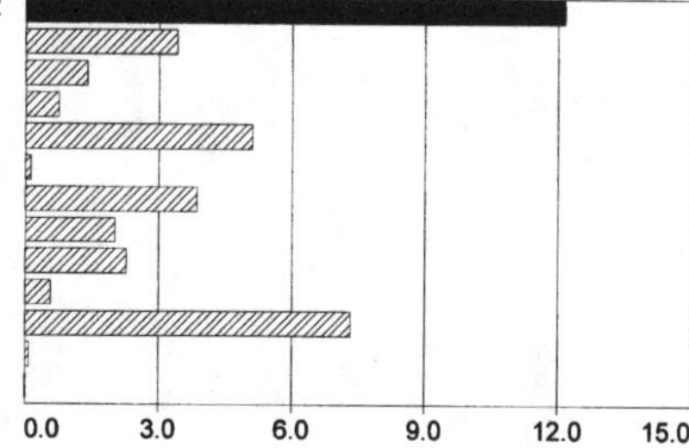

Schedule Months

Development Effort

Activity

Dev project management
Requirements
Funct analysis/design
Detail design & specs
Coding
Reusable code acquis
Unit testing
Function testing
System testing
Acceptance testing
User/maintenance doc
Installation
User training

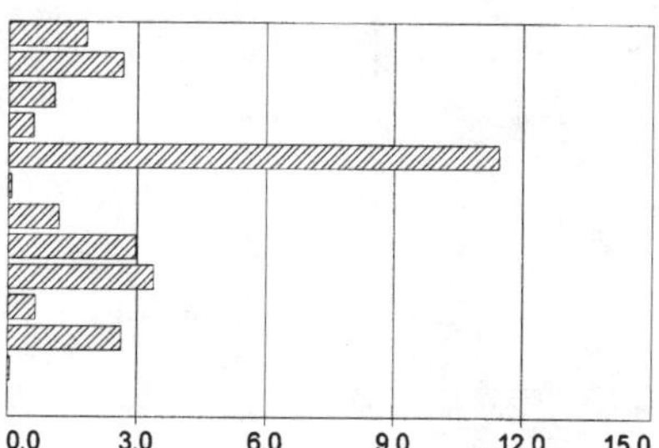

Effort Months

Security level NONE
Project s:\tmp\mcgraw
Version label MIS EXAMPLE: 320 FUNCTION POINT PAYROLL PROGRAM
Location BOSTON, MASSACHUSETTS

3/06/96 5:35:23pm
Page 8

DEVELOPMENT SCHEDULE / EFFORT / COST CHART (continued)

Development Staff

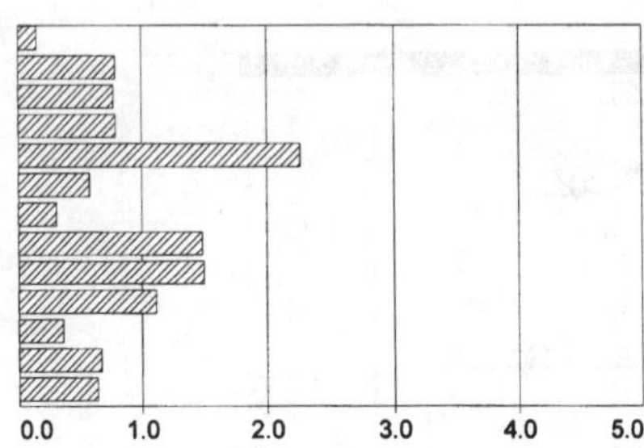

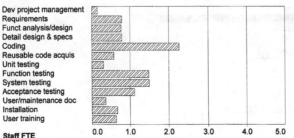

Development Cost

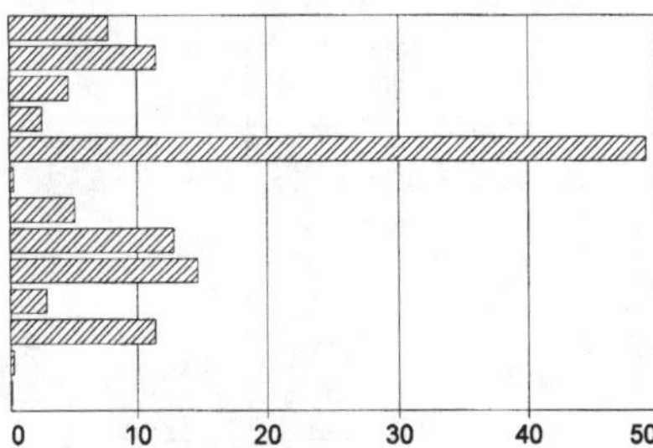

Security level NONE
Project s:\tmp\mcgraw
Version label MIS EXAMPLE: 320 FUNCTION POINT PAYROLL PROGRAM
Location BOSTON, MASSACHUSETTS

3/06/96 5:35:23pm
Page 9

DEVELOPMENT GANTT CHART

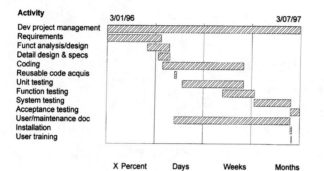

Activity
Dev project management
Requirements
Funct analysis/design
Detail design & specs
Coding
Reusable code acquis
Unit testing
Function testing
System testing
Acceptance testing
User/maintenance doc
Installation
User training

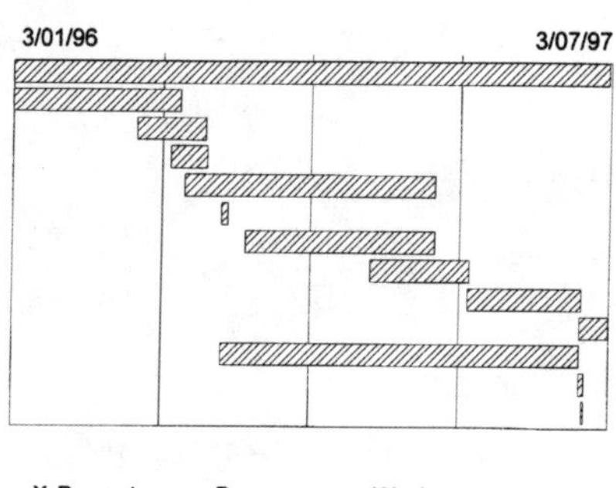

X Percent Days Weeks Months

DEVELOPMENT STAFFING BY MONTH

Year	Jan	Feb	Mar	Apr	May	Jun	Jul	Aug	Sep	Oct	Nov	Dec
1996	0	0	1*	1*	2*	4*	4*	4*	4*	5*	4*	2*
1997	2*	3*	1*	0	0	0	0	0	0	0	0	0
1998	0	0	0	0	0	0	0	0	0	0	0	0
1999	0	0	0	0	0	0	0	0	0	0	0	0
2000	0	0	0	0	0	0	0	0	0	0	0	0
2001	0	0	0	0	0	0	0	0	0	0	0	0
2002	0	0	0	0	0	0	0	0	0	0	0	0
2003	0	0	0	0	0	0	0	0	0	0	0	0
2004	0	0	0	0	0	0	0	0	0	0	0	0
2005	0	0	0	0	0	0	0	0	0	0	0	0

Security level NONE
Project s:\tmp\mcgraw
Version label MIS EXAMPLE: 320 FUNCTION POINT PAYROLL PROGRAM
Location BOSTON, MASSACHUSETTS

3/06/96 5:35:23pm
Page 10

DEVELOPMENT STAFFING BY MONTH CHART

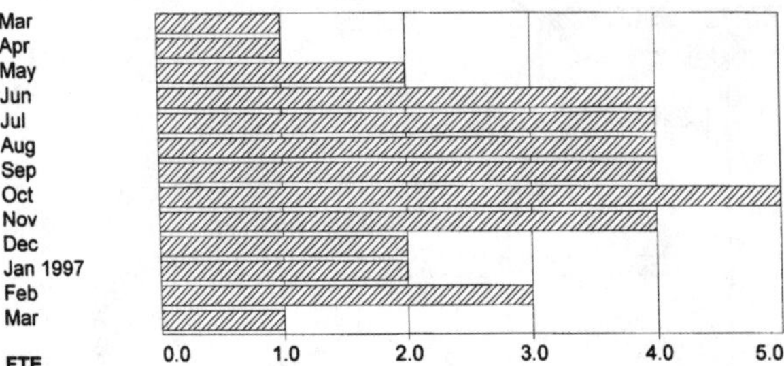

DEVELOPMENT COST PERCENTAGES

Phase	% Paper	% Q.A.	% Rvws.	% Test	% Code	% Mgmt.	% Other	Total
Planning & management	0.0*	0.0*	0.0*	0.0	0.0	6.4*	0.0*	6.4*
Requirements	9.3*	0.0	0.0*	0.0	0.0*	0.0	0.0*	9.3*
External design	3.8*	0.0	0.0*	0.0	0.0	0.0	0.0	3.8*
Internal design	2.1*	0.0*	0.0*	0.0	0.0	0.0	0.0	2.1*
Coding	0.0	0.0	0.0*	4.2*	40.1*	0.0	0.0	44.3*
Integration and test	0.0	0.0	0.0	24.6*	0.0	0.0	0.0*	24.6*
Documentation	2.4*	0.0	0.0*	0.0	0.0	0.0	6.9*	9.2*
Installation/training	0.0	0.0	0.0	0.0	0.0	0.0	0.3*	0.3*
Total %	17.6*	0.0*	0.0*	28.7*	40.1*	6.4*	7.2*	100.0*

Security level NONE
Project s:\tmp\mcgraw
Version label MIS EXAMPLE: 320 FUNCTION POINT PAYROLL PROGRAM
Location BOSTON, MASSACHUSETTS

3/06/96 5:35:23pm
Page 11

DEVELOPMENT COST PERCENTAGES CHART

Category

Paper
Quality Assurance
Reviews
Testing
Coding
Management
Other

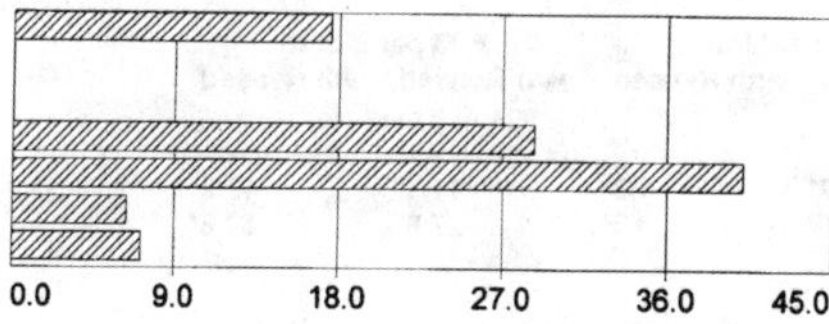

Percentage

TESTING SUMMARY

Task	**Test Cases Count**	**Test Cases per FP3**	**Test Cases per KLOC**
Unit testing	197*	0.65*	6.15*
New function testing	146*	0.48*	4.55*
System testing	61*	0.20*	1.90*
Acceptance testing	27*	0.09*	0.84*
Total	431*	1.43*	13.45*

Percent of development costs for testing 28.7* %

Security level NONE
Project s:\tmp\mcgraw
Version label MIS EXAMPLE: 320 FUNCTION POINT PAYROLL PROGRAM
Location BOSTON, MASSACHUSETTS

3/06/96 5:35:23pm
Page 12

PRODUCTIVITY RATIOS

Output Ratios

	KLOC per Month		FP3 per Month	
	w/o Reused	**with Reused**	**w/o Reused**	**with Reused**
Excluding unpaid OT				
All development	1.2*	1.3*	11.1*	12.3*
Coding	3.0*	3.3*	27.8*	30.9*
Including unpaid OT				
All development	1.0*	1.1*	9.5*	10.5*
Coding	2.5*	2.8*	23.7*	26.4*

Pages produced per calendar Month	29.2*
Average staff per calendar Month	2.8*
Thousands $ per calendar Month	11.9*

Headcount Ratios

	per Person	per Programmer
New FP3	38.9*	90.7*
Reused FP3	4.3*	10.0*
New KLOC	4.1*	9.7*
Reused KLOC	0.4*	1.0*
Document pages	50.9*	118.7*
Potential defects	56.9*	132.7*
Test cases	61.6*	143.7*

Security level NONE
Project s:\tmp\mcgraw
Version label MIS EXAMPLE: 320 FUNCTION POINT PAYROLL PROGRAM
Location BOSTON, MASSACHUSETTS

3/06/96 5:35:23pm
Page 13

USER TASK ANALYSIS

User Schedule / Effort / Cost

Activity	Begin Date	End Date	Schedule Months	Effort Months	Staff FTE	Cost $ Thousands
Requirements	3/01/96*	6/13/96*	3.42*	4.02*	1.19*	17.30*
Acceptance testing	2/17/97*	3/10/97*	0.69*	0.29*	0.43*	1.30*
User/maintenance doc	9/01/96*	10/17/96*	1.51*	0.59*	0.40*	2.54*
User training	2/19/97*	2/20/97*	0.03*	0.02*	0.65*	0.09*
Total			5.65*	4.93*	2.00*	21.23*
Overlapped schedule			12.29*		0.41*	
Unpaid overtime				0.72*		

User Schedule / Effort Percentages

Activity	Schedule %	Effort %
Requirements	28.1*	81.7*
Acceptance testing	5.6*	5.9*
User/maintenance doc	12.3*	12.0*
User training	0.3*	0.4*
Total	46.3*	100.0*

User Paid / Unpaid Effort

Activity	Paid Effort Months	Unpaid Effort Months	Total Effort Months
Requirements	3.4*	0.6*	4.0*
Acceptance testing	0.2*	0.0*	0.3*
User/maintenance doc	0.5*	0.1*	0.6*
User training	0.0*	0.0*	0.0*
Total	4.2*	0.7*	4.9*

Security level NONE
Project s:\tmp\mcgraw
Version label MIS EXAMPLE: 320 FUNCTION POINT PAYROLL PROGRAM
Location BOSTON, MASSACHUSETTS

3/06/96 5:35:23pm
Page 14

USER TASK ANALYSIS (continued)

User Productivity

Activity	FP3 per Month	KLOC per Month	Cost $ Thousands per FP3	Cost $ Thousands per KLOC
Requirements	75.05*	7.97*	0.06*	0.54*
Acceptance testing	1,032.74*	109.61*	0.00*	0.04*
User/maintenance doc	511.96*	54.34*	0.01*	0.08*
User training	14,388.34*	1,527.13*	0.00*	0.00*
Total	61.29*	6.51*	0.07*	0.66*

User Sizes / Scopes / Rates

Task	Size	Deliverable	Assignment Scope	Production per Month
Tradit requirmnts spec	109.00*	Internal Pages	54.50*	27.09*
Acceptance testing	27.00*	Cases	27.00*	144.50*
Acceptance testing rpts	53.00*	Internal Pages	53.00*	502.00*
User's guide	91.00*	External Pages	91.00*	154.27*
User training	36.00*	External Pages	36.00*	1,715.17*

Security level NONE
Project s:\tmp\mcgraw
Version label MIS EXAMPLE: 320 FUNCTION POINT PAYROLL PROGRAM
Location BOSTON, MASSACHUSETTS

3/06/96 5:35:23pm
Page 15

USER SCHEDULE / EFFORT / COST CHART

User Schedule

Activity

Requirements
Acceptance testing
User/maintenance doc
User training

Schedule Months

0.0 1.0 2.0 3.0 4.0 5.0

User Effort

Activity

Requirements
Acceptance testing
User/maintenance doc
User training

Effort Months

0.0 1.0 2.0 3.0 4.0 5.0

User Staff

Activity

Requirements
Acceptance testing
User/maintenance doc
User training

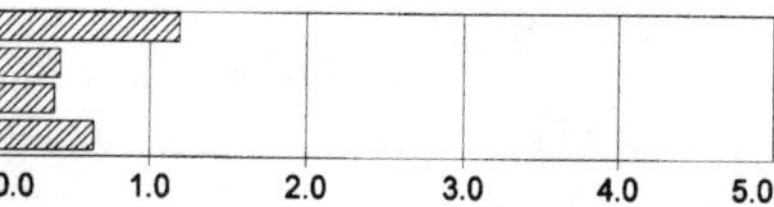

Staff

Security level NONE
Project s:\tmp\mcgraw
Version label MIS EXAMPLE: 320 FUNCTION POINT PAYROLL PROGRAM
Location BOSTON, MASSACHUSETTS

3/06/96 5:35:23pm
Page 16

USER SCHEDULE / EFFORT / COST CHART (continued)

User Cost

Activity

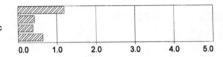

Requirements
Acceptance testing
User/maintenance doc
User training

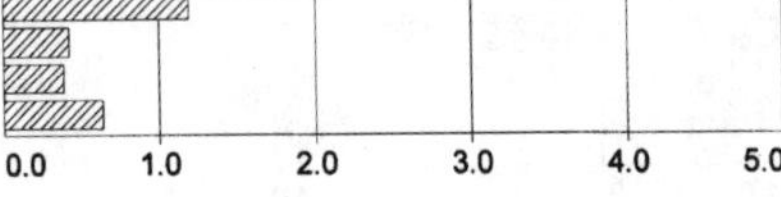

Cost $ Thousands

USER GANTT CHART

Activity

Requirements
Acceptance testing
User/maintenance doc
User training

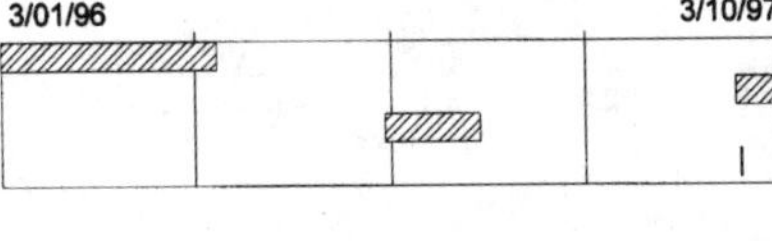

X Percent Days Weeks Months

Security level NONE
Project s:\tmp\mcgraw
Version label MIS EXAMPLE: 320 FUNCTION POINT PAYROLL PROGRAM
Location BOSTON, MASSACHUSETTS

3/06/96 5:35:23pm
Page 17

USER STAFFING BY MONTH

Year	Jan	Feb	Mar	Apr	May	Jun	Jul	Aug	Sep	Oct	Nov	Dec
1996	0	0	2*	2*	2*	1*	0	0	1*	1*	0	0
1997	0	1*	1*	0	0	0	0	0	0	0	0	0
1998	0	0	0	0	0	0	0	0	0	0	0	0
1999	0	0	0	0	0	0	0	0	0	0	0	0
2000	0	0	0	0	0	0	0	0	0	0	0	0
2001	0	0	0	0	0	0	0	0	0	0	0	0
2002	0	0	0	0	0	0	0	0	0	0	0	0
2003	0	0	0	0	0	0	0	0	0	0	0	0
2004	0	0	0	0	0	0	0	0	0	0	0	0
2005	0	0	0	0	0	0	0	0	0	0	0	0

USER STAFFING BY MONTH CHART

Month and Year

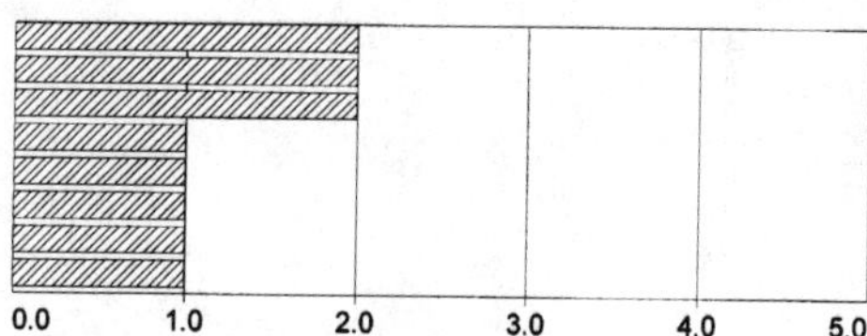

Security level NONE
Project s:\tmp\mcgraw
Version label MIS EXAMPLE: 320 FUNCTION POINT PAYROLL PROGRAM
Location BOSTON, MASSACHUSETTS

3/06/96 5:35:23pm
Page 18

MAINTENANCE STAFF / EFFORT / COST

Maintenance Summary

Year	Staff	Effort Months	Cost $ Thousands
1997	3*	14.6*	66.5*
1998	3*	14.1*	67.9*
1999	3*	14.3*	73.2*
2000	3*	13.9*	75.3*
2001	3*	13.5*	77.5*
2002	3*	14.1*	86.0*
2003	3*	13.6*	88.2*
2004	3*	13.4*	91.9*
2005	3*	14.3*	104.1*
2006	3*	14.1*	108.6*
Total		139.7*	839.1*

Maintenance effort per KLOC	4.4*
Maintenance effort per F.P.	0.5*
Maintenance effort per defect	0.5*
Maintenance cost per KLOC	26.2*
Maintenance cost per F.P.	2.8*
Maintenance cost per defect	3.2*

Security level NONE
Project s:\tmp\mcgraw
Version label MIS EXAMPLE: 320 FUNCTION POINT PAYROLL PROGRAM
Location BOSTON, MASSACHUSETTS

3/06/96 5:35:23pm
Page 19

MAINTENANCE STAFF / EFFORT / COST (continued)

Maintenance Cost by Activity

Year	Central Maintenance	Field Maintenance	Customer Support	Maintenance Management	Total $ Thousands
1997	47.0*	0.0	2.9*	16.6*	66.5*
1998	48.1*	0.0	2.8*	17.0*	67.9*
1999	51.8*	0.0	3.1*	18.3*	73.2*
2000	53.4*	0.0	3.1*	18.8*	75.3*
2001	55.1*	0.0	3.0*	19.4*	77.5*
2002	60.9*	0.0	3.6*	21.5*	86.0*
2003	62.7*	0.0	3.5*	22.0*	88.2*
2004	65.4*	0.0	3.5*	23.0*	91.9*
2005	73.7*	0.0	4.4*	26.0*	104.1*
2006	77.0*	0.0	4.5*	27.1*	108.6*
Total	595.0*	0.0	34.4*	209.8*	839.1*

Maintenance Effort by Activity

Year	Central Maintenance	Field Maintenance	Customer Support	Maintenance Management	Total Months
1997	10.3*	0.0	0.6*	3.6*	14.6*
1998	10.0*	0.0	0.6*	3.5*	14.1*
1999	10.1*	0.0	0.6*	3.6*	14.3*
2000	9.8*	0.0	0.6*	3.5*	13.9*
2001	9.6*	0.0	0.5*	3.4*	13.5*
2002	10.0*	0.0	0.6*	3.5*	14.1*
2003	9.7*	0.0	0.5*	3.4*	13.6*
2004	9.5*	0.0	0.5*	3.3*	13.4*
2005	10.1*	0.0	0.6*	3.6*	14.3*
2006	10.0*	0.0	0.6*	3.5*	14.1*
Total	99.1*	0.0	5.7*	34.9*	139.7*

Security level NONE
Project s:\tmp\mcgraw
Version label MIS EXAMPLE: 320 FUNCTION POINT PAYROLL PROGRAM
Location BOSTON, MASSACHUSETTS

3/06/96 5:35:23pm
Page 20

MAINTENANCE STAFF / EFFORT / COST (continued)

Maintenance Staff / Effort / Cost

Year	Central Maintenance	Field Maintenance	Customer Support	Maintenance Management	Total Staff
1997	1*	0	1*	1*	3*
1998	1*	0	1*	1*	3*
1999	1*	0	1*	1*	3*
2000	1*	0	1*	1*	3*
2001	1*	0	1*	1*	3*
2002	1*	0	1*	1*	3*
2003	1*	0	1*	1*	3*
2004	1*	0	1*	1*	3*
2005	1*	0	1*	1*	3*
2006	1*	0	1*	1*	3*
Average	1.0*	0.0	1.0*	1.0*	3.0*

MAINTENANCE DEFECT REPAIRS

Year	Valid Defects	Invalid Defects	Duplicate Defects
1997	29*	2*	0*
1998	26*	2*	0*
1999	27*	2*	0*
2000	25*	2*	0*
2001	24*	2*	0*
2002	26*	2*	0*
2003	25*	1*	0*
2004	24*	1*	0*
2005	28*	1*	0*
2006	27*	1*	0*
Total	261*	16*	0*
Valid defects per KLOC			8.15*
Valid defects per F.P.			0.87*

Security level NONE
Project s:\tmp\mcgraw
Version label MIS EXAMPLE: 320 FUNCTION POINT PAYROLL PROGRAM
Location BOSTON, MASSACHUSETTS

3/06/96 5:35:23pm
Page 21

YEARLY MAINTENANCE

Significant Ratios

Year: 1997	**Valid Defects**	**Invalid Defects**	**Duplicate Defects**
per KLOC	0.89*	0.06*	0.00*
per FP3	0.09*	0.01*	0.00*
per customer site	28.65*	2.00*	0.00*
per repair site	28.65*	2.00*	0.00*
per staff member	9.55*	0.67*	0.00*
per person Month	1.96*	0.14*	0.00*

Year: 1998	**Valid Defects**	**Invalid Defects**	**Duplicate Defects**
per KLOC	0.78*	0.06*	0.00*
per FP3	0.08*	0.01*	0.00*
per customer site	26.25*	2.00*	0.00*
per repair site	26.25*	2.00*	0.00*
per staff member	8.75*	0.67*	0.00*
per person Month	1.87*	0.14*	0.00*

Year: 1999	**Valid Defects**	**Invalid Defects**	**Duplicate Defects**
per KLOC	0.70*	0.05*	0.00*
per FP3	0.07*	0.01*	0.00*
per customer site	27.30*	2.00*	0.00*
per repair site	27.30*	2.00*	0.00*
per staff member	9.10*	0.67*	0.00*
per person Month	1.91*	0.14*	0.00*

Security level NONE
Project s:\tmp\mcgraw
Version label MIS EXAMPLE: 320 FUNCTION POINT PAYROLL PROGRAM
Location BOSTON, MASSACHUSETTS

3/06/96 5:35:23pm

YEARLY MAINTENANCE (continued)

Significant Ratios (continued)

Year: 2000	**Valid Defects**	**Invalid Defects**	**Duplicate Defects**
per KLOC	0.62*	0.05*	0.00*
per FP3	0.07*	0.01*	0.00*
per customer site	25.35*	2.00*	0.00*
per repair site	25.35*	2.00*	0.00*
per staff member	8.45*	0.67*	0.00*
per person Month	1.83*	0.14*	0.00*

Year: 2001	**Valid Defects**	**Invalid Defects**	**Duplicate Defects**
per KLOC	0.55*	0.05*	0.00*
per FP3	0.06*	0.00*	0.00*
per customer site	23.55*	2.00*	0.00*
per repair site	23.55*	2.00*	0.00*
per staff member	7.85*	0.67*	0.00*
per person Month	1.75*	0.15*	0.00*

Year: 2002	**Valid Defects**	**Invalid Defects**	**Duplicate Defects**
per KLOC	0.53*	0.04*	0.00*
per FP3	0.06*	0.00*	0.00*
per customer site	26.40*	2.00*	0.00*
per repair site	26.40*	2.00*	0.00*
per staff member	8.80*	0.67*	0.00*
per person Month	1.87*	0.14*	0.00*

Security level NONE
Project s:\tmp\mcgraw
Version label MIS EXAMPLE: 320 FUNCTION POINT PAYROLL PROGRAM
Location BOSTON, MASSACHUSETTS

3/06/96 5:35:23pm
Page 23

YEARLY MAINTENANCE (continued)

Significant Ratios (continued)

Year: 2003	Valid Defects	Invalid Defects	Duplicate Defects
per KLOC	0.48*	0.02*	0.00*
per FP3	0.05*	0.00*	0.00*
per customer site	24.90*	1.00*	0.00*
per repair site	24.90*	1.00*	0.00*
per staff member	8.30*	0.33*	0.00*
per person Month	1.83*	0.07*	0.00*

Year: 2004	Valid Defects	Invalid Defects	Duplicate Defects
per KLOC	0.44*	0.02*	0.00*
per FP3	0.05*	0.00*	0.00*
per customer site	23.85*	1.00*	0.00*
per repair site	23.85*	1.00*	0.00*
per staff member	7.95*	0.33*	0.00*
per person Month	1.78*	0.07*	0.00*

Year: 2005	Valid Defects	Invalid Defects	Duplicate Defects
per KLOC	0.45*	0.02*	0.00*
per FP3	0.05*	0.00*	0.00*
per customer site	28.05*	1.00*	0.00*
per repair site	28.05*	1.00*	0.00*
per staff member	9.35*	0.33*	0.00*
per person Month	1.96*	0.07*	0.00*

Security level NONE
Project s:\tmp\mcgraw
Version label MIS EXAMPLE: 320 FUNCTION POINT PAYROLL PROGRAM
Location BOSTON, MASSACHUSETTS

YEARLY MAINTENANCE (continued)

Significant Ratios (continued)

Year: 2006	**Valid Defects**	**Invalid Defects**	**Duplicate Defects**
per KLOC	0.41*	0.02*	0.00*
per FP3	0.04*	0.00*	0.00*
per customer site	27.00*	1.00*	0.00*
per repair site	27.00*	1.00*	0.00*
per staff member	9.00*	0.33*	0.00*
per person Month	1.92*	0.07*	0.00*

Assignment Scopes

Year: 1997	**KLOC**	**FP3**	**Valid Defects**	**Customer Sites**
Central maintenance	32.05*	302.00*	28.65*	1.00*
Field service	0.00*	0.00	0.00*	0.00
Customer support	32.05*	302.00*	28.65*	1.00*
Management	32.05*	302.00*	28.65*	1.00*
Total maintenance	10.68*	100.67*	9.55*	0.33*

Year: 1998	**KLOC**	**FP3**	**Valid Defects**	**Customer Sites**
Central maintenance	33.66*	317.10*	26.25*	1.00*
Field service	0.00*	0.00	0.00*	0.00
Customer support	33.66*	317.10*	26.25*	1.00*
Management	33.66*	317.10*	26.25*	1.00*
Total maintenance	11.22*	105.70*	8.75*	0.33*

Security level NONE
Project s:\tmp\mcgraw
Version label MIS EXAMPLE: 320 FUNCTION POINT PAYROLL PROGRAM
Location BOSTON, MASSACHUSETTS

3/06/96 5:35:23pm
Page 25

YEARLY MAINTENANCE (continued)

Assignment Scopes (continued)

Year: 1999	**KLOC**	**FP3**	**Valid Defects**	**Customer Sites**
Central maintenance	38.87*	366.25*	27.30*	1.00*
Field service	0.00*	0.00	0.00*	0.00
Customer support	38.87*	366.25*	27.30*	1.00*
Management	38.87*	366.25*	27.30*	1.00*
Total maintenance	12.96*	122.08*	9.10*	0.33*

Year: 2000	**KLOC**	**FP3**	**Valid Defects**	**Customer Sites**
Central maintenance	40.82*	384.56*	25.35*	1.00*
Field service	0.00*	0.00	0.00*	0.00
Customer support	40.82*	384.56*	25.35*	1.00*
Management	40.82*	384.56*	25.35*	1.00*
Total maintenance	13.61*	128.19*	8.45*	0.33*

Year: 2001	**KLOC**	**FP3**	**Valid Defects**	**Customer Sites**
Central maintenance	42.86*	403.79*	23.55*	1.00*
Field service	0.00*	0.00	0.00*	0.00
Customer support	42.86*	403.79*	23.55*	1.00*
Management	42.86*	403.79*	23.55*	1.00*
Total maintenance	14.29*	134.60*	7.85*	0.33*

Security level NONE
Project s:\tmp\mcgraw
Version label MIS EXAMPLE: 320 FUNCTION POINT PAYROLL PROGRAM
Location BOSTON, MASSACHUSETTS

3/06/96 5:35:23pm
Page 26

YEARLY MAINTENANCE (continued)

Assignment Scopes (continued)

Year: 2002	**KLOC**	**FP3**	**Valid Defects**	**Customer Sites**
Central maintenance	49.50*	466.38*	26.40*	1.00*
Field service	0.00*	0.00	0.00*	0.00
Customer support	49.50*	466.38*	26.40*	1.00*
Management	49.50*	466.38*	26.40*	1.00*
Total maintenance	16.50*	155.46*	8.80*	0.33*

Year: 2003	**KLOC**	**FP3**	**Valid Defects**	**Customer Sites**
Central maintenance	51.97*	489.70*	24.90*	1.00*
Field service	0.00*	0.00	0.00*	0.00
Customer support	51.97*	489.70*	24.90*	1.00*
Management	51.97*	489.70*	24.90*	1.00*
Total maintenance	17.32*	163.23*	8.30*	0.33*

Year: 2004	**KLOC**	**FP3**	**Valid Defects**	**Customer Sites**
Central maintenance	54.57*	514.18*	23.85*	1.00*
Field service	0.00*	0.00	0.00*	0.00
Customer support	54.57*	514.18*	23.85*	1.00*
Management	54.57*	514.18*	23.85*	1.00*
Total maintenance	18.19*	171.39*	7.95*	0.33*

Security level NONE
Project s:\tmp\mcgraw
Version label MIS EXAMPLE: 320 FUNCTION POINT PAYROLL PROGRAM
Location BOSTON, MASSACHUSETTS

3/06/96 5:35:23pm
Page 27

YEARLY MAINTENANCE (continued)

Assignment Scopes (continued)

Year: 2005	**KLOC**	**FP3**	**Valid Defects**	**Customer Sites**
Central maintenance	63.03*	593.88*	28.05*	1.00*
Field service	0.00*	0.00	0.00*	0.00
Customer support	63.03*	593.88*	28.05*	1.00*
Management	63.03*	593.88*	28.05*	1.00*
Total maintenance	21.01*	197.96*	9.35*	0.33*

Year: 2006	**KLOC**	**FP3**	**Valid Defects**	**Customer Sites**
Central maintenance	66.18*	623.58*	27.00*	1.00*
Field service	0.00*	0.00	0.00*	0.00
Customer support	66.18*	623.58*	27.00*	1.00*
Management	66.18*	623.58*	27.00*	1.00*
Total maintenance	22.06*	207.86*	9.00*	0.33*

Security level NONE
Project s:\tmp\mcgraw
Version label MIS EXAMPLE: 320 FUNCTION POINT PAYROLL PROGRAM
Location BOSTON, MASSACHUSETTS

3/06/96 5:35:23pm
Page 28

ENHANCEMENT

Enhancement Effort / Cost

Year	Staff	Effort Months	Cost $ Thousands	Complexity	
1997	1*	5.7*	28.1*	12*	
1998	1*	6.1*	31.4*	13*	
1999	1*	6.1*	33.4*	8*	Restructured
2000	1*	7.0*	40.9*	8*	
2001	1*	7.4*	45.7*	8*	
2002	1*	7.7*	50.6*	8*	Restructured
2003	1*	8.9*	62.1*	8*	
2004	2*	9.4*	69.3*	8*	
2005	2*	9.8*	76.7*	8*	Restructured
2006	2*	11.4*	94.2*	8*	
Total		79.5*	532.4*		

Enhancement Sizing

Year	FP3 Added	FP3 Deleted	Current FP3	Complexity	
1997	21.1*	6.0*	317.1*	12*	
1998	22.2*	6.3*	333.0*	13*	
1999	23.3*	6.7*	384.6*	8*	Restructured
2000	26.9*	7.7*	403.8*	8*	
2001	28.3*	8.1*	424.0*	8*	
2002	29.7*	8.5*	489.7*	8*	Restructured
2003	34.3*	9.8*	514.2*	8*	
2004	36.0*	10.3*	539.9*	8*	
2005	37.8*	10.8*	623.6*	8*	Restructured
2006	43.7*	12.5*	654.8*	8*	
Total	346.9*	99.1*			

Security level NONE
Project s:\tmp\mcgraw
Version label MIS EXAMPLE: 320 FUNCTION POINT PAYROLL PROGRAM
Location BOSTON, MASSACHUSETTS

3/06/96 5:35:23pm
Page 29

ENHANCEMENT (continued)

Enhancement Productivity

Year	FP3 Scope	FP3 per Month	Complexity	
1997	27.2*	4.7*	12*	
1998	28.5*	4.7*	13*	
1999	30.0*	4.9*	8*	Restructured
2000	34.6*	4.9*	8*	
2001	36.3*	4.9*	8*	
2002	38.2*	4.9*	8*	Restructured
2003	44.1*	4.9*	8*	
2004	23.1*	4.9*	8*	
2005	24.3*	4.9*	8*	Restructured
2006	28.1*	4.9*	8*	

Security level NONE
Project s:\tmp\mcgraw
Version label MIS EXAMPLE: 320 FUNCTION POINT PAYROLL PROGRAM
Location BOSTON, MASSACHUSETTS

3/06/96 5:35:23pm
Page 30

DOCUMENTATION ANALYSIS

Overall Documentation

Document Types	Pages per FP3	Pages per KLOC	Words per FP3	Words per KLOC
Planning	0.0	0.0*	0*	0*
Management	0.0	0.0*	0*	0*
Specification	0.7*	6.4*	272*	2,558*
Quality Assurance	0.2*	1.7*	88*	827*
External	0.3*	3.1*	162*	1,529*
Total	1.2*	11.1*	522*	4,914*

Diagrams	51.7*	Diagrams per 1000 words	0.3*
Document pages	356.0*	Words per page	442.4*
Total words	157,500.0*	Total words / source line	4.9*

Percent of development costs for paperwork 17.6* %

Specification Documents

	Pages
Traditional requirements specification	109*
Initial functional specifications	76*
Data design specification	20*
Total	205*

On-Line Specification Documents	Screens
Prototyping	0

Security level NONE
Project s:\tmp\mcgraw
Version label MIS EXAMPLE: 320 FUNCTION POINT PAYROLL PROGRAM
Location BOSTON, MASSACHUSETTS

3/06/96 5:35:23pm
Page 31

DOCUMENTATION ANALYSIS (continued)

Quality Assurance Documents

	Pages
Acceptance testing reports	53*
Total	53*

Defect Reports

	Pages
Pre-delivery defect reports	180*
Post-delivery defect reports	261*
Total	441*

External Documents

	Pages
Installation guide	7*
User's guide	91*
Total	98*

On-Line Documents

	Screens
Product input/output screens	94*
On-line error messages	30*
Total	124*

Security level NONE
Project s:\tmp\mcgraw
Version label MIS EXAMPLE: 320 FUNCTION POINT PAYROLL PROGRAM
Location BOSTON, MASSACHUSETTS

3/06/96 5:35:23pm
Page 32

STRENGTHS

Personnel

Strengths	Value
Project organization structure	2.00
Project team roles and responsibilities	2.00
Project team morale	2.00
Project management methods	2.00
Project management tools	2.00
Development personnel tool and method experience	2.00
Development personnel analysis and design experience	2.00
Development personnel programming language experience	1.00
Development personnel hardware experience	2.00
User personnel experience with software projects	2.00
User personnel experience with application type	2.00
User involvement during requirements	2.00
User involvement during design reviews	2.00
User involvement during acceptance testing	2.00

Technology

Strengths	Value
Project source code library	2.00
Support software novelty	2.00
Development platform novelty	2.00
Development hardware stability	2.00

Process

Strengths	Value
New function testing effectiveness	2.50
Automated restructuring effectiveness	1.00

Security level NONE
Project s:\tmp\mcgraw
Version label MIS EXAMPLE: 320 FUNCTION POINT PAYROLL PROGRAM
Location BOSTON, MASSACHUSETTS

3/06/96 5:35:23pm
Page 33

STRENGTHS (continued)

Environment

Strengths	**Value**
Legal and statutory restrictions	1.00
Security restrictions	1.00
Target hardware novelty	2.00
Development geography	2.00
Installation and production geography	1.00

WEAKNESSES

Personnel

Weaknesses	**Value**
Project managerial and technical cohesiveness	4.00
Pre-test defect removal experience	4.00
Maintenance personnel staffing	4.00
Maintenance personnel education	4.00

Technology

Weaknesses	**Value**
Design automation environment	4.00
CASE integration	5.00
Project documentation library	4.00

Security level NONE
Project s:\tmp\mcgraw
Version label MIS EXAMPLE: 320 FUNCTION POINT PAYROLL PROGRAM
Location BOSTON, MASSACHUSETTS

3/06/96 5:35:23pm
Page 34

WEAKNESSES (continued)

Process

Weaknesses	**Value**
Requirements clarity	4.00
Requirements methods	3.50
Prototyping methods	3.50
Analysis methods	4.00
System development methodology	4.00
Productivity measurements	5.00
Design defect removal training	4.00
Code defect removal training	4.00
Pre-test defect removal scheduling	4.00
Pre-test defect removal facilities	4.00
Testing function	4.00
Testing training	4.00
Quality assurance function	4.00
Quality assurance process	5.00
Quality and defect measurement	5.00
User and external document production	4.00
Field maintenance	5.00
Software warranty coverage	5.00

Environment

Weaknesses	**Value**
Office noise and interruption environment	4.00

Security level NONE
Project s:\tmp\mcgraw
Version label MIS EXAMPLE: 320 FUNCTION POINT PAYROLL PROGRAM
Location BOSTON, MASSACHUSETTS

3/06/96 5:35:23pm
Page 35

RISK / VALUE ANALYSIS

Risk / Value

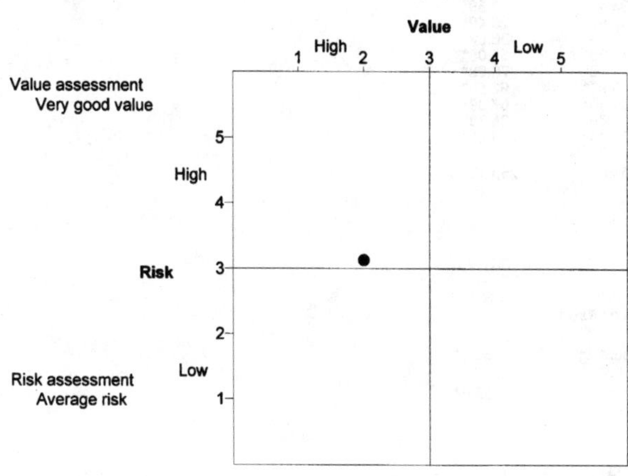

Security level NONE
Project s:\tmp\mcgraw
Version label MIS EXAMPLE: 320 FUNCTION POINT PAYROLL PROGRAM
Location BOSTON, MASSACHUSETTS

3/06/96 5:35:23pm
Page 36

RISK / VALUE ANALYSIS (continued)

Net Present Value

Year	Value $ Thousands	Expense $ Thousands	Present Value $ Thousands
1996	0.00	106.63*	-106.63*
1997	50.00	83.43*	-30.39*
1998	100.00	67.95*	26.49*
1999	125.00	73.19*	38.92*
2000	150.00	75.25*	51.05*
2001	200.00	77.48*	76.08*
2002	250.00	85.97*	92.59*
2003	200.00	88.16*	57.39*
2004	175.00	91.88*	38.78*
2005	125.00	104.14*	8.85*
Total	1,375.00	854.07*	253.13*

Payback and Net Return

Payback $ Thousands

Net return	520.93*
Payback in	1,998*

Rate of Return

Accounting	161.0*
Internal	36.6*

	per KLOC	per FP3
Total value	42.90*	4.55
Total costs	26.65*	2.83*
Net value	16.25*	1.72*

Security level NONE
Project s:\tmp\mcgraw
Version label MIS EXAMPLE: 320 FUNCTION POINT PAYROLL PROGRAM
Location BOSTON, MASSACHUSETTS

3/06/96 5:35:23pm
Page 37

PROJECT DESCRIPTION

Security level	NONE	SIC code	73
Organization	ABC COMPANY		
Location	BOSTON, MASSACHUSETTS		
Manager	J. DOE		
Completed by	C. JONES		
Current Date	3/06/96		
Formal request	/ / *	Project start	3/01/96
Planned delivery	/ /	Actual delivery	/ /

PROJECT CLASSIFICATION

Project nature

New program development

Project scope

Complete stand-alone program

Project class

Internal program, for use at a single location

Project type (primary)

Interactive database applications program

Project type (secondary)

Batch applications program

Checkpoint(R) 2.3.1 Input Report

Security level NONE
Project s:\tmp\mcgraw
Version label MIS EXAMPLE: 320 FUNCTION POINT PAYROLL PROGRAM
Location BOSTON, MASSACHUSETTS

3/06/96 5:35:23pm
Page 38

PROJECT GOALS

Project goals for estimating
1 Find the standard estimate of schedule, staff, and quality

PROJECT COMPLEXITY

New problem complexity
2.50 Algorithms and calculations of average complexity

New code complexity
3.00 Well structured (small modules and simple paths)

New data complexity
3.00 Multiple files, switches, and data interactions

New code cyclomatic complexity	12.00*
Cyclomatic complexity	12.00*

Security level NONE
Project s:\tmp\mcgraw
Version label MIS EXAMPLE: 320 FUNCTION POINT PAYROLL PROGRAM
Location BOSTON, MASSACHUSETTS

3/06/96 5:35:23pm
Page 39

FUNCTION SIZING

New SPR Function Points

Function Types					**Totals**
External inputs	20	x	4	=	80
External outputs	20	x	5	=	100
External inquiries	15	x	4	=	60
Internal logical files	5	x	10	=	50
External interface files	4*	x	7	=	28
Percentage reused	10.0 %				
Raw total					318
Adjustment					0.95
New F.P.					302*

Security level NONE
Project s:\tmp\mcgraw
Version label MIS EXAMPLE: 320 FUNCTION POINT PAYROLL PROGRAM
Location BOSTON, MASSACHUSETTS

3/06/96 5:35:23pm
Page 40

SOURCE CODE

Source Code Languages

Code Class	Language	Level	KLOC
New	COBOL	3.00	0.00*
Reused	COBOL	3.00	0.00*
Prototype	COBOL	3.00	0.00

PROJECT COSTS

						Cost $ Thousands
Average monthly salary		Burden rate				Average loaded salary
3.6	x	40.0	%	=		5.0*
Project hiring and relocation costs						0.0*
Project capital equipment costs						0.0*
Project travel costs						0.0
Marketing and sales costs						0.0*
Other project costs: fees, services						0.0*

Security level NONE
Project s:\tmp\mcgraw
Version label MIS EXAMPLE: 320 FUNCTION POINT PAYROLL PROGRAM
Location BOSTON, MASSACHUSETTS

3/06/96 5:35:23pm
Page 41

TASK SELECTION

Development Task Selection

☒ Automatic selection of tasks

Phase X Activity Task

Task	Selected
PLANNING AND MANAGEMENT	
Project planning	☐
Development project management	☒
Business functions	☐
Quality assurance	☐
Configuration control	☐
REQUIREMENTS	
Requirements	☒
Prototyping	☐
Purchase application acquisition	☐
EXTERNAL DESIGN	
System architecture	☐
Functional analysis and design	☒
Functional design reviews	☐
INTERNAL DESIGN	
Detail design and specifications	☒
Detail design reviews	☐
CODING	
Coding	☒
Reusable code acquisition	☒
Unit testing	☒
Code review	☐
INTEGRATION AND TEST	
Function testing	☒
Integration	☐
Integration testing	☐
System testing	☒
Field testing	☐
Acceptance testing	☒
Independent testing	☐
Indep. verification and validation	☐
DOCUMENTATION	
User and maintenance documentation	☒
Documentation reviews	☐
INSTALLATION AND TRAINING	
Installation	☒
User training	☒

Security level NONE
Project s:\tmp\mcgraw
Version label MIS EXAMPLE: 320 FUNCTION POINT PAYROLL PROGRAM
Location BOSTON, MASSACHUSETTS

TASK SELECTION (continued)

User Involvement Task Selection

☒ Automatic selection of tasks

Phase X Activity Task	
REQUIREMENTS	
Requirements	☒
Prototyping	☐
EXTERNAL DESIGN	
Functional design reviews	☐
INTERNAL DESIGN	
Detail design reviews	☐
INTEGRATION AND TEST	
Acceptance testing	☒
DOCUMENTATION	
User and maintenance documentation	☒
Documentation reviews	☐
INSTALLATION AND TRAINING	
User training	☒

Maintenance Task Selection

☒ Automatic selection of tasks

Phase X Activity Task	
MAINTENANCE	
Post delivery	☐
Central maintenance	☒
Field service	☐
Customer support	☒
Maintenance management	☒

Security level NONE
Project s:\tmp\mcgraw
Version label MIS EXAMPLE: 320 FUNCTION POINT PAYROLL PROGRAM
Location BOSTON, MASSACHUSETTS

3/06/96 5:35:23pm
Page 43

DEVELOPMENT CONSTRAINTS

Development Staff / Schedule Constraints

☐ Estimate with constraints

Development Activity	Staff Headcount	Schedule Months
Dev project management	0	0.0
Requirements	0	0.0
Funct analysis/design	0	0.0*
Detail design & specs	0	0.0*
Coding	0	0.0
Reusable code acquis	0	0.0
Unit testing	0	0.0
Function testing	0	0.0
System testing	0	0.0
Acceptance testing	0	0.0
User/maintenance doc	0	0.0
Installation	0	0.0
User training	0	0.0

Development Size Constraints

☐ Estimate with constraints

Development Task	Size
Personnel management	0 People
Tradit requirmnts spec	0 Internal Pages
Initl functional spec	0 Internal Pages
Data design spec	0 Internal Pages
Unit testing	0 Cases
New function testing	0 Cases
System testing	0 Cases
Acceptance testing	0 Cases
Installation guide	0 External Pages
User's guide	0 External Pages
Product I/O screens	0 Screens
On-line error messages	0 Screens
User training	0 External Pages

Security level NONE
Project s:\tmp\mcgraw
Version label MIS EXAMPLE: 320 FUNCTION POINT PAYROLL PROGRAM
Location BOSTON, MASSACHUSETTS

3/06/96 5:35:23pm
Page 44

DEVELOPMENT CONSTRAINTS (continued)

Development Overlap Constraints

☐ Estimate with constraints

Development Task	Overlap Task	%	Start Date
Personnel management	N/A	0	/ / *
Tradit requirmnts spec	N/A	0	/ / *
Initl functional spec	N/A	0	/ / *
Data design spec	N/A	0	/ / *
Coding	N/A	0	/ /
Reusable code acquis	N/A	0	/ /
Unit testing	N/A	0	/ /
New function testing	N/A	0	/ /
System testing	N/A	0	/ /
Acceptance testing	N/A	0	/ /
Installation guide	N/A	0	/ /
User's guide	N/A	0	/ /
Product I/O screens	N/A	0	/ /
On-line error messages	N/A	0	/ /
Installation	N/A	0	/ /
User training	N/A	0	/ /

Security level NONE
Project s:\tmp\mcgraw
Version label MIS EXAMPLE: 320 FUNCTION POINT PAYROLL PROGRAM
Location BOSTON, MASSACHUSETTS

3/06/96 5:35:23pm
Page 45

PERSONNEL

Project Management

Project organization structure
2.00 Small team project (less than four staff members)

Project team roles and responsibilities
2.00 Very clear and well-documented

Project team morale
2.00 Most team members are enthusiastic about the project

Project managerial and technical cohesiveness
4.00 Uncertain or ambiguous about goals, schedules, methods

Project management experience
3.00 Average: implemented some projects

Project management methods
2.00 PERT chart with CPM, milestones, and delivery dates

Project management tools
2.00 Partially automated and generally effective system

PERSONNEL (continued)

Development Personnel Experience

Development personnel application experience
3.00 Even mixture of experts, new hires, and novices

Development personnel tool and method experience
2.00 Majority of experts in the tools and methods

Development personnel analysis and design experience
2.00 Majority of experts in analysis and design methods

Development personnel programming language experience
1.00 All experts in the language(s) used for the project

Development personnel hardware experience
2.00 Majority of experts in the hardware used for this project

Pre-test defect removal experience
4.00 Most personnel inexperienced in reviews/inspections

Testing defect removal experience
3.00 Even mixture of experienced and inexperienced personnel

Security level NONE
Project s:\tmp\mcgraw
Version label MIS EXAMPLE: 320 FUNCTION POINT PAYROLL PROGRAM
Location BOSTON, MASSACHUSETTS

3/06/96 5:35:23pm
Page 47

PERSONNEL (continued)

User Personnel Experience

User personnel experience with software projects
2.00 All or a majority of users have software experience

User personnel experience with application type
2.00 All or a strong majority of users are experts

User involvement during requirements
2.00 Users are heavily involved during requirements

User involvement during design reviews
2.00 Users are heavily involved during design reviews

User involvement during acceptance testing
2.00 Users are heavily involved during acceptance testing

Maintenance Personnel Experience

Maintenance personnel staffing
4.00 Most maintenance done by development personnel

Maintenance personnel experience
3.00 Even mixture of experts, new hires, and novices

Maintenance personnel education
4.00 Some training in projects to be maintained is available

Security level NONE
Project s:\tmp\mcgraw
Version label MIS EXAMPLE: 320 FUNCTION POINT PAYROLL PROGRAM
Location BOSTON, MASSACHUSETTS

3/06/96 5:35:23pm
Page 48

TECHNOLOGY

Software Support

Design automation environment
4.00 Semi-formal design with text automation only

CASE integration
5.00 No integration

Project source code library
2.00 Partial (tracking or mgmt.) project library with automated support

Project documentation library
4.00 Manual documentation control

Support software novelty
2.00 Most support software is familiar and well understood

Support software effectiveness
3.00 Support tools and software usually effective

Program debugging tools
3.00 Full screen editor, traces, but little else

Security level NONE
Project s:\tmp\mcgraw
Version label MIS EXAMPLE: 320 FUNCTION POINT PAYROLL PROGRAM
Location BOSTON, MASSACHUSETTS

3/06/96 5:35:23pm
Page 49

TECHNOLOGY (continued)

Hardware Support

Development platform novelty
2.00 Most hardware is familiar and well understood by staff

Development hardware stability
2.00 Single vendor hardware with moderate compatibility

Response time of development environment
3.00 One to five second response time is the norm

Development computing support
3.00 Computer support is usually adequate and effective

Tools, equipment, and supplies
3.00 Tools and equipment for project already in use

Workstation environment
3.00 Individual workstations for all staff members

Maintenance Support

Maintenance computing support
3.00 Computer support is usually adequate and effective

Release control methods
3.00 Manual system controlled by naming convention with date and size

Problem tracking and reporting
3.00 Partially automated system

Replacement and restructure planning
3.00 Aging systems replaced as required

Security level NONE
Project s:\tmp\mcgraw
Version label MIS EXAMPLE: 320 FUNCTION POINT PAYROLL PROGRAM
Location BOSTON, MASSACHUSETTS

PROCESS

Development Methods

Requirements clarity
4.00 Incomplete or ambiguous user requirements

Requirements methods
3.50 Limited user input

Prototyping methods
3.50 Prototyping of a few outputs and inputs

Analysis methods
4.00 Informal or partial data analysis

Data administration
3.00 Data administration and passive data dictionary

System development methodology
4.00 Manual and cumbersome system development methodology

Productivity measurements
5.00 Incomplete or inaccurate productivity measures

Client/server architecture
N/A Not answered

Client/server strategies
N/A Not answered

Object-oriented analysis and design
N/A Not answered

Security level NONE
Project s:\tmp\mcgraw
Version label MIS EXAMPLE: 320 FUNCTION POINT PAYROLL PROGRAM
Location BOSTON, MASSACHUSETTS

3/06/96 5:35:23pm
Page 51

PROCESS (continued)

Quality Assurance Process

Design defect removal training
4.00 Very limited training for design reviews/inspections

Code defect removal training
4.00 Very limited training for code reviews/inspections

Pre-test defect removal scheduling
4.00 Some schedule pressure and rushed sessions

Pre-test defect removal facilities
4.00 Very limited availability of facilities for reviews

Testing function
4.00 Informal testing with no predefined goals or criteria

Testing methods
3.00 Effective scripted manual test bed used

Testing training
4.00 Very limited training for testing

Test planning
3.00 Test plans developed during Coding and informally reviewed

Quality assurance function
4.00 QA role is performed informally

Quality assurance process
5.00 No QA activities distinct from testing

Quality and defect measurement
5.00 No measures of quality and defects

PROCESS (continued)

Defect Removal Effectiveness

Testing Defect Removal

Unit testing effectiveness
3.00 Average

New function testing effectiveness
2.50 Average

System testing effectiveness
3.00 Average

Acceptance testing effectiveness
3.00 Average

Post-Release Defect Removal

Automated restructuring effectiveness
1.00 Excellent

Maintenance defect repairs effectiveness
3.00 Average

Security level NONE
Project s:\tmp\mcgraw
Version label MIS EXAMPLE: 320 FUNCTION POINT PAYROLL PROGRAM
Location BOSTON, MASSACHUSETTS

3/06/96 5:35:23pm
Page 53

PROCESS (continued)

Document Preparation

User and external document production
4.00 Text automation; manual graphics support

Documentation preparation
3.00 Mixed: users and analysts

Graphics production
3.00 Partially automated

Documentation output devices
3.00 Text laser printing

Documentation production
3.00 Microcomputer word processing

Documentation distribution to team members
3.00 Hard copy distribution to individual team members

Overall satisfaction with documentation methods
3.00 Average documentation methods

Security level NONE
Project s:\tmp\mcgraw
Version label MIS EXAMPLE: 320 FUNCTION POINT PAYROLL PROGRAM
Location BOSTON, MASSACHUSETTS

3/06/96 5:35:23pm
Page 54

PROCESS (continued)

Maintenance Process

Central maintenance
3.00 Informal defect repairs and update distribution

Field maintenance
5.00 No field maintenance for project

Software warranty coverage
5.00 No explicit or implicit warranties on software

Customer support
3.00 Informal telephone support; normal write-in support

Delivery support
3.00 On-site support for early customers

Security level NONE
Project s:\tmp\mcgraw
Version label MIS EXAMPLE: 320 FUNCTION POINT PAYROLL PROGRAM
Location BOSTON, MASSACHUSETTS

3/06/96 5:35:23pm
Page 55

ENVIRONMENT

Product Restrictions

Legal and statutory restrictions
1.00 No known legal or statutory restrictions

Security restrictions
1.00 No known security restrictions

Product performance/execution speed restrictions
3.00 Normal performance and execution speed restrictions

Product memory utilization restrictions
3.00 Normal memory utilization restrictions

Target hardware novelty
2.00 Most hardware is familiar and well understood by staff

Functional novelty
3.00 Even mixture of repeated and new features

Physical Environment

Individual office environment
3.00 60 to 80 square feet of enclosed space per worker

Office noise and interruption environment
4.00 Some background noise and frequent interruptions

Development geography
2.00 Multiple development departments within same site

Number of development locations 1

Security level NONE
Project s:\tmp\mcgraw
Version label MIS EXAMPLE: 320 FUNCTION POINT PAYROLL PROGRAM
Location BOSTON, MASSACHUSETTS

3/06/96 5:35:23pm

ENVIRONMENT (continued)

Maintenance Environment

Current system status
3.00 System is new, with few current customers

Long range project stability
3.00 New functions, data types, and hardware may occur

Program execution frequency
3.00 Daily or hourly runs

Installation and production geography
1.00 Single production site, in a single city

Number of system installation sites	1
Annual growth in installation sites (percent)	0.0
Number of system maintenance sites	1

Security level NONE
Project s:\tmp\mcgraw
Version label MIS EXAMPLE: 320 FUNCTION POINT PAYROLL PROGRAM
Location BOSTON, MASSACHUSETTS

3/06/96 5:35:23pm
Page 57

SPECIAL FACTORS

Risk / Value Analysis

Project Risk

Risk of high project novelty
3.00 Average risk

Risk of unstable user requirements
4.00 High risk

Risk of change in project architecture
2.00 Low risk

Risk of change in development hardware
2.00 Low risk

Risk of inadequate speed or memory capacity
2.00 Low risk

Risk of inadequate functionality
4.00 High risk

Risk of poor quality and reliability
4.00 High risk

Risk of significant usability problems
3.00 Average risk

Risk of significant schedule overruns
4.00 High risk

Risk of significant cost overruns
4.00 High risk

Security level NONE
Project s:\tmp\mcgraw
Version label MIS EXAMPLE: 320 FUNCTION POINT PAYROLL PROGRAM
Location BOSTON, MASSACHUSETTS

3/06/96 5:35:23pm
Page 58

SPECIAL FACTORS (continued)

Risk / Value Analysis (continued)

Project Risk (continued)

Risk of insufficient project staffing
2.00 Low risk

Risk of insufficient project skill levels
3.00 Average risk

Risk of excessive schedule pressure
4.00 High risk

Risk of high staff turnover and attrition
3.00 Average risk

Risk of major management disagreements
3.00 Average risk

Security level NONE
Project s:\tmp\mcgraw
Version label MIS EXAMPLE: 320 FUNCTION POINT PAYROLL PROGRAM
Location BOSTON, MASSACHUSETTS

3/06/96 5:35:23pm
Page 59

SPECIAL FACTORS (continued)

Risk / Value Analysis (continued)

Project Value

Project is mandatory due to law or policy
N/A Not answered

Value to human life or safety
N/A Not answered

Value to security or national defense
N/A Not answered

Value to morale and human relations
N/A Not answered

Value to enterprise prestige
N/A Not answered

Value to competitive advantage
N/A Not answered

Value to market share
N/A Not answered

Value to quality and reliability
N/A Not answered

Value to direct revenues from project
N/A Not answered

Value to indirect revenues from project
N/A Not answered

Security level NONE
Project s:\tmp\mcgraw
Version label MIS EXAMPLE: 320 FUNCTION POINT PAYROLL PROGRAM
Location BOSTON, MASSACHUSETTS

3/06/96 5:35:23pm
Page 60

SPECIAL FACTORS (continued)

Risk / Value Analysis (continued)

Project Value (continued)

Value to enterprise strategic plans
N/A Not answered

Value to enterprise tactical plans
2.00 High value

Value to enterprise operating costs
2.00 High value

Value to enterprise operating speed
2.00 High value

Value to related or future projects
2.00 High value

Project Yearly Value

Cost of capital 10.0 %

Year	Cost $ Thousands
1996	0.0
1997	50.0
1998	100.0
1999	125.0
2000	150.0
2001	200.0
2002	250.0
2003	200.0
2004	175.0
2005	125.0

Security level NONE
Project s:\tmp\mcgraw
Version label MIS EXAMPLE: 320 FUNCTION POINT PAYROLL PROGRAM
Location BOSTON, MASSACHUSETTS

3/06/96 5:35:23pm
Page 61

SPECIAL FACTORS (continued)

Contract Development

Contract award method
N/A Not answered

Contract origin
N/A Not answered

Domain of contract
N/A Not answered

Form of contract
N/A Not answered

Ownership of source code and deliverables
N/A Not answered

Location of contract work
N/A Not answered

Method of contract completion
N/A Not answered

Security level NONE
Project s:\tmp\mcgraw
Version label MIS EXAMPLE: 320 FUNCTION POINT PAYROLL PROGRAM
Location BOSTON, MASSACHUSETTS

3/06/96 5:35:23pm
Page 62

PROJECT SETTINGS

Project Mode				
	Quick Estimate			
	X Detailed Estimate			
	Measure			

Work metric			Cost metric	
	Hours	Days		Ones
	Weeks	X Months		X Thousands
	Years			Millions

Data entry level		Data display level	
	Project		Project
	Phase		Phase
	X Activity		X Activity
	Task		Task

Security level NONE
Project s:\tmp\mcgraw
Version label MIS EXAMPLE: 320 FUNCTION POINT PAYROLL PROGRAM
Location BOSTON, MASSACHUSETTS

3/06/96 5:35:23pm
Page 63

TIME ACCOUNTING

Business Year

Holidays	10
Other days not worked (weekends)	104

Average Employee's Year

Vacation and personal days	16
Sick days	4
Non-project days (education, travel)	20
Non-business days worked	20

Output (Per Year)

Business days	251
Project days	211
Productive hours	1,557

Project Accounting

Accounting hours per business day	8.00
Productive hours per project day	6.00
Overtime hours per project day	1.00
Overtime hours per non-business day	4.00

Security level NONE
Project s:\tmp\mcgraw
Version label MIS EXAMPLE: 320 FUNCTION POINT PAYROLL PROGRAM
Location BOSTON, MASSACHUSETTS

3/06/96 5:35:23pm
Page 64

AVAILABILITY

Development Availability

Development contract personnel	0.0	%
Development staff availability	100.0	%
Development unpaid overtime	100.0	%
Overtime premium rate	150.0*	%

Maintenance Availability

Maintenance contract personnel	0.0	%
Maintenance staff availability	100.0	%
Maintenance unpaid overtime	100.0	%

Security level NONE
Project s:\tmp\mcgraw
Version label MIS EXAMPLE: 320 FUNCTION POINT PAYROLL PROGRAM
Location BOSTON, MASSACHUSETTS

3/06/96 5:35:23pm
Page 65

POST DELIVERY

Maintenance years	10	
Annual new and changed code (percent)	7.0	%
Annual deleted code (percent)	2.0	%
Restructure interval (years)	3	
Annual inflation rate	6.0	%

DOCUMENTATION FORMAT

External documentation page format
3 Triple column

Internal documentation page format
3 Triple column

External documentation page size
3 U.S. Standard Civilian. (8.5 x 11) inches

Internal documentation page size
3 U.S. Standard Civilian. (8.5 x 11) inches

External documentation type size
3 Twelve point. (Equivalent to PICA type)

Internal documentation type size
3 Twelve point. (Equivalent to PICA type)

Security level NONE
Project s:\tmp\mcgraw
Version label MIS EXAMPLE: 320 FUNCTION POINT PAYROLL PROGRAM
Location BOSTON, MASSACHUSETTS

3/06/96 5:35:23pm
Page 66

INTERNATIONAL

Date format	MM/DD/YY
Thousands separator	,
Decimal separator	.
Country	USA
Currency name	Dollar
Currency symbol	$
Exchange rate US $1 =	1.00

SOFTWARE METRICS

Output software metric	Function Points (IFPUG release 3)
New code software metric	SPR Function Points
Reused code software metric	% of New Functionality

Security level NONE
Project s:\tmp\mcgraw
Version label MIS EXAMPLE: 320 FUNCTION POINT PAYROLL PROGRAM
Location BOSTON, MASSACHUSETTS

3/06/96 5:35:23pm
Page 67

IFPUG COUNTING RULES CONVERSION

Recommendation Use of IFPUG conversion algorithm is RECOMMENDED for interactive applications like this project.

Conversion algorithm

None X IFPUG Custom

[FP rlse 4] = 31.838 + 0.758 x [FP rlse 3]

IFPUG Counting Rules Used

New X Release 3 Release 4

Reused X Release 3 Release 4

Appendix

D

Example of an Annual Baseline Report

Introduction

The following is an example of an annual baseline report on software productivity and quality. The report is derived from the contents and formats of several actual reports produced by major corporations. The data, although abstract, is typical of the kinds of information presented. The productivity and quality rates are derived from actual studies of real projects. Reports such as this are normally produced in the first quarter of a year, and they are based on the data of all projects which the enterprise completed in the preceding year. Thus, this report for the year 1990 would have been produced in the first quarter of 1991. Although the second edition is being published in 1996, the form and content of the baseline report are still valid and useful.

In large corporations, responsibility for such reports normally resides with a permanent measurement department. The group would typically report to a vice president or director, and it would include measurement specialists, statisticians, systems analysts, and sometimes writers.

The data itself would be gathered from the individual projects in the course of the year. The very first time such a report is produced, it will usually be necessary to expend considerable effort in both collecting and validating the data. Once annual reports become standard business practices, both the speed with which the data can be gathered and the accuracy of the numerical information improve.

Although large corporations produce thousands of them, small programs are often excluded from annual reports for reasons of policy. The exclusions are especially common in European and multinational corporations because recording performance data against individual workers may violate either national law or internal work rule regulations. This example, based on typical large-company, multinational practice, omits projects smaller than 2 person-years of total effort.

The distribution of annual baseline reports will vary, but in every case it will include all of the senior executives of the enterprise. The information provided is useful at all levels, and fairly wide distribution through an enterprise is normal. This kind of information would obviously be valuable to competitors, so security classifications such as INTERNAL USE ONLY and COMPANY CONFIDENTIAL would be normal.

Finally, this example uses the hypothetical name, ABC Corporation. It is intended to be abstract, and it certainly is not intended to identify any real corporation.

ABC CORPORATION 1990 SOFTWARE BASELINE REPORT

ABSTRACT

This report contains the results of the productivity analysis of the ABC software projects which entered production in calendar year 1989. The report is the first ABC annual report to express its results in the new Function Point and Feature Point metrics. ABC made substantial productivity gains across the board, and generally good quality gains with the exceptions that are noted in the text.

PREPARED BY:
ABC Software Metrics Department
J. Doe, Director
March 30, 1991

TABLE OF CONTENTS

Executive Overview of the 1990 Software Baseline Report

The ABC Corporation has four discrete software environments: (1) Real-time military software, (2) real-time commercial software, (3) support software, (4) information systems. Since these four environments produce different kinds of software, use different tools and methods, and report to different executives, it is desirable to show their productivity and quality data separately.

The year 1990 showed continued improvements in software productivity rates for all four operating areas of the ABC Corporation and improvements in quality for all operating areas except that of internal support software. Corrective actions have been put in place to bring support software quality up to adherence of ABC's corporate quality goals.

The 1990 report introduces the use of function point and feature point metrics for normalization purposes. The older "lines of code" normalization will continue to be used for comparative and historical purposes.

Software productivity gains in 1990

Figure 1 shows the net improvement in software productivity by area between 1989 and 1990. All areas experienced improvements, with information systems having the highest overall percentage gain of 29.4%. The overall corporate gain was 19.4%, which reflects the cumu-

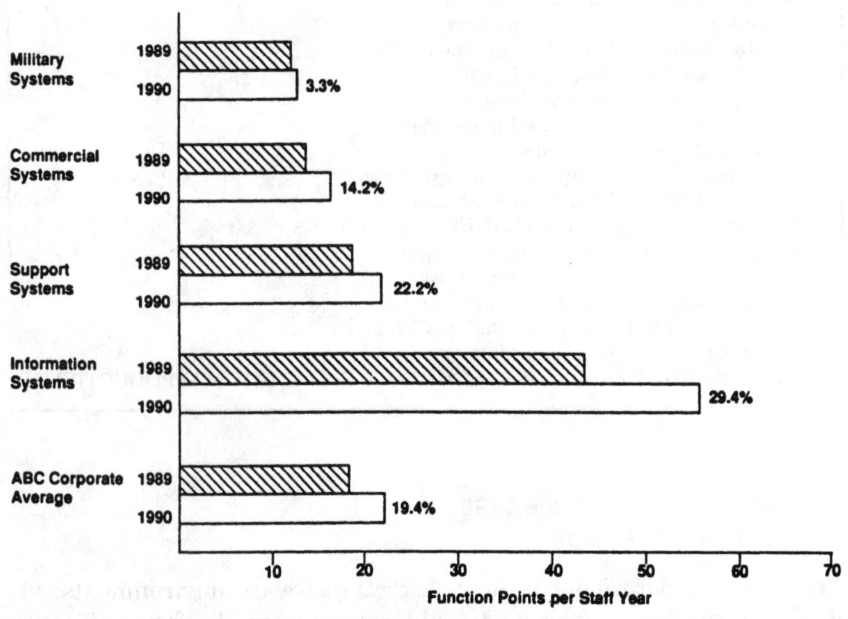

Figure 1 ABC software productivity rates in 1989 and 1990, by area.

lative results of the last several years of ABC software technology improvements.

ABC's military projects area had the lowest gain of 3.3%. Since military specifications determine many of the deliverables and much of the kind of work which must be performed, military software is more difficult to improve than the other classes of ABC projects.

Software quality and defect levels in 1990

Figure 2 shows the net improvement in user-reported software defect rates between 1989 and 1990. All areas except that of internal support tools experienced defect reductions and quality improvements in 1990. The ABC information system area had the greatest reduction in defects at −17.9%. The overall ABC performance reflected a reduction of −5.5% in user-reported defects. While such a reduction is encouraging, it is desirable to reduce defect rates still further in 1991.

The unfortunate increase in defect rates for internal support tools of 16.6% in 1990 was due to schedule pressure interfering with the usage of reviews and inspections. Corrective actions have been put in place for 1991.

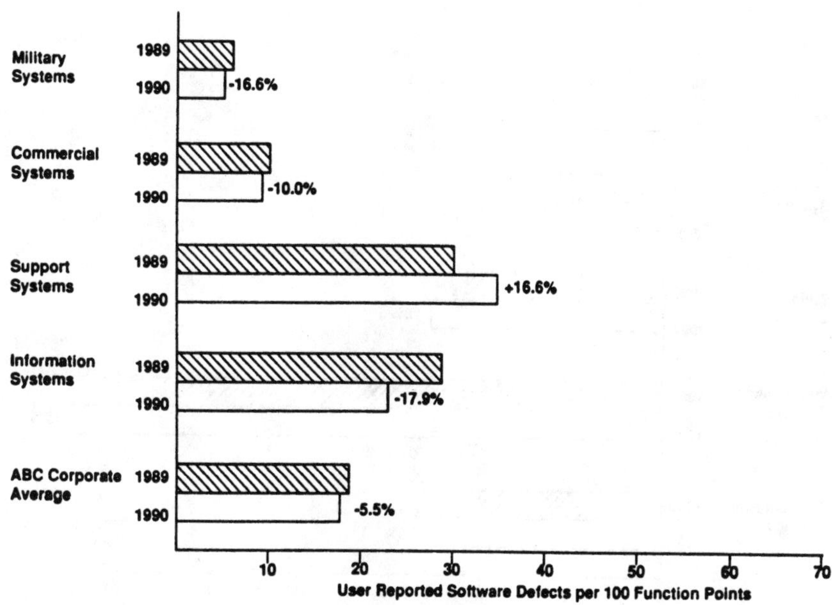

Figure 2 ABC user-reported defect rates in 1989 and 1990, by area.

Summary of overall productivity and quality results

Overall, ABC is continuing to make progress in both software productivity and quality. However, in 1991 the ABC Corporation should achieve even better results than were accomplished in 1990, due to the continued improvements in methods and to new tool sets to be installed.

ABC Productivity and Quality Targets for 1991

As the software methods and technologies at ABC continue to improve, the year 1991 should see significant gains in both productivity and quality. The improvement goals are based on the empirical observations of what major corporations have been able to accomplish. Although the goals are challenging to both managers and technical staff, they are not impossible to achieve.

Figure 3 shows the 1991 productivity improvement targets, which establish an overall goal of 14.4%. Figure 4 shows the overall 1991 quality and defect rate target, which calls for a 53.0% overall reduction in user-reported defects. This reduction, although comparatively high, is within the capabilities of the ABC staff and technology sets.

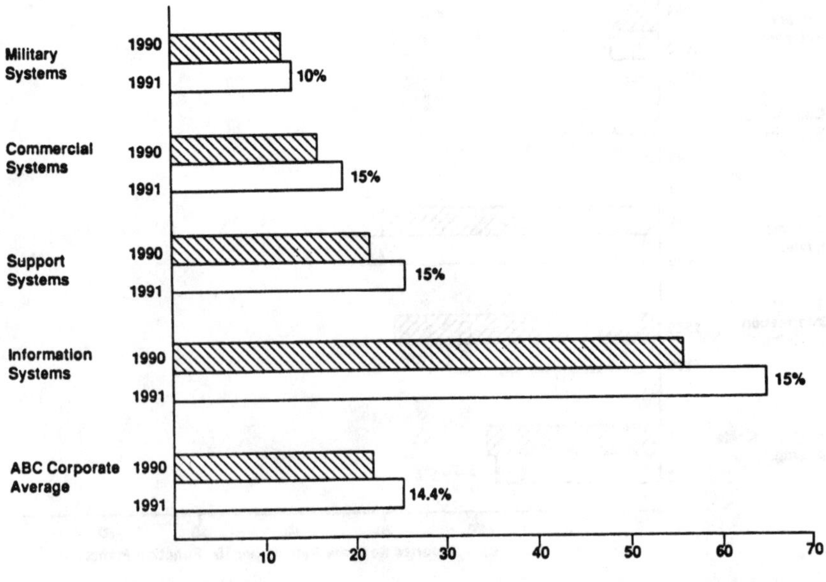

Figure 3 ABC software productivity targets for 1991, by area.

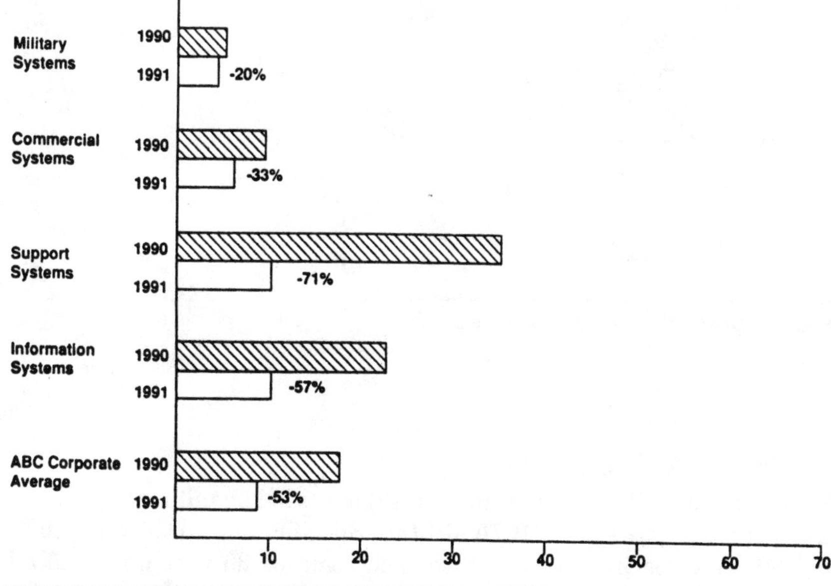

Figure 4 ABC user-reported defect targets for 1991, by area.

ABC software demographics

The overall distribution of the ABC software population stayed relatively constant between 1989 and 1990. The net voluntary attrition rate of software personnel has stayed relatively constant at 4.0% per year since 1985. The new-hire growth rate of ABC personnel between 1989 and 1990 was 8.0%. When the attrition and new-hire rates are considered together, it is seen that the software staff of ABC grew by a net of 4%. The new-hire growth rate is targeted to be approximately 5% in 1991. If the attrition rate stays constant, then ABC should experience a 1% net growth next year. Net growth (new hires−(voluntary + involuntary attrition)) is now at 4%.

Figure 5 shows the overall distribution of the ABC software professional and management staff.

Analysis of the Four ABC Software Environments

The factors which cause the variations among the four software environments have been identified by multiple-regression techniques, as have the factors which are yielding productivity and quality improvements.

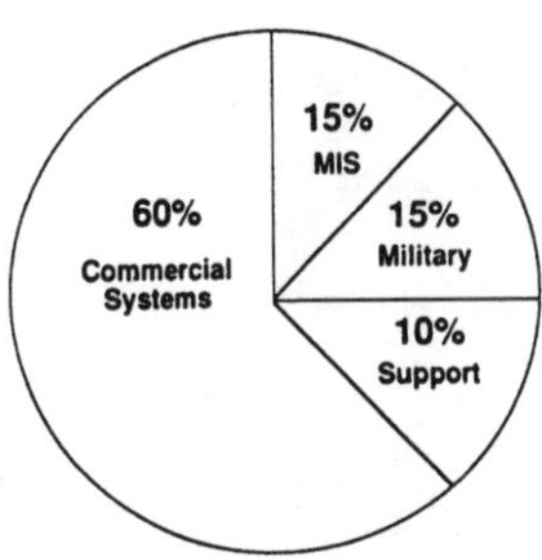

Figure 5 Distribution of ABC software personnel, by area.

The real-time military environment

The real-time military environment is dominated by military specifications, including the new 2167A Military Specification on software quality. Military specifications require such rigorous documentation of all phases and activities that approximately 45% of all military software costs are associated with paperwork. In addition, the military requirements for independent verification and validation and independent testing add activities to the development chart of account that are not present for other classes of software.

Approximately 30% of military software costs are associated with defect removal and quality control. The code itself approximates 20% of military software costs. The special military requirements are placed on top of the high complexity of telecommunications software and the known difficulties of building software on hardware that is itself unstable and being developed simultaneously. Military projects have the lowest productivity rates of all forms of software, and this situation will probably continue indefinitely. Military software quality, however, is often significantly better than average.

The improvements between 1989 and 1990 are attributable to the introduction of an integrated design environment providing full graphics and text support coupled with a data dictionary.

The real-time commercial environment

The real-time commercial environment is dominated by the impact of highly complex algorithms, unstable hardware, and severe timing and performance constraints. The need for high quality and reliability for real-time commercial software is extreme. The combination of these factors requires careful development with complete specifications, full design and code inspections, exhaustive testing, and substantial modelling and simulation during the development phase.

The volume of paperwork is smaller for commercial software than for military, but it still amounts to some 30% or more of the total development expense. Quality control and the sum of all defect removal activities for real-time commercial software comprise some 35% of all development expenses. The code itself typically comprises some 30% of the development expenses for real-time commercial software.

The improvements between 1989 and 1990 are attributable to the introduction of full design and code inspections, plus the new integrated design environment offering full graphics and text support and a data dictionary.

The support environment

Internal support software, such as engineering aids or software test tools, is dominated by the need for short development cycles, since the tools are usually on the critical path for other projects. Internal systems software that is not intended for external customers is usually sparsely documented, and the major concentration of effort is found during coding, integration, and testing. Typically, paperwork for internal systems software comprises 20% or less of the total development expenses, coding comprises more than 40%, and the sum of defect removal activities would comprise some 25% or less.

The improvements in productivity between 1989 and 1990 reflect the introduction of the new integrated design environment offering full graphics and text support and a data dictionary. The small decline in software quality reflected in the increased defect levels in 1990, and the less than satisfactory quality over the past few years, implies a need to use inspections on ABC's internal systems software development. It is also suggested that internal systems software be required to achieve quality goals similar to those established for commercial and military software: less than 0.5 valid unique defect reports per KLOC per year, or the equivalent metric of no more than 10 delivered defects per 100 feature points.

The management information systems environment

The MIS environment is dominated primarily by user requirements and secondarily by the fact that the bulk of MIS work tends to be maintenance and enhancements. Because user requirements are often ambiguous and rapidly changing, the observed variations in MIS software costs are far greater than for the other three classes of software. Typical MIS projects will average 20% to 30% of all development costs in requirements, specifications, and paperwork. Coding costs will average 30% to 45%, while defect removal costs will average 15% to 35%. The large range of uncertainty is typical of the MIS environment.

The improvement in MIS productivity and quality between 1989 and 1990 is attributable to a multifaceted approach including: (A) the introduction of the Joint Application Design (JAD) methodology for creating the user requirements; (B) the restructuring and geriatric care given to the older applications in the ABC production library; (C) the introduction of leading-edge design methods featuring integrated graphics/text support and a data dictionary; (D) the introduction of application generators, query languages, and database methods on selected projects which significantly improved function point productivity rates. Improvements in productivity caused by very high level languages such as SQL or QBE or with application generators are not directly measurable with lines of code metrics.

However, the fact that MIS quality is still significantly worse than the other classes of software produced by ABC implies that more changes will be necessary. It is recommended that design and code inspections be introduced in 1991 for critical MIS applications, and that MIS software be required to achieve the same quality levels as our commercial software: no more than 0.5 annual defect per KLOC per year for applications in production, or the equivalent metric of achieving no more than 10 delivered defects per 100 function points.

This quality goal for MIS should also benefit productivity, since the target can only be achieved by minimizing one of the more expensive activities of all software; i.e., defect removal.

Overall trends and conclusions

The ABC Corporation has continued to make significant improvements in software productivity in 1990. The 1987, 1988, and 1989 investments in new design tools and methods appear to have been effective, as does the introduction of the JAD requirements method. The adoption of function points and feature points is beginning to provide new levels of economic understanding of software.

Quality, although better than industry norms, needs continued improvement in 1991. An increased emphasis on design and code inspections for support software and MIS applications will accomplish this target.

Background of the 1990 Baseline

This baseline is the fourth annual report produced by the ABC corporation, and the first to adopt the use of functional metrics. The ABC management committee recognized that software was becoming a critical aspect of ABC operations in 1985, and issued a request for more complete software information. The result of that request was the first ABC baseline, produced in 1987 and covering the year 1986.

As a manufacturer of telecommunications equipment and private branch exchanges (PBX), the products of the ABC corporation have software as part of the critical path leading to delivery. Once installed, the reliability of the equipment in the perception of users is significantly related to the quality of the software itself. In addition, ABC also produces much of its own test and engineering support software, and many of its own management information systems. The ABC government systems division also produces ruggedized and portable telecommunications equipment for U.S. military and defense agencies and for the NATO countries.

This corporate measurement report is produced annually at the request of the ABC management committee, and it highlights the importance of achieving the highest possible levels of software quality and achieving optimum productivity at the same time. By corporate policy, projects totalling less than two person-years of effort have been excluded as separate projects from this report. Small projects are handled as aggregates by summing their sizes, effort, and quantified results.

The ABC corporation has four distinct programming environments, and each environment has its own characteristic productivity and quality profile: (1) real-time telecommunications software embedded within the ABC military products; (2) real-time telecommunications software embedded within the ABC commercial and consumer products; (3) systems software produced internally to aid the ABC engineering and software engineering populations; (4) management information software produced to aid in the operation and management of ABC.

Table D.1 shows the 1989 and 1990 annual productivity rates for these four software environments, expressed in "source statements per person-year" measured to the ABC standard chart of accounts.

Table D.2 shows the 1989 and 1990 annual user-reported defect rates for the same four software environments. The unit of measure is "unique valid defects per KLOC reported by users in one calendar year."

TABLE D.1 1989 and 1990 Annual Software Productivity Rates in Source Statements per Person-Year

Environment	1989	1990	Change	Percent
Real-time military	1500	1550	50	3.3
Real-time commercial	1750	2000	250	14.2
Systems and support	2250	2750	500	22.2
Information systems	3500	4250	750	21.4
ABC corporate average	2025	2345	320	15.8

TABLE D.2 1989 and 1990 Annual User-Reported Software Defect Rates per KLOC

Environment	1989	1990	Change	Percent
Real-time military	0.5	0.4	−0.1	(20.0)
Real-time commercial	0.8	0.7	−0.1	(12.5)
Systems and support	2.5	2.8	0.3	10.7
Information systems	3.5	3.1	−0.4	(11.4)
ABC corporate average	1.5	1.4	−0.1	(6.6)

As can be seen from Tables D.1 and D.2, ABC enjoyed substantial improvements in both productivity and quality with the exception of the quality levels for "Systems and support," for which improvement plans have been made.

ABC Migration to Function Points and Feature Points

Because the four discrete ABC environments use many different programming languages and measurements based on "source code statements" are known to be paradoxical and unreliable in mixed language environments, the ABC corporate measurement department decided to adopt the IBM function point metrics for information systems measurements and the extended SPR feature point metrics for the real-time and systems measurements. This decision was made in November of 1990, and it reflects the growing international trend toward function-based metrics for software.

Previous attempts at ABC to use function points in 1985 had not yielded satisfactory results for real-time software, because that technique was perceived as being optimized for information systems. The extended SPR feature point technique, originally developed in 1986, is suitable for real-time software, however. Tables D.3 and D.4 contain the ABC productivity and quality rates for 1989 and 1990 expressed in these new metrics.

Because functional metrics are free of the distortions and paradox associated with "lines of code," they provide a much clearer picture of economic productivity than was previously possible. When comparing Table D.3 with Table D.1, note that the improvement in ABC's economic software productivity was substantially greater than revealed by Table D.1. This was due, in part, to the expanded use of application generators and query languages by the ABC Information Systems group. The productivity impact of higher-level languages was masked and distorted by the former "lines of code" metric.

TABLE D.3 1989 and 1990 Annual Software Productivity Rates Expressed in Feature Points and Function Points per Year

Environment	1989	1990	Change	Percent
Real-time military	12.0	12.4	0.4	3.3
Real-time commercial	14.0	16.0	2.0	14.2
Systems and support	18.0	22.0	4.0	22.2
Information systems	43.8	56.6	12.8	29.4
ABC corporate average	18.6	22.2	3.6	19.4

TABLE D.4 1989 and 1990 Annual User-Reported Software Defect Rates Expressed In Defects per 100 Function or Feature Points per Year

Environment	1989	1990	Change	Percent
Real-time military	6.0	5.0	−1.0	(16.6)
Real-time commercial	10.0	9.0	−1.0	(10.0)
Systems and support	30.0	35.0	5.0	16.6
Information systems	28.0	23.0	−5.0	(17.9)
ABC corporate average	18.0	17.0	−1.0	(5.5)

TABLE D.5 1989 and 1990 Annual User-Reported Software Defect Rates Expressed as Feature and Function Points per Reported Defect

Environment	1989	1990	Change	Percent
Real-time military	16.1	20.2	4.1	25.0
Real-time commercial	10.0	11.4	1.4	14.0
Systems and support	3.2	2.9	−4.0	(9.4)
Information systems	3.6	4.3	0.7	19.5
ABC corporate average	5.5	6.0	0.5	9.1

Because quality is a positive matter, the ABC Measurement Department also recommends that software quality be expressed by using the unit of measure "Feature Points Delivered per Defect." This unit expresses the number of feature (or function) points which are associated with a single user-reported bug. This metric yields progressively larger values as quality improves. Table D.5 shows the ABC Corporation's 1989 and 1990 quality data with this metric.

Since the overall goal of the ABC Corporation's productivity and quality improvement program is to deliver more functionality to users with higher quality at the same time, this new metric of feature points per defect will become an auxiliary corporate quality measure.

ABC Defect Removal Efficiencies

Table D.6 shows the overall defect removal efficiency rates for the four environments, using the ABC standard formula for removal efficiency:

$$\text{Removal efficiency} = \frac{\text{prerelease defects}}{\text{prerelease defects} + 1 \text{ year of user defects}}$$

The defects counted are valid unique defects. Duplicate defects and invalid defects (user errors, hardware faults, etc.) are excluded from the efficiency calculations. The efficiency calculation includes the sum of all four severity levels from Severity 1 (total failure of software) through Severity 4 (superficial error).

Because the formula requires one year of user-reported defect reports before efficiency can be calculated, Table D.6 shows the overall efficiencies for 1989 rather than for 1990. The 1990 efficiencies will be included in the 1991 annual report:

Although the ABC results are within approximate industry averages as reported by Software Productivity Research, it is obvious that the systems and support environment and the IS environment are not as rigorous in defect removal as the two real-time environments. Increased utilizations of inspection technologies will be necessary to achieve significant quality increases in 1990.

Differences in the Work Content of the Four ABC Environments

Prior to the utilization of the Software Productivity Research tool set, ABC had planned to develop a single "life cycle" systems development methodology (SDM) across all of its four environments. That would not have been beneficial due to the differences in work content performed across the four main classes of ABC software. Figure 6 shows the average tasks performed in each ABC environment class.

TABLE D.6 1989 Defect Removal Efficiencies of ABC Environments

ABC software domain	Overall efficiency, %
Real-time military environment	96.5
Real-time commercial environment	95.0
Systems and support environment	78.0
Information systems environment	80.0
ABC corporate average	90.3

Cost Accumulators	Environment			
	MIS	Sup	Sys	Mil
1. Requirements	X	X	X	X
2. Prototyping	X		X	X
3. Architecture			X	X
4. Formal Plans and Estimates			X	X
5. Initial Analysis and Design	X	X	X	X
6. Detail Design	X		X	X
7. Formal Design Reviews			X	X
8. Coding	X	X	X	X
9. Reusable Code			X	X
10. Purchased Package Code	X	X		X
11. Formal Code Inspections			X	X
12. Independ. Verif. & Valid.				X
13. Formal Configuration Mgt.			X	X
14. Formal Integration	X		X	X
15. User Documentation	X	X	X	X
16. Unit Testing	X	X	X	X
17. Function Testing	X	X	X	X
18. Integration Testing			X	X
19. System Testing	X		X	X
20. Field Testing			X	X
21. Acceptance Testing	X	X		X
22. Independent Testing				X
23. Formal Quality Assurance			X	X
24. Installation & Training	X	X	X	X
25. Project Management	X	X	X	X
Total activities	13	10	21	25

Figure 6 Average tasks performed for MIS, support, systems, and military projects within ABC.

The importance of Fig. 6 is significant in terms of both ABC's productivity and quality goals. The difference in tasks performed is one of the key contributors to the overall differences in productivity. MIS and support software would benefit from the utilization of additional tasks that benefit quality, while military projects are constrained to perform tasks that appear perhaps unnecessary but are required by military specifications.

In all four ABC environments, substantial flexibility exists in both the maximum and average numbers of activities performed. For MIS projects, the smallest number of activities recorded was three and the largest was 17. For support software, the smallest number was 1 and the largest number was 6. For commercial systems software, the smallest number recorded was 5 and the largest number was 23. For military projects, the smallest number recorded was 19 and the largest was of course all 25.

Variation in the number of activities performed is a significant reason for productivity rate differences between large and small projects and also between project classes.

Differences In Software Specialization at ABC

Not only are there significant differences in the tasks performed among the four ABC software environments, but there are also significant differences in the kinds of staff specialists utilized. The significance of this factor is only just starting to be researched, and this is the first time occupation groups have been included in the ABC baseline report. Figure 7 shows the various specialists identified within ABC.

It is apparent from Fig. 7 that both the ABC information system groups and the internal tool development might benefit from the specialist skills used elsewhere within the company. In particular, it may also be useful to make some of the special skills available for MIS projects, such as human factors and integration.

ABC Software Productivity and Quality Goals for 1991

The year 1990 marks the last year that the older "source code statements" metric will be used as the primary metric for expressing software productivity and quality goals, although data will continue to be normalized to this base for several more years as a courtesy to those not yet familiar with function points and feature points.

The 1991 productivity and quality goals will be expressed in terms of the new function point/feature point metrics. The main productivity target for 1991 will be expressed as "function or feature points delivered per staff year." The main quality target for 1991 will be expressed as "User-reported defects per 100 feature/function points per year." Table D.7 contains the new 1991 productivity goals, and Table D.8 contains the new 1991 quality goals.

The technologies and methods that will allow these goals to be achieved include the normal ramp-up in the learning curve of the new

Occupation Groups	Environment			
	MIS	Sup	Sys	Mil
1. Application Programmers	X	X		X
2. Systems Programmers		X	X	X
3. Systems Analysts	X		X	X
4. Database Programmers	X			X
5. Database Administrators	X			
6. Proposal Specialists				X
7. Cost-Estimating Specialists				X
8. Measurement Specialists	X		X	X
9. Purchasing Specialists	X			X
10. Integration Specialists			X	X
11. Testing Specialists			X	X
12. Configuration Specialists				X
13. Quality Assurance			X	X
14. Technical Writers			X	X
15. Network Specialists	X		X	X
16. Human Factors Specialists			X	X
17. Microcode Specialists			X	X
18. Maintenance Specialists			X	X
19. Marketing Specialists			X	X
20. Contracts Specialists			X	X
21. Education Specialists			X	X
22. Customer Support	X		X	X
23. Field Service			X	X
24. Research Specialist			X	
25. Project Managers	X	X	X	X
Total	9	3	17	23

Figure 7 Average sets of specialists utilized for MIS, support, systems, and military projects within ABC.

JAD requirements method and the integrated graphics/text design tools introduced in 1990. Another and major contributing factor will be increased utilization of reusable code and the creation of a library of "blueprints" or reusable designs, commencing in late 1990.

Although the overall corporate defect reduction required for 1991 exceeds 50%, the technology for accomplishing this target has been in existence for many years and has demonstrated its effectiveness: The target essentially requires that internal systems and support software

TABLE D.7 1990 Actual and 1991 Target Software Productivity Rates Expressed in Feature Points and Function Points

Environment	1990	1991	Change	Percent
Real-time military	12.4	13.6	1.2	10.0
Real-time commercial	16.0	18.4	2.0	15.0
Systems and support	22.0	25.3	4.0	15.0
Information systems	56.6	65.1	8.5	15.0
ABC corporate average	22.2	25.4	3.2	14.4

TABLE D.8 1990 Actual and 1991 Target User-Reported Software Defect Rates Expressed as Unique Valid Defects per 100 Function or Feature Points

Environment	1990	1991	Change	Percent
Real-time military	5.0	4.0	−1.0	(20.0)
Real-time commercial	9.0	6.0	−3.0	(33.3)
Systems and support	35.0	10.0	−25.0	(71.0)
Information systems	23.0	10.0	−13.0	(57.0)
ABC corporate average	17.0	8.0	−9.0	(53.0)

and the ABC corporate information systems use formal design and code inspections.

Formal design and code inspections for internal systems and for IS projects had been rejected in 1985 due to the assumption that the inspection process would delay delivery of these tightly scheduled projects. The ABC corporate productivity and quality measurements since then have shown this assumption to be unjustified. The projects that use careful reviews and inspections tend to have shorter schedules than those that do not. Similar findings have been reported from other enterprises, including IBM itself.

The introduction of design and code inspections for all project classes within the ABC Corporation will allow a new corporate goal to be set: All classes of software should achieve at least a 95% cumulative defect removal efficiency rate, using the standard corporate formula of defects found prior to delivery plus defects found during the first year of production. This goal will become effective for projects delivered in 1988.

ABC Corporation Enterprise Demographics

Table D.9 summarizes the 1990 ABC overall demographics in terms of software staffing, function and feature points produced, source code produced, and user-reported unique valid defects:

TABLE D.9 Overall 1990 ABC Corporation Software Demographics

Environment	Staffing in 1990	Lines of source code	Function/feature points	Defects reported by users
Real-time military	75	116,250	930	46
Real-time commercial	300	600,000	4,800	420
Systems and support	50	137,500	1,100	385
Information systems	75	318,250	4,250	988
ABC totals	500	1,712,000	11,080	1,839

TABLE D.10 Size Ranges of Software Projects Completed In 1990

Size range in KLOC		Projects complete	Percent of projects
Very large	> 512 K	0	0.0
Large	256–512 K	1	0.5
Medium	64–256 K	4	2.0
Small to medium	16–64 K	15	7.5
Small	2–16 K	40	20.0
Very small	< 2 K	140	70.0
Totals		200	100.0

TABLE D.11 Effort Ranges of Software Projects Completed In 1990

Size range in KLOC		Labor-years of effort	Percent of effort
Very large	> 512 K	0	0.0
Large	256–512 K	150	20.4
Medium	64–256 K	250	34.0
Small to medium	16–64 K	200	27.2
Small	2–16 K	100	13.6
Very small	< 2 K	35	4.8
Totals		735	100.0

Table D.10 gives the size distribution of the programs, systems, and applications completed in calendar year 1990. As can be seen, 90% of all projects delivered in 1990 were small or very small in size.

It is surprising to compare Table D.10 and Table D.11. From Table D.10, it would appear that the bulk of the work at ABC is concentrated on small to very small programs, since those sizes constituted some 90% of the ABC software projects in 1989. However, when Table D.11 is viewed, those same sizes accumulated less than 20% of the ABC effort.

Table D.11 gives the development effort distribution of the programs, systems, and applications completed in calendar year 1990. Note that, although the projects were completed in calendar year 1990, or otherwise they would not be in this report, the starting dates often were prior to 1990. The single large project, for example, started in 1984. This explains why the total effort for projects installed in 1990 is larger than the total software staff in 1990.

As can be seen, some 54%, or the bulk of ABC's corporate programming effort, was concentrated in the large and medium categories.

Table D.12 gives the volume of source code and the percentage contribution of each size range to the overall 1990 deliveries. As can be seen, 57.9% of the delivered code was concentrated in the small to medium and medium-size categories.

Table D.13 gives the 1990 overall ABC Corporation's software population by job category.

Table D.14 shows the net change due to attrition, plus new hiring.

Analysis of Factors Which Cause Variations

The ABC Corporate Measurement Department has been licensed to use a set of software measurement methods and tools developed by Software Productivity Research, Inc., of Burlington, Mass. The SPR proprietary measurement technique contains two major elements:

1. A questionnaire that includes all of the known soft factors that can impact software projects by as much as 1 percent.

TABLE D.12 Volume of Source Code for Software Projects Completed in Calendar Year 1990

Size range in KLOC		Source code delivered	Percent of total code
Very large	> 512 K	0	0.0
Large	256–512 K	260,000	15.2
Medium	64–256 K	512,000	29.9
Small to medium	16–64 K	480,000	28.0
Small	2–16 K	320,000	18.7
Very small	< 2 K	140,000	8.2
Totals		1,712,000	100.0

TABLE D.13 Overall 1990 ABC Software Employment Distribution

Category	Number of personnel	Percent of personnel
Director(s)	1	0.2
3rd-line management	3	0.6
2nd-line management	12	2.4
1st-line management	34	6.8
Management subtotal	50	10.0
Senior software engineers*	25	5.0
Senior systems analysts	10	2.0
Programmer/analysts	35	7.0
Software engineers*	250	50.0
Software quality assurance	15	3.0
Software technical writers	15	3.0
Technical subtotal	400	80.0
Planning/estimating	10	2.0
Measurements	15	3.0
Administration/support	25	5.0
Administrative subtotal	50	10.0
ABC 1990 total	500	100.0

*The job title "software engineer" has been utilized by ABC as a generic title for as many as 10 different subspecialties, including testing specialists, maintenance specialist, and many others. This situation is common in high-technology and telecommunication companies, but it is not adequate to meet current needs. (Indeed, some telecommunication companies use the title "member of the technical staff" for more than 50 occupations.) Expanded job descriptions and position codes are being developed by the ABC personnel department, and they will be used in the next annual report.

TABLE D.14 Annual Personnel Changes In 1989

	Number	Percent
1990 Attrition	20	4.0
1990 New hires	40	8.0
1990 Net change	40	4.0

2. A measurement tool that collects the hard staffing, effort, cost, and schedule data by activity using a standard chart of accounts for 25 development/enhancement activities. (Supplemental charts of accounts are used for capturing user effort, commercial software maintenance effort for field service and customer support, and package evaluations.)

The SPR measurement methodology generates several reports that allowed our ABC statisticians to use multiple-regression techniques to isolate the factors that cause productivity and quality variations. Our statisticians were able to derive the correlations that explained variations in hard data by using multiple-regression techniques on the soft data. This section summarizes the key findings, dealing first with individual factors and then with composite sets of factors. The results throughout are shown in two ways.

1. Lines of source code per man-year (abbreviated LOC/MY)
2. Feature points per man-year (abbreviated FP/MY)

Single-Factor Influences

Following are discussions of the major individual factors which have been demonstrated to cause significant changes in productivity or quality.

Concurrent hardware and software development

This factor is very significant when it occurs, but it occurs primarily only for the real-time communications projects where the communications hardware is being built simultaneously with the software. This factor seldom or never affects MIS projects. Unstable hardware was noted on 20 of the 200 projects delivered in 1990, and yielded the results listed in Table D.15.

Constraints on performance or memory utilization

Real-time performance constraints and tight memory requirements degrade productivity when they occur, because of the extra effort needed to tune the software. Memory and performance constraints occurred primarily on the real-time communications and military projects. This factor seldom affects MIS projects. Constrained memory and performance requirements were noted on 30 of the 200 projects delivered in 1990, and yielded the results listed in Table D.16.

TABLE D.15 Annual Software Productivity with Stable and Unstable Hardware

Factor	Source code production (LOC/MY)	Feature point production (FP/MY)
Stable hardware	3000	24
Unstable hardware	1500	12

TABLE D.16 Annual Software Production with Constrained Performance and Memory Utilization

Factor	Source code production (LOC/MY)	Feature point production (FP/MY)
No constraints	2700	22
Severe constraints	1800	15

TABLE D.17 Annual Software Production with Low, Medium, and High Volumes of Difficult, Complex Code

Factor	Source code production (LOC/MY)	Feature point production (FP/MY)
Low complexity	4500	50
Medium complexity	2500	25
High complexity	1200	10

Volume of difficult and complex code

Complexity of software is partly subjective, but the McCabe essential complexity metric provides reasonably effective insights into code structural complexity. Highly complex or difficult code degrades productivity, as may be expected. Whether or not any given program needs to be complex, or whether the complexity is caused by inexperience or haste, is a more difficult question. Complexity occurs often in software, and 80 of the 200 projects delivered in 1990 had significant amounts of complex, difficult code within them. For 25 of the projects, complexity appeared to derive from the nature of the problems themselves. For 55 of the projects with high complexity, the complexity appeared to be accidental (Table D.17).

Unstable or uncertain user requirements

Unstable and uncertain user requirements are a widespread phenomenon (Table D.18) and prior to the introduction of the joint application design (JAD) methodology in 1988, some 70% of the ABC projects cited unstable requirements. Even though the JAD method works effectively for MIS projects, it is not as easy to apply to commercial or military software where the project does not meet the needs of a single identified set of customers, and where the customers are not employees of ABC. In 1990, unstable requirements remain a problem, and 90 projects out of the 200 delivered cited this factor.

TABLE D.18 Annual Software Production with Stable and Unstable User Requirements

Factor	Source code production (LOC/MY)	Feature point production (FP/MY)
No constraints	3500	40
Severe constraints	1700	18

TABLE D.19 Annual Software Production with Experienced, Average, and Inexperienced Development Staffs

Factor	Source code production (LOC/MY)	Feature point production (FP/MY)
Experienced staff	4000	50
Average staff	3000	27
Inexperienced staff	1600	15

Development team experience levels

The experience levels of the development teams vary from leading experts through novices. As might be anticipated, productivity rates vary accordingly. From the 1990 data, 10 projects out of 200 asserted that the development team was uniformly high in experience; 25 projects asserted that the development team was new to the application area; and 165 stated that the development team was of mixed experience levels (Table D.19).

New development versus enhancement projects

As the industry and the ABC corporation mature, the quantity of aging software that needs enhancement grows larger each year. In 1990, the ABC corporation's production library consisted of some 5500 identifiable programs and 200 systems, with an aggregate total of 15,000,000 source statements in various languages. The function/feature point total for the production library is 135,000. A substantial amount of the total ABC software effort goes into the maintenance and enhancement (and replacement) of aging software. In 1990, 120 projects out of the 200 delivered involved enhancing or maintaining existing applications. Some 15 projects out of 200 were complete replacements of older programs. The observed productivity rates and curves for enhancement projects are sufficiently different from development to require their own analysis. Because of the overhead costs of analyzing the existing software, regression testing it, and recompiling it, enhancement productivity rates are normally lower than producing an equivalent amount of new code (Table D.20).

Small versus large software projects

Enhancement projects and new development projects follow different patterns when considering size. Small development projects are significantly more productive than large. However, small enhancement projects are usually low in productivity, due to overhead costs of recompiling, regression testing, etc. Small projects are less than 16 K source statements, and large projects are greater than 64 K (Table D.21).

The impact of programming languages

One of the primary reasons for adopting function points and feature points is that source code metrics penalize high-level languages. The penalty is caused by a well-known phenomenon that has been understood for more than 200 years by manufacturing managers, but unfortunately not by software managers. When a manufacturing process includes a significant percentage of fixed costs and there is a decline in the number of units produced, the cost per unit will go up. For software, there are many fixed and inelastic costs. When migration occurs to a

TABLE D.20 Annual Software Production Rates for Development and Enhancement Projects

Factor	Source code production (LOC/MY)	Feature point production (FP/MY)
New projects	3200	37
Enhancements	2500	23

TABLE D.21 Annual Software Production Rates for Small versus Large Development and Enhancement Projects

Factor	Source code production (LOC/MY)	Feature point production (FP/MY)
Small development	5000	60
Large development	2500	24
Small enhancement	1750	15
Large enhancements	3000	28

higher-level language, the results are mathematically equivalent to a manufacturing process with fewer units produced, since high-level languages require fewer statements to implement functions.

The 1990 report is the first ABC measurement report to segregate productivity rates by language, and the new SPR feature point technique (used on real-time and military projects) and IBM function point technique (used on MIS projects) illustrated the hazards of "lines of code" metrics when projects are measured to a standard life cycle with a high percentage of paperwork and overhead costs included. In Table D.22 are the 1990 data by language. At least 10 projects were developed in each of the languages shown from the 1990 data.

The impact of physical office environments

This is a new study topic included for the first time in the 1990 report. Analysis outside the ABC Corporation by Gerald McCue, Dean of Architecture at Harvard, and Tom DeMarco and Tim Lister, of the Atlantic Systems Guild, indicated that the physical office environment would have a strong impact on software development productivity. Office space of more than 78 square feet was often associated with high software productivity, while office space of less than 44 square feet or open office arrangements was often associated with low software productivity (Table D.23). Since the SPR questionnaire captures data on office space, it was decided to explore this factor. The results were ambiguous in ABC since all except for 50 of the personnel worked in a temporary rented office building, where they averaged 75 square feet of enclosed space, and all of the other office space was between 40 and

TABLE D.22 Annual Software Production as a Function of the Programming Language Used for Development

Language	Source code production (LOC/MY)	Feature point production (FP/MY)
Assembly language	4000	18
C	3500	24
Cobol	3000	28
Ada	2500	33
APL	1500	45
Objective-C	1250	47
Query language(s)	1000	77

Note: This table clearly reveals why function points and feature points are superior to "line of source code" metrics for economic analysis and productivity studies. The older "lines of source code" metrics penalize high-level languages, and they always achieve their highest rates for the least productive languages.

TABLE D.23 Annual Software Production as a Function of the Size of the Programming Office

Factor	Source code production (LOC/MY)	Feature point production (FP/MY)
> 75 square feet	3500	37
50 to 75 square feet	3200	32
< 50 square feet	2400	27

70 square feet per technical staff member. Although trends were noted, the 0% availability of larger office environments meant that the high-end benefits could not be explored.

Since office space is a new topic in this year's survey, a total of 125 ABC software personnel were interviewed regarding their perceptions of the ABC office environment. The results were unambiguous: All occupants of crowded office space felt their performance suffered as a result. Several enjoyed the social advantages of working with colleagues, but none who had moved from smaller to larger office space wished to return to the previous environment. This is a factor which deserves more extended study in the future.

The impact of reusable code

"Reusable code" is defined as independent functional modules that can be linked or included in a program without requiring any internal modification. Examples of reusable code include calendar routines, date conversion routines, square root routines, and routines for handling pull-down menus, standard input validation routines, and the like. Code that is borrowed from other applications can be classed as reusable if it does not require modification. If borrowed code does require minor or major change before use, it should be termed "modified code." Some 50 projects out of 200 reported various degrees of reusable code. Because of the very high productivity impact of reusability, this technology should be extended in 1988 (Table D.24).

TABLE D.24 Annual Software Production Rates as a Function of the Amount of Reused Code In the Application

Factor	Source code production (LOC/MY)	Feature point production (FP/MY)
> 50% reusability	9500	87
25% to 50% reuse	4500	42
10% to 25% reuse	3500	32
< 10% reusability	3000	28

Since this factor had the largest impact of any factor in the baseline, it is apparent that ABC should institute an aggressive campaign to achieve higher levels of reusability in all four ABC environments.

The impact of project organization structures

This is a new topic studied for the first time in 1990. Observations from other companies such as GTE and ITT had indicated that matrix management for large software projects had a negative effect on productivity. The ABC data tends to confirm this hypothesis. Of the 200 projects reported, 20 used a matrix management organization, 25 were hierarchically organized, 65 were small team projects (2–3), and 90 were individual projects (Table D.25).

The impact of CASE tools and workstations

The acronym "CASE" stands for the term "computer-aided software engineering" and refers to loosely integrated tool sets that are intended to provide continuous support from design through development. The ABC CASE environment, experimental in 1990, includes a graphics/text design tool with an integrated data dictionary, an application generator coupled to the design engine, and a workstation optimized for these tools. (*Note:* Vendor names are deliberately omitted from this report.) Since the ABC CASE environment was experimental in 1990, it was used on only five small projects out of 200 (Table D.26). To equalize the comparisons,

TABLE D.25 Annual Software Production Rates as a Function of Project Organization Structure

Factor	Source code production (LOC/MY)	Feature point production (FP/MY)
One-person projects	5500	50
Small teams (2–3)	4250	39
Hierarchical	3750	34
Matrixed	2800	25

TABLE D.26 Annual Software Production Rates Using Experimental CASE Tool Suites and Workstations

Factor	Source code production (LOC/MY)	Feature point production (FP/MY)
CASE development	6000	55
Non-CASE projects	4000	36

the CASE results are reported against 10 projects of similar sizes and attributes.

The Impact of Composite Multiple Factors

This section deals with the impact of simultaneous changes in several factors at once. Because of the large number of possibilities, the organizing principle for this section is in declining order of results. The factors associated with successful projects are discussed first, and then the factors associated with various problems, ending with the factors most often associated with canceled projects and disasters.

Factors associated with successful projects

The word "successful" in the context of this report means three things: (1) the project was completed on time and within budget; (2) the first year of production revealed acceptable levels of quality and reliability; (3) users were generally satisfied with the functionality and ease of use of the software. All three of these items must be present for a project to be considered a success. An "average" project is one where at least one and sometimes two of the criteria were met. An "unsuccessful" project is one where none of the three criteria were met but the project was finished and delivered anyway (Table D.27).

The factors most often associated with success include but are not limited to the following: (1) stable and unambiguous requirements; (2) stable and well-understood hardware; (3) well-seasoned, experienced development teams; (4) no excessive schedule pressure on the managers or developers; (5) adequate computer availability and response time; (6) full reviews and inspections of major deliverables; (7) careful design and specification; (8) automation of design and documentation.

Of the 375 projects reported over the last two years in the 1989 and 1990 reports, some 30 (or 8%) meet the above criteria for being termed "successful." It is interesting and statistically significant that successful projects are often record-setters for productivity and quality simultaneously.

TABLE D.27 Annual Software Production for Successful, Average, and Unsuccessful Projects

Factor	Source code production (LOC/MY)	Feature point production (FP/MY)
Successful projects	4250	39
Average projects	2500	23
Unsuccessful projects	1100	12

Factors causing customer dissatisfaction

In reviewing several hundred letters and attending a number of meetings with customers and customer organizations, the major factors that cause dissatisfaction appear to be these: (1) poor quality and reliability; (2) inadequate functionality; (3) hard to use or irrational commands and menus; (4) poor user documentation; (5) poor customer support; (6) late delivery of promised functions.

Conversely, the factors cited most often by users who like software products are these: (1) intuitive command and menu structure; (2) excellent functionality; (3) excellent quality and reliability; (4) good or excellent user documentation; (5) good or excellent customer support.

The controllable factors which development managers and staff can utilize to achieve high levels of user satisfaction are these: (1) joint application design (JAD) requirements development where possible; (2) prototyping where possible; (3) reviews and inspection; (4) professional writers.

Of the 375 projects reported in 1989 and 1990, some 40, or 10.6%, had high levels of user satisfaction, while 65, or 17.3%, had significant user complaints after delivery. As it turns out, projects with high levels of user satisfaction are usually more productive than projects that lack this attribute, as can be seen in Table D.28.

Factors causing cost and schedule overruns

The primary factor causing cost and schedule overruns is the common occurrence that the schedules and development costs were set before the project was defined. Of the 375 projects reported in 1989 and 1990, some 135, or 36%, had their schedules and budgets assigned prior to the completion of requirements while the project scopes were still unstable.

The second most common reason for cost and schedule overruns is new functionality added to a project after the requirements are nominally frozen. Some 60 out of 375 projects (16%) reported that substantial new functions were added during the design and development period. In the most extreme case, a project was initially sized at 80,000 source

TABLE D.28 Annual Software Production Rates for Projects with High and Low User Satisfaction

Factor	Source code production (LOC/MY)	Feature point production (FP/MY)
High user satisfaction	3850	36
Low user satisfaction	3200	29

TABLE D.29 Annual Software Production Rates for Projects That Met Cost and Schedule Estimates Versus Projects That Overran Their Cost and Schedule Estimates

Factor	Source code production (LOC/MY)	Feature point production (FP/MY)
Estimates met	4250	39
Estimates not met	2650	22

statements. New functionality ordered by the executive vice president, who was the customer for the project, brought the delivered size of the application up to 195,000 source statements: an increase of 144%.

The third most common reason for cost and schedule overruns is inaccurate sizing and estimating. There are more than 30 commercially available software estimating programs in the United States in 1990, but only 25 projects out of 200 (12.5%) reported using a formal estimating approach.

The fourth most common reason for cost and schedule overruns is a complex of multiple factors: (1) inexperience of the development team; (2) unstable hardware; (3) unexpected attrition of key project personnel; (4) failure to consider topics such as multisite development; (5) poor morale; (6) management disputes regarding the project; (7) inadequate tools, workstations, computer availability, or response time.

As may be expected, the projects overrunning their estimated costs and schedules had lower productivity than those which met their cost and schedule estimates, as can be seen in Table D.29.

Factors causing quality and reliability problems

In all major studies to date, there is an almost perfect correlation between quality and productivity. Those projects that aim at high quality will also achieve shorter development schedules and higher productivity rates than yielded by any other target. The reasons for this phenomenon are straightforward: Defect removal has been the most expensive aspect of software development since the software industry began in 1946. Projects that utilize a well-chosen combination of defect prevention and defect removal methods will simultaneously optimize both quality and productivity.

The defect prevention methods most often associated with high quality and high productivity include but are not limited to the following: (1) JAD or joint application design requirements methods; (2) prototyping; (3) user involvement during requirements and design; (4) fully automated design tools with graphics and text support and an integral data dictionary; (5) formal analysis and design methods such as Warnier-Orr design, Jackson design, structured design, state transition diagramming, etc.; (6) reusable code and standard functional modules; (7) structured programming techniques; (8) restructuring of aging Cobol applications via one of the commercial restructuring engines; (9) tracking of defects and quality.

The defect removal methods most often associated with high quality and high productivity include but are not limited to the following: (1) formal design and code inspections; (2) structured walk-throughs; (3) formal test departments staffed by testing specialists; (4) tracking of defects and quality (this is both a prevention and removal technique); (5) formal test libraries; (6) quality assurance reviews of key deliverables.

The methodologies most often associated with low quality and low productivity include but are not limited to the following: (1) no reviews or inspections at all; (2) no significant user involvement during requirements and design; (3) no formal requirements and design methods; (4) no quality tracking at all; (5) no formal test library; (6) no quality assurance organization at all; (7) no quality goals for managers or key projects; (8) corporate emphasis on schedule adherence rather than quality; (9) no testing specialists at all.

The phrase "high quality" (Table D.30) means meeting or bettering the ABC corporate targets for annual user-reported defect rates plus achieving good to excellent user reports on functionality and usability. Of the 375 projects reported in 1986 and 1990, some 20 (10%) had high quality, while 40 (20%) had low quality.

The phrase "low quality" means the bottom quartile of annual user-reported defects (i.e., the largest quantity of defect reports) plus achieving low to very low user satisfaction reports on functionality and usability. Of the 375 projects reported in 1989 and 1990, some 40 (20%) had low quality.

Factors causing project cancellations

In 1989 and 1990, some 375 software projects were completed and included in the two annual ABC productivity reports. There were also 40 projected canceled over that same time period, or 10.6% of all proj-

TABLE D.30 Annual Software Production Rates for Projects That Have High Quality Versus Projects with Low Qualities

Factor	Source code production (LOC/MY)	Feature point production (FP/MY)
High-quality projects	4000	38
Low-quality projects	2200	28

ects begun. The factors which were associated with the cancellations are these:

1. *Change in business environment:* Closing of a business unit negated the need for projects. This factor caused 15 out of 40 cancellations.

2. *Costs exceed value:* The anticipated cost to complete the projects versus the anticipated value of the projects did not meet the corporate requirements for internal rates of return. This factor caused 10 out of 40 cancellations.

3. *Stronger project selected:* Two similar projects were in simultaneous development. When this fact became known, one of the projects was terminated. This factor caused 5 out of 40 cancellations. This factor is not uncommon in large enterprises, and it implies a need for more careful project screening and justification.

4. *Unachievable objectives:* The project requirements were unimplementable by using available technologies, and the project was terminated by joint agreement of users and development management. This factor caused 5 out of 40 cancellations.

5. *Miscellaneous causes:* These projects were canceled for various reasons, including (A) the primary sponsor and user of the project left the company; (B) a purchased package became available that performed the same functions; (C) hardware changes negated the need for project. These factors caused 5 out of 40 cancellations.

Because the projects were canceled, their complete productivity data is not known. It is significant, however, that the accumulated effort on the 40 canceled projects amounted to 125 person-years, or 12.5% of the available staff time for 2 years.

Summary and Conclusions about Factors Affecting Productivity

There are more than 200 individual factors that are known to affect software productivity and quality. These factors exert both an individual impact, and of course combinations of factors can exert synergistic impacts.

This report highlights some of the major and better understood factors as they relate to productivity and quality. Other topics, no less important, have been omitted in the interest of conciseness from this year's report and will be dealt with in the future.

The ABC Corporation in 1990 can be defined as a better-than-average enterprise in overall quality and productivity at present. Further, because of strong executive, management, and staff desire to improve, our rate of change is much faster than normal. The prognosis for 1991 and the future is excellent.

Appendix

E

Example of an Executive Briefing on a New Baseline

Introduction

When software measurement programs get underway in an enterprise, the information is obviously of vital importance to senior management and executives. Not only do the software executives have an interest in the results, but so do senior corporate executives up to the levels of the CEO and indeed the board of directors.

Although printed baseline reports such as the one illustrated in Appendix D are distributed to executives, it is normal practice to supplement the printed baseline report with a presentation in either overhead or 35-mm slide format. That allows the executives to interact directly and ask questions about topics that may be outside the scope of the printed baseline.

For the example baseline shown here, a half-day working session is normally reserved to give executives a chance to fully explore the issues that are raised. It often happens that the half day expands to a full day if major issues are surfaced that need extended discussions. This presentation is normally given to management by the director or senior manager who is responsible for carrying out the baseline. In large corporations such as IBM, ITT, AT&T, and Hewlett-Packard, the executive briefing may be given many times in many different laboratories and locations. For example, the annual IBM, ITT, and Hewlett-Packard baseline presentations were given internationally at more than 20 locations within the respective companies.

The following is an example of an executive briefing on an initial software baseline. In this case the baseline was prepared by the consulting staff of Software Productivity Research. (To ensure confidentiality, excerpts from several actual baselines have been melded together rather than using data prepared for a single enterprise.)

Context of the Example

The sample baseline presentation in this appendix is typical of an annual baseline when a company first starts its measurement program. Since measurement itself is new in such a situation, the baseline presentation must provide some background information about the measurement process itself, as well as about the findings of the baseline study.

In later years, the baseline presentations may eliminate the background information on measurement and concentrate only on the findings. However, when an initial baseline is prepared, executives will have as many questions about the measurement process as they have about the findings, so it is important to include some background information. Indeed, if the executive questions about the measurement process are not answered clearly and precisely, the results of the baseline may not be credible.

The example baseline is a divisional MIS baseline for one unit of a manufacturing company, identified in the example as "XYZ company." Note that this is a hypothetical example and is not intended to represent any actual company. The initial baseline was created from the analysis of 19 MIS projects which spanned the nature, size, and scope of the division's software work. The projects were a mixture of new development, enhancement, and maintenance work. The sizes ranged from small to large, and the platforms on which the projects were developed ranged from microcomputers to mainframes.

Some of the kinds of projects included were an order entry system, an accounts receivable system, a human resources system, and a benefits tracking system. The data collected for the projects themselves was derived from structured interviews by using a proprietary questionnaire. The interviews were conducted with the project managers and teams, augmented by data from the company's project-tracking system. (Tracking system data is seldom accurate enough to be relied upon, however.)

The interview sessions averaged about 3½ h per project, and the data collection was spread over a period of about 2 weeks. The interview process itself normally arouses some apprehension ahead of time, since the project managers and teams may be uncertain as to the intent. This apprehension disappears immediately once the sessions begin, and it becomes obvious that the purpose is to find out what the project staffs really think about the suitability of the tools, methods, and environments that are available to them.

Components of the Executive Briefing

The normal format of a baseline executive briefing includes the following sections and contents:

1. *Introduction (normally 5 to 10 pages)* Brief discussion of how measurements were taken and what projects were measured.
2. *Executive summary (normally 5 to 15 pages)* Highlights of key findings in 10 min or so.
3. *Findings (normally 10 to 30 pages)* Significant strengths and weaknesses derived from the interviews and both the soft and hard data collected.
4. *Conclusions (normally 10 to 30 pages)* How the organization stacks up in both an absolute sense and compared to other companies in the same lines of business (if known) and to U.S. norms.
5. *Opportunities (normally 10 to 20 pages)* The word "opportunity" is a polite way to point out problems that need to be fixed.
6. *Next steps (normally 5 to 20 pages)* The next step after an initial baseline report is normally to produce an improvement plan aimed at correcting the key deficiencies noted.
7. *Appendix (normally 10 to 20 pages)* Backup data in substantial amounts should detailed questions be asked.

Assuming that the baseline presentation will be given to somewhere between 3 and 10 executives at a sitting, and that there will be a normal volume of questions and dialog between the presenter and the executives, a briefing such as the following will take between 2 and 4 h to present. However, for the very first sets of briefings when a company is just getting started with measurement, it is desirable to plan on at least half a day and sometimes a full day for the session.

Preparation of the Executive Briefing

There are a number of alternative ways to reach the same end when it comes to baseline presentations and reports. ITT, for example, used Focus as the database for holding its baseline information, SAS for the statistical analysis, and Merganthaler phototypesetters for report preparation.

The baseline presentation shown in this appendix was prepared from data collected by using the proprietary CHECKPOINT® data collection tool and the associated interview questionnaire. The results of the projects were aggregated and statistically analyzed using proprietary tools developed by Software Productivity Research. The presentation itself was produced using ordinary laser printers.

In addition to the basic statistical analysis, the consultants who gathered the data discussed the findings among themselves and with both the clients and the consulting staff of SPR. It is normal when outside consultants collect the data to produce intermediate reports to apprise the clients of the early findings. The final report, included here, should not contain major surprises which no one in the client organization realized would be forthcoming.

The aggregation, statistical analysis, and report preparation took about two calendar weeks and somewhat more than 2 weeks of effort, since it involved both consulting and production personnel. The moral of the story is simple: Allow adequate time for both thoughtful analysis and for final production.

Problems Widely Reported via Executive Briefings

To the management and staff of any given company, the problems identified in a baseline presentation will no doubt seem unique. However, to management consultants who work with many different companies, certain problems occur repeatedly in many different organizations. Just as physicians tend to see quite a large number of similar medical conditions such as influenza or hay fever, consultants tend to see quite a lot of similar software problems.

The baseline presentation shown here contains a typical volume of problems that are widespread in MIS organizations throughout the United States. Following are six very common problems observed in the U.S. as a whole, and in this report in particular:

1. Quality control is not very good.
2. Schedule pressure is the strongest driving force.
3. Requirements are seldom stable, so that projects grow significantly late in development.
4. There is little consistency from project to project in the tools or methods used.
5. The physical office space is cramped and noisy.
6. Prior to the baseline itself, there was no meaningful measurement program of either quality or productivity.

Fortunately, there are available solutions for all six of these common problems, although the solution to problem 5 is normally very expensive. For example, office space in urban areas such as Boston, San Francisco, and New York is currently renting for about $35 per square foot. To double or triple the space per staff member is not a trivial expense.

However, until the impact of problems such as these six is quantified, they can exist (and have existed) for many years. When the problems and their implications are measured in a formal baseline presentation, it becomes possible to move toward their solution in a reasonable and well-planned fashion.

There will also be problems that are in fact unique to an enterprise that will require customized solutions. As a rule of thumb, about 70 percent of observed problems are fairly standard but perhaps 30 percent of the observed problems will be unique to the specific enterprise or location.

Executive Responses to the Briefings

For many years, senior management has experienced frustration that is due to an inability to bring software projects under full management control. Although there may be aspects of discomfort if some of the problems found and reported are serious, the normal response by senior management to a baseline presentation is a compound of surprise, interest, and relief. The surprise is because they may never before have seen a rational, quantified depiction of software. The interest is because they finally have something tangible that allows them to exert management judgment about needed improvements. The relief is because they can finally see the light at the end of the tunnel: Software is no longer an esoteric discipline but is now capable of being a true business function.

There is one almost universal executive reaction to an initial baseline presentation. The executives will want the same kind of information, or even more, on a continuing basis. A surprisingly large number of measurement specialists, including both A. J. Albrecht and the author, did not originally plan long-term careers in the measurement domain. The requests by IBM's senior executives for more and more quantified information on MIS projects (in the case of Albrecht) and systems software (in the case of the author) led to continuing measurement studies and eventually into new permanent careers that centered around software measurement. This same phenomenon can be observed in other large enterprises as well. Once solid, reliable, and quantified information on software becomes available, executives will never want to go back to the previous situation of "unmeasured and therefore unmanageable."

A software baseline study and the associated presentation and written report are key steps in bringing software out of the dark ages and into the light as both a true engineering discipline and a valuable component of modern business.

and their implications are measured in a formal baseline presentation, it becomes possible to move toward their solution in a reasonable and well-planned fashion.

There will also be problems that are in fact unique to an enterprise that will require customized solutions. As a rule of thumb, about 70 percent of observed problems are fairly standard but perhaps 30 percent of the observed problems will be unique to the specific enterprise or location.

Executive Responses to the Briefings

For many years, senior management has experienced frustration that is due to an inability to bring software projects under full management control. Although there may be aspects of discomfort if some of the problems found and reported are serious, the normal response by senior management to a baseline presentation is a compound of surprise, interest, and relief. The surprise is because they may never before have seen a rational, quantified depiction of software. The interest is because they finally have something tangible that allows them to exert management judgment about needed improvements. The relief is because they can finally see the light at the end of the tunnel: Software is no longer an esoteric discipline but is now capable of being a true business function.

There is one almost universal executive reaction to an initial baseline presentation. The executives will want the same kind of information, or even more, on a continuing basis. A surprisingly large number of measurement specialists, including both A. J. Albrecht and the author, did not originally plan long-term careers in the measurement domain. The requests by IBM's senior executives for more and more quantified information on MIS projects (in the case of Albrecht) and systems software (in the case of the author) led to continuing measurement studies and eventually into new permanent careers that centered around software measurement. This same phenomenon can be observed in other large enterprises as well. Once solid, reliable, and quantified information on software becomes available, executives will never want to go back to the previous situation of "unmeasured and therefore unmanageable."

A software baseline study and the associated presentation and written report are key steps in bringing software out of the dark ages and into the light as both a true engineering discipline and a valuable component of modern business.

XYZ COMPANY

SOFTWARE MEASUREMENT BASELINE STUDY

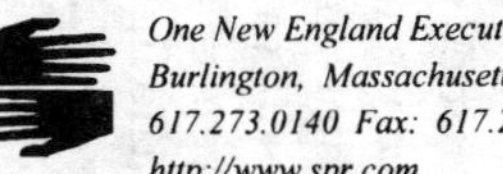

One New England Executive Park
Burlington, Massachusetts 01803
617.273.0140 Fax: 617.273.5176
http://www.spr.com

TABLE OF CONTENTS

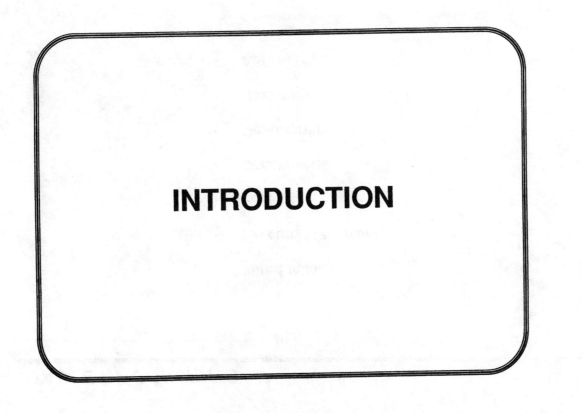

INTRODUCTION

C00037/3

FOUR AREAS NEED TO BE MANAGED TO IMPROVE SOFTWARE QUALITY AND PRODUCTIVITY

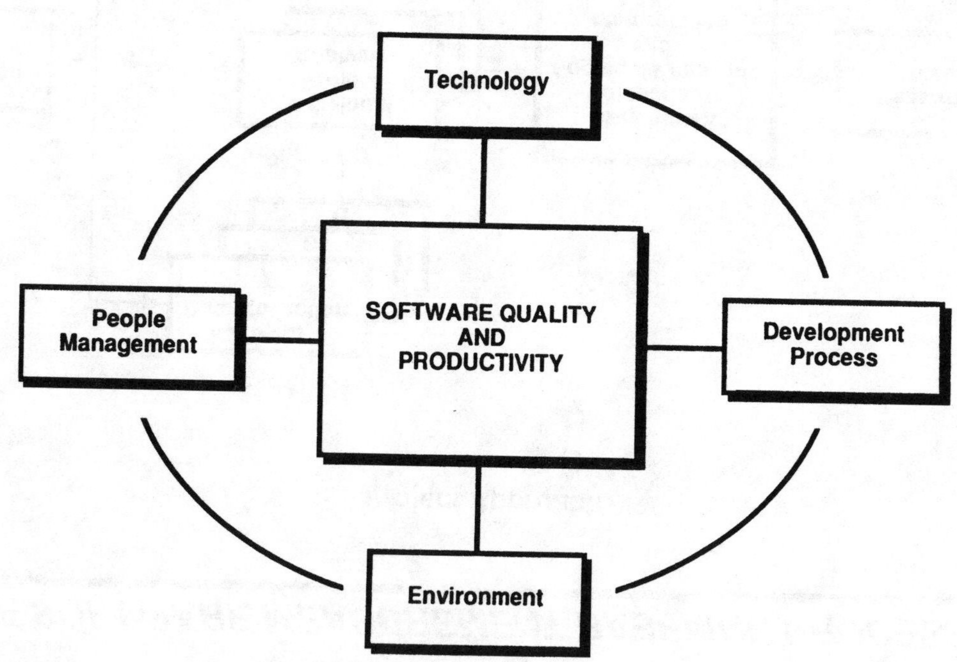

THE SOFTWARE MEASUREMENT BASELINE PROCESS

Project Approach

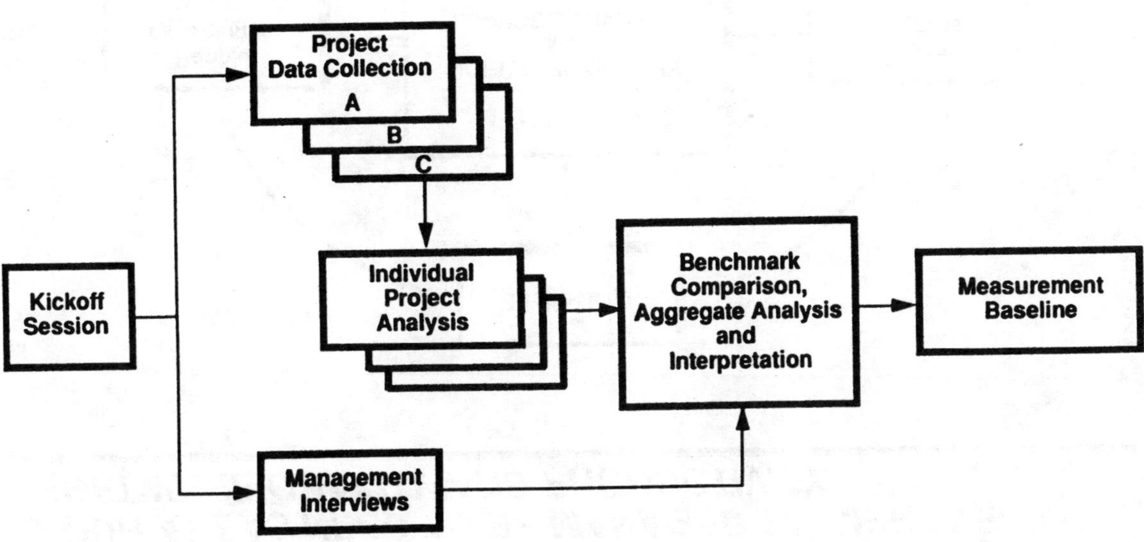

SOFTWARE QUALITY AND PRODUCTIVITY MEASUREMENT LEADS TO NEW STRATEGIC DIRECTION AND MANAGEMENT PLANS

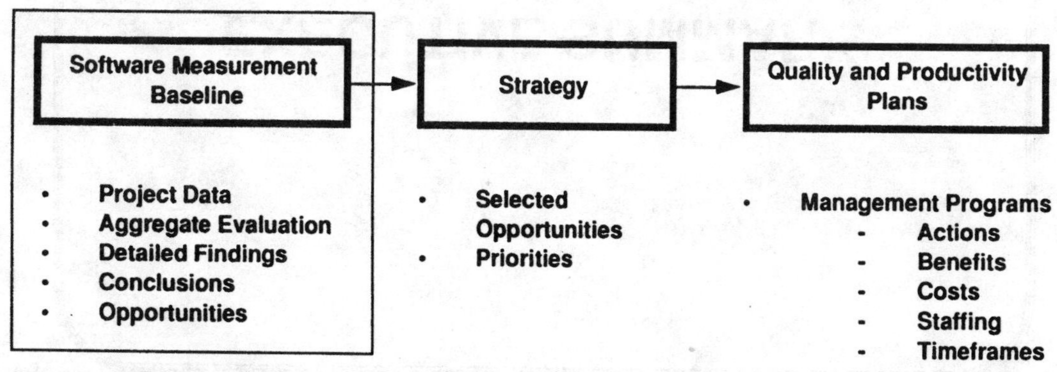

EXECUTIVE SUMMARY

PROJECT SCOPE

Project review included 19 applications, varying in type, size, and technology.

CODE	PROJECT I.D.	TYPE	SIZE	TECHNOLOGY
A	Purchase Order Entry	D	L	MF
B	Securities Handling	D	S	MF
C	Claims	D	S	MF
D	Automatic Teller	E	S	MF
E	Human Resources	D	S	MF
F	Payroll Front-End	D	M	MF
G	Distribution Systems	M	M	MF
H	On-Line Agent	E	L	MF
J	Merchandising Systems	D	M	PC
K	Accounts Receivable	E	M	MF
L	Benefits	E	S	MF
M	Long Term Care	E	S	PC
N	Manufacturing Systems	D	S	MF
P	Confirmation	E	L	PK
Q	Prototype	E	L	MF
R	Financial Analysis	M	L	MF
S	Systems Conversion	D	S	MF
T	Checkpoint	D	S	MF
U	On-Line Inquiry	E	M	PC

KEY:

1. TYPE	2. SIZE	3. TECHNOLOGY
D = Development	L = Large (>500 FP)	MF = Mainframe
E = Enhancement	M = Medium (200-500 FP)	PC = Micro
M = Maintenance	S = Small (<200 FP)	PK = Package

C00037/9

EXECUTIVE SUMMARY

- **I/S needs to develop a greater awareness of business problems and strategies, and focus their efforts on tactically supporting those strategies.**

- **People Management includes an I/S staff with strong, technical expertise. High morale and company loyalty are prevalent. It is necessary to move forward in new directions:**

    - **The Need to Increase Business Knowledge**
    - **Manage Customer Expectations**
    - **Develop Project Management Skills**

- **Technology includes the lack of consistent use of development methods, techniques, and tools reducing productivity and increasing project risk. Use of tools needs to be propagated using the following:**

    - **Enforcement/Standards**
    - **Newsletters**
    - **Tool Assessment/Feedback**

HARD DATA FINDINGS

INDIVIDUAL PROJECT DATA WAS COLLECTED AND COMPARED TO INDUSTRY STANDARDS.

- **Staffing Levels**
- **Project Schedules**
- **Documentation Volumes**
- **Productivity Levels**
- **Defect Removal**

PROJECT STAFFING LEVELS ARE HIGH EMPHASIZING THE PUSH FOR QUICKER SYSTEMS DELIVERY

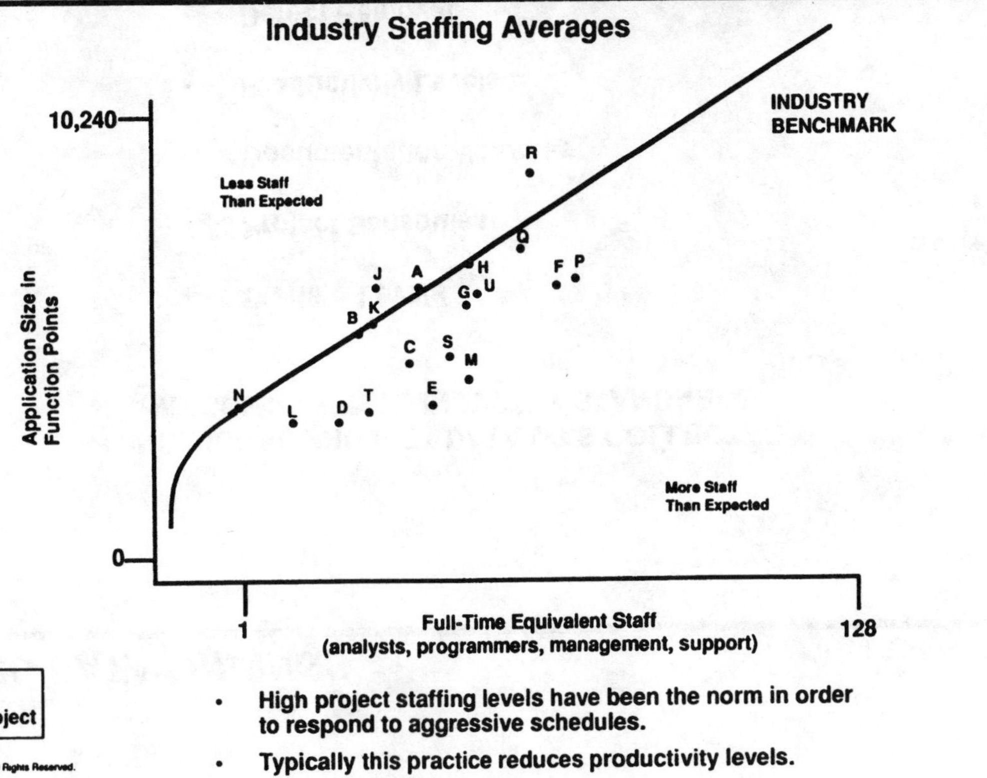

- High project staffing levels have been the norm in order to respond to aggressive schedules.
- Typically this practice reduces productivity levels.

Copyright © 1990, All Rights Reserved.

SHORTER SCHEDULES REFLECT THE DEADLINE DRIVEN ENVIRONMENT

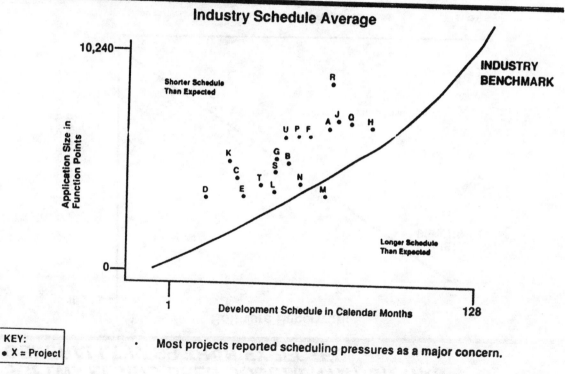

Industry Schedule Average

10,240

0

Application Size in Function Points

Shorter Schedule Than Expected

INDUSTRY BENCHMARK

R

J A Q H

U P F

K G B

C S

T L N

D E M

Longer Schedule Than Expected

1

Development Schedule in Calendar Months

128

- Most projects reported scheduling pressures as a major concern.

Copyright © 1990, All Rights Reserved

SOFTWARE AND USER DOCUMENTATION WAS GENERALLY LESS THAN EXPECTED

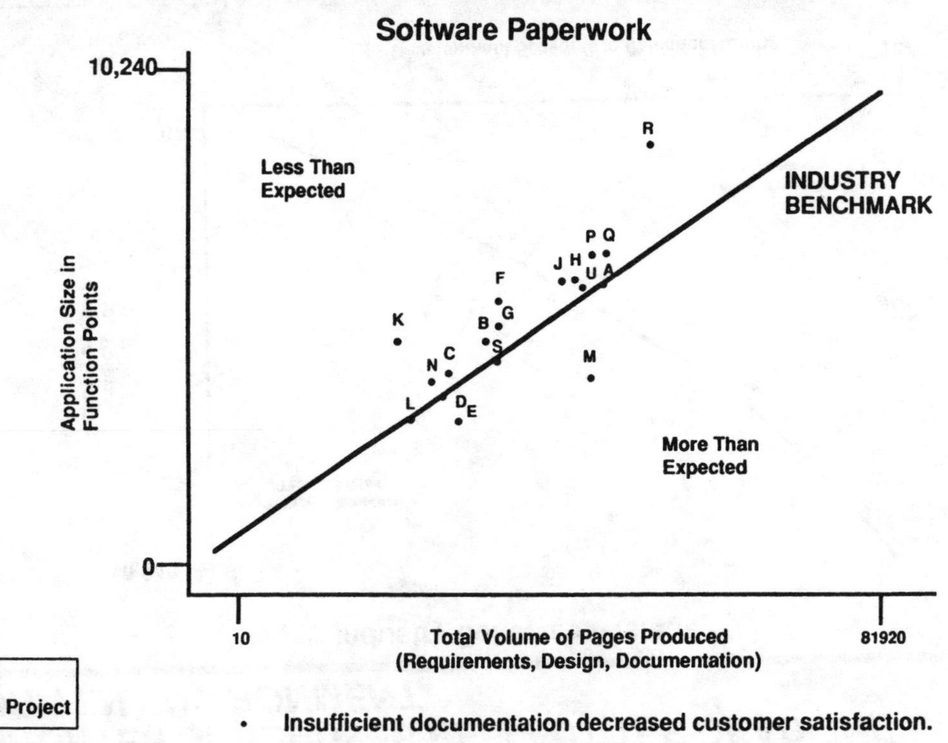

KEY:
● X = Project

- Insufficient documentation decreased customer satisfaction.

Copyright © 1990, All Rights Reserved.

OVERALL PRODUCTIVITY LEVELS VARIED SIGNIFICANTLY

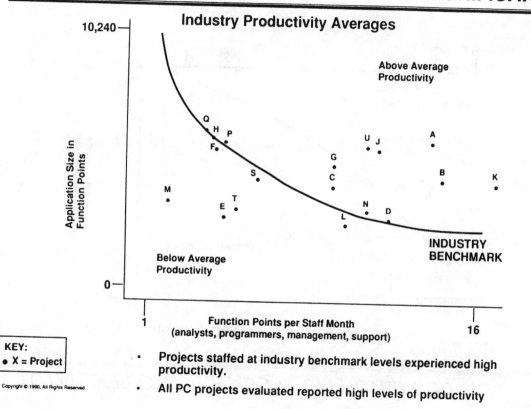

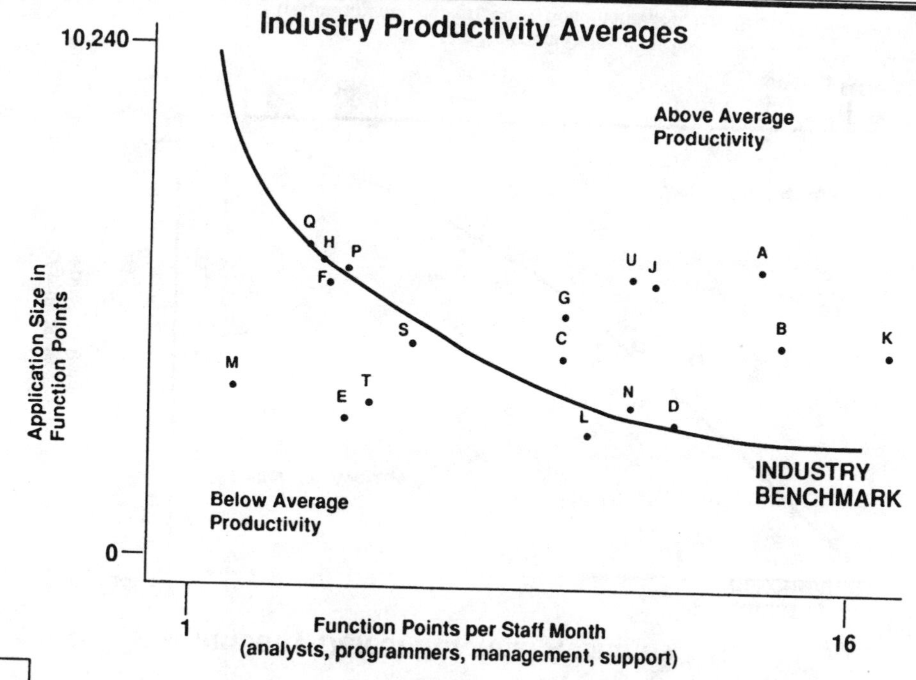

KEY:
● X = Project

Copyright © 1990, All Rights Reserved.

- Projects staffed at industry benchmark levels experienced high productivity.
- All PC projects evaluated reported high levels of productivity

TOTAL DEFECTS ARE ABOVE EXPECTED COUNTS

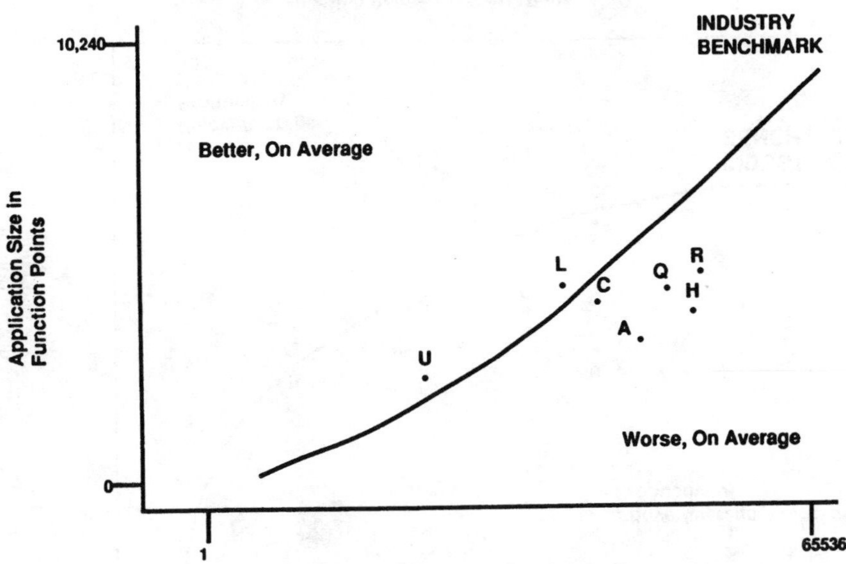

Copyright © 1990, All Rights Reserved.

DEFECT FORECASTING SHOULD BE PERFORMED TO PREDICT DEFECT COUNTS

Industry Delivered Defect Averages

Expectations Based on Size Shown

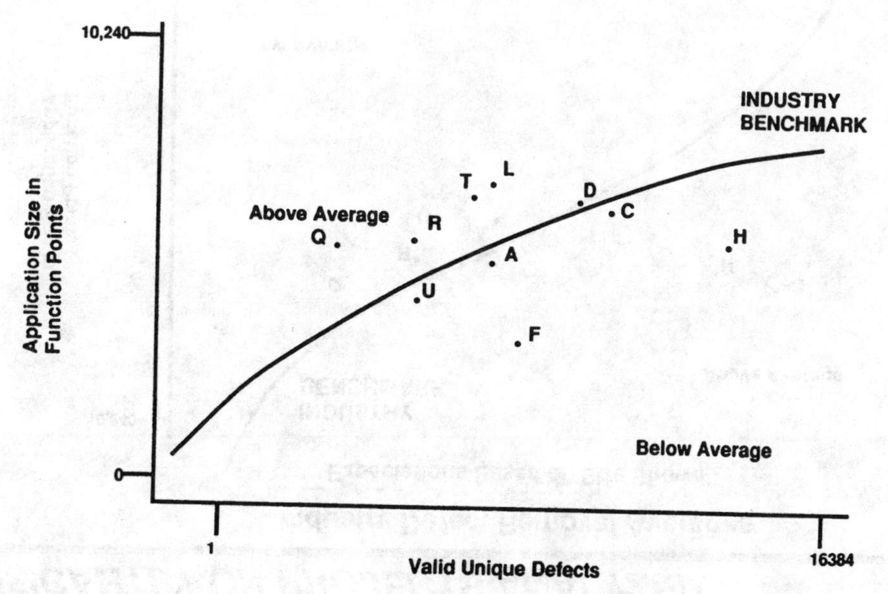

Copyright © 1990, All Rights Reserved.

DEFECT REMOVAL EFFICIENCY RATES VARIED SIGNIFICANTLY ON PROJECTS ANALYZED.

Industry Defect Removal Averages

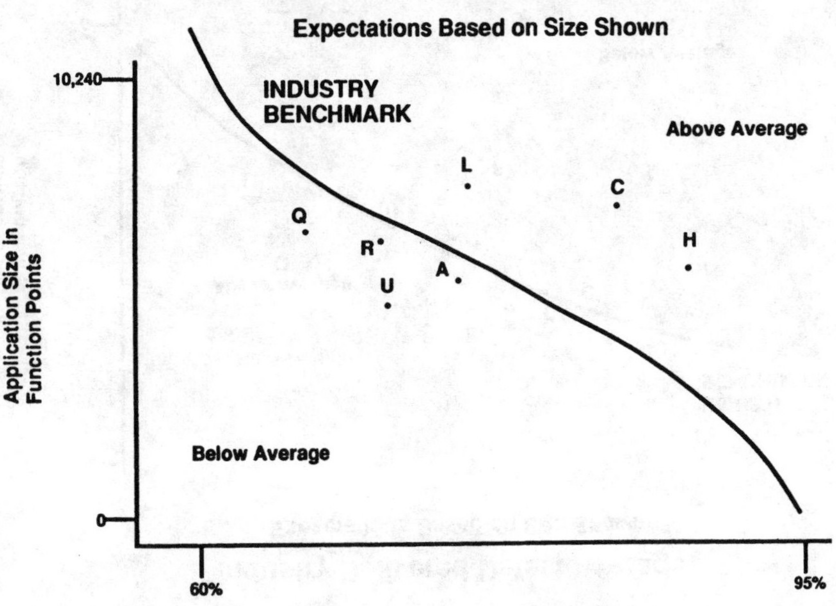

Cumulative Defect Removal
(reviews, inspection, all testing)

Copyright © 1990, All Rights Reserved.

CUSTOMER PERCEPTION OF SYSTEMS QUALITY WAS SURVEYED

2 Perspectives Were Sought

Survey	CUSTOMERS End User	CUSTOMERS Project Team
Data Accuracy	✓	
System Availability	✓	
Functionality	✓	
Reliability	✓	
Screens/Reports	✓	
Documentation	✓	
Training	✓	
System Design		✓
Estimating/Planning		✓
Project Controls		✓
Computer Support		✓
Development Techniques		✓
Development Tools		✓
Technical Knowledge		
Resource Availability		

C00037/24

END-USER CUSTOMERS ARE GENERALLY SATISFIED WITH DELIVERED SYSTEMS

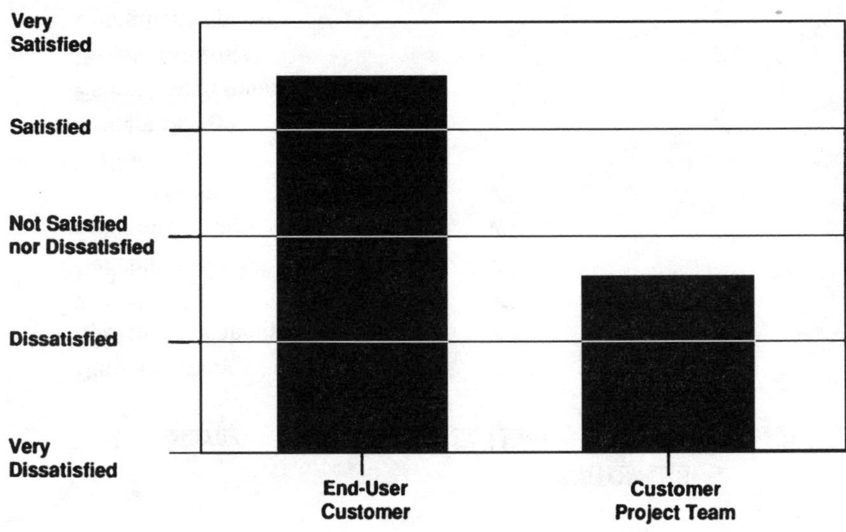

- **Customer project team members were less than satisfied with development activities.**

END-USER CUSTOMER CONCERNED WITH QUALITY AND QUANTITY OF DOCUMENTATION

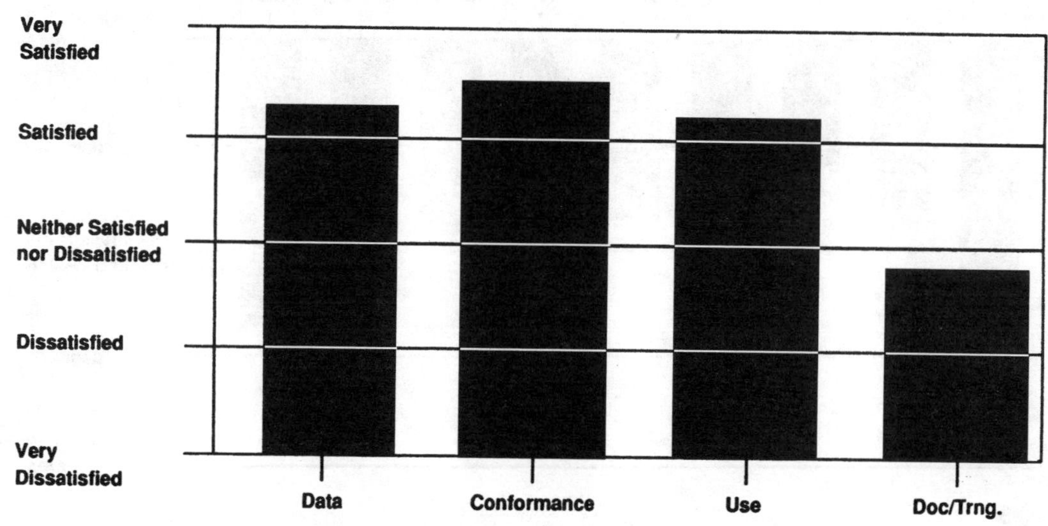

- Support documentation was of poor quality.

C00037/26

PROJECT TEAM CUSTOMERS FOCUS ON PLANNING, AND DEVELOPMENT TOOLS AND TECHNIQUES, AS AREAS FOR IMPROVEMENT

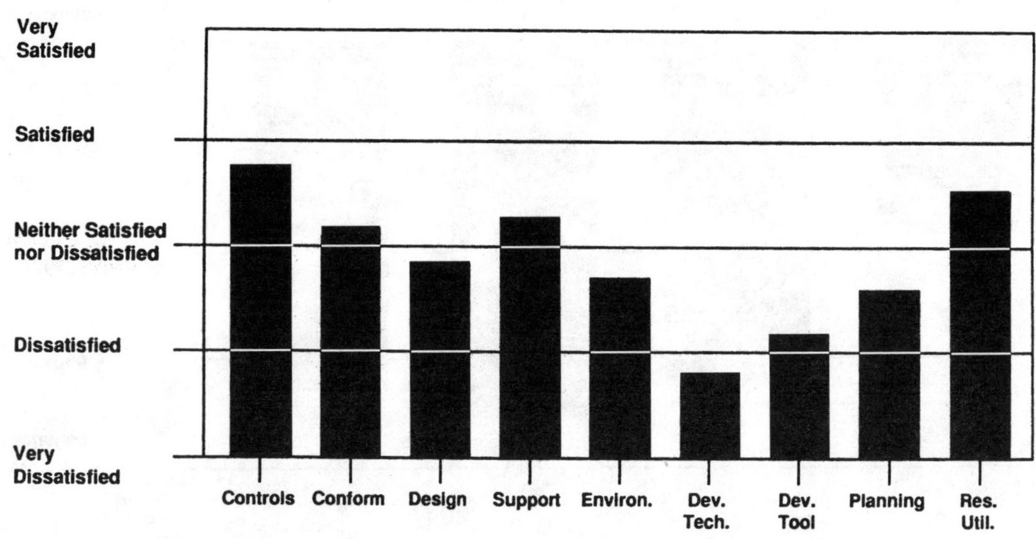

- Customers are not satisfied with the accuracy of estimates and project plans.
- System documentation and testing sign-off procedures are not adequate.
- Customers are less than satisfied with development techniques and tools.

C00037/27

SOFT DATA FINDINGS

PROJECT WORKSHOPS WERE CONDUCTED, FOCUSING ON A BROAD RANGE OF MEASURES.

- **Experience Levels**
- **Tools/Methods**
- **Defect Removal Activity**
- **Project Management**
- **Environment**
- **Maintenance & Enhancement Support**

C00037/28

A HIGH LEVEL OF DEVELOPMENT EXPERIENCE MAY BE OFFSET BY LIMITED USER INVOLVEMENT AND EXPERIENCE

Staff/Customer Experience

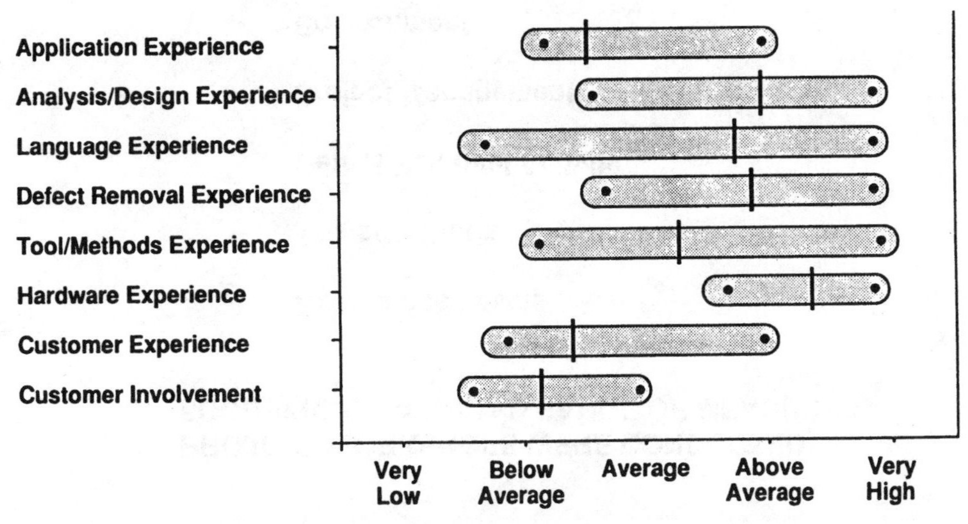

KEY:

| Average

• Project Range

- Non-technical, application experience (business knowledge) was rated lowest among skill areas.

C00037/29

A SYSTEMS DEVELOPMENT METHODOLOGY EXISTS BUT IS USED SPARINGLY ACROSS PROJECTS

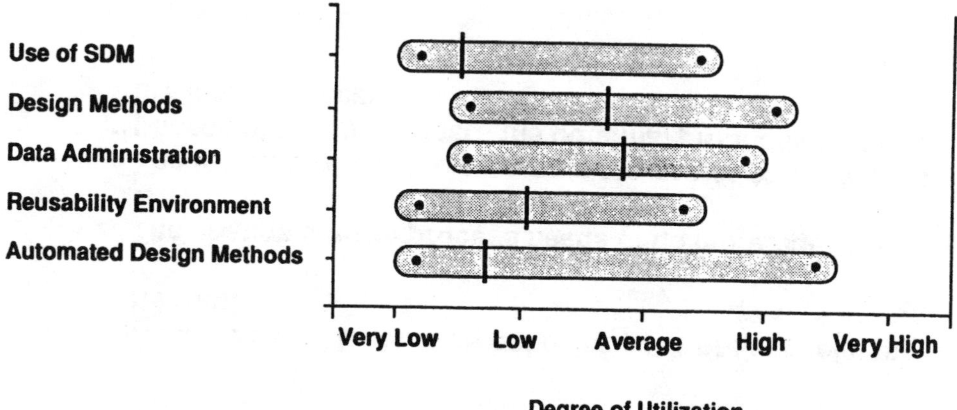

KEY:

| Average
• Project Range

- Development techniques are used inconsistently from project to project.
- Automated methods are used infrequently.
- Use of SDM's and automated design methods are not enforced.

C00037/30

Additional Findings

- A stable set of tools does not exist, each project selects its own.
- The change control process needs to be more rigorous.
- The majority of productivity tools are geared towards later phases of life cycle where the potential productivity gains are less significant.

BASELINE DATA

BASELINE DATA - PROJECT KEY

PROJECT I.D.

Purchase Order Entry
Securities Handling
Claims
Automatic Teller
Human Resources
Payroll Front-End
Distribution Systems
On-Line Agent
Merchandising Systems
Accounts Receivable
Benefits
Long Term Care
Manufacturing Systems
Confirmation Prototype
Financial Analysis
Systems Conversion
Checkpoint
On-Line Inquiry

EXPLANATION OF NORMALIZED SCALE

The scale used for the soft data on the following pages normalizes the Checkpoint Questionnaire Scale by exactly reversing it (e.g., 3.2 becomes 2.8).

The Normalized Scale facilitates statistical analysis and graphical representation of the data.

Checkpoint Questionnaire Scale		Normalized Scale
5.0 - 4.5	Poor	1.0 - 1.5
4.5 - 3.5	Below Average	1.5 - 2.5
3.5 - 2.5	Average	2.5 - 3.5
2.5 - 1.5	Above Average	3.5 - 4.5
1.5 - 1.0	Leading Edge	4.5 - 5.0

C00037/53

BASELINE DATA - END-USER CUSTOMER SATISFACTION

ATTRIBUTE

CODE	SYST. DATA	SYST. CONF.	SYST. USE	SYST. DOC/TRNG.	TOTAL
A	3.75	3.29	3.33	3.63	3.48
B	2.90	2.26	2.75	3.00	4.00
C	3.84	3.79	4.15	3.60	3.89
D	3.75	2.71	2.38	1.75	2.77
E	4.00	4.00	3.75	3.55	3.20
F	3.45	3.70	3.87	2.00	3.25
G	3.00	3.00	3.87	2.00	3.00
H	3.90	3.82	3.88	3.15	3.71
J	3.70	3.70	4.00	2.10	3.50
K	4.14	4.00	3.45	2.33	3.60
L	3.60	3.27	3.96	1.65	3.20
M	4.46	4.23	4.13	3.88	3.05
N	5.00	5.00	4.09	5.00	4.69
P	3.38	3.13	3.29	2.75	3.15
Q	4.00	3.95	3.88	3.39	3.81
R	4.05	4.17	3.93	1.73	3.00
S	4.00	3.75	3.86	3.50	3.78
T	5.00	4.86	4.92	2.00	4.00
U	4.43	4.50	4.44	1.95	3.10
CLIENT AVG.	4.20	4.45	4.15	2.88	3.92

C00037/54

BASELINE DATA - PRODUCTIVITY

37421 McGraw

ATTRIBUTE

CODE	TECH	TYPE	FP	EFF	SCH	FTE	DOC	FP/MO
A	MF	D	588	40.3	10.5	3.8	1969	14.58
B	MF	D	193	13.8	6.0	2.3	199	13.99
C	MF	D	145	16.0	3.5	4.6	166	9.06
D	MF	E	63	5.2	2.0	2.6	163	12.12
E	MF	D	69	16.2	3.7	4.4	174	4.26
F	MF	D	437	110.0	8.0	14.4	335	3.80
G	MF	M	288	30.8	5.3	5.9	380	9.36
H	MF	E	604	164.3	22.0	6.6	1000	3.68
J	PC	D	392	34.0	11.0	3.1	914	11.53
K	MF	E	202	12.2	2.5	3.2	67	16.50
L	MF	E	57	6.2	5.0	1.5	108	9.83
M	PC	E	80	50.0	11.3	6.3	1407	1.60
N	MF	D	79	7.1	7.0	1.0	121	11.06
P	PK	E	513	104.4	7.0	14.9	1181	4.91
Q	MF	E	671	186.9	16.0	11.7	1541	3.59
R	MF	M	3162	120.0	12.0	10.1	2136	25.98
S	MF	D	158	28.5	5.7	4.8	450	5.54
T	MF	D	63	14.2	4.3	3.3	110	4.44
U	PC	E	405	35.0	5.3	7.0	1195	10.95
CLIENT AVG.			429	52.4	7.8	6.0	716	9.30

KEY:

CODE
Identifies Projects on graphs

TYPE
D = Development
E = Enhancement
M = Maintenance

TECHNOLOGY
MF = Mainframe
PC = Micro
PK = Package

FP = Function Points
EFF = Effort (Person-Months)
SCH = Schedule (Elapsed Months)
FTE = Staff (Full-Time Equivalents)
DOC = Documentation (Pages)
FP/MO = Productivity (Function Points per Person-Month)

C00037/55

BASELINE DATA - PEOPLE MANAGEMENT

ATTRIBUTE

CODE	APPL. EXP.	ANAL. DSN. EXP.	LANG. EXP.	DEF. REM. EXP.	USER EXP.	USER INVOL.	H/W EXP.	PROJ. ORG. STRCT.	MORALE	TEAM COHES.	TOOL/ METH. EXP.	MAINT. PERS	TOTAL
A	3.0	5.0	5.0	4.5	4.0	2.0	4.5	2.0	5.0	5.0	3.0		4.1
B	2.0	2.0	4.5	2.5	4.0	2.0	4.5	4.5	4.5	4.0	4.5		3.7
C	2.0	3.0	4.0	3.0	2.5	6.5	4.0	2.0	5.0	4.5	2.5		3.3
D	2.0	3.0	3.0	4.5	3.5	2.0	5.0	2.0	4.0	5.0	4.5		3.7
E	4.0	4.0	5.0	4.5	2.3	2.0	5.0	4.0	3.0	5.0	5.0		4.1
F	3.0	3.0	3.0	3.0	4.0	2.0	4.0	1.0	1.0	3.0	3.0		2.9
G	3.5	3.5	4.0	4.0	1.8	1.7	5.0	2.5	5.0	4.5	3.0		3.7
H	3.5	4.0	3.5	3.0	4.0	41.0	3.5	3.0	3.0	5.0	3.0	3.6	3.6
J	2.0	3.0	3.0	4.0	3.0	3.0	5.0	3.0	5.0	4.0	2.0	3.7	3.4
K	4.5	5.0	4.0	5.0	4.0	2.0	5.0	4.0	5.0	5.0	5.0	4.0	4.5
L	2.0	3.0	4.0	3.5	3.0	2.0	4.0	3.0	4.0	4.0	4.0		3.5
M	2.0	4.0	4.0	3.0	4.0	3.5	4.0	3.0	4.0	3.0	2.5		3.4
N	5.0	3.0	1.5	4.0	3.5	2.0	5.0	4.0	3.5	5.0	2.0		3.7
P	3.0	4.5	4.0	3.3	3.0	2.0	4.0	1.0	3.0	1.5	3.0		3.1
Q	3.0	2.0	4.0	4.0	2.5	1.9	4.0	3.0	5.0	4.0	2.5		3.3
R	4.0	3.0	3.0	4.5	4.0	4.0	4.0	3.0	3.0	4.0	4.0	4.0	3.7
S	3.0	4.0	4.0	3.3	4.0	2.0	4.0	3.0	4.0	4.5	3.5		3.8
T	2.5	5.0	5.0	5.0	3.0	2.0	4.0	4.0	4.0	4.0	2.0		3.9
U	3.0	4.0	2.0	4.5	3.3	2.0	4.0	3.0	2.5	3.0	3.0		3.3
CLIENT AVG.	2.5	3.7	3.6	3.7	2.5	2.0	4.3	2.9	3.6	4.1	3.3	3.8	3.6

KEY:

Poor	1.0 - 1.5
Below Average	1.5 - 2.5
Average	2.5 - 3.5
Above Average	3.5 - 4.5
Leading Edge	4.5 - 5.0

C00037/56

BASELINE DATA - TECHNOLOGY

ATTRIBUTE

CODE	RESP. TIME	DEV. COMPTR. SUPPORT	PROJ. LIB./EQUIP.	MAINT. COMPTG. SUPPORT	HDWRE. NOVELTY	SUPPORT S/W NOVELTY	AUTO. METH.	TOTAL
A	3.0	4.8	2.8		5.0	1.0	1.0	2.9
B	3.0	4.8	3.5		5.0	3.8	3.0	3.8
C	3.0	4.8	2.5		4.0	3.0	4.5	3.6
D	3.0	3.8	3.5		5.0	5.0	2.0	3.7
E	3.0	4.5	2.5		5.0	5.0	1.0	3.5
F	3.0	5.0	3.0		5.0	5.0	1.0	3.7
G	3.0	4.4	3.5		5.0	4.0	3.0	3.8
H	3.5	4.8	3.0	4.0	5.0	5.0	1.0	3.8
J	5.0	4.4	3.5	5.0	5.0	4.0	1.0	4.0
K	3.0	5.0	3.0	5.0	5.0	5.0	1.0	3.9
L	3.0	5.0	3.5		4.0	4.0	1.0	3.4
M	5.0	4.3	2.5		5.0	3.0	1.0	3.5
N	3.0	4.1	3.8		4.0	3.0	1.0	3.1
P	4.0	4.5	3.0		5.0	3.0	3.0	3.8
Q	3.0	4.8	3.5		5.0	4.0	1.0	3.5
R	3.0	4.8	3.0	5.0	5.0	5.0	1.0	3.8
S	3.0	4.8	3.0		5.0	4.5	1.0	3.5
T	3.0	4.8	3.0		5.0	3.0	4.0	3.8
U	5.0	4.4	2.5		4.0	5.0	2.0	3.8
CLIENT AVG.	3.4	4.6	3.1	4.8	4.8	4.0	1.8	3.6

KEY:

Poor	1.0	-	1.5
Below Average	1.5	-	2.5
Average	2.5	-	3.5
Above Average	3.5	-	4.5
Leading Edge	4.5	-	5.0

C00037/57

BASELINE DATA - DEVELOPMENT PROCESS

ATTRIBUTE

CODE	PRODVTY. MEASURES	USE OF SDM	DESIGN METHODS	DATA ADMIN.	REUSEABILITY ENVIRONMENT	QA FUNCT. EXISTS	QUAL. MEAS. DB EXISTS	DEF. REM. ENVIRON.
A	1.0	2.5	4.0	3.0	2.0	1.0	1.0	3.5
B	1.0	1.5	2.3	4.5	5.0	1.0	1.0	2.0
C	1.0	3.0	4.0	2.0	2.5	2.0	2.0	3.0
D	1.0	3.0	1.7	3.0	2.0	1.0	1.0	2.0
E	1.0	1.0	2.0	4.0	1.0	1.0	1.0	3.0
F	1.0	2.0	2.3	2.0	2.0	1.0	1.0	3.5
G	1.0	2.5	3.5	2.5	5.0	1.0	1.0	3.5
H	1.0	1.0	2.0	4.0	2.0	2.0	2.5	3.8
J	1.0	3.0	2.7	3.0	2.5	2.0	1.0	3.0
K	1.0	2.5	2.3	5.0	3.0	1.0	1.0	3.0
L	1.0	1.0	2.7	5.0	1.0	1.0	1.0	3.5
M	1.0	3.0	2.7	3.0	2.5	3.0	1.0	3.0
N	1.0	2.0	3.0	1.0	4.0	3.0	1.0	2.5
P	1.0	3.0	2.0	1.0	2.5	1.0	1.0	2.5
Q	1.0	1.5	2.3	1.0	5.0	1.0	1.0	2.5
R	1.0	1.0	2.3	3.0	3.5	1.0	1.0	3.3
S	1.0	3.0	2.0	1.5	2.0	1.0	1.0	2.5
T	1.0	2.0	4.2	4.0	2.0	1.0	1.0	3.0
U	1.0	2.0	4.2	1.0	3.0	1.0	1.0	3.5
CLIENT AVG.	1.0	1.5	2.7	2.8	2.0	1.4	1.1	3.0

KEY:	
Poor	1.0 - 1.5
Below Average	1.5 - 2.5
Average	2.5 - 3.5
Above Average	3.5 - 4.5
Leading Edge	4.5 - 5.0

C00037/58

BASELINE DATA - DEVELOPMENT PROCESS (CONT)

ATTRIBUTE

CODE	DEF. REM. SCHED.	TOOLS/ TESTING FUNCTION	CUSTOMER SUPPORT	L-R PLANNING/ STABILITY	DOC TYPE SIZE/ FORMAT	AUTO. DOC. PREP.	DOC. METHODS	DOC. OUTPUT DIST.	TOTAL
A	2.0	4.0			2.0	4.2	4.0	3.0	2.7
B	3.0	4.5			2.0	2.3	4.0	2.8	2.7
C	2.0	3.8			2.0	2.3	3.5	1.8	2.6
D	2.0	4.0			1.0	2.7	3.0	3.0	2.3
E	3.0	4.5			4.0	2.7	4.5	3.0	2.5
F	1.8	4.5			2.0	2.3	2.0	3.3	2.2
G	2.0	4.0			2.0	3.3	4.5	2.0	2.7
H	2.0	4.0	4.5	2.5	4.0	2.3	3.0	3.3	2.7
J	2.0	3.5	4.3	1.5	2.5	2.7	5.0	3.0	2.7
K	2.5	3.5	3.7	2.0	2.0	3.2	3.0	3.0	2.6
L	2.0	3.5			1.0	2.7	3.0	3.0	2.2
M	2.0	3.5			2.0	2.0	4.0	3.0	2.6
N	1.0	4.5			4.0	2.7	4.0	2.3	2.3
P	3.0	4.0			3.0	3.0	3.0	3.0	2.8
Q	3.0	4.0			2.0	2.3	3.0	2.5	2.3
R	3.0	3.5	4.5	2.0	2.0	3.2	3.0	3.0	2.6
S	1.5	4.0			3.0	2.7	3.0	3.0	2.2
T	5.0	4.0			1.0	3.7	4.0	2.5	3.0
U	2.0	3.0			1.0	2.7	3.0	3.5	2.3
CLIENT AVG.	2.4	3.9	4.3	2.0	2.2	2.8	3.5	2.8	2.5

KEY:

Poor	1.0 - 1.5
Below Average	1.5 - 2.5
Average	2.5 - 3.5
Above Average	3.5 - 4.5
Leading Edge	4.5 - 5.0

C00037/59

BASELINE DATA - ENVIRONMENT

ATTRIBUTE

CODE	FUNC. NOV.	PROD. REST.	LEGAL/ STAT.	PROG. COMP.	PROD. FACT.	DEV. GEO.	OFFICE ENV.	NOISE/ INTER.	MAINT. AVAIL.	TOTAL
A	1.0	5.0	5.0	3.0		4.0	2.3	3.0		3.3
B	1.5	3.0	5.0	2.3		5.0	2.3	2.0		3.0
C	5.0	3.0	5.0	3.8		4.0	2.3	3.0		3.7
D	4.0	3.0	5.0	3.0		4.0	2.3	1.0		3.2
E	3.0	2.5	5.0	2.5		5.0	2.3	2.0		3.2
F	3.0	3.0	3.0	1.5		4.0	2.3	2.0		2.7
G	4.0	3.0	5.0	4.0		5.0	2.0	2.0		3.6
H	4.0	3.3	3.0	2.5	3.5	4.5	2.3	1.0	1.0	2.8
J	2.0	2.5	5.0	2.7	2.5	5.0	2.3	3.0	3.5	3.2
K	3.0	3.0	5.0	2.0	2.5	5.0	2.3	1.5	3.0	3.0
L	4.0	2.0	5.0	3.2		5.0	2.3	5.0		3.8
M	3.0	2.5	3.0	3.5		3.0	2.3	2.3		2.8
N	4.0	2.8	3.0	3.3		4.0	1.5	1.5		2.9
P	4.0	2.8	5.0	4.2		5.0	2.3	1.0		3.5
Q	4.0	3.0	3.0	2.8		5.0	2.0	2.0		3.1
R	3.0	3.0	5.0	2.2	2.5	5.0	2.3	1.5	1.0	2.8
S	4.0	5.0	5.0	3.0		5.0	2.3	2.0		3.8
T	2.0	3.0	5.0	4.0		3.0	2.3	2.0		3.0
U	2.5	2.3	5.0	2.3		5.0	2.5	4.0		3.4
CLIENT AVG.	3.2	3.0	4.5	2.9	2.8	4.5	2.2	2.2	2.1	3.2

KEY:	
Poor	1.0 - 1.5
Below Average	1.5 - 2.5
Average	2.5 - 3.5
Above Average	3.5 - 4.5
Leading Edge	4.5 - 5.0

C00037/60

FINDINGS BASIS

C00037/61

FINDINGS BASIS - PRODUCTIVITY

ATTRIBUTE

CODE	% DEVIATION FROM INDUSTRY AVERAGE SCH	FTE	DOC	FP/MO
A	60	-207	-51	12
B	58	-189	73	0
C	138	-260	-82	14
D	110	10	-10	266
E	-14	-50	54	-62
F	14	-340	2	-54
G	422	-52	-93	333
H	92	-15	-69	126
J	608	72	-95	N/A
K	-2	-27	-60	-12
L	41	-80	-52	-14
M	65	-136	-52	62
N	40	-197	-28	-21
P	0	-230	-20	-56
Q	48	-19	-40	144
R	76	-75	-42	180
S	49	-58	-26	46
T	70	-148	-51	8
U	-8	0	-35	16

KEY:

- SCH = Schedule
- FTE = Staff (Full-Time Equivalents)
- DOC = Documentation
- FP/MO = Productivity (Function Points per Person-Month)

FINDING

- Schedule is much shorter than expected on vast majority of projects (79%).
- Staff levels significantly higher than expected on virtually all projects (84%).
- Documentation less than expected for nearly all projects (84%).
- Productivity levels tended toward norm: half of projects within 21% of industry average.

EXPLANATION OF TABLE:

% Deviation From Industry Average indicates how much better (positive %) or worse (negative %) the measured attribute is compared to the industry average.

For example, project A in the *Baseline Data - Productivity* table was sized at 132 Function Points and had a schedule measured at 3.5 months. The industry average schedule for a project with 132 Function Points is 8.8 months. Therefore, project A's schedule is (8.8 - 3.5) ÷ 8.8 = 60% better than the industry average.

C00037/62

FINDINGS BASIS - CUSTOMER SATISFACTION

FINDING	SUPPORTIVE DATA
STRENGTHS	
• Customers Generally Satisfied With Systems	Interviews
- End User Customers	4.65
- Project Team Customers	2.50
WEAKNESSES	
• Project Team Customers Not Completely Satisfied With:	
- Project Controls	3.44
- System Design	3.39
- Development Techniques	3.34
- Development Tools	3.18
• Customers Express Loss of Control and Doubts About I/S Productivity	Interviews

KEY:

Very Dissatisfied	1.0 - 1.5
Dissatisfied	1.5 - 2.5
Not Completely Satisfied	2.5 - 3.5
Satisfied	3.5 - 4.5
Very Satisfied	4.5 - 5.0

C00037/63

FINDINGS BASIS - PEOPLE MANAGEMENT

FINDING	SUPPORTIVE DATA
STRENGTHS	
• Above Average Hardware Experience	4.3
• Above Average Team Cohesiveness	4.1
• Above Average Analysis/Design Experience	3.7
• Above Average Language Experience	3.6
• Above Average Defect Removal Experience	3.7
• Very Good Employee Loyalty	Interviews
WEAKNESSES	
• Below Average User Experience	2.0 - 2.5
• Extensive Use of Generalists vs. Specialists	Interviews
• Reluctance to Change	Interviews

KEY:

Poor	1.0 - 1.5
Below Average	1.5 - 2.5
Average	2.5 - 3.5
Above Average	3.5 - 4.5
Leading Edge	4.5 - 5.0

C00037/64

FINDINGS BASIS - TECHNOLOGY

FINDING	SUPPORTIVE DATA
STRENGTHS	
• Above Average Hardware Novelty	4.8
• Above Average Maintenance Computer Support	4.8
• Above Average Development Computer Support	4.6
• Support Software Novelty Above Average	4.0
WEAKNESSES	
• Poor Automated Design Methods	1.8
• Maintenance Lifecycle Not Closely Managed	Interviews
• Insufficient Technology Transfer Communications	Interviews

KEY:

Poor	1.0 - 1.5
Below Average	1.5 - 2.5
Average	2.5 - 3.5
Above Average	3.5 - 4.5
Leading Edge	4.5 - 5.0

FINDINGS BASIS - DEVELOPMENT PROCESS

FINDING	SUPPORTIVE DATA
STRENGTHS	
• None	
WEAKNESSES	
• Poor Productivity Measures	1.0
• Poor Quality Measurements	1.1
• Poor QA Existence	1.4
• Poor Reusability Environment	2.0
• Poor Long Range Planning Stability	2.0
• Below Average Documentation Format	2.2
• Below Average Defect Removal Scheduling	2.4
• User Generated Documentation	Interviews
• Insufficient SDM Enforcement	Interviews

KEY:

Poor	1.0 - 1.5
Below Average	1.5 - 2.5
Average	2.5 - 3.5
Above Average	3.5 - 4.5
Leading Edge	4.5 - 5.0

C00037/66

FINDINGS BASIS - ENVIRONMENT

FINDING	SUPPORTIVE DATA
STRENGTHS	
• Above Average Legal/Statutory Requirements	4.5
• Above Average Development Geography	4.5
WEAKNESSES	
• Below Average Maintenance Availability	2.1
• Below Average Office Environment	2.2
• Below Average Noise Suppression	2.2
• Culture of Quantity vs. Quality	Interviews
• Culture of Complacency and Limited Accountability	Interviews
• Higher Degree of Business Urgency than Perceived I/S Urgency	Interviews

KEY:

Poor	1.0 - 1.5
Below Average	1.5 - 2.5
Average	2.5 - 3.5
Above Average	3.5 - 4.5
Leading Edge	4.5 - 5.0

C00037/67

HIGH PRODUCTIVITY PROJECTS CONSISTENTLY USED A COMBINATION OF TOOLS AND METHODS

Productivity Factors

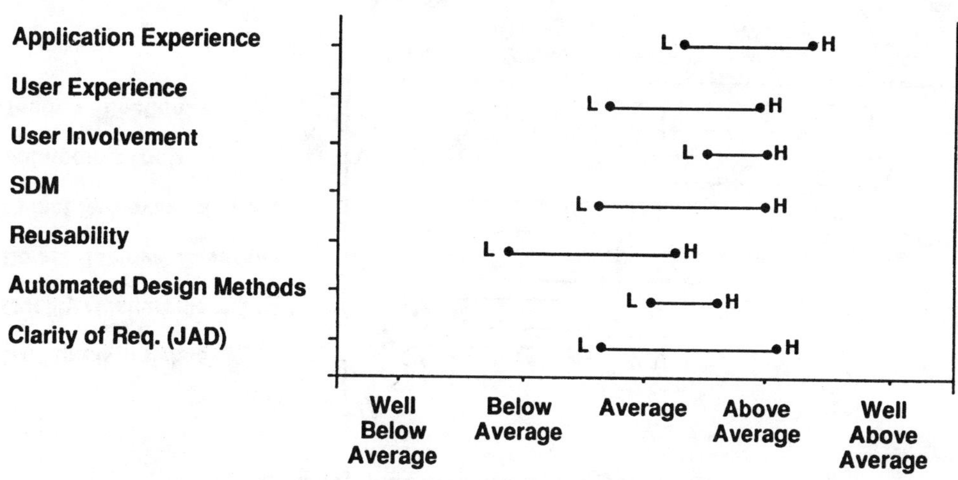

- **User involvement was a key factor in productivity gains.**

L = Low Productivity Projects
H = High Productivity Projects

C00037/32

INFORMAL QUALITY ASSURANCE ACTIVITIES ARE TYPICALLY PERFORMED BY DEVELOPMENT TEAM

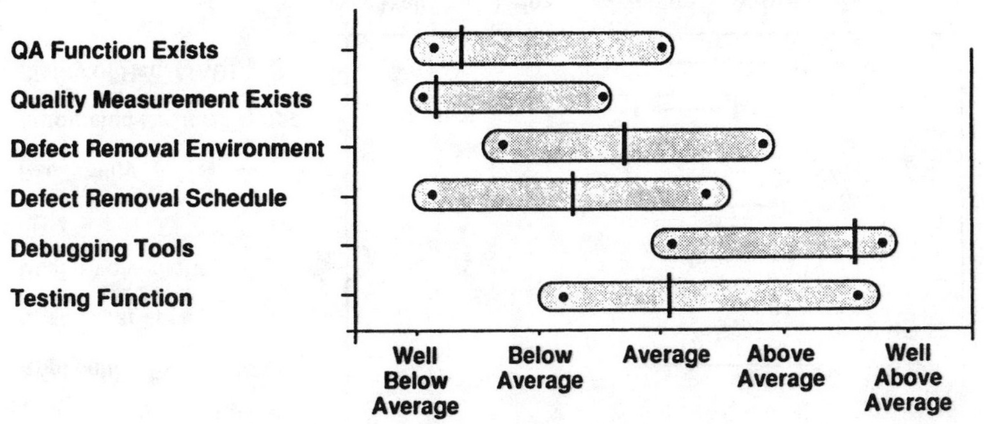

KEY:

- Average
- Project Range

- Defects are recorded and tracked but are not analyzed across the lifecycle.
- Defect removal activities are often impacted by tight schedules impacting the ability to do adequate reviews/inspections.
- Testing is often viewed as more important than pre-test reviews.

C00037/33

A NUMBER OF KEY DEFECT REMOVAL ACTIVITIES ARE NOT PERFORMED

Defect Removal Activity

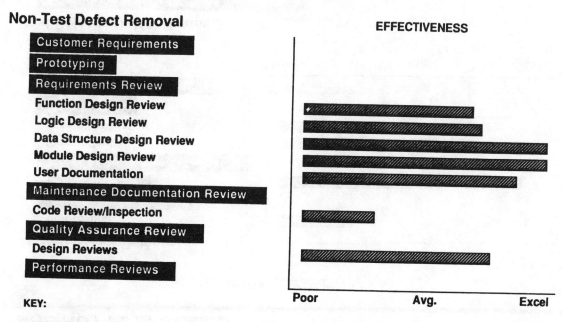

Non-Test Defect Removal

Customer Requirements
Prototyping
Requirements Review
Function Design Review
Logic Design Review
Data Structure Design Review
Module Design Review
User Documentation
Maintenance Documentation Review
Code Review/Inspection
Quality Assurance Review
Design Reviews
Performance Reviews

EFFECTIVENESS

Poor Avg. Excel

KEY:

Performed
Not Performed

C00037/34

A NUMBER OF KEY DEFECT REMOVAL ACTIVITIES ARE NOT PERFORMED

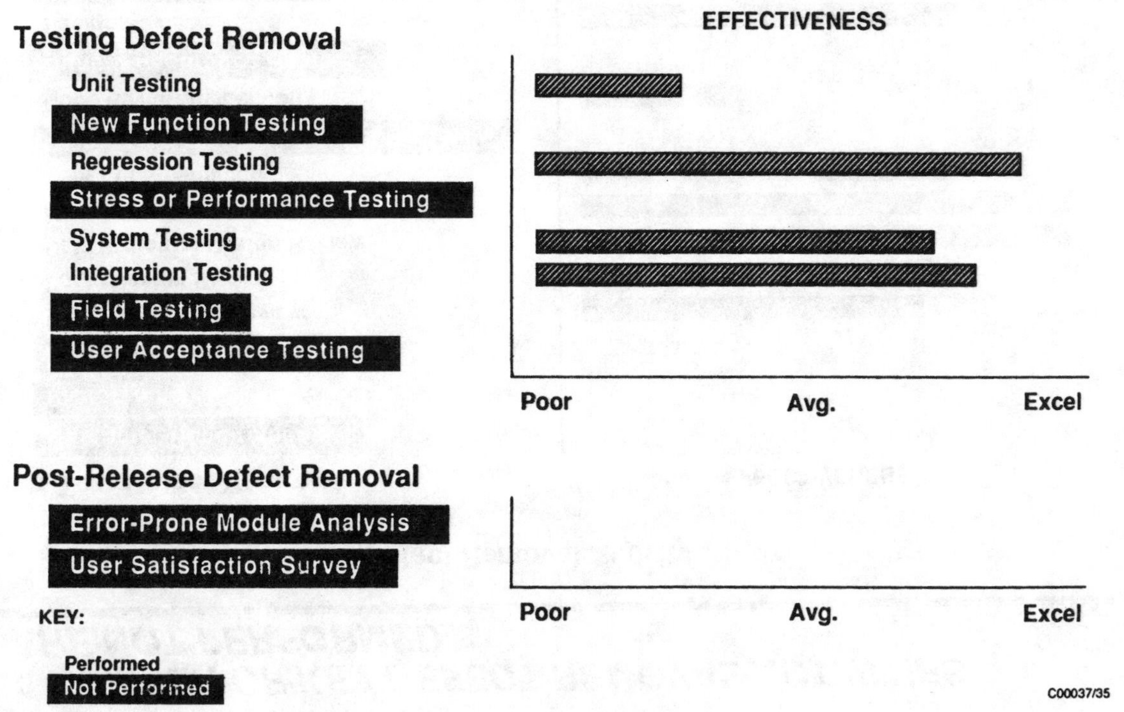

PRODUCTIVITY MEASURES ARE INCOMPLETE AND INCONSISTENT

Project Management Environment

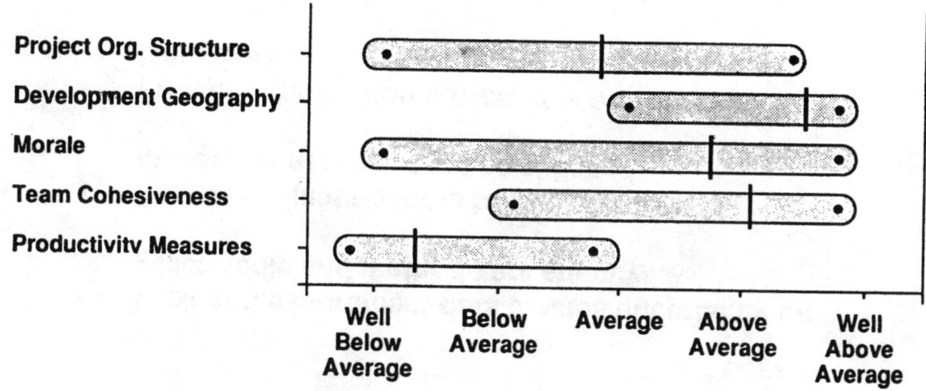

KEY:

| Average

● Project Range

- A number of projects reported a matrix organization which can impact productivity negatively.
- Morale varies significantly by project.

PROJECT MANAGEMENT ENVIRONMENT

Additional Findings

- Lack of measurement data creates uncertainty on which tools and methods are effective.
- Project estimating tools to assist project management are not yet established.
- Project organization structure is not conducive to team work.

PHYSICAL ENVIRONMENT IS NOT CONDUCIVE TO HIGH PRODUCTIVITY OR QUALITY

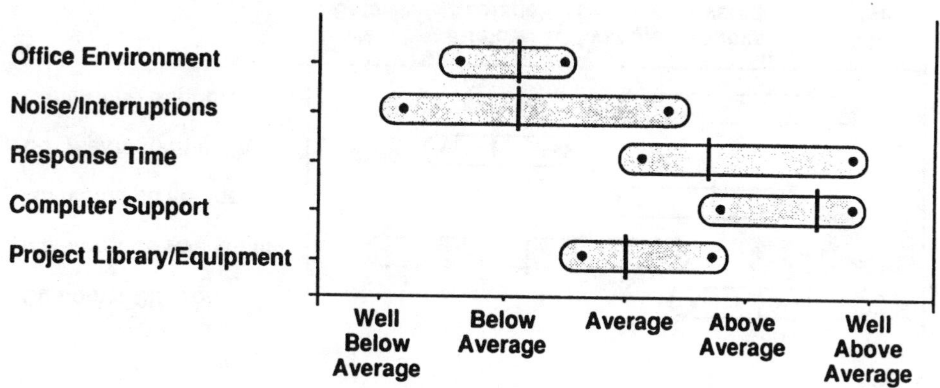

KEY:

| Average

• Project Range

- Individual offices are not enclosed contributing to noise, distractions, and frequent interruptions.
- Computer support and response time is reliable and effective.

C00037/39

LONG RANGE SYSTEMS PLANNING IS NOT YET A PART OF THE COMPANYS' OVERALL BUSINESS STRATEGY

Maintenance and Enhancement Support

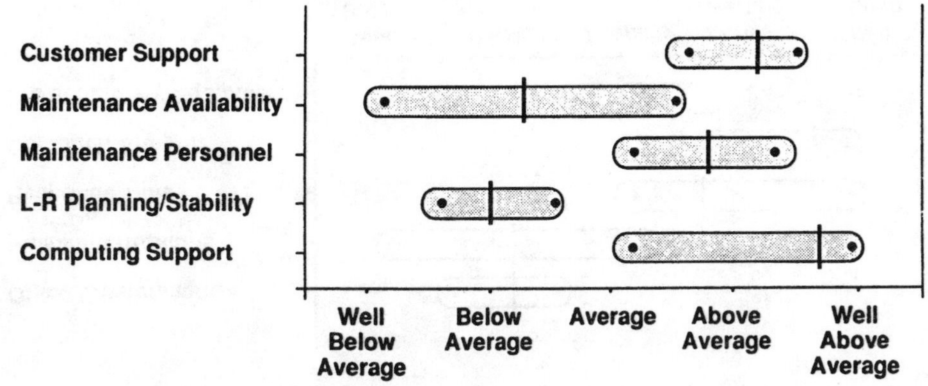

KEY:

| Average
● Project Range

- Customer support is well staffed with experienced people.
- Frequent changes to software and limited long range planning has resulted in a low stability rating.
- Systems are not being analyzed for possible improvements through restructuring.

C00037/40

SCHEDULE PRESSURE AND UNCLEAR USER REQUIREMENTS WERE HIGH RISK FACTORS ON MOST PROJECTS

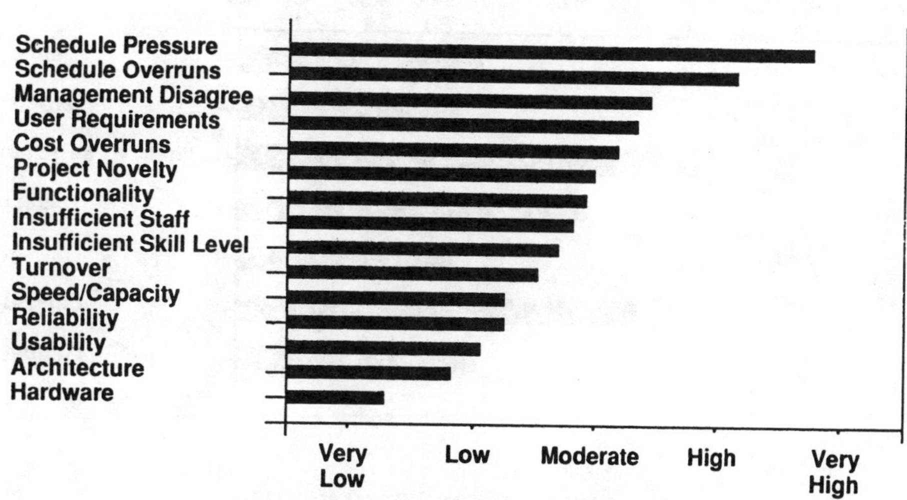

KEY:

■ AVERAGE

- User requirements are frequently unstable.
- Management disagreements on most projects should be a concern.

C00037/42

END-USER DOCUMENTATION IS VERY LIMITED

Percent of Expected Documents

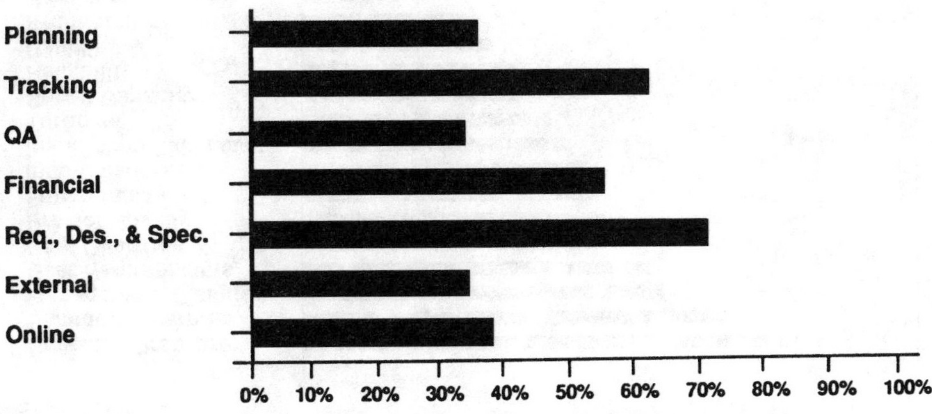

C00037/41

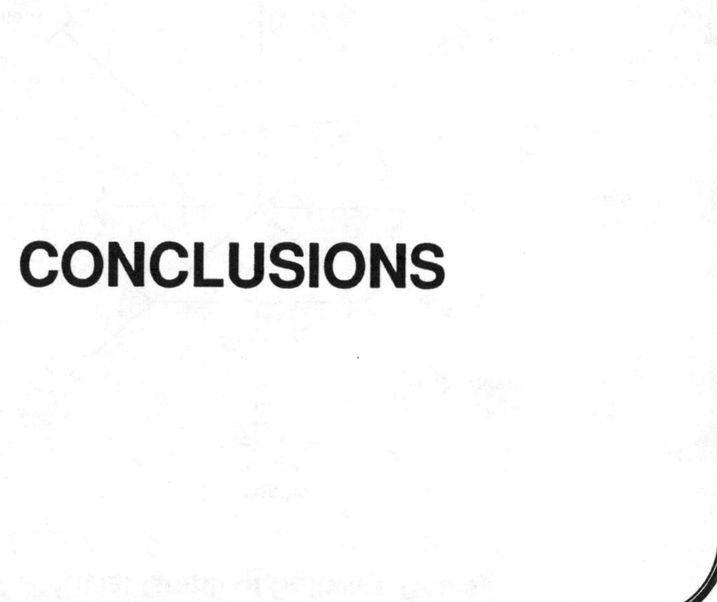
CONCLUSIONS

A MULTIFACETED IMPROVEMENT PLAN IS REQUIRED TO EFFECTIVELY ORCHESTRATE CHANGE

Kiviat Graph of Software Goals

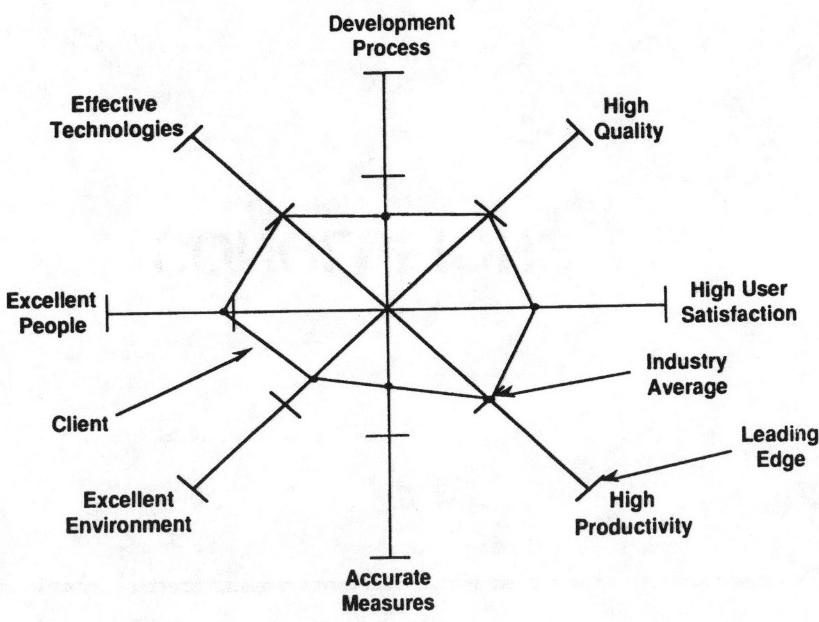

C00037/44

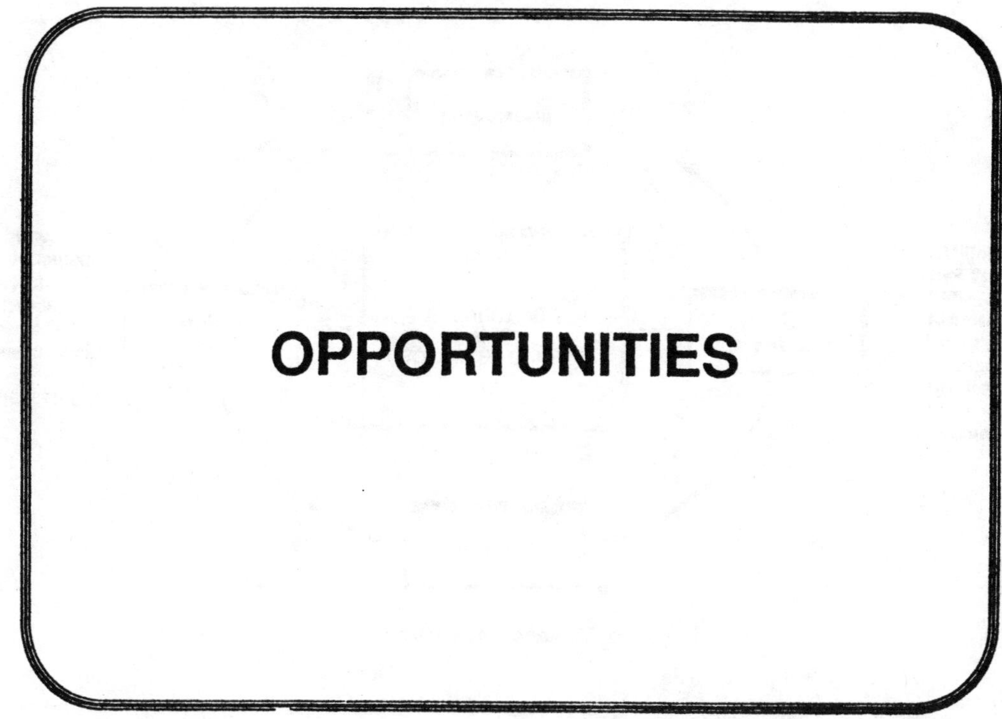
OPPORTUNITIES

SUMMARY OF OPPORTUNITIES

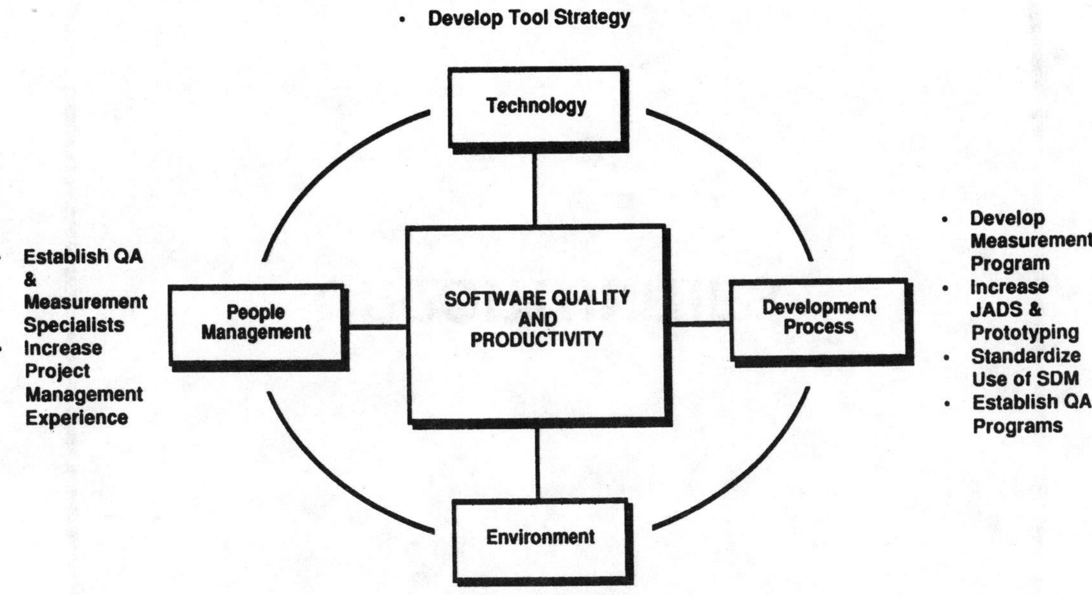

- Establish Communication Programs
- Improve Physical Office Space
- Improve Partnership with Customers

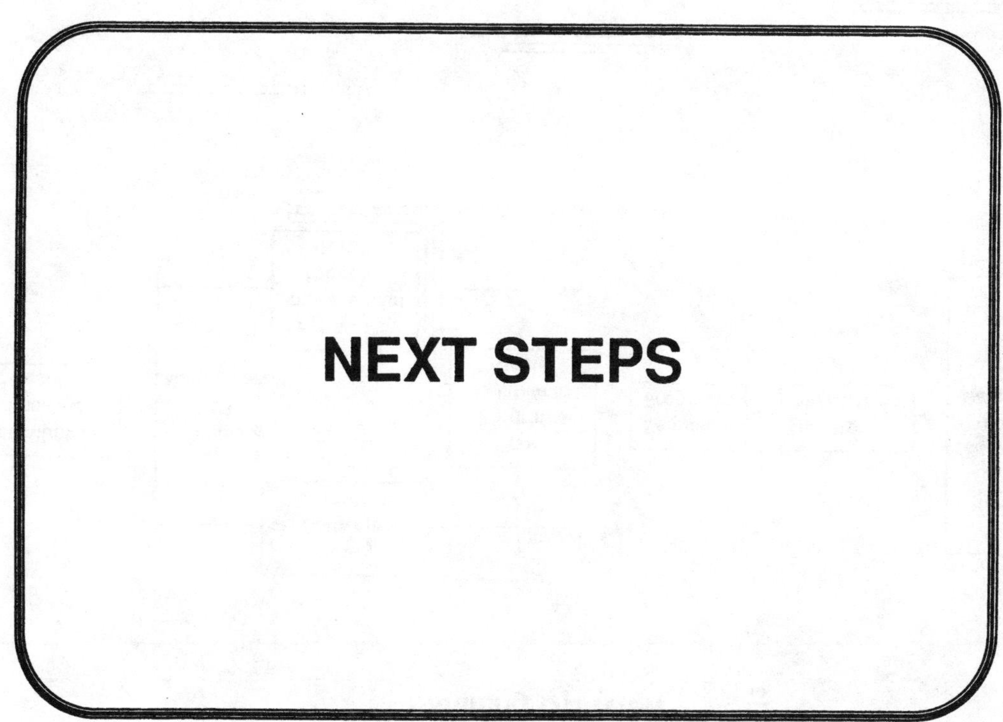

C00037/47

NEXT STEPS DEVELOP A QUALITY/PRODUCTIVITY PLAN

Planning Overview

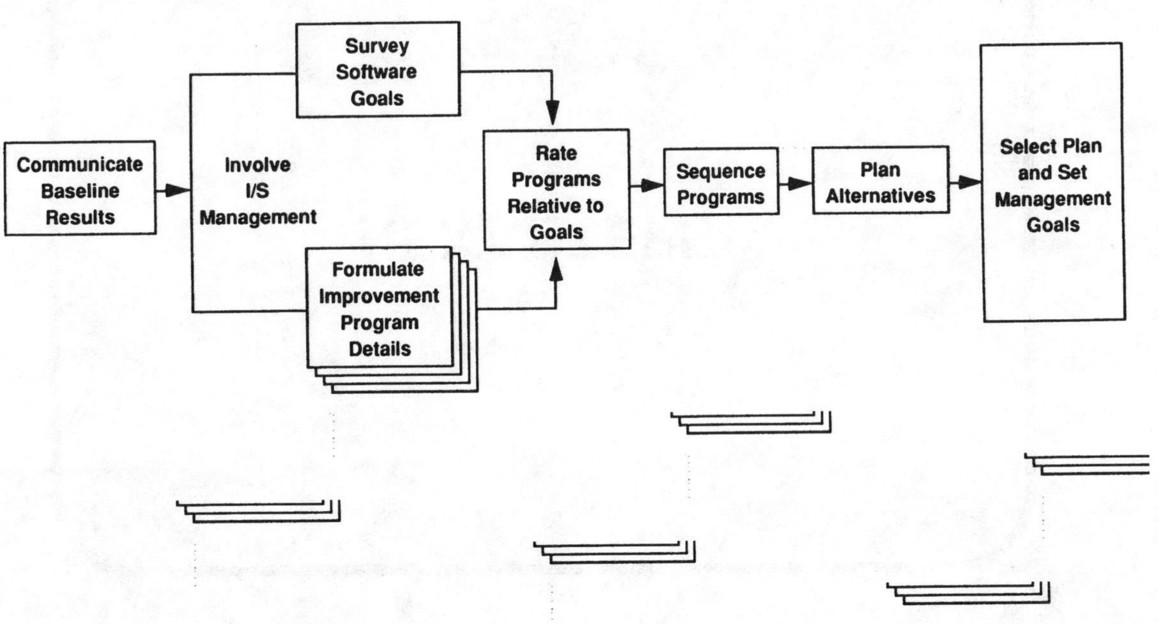

NEXT STEPS

- Conduct software goals survey.
- Gain management acceptance of baseline results.
- Identify and involve I/S management in program planning to formulate program details.
- Develop plans and set goals.

C00037/49

APPENDIX

C00037/50

APPENDIX

- **Baseline Data**
- **Findings Basis**

Index

ABOUT THE AUTHOR

T. Capers Jones is widely considered a founding father of functional analysis, and is a highly respected figure in the field of software engineering. He is the founder and chairman of Software Productivity Research, a prestigious consultancy that works with both technical and business management on productivity issues. In addition to the groundbreaking First and Second Editions of *Applied Software Management*, Mr. Jones is also the author of several other books and numerous articles. He lives in Burlington, Massachusetts.